Counseling Teenagers

The complete Christian guide to understanding and helping adolescents

Dr. G. Keith Olson

Group Books

Loveland, Colorado

Counseling Teenagers (paperback)
Copyright © 1984 by Thom Schultz Publications, Inc.

Fourth Printing, 1993

Library of Congress Catalog No. 83-81450
ISBN 0-931529-67-0

For the sake of privacy, all people named in the case histories in this book are composites, with names and details sufficiently altered to make them unidentifiable.

CREDITS
Designed by Jean Bruns

The scripture quotations in this publication are from the Revised Standard Version of the Bible, copyrighted 1946, 1952 © 1971, 1973. Used by permission.

The illustration on page 40 is from *Patterns in Moral Development* by Catherine M. Stonehouse, Word Educational Products Division, Word, Inc., P.O. Box 1790, Waco, Texas 76796. Used by permission.

The illustration on page 57 is from "Parents and Problems: Through the Eyes of Youth" by Dr. Fred Streit, 168 Woodbridge Ave., Highland Park, N.J. 08904. Used by permission.

The illustration on page 353 is from *Christian Counseling: A Comprehensive Guide* by Gary R. Collins, Word Educational Products, P.O. Box 1790, Waco, Texas 76796. Used by permission.

The first illustration on page 376 (illustration 36) is reprinted with permission of author and publisher from: Devries, A.G. A potential suicide personality inventory. PSYCHOLOGICAL REPORTS, 1966, 18, 731-738.

The illustration on pp. 376-379 (illustration 37) has been reprinted from *The Prediction of Suicide* edited by Aaron T. Beck, H. Resnik and D. Lettieri with permission from Charles Press Publishers, Philadelphia, PA 19102.

Printed in the United States of America

To my wife, Betty,
who has contributed so much for this project's completion,

and

To my son, Ryan,
who thinks that his father should practice what he preaches.

■ Contents

■ Preface

There is a wide variety of books on parenting teenagers, from both Christian and the secular perspectives. These volumes are primarily oriented to parents, and do not focus primarily on the psychology of adolescence. Their main purpose is to present just enough of an understanding of adolescence to help parents more effectively raise their children.

In the realm of clinical psychology and psychiatry, there are several excellent works on adolescent psychology and counseling, from both Christian and secular perspectives. These volumes, however, are usually more academic and technical rather than practical.

Counseling Teenagers is an integrative effort. Its goal is to integrate:
●Christian thought with psychological perspectives;
●several counseling theories with specific guidelines for counseling adolescents; and
●understanding of adolescent counselees with specific guidelines on how to work with these young people.

Counseling Teenagers is built on the foundation that all truth is from and consistent with God. Counseling is viewed as a healing process that occurs between two or more people in any setting. Counseling is viewed as a specific activity that is different from preaching, teaching and parenting. Counseling is also different from being a friend. However, these activities can be enhanced by developing and maintaining effective counseling skills.

This book is intended to be used as an introduction to adolescent psychology and counseling. It is a suitable text for classrooms. It also has a place on the reference shelf of anyone who works closely with teenagers. Pastors, youth ministers, youth group sponsors, Sunday school teachers, lay counselors and parents will discover their needs met time and again as they work, lead and encourage youth.

The contents of *Counseling Teenagers* have been arranged in a manner that supports its underlying integrative philosophy. The introductory chapter, "You Are the Main Ingredient," explores the concept that effective counseling with teenagers depends mainly upon the personal nature and quality of the counselor. Part I, "Understanding Teenagers," focuses upon adolescence as a developmental stage of life. It explores adolescent physiological changes, intellectual and moral development, psychological tasks, expected behaviors and the effect of the family. Part II, "A Christian Approach to Counseling Teenagers," presents an overview of secular and Christian counseling perspectives, followed by an approach that integrates psychological understanding with Christian perspective. Specific counseling techniques, important counseling-related considerations and family, group and crisis intervention counseling are examined. Part III, "Special Issues in Counseling Teenagers," surveys the wide variety of psychological, interpersonal and behavioral problems that teenagers commonly experience. Specific counseling approaches to each problem are suggested, thereby integrating the foundational work that was laid in the first two parts.

A deep sense of gratitude is felt for the people whose love, encouragement and assistance made this book a reality. Many thanks to Cindy Hansen for her help with editing and laborious typing of the original manuscript from my not-too-legible handwriting. Appreciation is also felt for Mary Stubbe for her careful typesetting of the entire volume. Lee Sparks, as editor, has made this project pleasurable and challenging. His warm support, kind encouragement, advice and well-placed insistence that deadlines really are important, were all valued sources of help. And to Thom Schultz, gratitude is expressed for providing the opportunity, patience and confidence which made this publication possible. A number of friends and associates were particularly encouraging, and my grateful thanks is expressed to each one. Special appreciation is also felt for my clients' understanding when my counseling schedule was disrupted in order to complete this task. And loving gratitude to my wife, Betty, and son, Ryan, for their many months of support and patience so that *Counseling Teenagers* could be completed.

■ You Are the Main Ingredient

Imagine yourself driving on a Sunday afternoon out to a park a few miles from your church. You are on your way to pick up 17-year-old Jared, one of the young people in your church. Earlier that day he approached you after the morning service and asked if he could talk with you. "Sure, I'll pick you up after lunch. We can go get a Coke and spend some time together."

As you are driving, you begin to ask yourself some very important questions: "How can I best help Jared?" "I wonder what it is that he needs from me?" "Why did he ask *me* for help?" "What personal gifts has God given me that can be used to help others?" "Is it sometimes hard for me to help others?"

These are indeed some very important questions. Important, because they all lead back to you. You are the main ingredient in counseling. The effectiveness of your counseling is determined primarily by the quality of your personality. The techniques that you use and the skills you possess, although important, are secondary to the quality of your being. Let us explore some answers to the question, "What are the personal characteristics that will help me to counsel teenagers more effectively?"

Primary Counseling Ingredients

The search to discover what makes some counselors successful and some unsuccessful (and some even harmful) has led researchers to an overwhelming conclusion. There are certain personality characteristics that provide the core of effective counseling when adequately integrated within the counselor's person.

Techniques are important. Professional therapists spend years in graduate schools, training seminars, weekend workshops, group supervision experiences and countless hours in reading and studying in order to perfect their skills. They immerse themselves in the study of personality development, abnormal behavior, theories and psychotherapy. They model their beliefs about personality and therapy after one or more traditional theories. Then they develop their own therapeutic approach. Some are reality therapists, some are Gestalt psychologists, others are psychoanalytic in their approach, while others are existentialists and so on. Each therapist blends his or her therapeutic orientation with his or her own personality. The result: a unique style of therapeutic helping and caring that reflects each counselor's personality, belief system and value structure.

If you are a lay counselor, your path will be much the same, only with less investment of time and energy. You will probably read several books, attend several classes and workshops, even participate in a counseling supervision group. Your emerging counseling style will reflect what you have learned, what you have observed and what you have practiced. But even more, the way you counsel with teenagers will reflect who you are.

God was present at the time of your creation (Psalms 139:13-16). He was involved in the selection of your genetic inheritance. He has been with you as you have progressed through the events of your life. Your personality today is the result of your genetic endowment impacted and developed by your environmental experiences. You must start your quest for an effective counseling ministry by knowing yourself more fully.

We will examine the various personality characteristics that help people become effective counselors. Your task will be to evaluate your own personality in light of these characteristics. Your increased awareness and knowledge will start you on the path of your own growth.

To start on your road to increased self-discovery, try this reflective exercise. Make three columns on a sheet of paper. Label the first column, "Helping Person"; the second column, "Their Helping Quality" and the third column, "My Response."

In the first column record the names of the people who have had the greatest healing impact in your life. In the second column write down their personal characteristics that have had a positive effect on you. In the third column state your own personal response to their help. Remember to include your emotional or feeling response as well as your behavioral response (what you actually did as a result of each person's help).

As you complete this exercise you are already increasing your awareness of the personal characteristics that facilitate effective counseling.

A very important research project studied the impact of psychotherapy on psychiatric inpatients. Some patients got better. Some showed no change. And others even grew worse, partly because of the therapy they were receiving. The patients who improved had therapists who exhibited high levels of accurate empathy, warm acceptance and genuineness in their self-expression. The patients who showed no change or even a worsening in their condition had therapists who lacked in these three qualities.[1]

Subsequent research has reinforced the validity of these findings both for inpatient and outpatient groups.[2] The implications are clear. Regardless of the setting—on the hospital neuropsychiatric ward, in the psychologist's office, in the pastor's study or under a tree on the high school campus—counseling is most effective when the counselor possesses three personal characteristics: accurate empathy, non-possessive warmth and genuineness.

Accurate empathy. Fifteen-year-old Anne is struggling to tell her story to her counselor. Three days ago she had her first sexual experience. She was raped. Filled with violent conflicting feelings, fighting back uncontrollable nausea and experiencing utter confusion, she haltingly tells her story. How does the counselor help her? Platitudes will not work. Reassurances that "everything will be okay" fall meaninglessly to the floor. Reading scripture to her would probably increase her sense of worthlessness. And praying with her too soon would likely cause her to feel isolated.

What then can the counselor say to help her? Typically, the most helpful initial responses are empathic expressions of understanding: "It's terribly hard to put such strong feelings into words." "It makes you sick to your stomach every time you think about what happened." "Everything seems so confused now." "You were so scared." "You felt so alone, defenseless and helpless." "You wish you could wake up and find that it was only a bad dream."

Such responses tell her immediately that the counselor is not only hearing her words but also her feelings (physical and emotional), her thoughts and wishes. She will feel understood and accepted. She will be warmed by her counselor's empathy. Her awful story will be expressed more easily in this relationship that now feels more safe and supportive. Empathic understanding is a three step process: sensing, experiencing and expressing.

1. Empathic sensing. The word "empathy" is translated from the German word "emfulung" which means "feeling into." Accurate empathy requires that the counselor attend carefully to all of the counselee's behaviors. Words, voice tone, inflections, rate of speech, posture, gestures and eye movements all carry meaning. The counselor who listens and watches attentively can gather key information bits that would otherwise be lost.

Do you remember the last theatrical performance you attended? The spots broadly washed the stage with light. Then the soloist moved to front-stage-center. The spot focused all of its light into one intense beam, illuminating every detail of the performer's appearance. Accurate empathic sensing requires attention that is so intensely focused that peripheral details are not noticed. The counselor's hearing, seeing, thinking and feeling are centered on the counselee. Sustaining this level of attending requires that the counselor's own psyche is relatively conflict-free and that the general intrapsychic movement is toward resolution and integration. This is not to say that the mind and soul of the counselor should be totally at rest. Not at all. A certain level of dynamic tension seems to be required to launch us into energized problem-solving and decision-making activities. But one must operate with a certain level of internal calm to transcend the confines of the self and become adequately invested in the counselee. This is the kind of peace or internal resting that Christ spoke of in Matthew 11:28-30.

2. Empathic experiencing. It is impossible for one person literally to feel another person's feelings. When your counselees feel sadness, pain, relief or joy, it is their experience. You cannot feel their emotions. What you can do is accurately sense what they are feeling and then fully experience your own emotional response. The empathic counselor identifies with the counselee and at the same time reaches within to find his or her own emotional responses.

It is this transcendent quality that separates empathy from sympathy. Rollo May presents us with a most interesting concept. "The counselor works basically through the process of empathy. Both he or she and the counselee are taken out of themselves and become merged in a common psychic entity. The emotions and will of each become part of this new psychic entity. Consequently the problem of the counselee is dumped on the 'new person' and the counselor then bears half

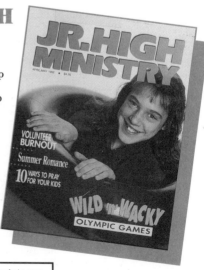

BUSINESS REPLY MAIL
FIRST CLASS MAIL   PERMIT NO. 25   MT. MORRIS, IL

POSTAGE WILL BE PAID BY ADDRESSEE

Group®
Box 202
Mt. Morris, IL 61054-9816

BUSINESS REPLY MAIL
FIRST CLASS MAIL   PERMIT NO. 26   MT. MORRIS, IL

POSTAGE WILL BE PAID BY ADDRESSEE

JR.HIGH MINISTRY
Box 407
Mt. Morris, IL 61054-9814

of it. And the psychological stability of the counselor, his or her clarity, courage and strength of will will carry through to the counselee, thus lending great assistance in the personality struggle."[3]

3. Empathic expressing. The counselor's empathy has a healing impact on the counselee when it is sensitively expressed in words that correspond to the counselee's feelings. "But, you don't understand" is a recurring complaint from teenagers. Because they so often feel alienated, accurate expressions of empathic understanding are absolutely vital. Hearing a counselor's responses that reflect a deep understanding of the troubled counselee's private world engenders a sense that maybe someone really does understand. Maybe someone really does care. Fortressed with the strength of the counselor's empathic understanding, life no longer feels as lonely and frightening.

Non-possessive warmth. Non-possessive warmth is shown most clearly in the gift of salvation that we freely receive through Jesus Christ. "But God shows his love for us in that while we were yet sinners, Christ died for us. For if while we were enemies we were reconciled to God by the death of his Son, much more, now that we are reconciled, shall we be saved by his life" (Romans 5:8, 10). Who could be better equipped to continue expressing this gift of unconditional love than a counselor who is a child of God?

The effective counselor genuinely cares about the happiness and well-being of the counselee. There is a sense of liking that begins to win the teenager's trust. More importantly, as he or she experiences being valued and cared about, the counselee begins to develop an internal basis for self-value and self-love. "If my counselor cares about me, then maybe I am worth something after all."

Non-possessive warmth is non-judgmental. It is neither approving nor disapproving. Rather it accepts the individual, not requiring change or growth in order to invest time and energy in him or her. The issue here is acceptance, not evaluation. Approval is still a judgment. A positive evaluation may turn into a negative or disapproving judgment if the client's behavior or attitudes change.

Non-possessive warmth is a freeing kind of love. It frees the teenager from the tyranny of pleasing the counselor in order not to feel guilty. It frees the teenager to be his or her own person, rather than the person someone else wishes. Some of the teenager's behavior may be self-destructive. Maybe the counselee turns other people off by attitudes and actions. Some of his or her life might disobey God's laws. The effective counselor seeks to help the counselee solve these problems by encouraging the growth of internal strength.

Paul Halmos, professor of sociology at the University of Wales, wrote a book titled *The Faith of the Counsellors*. He states, in essence, that the healing impact of counseling depends on the strength and quality of the love the counselor expresses. Central to the counselor's faith is the belief that love will triumph over hatred.[4]

Genuineness. The third therapeutic ingredient in the counselor's personality is genuineness or self-congruence. Self-congruence is the relationship between the counselor's behavior and his or her thoughts and feelings. " 'Being himself' simply means that at the moment the therapist is really whatever his (or her) response denotes. It does not mean that the therapist must disclose his (or her) total self, but only that whatever the counselor does show is a real aspect of him or herself, not a response growing out of defensiveness or a merely 'professional' response that has been learned and repeated."[5]

Fourteen-year-old Bill is a tall, lanky youngster who hasn't quite figured out how to make the parts of his body all work together to accomplish the same goal. The way he interacts with others is just as confusing and inefficient. His father abandoned their family six years ago and Bill's intense pain and anger is repeatedly projected onto friends and family. His fear of being rejected again has evolved into a formidable wall that holds back anyone who might offer him the gifts of love, acceptance and closeness.

Young Bill, like the rest of us, does not live in a vacuum. He learns who he is largely from how other people treat him. His father's desertion has taught him a lie. His false conclusion goes like this, "If I was a better kid, Dad wouldn't have left. If I was lovable and important, he would have stayed with me."

Bill needs his counselor to be genuine. If he gets honest, negative (but not judgmental) responses from the counselor to his offensive and inappropriate behavior then he can more readily believe the counselor's positive and affirming responses. Sometimes Bill knows very well that he is being obnoxious, which makes the counselor's reactions ring even more authentically. In other words, the counselor is believable! The positive responses to Bill are also more believable. He stays, he meets regularly with the counselor, and he invests energy and interest when they are together. Bill has a chance to learn some very valuable things about himself; that he is a very energetic, interesting, likable and lovable young man.

Accurate empathy, non-possessive warmth and genuineness are the three most important personal ingredients that help people to be more effective counselors. Teenagers will grow and optimally develop when they feel deeply understood, experience unconditional loving and acceptance, and when they trust the honesty and genuineness of their adult counselors.

Additional Characteristics of Effective Counselors

"For as in one body we have many members, and all the members do not have the same function, so we, though many, are one body in Christ, and individually members one of another. Having gifts that differ according to the grace given us, let us use them: if prophesy, in proportion to our faith; if service, in our serving; he who teaches, in his teaching; he who exhorts, in his exhortation; he who contributes, in liberality; he who gives aid, with zeal; he who does acts of mercy, with cheerfulness" (Romans 12:4-8).

What are your functions in the body of Christ? What are your gifts that you can use to help the rest of us? Which are the specific interpersonal ministries that you can best perform? The answers to these questions largely depend on the nature of the gifts God has created within you. Perhaps one of your functions within the body of Christ is counseling. If so, the personal characteristics presented here are important for you to develop. They represent the personality traits that are most important for being able to establish effective counseling relationships. Each is a healthy personality trait in itself. But their collective impact is invaluable for developing helping relationships.

Spiritual sensitivity and vibrance. The counselor who sincerely seeks contact with God may become more open to learning about himself or herself as a result of this search. Seeking the Holy Spirit's revelation of truth about ourselves can greatly increase our awareness of internal strengths, areas needing further growth, hidden pain and unresolved conflict. Practicing openness before the Lord can create greater vulnerability in our human relationships.

The Christian counselor recognizes God as his or her foundation. "The fear of the Lord is the beginning of wisdom, and the knowledge of the Holy One is insight" (Proverbs 9:10). Being a Christian does not give a counselor some mystical power for healing people's psychological brokenness. It does, however, bring him or her into conscious spiritual living. Being a Christian opens us to the possibility of living our lives at a higher level of personal integration. Spiritual and psychological energies can be focused together for more effective counseling.

Active interaction with God requires a lively movement between prayer and reading scripture. A dynamic prayer life includes praise, thankfulness, intercession, confession and supplication. But prayer without an adequate and growing life-related knowledge of the Bible is an incomplete process. We learn about God's identity, the characteristics of our created being and the nature of our relationship with him from scripture. "All scripture is inspired by God and is profitable for teaching, for reproof, for correction and for training in righteousness, that the man of God may be complete, equipped for every good work" (2 Timothy 3:16-17). The prophet Jeremiah reminds us of the pleasure that is ours through belonging to God and he calls our attention to the joy and nourishment we receive from digesting his words. "Thy words were found, and I ate them, and thy words became to me a joy and the delight of my heart; for I am called by thy name, O Lord, God of hosts" (Jeremiah 15:16).

Being a Christian does not guarantee being a good counselor. But being alive to spiritual reality within yourself can help you assist young counselees in their spiritual and psychological growth.

Humble spirit. Many university students select psychology as their major focus. Most of these psychology majors fall prey to an infectious and temporarily debilitating disease called "junior psychologistitis." Who was it that coined the well-worn phrase: "A little knowledge is dangerous"? Seldom is that phrase more true than in the study of counseling.

Another phrase is: "Knowledge is one form of power." Accurately learning how to read body language, understanding voice tone and intonations, and empathically hearing what a person is "really saying" can give a counselor a sense of power. Unfortunately, too many counselors thrive on this experience of power over others. Professionally trained therapists are not immune. But young lay counselors are particularly vulnerable to developing symptoms of "junior psychologistitis."

Most all youth workers and pastors experience periodic feelings of insecurity. "Is my ministry really changing people's lives?" "Do people respect me?" "Do they really like me or are they just being kind?" "Our group seems to be getting smaller. Maybe I'm losing touch." It is extremely important not to seek a position of power or control over counselees in order to stroke our hurting egos.

Procuring excessive dependence from counselees is another expression of a counselor's struggle for personal significance. Some counselors try to compare their "success rates" with others in order to affirm confidence in their skills. The temptation to break confidentiality in order to tell people's stories that are particularly exciting, arousing or unusual is of particular danger here. Insecure counselors feel more important when counselees confide material that is especially personal or unusual.

A humble spirit emanates from a psyche that is well-established, centered around the knowledge of who the counselor is and grounded in an enduring sense of internal strength. A humble spirit is not overly eager to give advice. The counselor supports the teenager's search for his or her own answers and direction. A humble spirit focuses the counseling around the thinking and feeling experience of the counselee. Little attention is centered on the skill, expertise or wisdom of the counselor.

The counselor with a humble spirit recognizes his or her own weaknesses, understands personal inadequacies and is well-acquainted with the need for continuing growth. The counselor identifies with a young counselee as a fellow human being, uniquely and wonderfully made by God. He or she recognizes that both have strengths and weaknesses, skills and inadequacies, love and anger. With a spirit of humility the effective counselor seeks and waits for an invitation to help. He or she recognizes that the only right to be in such an intimate place is by the request that comes from the counselee.

Emotional balance and integration. Often it is the teenagers' tumultuous, emotional reactions that lead them to seek counseling. They are on an internal roller coaster ride that is at times exhilarating and at other times terrifying. An anchor is needed. A point of reference. A place of stability that can be depended upon to hold fast against the swing of radical change. The counseling relationship might well be the teenagers' foothold in granite, refuge from the strong winds of their everchanging emotionality.

Counselors must be able to deal constructively with their own emotions in order to provide this place of stability. An accepting attitude, personal emotional control, and balanced integration of emotions are required characteristics of the effective counselor.

Acceptance. Empathic sensitivity to the counselee's expression of pain, sadness, sexual arousal or fear will bring emotional responses from within the counselor. These reactions are sometimes uncomfortable and even frightening. At times they surge up from within with a great force. Sometimes their subtlety causes us to miss their presence entirely.

Counseling is stopped cold if counselors cannot accept their own emotional responses to the counselees and the material they are sharing. Repression of the counselors' emotional responses blocks their awareness of the counselees' emotionality. Repression and denial lead therapists further away from understanding why they respond to the counselees the way they do. Counselors must be freely accepting of the full range of their emotional experiences. They must be able to readily admit, "I'm angry," "I feel so sad and empty," "I'm really turned on," "I'm greatly disappointed," "I feel awfully lonely," "I'm feeling very warm, tender and loving."

It is not the presence of an emotion that is good or bad. Rather it is what we do with the emotion that is righteous or unrighteous. Our actions are moral or immoral, not the presence of an emotion. Emotions, like the various parts of our anatomy, are simply the created parts of our humanity. My hands are neither moral nor immoral. By God's own declaration, they are "very good" (Genesis 1:31). God created our emotional selves and his same positive sanction applies to them as well.

Control. To openly experience an emotional response does not imply a spontaneous direct expression of it. Individuals who give uncontrolled vent to their feelings express immaturity, egocentricity and lack of love and respect for themselves and others.

Counseling requires effective control over one's emotions. To be in the relationship in a healing, nurturing posture is to be there primarily for the good of the counselee. It means sometimes not showing disgust, indignation or displeasure. It means not telling your counselee that you're sexually turned on. It may mean not telling the young person that you feel frightened for him or her. It means saying "no" to your immediate and spontaneous impulse in order to determine what expressions would be most appropriate for the situation.

Integrated action. After the counselor controls his or her spontaneous emotional reaction, the response that best fits the counseling goals must be chosen. John Powell presents a simple graph for integrating emotions, intellect and will.[6] It involves a three-step process.

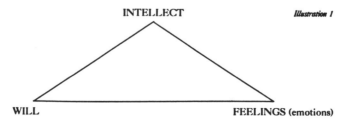

INTELLECT   *Illustration 1*

WILL   FEELINGS (emotions)

First, we must openly admit to ourselves the emotion we are feeling. *Second,* we should seek as full an understanding of the emotion as we can. "When have I felt this way before?" "What is it that I am reacting to?" "What have I done before when I felt this way?" "How did it work out last time?" Then we decide how to respond to our feeling. *Third,* we purposefully determine to carry out the decided-upon action.

Balanced personality characteristics. Everett Shostrom, a well-known psychologist, suggests that people possess essentially the same personality characteristics.[7] Individual differences are caused by the varying degrees of intensity with which these characteristics are exhibited. Two personality inventories which Dr. Shostrom has developed are the Personal Orientation Dimensions[8] and the Personal Orientation Inventory.[9] Both of these psychological instruments contain items that measure personality correlates on two bipolar scales: strength-weakness and love-anger. These scales are placed in an almost perpendicular juxtaposition with each other, overlaid so that their respective midpoints coincide.

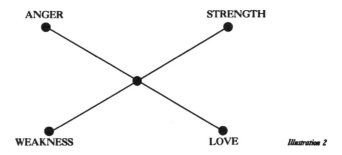

ANGER STRENGTH

WEAKNESS LOVE *Illustration 2*

This section of the instruments produces four scores, one each for anger, strength, love and weakness. The person's anger score indicates his or her openness to experience and willingness to appropriately express anger. The strength scale measures the individual's capacity for and expression of a sense of personal worth, competence or power. The degree to which a person can feel and express warmth, love and affection is measured by the love scale. The weakness scale indicates an individual's openness to experience and to express his or her human imperfection, vulnerability and inadequacies.

The person's scores are evaluated to determine if the respective personality characteristic is expressed with inadequate, sufficient or exaggerated intensity. The four scores are then compared in order to assess the degree of balance or imbalance within the individual's personality structure.

Dr. Shostrom suggests that healthy or self-actualizing people are able to express their feelings with appropriate intensity. Some people live their lives on the barren plain of emotional flatness. They are restricted in their ability both to give to and receive from others.

"For many people, this is a new idea. The middle (the golden mean) is generally agreed upon as the place to be. The 'middle of the road' metaphor is commonly used. Yet the poet Robert Frost complained that 'the middle of the road is where the white line is, and that's the worst place to drive.'

"The middle may be all right for a society, striking balances between competing feelings strongly held between various groups, but for an individual it becomes a place of indifference for canceling out of feelings. The middle becomes a natural hiding place for the uninvolved and the disinterested. If one feels, then one cares, and actualizing means involvement and caring. The actualizing person must be willing to express the natural extremes of feeling that come with involvement and interest in living."[10]

In order to respond adequately to the wide variety of situations that adolescent counselees present, their counselors must be able to respond out of anger, strength, weakness and love. Sometimes confrontation and an open expression of the counselors' anger is just what counselees need in order to take responsibility for their actions. Young counselees often need strength, leadership and assertiveness from counselors in order to increase their own self-confidence. At other times it is the counselors' expression of warmth, caring and support that encourages the counselees' much-needed self-acceptance. And sometimes it is the counselors' willingness to reveal their own incomplete knowledge or their own experiences with failure that help the young persons realize that they don't have to be perfect in order to be successful.

The effective counselor is able to perceive what is needed and is capable of giving a wide variety of counseling responses whenever the teenager requires them. His or her own internal psychic state is well-integrated so that the counselor is able to respond more to the counselee's needs than to his or her own feelings.

Hope and expectation for change. A widely held belief is that people have a greater chance of accomplishing their goals when they have a high level of faith that they will succeed. Students who believe in their academic skills have a better chance of making A grades than if they lack confidence. Athletes produce their best performances when feeling a positive or exaggerated evaluation of their abilities. When filled with self-doubt or fears, the athlete is his or her own worst enemy.

Research has produced some interesting indications regarding expectation for change and counseling success. One study investigated the relative effect of counselors' expectations and clients' expectations of change upon actual client change.[11] It was found that the counselors' expectations of client personality change had a relatively greater impact than the clients' expectations of their own change.

Many young people are discouraged and feel frightened or hopeless about their future. Nineteen-year-old Irene has suffered too much trauma in her young life. She was physically and emotionally abused as a young child, her parents have continued to be cruelly rejecting. She was raped, had an abortion, and has been married and divorced from a man who physically abused her. The outward expression of her rage toward the cruel world is blocked by her experience of impotence. The only remaining avenue to express her overwhelming anger is toward herself. Slicing her arms and legs with razor blades, overdosing on medication, depriving herself of food and sleep, and inducing infections in her body are weekly expressions of immense rage and frustration. She feels virtually no hope for the future. Often, it is only the therapist's hope, positive expectation for Irene's future and caring acceptance that forestalls her personal devastating attacks.

Though Irene's case is extreme, the principle is true for many. Permit your young counselees to see their future through your eyes of hope. Help them draw strength from your faith. They need you to have the courage to hope. They need to hear in your life the echo of David's proclamation, "But I will hope continually" (Psalms 71:14a).

Frank openness. Psychologists use the term "self-disclosure" when referring to the therapist's open and honest expression of his or her own thoughts and feelings toward the client. Teenagers need role models. They need to see how successful adults view life, solve problems, make decisions and build healthy relationships. The detached, nonresponsive and unemotional counselor is virtually useless as a role model.

In Christian terminology we're talking about confession—the outward expression of the inward experience. It is in this process of becoming open, real and honest with the counselee that the counselor may face his or her greatest feelings of threat. By dropping the guards of cold professionalism and quiet detachment, you are much more free to touch your young counselee where he or she is hurting. But you are also more open to the counselee's gaze and reaction. Suddenly your authoritative superiority has melted. The relationship is more reciprocal. Now you can be affected by your counselee's remarks and actions as he or she can be affected by yours. It comes as no surprise that psychological research has found that people with positive self-concepts tend to self-disclose more than people with poor self-concepts.[12]

Another researcher found that when interviewers shared openly about themselves, their subjects were more open with intimate, personal information.[13] This result was found to be even more powerful than when the interviewers specifically reinforced their subject's self-disclosing statements. Nothing seems to help a counselee share more fully than honest and open self-expressions from the counselor.

We can differentiate between two types of counselor self-disclosures:

1. The counselor can relate personal past events that he or she thinks might be helpful to the counselee. This type tends to be the least effective form of self-disclosure and should be used only rarely. It tends to transfer the focus from the counselee to the counselor. Overuse of this form of self-disclosure results in storytelling which is designed to stroke the counselor's ego more than help the counselee.

2. The counselor can confess or disclose his or her current feelings to the teenager. Young people care so very much about how others view them. Yet they seldom get the straight feedback from adults that they need. This is the most valuable form of self-disclosure because the primary focus is maintained on the counselee. The teenager gains an honest report of how an important person views and responds to him or her. And the counselee receives this otherwise hurtful message in a supportive atmosphere of love.

You may have already noticed that congruence and self-disclosure are similar yet different aspects of the counselor's responsiveness to his or her counselee. Congruence simply suggests that whatever the counselor is saying or doing on the outside is representative of what he or she is feeling or thinking on the inside. The counselor may or may not be telling the counselee something specific about his or her personal history, thoughts or feelings. Self-disclosure, on the other hand, is a specific verbal message that tells the other person something about the counselor—an experience he or she has had in the past, a current thought about what the counselee has just said, or a here-and-now feeling that he or she is experiencing toward the counselee.

Personal transcendence. The counselor who effectively helps teenagers grow and change is able to reach outside of himself or herself. The counselor is able to reach beyond the confines of his or her own identity and become emotionally responsive to the counselee. He or she identifies with the experience of the counselee to some degree. This quality of personal transcendence underlies the process of empathic understanding. Beyond this, it allows the counselor to become intimately involved in the young person's life so that the counselor's healthy personality can have a profound impact within the counselee's personality.

The word "transcendent" is defined as "exceeding usual limits . . . extending or lying beyond the limits of ordinary experience."[14] The transcendent counselor is able to move beyond the limits of his or her own usual experience, into the experiencing realm of the counselee.

Where could a clearer, more forceful picture of transcendent love be found than in the person of Jesus Christ? The four Gospel accounts of his life are filled with reports of his ability to reach outside of himself into the lives of spiritually, physically and psychologically sick people. And he did so with dramatic, healing impact.

Elizabeth Skoglund, a California marriage and family therapist, suggests the following insights: "The end result of the relationships Christ formed was usually a positive personality change in the people he knew. Nowhere is this shown more clearly than in the lives of the disciples with whom he was closest. They were, to start with, ordinary men . . . it is impossible to overemphasize the place of the spiritual in the changes of these men. The Bible clearly states that their lives were transformed by the power of God through the indwelling Holy Spirit. Yet it is also impossible to think that the formation of a close, trusting relationship with Jesus as he walked on this earth had no effect on the self-esteem of his disciples."[15]

Another effect of the transcendent quality of counseling is the degree of involvement that you are able to have with your counselees. The greater your capacity for transcendence, the deeper your involvement. There are several prerequisites for developing this life-changing capacity for transcendence. A high level of personality integration and resulting personal stability are important. When a relative sense of internal peace rather than conflict is present, there is more psychological energy that can be released to power the transcendence function. Being comfortable with your identity, feeling fulfilled in your family and social relationships, and experiencing satisfaction with the pace and direction of your own growth all release energy that can be expressed in transcendent love.

We have examined the fact that you are the primary ingredient in determining the degree of success that you will experience as a counselor. The quality of relationships that you develop with your young counselees will depend largely upon the presence and expression of certain characteristics in your personality.

In counseling it is the relationship that brings healing to suffering people. And so, along with psychologist Carl Rogers, we ask the question, "How can I create a helping relationship?"[16] To help us understand this larger question he asks 10 more specific queries:

1. Can I be perceived by the other person as trustworthy, dependable or consistent in some deep sense?

2. Can I be expressive enough as a person so that what I am will be communicated unambiguously?

3. Can I let myself experience positive attitudes toward this other person—attitudes of warmth, caring, liking, interest, respect?

4. Can I be strong enough as a person to be separate from the other?

5. Am I secure enough within myself to permit the counselee his or her separateness?

6. Can I let myself enter fully into the world of the counselee's feelings and personal meanings and see these as he or she does?

7. Can I be acceptant of each facet of this other person which he or she presents to me?

8. Can I act with sufficient sensitivity in the relationship that my behavior will not be perceived as a threat?

9. Can I free him or her from the threat of external evaluation?

10. Can I meet this other individual as a person who is in the process of becoming, or will I be bound by his or her past and by my past?

We seek to be healers. We seek to bring quiet to anguished hearts. We seek to bring peace to troubled relationships. We have begun.

Notes

1. Carl R. Rogers et al., *The Therapeutic Relationship and Its Impact* (Madison: University of Wisconsin Press, 1967).

2. Allen E. Bergin and Sol L. Garfield, *Handbook of Psychotherapy and Behavior Change: An Empirical Analysis* (New York: Wiley, 1971).

3. Rollo May, *The Art of Counseling* (Nashville: Abingdon, 1978), p. 81.

4. Paul Halmos, *The Faith of the Counsellors: A Study in the Theory and Practice of Social Case Work and Psychotherapy* (New York: Schocken Books, 1966).

5. Charles B. Truax and Robert Carkhuff, *Toward Effective Counseling and Psychotherapy: Training and Practice* (Hawthorne, N.Y.: Aldine Publishing, 1967), ch. 2.

6. John Powell, S.J., *Why Am I Afraid to Tell You Who I Am?* (Chicago: Argus Communications, 1969), pp. 72-73.

7. Everett Shostrom, *Freedom to Be* (New York: Bantam Books, 1972).

8. Everett Shostrom, *Personal Orientation Dimensions* (San Diego: EdITS, 1975).

9. Everett Shostrom, *Personal Orientation Inventory* (San Diego: EdITS, 1963).

10. Everett Shostrom, *Actualizing Assessment Battery: Interpretation Brochure* (San Diego: EdITS, 1975), p. 6.

11. Arnold P. Goldstein, "Therapist and Client Expectations of Personality Changes in Psychotherapy," Journal of Counseling Psychology 7 (Fall 1960):180-184.

12. Arnold Shapiro, "The Relationship Between Self-Concept and Self Disclosure," Dissertation Abstracts 29 (1968):1180-1181.

13. G. Keith Olson, "The Effects of Interviewer Self-Disclosing and Reinforcing Behavior Upon Subject Self-Disclosure" (Ph.D. dissertation, University of Arizona, 1972).

14. *Webster's Seventh New Collegiate Dictionary* (Springfield, Mass.: G. and C. Merriam, 1963).

15. Elizabeth Skoglund, *Can I Talk to You?* (Glendale, Calif.: Gospel Light Publications, 1977), p. 83.

16. Carl R. Rogers, *On Becoming a Person* (Boston: Houghton Mifflin, 1961), pp. 50-56.

PART I

Understanding Teenagers

◼ CHAPTER 1

Teenagers:
People in Transition

Before we can counsel a teenager, we must understand the psychology of adolescence. Otherwise the counseling is less effective and sometimes even destructive.

A musician performing before a teenage audience said something destructive that illustrates our need to understand young people. "A high school senior wrote a letter to me," the singer said. "In it he explained that he was the president of his school class, president of his church youth group and a success at whatever he attempted. He proclaimed himself to be a Christian and stated that everyone around him thought that he led an immensely successful, consistent Christian life. Let me read a couple lines of the letter: 'They don't see the aching emptiness and awful inconsistencies within me that make my life such a roller coaster experience. I'm nothing but a phony and I don't know how to be real.'

"I responded to that letter with, 'If your life goes up and down, on and off, is inconsistent, and if you're pretending to be one thing on the outside while being something else on the inside, then there is one thing you need to know: You're probably not really a Christian at all!' "

Though it is possible that the distraught young man who wrote the letter was not a Christian, it is at least as likely that he was simply struggling with normal adolescent internal conflicts. If the performer had better understood what it means to be a teenager, he would have responded entirely differently to his young audience.

Effective counseling requires more than a loving desire to help. Positive motivation must be paired with an adequate understanding of the young people whom we seek to serve. Without this deeper level of understanding, our finest intentions can create worse problems and more confusion. Our young letter writer may have gone away feeling less affirmed, experiencing greater self-doubt and wondering why he has to repeatedly accept Christ into his life when the Bible says that once is enough.

One of the healing aspects of the counseling process is that the counselee feels intimately known and fully accepted by the counselor. To know a teenager, one must have some knowledge of teenage psychology.

The adolescent years have long been considered as an age marked by change, transition and tumult. Early American psychologist G. Stanley Hall wrote in 1904 that adolescence is a time in life characterized by "storm and stress."[1] This chapter presents a developmental perspective on the physiological and psychological changes common to most teenagers. These changes produce the erratic behavior patterns that often cause focused and apprehensive concern from adults.

Defining Our Perspective

What is meant by the term "developmental perspective"? The phrase essentially connotes a view of life that appreciates the meaningful interrelatedness of the past, present and future. It is a "longitudinal view of human behavior" that seeks to understand our life experience as a progressive movement.[2]

Development normally proceeds in the direction of actualizing or fulfilling the created potential. Under healthy conditions the teenager will move naturally toward developing spiritual, psychological, physical and interpersonal areas of living to his or her full potential.

Development usually proceeds in an orderly fashion and is therefore generally predictable. Growth rate is uneven, marked by plateaus, spurts and regressions. Knowledge of the overall pattern of human development helps the counselor to anticipate a teenager's next step in his or her development.

Development is seen as a progression through different stages. Each developmental stage is characterized by certain tasks that must be accomplished. Each life stage from conception to death brings with it a new set of problems and challenges. The specific developmental tasks of adolescence will be discussed later in this chapter.

Effective accomplishment of any particular developmental task depends upon the quality of previous developmental work, and in turn provides the foundation for future growth. Growth is marked more by continuity than by segmentation. As the tasks of one developmental stage are being completed, the person begins to work on the tasks of the next stage. Failure to successfully solve the challenges of any one stage of development will seriously impede future growth.

Developmental changes and stagnation in any one sphere of the person's life will impact the growth process in every other sphere of the individual's life. There is an interdependency between each sector of a person's life. For example, the teenager who does not reach puberty until age 17 will be seriously hampered in social development as well. On the other hand, the girl who develops a sexually attractive physique at age nine may have to struggle with sex-oriented attention from men and boys before she is psychologically able to deal with this kind of interpersonal interaction.

There are both shared characteristics and differences between the developmental experiences that people go through. We all proceed through the same stages in the same order. But the rate and timing of growth, the particular patterns of change, and the outcomes of development vary widely between people.

The development from conception to maturity is characterized by a movement toward increasing differentiation, integration and complexity. The older adolescent is capable of a greater variety of responses in different kinds of interpersonal situations than is the shy, self-conscious junior higher who tends to act the same embarrassed way around everyone.

The older teenager is also usually more coordinated, physically poised, and comfortable with his or her sense of identity that integrates his or her spiritual, physical, intellectual and emotional aspects. Finally, this growing integration of the differentiated parts allows for the staggering complexity in mature adult functioning. It is this complexity that allows us to be capable (though we may question our capability) of the task for which we were created. "And God blessed them, and God said to them, 'Be fruitful and multiply, and fill the earth and subdue it; and have dominion over the fish of the sea and over the birds of the air and over every living thing that moves upon the earth.' And God said, 'Behold, I have given you every plant yielding seed which is upon the face of all the earth, and every tree with seed in its fruit; you shall have them for food. And to every beast of the earth, and to every bird of the air, and to everything that creeps on the earth, everything that has the breath of life, I have given every green plant for food.' And it was so" (Genesis 1:28-30).

It is this complexity that allows us to appreciate the infinite grandness and complexity of the One in whose image we are crafted. "So God created man in his own image, in the image of God he created him; male and female he created them" (Genesis 1:27).

Now the question arises, "When is a person an adolescent?" Like most significant questions, there is not an easy or simple answer. There are three ways of defining the adolescent stage of development.[3] First, by using physical developmental changes, adolescence starts with the puberty-related growth spurt and appearance of primary and secondary sex characteristics, and ends with the completion of the major physical growth changes. A second way of defining adolescence is to assign a specific age span, for example, ages 11-19. The third definition uses socio-cultural concepts like the transition from child roles to adult roles and status.

It is acceptable to use some combination of these three approaches to define adolescence.[4] This flexibility is important as we counsel with teenagers. We need to understand their psychological, intellectual, emotional and sociocultural dynamics that identify them as people working through the adolescent process.

Our task in defining and understanding adolescence is even more difficult as we seek to appreciate the wide range of maturity represented by the attitudes, behaviors and thinking patterns exhibited by adolescents.

Let's take a look at 12-year-old Johnny B. His body is just beginning to experience the growth spurt, signaling the onset of puberty. He occasionally sleeps with his favorite stuffed animal and enjoys the physical warmth and emotional security of cuddling close to his mother when no one else is nearby. He is shy in groups, does not know quite how to respond to adults who speak to him, and passes through several hours each day in his own fantasy world, alternating between gallant hero and rescued victim. Young Johnny is an adolescent.

Now, let's get acquainted with 19-year-old Deborah, a young woman who in form, poise and overall appearance could be accepted easily as a woman in her mid-20s. Deborah has adjusted to her parents' divorce. She has graduated from high school and is completing her first year at a state university. Her major is biology and she is making good progress toward her long-term goal of becoming a physician. She lives in her own apartment, works part time and has received a partial scholarship for tuition. Though Deborah has been sexually active in the past, she is now trying to pace the sexual expression of her love for her boyfriend in a manner that is consistent with her Christian moral code. Deborah is also an adolescent.

Dividing the adolescent developmental stage into three stages or phases helps to clarify the widely divergent maturity levels exhibited by adolescents.[5] The three phases help us to understand the characteristics exhibited by young people as they grow through this difficult transition period.[6]

Early adolescence. This stage begins with the physiological changes that alter hormonal functioning and related psychological changes. This period begins just prior to onset of puberty and lasts usually 18 to 24 months. During this time the young person is becoming far more motivated by peer pressure than by parental pressure. While girls experience menarche (onset of menses), boys experience their first ejaculations and a sharp increase in the frequency of erections. Both boys and girls develop secondary sex characteristics including increase in body hair, growth and breast development. Clumsiness is typical of this age and is caused by the rapid growth spurt prior to and at the time of puberty.

Mid-adolescence. This stage is characterized by additional physical and sexual development and is accompanied, especially in boys, by an increasing sexual desire and responsiveness to sexual stimuli. During this phase there is a decreased interest in same-sex peer groups and an increased focus upon building friendships and dating relationships with members of the opposite sex. Movement away from parental influence is facilitated by adhering to the norms and values of groups and organizations that are on the parents' non-approval list.

Late adolescence. This stage marks the transition into early adulthood. Major physical growth and sex changes have been accomplished and the young person is feeling more comfortable living within his or her "new" body. Energies are now being focused on future issues. "What vocational commitments and what relationship commitments should I be making?" "Does my future look promising and secure enough to really burn my bridges behind me?" These are the questions of the late adolescent.

Now go back earlier in this chapter and read again the descriptions of 12-year-old Johnny and 19-year-old Deborah. Now we can understand why both are adolescents even though they are very different from each other.

Major Changes in the Body

The adolescent developmental stage is commonly thought to begin with the onset of puberty. Because the physiological changes during this stage have such a dramatic effect on the teenager's self-concept and behavior it is important for us to have a solid understanding of the physiology of adolescence.

Pubescence begins with a complex series of changes in the rate of production and secretion of several hormones. Accompanying these changes is an altered sensitivity to hormones in various target organs.[7] These two interacting sets of altered physical functions set the stage for all of the physical, emotional and interpersonal changes that we call "adolescence."

The first observable anatomical changes in boys at puberty are growth of testicles and slight growth of the penis. In girls, puberty is heralded by the onset of menarche, appearance of pubic hair and development of breast buds. As puberty continues, the boy's penis continues to grow, pubic hair develops followed by axillary hair, facial hair and sweat gland development. His voice deepens, his height increases rapidly and he increases dramatically in muscular strength. As a girl continues through puberty, her breasts continue developing, the shape and curvature of the pelvis and hips change, vaginal tissues develop and begin secretions, a physical growth spurt is realized, pubic hair develops further, axillary hair appears and sweat gland activity increases.

Primary sexual characteristics of puberty are those that affect reproductive capability. Boys begin producing spermatozoa and the first ejaculation occurs. However, the first ejaculations may contain few or no live mature spermatozoa. In girls, menarche indicates maturing ovarian functioning. However, the first 12 to 18 months of menstrual cycles may be anovulatory (no ovum is released) so that the girl can be infertile for some time following onset of menses.[8]

Secondary sexual characteristics include all of those puberty-related physical changes that do not affect fertility. Pubic and axial hair growth, increased sweat gland activity, growth spurts, weight gain and increases in physical strength, are all secondary sexual changes that both boys and girls experience. Boys also develop facial hair and a voice change. It should be noted that about one-third of boys also experience some breast enlargement during mid-pubescence that can last from about 12 to 18 months.[9]

People who work with junior and senior high school youth are involved in an arena of human development that is at the same time fascinating and confusing. An apparent disarray of physical growth spurts, regressions to childhood behavior, mature rational thinking, moodiness and depression, sexually mature bodies and childlike innocence provide a continually changing and always challenging environment. Much of the confusion about these years of rapid change can be alleviated by an awareness of how boys and girls mature differently from each other.

Onset of menarche usually occurs between the ages of 10 and 16½, with the highest frequency at about age 13. The average age that menses begins in Western civilization seems to be lowering by about four months every decade.[10] The earliest stage of puberty (pubescence) usually begins at about age 10 in girls and at about age 11 in boys.[11] The average girl of nine to 13 years is taller than her male counterpart of the same age. This is the only age that girls are taller than boys (and this causes some of the awkwardness between the sexes).

Boys' physical strength doubles between the ages of 12 and 16 and continues to increase through early adulthood.[12] Girls, however, experience the greatest increase in strength at menarche and reach their maximum level of muscular strength during late adolescence. Girls' superiority over boys in physical strength, then, is very short lived.

The Adolescent's Developmental Tasks

Central to the developmental perspective of human growth is the belief that each life stage requires the successful completion of one or more developmental tasks.[13] Teenagers' behavior often appears to have no understandable goal or meaning. Why is it sometimes so difficult to get them to quiet down before a youth meeting? Why is it so hard for them to see beyond their own needs? Why do they sometimes refuse to have anything to do with adults? Why are they so inseparable from their friends? Why do they get so depressed when things don't work out well for them?

As you think of the teenagers that you know and perhaps work with, consider their actions in light of the developmental tasks which are theirs to accomplish. There are essentially three psychological tasks that today's teenagers need to accomplish:

1. To develop a sense of personal identity that consistently establishes who he or she is as an integrated individual throughout each life role, separate and different from every other person.

2. To begin the process of establishing relationships that are charac-

terized by commitment and intimacy.

3. To begin making decisions leading toward training and entry into a particular occupation.

It is understandable that adolescence is important in the process of developing into adulthood. So much of what an adult accomplishes or fails to accomplish is determined by successful completion of these adolescent tasks. Those who work most successfully with teenagers understand how teenagers' behavior is meaningfully related to their attempts to accomplish these goals.

Identity development. If adolescence is of pivotal importance to developing into healthy adults, then identity development is just as central a prerequisite for accomplishing the other two adolescent developmental tasks.

Perhaps the first component in establishing identity is really a carry-over function from childhood. Identity formation requires a *self-ideal* to strive toward. Elementary-aged children are great hero worshipers. Ask them the name of their city's first-string quarterback. They'll probably not only tell you his name, but be able to rattle off his statistics, too. They know the names of child actors and actresses on television. And watch Saturday morning cartoons. Now *there* is rich food for hungry little hero worshipers.

Pubescent young people and early to mid-adolescent teenagers bring more maturity to this theme of hero worshiping. The content changes from Superman or Wonderwoman to a current rock star, movie star or athlete. For some, the focus may be on a favorite teacher, pastor or even a scientist. As the teenager matures, the idealized object and the young person become more similar to each other. Idealized symbols that represent more attainable characteristics begin to be selected. The teenager also tries to become more like his or her idealized model.

In addition to hero worship, the maturing adolescent begins to develop a collection of desirable traits to emulate. This more sophisticated self-ideal development requires a capacity for higher levels of abstractions. The self-ideal then becomes more personally identified rather than embodied in the image of another person. The young person concentrates on the question, "Who or what do I wish to be in life?"

The second aspect of identity that we will consider is the *self-concept*. This is the person's perception of what he or she is really like. In this aspect of identity formation, the adolescents leave the glamorous halls of fantasied ideals and bump, often painfully, into their perception of the reality of who they are. The word "perception" is extremely important in this discussion, because the only "real self" that the teenager (or any of us) knows is the perception of his or her real self.

Adolescence, particularly the early and middle phases, is an extremely egocentric period in life. Young persons' focus is heavily placed on themselves. "How do I look?" "Will they like me?" "Am I too pushy?" "Will they think I'm stuck up?" Endless streams of self-focused questions flow through their minds, mostly relating to how their peers will perceive and respond to them. This egocentricity, though it appears to be quite the opposite of Christianity's emphasis on loving and valuing others, is really a very important step in the process of developing a stable sense of identity. This intense surge of egocentric energy enables the young teenager to establish a clearer, more stable concept of who he or she really is.

However, by the very nature of their egocentricism, teenagers tend to block out much of the potentially helpful feedback that is offered to them. Responses from adults, particularly parents, are especially subject to being discounted as irrelevant and meaningless. As a result, the teenager is left swimming in rather confused circles of thoughts, feelings and fears. All too often the growing self-concept becomes increasingly divergent from reality as it becomes clearer and more defined. One of the most vivid examples of this dynamic is the tragic picture of the anorexic's inaccurate yet unwavering perception that her (most anorexics are female) unhealthy, frail starved body is repulsively fat.

Inaccuracy can occur in either the direction of underrating or overrating the self. Virtually all teenagers experience painful times of focused attention on their self-perceived ugliness, awkwardness, stupidity, immaturity, sinfulness and unacceptability. These ruminations typically represent an exaggerated concentration on one or more personal imperfections. The overreaction is powered by the youth's fear that a blemish is certain to bring ruin and tragedy, probably in the form of being alienated from peers.

Overestimations and grandiosity in the self-concept emanate from the same pool of feared doom that produces the self-depreciating thoughts which have been discussed. Grandiose perceptions of one's intelligence, physical attractiveness, sexual appeal, popularity, physical strength, spiritual excellence and financial future are overcompensations for the fears harbored secretly inside. The need to convince others of personal greatness is both tool and byproduct in the process of trying to convince the self to believe in that same greatness. Self-concept, then, whether accurate, overrated or underestimated, answers the question, "Who am I and what am I really like?"

The third aspect of identity results from an interaction of the first two. While self-concept refers to what the person thinks he or she is really like, *self-evaluation* involves the judgments and emotional reactions to these self-related thoughts. Psychological testing with teenagers indicates that their self-evaluations are typically more negative when there exists a greater gap between this self-ideal and self-concept. When the gap seems too wide to cross, the teenager will often turn away from life in despair and discouragement, make flailing, ineffective attempts to grow, feel incompetent and worthless, reach outwardly in rebellious aggression at the world that allows such pain to exist, or repress his or her personal pain and fear and overcompensate in other ways.

This gap between the self-concept and self-ideal can be caused by either unrealistically high expectations and demands for the self or by an inaccurately low perception of the self. Counseling with a teenager who is suffering from a painfully negative self-evaluation can involve therapeutic downward adjustment of the youth's self-ideal and upward adjustment of the self-concept. The specific counseling decision will be determined by the location of the problem. The counselor needs to understand both the real and ideal self-perceptions and determine which is most inaccurate and which shows least resistance to movement. The teenager's self-evaluation answers the question, "What judgments do I place on myself and how do I feel about being me?"

A fourth element in the teenager's identity can be labeled *self-control* or *self-power*. When Tim was born, he was totally dependent on his parents. He couldn't sustain his own life. He had to be fed, bathed, diapered, cleaned and rediapered, clothed for warmth, positioned for sleep and held for physical contact in order to stay alive and grow. As he progressed through childhood, he became less dependent on external sources and took over more self-sustaining functions himself. Now, at age 15, Tim is capable of feeding himself, choosing his friends, earning some of his own money, arranging for his own transportation, and developing an intimate relationship with a girl. He will soon be transporting himself and friends in his own vehicle, living away from his parents, training for and entering his own occupation, and establishing his own separate family unit.

Adolescence is a time for dramatic movement of the focus of power and control from external sources (like parents and teachers) to the internal domain of the young person. How the teenager accepts and begins to experiment with this increasing power depends on the interaction of several factors, including physiological pace of maturation, parents' attitudes and parenting style, quality of family relationships, cultural background and expectations, peer group activities and expectations, and the nature of his or her self-evaluation. Successful adolescent development requires that the teenager accept responsibility for this increasing personal power. The teenager learns how to use this power constructively through experimentation. Inadequate development in this aspect of identity formation can result in either overly dependent or excessively authoritarian behavior in adulthood. Self-power or self-control then answers the question, "What decisions can I actually make and implement about my life and my future and how much can I really control in my environment?"

A fifth and final element of identity is somewhat broader and more philosophical in scope. *Self-valuation* involves the teenager's beliefs about the value of being human. The teenager who struggles alone without adequate guidance for a sense of significance and meaning can quite easily become disillusioned about the value of being alive. Materialistic reductionism teaches that human life holds no value different from any other form of life on earth. We are, according to this teaching, at one with and a part of all matter and that our concepts of mind and spirituality are simple illusory productions of materialistic functions. With such teaching, it is difficult for a teenager to experience and respond to a teleological pull toward greatness and significance.

Spiritualistic reductionism holds just as much danger as its materialistic counterpart. Adolescent idealism can be dangerously excited by overemphasizing the spiritual aspects of life and downplaying the material or physical part of life. Remember that God created all of life and judged all of it as good. "And God saw everything that he had made, and behold, it was very good" (Genesis 1:31a). Teenagers struggling with their rapidly changing bodies, emerging sexuality, moodiness, frightening impulses, and changing interpersonal relationship patterns can find an all-too-inviting escape from these important developmental issues in an overly spiritualized presentation of reality.

Spiritual reductionism can lead to the same sense of self-depreciation as materialistic reductionism by implying that the body and mind are at least worthless if not absolutely evil. Teenagers are especially vulnerable because of their tendency toward idealism as a defensive maneuver against rising anxiety about internal physiological and psychological changes.

Self-valuation answers the question, "What, if any, is the value of being alive as a human?" Developing an adequate sense of identity is an extremely complex process. Failure to accomplish a consistent, unified, and growing sense of identity results in role diffusion and sometimes identity panic. Older adolescents and young adults are sometimes unable to find any identifying links between their roles in life. There is no sense of self, no sense of personal integration that meaningfully pulls together all of their different functions into a form that they can identify with their name. The anxiety from this awareness can reach panic proportions, overwhelming the person with confusion, desperation and disturbed contact with reality. Working with teenagers enables adults to assist young people in their identity formation.

Establishing intimate relationships. Much attention, often humorous, has been attracted to the arena of adolescent relationships. Chart the sociometric history of almost any group of teenagers. Watch their interaction patterns, to whom they draw closer and from whom they distance themselves. Monitor the varying levels of intensity found in their relationships and then try to predict their future relationship patterns. You will notice a continually changing and fluctuating array of pairings, groupings and separations.

This inconsistency in interpersonal relationship patterns is largely due to teenagers' struggle toward identity. Being intimate with another is defined as establishing a relationship "marked by a warm friendship developing through long association."[14] The continuous personal change and adjustment that characterizes teenagers' lives makes the establishment of "long associations" a very elusive goal. Without these long-term relationships, intimacy is a difficult goal to realize. Yet intimacy is an important task that adolescents must strive to accomplish.

During early adolescence the most significant movement is from parents and family to peers as the reference group. This movement is of vital importance because the young person begins looking primarily toward peers for feeling accepted, for confirmation of personal okayness and for agreement concerning values, beliefs, ideas and feelings. This transition is made primarily to groups of peers rather than to individual peers. Part of this transition is a movement away from authority represented primarily by parents, parent figures, teachers and sometimes church youth workers. The youth's allegiance to authority is really being transferred from these individuals to his or her group. Unfortunately, then, authority is composed of others, like the young person, who are involved in a rather confused quest for identity.

One of the important benefits that an adolescent peer group offers is the opportunity to establish long-term individual contacts with one or more of its members. The more significant relationships that a teenager develops often evolve from his or her group interactions. The primary motivation for a young person to attend school activities is probably not academic, nor is the typical teenager involved in a church youth group for primarily spiritual reasons. Adults who are sensitive to the primacy of social interest can integrate that drive with the spiritual, academic and other values that the group represents.

As the teenager progresses through mid-adolescence and into late adolescence, increased energy is focused on developing significant relationships with same-sex "buddies" and romantic relationships with opposite-sex peers. Less time and energy is invested into the group and more emphasis is placed on being alone with the significant other person. Often these relationships will endure for many years, impacting the person's life throughout adulthood. When young people fail to establish significant relationships with other individuals, they tend to become increasingly dependent on their group for a sense of belonging and identity. Overidentification with the group can become a hiding place and a regressive withdrawal from the anxiety generated from feeling left out and unwanted.[15]

A common misconception is that teenagers need relationships only with peers. They also need to have stable relationships with adults during the mid-adolescent phase.[16] These important relationships provide a secure emotional anchor during a time of rapid transition and tumultuous growth. The adult, along with his or her values and morals, may be held at a suspicious distance. But the teenager feels more secure and experiences less trauma and disruption knowing that the caring adult is there.

The teenager who fails to establish adequate membership in one or more peer groups and who fails to develop significant relationships with at least one friend will suffer feelings of isolation and alienation. His or her developmental failure is often the cause for depression, anxiety symptoms, aggressive acting-out behavior and delinquent reactions. Adjustment into adulthood will be severely hampered until the ability to establish meaningful relationships with increasing intimacy is accomplished.

Making career choices. A third developmental task facing adolescents is to make progress toward the selection of an occupation. Economic level, cultural heritage, available adult role models, and real opportunities for education and training create very different environments in which teenagers confront the task of selecting occupational orientations. A full analysis of these factors' impact is beyond our current focus. Our task here is to understand the psychological issues confronting a typical teenager in relation to selecting an occupation.

Researchers who study the development of vocational choice understand that the process of choosing a career begins in childhood and proceeds throughout life. One group of researchers describes this process as occurring in three stages.[17]

1. Fantasy period. Most children relate to occupational choice from this initial orientation until about age 11. During this time the child assumes that he or she can become anything. There is no reality testing of occupational choices according to intellectual and personal qualifications, realistic opportunities, or educational and training requirements. Children try out occupations in their play as they identify with their parents, adult friends, and role models from television and the movies.

2. Tentative period. This stage, lasting from about age 11 to 17, is the first time that the young person realizes that he or she will actually have to make a future decision about selecting an occupational direction. This stage essentially covers early and mid-adolescence. During this time young people begin to assess their own interests, values and abilities. As this stage progresses they begin to assess seriously their intellectual capabilities, academic success and training opportunities in relationship to occupational choices.

3. Realistic choice stage. Adolescents reach this stage of occupational development at about the same time that mid-adolescence is giving way to late adolescence. This is the time that self-evaluation and awareness of the occupational world must come together in specific choices about work. Unrealistic dreams clash with realities of pay, living standards, college entrance requirements and job availability. This stage involves three processes: *exploration*, or the acquisition of information about job possibilities and work experiences; *crystallization*, or the narrowing of alternatives as movement is made toward a career choice; and *specification*, or pairing commitment with decision to pursue a particular occupational choice.

Adolescent Sexuality

When Susan was 10 years old, she enjoyed playing with dolls, jumping rope and climbing trees. Her little pre-puberty body was slim and lithe, giving no hint to the sexual revolution about to erupt. By age 12, she was having periods that were beginning to approximate a monthly cycle and her breast development had significantly altered her shape. Some of her girlfriends envied and complimented her on her shape, while others displayed obvious jealousy. Boys began responding to her differently, some teasing, and some boys (as well as some men) showing her obvious sexual interest.

Between the ages of 14 and 18, Susan's figure developed fully to that of a sexually mature woman. Most of her interests, activities and concerns centered around ways to be attractive to boys and her desire to be loved by a boy. Her desire to be loved led her through several relationships with boys. Each relationship was different. Some were just friendships while others developed into passionately sexual, romantic involvements. In just a few years Susan grew from being an apparently asexual little girl to being a fully sexual young woman.

The teenager's sexual development is initiated and impacted by biological changes, peer pressures, family influences and religious convictions. Girls have to adapt to the onset of menarche. Pain, cramping and discomfort need to be accepted by many as normally occurring events in their lives for many years to come. Body image changes need to be made in order to incorporate sexually maturing form and new body sensations. Girls also must learn to cope with changes in emotions as menstrual cycles become more regular.[18] During the first two weeks of the cycle, estrogen predominates and females are apt to feel very loving toward others. During the next two weeks, progesterone predominates and they will tend to feel quite insecure, requiring reassurances of others' love. Then, just prior to the start of menses, they are apt to feel depressed, irritable, moody and withdrawn from social contact.

For boys, the onset of puberty brings an intense rise in sensitivity to sexual stimulation. He experiences erections throughout his teenage years in response to very little physical or mental stimulation, and at very inappropriate and embarrassing times. Androgen production reaches its peak level during the late teens and the sex drive will probably never again be as strong as it is at this age for the boy.

Middle- and upper-class boys usually accept masturbation as an acceptable way to achieve orgastic relief in addition to nocturnal emissions and sexual intercourse with girls. A less accepted but fairly common release is through homosexual experimentation. Lower-class and blue-collar-class boys are more likely to view masturbation as unmasculine. The ability to sexually possess a girl is viewed by lower-class boys as a sign of their manhood and any alternative means for sexual release is shunned.

While boys typically view sexual gratification and love as separate experiences, girls tend to see them as meaningfully related. For boys, sex represents sought-after pleasure, experimentation with manhood affirmation of masculinity. Girls usually associate sexual activity with giving or receiving love, feeling valued or being assured of her attractiveness.

Teenage boys and girls experience tremendous peer pressure to become sexually active. This external pressure mixed with media saturation of sexually focused messages presents a tremendously difficult task for teenagers who seek to keep their sexual expression in line with their Christian values and moral code. Because peer group influence is so great it is advantageous for young people to be involved with groups that reinforce the values of reserving genital sexual involvement for the marriage relationship. Parental and church influence can sometimes be best exerted by encouraging participation in such groups.

Anthropologist Ashley Montagu refers to "sexual responsibility" as a moral involvement in the life of the other person who is a possible sexual partner.[19] Another researcher Elizabeth Hurlock suggests that when people attain psychosexual maturity, they are able to make adequate heterosexual adjustments, possess healthy attitudes toward sex, form appropriate relations with members of their own sex, and have a healthy identification with their own sex role.[20]

Adolescent Emotional Development

The emotional world of the adolescent is typically fast and intense. Remember that adolescence is a period of transition. A prevailing characteristic of change, whether psychological, spiritual or chemical, is instability. When something is going through a transition it is less structured internally. A less powerful stimulus will trigger a more intense reaction. What a description of adolescence!

6:30 a.m. - Bonnie wakes up reluctantly, dreading this day that she is absolutely positive will be awful.

6:50 a.m. - She is elated because she can still fit into her favorite dress. She'll wear it to school.

7:00 a.m. - She is upset because her hair will not curl properly. She knows she will feel humiliated when the other kids see her.

7:30 a.m. - She is both thrilled and apprehensive because Jeff called, asking to drive her to school that day.

7:50 a.m. - Pride, even arrogance, is what she feels as her friends see her driving into the school parking lot, snuggled close to Jeff.

7:55 a.m. - She feels indignant and angry as she sees her friends walk off to class ahead of her after making a snippy remark about her special transportation.

In just 90 minutes Bonnie experienced intense feelings of reluctance, dread, elation, upset, humiliation, thrill, apprehension, pride, arrogance, indignance and anger. Girls are especially prone to experience more intense emotional reactions because of cultural and social influences that encourage girls to express their feelings. Cultural influences discourage emotional expression in boys.[21] This effect is often compounded by the hormonal changes that occur along with the menstrual cycle.

Increased emotional reactions are experienced by boys and girls because they are learning to cope with new roles, new relationships, new expectations and new responsibilities. All of these challenges are encountered at a time when some of the old comfortable supports have been left behind. It is not quite as okay to go to mom and dad for help.

The most common negative emotions or feelings that teenagers experience are anger, apathy, boredom, sadness, depression, guilt, fear and anxiety.[22] An important note here is that these emotions are labeled "negative" not because they are bad. Emotions are amoral and therefore should not be labeled as evil or righteous. Rather, they exist as a part of our human experience. It is only our response to a given emotion that is morally good or morally bad. The emotions listed above are negative only because they are unhappy, difficult or unpleasant to experience. They are the emotional reactions that have the highest probability of causing distress in the teenager's life. A more in-depth discussion of the nature, causes, and recommended counseling approach for these emotional reactions will be presented later.

Intellectual Development

Up to this point our attention has been focused on the biological, emotional and relational changes that characterize adolescent growth. There are intellectual changes, too. During the childhood years thinking is tied to the manipulation of concrete facts and observations. Around 11 or 12 years of age, young people move from this concrete operational period into the beginnings of abstract thinking and formal reasoning or propositional thinking. The young adolescent can think in "if . . . then" patterns. The maturing teenager becomes more adept at imagining alternatives, anticipating consequences of the possible choices, and systematically reasoning his or her way through complex problem-solving and decision-making tasks. Some researchers have found that intellectual growth reaches its highest potential during mid- to late adolescence though others believe that certain aspects of intelligence continue to develop into later years.[23]

It has been proposed that developing the capacity for abstract thought is a major developmental task for young adolescents.[24] Their ability to reason, predict and plan ahead certainly affects their academic performance, vocational decisions, relationships with parents and most of the other tasks of this life phase.[25]

Young adolescents' abstract thinking abilities enable them to imagine ideal possibilities and to compare the reality around them to these fantasized states of perfection. The result is often criticism of parents, church, society and friends. This process helps the teenagers' development by: assisting the process of separating from parents and other authority; helping them become increasingly independent; sharpening their thoughts and ideas about the personal qualities they do and do not wish to develop; and allowing them the opportunity to try out new ideas while still in a safe environment.[26]

This critical attitude is not reserved only for those surrounding the teenager. They tend also to perceive themselves in a very critical manner. This ability to focus on themselves gives rise to a form of egocentricism characteristic of adolescence.[27] They can conceptualize their own thoughts and also anticipate what others are thinking. They tend to believe that others are thinking the same thing that they are. Since teenagers' focus is so often centered on themselves, they usually assume that others' attention is focused on them, too. When young persons feel good about their looks, poise or some performance, they tend to believe that others also are pleased with them. But when there is self-doubt or self-criticism, they are absolutely sure that others view them with the same degree of negativity. This self-focus brings much of the embarrassment so common to early and mid-adolescence. The older adolescent increases in his or her ability to differentiate between self-perceptions and others' thoughts and perceptions. This process opens the way for more mature relationships that can allow for mutual individuality without excessive projection of one person's identity upon the other.

Values and Moral Development

A reading of the previous section on intellectual development suggests similar direction in teenagers' moral development. Piaget formulated that there are two stages of moral development in childhood with an intermediate third stage.[28] He described the direction of this movement from a rigid sense of justice toward a more flexible concern for appropriate standards in light of relevant circumstances.

Building on this foundational work, Kohlberg hypothesized that there are three levels of moral development, each of which contains two stages.[29]

Level I: Preconventional or Premoral

Stage 1: Response to cultural labels of good and bad with focus on unquestioning obedience to authority and automatic punishment for disobedience.

Stage 2: Market place morality in which doing right consists of meeting one's own needs and sometimes the needs of others. Reciprocity means only "scratching each other's back."

Level II: Conventional or Role-Conformity Morality

Stage 3: The "good boy—good girl" orientation in which good behavior is that which helps others and gains their approval. Behavior is judged by its intentions rather than solely by its consequences.

Stage 4: The law and order orientation with strong respect for authority. A sense of personal investment exists in maintaining law and order.

Level III: Postconventional or Self-Accepted Morality

Stage 5: Social-contract orientation in which laws are recognized values. Personal opinions and values are also respected. Law is emphasized and the possibility of changing the law for the social good is also realized.

Stage 6: Self-adopted abstract ethical principles that are not behavioral prescriptions enforced by society, but are rather universal, abstract principles like the golden rule.

Many early teenagers have developed to the conventional or role-conformity level of moral functioning.[30] They, like Charlie Brown, are very interested in being nice to others and are as concerned about others liking them. Stage 4 adolescents still consider law to be unchangeable but do feel a need to do their part to maintain social order out of a sense of duty to society. Some (but certainly not all) late adolescents reach the Stage 5 level of moral reasoning. These young people believe that breaking a law is justified if they think that the law is unjust and if they anticipate that breaking the law will help to change it.

The table reprinted below presents what Level I, II and III people believe about definitions of right and wrong, intentions, justice, the value of persons, the stimulus to right action and their ability to take another person's perspective. Most younger adolescents are functioning in the range between Level I and Level II, while older adolescents will typically display Level II or Level III moral functioning. It is also important to note that an individual's moral judgment and moral behavior will probably represent more than just one stage at any one time. However, one stage will probably be more predominant than the others.[30]

	LEVEL I	LEVEL II	LEVEL III
SOURCE OF AUTHORITY	*Self-interest*	*External standards —models and rules*	*Internal principles*
Definitions	Right is what adults command or what brings reward.	Right is what good people do or what the law says one should do.	Right is living our moral principles and being just.
	Wrong is what I am punished for—what brings pain.	Wrong is what good people do not do or what the law says one should not do.	Wrong is violating a moral principle and being unjust.
Intentions	Oblivious to intentions	Make allowances for intentions. Lenience tempered by sense of duty.	Consider intentions but also concerned about justice.
Justice	What adults command. Later, equal treatment.	Defined by society.	Equal consideration for all.
Value of Persons	Valued in material terms. "Persons are valuable for what they do for *me.*"	Valued because of relationships of affection and for their contribution to society.	Valued because they are persons. Human life is sacred.
Stimulus to Right Actions	Fear of punishment and desire for reward.	Desire to please important persons and perform one's duty to society.	To be true to oneself one must act upon the moral principles to which one is committed.
Ability to Take Another's Perspective	Understands the perspective of persons in situations which he has experienced.	Understands the perspective of friends, family, and eventually society.	Understands the perspective of a wide range of persons including minority groups.

Illustration 3

The specific values held by an adolescent and his or her moral behavior are largely determined by the family's influence on the teenager when he or she was a child.[31] The child's cultural heritage, social environment, primary role models, and early treatment as a person will have tremendous impact on the specific values that will be adopted and on the timing and rate of development through the teenage years. During these adolescent years, even though there is typically a pushing away from parental influence, family-held values can still prove to be valuable guidelines for the growing teenager.

Notes

1. G. Stanley Hall, *Adolescence: Its Psychology and Its Relations to Physiology, Anthropology, Sex, Crime, Religion and Education*, vol. 1 (New York: Appleton, 1904).

2. Leland E. Hinsie and Robert J. Campbell, *Psychiatric Dictionary* (New York: Oxford University Press, 1970).

3. Charlotte Buhler, Patricia Keith-Spiegel, and Karla Thomas, "Developmental Psychology," in *Handbook of General Psychology*, ed. Benjamin B. Wolman (Englewood Cliffs, N.J.: Prentice-Hall, 1973), p. 883.

4. Gene R. Medinnus and Ronald C. Johnson, *Child and Adolescent Psychology* (New York: John Wiley, 1969).

5. Carl P. Malmquist, *Handbook of Adolescence* (New York: Jason Aronson, 1978).

6. Paul D. Meier, Frank B. Minirth, and Frank Wichern, *Introduction to Psychology and Counseling* (Grand Rapids, Mich.: Baker Book House, 1982).

7. Malmquist, *Handbook of Adolescence*.

8. Ibid.

9. Ibid.

10. J.M. Tanner, "Earlier Maturation in Man," Scientific American 218 (1968):21-28.

11. Derek Miller, *Adolescence: Psychology, Psychopathology and Psychotherapy* (New York: Jason Aronson, 1974).

12. Elizabeth Hurlock, *Developmental Psychology: A Life-Span Approach*, 3rd ed. (New York: McGraw-Hill, 1968).

13. Erik H. Erikson, "Identity and the Life Cycle," Psychological Issues, no. 1 (1959).

14. *Webster's New Collegiate Dictionary* (Springfield, Mass.: G. and C. Merriam, 1977).

15. H.H. Remmers and D.H. Radler, *The American Teenager* (Indianapolis: Bobbs-Merrill, 1957).

16. Miller, *Adolescence: Psychology, Psychopathology and Psychotherapy*.

17. Eli Ginzburg, *The Development of Human Resources* (New York: McGraw-Hill, 1966).

18. Meier, Minirth, and Wichern, *Introduction to Psychology and Counseling*.

19. Ashley Montagu, "The Pill, the Sexual Revolution, and the Schools," Phi Delta Kappan (May 1968):480-484.

20. Hurlock, *Developmental Psychology*.

21. Bruce Narramore, *Adolescence Is Not an Illness* (Old Tappan, N.J.: Fleming H. Revell, 1980).

22. Don Dinkmeyer and Gary McKay, *Systematic Training for Effective Parenting of Teens: Parent's Guide* (Circle Pines, Minn.: American Guidance Service, 1983).

23. W. F. Dearborn and P. Cattell, "The Intelligence and Achievement of Private School Pupils," Journal of Educational Psychology 21 (1930):197-211.

24. David Elkind, "Egocentrism in Adolescence," Child Development 38 (1967):1025-1034.

25. P.H. Mussen, J.J. Conger, and J. Kagan, *Child Development and Personality* (New York: Harper and Row, 1969).

26. Gardner Lindzey, Calvin Hall, and R. Thompson, *Psychology* (New York: Worth Publishers, 1975).

27. Elkind, "Egocentrism in Adolescence."

28. Jean Piaget, *The Moral Judgment of the Child* (New York: Harcourt Brace Jovanovich, 1932).

29. Lawrence Kohlberg, "Stage and Sequence: The Cognitive-Developmental Approach to Socialization," in *Handbook of Socialization Theory and Research*, ed. D.A. Goslin (Chicago: Rand McNally, 1969).

30. Lindzey, Hall, and Thompson, *Psychology*.

31. M.W. Riley and M.E. Moore, "Adolescent Values and the Riesmann Typology: An Empirical Analysis," in *Culture and Social Character*, eds. S.M. Lipset and L. Lowenthal (New York: Free Press, 1961).

■ CHAPTER 2

Characteristics of the Age

A concerned parent recently called a psychologist expressing fear that something was seriously wrong with her 15-year-old son. As the therapist questioned her about her son's symptoms and behavior the story gradually unfolded.

"Terry has always been a bright, talkative boy," the mother began. "He is our middle child. We have three. Ever since he was a baby he has been the happiest, best-natured little boy you could ask for. He always liked being with the family and eagerly enjoyed whatever we did together. As far as Sunday school, he loved it. He learned his Bible stories, sang the songs and even enjoyed memorizing verses. When he started to school he was a little nervous. But as soon as he got over being scared, everything was great. All of his teachers have commented on what an interested and well-mannered little boy he is, that is, up until a few years ago. About the time he started junior high school things changed. Boy, did they change! He started getting sullen and moody. You don't dare say anything or he'll bite your head off. I feel like half the time I'm walking on egg shells. He's especially mean to me. I don't think he even likes me anymore." No longer able to hold back her tears, she began to release her pain along with her worry.

"His father and I have invested so much in him. And right now it all seems lost. His older brother didn't act this way! Terry couldn't seem to care less about his schoolwork anymore. He just acts dumb. But I know he isn't. He just doesn't care about studying anymore. He's lazy.

And he doesn't realize it's going to hurt his chances for having a good future."

A pause, more tears, and then she continued with some difficulty. "I guess the part that hurts most is that he just doesn't seem to care about his own family anymore. I mean his own family! He gulps his dinner down in five minutes and sits there with that pained look on his face, like he's being tortured having to be with us until he's excused from the table. Whenever he's at home—and that's not much—he's always in his room with the door closed. He listens to loud music on his stereo and who knows what else he's doing. The rest of the time he's with his friends. That's the only time he seems to be happy at all.

"I don't know. What's happening to him? We can't seem to reach him anymore. He won't let us. His father and I are scared. He's out of our control."

The therapist was able to tell this concerned, frightened mother that her son was really a very normal teenager. His behavior patterns, emotional reactions and changes are symptoms, not of an illness, but of adolescence. This does not imply that there is no need to worry or be concerned. Because the teenage years are a drastic transition, the young person experiences a vulnerable unstable condition. While passing through this phase, the teenager is quite susceptible to environmental pressures and the impact from the many emotional crises common to the age.

But be reassured. It is through this developmental process that one must pass in order to mature successfully into adulthood. Remember that God is the architect of our design. His spirit dwells within our Christian teenagers as they pass through this difficult period. And he is able to minister fully to the needs and impact the lives of adolescents who don't even know him.

Adolescence, then, is normal. Understanding the normal behaviors for adolescence is a great help to us as we parent and counsel with teenagers. The purpose of this chapter is to specify normal adolescent behaviors and reactions and to alert us to abnormal behaviors that may indicate the existence of psychological problems.

Age-Appropriate Behavior

There are many behaviors that are typical, usual and understandable as a part of the adolescent developmental process. Were they to occur in earlier childhood or during the adult years they would certainly be considered as abnormal behavior and symptomatic of psychopathology or maladjustment. Let's take a closer look at some of these age-appropriate adolescent bahaviors.

Typical goals. A basic premise underlying the psychological understanding of human behavior is the belief that all behavior is goal directed. Everything that we do is motivated to meet a certain need, accomplish a task or to produce a desired result. Because the developmental tasks are different for each age group, the behavioral goals also vary.

Alfred Adler, a well-known psychologist who was one of Sigmund Freud's students, provided the theoretical foundation for some very important study of childhood behavior.[1] More recent work brings specific applications to teenagers and helps us to understand the goals that motivate most of adolescent behavior.[2]

Establishing a sense of belonging is a basic goal from early childhood through maturity. The specific way a young person seeks this sense of belonging is shaped by his or her genetic inheritance, parents' attitudes and behavior, ordinal position in the family (oldest, middle, youngest), cultural and socioeconomic influences, and the child's own developing style of responding to the world. The following five goals account for most adolescent behavior (both positive and negative). Please keep in mind that most behavior represents a combination of two or more goals.

1. Attention. Attention-getting behavior is an almost universal characteristic of young children. Being attended to gives them a sense of personal significance and importance. By the time a person reaches the teenage years, attention getting is usually a less prominent goal than in earlier childhood. When it is seen, it is most often in the arena of peer relationships rather than within the realm of the family. Two high school boys swapping escalating accounts of their physical prowess athletic feats or dating exploits are seeking attention. The low rider cruising Main Street in his 50s vintage Chevy and the off-road enthusiast laying rubber in the high school parking lot are two more examples of teenagers seeking attention.

When a teenager feels insecure about his or her belonging, especially with peers, there is a greater likelihood of more extreme attention-getting mechanisms (AGMs). These behaviors are sometimes positively directed. For example, some adolescents are obsessive about their dress, always having to wear the finest labels, the most "in" fashions and meticulously caring about fabric and color coordination. The young "stud" who never walks but always struts, usually is seen flexing, and seldom misses an opportunity to go shirtless in order to display his torso, pectorals and biceps is another example of positive AGM behavior.

An increasing sense of discouragement and anger often elicits negatively directed AGM behavior. Disruptive playing of the stereo, talking loudly at inappropriate times and consistently leaving clothes, school materials and other possessions strewn about the house are examples.

Teenagers who use AGMs, whether positively or negatively, and whether active or passive in nature, are essentially making the statement, "When you attend to me I feel important and when I feel important, I am more confident that I really do belong. Therefore I must constantly seek ways of keeping your attention on me."

2. Power. Power-seeking behavior is very common among teenagers because a significant aspect of successful adolescent identity formation is experiencing movement in the locus of power from the external environmental domain to the internal intrapersonal domain. Much of the transition from helpless child to effective adult takes place during the teenage years. Active, energetic and courageous teenagers are most apt to seek a greater sense of power. This drive for power is another goal that can produce both positively and negatively directed behavior.

Teenagers who consistently seek positions of leadership (class president, church group song leader, drum major for the school band and head cheerleader) are examples of youth whose behavior is positively directed toward the goal of increasing power.

When teenagers are feeling insecure or unsure about their worth and angry about not feeling valued, they are more apt to express their power-oriented behaviors in negative ways. Taking the car without permission, installing a lock on their own bedroom door and lighting up a cigarette on church property are examples of seeking power through negative behavior.

This form of behavior represents a challenge to authority, and as such, it is usually directed toward adults. It is associated with teenagers' natural, healthy need to rebel; to push away somewhat from tradition and authority in order to establish their own sense of identity.

Teenagers who are involved in power-oriented behavior, whether positively or negatively directed, are essentially saying, "I feel significant and valuable only when I am winning and when I am in control. When you win I feel put down and when you tell me what to do I feel angry. Therefore, I will always seek to be in control."

3. Excitement. Arousal-seeking behavior is activity that pumps in-

creased amounts of adrenalin into the blood. Glandular and muscular activity is, in turn, increased and the individual feels excited, turned on, hyper or aroused. Seeking excitement is often associated with the pleasure of developing new abilities and talents. Expanding the limits is a central part of the adolescent experience. Arousal and excitement are also closely associated with the increased physical strength and sexual maturation beginning with the onset of puberty.

Positive forms of arousal or excitement-seeking behavior include trying to run faster or longer distances, developing increasing physical intimacy with the opposite sex within moral guidelines, and engaging in various sports like hiking, skiing, surfing, motorcycling, skin diving, sky diving, flying or any other activity that is associated with a sense of thrill, danger or extending the limits of one's behavior. These are all positive behavior, because they help teenagers learn more about their strengths and abilities without causing negative or unhealthy consequences.

Negative forms of arousal-seeking behaviors include the above activities when they are followed through to an immoral, unhealthy or excessively risky extreme. Teenagers who see themselves as academically unsuccessful, unpopular with their peers or who suffer low self-esteem for any other reason are apt to engage in the most potentially damaging, life-risking types of arousal-seeking activities. Abusive use of drugs, stealing, truancy, arson and other forms of delinquent behavior are not considered age-appropriate behaviors for teenagers or any other age group.

Teenagers who are involved in excitement-seeking behaviors, whether positively or negatively directed, are essentially saying, "I feel important when I am doing something that feels daring, risky, new and exciting."

4. Peer acceptance. Much of a teenager's self-evaluation is formulated by acceptance among peers although some researchers include peer acceptance as one of the driving goals of adolescence, it is actually a goal of a different order.[3] For instance, a young person might seek more attention or power in order to feel accepted by peers. Conversely, increased peer acceptance will help a teenager acquire positive attention and more interpersonal power. Therefore the topic of peer acceptance will be discussed later in this chapter as it relates to the teenager's movement toward his or her peers.

5. Superiority. The goal of superiority is a common motivator for many teenagers. Their quest for identity often propels them toward

identification with hero images. Wanting to be just like or desiring to possess the attributes of an idealized hero represents the teenagers' striving for excellence, superiority and a sense of significance. Some strive for academic or spiritual excellence, but most will be drawn toward superiority strivings in attractiveness, athletics and popularity.

The healthfulness of the individual's drive for superiority is partially determined by the relationship between the young person's personal talents and the kind of superiority that is desired. A teenager who strives for excellence in a skill for which he or she is qualified is likely to feel successful and encouraged. A teenager who unrealistically strives for superiority in activities where there is little natural aptitude or opportunity is probably destined for a sense of failure and discouragement.

Discouraged youth will tend to seek superiority, not simply in the sense of experiencing excellence, but also by trying to be better than others. Being a good pass receiver, pitcher or skier isn't quite good enough. Having a good tan, an attractive body or a good intellect doesn't quite make it. Discouraged youth often must perceive themselves as better than everyone else around them in order to accept themselves. One unfortunate result of this orientation is that relationships become fields of competition in which friends' successes represent threats to one's own self-esteem. Discouraged teenagers will sometimes seek superiority in destructive ways, like driving faster, drinking more beer or scoring more sexual conquests than anyone else.

Striving for superiority as a sign of personal excellence within a teenager is essentially saying, "I only feel worthwhile and valuable when I am at the top. If I am not the best in at least something, then I'm not sure that others will like me." When the goal of superiority takes on more competitive tones, the teenager's statement is more like, "It hurts me inside when I see someone better than me. I've got to be better than all the rest in order for me to know that I'm okay."

Common emotions. Two of the more characteristic adolescent behaviors are frequent fluctuations in mood and extreme emotional reactions. Teenagers commonly go through one or more mood-swing cycles per day. And these moods are often experienced in extreme forms, rarely in moderation. Emotional reactions are also commonly extreme. But the teenager often recovers from these extreme reactions fairly quickly.

Physiological changes, hormonal imbalances and the psychological stress of accomplishing the adolescent developmental tasks set the stage for a great deal of emotional reactivity. It is often difficult to work with teenagers who are expressing strong emotional reactions. Keeping three points in mind will be helpful:

1. Emotions are amoral. Emotions themselves are neither good nor bad from a moral perspective. It is what we *do* with our emotions, how we respond to them, that can be judged righteous or evil, good or bad.

2. Strong emotional reactions are age-appropriate for teenagers. Teenagers often experience very high "highs" and very low "lows." Understanding this removes some of the confusion we feel when teenagers overreact to apparently small issues.

3. Teenagers sometimes use their emotions to get what they want. The emotions themselves are not bad, they are simply used toward a desired end. Young people need supportive help to learn how to express their emotions honestly and openly without manipulative intent. It will be helpful for us to understand more about the emotions so commonly experienced by teenagers.

Anger. Children often store up a great deal of anger during their earlier years because they do not have an adequate means of releasing feelings of frustration, confusion and helplessness.[4] Teenagers, however, have greater opportunity and ability to release these energy-charged feelings. Often they come out in the form of anger, precipitated by some current provocation. The combined force of past anger and current anger sometimes produces excessive reactions. Another cause for extremely intense reactions is a transient hormonal imbalance, most clearly seen in young adolescent girls just prior to menses.

Adolescent anger is often closely associated with the need to rebel or push away from parents and other authority figures. Energy from the anger is used to strengthen the pushing-away process. Angry reactions also express the youth's need to regain more of a sense of control over his or her life. These reactions, although uncomfortable and often scary to deal with, are completely normal and healthy (unless destructively intense).

Apathy. Not caring or withdrawing emotional investment often expresses the belief that teenagers are powerless to have any effect on their lives or situations. It represents a kind of giving up when life becomes too painful. "If I just don't care, then it doesn't hurt so much." Anger is often mixed with apathy because the teenager does not like what is happening. Apathetic teenagers are too discouraged to express their anger openly. Although some apathy is normal, a serious problem occurs when it becomes either chronic or manipulative ploy.

Boredom. This is another pseudo-emotion, similar to apathy, in that there is a very low energy level and often an accompanying anger component: "There's nothing to do around here." The bored teenager can sit in the midst of assorted athletic equipment, color television, home video games, stereo, guitar, reading material and various arts and crafts supplies, and feel at a total loss for anything to do.

Young people who have the greatest propensity to boredom are those who have not yet developed their own creativity and a sense of responsibility for themselves. Their strong need for contact with peers adds to their difficulty with boredom. As teenagers continue developing, they normaly become increasingly well-equipped to create or provide activities for themselves.

Sadness. This does not mean serious or clinical depression, but only mild depression or sadness commonly experienced at quite frequent intervals by teenagers. Feeling blue, loss of energy, wanting not to be around people, irritability and refusing to be consoled are all symptoms of sadness. Elements of anger, apathy, and boredom are commonly experienced with sadness and are sometimes its cause.

Teenagers experience sadness in response to a variety of situations and experiences. Trying out for the cheerleading squad or athletic team and not making it, losing a boyfriend or girlfriend, overhearing parents fighting, being concerned about the future, the death of a pet and feeling badly about one's physical appearance are some of the causes of sadness.

This kind of mild depression represents a kind of "time out" from life.[5] It is a respite from the pressure of coping and can sometimes provide the adolescent with regenerative time. Teenagers who are sad will often retreat to their room, sit alone in the backyard, or sometimes seek the company of a special friend.

Guilt. Teenagers experience several different kinds of guilt. Real guilt is a situation or condition of fact more than a feeling. Real guilt is experienced when a person has actually sinned, committed a crime, or purposefully wronged someone by an act or a consciously neglected act. Scripture gives us some very clear solutions for resolving this form of guilt.

There are two other forms of irrational guilt. Irrational guilt can be defined as guilt that is without sin or wrongdoing and therefore has no rational basis for the guilt feelings. An example of this is the guilt that one feels after innocently saying or doing something that results in hurting other person's feelings. Most of us can recall those socially awkward experiences when we made a serious faux pas, acted in a socially insensitive manner or suddenly realized that we had said something that hurt another. Teenagers can feel guilt with stabbing intensity even when they intended no pain or harm to anyone. Sometimes this kind of guilt is also experienced along with fears of being ostracized because of one's mistakes.

The second kind of irrational guilt is a negative feeling directed toward the self. Statements like, "I'm not smart enough," "I'm such a klutz," "I'll never be anybody important" and "Nobody will ever fall in love with me" represent the thinking that underlies this type of guilt.

Fear and anxiety. Fear is strong apprehension or frightened anticipation of a specific object, experience or person. Anxiety is the experience of a more generalized fear or agitation and felt toward several experiences, objects or people. For example, 17-year-old Jan may fear failing a certain math test or she might have test anxiety or a math block. Previous painful or frightening experiences or hearing others' "war stories" usually cause the formation of anxieties. The experience of anxiety often causes teenagers to avoid confronting the feared event. Each time, for example, that 16-year-old Mark avoids asking an attractive girl for a date, his avoidance relieves his anxiety and reinforces his avoidance response. Anxiety often causes young persons to feel so much tension that their functioning is severely impaired. When Mark finally does ask a girl for a date, he is so nervous that his tongue feels paralyzed and his movements don't feel under control. He comes across stiffly, awkwardly and so poorly that he gets a negative response, again reinforcing and intensifying his anxiety.

There are so many challenges, new experiences and changes that require adjustments during adolescence that anxiety is a very common companion for the teenager. Excessive anxiety reveals an underlying lack of self-confidence. A great deal of encouragement combined with a series of significant successes will help overcome anxiety.

Stress. Many of us think of the teenage years as a happy-go-lucky, playful time in life that is relatively free from responsibility, struggle and pain.[6] Yet teenagers often have very hectic, full schedules with many different kinds of activities. Striving for grades, learning how to relate with the opposite sex, confronting their own sexuality and moving from dependence to independence are only some of the dynamics that create pressure in teenagers' lives.

Stress is not actually an emotion. It is, rather, the person's response to the pressures that he or she is experiencing. Many of the negative emotional reactions and destructive behavioral acting-out experienced during adolescence result from strong stress reactions. Teenagers who become discouraged, feel a lack of control over their lives and anticipate their futures without optimism are most likely to exhibit stress symptoms. Such symptoms include anger, irritability, social withdrawal, nervousness, stomach problems, sleeping problems, high blood pressure, headaches, skin problems, nervous tics and many others. A mild to moderate degree of stress symptoms are expected periodically during adolescence.

Joy and elation. In the same way that teenagers are capable of feeling strong negative or unhappy emotions, they are equally able to feel extremes of joy, elation and happiness. Winning a ball game, getting a date with that special boy or girl and getting just what they wanted on their birthday are experiences that can draw tremendously happy reactions from young people.

Church youth groups are known for spiritual highs after coming down the mountain from summer retreat or returning from choir tour. Unfortunately, they are also well-known for spiritual valleys between these special events. This characteristic cycling between mountaintop highs and valley lows is usually not so much a sign of unhealthy spirituality as it is a product of adolescent emotional lability.

Effusive spiritual excitement in teenagers is as expressive of their emotional high as it is of the richness in their contact with God. This is another reminder of the interrelatedness of our spirit, emotions and intellect. It is unrealistic to expect spiritually and emotionally "up" teenagers to be that way all year long. Respond positively and with encouragement to their emotional highs. Be equally certain not to engender a sense of guilt or shame when they feel down.

Love. "Isn't that cute? But they're really not in love. It's just 'puppy love.'" Such disclaimers of teenagers' ability to love can cause adults to underestimate seriously the depth of emotion and sincerity that is so much a part of teenagers' loving.

It is true that adolescents cannot love as completely as adults can. Their incompletely developed identities limit the maturity of their love. But that does not limit the sincerity or reduce the meaning that love has in their lives.

During adolescence, interpersonal warmth and love are especially directed toward peers. This is particularly true during mid- and late adolescence when teenagers are trying to reach out beyond themselves. They are trying to overcome the egocentricity of early adolescence.

Heterosexual pairings and the development of intense "buddy" friendships with members of the same sex provide the most common opportunities for developing loving in relationships.

Both types of relationships are important to growing adolescents. The former provides opportunities to learn about the opposite sex, to explore their own developing sexuality, to experiment with building relationships that will help prepare them for marriage and to better define their own emerging identity. The latter provides experiences that reinforce their masculine or feminine sex roles, encourages movement from dependence on parents toward independence, and supports the exploration of virtually every fact of their developing identity.

One aspect of adolescent loving is particularly painful for adults. As they move closer toward separating from parents and other authority figures, teenagers typically withdraw some of their emotional attachment, loving and dependency from these figures. This process usually involves angry expressions from the teenager and in some cases temporary episodes of actual hatred. The extremes of their intense loving and anger express the inconsistencies of the age.

Experimentation with new behaviors. There is no other age, with the exception of the first two years of life, that brings more experimentation with new behaviors than adolescence. During the early teenage years, childhood interest, activities and hobbies are gradually dropped. Along with physiological and emotional changes come new activities, new interests and expanded possibilities.

Teenagers have an almost endless supply of energy for experimenting with new behavior and exploring new boundaries for possible involvement. Much of this experimenting aids in the young person's identity development. It is a sort of trying on of new behaviors to see how they feel. "Is being more assertive or more passive best for me?" "I wonder if I'll enjoy a team sport like football or more of an individual sport like gymnastics better?" "If I try to flirt, I wonder if boys will laugh or will they be attracted to me?" "I wonder if I will feel guilty or strong and independent if I tell my parents that I don't want to go on vacation with them?" Answers to these kinds of questions are produced only by trying on the new behaviors.

The most significant area of experimenting with new behavior is in developing heterosexual relationships. With sexual maturation comes the ability to establish relationships with the opposite sex that involve romantic attachment, sensual arousal and sexual involvement. These new abilities and the available intense pleasures lead the young person into ongoing heterosexual experimentation. This experimentation helps the growing adolescents to develop their masculine and feminine roles. It is from this process that adult sexuality and the readiness for marital commitment emerges.

Egocentric self-focus. During early and mid-adolescence, young people are extremely egocentric. That is, they are consumed with self-focus. It is an age of narcissism. Young teenagers find it almost impossible to respond to others' needs above their own. The monumental changes occurring within the teenager require most of his or her energy and focus. The added insecurity of the age increases teenagers' difficulty in seeing beyond themselves. And sometimes it is not simply insecurity, but actual feelings of self-hatred and serious self-esteem problems that intensify their egocentricity.[7]

Idealism. Adolescent idealism springs from the intellectual growth of concrete thinking during childhood to the more mature capacity for abstract thought. The ability to conceptualize ideals provides both positive and unpleasant adolescent characteristics. It enables young people to begin establishing marriage, vocational and spiritual goals for their future. Early and mid-adolescence is a time for idealistic goal-setting. Late adolescence is a time for adjusting these goals to a more realistic level.

The young adolescent thinks freely without the binds of reality testing: "What do I want to be when I grow up?" Brain surgeon? Astronaut? Pastor? Football star? Idealistic fantasy is not bound by thoughts of realistic limitations. Thus, a rich variety of possibilities are considered and later provide a wide range of options from which to choose.

The same idealism sometimes helps the young adolescent to make deeply meaningful and long-lasting spiritual commitments.[8] Spiritual ideals are particularly attractive to youth because belief in an all-powerful, all-loving God and eternity provides the greatest perceived avenue for the grandest of hopes and dreams. "Trust in the Lord with all your heart, and do not rely on your own insight. In all your ways acknowledge him, and he will make straight your paths" (Proverbs 3:5-6). Scriptures like this provide form and direction for youth's ideals. Understanding this beautiful characteristic can help those who work with teenagers. It is most important to resist the temptation to exploit their spiritual sensitivity for evangelistic or other purposes.

One of the unfortunate aspects of adolescent idealism is the extreme self-criticism that it fosters. Being able to conceptualize the ideal also enables young persons to compare this idealized picture with their own perceived reality. Since they can conceptualize their own thoughts, they also are able to contemplate the thoughts of others. Teenagers usually believe that others think of them in the same way that they think of themselves.[9] Unfortunately, this type of egocentrism most often reinforces negative self-criticism rather than positive and self-affirming thoughts.

Another unpleasant effect of adolescent idealism is an overly critical attitude toward parents, teachers and other authority figures.[10] This extreme intolerance of even minor faults or shortcomings in parents and adults is often a projection of their own self-hatred. They tend to feel critical because of their own weaknesses. Unable to live with such intense self-criticism, the anger is unconsciously directed at others who are "supposed to be perfect." This use of projection aids teenagers in their movement away from parent figures in order to establish their own identity.[11]

Movement away from parents. Some of the most developmentally significant adolescent behavior is also disconcerting for adults. Successful adolescent growth requires that they move away from childhood dependence upon their parents. This growth toward independence involves every area of life, finally enabling them to live a fully adult lifestyle. Examining specific breaking away behaviors helps us to understand the psychological meaning of these otherwise confusing and threatening actions.

1. Teenagers require a lot of time alone and with friends. While alone they think through problems and plan out how they want to act in upcoming situations. They ponder what went wrong yesterday and try to sort out the okayness of their emerging identities. Time with friends is spent exploring new relationships, learning new interpersonal skills, establishing their masculine and feminine roles, and becoming more comfortable with their new sexuality.

Teenagers will normally spend less time at the table, not want to go on family outings, and will generally find home a rather boring and uneventful place to be.

2. Teenagers may withdraw. When children who have been raised in the church reach adolescence, it is quite normal for them to become less involved, to not want to attend church and even to become overly cynical of the church and its people. The more highly the parents value church attendance the more likely this subject will become a battleground unless it is handled in an adept manner. Sometimes teenagers

don't like church simply because there is little there to interest them. If there is not much of a youth group, if the preaching and teaching is not very interesting and if there are few special activities for youth, then is it any surprise that a teenager would lose interest in attending? Some adolescents will fight going to church because they dread being teased or rejected by their non-Christian friends at school. Keep in mind the tremendous impact of peer opinion during adolescence.

3. Teenagers may be secretive around parents. Another expression of teenagers' need to pull away from their parents is their tendency to not confide in them. Information is a form of power and the holder of valued data often has a sense of control. Since control is a basic issue during adolescent growth, holding information away from the grasp of parents enhances the sense of control that the teenager feels. Unhappily, the more desire parents have for their youth to share with them, the more control the teenager experiences by saying "no" to their request.

4. Teenagers are very reluctant to accept advice or criticism from parents. Teenagers' insecurities are magnified by the suggestion that they might be able to benefit from an adult's input. "I know, I know," is so often the immediate response as soon as a would-be helper opens his or her mouth. Low self-esteem, uncertain identity and feared loss of control are the underlying issues to this extreme sensitivity.

5. Teenagers tend to have a difficult time coping with discipline. Adolescents tend to resist discipline for the same reasons they resist advice and criticism. The potential for loss in self-esteem, increased insecurity about their identity and loss of personal control is even greater when faced with being disciplined. An angry, "You don't have the right to do this to me," is a very common reaction to discipline.

6. Teenage rebellion is normal. Rebellion in some form against authority is an often unpleasant but necessary part of adolescent development. External control must be thrown off enough to allow sufficient space for the growth of internal controls. This rebellion typically takes place over a period of several years and it usually does not have to cause a great deal of disruption. However, if the teenager is very unsure of his or her strength, an exaggerated rebellion may occur. Parents who have a very difficult time letting go of their teenagers will also tend to draw more severe rebellious reactions from them. The more frustrated a young person feels, the more angry will be the rebellion.

Movement toward peers. As teenagers develop away from parents, church and other traditional sources of authority and support, they strongly gravitate toward peers. During early and mid-adolescence this movement is primarily toward the peer group. During the late teenage years, allegiance and commitment is shifted more to individual peers, of both the opposite and the same sex. The strength of this transition on a teenager's life is illustrated in the following chart:[12]

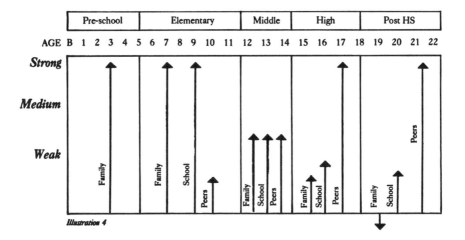

Illustration 4

Increased involvement with peers often creates anxiety for parents. Evenings spent talking on the telephone and constant demands to be with friends are the norm. Changes in manner of dress, speech, musical taste, enjoyable activities and general behavior are usually related to the peer group.

Adults often view the teenager's move toward independence more as a transference of dependency from one source to another. That's true. But from the adolescent's perspective it is also a monumental move toward self-reliance. To say "no" to the source of care, support and guidance that has been trusted and comfortably enjoyed for about 12 years takes a great deal of courage. Teenagers are not equipped to stand totally alone (none of us are) in a new and challenging world. They need mutual support and that is the purpose behind their strong demands for conformity. "If we're all pretty much alike then we must be okay. How can we all be wrong? I guess our parents just don't understand." As the teenager gains strength in his or her self-concept, more mature and interdependent relationships are possible, enabling the young person to form more intimate attachments with their peers.

Notes

1. Rudolph Dreikurs and Vicki Soltz, *Children: The Challenge* (New York: Hawthorn Books, 1964).

2. Don Dinkmeyer and Gary McKay, *Systematic Training for Effective Parenting of Teens: Parent's Guide* (Circle Pines, Minn.: American Guidance Service, 1983).

3. Ibid.

4. Peter Buntman and Eleanor Saris, *How to Live With Your Teenager* (Pasadena, Calif.: Birch Tree Press, 1979).

5. Dinkmeyer and McKay, *Systematic Training for Effective Parenting of Teens.*

6. Bruce Narramore, *Adolescence Is Not an Illness* (Old Tappan, N. J.: Fleming H. Revell, 1980).

7. Ibid.

8. Paul Meier, *Christian Child-Rearing and Personality Development* (Grand Rapids, Mich.: Baker Book House, 1977).

9. David Elkind, "Egocentrism in Adolescents," Child Development 38 (1967): 1025-1034.

10. Paul D. Meier, Frank B. Minirth, and Frank Wichern, *Introduction to Psychology and Counseling* (Grand Rapids, Mich.: Baker Book House, 1982).

11. Gardner Lindzey, Calvin Hall, and R. Thompson, *Psychology* (New York: Worth Publishers, 1975).

12. Fred Streit, *Parents and Problems: Through the Eyes of Youth,* quoted in Buntman and Saris, *How to Live With Your Teenager*, p. 14.

■ CHAPTER 3

A Closer Look at Families With Teenagers

By the time young people have reached adolescence they have spent their most vulnerable, impressionable years within a specific environmental structure—the family. The adolescent's identity and how he or she deals with the teenage years and matures into adulthood will be heavily impacted by what is happening at home. The family is worthy of our close attention because of its importance in adolescent development.

The Generation Gap

There has probably always existed a generation gap between teenagers and their parents. It does seem, however, that in our society it is widening and that it is showing up when children are at a younger age than before.[1]

The Robinsons were participating in family counseling with their pastor. The pastor had met with the parents twice and twice with their two children, Cari, 17, and Glen, 15. All four of these sessions were very positive. Trust relationships were established between the pastor and each family member. The relevant background information was obtained, commitments to work together for the family's benefit were extracted and all were ready for the first family session.

The night of the first scheduled meeting, the waiting room outside of the pastor's study was charged with tension. One by one the family members filed into his study, took their seats and waited. "I'm glad that you could all make it tonight. It seems like everybody is pretty tense. Would someone like to share with me what is happening?"

Then it all came out. Two days before, Glen had been caught smoking at school for the third time, resulting in mandatory suspension for three days. Mr. and Mrs. Robinson were frustrated, embarrassed and angry, and added a month's restriction onto Glen's suspension as extra punishment. In turn Glen reacted, "You don't have any business restricting me at home. I didn't smoke at home. It was at school. It's none of your business. It's between me and the school. I just wish you'd get off my back. Why don't you mind your own business?"

Dad took the bait and responded to the fiery challenge. "All right! I've had it. If you are no longer our business, then you just take care of yourself, big shot. Buy your own food, cook your own meals, take care of your own clothes, provide your own transportation. At least maybe this'll get you up off your lazy tail! You won't do anything for us. You're too selfish. I'm not even sure you'll do it for yourself."

The raging went on, back and forth for most of the session. Their pastor's attempts to bring some sense of constructive order were always squelched by Mom, Dad or Glen. Finally Cari, who had been sitting in a corner looking very bored and long suffering, announced with audible indignation, "I'm sick of this. It's all our family ever does. Fight, fight, fight. You did it with me. Now you're doing it with Glen. I sure am glad I'm almost gone. Nobody can be happy around here."

The session finally ended with tempers somewhat cooled, or at least vented. Unfortunately the same thing happened the following week at the second family session. Different problem areas were talked about but the same rage and lack of real communication prevailed. Possible referral was discussed, agreed upon, and made for family counseling with a professional therapist.

The Robinson family presents us with a very clear picture of a generation gap. Adolescents are becoming increasingly sophisticated, more powerful and freer to express themselves openly. This increased assertiveness, though in ways very positive, adds more stress to family living which is already quite demanding. In many families, the times that parents and teenagers spend together become filled with frustration, outrage, humiliation, sullenness, resentment and despair.[2]

A lack of mutual understanding and (in more severe cases) a loss of desire to understand marks a generation gap.[3] Parents and teenagers are at completely different places in their lives. Adolescents are confronting their sexuality, separating from family, developing peer relationships, establishing an independent sense of identity, and formulating career goals. Parents of teenagers are usually in their middle-adult years and are facing developmental tasks, such as: achieving a level of social responsibility, establishing and maintaining a certain economic standard of living, parenting teenagers, developing adult recreational activities, adjusting to their own and their spouse's physiological changes, and responding to the needs of their aging parents.[4] Teenager and parent are both responding to demanding changes and crises that can leave little energy for reaching out in understanding each other.

The Important Role of Parents

The quality of parenting has a great influence on a person's adolescent experience. Unfortunately, children go through adolescence at about the same time their parents go through a major period of developmental adjustment.[5] During their 40s and 50s most parents cope with a mid-life crisis that requires significant emotional energies. At a time when parents are reevaluating their values, beliefs and morals, their adolescent children are also questioning and doubting. Mature and well-integrated adults continue to grow, partly from the stimulation from their teenagers.[6] When adolescent challenges are felt as threatening to parents, they will often rebuff their child in ways that imply that the teenager's ideas are stupid and bothersome. These rebuffs harm the teenager's self-esteem and cause resentful rage or withdrawal into depression.

Parents of teenagers often question their own sexuality. As they age and lose the last vestiges of youthful sexual attractiveness, they must readjust their body image and self-concept in order to accommodate their body changes. Resentments about unhappy marital sexual relationships also often flare up during the mid-life years. As these internal sexual struggles are brewing, parents' teenage sons and daughters rapidly develop new and intense sexual urgings. Sexually unhappy parents will sometimes consciously, though usually unconsciously, encourage their children to be sexually active.[7] Women who are unable to enjoy sex sometimes live vicariously through their sexually promiscuous daughters.[8] Fathers who struggle with their own declining potency sometimes seek vicarious pleasure through their sons' sexual exploits and conquests.

In addition to the parenting problems caused by adult developmental struggles, many parents simply do not know how to respond to their adolescent children. Ironically, this problem has been intensified by the proliferation of Christian "how to" parenting books. Christian readers seem to think that if it is written by a Christian author, then it is believable. If a book sounds biblical, especially if it is full of scripture references, then it has to be true. Critical reading tells us, however, that Christian authors do not always agree.

When parents follow through with what an author recommends and the results are not the same as was indicated in the book, they feel more frustrated, dismayed and lost. Three factors account for the differences between the promised and actual outcomes. First, even though parents think they are following the author's recommendations, there may be subtle but very important differences, such as voice tone and facial expression. Second, the author's advice, though perhaps valid and very useful, might not apply to the specific situation where it was applied by the parents. Third, some authors tend to oversimplify very complex dynamics of human behavior and interpersonal relationships. They dogmatically offer simplistic answers that will work successfully with only a few people part of the time. All too often, the advice we are given is that which we know to do but feel unable to accomplish. "I know I shouldn't give in to my son's rage, but I just don't seem to be able to keep hanging in there," said a frustrated mother.

Parents may struggle in their relationships with teenagers because of stereotyped images of adolescence. The hearing of other parents' war stories and the exposure to the current myths about adolescence is apt to create a variety of attitudes, perceptions and responses to teenagers.[9] One current myth portrays adolescents as excessively powerful and threatening. They are described as being "explosive," "a seething cauldron," "totally out of control" or as a "train on the loose." These phrases tell us more about adults' fears than they do about their children.

A second common myth sees adolescents as engulfed in their own sexual desires and hopelessly driven to tempt others into sexual activity. This reaction comes from insecure, narcissistic parents who feel threatened at any sign of maturing in their children. These parents tend to need their children to depend on them. Visible sexual maturation is perceived as a threat to this need to be needed.

Parents who have ongoing, unresolved, internal sexual conflicts will often project their fears onto their teenage children. Other insecure parents may feel reaffirmed in their own sexual adequacy by comparing themselves with the more clumsy, awkward and hesitant sexual expressions of their children.

A third myth is that adolescence is essentially psychopathological, that it is a period of transitory sickness. We chuckle and welcome the titles of books about teenagers, such as: *Adolescence Is Not an Illness.*[10] Many typical behaviors of teenagers would probably be judged as sick at any other age, but for adolescents they are appropriate.

One attitude that parents have of adolescence is envy. Many middle-aged mothers feel jealous of their daughter's firm and beautiful shape. Dads, caught in lives of routine and never-ending demands, can become resentful of their son's apparent freedom to do whatever he wishes. In extreme cases the parent becomes competitive. Mother starts dressing in her daughter's style and flirts with her girl's boyfriends. Dad tries to recapture his youth by taking excessive time away from work, having his hair permed, buying a sports car and getting back into athletics.

Another attitude toward adolescence is the mourning of the loss of identity as a parenting figure. Onset of adolescence signals the beginning of the end to many parents. If they are not able to find new values, invest themselves into new interests and deepen other relationships, they will experience serious problems in the future.

The last response that we will discuss is viewing teenagers from a safe distance as objects of curiosity. Parents who have deep conflicts and who fear the pain that can result from emotional intimacy never really let themselves (physically or emotionally) touch or be touched by their children.

Most parents seek to do their best in raising children. But every parent has his or her limitations. Parents will exhibit certain reactions that are damaging to the relationship with their teenager, particularly when under stress. By spotting these patterns of damaging (dysfunctional) parenting, counselors can better understand the origins of teenagers' behavior problems. There are nine patterns of dysfunctional parenting styles that will be discussed here:[11]

The perfectionistic parent. Teenagers of the perfectionistic parent can never seem to do anything right. If there is a compliment it is always followed by a disclaimer or a qualifying statement. "You played a good game, son, but weren't you running a little slowly today?" "Your art work is very pretty, Peggy, but I really wish you would put more importance on your real schoolwork." Good is never enough. Perfect is only okay for today. It better show improvement tomorrow.

Discouragement, feelings of inadequacy, self-hatred and depression are common for most adolescents of perfectionistic parents. The teenagers have learned to set the same kinds of standards for themselves. These goals can never be reached or accomplished and further despair is the usual result. Only with great internal strength of character or ample encouraging and support from others can these teenagers bounce back to believe in themselves.

The rejecting parent. The damaging effect of this kind of parent is worse than the perfectionistic parent. It is worse because the rejection is directed squarely at the child, instead of being directed toward the teenager's performance. Since there is no apparent reason for the rejection, the young person assumes that there is something personally very wrong. The parents avoid contact with their child whenever possible. And when contact cannot be avoided, it is usually hostile, demeaning and abusive. "You're not good for anything." "It's gonna be one happy day around here when you finally move out." "You've been a problem to me ever since the day you were born." More subtle forms of rejection come in the form of putting the teenager off with phrases like, "not now," "after awhile" and "maybe next time." Although most teenagers will hear these statements from their parents occasionally, they should not be the usual response. The most extreme expression of rejection is physically abusing the child.

Teenagers assume that if their parents do not love them, then nobody must love them. The reaction in the adolescent is typically a strong one. They will demand attention from adults in any way that works, even if the only attention that they get is negative. Adolescent delinquent and overt antisocial behavior reflects the way they were taught to view themselves.

The overprotective parent. This type of parent continues to do things for the child long after such help is necessary. They break one of the cardinal rules for effective parenting: The parent should not continue to do something for the child that the child can begin to do. This is difficult for overprotective parents because they usually tend to be perfectionists and would rather do things "right" than let the child do them in a less efficient and less perfect manner. These parents differ from the perfectionistic parents in that they are not critical of the child's performance, they are uncomfortable with it.

Overprotective parents can be very loving, well-meaning people who simply have a difficult time letting go. They project their own insecurity and need for support onto their children, gaining a sense of security by exerting more control over their children's lives, which in turn fosters more dependency back onto the parent. Through this dynamic, insecure parents beget insecure children. For some parents, overprotective patterns reveal a deep-seated hostility which is indirectly and passively expressed through their extreme control over their children.

Many children allow their parents to wait on them and develop a very demanding attitude, growing angry quickly when things do not automatically go for them the way they wish. They have little personal courage, quickly give in to pressure and give up when faced with a difficult challenge. Deep within overprotected adolescents is an aching feeling of inadequacy and helplessness. They believe that they never can do things well enough and that they will never gain the genuine approval of others. Hopes for affirmation wane and deep-seated guilt and angry resentment build.

Adolescence is a crucial period for the overprotected child. Will he or she choose strength and independence? Or are the challenges and fears too great? The parents will not change the pattern because (for the moment) it works so well for them. It's up to the teenagers to gain more and more responsibility in that challenging world out there. They will need the support of friends and the respecting affirmation of an adult to help them in the process.

The overindulgent parent. This type of parent shares many of the dynamics of the overprotective parent but the primary expression is through giving too many things to the child. This overabundance of giving is an attempt to overcompensate for the parents' experience of lacking things during their childhood. It also reflects the parents' fear of their child's rage should they say "no." Beneath other parents' overindulging ways is the desire to maintain control over their child upon whose dependency they themselves are dependent.

Teenagers of the overindulgent parent are likely to suffer significant damage. They do not learn the value of working hard to attain a goal, nor do they experience the pleasure of attaining a sought-after outcome. Instead, overindulged teenagers are selfish and demanding, believing that parents, friends and everyone else owe them whatever is desired. They often fail to cope with even the simplest of day-to-day frustrations because they have never learned to deal with delayed gratifications. They become virtually incapable of being responsible or accountable to anyone. They perceive themselves as the center of existence and the external environment exists to serve their immediate pleasure alone. Rage and rebellion are the inescapable results during adolescence or early adulthood. Continuing the overindulgence only postpones the inevitable to a time when the person is stronger and the reaction more powerful.

The overpermissive parent. Where do spoiled brats come from? That is right. Overpermissive parents. They are often well-intentioned parents who want to provide a very free, happy childhood for their offspring. They have determined not to frustrate or discourage their children with too many rules and restrictions. But they have overcompensated. By taking away virtually all rules, limits and expectations, the child never learns to live in a system where there are rights and wrongs, rules and limits, expectations and consequences. Overpermissive parents do their children no favor at all.

Adolescents who are raised in this kind of a system usually make a disastrous interpersonal adjustment because they are not accustomed to adjusting to anyone. As peers demand mutual respect and tolerance, this kind of teenager will react with extreme frustration and a deep sense of alienation because he or she does not know the rules for healthy interpersonal relating.

The severe parent. Severe parents are those who carry an acceptable form of parenting behavior to such an extreme that it becomes excessively harsh or severe. Instead of receiving a spanking, Mark was whipped with a belt until his back was bleeding. Charlene was not only restricted, but was locked in her room with her windows nailed shut during one summer month, being let out only to eat and go to the bathroom. Millie's crying was stopped by being beaten to unconsciousness because her father lost control.

Are these parents hopelessly evil? Should we despise them? No. They usually love their children very much, like other parents do. But they have a serious impulse control problem that renders them unable to deal with the daily frustrations common to most households. Many of them had severe parents and it was during their own childhood that the problem began.

In order to escape severe psychological and sometimes physical damage the teenager must have help from adults outside of the home. Two factors make seeking this help very threatening. First, many adults will tend not to believe the teenager's story. They will interpret it as a part of the adolescent's rebellion and therefore not want to get involved. They may know the parents as outstanding church members and otherwise excellent citizens. Many well-meaning adults will express their concern by telling the parents what their child confided and then the young person is in a worse situation. The second factor that makes it difficult to seek help is a sense of guilt that the teenager is betraying his or her parents and is therefore a bad person. The person feels like a helpless victim bound by fear and guilt.

The inconsistent parent. This kind of parent typically shifts from one pattern to another without any logical rationale. One day they can be very loose and flexible, and the very next day they can be sticklers about even the smallest details. The confused parenting pattern is only one expression of an adult who is out of control of his or her life. These parents do not establish personal or family goals, and if they do set goals, there is seldom a consistent plan for reaching them.

Adolescents who are raised by inconsistent parents do not know what is expected of them. Their abilities to establish a strong moral basis to their lives is severely damaged. Their conscience development is stunted and they become skilled manipulators to get what they want. They assume that there is no absolute right or wrong, good or bad. Therefore, every situation and every decision can be changed if they find the right pressure points. They often become superb "con artists" who try to make it through life without ever squarely confronting reality. Their sense of identity is vague and they usually fail at being dependable friends, spouses and parents. People in relationships with them typically feel used, uncared for and angry.

The faulty parental model. One of the greatest impacts that parents have on their child is the modeling that they provide. Every parent models some kind of behavior, attitude or value. When parents model criminal or antisocial behavior, they are literally teaching their children the value of illegal conduct. Young children are literalists. They are concrete thinkers. What parents say is believed to be true and what they do is believed to be right. The children have already learned their parents' value system and behavioral patterns long before the teenage years.

Adolescents who see themselves as different from the majority of law-abiding, rule-complying citizens will usually seek out peers who view themselves in the same way. They look at law-abiding citizens with contempt and perceive them as stupid and weak. Their feeling of tough superiority is a mask that conceals internal pain, loneliness and helplessness. They dare not be emotionally vulnerable or let anyone get very close because people are viewed with suspicion.

The double-binding parents. "Yes, dear, you can go out with Tom tonight. Have a good time. Dad and I will just sit here at home again without anyone to talk with." "Son, your grades are really good this semester. Just think what you could do if you developed some halfway decent study habits." "Judy, you're doing so well in gymnastics, I'm afraid all those muscles are going to make you look more like a boy than a girl." "I'm so proud of you, Don, for landing that job. I guess now I'll have to hire someone to do all the work that's piling up around here in the yard."

Double-binding is a subtle and insidious way for parents to keep control over their teenagers. It expresses angry disappointments or resentments that the parents feel about their lives that may or may not have anything to do with the teenager.

Double-binding is very dangerous for teenagers and difficult to deal with, because it traps them in a position where there is no way for them to win. No matter what they do, they cannot feel good. If Judy continues in gymnastics she has to worry about her femininity. But if she accentuates her feminine softness she has to give up gymnastics. It is obvious which decision would please her parent. The parent's wishes are made known, but they never own them or admit to them as such. At such a crucial time of identity formation, the young person is lead into frustration, self-doubt and distrust in his or her thoughts and feelings of worth, value and purpose.

Double-bound teenagers usually need someone to help them see the reality of what is happening more clearly. They need help to focus on and respond to the positive portion of statements, such as: "Yes, dear, you can go out with Tom tonight." "Son, your grades are really good this semester." "Judy, you're doing so well in gymnastics." "I'm so proud of you, Don, for landing that job." And double-bound teenagers need help to avoid getting hooked by: "Dad and I will just sit here at home again without anyone to talk with." "Just think what you could do if you developed some halfway decent study habits." "I'm afraid all those muscles are going to make you look more like a boy than a girl." "I guess I'll have to hire someone to do all the work that's piling up around here in the yard."

Another important issue in parenting is the use of parental authority. It is quite clear from scripture that God grants a role of authority to parents. Paul writes, "Children, obey your parents in the Lord, for this is right. 'Honor your father and mother' (this is the first commandment with a promise) 'that it may be well with you and that you may live long on the earth.' Fathers, do not provoke your children to anger, but bring them up in the discipline and instruction of the Lord" (Ephesians 6:1-4).

How can parents best use their authority in order to provide the greatest help and good for their teenage children? Psychological research tells us that both too much and too little parental involvement in adolescents' lives will hamper their growth toward autonomy and adult maturity.[12] The parenting options that are best for the continuing growth and well-being of teenagers lie somewhere between the extremes of excessive authoritarianism and extreme permissiveness.[13]

The authoritarian style of leadership in the home has its roots planted deeply in the belief that humanity is basically sinful. Adolescent behavior, especially behavioral problems, are viewed as resulting from this sinful nature. Thus, the goal is to force the teenager to obey the authority (parents) that God has established. The primary focus is an external one, which emphasizes behavioral conformity and obedience above all else. Conformity is attained through the use of strict discipline measures, fear of punishment, and sometimes the offer of rewards for "good" behavior. This type of leadership in the home is prevalent today. In a recent survey, almost 30 percent of the adolescents who were questioned described their parents as being authoritarian.[14]

Authoritarian parenting of teenagers has several major problems. First, it is based on the belief of humanity's sinfulness without taking into account that we were originally designed in God's image, blessed and given dominion over the rest of his creation (Genesis 1:26-31). Neither does the authoritarian parent give adequate acknowledgment to the power of the Holy Spirit to change a teenager from within. Paul writes, "Therefore, if any one is in Christ, he is a new creation; the old has passed away, behold, the new has come" (2 Corinthians 5:17).

Second, since authoritarian parenting is based upon total obedience to an external force, it operates in opposition to the adolescent process of developing independence and internal identity. By keeping the focus on pleasing mother and father the teenager's development of good judgment, problem-solving, decision-making and reasoning skills are seriously impaired. The force to obey is so strong that there is little room to develop positive behavior patterns that spring forth from love. Christ said, "If you love me, you will keep my commandments" (John 14:15).

Third, the excessive use of force and dependency upon external controls creates within the normal teenager an unhealthy, rigid defense that is destructive both to the teenager and to the family. This defense consists of overdependency, angry rebellion, crippled development of self-esteem, inability to develop healthy relationships, and deep feelings of unworthiness and guilt about themselves.

At the other extreme of parental authority lies the permissive style of parenting. Permissive parenting of adolescents assumes that people are naturally good. This belief is too narrow and one-sided. Both Old and New Testament writers speak of our sinfulness. David confesses, "Behold, I was brought forth in iniquity, and in sin did my mother conceive me" (Psalm 51:5). And Paul tells us, "None is righteous, no, not one" (Romans 3:10).

In the permissive parenting model, adolescent behavioral problems are thought to be caused totally by poor parenting, inadequate education, poverty or interpersonal stress. Permissive parenting is an attempt to provide an environment that is totally free of restraints, controls and limits. Within such an environment it is believed that the teenager will naturally grow in positive directions that will be good ultimately for the family and society. The primary focus is internal. How does Karla feel about what is happening? What is Tommy's attitude? Of less concern is what Karla and Tommy are doing. Positive behavior is encouraged and the use of rewards and punishments is discouraged. In the previously cited survey, about 10 percent of adolescents describe one or both of their parents as being permissive.[15]

Permissive parenting of teenagers can produce some very unhappy results. First, when adolescents interact with the world outside of the home (school, jobs, friends) they are poorly prepared to cope with the demands, limits and expectations placed upon them. The shock of this reality has a devastating impact on their self-esteem. Second, because permissively raised teenagers have not had to deal with authority figures in their homes, when they do encounter authorities (police, teachers, bosses) they typically react with rage, rebellion, or a compliance that indicates bewilderment and giving up. Third, these adolescents lack the opportunity to develop strong internal controls. They have a very difficult time saying "no" to their desires and delaying gratification, even when they can see that it is in their best interest.

Most parents are neither completely authoritarian nor permissive with their teenagers. They would find their place somewhere between these two extremes. Exactly where a parent is located on this continuum is probably dependent upon three interrelated factors:[16]

1. Parents tend to raise their children in a manner that is similar to the way they were parented. If they tend to be more authoritarian in

their approach, their parents probably were also. If they are quite permissive, then their own parents probably raised them in a permissive manner.

2. Parenting is usually heavily influenced by the most accepted contemporary practices and theories. A major shift from authoritarian to permissive approaches to child rearing came in the 1940s and 1950s. During the late 1970s and early 1980s there seems to be a shift in the reverse direction, toward democratic and moderated authoritarian parenting models.

3. Parenting style is heavily influenced by the individual's beliefs about the nature of humanity. Often, more can be discerned about an adult's theology and philosophy by observing actions (parenting behavior) rather than listening to words.

Democratic parenting represents a significant and positive attempt to improve some of the problems of the permissive model.[17] The democratic approach is very sensitive to the teenager's need to express feelings, make decisions, solve problems and develop self-esteem and independence and at the same time it teaches the value of parental authority.[18] Authority is expressed by setting limits rather than giving directions; by structuring choices rather than declaring "yes" or "no"; by disciplining through natural and logical consequences rather than punishing; and by encouraging rather than praising. Heavy emphasis is placed upon communication, responsibility, accountability, teaching, working together, and loving and valuing each other as equals. The family meeting is one of the places where much of the action occurs.

There are several variations of the authoritarian model of parenting. One is the "loving" or "benevolent" authority variation.[19] It is also called the "authoritative" style of family leadership.[20] This model retains a very high value on parent-as-authority while also elevating the value of the child and his or her interests, needs, thoughts and feelings. Authority is expressed directly by delegation, training and discipline. Heavy emphasis is given to the love, support and nurturance of the child.

The following chart shows how these parenting models compare with each other.[21] It is important to note that few parents operate exclusively from one model. Particular parenting styles are coalitions of two or more of the four models. The healthiest parenting styles will be primarily characterized by the benevolent authority/authoritative and democratic models. Counseling with teenagers or with a family requires an understanding of the parenting dynamics because they levy a major impact on the psychological adjustment of the adolescent.

Comparison of Parenting Models

PARENTING MODELS

FACTOR COMPARED	Authoritarian	Benevolent Authority/Authoritative	Democratic	Permissive
Primary Goals of Parenting	External conformity and obedience of behavior.	Healthy attitudes that readily result in acceptable behavior.	Healthy attitudes and feelings that eventually result in positive behavior.	Healthy attitudes and feelings that result in behavior that the child judges as good.
Use of Parental Authority	Parent has complete authority and children have no recourse.	Parent has complete authority, some of which is delegated at the parent's discretion.	Parents and children share authority within limits set by parents.	Parental authority used only in extreme cases regarding safety, provision of basic needs, etc.
Motivation Primarily Used by Parents	Fear, pressure, power, coercion, threat, guilt and rewards.	Fear, pressure, power, punishment, rewards, praise, encouragement, cooperation and consequences.	Encouragement, consequences, love, group cooperation.	Love, cooperation, promises, encouragement, praise and rewards.
View of Human Nature	Basically sinful.	Created in God's image, yet also sinful.	Basically good, yet capable of destructive behavior.	Basically good.
Parent's Attitude Toward Teenager	Teenagers are to obey, not cause problems for adults and must be tightly controlled.	Teenagers are valued as God's creation who are also sinful and often rebellious. They must be kept under as much control as deemed necessary by the parent.	Teenagers are respected as equals who can be trusted to try to behave in a manner which is good for everyone, yet sometimes needing guidance and limits.	Teenagers are respected as equals who can be trusted to act in good will.
Resulting Adolescent Behavior	Passive conformity, angry acting-out, overt rebellion and/or social withdrawal.	Passivity, conformity, cooperation, assertiveness and/or rebellion.	Conformity, cooperation, assertiveness and/or rebellion.	Angry acting-out, overt rebellion and/or social withdrawal.
Resulting Adolescent Feelings and Emotions	Rage, anger, frustration, resentment, fear, depression, despair, helplessness and/or alienation.	Anger, fear, security, love and self-respect.	Anger, security, love and self-respect.	Rage, anger, resentment, frustration, anxiety, fear, depression, despair, isolation and/or alienation.

Illustration 5

Even though teenagers are separating from parents and pulling closer to their peers, they continue to have a strong need for ongoing relationships with adults.[22] But because they are unsure and distrustful of themselves they tend to be very cautious around adults, including parents, pastors, therapists and counselors. They will keep at a safe distance, watch, evaluate and determine to what extent the adult can be safely trusted. We will take a look at 20 personal characteristics that help adults to be the healthy, well-adjusted kind of parents that adolescents need.[23]

Feelings of worth. Parents who feel secure about themselves, affirmed in their own identities and needed by their families, friends and colleagues are more able to give generously of themselves to their teenagers.

Self-respect. Healthy self-respect enables parents to value and respect their children.

Satisfaction at work. Parents who are fulfilled in their work and are getting some of their personal needs met there are better able to give emotionally to their adolescent children even if the teenagers give little or nothing in return.

Sense of humor. An adequate sense of humor helps parents to get through upsetting and painful parenting experiences. Humor helps to release tension and frustration, preventing its development into anger.

Honesty. Consistent honesty reveals a well-developed personal integrity and suggests a high level of personal maturity.

Stability. Stability requires the ability to think through difficult problems without reacting in a destructive manner.

Optimism. Optimism suggests an orientation to life that expects a positive outcome. This is an important trait for teenagers to learn from a parent.

Meaningful goals. Parents whose lives are organized around important goals and values are characterized by meaning and purpose.

Inquisitiveness. An inquiring mind sets a good example for becoming a self-motivated learner.

Respect for others. Parents who have a consistent, genuine respect for others' rights help to lead adolescents from their age-appropriate egocentricity toward an adult ability to love others more selflessly.

Positive attention. Teenagers need a great deal of positive attention in order to reinforce their developing identities and to affirm them when they are feeling unsure of themselves.

Reasonableness. "Because I'm your parent" isn't a good answer to a teenager's honest request for a reason or explanation. The use of reason stimulates growth while excessive force hinders development and produces resentment.

Thoughtfulness. Teenagers need to feel respected and valued. They need to be encouraged to think about themselves and their world.

Loving attitude. Seeing their mother and father expressing love to each other helps teenagers to develop healthy attitudes toward the opposite sex. Adolescents also need to be able to give and receive love from their parents.

Social skills. Parents who work to develop social skills, who enjoy relating with people and who build healthy friendships are displaying important behaviors for their children to learn.

Flexibility. Adolescence brings a great deal of change to the whole family. Parents who adjust comfortably to change help their teenagers feel more self-confident as they go through these changes.

Responsibility. Teenagers learn to value the trait of responsibility when they enjoy the benefits such as dependability and reliability within their own parents.

Knowledge of limitations. Teenage children begin to realize the faults, inconsistencies and limitations of their parents. When adults can nondefensively admit their shortcomings, they help their adolescents feel even more esteem, respect and acceptance.

Sense of purpose. Parents who have a purpose and method for attaining their goals will be far more effective in their parenting than those who are deeply conflicted, anxious or confused.

Openness. Parents who share their problems and personal pain with a friend allow themselves to learn new approaches to difficult situations. Adolescents gain both directly and indirectly from having parents who do not pretend to know all the answers.

When counseling with parents, these 20 traits can be used either formally or casually as a way of estimating how well they are adjusting to the task of parenting teenagers.

Common Areas of Conflict

It is possible to grow through the adolescent years without a great deal of disruption in relationships with family members. However, it will be helpful now to give special attention to certain "hot spots" in which conflict occurs far more often than others.

1. Selection of friends. Parents learn very quickly how important friends are to their youngsters, because they talk about them a lot if they feel secure from parental judgment and criticism. What their friends think, like and dislike, what clothes they wear, how they fix their hair, what kind of car they drive, and who they like (and don't like) are some of the seemingly endless list of adolescents' fascinations with friends.

One discomfort that parents feel about this movement toward friends is their teenager's converse movement away from their sphere of control and influence. As youth ascribe more closely to the beliefs, morals, attitudes and activities of their friends, parents are forced to rely more heavily on the effects from their previous parenting and in their faith and trust in their son or daughter.

A second major discomfort that parents feel concerns the particular friends chosen by their teenager.

The mother of 20-year-old Laura expressed her pain over the past three years as she watched her daughter's relationship with a boyfriend gradually limit and alter the direction of her life. As the relationship with her boyfriend deepened, Laura moved further away from her friends. Though she did attend her best girlfriend's wedding, she turned down her request to be a bridesmaid and didn't stay for the reception because she "had to get back to her boyfriend." Her boyfriend neither drives nor works. Laura provides most of his transportation and money while he provides her the security of having someone there.

A binding relationship of mutual neediness has effectively pulled Laura away from her parents' love and influence as well as her friends. Such heart-rending stories can cause us to fear the impact of peer friendships. But an accurate response to the effect of peer relationships must also include their many positive benefits. It is often the voice of a friend, not an adult, that turns a young person away from dangerous experimentation with drugs, alcohol or sex. Proverbs 13:20 carries promise as well as warning: "He who walks with wise men becomes wise, but the companion of fools will suffer harm."

Parents are, fortunately, not helpless when it comes to who their teenage children select for friends. But much of what parents can do to steer their teenagers toward positive influences must be accomplished prior to the adolescent years and then maintained through them. People tend to select friends who reflect the image that they have of themselves. Teenagers who feel especially frightened and insecure about rejection will usually seek acceptance from other frightened and insecure kids. Those with a strong sense of self-esteem will take the necessary risks to seek friendship from the most desirable young people. This confidence building must begin early and be carried on through the adolescent years. The more effectively the parents foster a healthy self-esteem within their children, the greater the chances are that they will seek association with a peer group that reinforces positive growth.

Parents who display a warm, accepting and valuing attitude toward their children's friends accomplish several valuable goals.[24] Friendships with age peers are very important to adolescents, yet making friends does not come easily and naturally to all teenagers. Parental encouragement and support can help a frightened and insecure teenager develop some friendships. By welcoming children's friends into the home, parents put themselves on the line and give visible evidence of their value on friendship. They also learn much more about their children's friends and, as a result, will probably become less fearful of their influence on their own child.

A common counseling issue for families with teenagers is disagreement between parents and teenagers over the selection of a particular friend or group of friends. There are few issues that lend themselves so naturally to a battleground for fierce parent-teenager warfare. Parents do well not to panic. Before even suggesting a critical or negative observation about a young person's friend, parents might try to draw out their son's or daughter's own feelings, attitudes and thoughts about a particular friend. "What is it that you think people like about Jayne?" "Does George have really good friendships that last quite a long time?" "Have you ever thought about where Stan seems to be headed in his life?" "What do you suppose are Vicki's goals?" Questions like these, especially if asked before the teenager becomes defensive, can help him or her develop thoughts and opinions which may display a great deal of wisdom. Pastors, counselors and parents can have a great impact by stimulating a teenager's own thoughts before presenting their own criticisms and judgments.

By the time disagreement about selection of friends reaches the counseling office, the situation is probably very intense and emotionally charged. Counselors and parents will make little or no progress through frontal attack. "You're not allowed to see him anymore." "She's a bad influence on you. All you're going to get out of that relationship are bad grades and a ruined life." "I thought you had better sense than to run around with somebody like that." These demeaning types of statements will produce more rage, defensiveness or passive withdrawal.

It is far more productive to seek reasons for the teenager's choice of friends. Often it is because of a lack of a warm, loving and secure home. Lack of loving contact in the home exaggerates the adolescent's already strong need for peer approval. The need becomes an obsession.

Often these young people seek friendship in the places where it is least threatening to find it. Other teenagers who are hungry for contact, who feel insecure about themselves and who have lowered their standards for acceptance can become very attractive to an insecure adolescent. Teenagers with low self-esteem expect almost certain rejection from young people who are physically attractive, successful in academics, outstanding in sports, leaders in school or youth group, or who are just mature, likable and popular.

Another parental attitude and response that can reinforce the selection of questionable friends is an overprotective or oppressive parenting style. Teenagers who are prevented from experiencing a gradual increase of power in their lives will often rebel in hurtful ways, such as choosing friends that will anger, frustrate and hurt parents.

As the underlying causes are discovered, understood and addressed by the family, the teenager has more personal freedom to change his or her selection of friends. Winning the power struggle with parents or facing rejection from peers is no longer the issue. As these negative barriers are cleared away, adolescents are then freer to select companions with healthier goals in mind.

2. Dating and sexual activity. A second common area of family conflict comes as adolescents become involved with the dating process. Teenagers' dating experiences can provide great opportunities for enjoyable and profitable interaction with their parents. Young people who can freely confide in their parents have a marvelous opportunity to learn from them. And they give their parents a chance to share in one of the most exciting times in their lives.

But this positive, happy picture does not automatically occur in every family. Open communication with adolescent children is usually the result of an ongoing pattern of healthy interaction between parent and child. It is a pattern of mutual trust, respect and openness that has been reinforced many times in the child's life. Beginning around first grade (or earlier) parents can stimulate children to begin thinking about the qualities in their peers that they like or don't like. A great starting place is, "Who do you want to invite to your birthday party?" An animated discussion may follow about why certain boys and girls are liked more than others, what makes some kids fun to be with and others not so enjoyable, and so on.

This kind of interaction (at a more mature level) with adolescents can focus on friends, dates or potential dates. "What is it about Joel that you enjoy so much?" "Son, you've been out with Mary and Barbie both about four or five times. Who's winning?" "Vera, is Joe a fun date or more of a serious relationship?" These kinds of questions, presented in a friendly manner are likely to produce energized responses. Teenagers want to talk but often tend not to because they fear challenging questions, disapproval or condemnation from adults.

One reason why the issue of dating so often causes problems between teenagers and parents is that adults are reacting to their own past as they try to deal with their children. Parents whose early dating experiences were seriously limited by their own shyness, excessive restrictiveness imposed by their parents or church, or other reason will tend to do one of two things. Some will overcompensate by pushing their child too quickly into relationships that they are not prepared to handle adequately. Others, still fearing the "danger" of teenage dating, will be just as overprotective and oppressive as their parents were with them. In either case teenagers suffer, having to tailor their dating behavior to meet the needs of the parents, and not their own.

The dating issue that often causes the greatest conflict is the timing of dating freedoms and limits. The fact that there is far more gray than black or white makes this a particularly difficult issue for parents to face with strength and sensitivity. Teenagers need limits. They require structure. And they need a structure that allows for gradual and purposeful change. They need a structure that they have a part in determining and that they can play a role in altering.

Each person matures at a different rate and in a diferent manner. Some 14-year-old girls live in the body of a 19-year-old while responding and making decisions with emotions and mentality of a 12-year-old. The reverse can be just as true. Each young person needs to be treated as an individual. But there are some broad guidelines that might be helpful for parents, pastors and counselors who work with adolescents.

During junior high school (generally ages 12 and 13) young people are in the midst of early adolescence. A driving need at this age is to be with their peer group. The process of pulling away from parental and family influence is underway. Though girls of this are often very interested in boys, the latter usually begin to get interested in the opposite sex at around age 14 or 15.

Group activities that involve both sexes seem to be the best beginnings for the dating process. Church youth group activities, school dances and chaperoned private parties (birthdays, Christmas, end-of-school) all provide ideal opportunities for boys and girls to get to know each other better on a social level. Though young teenagers typically come to these events individually, it is not uncommon for couples to begin to pair off. Attractions are experienced, assertions of interest are ventured (usually quite tentatively), and though some rejections are experienced, the beginnings of movement toward heterosexual intimacy have started. But most early adolescents are not mature enough for more intense forms of real dating.

During the first two years of high school (usually 14 and 15 years of age) young people become more assertive and purposeful in the dating process. Being with the group is okay, but they are now more interested in spending time with that special boy or girl. If, for some reason, they cannot sit together, eat together or talk with each other, then the evening is mostly ruined.

The beginnings of formal dating are usually seen during this stage of development. During eighth and ninth grades the boy's parents will probably be called upon to provide transportation to and from the movies, the school dance, miniature golf or Friday night's football game. Having Mom or Dad in the car loses its charm very quickly, though. This is where double dating is usually helpful. With four instead of only two, there are fewer chances that the conversation will stagnate at those deadly silent spots. And going out with another couple is far less embarrassing than cruising town with Mom or Dad.

Some teenagers at this age, however, still have little or no interest in the opposite sex. But that does not mean there is anything to worry about. Some young people simply mature a little slower than others. Many freshman and sophomore girls easily form crushes on boys who are juniors, seniors or even high school graduates. This can be a problem because most young teenage girls are not fully mature or experienced to adequately deal with the sexual demands and emotional intensity that boys of that age typically expect of their dates. Young girls, particularly those who developed sexually at an early age, overestimate their dating abilities. Setting limits in this situation is often a very painful but absolutely necessary process.

During the last two years of high school (usually ages 16 to 18) young people move from mid-adolescence to late adolescence. Formal single dating is the norm at this age.

It is best if a boy or girl can date several members of the opposite sex more than once. This gives them an opportunity to meet several people. Contrary to some advice, dating should not be restricted only to perceived potential marriage partners. That limitation can make the dating process far too heavy, serious and limiting. Adolescence is a time of high energy, excitement, fun and adventure. Dating should reflect these same characteristics. Caution should be used to forbid dates with people who might threaten real physical danger (reckless driving, for example) or moral danger.

Youth at this age will often begin dating one person exclusively for months or even several years. These long-term relationships provide settings for intimacy, sharing and commitment. Parental limits need to be broad enough to allow older teenagers the freedom to begin developing these more serious relationships while maintaining a position of influence in their teenager's thinking. By this stage, parents have had about 16 or so years to shape, mold and influence their children with morals, values, spiritual beliefs and ethical standards. Now it is time for the teenagers to test their own maturity and values in the real world. Some teenagers have to push further away from parents. Their dating practices will probably reflect this disparity between their own and their parents' beliefs.

Some parent-teenager conflict is typical at this age level. In the later high school years parents still need to be involved in establishing certain limits. Determining curfew, frequency of nights out, types of dating events and dating partners are all decisions in which parents should be able to participate. The degree of parent participation will depend on general parenting style, maturity level of the adolescent and the teenager's past dating history.

About the time an adolescent graduates from high school and turns 18, parents should diminish their control to the zero point. It is hoped their influence will remain strong, but the actual control should disappear. This allows late adolescents to be fully responsible for their dating behavior before being totally on their own. The consequences of poor judgment and mistakes will be easier to deal with if a supportive family is still there. Such times can be trying and frightening for parents. Parents often experience conflicting emotions, feel out of control, try to let go and struggle to express love and concern. It is easy to understand why everyone in the home is often relieved when the late adolescent moves away from home.

A particularly stressful dating issue for many teenagers and their parents is sex. Sexual awareness increases with dating activity. Concerned parents want to help their teenagers go from pre-puberty innocence through adolescence and finally to young adult maturity as normally and naturally as possible.

Discussing sex with adolescents can be a valuable, comforting and enjoyable experience. They are open, honest and motivated inquirers, especially if their parents have encouraged them to ask questions throughout childhood. All discussion about this topic is best brought up in a light, friendly manner. The heaviness and seriousness of a summit meeting will likely sabotage any possibility of a relaxed, open dialogue.

It is important to remember that while Mom and Dad are ready to talk, it doesn't mean that their sons or daughters will want to open up right at that moment. Being sensitive to their needs and timing is absolutely imperative. This sensitivity expresses respect and models the attitudes parents want from their children.

Some parents are able to be open with their sons and daughters about their own frustrations, temptations and experiences while they were teenagers. As adults disclose more of themselves they become more human, and more trusted by young people.[25] But do not get carried away with storytelling. Stories tend to be most appreciated by the teller, so keep in mind why the discussion is taking place. What are the goals? Personal accounts are helpful only when their telling is meaningful to the youthful hearer. Avoid graphic detail in order to keep the focus on the points that matter. And follow through by drawing out the teenager: "What do you think I should have done?" "If you were my parent, what would you have advised me?" "How would that have made you feel?"

Discussion about limits to sexual expression is very important. Healthy young people really do want to do what is right for themselves and their dating partners. They do wish to please their parents and other valued adults. But offsetting these wishes are their sometimes overwhelming impulses for sexual release and pleasure, the joy of feeling valued and desired and the craving for an intimate relationship.

Donna, an eighth grader, shared recently with her parents and close family friends that at parties, some of the kids pair off and "start kissing pretty heavily." Such is the nature of typical early sexual explorations. Unfortunately, some junior highers are already having regular sex while others haven't developed any interest in the opposite sex at all. But most early adolescents are beginning to do some occasional kissing and holding hands. Parents need to be able to accept these behaviors as normal and healthy, not as dirty and sinful. But early adolescents are not equipped with enough maturity to handle much sexual arousal, so opportunities for this kind of exploration with intimacy need to be monitored closely.

A very attractive 15-year-old client recently shared with her therapist, "For the first time I dated a boy that I didn't have to push away. Always before I felt that the only reason why guys took me out was because of sex. After one date, they usually don't ask me out again. But Bill is different. He really cares. He asks me about my problems, says he prays for me. He cares about me as a person. I mean, he's not weird or anything. We do kiss and stuff. But it's just different. It's really neat!"

Parental limitations, discussions, rules and guidelines, and most of all, consistent availability, provide mid-adolescents with the necessary structure and supportive environment for dating. Parental involvement also helps teenagers develop the sexual responsibility of saying "no." Mid-adolescents must say "no," "wait" and "only a little," both to their own inner urgings as well as to their dating partners. This aids conscience development, builds self-control and self-esteem. It also helps the young person confront a terrible fear: "If I don't do what they want me to, will they reject me?" Sometimes we are rejected when we tell someone "no." And so an even deeper and more haunting fear is confronted: "If he or she rejects me, can I ever face myself again as a person of value and worth?" Supportive parents and a loving family help the hurting teenager to rebound with a resounding "yes."

Late adolescence is characterized by much more sexual activity, corresponding to the increase in formal single dating, exclusive dating, and long-term intimate relationships that sometimes lead to marriage. Parents need to understand that they have less control over their teenagers at this age. They have about as much control as their children allow them to have. Parents whose teenage children have run away experience that unsettling sense of powerlessness in one of the most devastating ways. Their mobility and network of friends enable them to have far greater freedom from parental supervision than ever before.

During this age, parents are forced to rely heavily on the influence that they have developed through the years of parenting their child. Their hope is that spiritual principles, moral values and ethical standards have been planted deeply enough within their children's souls that they will become increasingly self-governing without serious negative results. This is not to imply that parents should not or cannot exert control over their 16-, 17- and 18-year-olds. They certainly can and should. But without the prevailing strong influence reinforced by past years, parents' control is seriously handicapped.

As late adolescents graduate from high school and reach that magic 18th birthday, they usually step into responsibility for their own decisions about sexual expression. Ideally, sex is viewed as a very beautiful expression of love and commitment within the marriage relationship. Though parents can still make suggestions, share their views and ask pertinent questions, the decisions belong to their children. Parents do best to handle their concerns about premarital sex, pregnancy before marriage, venereal diseases and premature marriage primarily through prayer, and secondarily through discussion.

3. Alcohol and other drugs. The use and abuse of drugs by teenagers has created a great deal of conflict in families over past decades. Because of its long-term acceptance among adults and more recent growing acceptance among Christian adults, alcohol is often thought of as something other than a drug. Since most other drugs are usually in the form of pills, capsules, injections and powder, alcohol is thought of as somehow different. Our government (along with most other governments of the world) has legalized its use, while making the access to other drugs illegal.

Tobacco and coffee are also consumed commonly by adults for their drug properties. Their use is now being discouraged because of overwhelming medical evidence of their harmful effects on our bodies. In many geographic areas of our nation tobacco is not an accepted drug in Christian circles. Coffee is usually served at church socials, in most Christians' homes, in adult Sunday school classes and during Sunday morning fellowship breaks. Parents need to recognize possible inconsistencies in their own attitudes and behaviors regarding drugs that reach beyond the issue of legality-illegality. We need not punish ourselves for our own inconsistencies, but we should be able to face our own drug usage with at least the same honesty and degree of responsibility that we expect from adolescents regarding their use of drugs.

Most Christian parents expect their teenagers to abstain from experimentation and usage of drugs. Yet, as they hear of the frequent and often daily use of drugs by large percentages of young people, even at the elementary school level, they question the reasonableness of their expectations. But remember that there are many teenagers who have never even tried drugs. Fears of the unknown and going against parental and church values stop some. But others refrain from drug experimentation because they have decided to refrain. They have determined not to go against the values and ethics that they have learned and adopted from their parents.

Other teenagers, as an expression of normal adolescent rebellion, will engage in mild, infrequent experimentation with drugs, usually of the more innocuous varieties. Understand that simply because a behavior is part of a normal developmental process, it does not follow that it is okay or justified. Not at all. But it is important for parents to understand what their children's drug use is saying. Is it simply a part of his or her experimentation with life, learning how to make decisions? Is the drug use because of peer pressure? Is this a pattern of rebellion that is showing up in other behaviors as well? Does his or her drug usage seem to be self-destructive or more to have a good time?

When parents discover that their teenager has been using drugs, shock and denial are typically the first reactions. Then comes a crucial choice. The wise parent asks some vitally important questions before reacting to the teenager. "What do I want to accomplish in this situation?" "What am I feeling right now?" "Am I going to be able to control my feelings and not react out of anger and rage?" "What is my son or daughter needing from me?" Taking time out to ask and seek answers to these questions will lead to a more positive conversation.

When drug usage becomes more chronic and when it involves the more dangerous kinds of substances, more than mere adolescent experimentation is involved. Such usage is sometimes a symbol of peer pressure levied by a group of friends whose acceptance is particularly valued by the teenager. At other times it expresses a deep sense of discouragement and the view that one is a failure with no realistic hope for success or happiness. In other instances the teenager is seeking to strike back at parents, causing them pain and embarrassment even though his or her actions may cause personal harm. Perhaps the most desperate motivation underlying drug abuse is the desire to be self-destructive as an expression of deep-seated depression and self-hatred.

When drug abuse is expressive of any of these more serious motivations, parents alone are not going to be able to reach their teenagers effectively. They should seek out a professional therapist or youth counselor who is trained to work with adolescents with drug and family problems.

4. Money. Learning how to take care of financial obligations is an integral part of adolescent growth toward maturity. Parents can greatly help in this process or hinder it. Most parent-teenager conflicts over money come about because the parents have not established a policy with their teenagers for handling finances. Or, they changed the existing policy without adequately consulting with their teenagers. Or, they established an excessive, burdensome policy for their teenagers. A respectful attitude and an awareness that having money is important to teenagers can usually prevent serious conflicts.

There are four common methods for handling the issue of money with teenagers.[26] The first method involves no structure at all. Whenever the teenager wants money for something, a request is made and the parents decide whether or not to provide the requested money. The main advantage to this plan is that since the teenager does not have to work for money, he or she has plenty of time for schoolwork, church activities, school social activities, having fun with friends, relaxing with other family members, and pursuing hobbies and interests.

But the disadvantages probably outweigh the advantages. Adolescence is a time of growth toward adult responsibility. In this "handout" system the teenager has no responsibility. There is no opportunity to learn how to manage funds or to learn about stewardship of God's money. Another disadvantage is that it places the adolescent in an ongoing dependency upon the parents. It repeatedly places both adolescent and parent in a vulnerable role. The teenager can never plan on a certain amount of money being available. There is always a big question mark when trying to make plans with friends. Mom or dad has to be consulted first in order to see if they can get the money. This method seems to run counter to normal adolescent developmental needs.

Another approach involves even less of a structure between the parents and teenagers. In this second plan the parents provide nothing other than room, food, clothing and maybe the absolutely essential school costs. The teenagers are responsible for everything else. If they want something, they have to pay for it. If they cannot swing it, they do not get it. Money can be earned by getting part-time jobs, summer jobs and by working around the house for an agreed-upon amount of money.

On the positive side, this approach definitely teaches young people to budget responsibly. If they do not, reality can hit pretty hard. And they have to bail themselves out. This plan also relieves parents from always having to make difficult choices about whether or not to give the money. Unfortunately, the disadvantages outweigh the advantages of this approach.

During the adolescent years, young people need to spend ample time socially with friends. And that means having some free weekends and evenings. Because teenagers usually don't get paid adequately, they have to work quite a few hours per week in order to pay for the things and activities they enjoy. All too often the job itself presents a time conflict. But without the job there is no money to pay for participating in the desired activities. So the teenager is really caught in a bind. And where are Dad and Mom? That is another problem. They're too far out of the picture. Though adolescence is a time for growth toward independence, teenagers also need to feel the solid support of their parents in order to be able to handle increasing responsibilities. Being totally dependent on their own earning power for "extras" thrusts a teenager out into harsh adult reality too early. Too many important social, spiritual, athletic and other opportunities will be lost. Jim can't go to his school class ski weekend because he has to work. Sonja has to miss the church youth retreat because she does not have enough money. These kinds of ongoing pressures can cause depression, frustration, anger, discouragement and an overly serious attitude about life.

A third and very common method of helping teenagers handle money is by giving them an allowance. The same amount of money is given to the young person every week (or whatever schedule is preferred, such as biweekly or monthly) without consideration of his or her contribution of help at home. The allowance is not a payment for chores completed. Rather, it is simply guaranteed income.

This system's advantages probably outweigh its disadvantages. The young person has a regular income to learn budgeting responsibilities. There is also ample time for enjoying the teenage years. However, one disadvantage is that the teenager does not learn the link between work and earned money. The funds come from the parents' pockets and the adolescent therefore feels no responsibility for earning it. Finally, it is assumed that the allowance will take care of whatever extras the teenager will want or need. What happens if Mary's budgeting error leaves her short $20 for choir tour or summer camp? She learns a hard lesson but also misses out on an important and enjoyable event in her life.

The fourth and final approach is really a combination of the first three. Its primary feature is an allowance that is freely and regularly given. But the teenager also works part time, cuts lawns, baby-sits or takes summer jobs. Flexibility is allowed for special occasions and unexpected problems. In this plan the teenagers have a regular income that can be budgeted under their control. But they are also encouraged to learn the value and pleasure of being paid for their work. And parents are close at hand to help work out solutions to financial problems.

Whichever system is used in the home, parents need to teach fiscal values that they deem important. The values and practices of budgeting, saving, gift-giving, tithing and investing can become a part of adolescent financial behavior if adequately taught, encouraged and modeled by the parents.

5. School. The primary source of conflict in this area centers around academic performance. Most parents have a strong desire for their children to do well in school. They see academic success as a prerequisite for future occupational success. Parents' ego and pride are often involved in their children's success. They feel pride and accomplishment when their children do well. Conversely, they feel embarrassed, angry and frustrated when their teenagers experience academic difficulty or failure. It is usually this overinvestment in their adolescent's performance that sets the stage for conflict.

In this situation students feel the pressure to do well not only for their own sake but also for the benefit of the parents. Poor grades mean not only personal disappointment, but the additional burden of their parents' disappointment. Young people normally want to please their parents. But when the load gets too heavy or the discouragement grows too strong, teenagers can cave in and give up trying. When adolescents are angry at their parents they will sometimes flunk or do poorly as an expression of that anger. The parents' wish for their teenager's success then becomes a tool for the adolescent to use against them.

As a part of their movement toward independence teenagers need to feel a sense of ownership and responsibility for their own grades. It is great when parents express concern and caring about their son's or daughter's progress. But when parents "need" their teenagers to do well, serious problems may be at hand.

6. Disinterest in church. A very common adolescent reaction is loss of interest in church. As concerned parents try to encourage their youth to get involved more in church the reaction is sometimes anger and more antagonism. "Do I allow my son to stay away from church or do I make him go even if he just sits there, sullen and angry?" A difficult dilemma, but one that is usually able to be prevented or at least partially diverted. Indications of failing interest in church usually are first seen during the pre-teenage years. Responding positively to these feelings at such an early stage can usually bring about good results.

Adolescence is normally a time of very high energy. Sitting on Sunday morning listening to a Sunday school lesson and sermon may have little interest to a teenager. This does not automatically mean that these teenagers are less spiritual than others. Some who stay heavily involved in church do so primarily to please parents. Others center all of their activities within the safe familiar confines of church and youth group circles because of the insecurity that they feel elsewhere among non-churched youth. This is not to imply that there are no teenagers who have strong spiritual motivations for their church attendance. Certainly there are! But we must be aware of underlying motivations, not only outward behavior.

When teenagers give signals that church is no longer an enjoyable experience, try to find out why. We need to understand what they are feeling. "Hey, Rhonda, you've seemed pretty down the last several weeks on the way home from church. Something going on there that you feel unhappy about?" "Frank, the last few weeks you've been complaining about having to go to youth group. Let's talk about it." Show interest in what the teenager is feeling and experiencing. Parents need not do what kids expect them to do: panic, get upset, angry and demand forcefully that "you kids will go to church and that's that." Before reacting, find out why. They might have a very good reason for their reluctance.

It might be that the meetings are boring and uninteresting for them. Perhaps the kids in the group are unattractive or unpleasant to be with for some reason. Or possibly the youth group kids have a bad "out of it" reputation at school. There also may be a conflict between the teenager and the youth pastor, a youth sponsor or Sunday school teacher. Few things will turn off a teenager faster than feeling disliked. The problem might also be spiritual in nature. Teenagers can feel pretty uncomfortable in church if they are cheating at school, using drugs behind their parents' back, secretly having sex, or committing some other sin that creates a condition of real guilt.

Finding out why the teenager does not want to go to church directs us to possible solutions for the problem. If the church service and youth meetings really are boring and not adequately designed or presented for adolescents, the parents could try to do something about it. They could talk with the pastor or youth pastor. They could volunteer to become youth sponsors, invite the group over periodically for backyard barbecues, swims, game nights or Bible studies. This kind of involvement says a lot to a young person.

Some youth groups are, unfortunately, almost lost causes. The handful of teenagers there may have little spiritual motivation and attempts to salvage the group seem to fail. In these sad situations parents need to consider moving to a different church. This is not a decision to be made lightly. It should be the focus of much prayer, thought and family discussion. Such a move can uproot adult worship patterns, church service functions and friendship contacts. Yet such action is a message of love to a confused teenager.

When interpersonal problems are the basis for withdrawing from youth group, the teenager needs to be encouraged to confront the difficulty and try to deal with it rather than running away. Parents must be sensitive to their adolescent's feelings and words. There are those times and situations where a youth pastor or adult leader is so legalistic or rigid that there is little or no room for individual differences. Teenagers feel very reluctant to open themselves up or to reveal themselves in any significant way in this kind of environment. Only correction and judgment would be given, and that is not sufficient for healthy growth and change.

Another solution (one that is less drastic than changing churches) is particularly appropriate when the teenager resists attendance not because of inadequacies or problems with the church's youth ministry, but because of personal reasons. Be willing to compromise on the number of church activities per week at which attendance is expected. Some parents demand that their teenagers be present at Sunday school, Sunday morning worship service, Sunday evening youth meeting, Sunday night church, mid-week Bible study and other church meetings. Now there is nothing intrinsically wrong with that kind of schedule except it is too busy. Adolescents need time alone and ample unstructured free time with their friends.

Some teenagers will respond well to the idea of ranking church-related meetings from "meetings I like most" to "meetings I like least." Parents can reduce the number of meetings per week at which attendance is required using their teenager's list. A non-denominational campus-related meeting might also supplement the church meeting schedule. Adolescents will usually respond positively to genuine efforts from parents to help work out church attendance problems. An excessively hostile and rejecting attitude indicates that the real problem lies somewhere other than with attending church. That is only one expression of a much deeper issue and until that issue is resolved little or no progress will be made regarding church involvement.

Communication in the Family

Feeling alienated and isolated from other family members is one of the most unhappy, yet common, experiences in families with teenagers. Adolescents struggle for greater independence and parents sometimes react by feeling threatened, uncared for and confused. Solomon tells us that, "A bad messenger plunges men into trouble, but a faithful envoy brings healing" (Proverbs 13:17). Reliable family communication is absolutely imperative for healthy progress through the adolescent years.

During the past two to three decades much research has been done in the study of communication. Some reliable and valid results have direct application in helping families with this process. Clinical psychologist Sven Wahlroos presents 20 rules for effective communication in families:[27]

Remember that actions speak louder than words. Non-verbal communication is more powerful than verbal communcation. A familiar saying that underscores this point is, "Your actions are yelling so loudly that I can't hear a word you're saying."

Define what is important and stess it; define what is unimportant and ignore it. Too many parents exhaust themselves and wear out their relationship with their adolescent because they expend far too much time and energy focusing on minor issues.

Make your communication as positive as realistically possible. It is so easy to get into the habit of starting sentences with, "I wish you wouldn't . . .," "Do you really have to . . .," "Isn't there any other way . . .," "Must you . . ." and other endless phrases that immediately set up the teenager to feel defensive.

Be clear and specific in your communication. Major family blowups often are the result of unclear communication or statements that are too general.

Be realistic and reasonable in your statements. Parents need to take time out to remember what life was like when they were teenagers. Adolescent behavior, not adult-like actions, should be expected of teenagers. Young people need to accept imperfection in their parents also.

Test all your assumptions verbally. Get your partner's okay before you act. Solomon warns, "By insolence the heedless make strife, but with those who take advice is wisdom" (Proverbs 13:10). We feel angry and misunderstood when someone assumes we think a certain way, but does not check with us first.

Recognize that each event can be seen from different points of view. It is so easy to fall into the myopic trap of believing that ours is the only valid perspective.

Recognize that your family members are experts on you and your behavior. In addition to the fact that lying, deceit and covering up are destructive to family process, they do not work for very long because we are so well-known by our family members.

Do not allow discussions to turn into destructive arguments. Though some arguing is okay and necessary in communication, take a "time out" if the argument becomes hostile, blocked or hurtful. Then come back to the issue after lunch, an hour or the next day.

Be open and honest about your feelings. Bring up all significant problems, even if you are afraid that doing so will disturb your partner. Some people seek to be "nice," they try not to "rock the boat," and in so doing exhibit a lack of trust that they and their family will be able to handle their feelings adequately. Avoidance reinforces the fear and seriously handicaps family growth.

Do not use unfair communication techniques; do not engage in "dirty fighting." The following 14 unfair techniques are designed not to draw the other person closer, but rather to defeat the other family members:[28]

1. Pretending that the other person had made an unreasonable statement or demand.

2. Mind reading, psychologizing, jumping to conclusions. Pretending that one single motive constitutes complete motivation.

3. Switching the subject. Using counteraccusations.

4. Bringing up more than one accusation at a time (the kitchen sink attack).

5. Bragging or playing the numbers game.

6. Using logic to hide from emotional reality.

7. Interrupting.

8. Using the atom bomb. The bull in the china shop. Intimidating. Yelling, screaming and exploding.

9. Blaming the partner for something that is not his or her fault. Refusing to forgive.

10. Humiliating the partner. Using insults and epithets. Rubbing in. Exposing dirty linen in public. Comparing.

11. Crazy-making. "Bugging." Unpredictability.

12. Having one's feelings hurt at the drop of a hat. Guilt induction.

13. The use of sarcasm and ridicule.

14. Silence, ignoring, sulking, pouting, "cold shoulder treatment."

Let the effect, not the intention, of your communication be your guide. People who are repeatedly saying, "You misunderstood me," "That's not what I meant . . .," "You took it all wrong . . ." are failing to communicate with the hearer. The hearer probably recognizes feelings, motivations and attitudes of which the speaker is unconscious.

Accept all feelings and try to understand them; do not accept all actions, but try to understand them. Feelings and emotions are facts and need to be accepted as such. Trying to argue family members out of their feelings or telling them how bad they are for feeling as they do is destructive.

Be tactful, considerate and courteous, and show respect for your partner and his or her feelings. Honesty must be regarded as a high value. But there is an even higher value. Jesus said, "You shall love the Lord your God with all your heart, and with all your soul, and with all your mind. This is the great and first commandment. And a second is like it, you shall love your neighbor as yourself. On these two commandments depend all the laws and the prophets" (Matthew 22:37-40).

Do not preach or lecture; ask questions instead." Preaching, lecturing and unnecessary repeating are sure ways of inflicting teenagers with "parent-deafness."

Do not use excuses and do not fall for excuses." Giving and accepting excuses is dangerous for family relationships because it reinforces irresponsibility and can lead to more overt forms of dishonesty.

Do not nag, yell or whine. All of these push others away and create chasms rather than bridges.

Learn when to use humor and when to be serious. Do not subject your partner to destructive teasing. Humor has a valuable place in family communicating. It can relieve tensions and maximize the pleasure of having fun together. But it can be deadly when mixed with anger that is not admitted and owned.

Learn to listen. Probably the most difficult, threatening and yet most powerful communication tool is intent listening.

Beware of playing destructive games. Social interaction games are necessary and helpful to family functioning.[29] But caution must be taken to insure that these patterns are constructive to each family member and are not run out at anyone's expense.

One of the most often heard cries of contemporary adolescents is, "But they don't understand me." Even more painful than the feeling of not being understood is the perception that parents sometimes do not want to understand them.[30] Sometimes parents get so exhausted with, "Why?" "Yes, but . . .," "No way . . .," etc., that they do not dare try to communicate understanding lest they lose another battle.

"You never listen to me" is a similar complaint heard from both parents and teenagers. Many people mistakenly view listening as a passive process. They think that they can accurately listen to their 16-year-old son at the same time they read the evening newspaper. Fourteen-year-old Jennie wonders why her mom is so uptight just because she is doing her homework and watching TV while "listening" to her. Paul Tournier writes, "It is impossible to overemphasize the immense need humans have to be listened to. Listen to all the conversations of our world, between nations as well as those between couples. They are, for the most part, dialogues of the deaf."[31]

Effective listening requires a great deal of concerted effort. Imagine yourself hiking up a mountain trail with a camera in hand. Next, imagine a beautiful flower along the side of the path. You have two types of lenses for your camera that you may use to take a picture of this flower. You may use the wide-angle lens, but it takes in the full range of the surrounding area. The whole environment is included—twigs, leaves, rocks, the path, etc. Or you can use the telephoto lens. This lens allows you to narrow in on the flower for a crisp, clear, sharp focus of its specific details.

Good listening is much the same. It is not a passive or shallow scanning of the environment. Rather, it requires focusing all our attention on the person we are hearing. It means turning off the TV or radio, putting down the paper, deciding to stop bouncing the basketball, turning around, making direct eye contact and focusing on the person.

Part of the difficulty with listening is that we must attend to far more than the spoken words. A study from the University of Pennsylvania found that when one person is speaking to another, 70 percent of the message is in his or her body language, 23 percent of the message is in voice tone and inflection and only seven percent of the message is in the specific spoken words.[32] When counseling families, it is important to spend significant time training them how to listen. There are some published models that pastors and counselors can use to aid in this training process. Dr. Haim Ginott emphasized the tremendous importance of understanding the inner world of the child and adolescent.[33] Their words are encoded messages from their private world that adults must hear from the child's perspective in order to really understand.[34] In 1970, Thomas Gordon published *Parent Effectiveness Training* that teaches a structured approach to listening called, "active listening."[35] In 1976, *Systematic Training for Effective Parenting* reached the market.[36] It also had a training focus on listening. These same authors added a training program in 1983 specifically for parents of teenagers called *Systematic Training for Effective Parenting of Teens*. This latter training program uses the phrase, "reflective listening." A third parent training program that focuses on the importance of listening is *How to Live With Your Teenager* which was written by two therapists.[37] They propose the phrase, "attentive listening." All of these training concepts treat listening in similar ways.

In all of these approaches the listener plays an active role in drawing out the fullest meaning of what the speaker just said. The listening parent makes every effort to understand what his or her teenager is feeling and thinking, rather than reacting to the first words out of the child's mouth. Parents react to the non-verbal portions of the communication, too, not the words only. Let us look at an example. Mom and Dad are watching the 6 p.m. news when 15-year-old Jeremy comes home from football practice. Slamming the door shut behind him, he crashes his helmet onto the tile floor of the entryway and kicks it down the hall, yelling in an enraged voice, "That Coach Thomas makes me sick! He's such a stupid idiot. To hell with him!"

Mom (swirling around, pointing a finger and yelling at Jeremy): "Jeremy Bosort, I've told you a hundred times not to use language like that. What do you mean, bursting in here like that? Don't you care about anyone but yourself? We have to live here, too, you know."

Jeremy (shoulders stooped, visibly upset, trying to control his anger and keep his cracking voice this side of yelling): "But Mom, you don't understand."

Mom (interrupts): "I understand that you came storming in here, cussing and swearing and throwing things around. Why don't you act your age for a change?"

Jeremy (near tears, red faced and almost whining): "But Mom, let me explain."

Mom: "There are no excuses for behavior like that. Now go to your room, cool down and when you think you can be civilized, you can come out and be with us."

Mom reacted to the awkward, impulsive way that Jeremy acted. In doing so, she failed to hear and respond to his clear verbal and non-verbal expression of hurt, bewilderment and exasperation. Too often parents expect adult-level skill in adolescent expressions of emotion. It does not happen without years of learning, practice, effective modeling and plenty of encouragement.

Let us revisit the same scene with young Jeremy and his parents. But this time, Dad responds.

Jeremy: "That Coach Thomas makes me sick! He's such a stupid idiot. To hell with him!"

Dad (startled and turning around to face Jeremy): "Hey, son, something big must have happened. You're really angry!"

Jeremy (turning to face his dad, red faced, almost crying and visibly very upset): "Dad, I couldn't believe it. He was so mean. It was the first time I was late to practice. It's just not fair" (starting to cry).

Dad (concerned expression on his face, walking over to Jeremy): "You're really feeling hurt about something that Coach Thomas did."

Jeremy (crying and hurt but no longer angry): "It was so crummy. He yelled at me in front of everyone. Made me run laps and sprints during the whole practice."

Dad: "I guess you felt pretty embarrassed in front of your team like that. I'll bet it makes it hard to still like Coach Thomas."

Dad has Jeremy engaged in a productive, close conversation. He did not react to the angry, noisy blast that announced something awfully important had happened in his son's life. Instead, by carefully and gently responding to what Jeremy was really feeling, his son felt understood and safe enough to be more vulnerable (he let the tears go that he had been holding back all afternoon). With his dad's sensitive help he was able to release the pain his anger had been masking.

Pastors and counselors can help parents and teenagers practice effective listening responses during family counseling sessions. Incorporate the responses as a part of your own counseling style. Help the parents overcome the awkwardness of trying out a new behavior while still in the counseling session. The more comfortable they feel, the greater the chances that they will practice the new responses at home. Explore with them the variety of listening responses: "You're feeling . . .," "Seems to me that . . .," "I wonder if . . .," "Sounds like . . .," "Maybe you . . .," "It could be that you . . ." and "Perhaps you're feeling . . ." are a few of the many variations. Tell the parents and teenagers that it will feel awkward for a while (like any new behavior) and then it will become a natural part of their dialogue within their family.

An unhappy characteristic about many homes is that the family members really do not know each other. "But the Lord called to the man, and said to him, 'Where are you?' And he said, 'I heard the sound of thee in the garden, and I was afraid, because I was naked; and I hid myself'" (Genesis 3:9-10). Ever since Adam and Eve's first attempts at hiding from themselves and God, people have become increasingly sophisticated in the ways of self-concealment.

John Powell helps us to understand how family members, after living together 20 and more years, must honestly confess, "I really don't know you very well." Powell describes five levels of communication, the fifth level representing the least communication; the first level representing the most communication of the inner self.

Level five: cliche conversation. Cliche interaction is often used in first-time communication. "Hi, how are you?" "Nice day, isn't it?" "This weather is something else." "I can't believe how fast time goes by." Nothing is really given of the self. No risk is taken, yet some interaction has taken place. It is a kind of "social grease." We slip by each other comfortably and easily, yet we never really touch. Families who use cliche conversation most of the time are in real trouble.

Level four: reporting external facts. At this level, virtually nothing of the self is communicated. All that is learned about the person is what he or she observed or heard. We know nothing of his or her personal thoughts, attitudes or feelings about the event. "Tom cut the lawn today." "Dad, the fender on your car got crumpled today." "Betsy got a D in Spanish on her report card." Facts are important but much is lacking without personal responses.

Level three: reporting personal ideas, judgments and opinions. Now we are getting somewhere. Risks are taken at this level because our personal beliefs can draw angry, hurt and other reactions squarely toward us. "I think Tom was really trying to cooperate by cutting the lawn today." "Dad, even though the fender on your car got crumpled today, I don't think it'll cost very much to get it repaired." "Betsy got a D in Spanish on her report card, and I think she ought to be grounded." A lot of parent-adolescent conflict occurs over personal ideas, opinions and judgments because parents and adolescents typically see the world from very different perspectives.

Level two: reporting feelings and emotions. This is "gut level" communication, the level where the greatest risk is felt. Sharing your feelings with others leaves you far more vulnerable than simply sharing thoughts. Someone might disagree with an opinion without even a hint of personal judgment. But feelings can only be accepted or rejected. And if your feelings are rejected, you are rejected in part too. "I feel so happy that Tom was willing to cut the grass today." "Dad, I feel so scared and guilty because I crumpled your car's fender today." "I am so frustrated because Betsy got a D in Spanish on her report card." Family members must share much more than the facts with each other. Healthy, vibrant family communication requires this level of sharing on a consistent basis.

Level one: peak communication. Consistent, open, mutual communication of feelings between two people will periodically bring about spontaneous moments of what feels like perfect, mutual empathic understanding. You know the other person at the same time they know you. These are beautiful moments to be savored, with the understanding that they cannot be preplanned or enjoyed forever. Peak-communication experiences create warm memories that family members can recall with mutual pleasure.[38]

Communication is a two-step process. We have already looked at listening, which is the process of receiving another's messages. The other step in the communication process is sending messages to the other person. Our thoughts, feelings, attitudes and perceptions are encoded into verbal and non-verbal cues and are then transmitted to the listener. The task of the person speaking is to use words and behaviors that most accurately represent the message he or she wants to convey. It is equally important to use words and behaviors that the listener will be able to understand and receive without defensiveness.

Too often parents and their teenagers communicate in a reciprocal blaming fashion, such as:

Dad: "You left the window open all day."

Todd: "Yeah, but it wasn't open very wide. Besides, you told me I could have it open on hot days."

Dad: "Don't you smart back to me, kid. You never accept responsibility when you do things that are wrong."

And so it goes—blame, defend, counterattack, and so on. Families with teenagers need not be a war zone. Parents and their young people can learn how to get their points across while inviting positive responses rather than defensive reactions.

The main problem in the little example noted above is that it was a series of "you-messages."[39] This kind of interaction is commonly heard during family counseling sessions. Counselors need to alert parents and teenagers to the negative effect of this kind of communication. "You-messages" send a criticism, complaint, threat or put-down. The sender of the message does not really give anything personal. All of the negative focus is placed on the other person.

When people learn to use "I-messages" they own their feelings. They do not attempt to blame the other family member for making them feel that way. Indeed, there is *no* attempt to blame, criticize, put down or threaten. The only intent is to communicate our genuine feelings expecting that the receiver will respect them.

The basic "I-message" looks like this: "I feel . . . " or "I am feeling . . . ."[40] This formula has been expanded in order to communicate more fully while still avoiding the trap of criticizing and accusing.[41] The complete formula looks like this: "I feel . . . when . . . because . . . ."[42] The format can be varied. For example:

"I feel angry when the window is left open because the air conditioner runs too much." "I feel angry because the air conditioner runs too much when the window is left open." "When the window is left open I feel angry because the air conditioner runs too much." "When the window is left open the air conditioner runs too much and then I feel angry." "Because the air conditioner runs too much when the window is left open, I feel angry." "Because the air conditioner runs too much, I feel angry when the window is left open."

Parents and teenagers who are in counseling can be encouraged to practice "I-messages" with the counselor and with each other so that it becomes natural and comfortable. Make sure that not only the words, but also the attitudes are adopted:

1. "My intent is not to blame or criticize you."

2. "It does not matter at all who caused the problem. It is only important to me that the problem is solved."

3. "I respect your feelings and I also desire for you to respect mine."

4. "Our relationship is the most important thing to me."

Here is one last point before leaving the important issues of family communication. "Quality time" is a phrase that has been heard a great deal during the last decade or so. The implication sometimes seems to be that it is okay if the family does not spend much time together, as long as the time that is together is "quality." Well, you can not have quality without quantity. Deep, loving relationships do not happen in real life within 25 or 55 minutes like they do on television. Regular and generous amounts of contact between family members is a prerequisite for healthy functioning families. This contact should be in the forms of time and touch.[43]

When parents and teenagers spend time together they are communicating that they value each other. Many parents get frustrated and hurt because teenagers often reject their offers to do something together. Remember that adolescence is a period of pulling away from parents. But even though they may say "no," the fact that Mom or Dad offered has a positive effect.

Touching is probably just as important as time. Many parents find it very natural to touch, hold and cuddle their infants and little children. But as they grow out of their "little cuteness" and into later childhood and adolescence, that freedom to touch and be touched is often lost by parents. This is particularly true between dads and their daughters. As girls develop into adolescence fathers very commonly experience feelings of sexual attraction to them. Though these feelings are completely normal, many fathers experience anxiety and guilt about them. The following are three common types of responses that dads have to this situation:

1. Some fathers feel so anxious and guilty that they stop hugging and cuddling their daughters altogether. Some try to avoid being around or talking with their girls, who perceive this change in behavior as rejection. They think that for some reason dad is mad at them or that he just does not like them anymore. Some girls sense their father's sexual discomfort around them, and as a result judge their own sexual development and any sexual feelings as bad, dirty or evil. Such reactions can have negative effects on their self-esteem, body image and future ability to develop and enjoy a healthy sexual relationship.

2. Some men take advantage of the situation and form an incestuous relationship with their daughters. Some incestuous fathers never actually have sexual intercourse or even sex play with their teenage daughters. But they do act seductively with their girls, make playful passes, initiate an exaggerated amount of physical contact, get overly involved with the selection and coordination of their clothing and show an exaggerated interest in their girlfriends and dating activities. Other fathers show even less self-control and do initiate sexual contact with their daughters.

3. Other dads are able to accept their own sexual feelings as being normal, knowing that they neither have to hide from them, nor do they have to act them out. These dads are able to enjoy their daughter's attractiveness and developing sexuality, not as a potential lover, but as a proud, loving father who is happy to see his little girl growing up to become a young woman. Hugs, kisses and cuddles continue with a sense of ease and comfortableness without intrusions of powerful sexual impulses. This pattern helps the girl to accept and feel good about her sexuality, and to learn how to interact with boys and men.[44]

The combined effects of spending adequate time with teenagers and maintaining caring touch, provide a strong foundation for building a healthy communicating relationship.

The Role of Discipline in Adolescent Development

The issue of discipline sometimes becomes the focus of a family counseling session. Parents find that their usual methods of disciplining cease to be effective as their children develop into adolescents. As parents get more frustrated they tend to cling to what they have already been doing, only doing it more frequently or more intensely. Pastors and counselors can help parents ask themselves the question, "Is it working?" If not, change. Sounds simple doesn't it? But we all know that parenting and disciplining are not easy at any age, let alone with adolescents.

Let us look at two approaches to the issue of discipline during adolescence: praise/punishment and encouragement/natural and logical consequences.

Praise/punishment. This method of discipline is the more traditional of the two. It is used heavily in authoritarian families and moderately in authoritative homes. Democratic parents seldom dispense praise or punishment and it is virtually non-existent in permissive homes. This system is heavily founded in the philosophical beliefs that people are basically evil and that blind obedience to God and his delegated authorities (parents, teachers, police, etc.) is necessary for the development of constructive behavior patterns.

Parents who employ this approach usually view the anger and rebellion that are often a normal part of adolescence as sinful, negative or at least unnecessary. Strong emphasis is placed upon self-control, little acting-out behavior is tolerated, and experimentation is watched closely and with some suspicion.

Constructive, positive behavior is rewarded by dispensing both verbal and non-verbal reinforcers. "You did a really good job on the lawn." "Jennie, the house looks so nice since you cleaned it." "Paul, I'm really proud of you. You have done so well in school this year." These are all verbal reinforcers for doing things that please Mom and Dad. Non-verbal reinforcers are also effective. Hugs, pats on the back, smiles, money, new privileges, increases in allowance and a later curfew are some commonly employed non-verbal reinforcers. When parents use praise or positive reinforcers they are essentially saying, "We like what you are doing. Your behavior pleases us. We want to let you know that in a way that benefits you so that you will be most apt to continue in this direction in the future."

Destructive, negative behavior draws punishing responses from Mom and Dad. These responses are both verbal and non-verbal. "I don't like what you're doing." "Sarah, you're not showing good sense. I'm very displeased that you stayed out so late last night." "You didn't even try out there on that field today. I'm surprised that coach let you play as much of the game as he did." "Valerie, these are the worst grades that you have ever brought home. Now something has got to be done. This has to stop!" These are all verbal forms of punishment. Non-verbal punishers include spanking, being sent to their room, restriction from use of the television, telephone, stereo or car, being grounded, loss of allowance, restriction from certain friends and extra work assignments. When parents use punishment they are essentially saying, "We don't like what you are doing. Your behavior displeases us. We want to cause you some discomfort, inconvenience or pain so you will be least apt to do the same thing in the future."

Encouragement/natural and logical consequences. The use of encouragement involves giving verbal responses that are designed to help teenagers feel good about themselves. The focus is on the person rather than behavior. Proponents of this approach believe that constructive behavior will follow when adolescents feel amply good about themselves. "I'll bet that felt awfully good when you hit that home run last night." "You must feel very satisfied having all A and B grades on your report card." "Doesn't it feel great to know that your chores are all done and the rest of the day is yours to enjoy?" Each of these is an encouraging statement because it focuses on the teenager's accomplishment, effort and positive feelings.

The use of natural and logical consequences is a discipline approach used primarily in democratic families and to varying degrees by authoritative parents.[45] Permissive parents tend not to discipline at all but when they do this would be their preferred choice. This method is founded in the philosophy that people are capable of both good and evil and that they will generally exhibit constructive behavior. Negative or destructive behavior occurs when teenagers get too discouraged or frustrated by environmental pressures. Some anger, acting-out, and rebellion are accepted as normal and healthy for adolescents as they work through the process of becoming an independent person. Though self-control is valued, the limits on emotional and behavioral expression are broad and more relaxed.

Parents who discipline using this approach try to structure situations so that their teenagers' misbehavior results naturally or logically in certain consequences for them. Since so much of adult life is structured along these principles the goal is to give young people plenty of practice learning to live with the same system. (Too many traffic tickets lead to a high insurance premium. Poor personal hygiene leads to poor health, etc.)

Natural consequences are those that occur through the laws of nature and social systems without parental contrivance. When Jamie decides not to study for his geometry test, he will probably get a poor grade. His poor grade is a natural consequence of his decision not to study. Sheri wants to wear her new summer outfit but the weather has turned cold and stormy. By letting her make the decision, she experiences the rather obvious results that follow naturally from her choice.

Logical consequences occur when the teenager goes against the order that has been established within the family. Twelve-year-old Bonnie knows that dinner is served at about 5:30 p.m. She chose to come home from her friend's house at 6:15 p.m., missing the meal. Logical consequences could be either waiting to eat until breakfast or being responsible to prepare her own dinner and clean up the kitchen after herself. The parent's task is to structure consequences that follow logically from the youngster's behavior, and that involve as little parental intervention as possible.

Differences between the two approaches. Praise and encouragement differ from each other in several ways:

1. Praise focuses on behavior. "Melinda, the dress you sewed looks so pretty."

Encouragement focuses on internal feelings. "Melinda, I'll bet you feel good knowing how hard you have worked on that dress."

2. Praise is usually a reward given by an authority figure. "Carlos, your speech was excellent. I'm proud of you."

Encouragement acknowledges and recognizes and is a gift that can come from anyone. "You have worked so long and hard on that speech, Carlos. You're really some kind of a guy!"

3. Praise is given to teenagers when they do what is pleasing to parents. "Marcie, you did a really good job getting home before your curfew tonight."

Encouragement helps teenagers to feel good about their efforts to be independent and responsible for their own behavior. "Marcie, I've noticed that you're really trying to be responsible about when you're getting home at night."[46]

There are also some important differences between punishment and logical consequences:

1. Punishment emphasizes parental authority and usually makes a demand. "Jerry, it's late. Your stereo is keeping us awake. It's time to turn it off now."

Logical consequences focus on making decisions that work well for everyone in the family. "Jerry, I understand that you are enjoying your stereo, but we're having a hard time getting to sleep. You can either turn it down low or turn it off. Whichever you choose is okay."

2. Punishment is often arbitrarily decided upon, not really making logical sense in relation to the misbehavior. "Cheryl, you said that you were going to have the car back two hours ago. I've been needing it. You're grounded for two weeks."

Logical consequences are directly related to the unacceptable behavior. "Cheryl, we've already discussed what would happen the next time something like this occurred. So you can give me your keys and next week you can have them back and give it another try."

3. Punishment equates the behavior with the person. Judging the behavior as bad implies a judgment of the person. "Your grades are horrible. If you can't do any better than this, then you can forget television for the rest of the year."

Logical consequences are directed toward the action without any disparaging implications toward the person. "These grades are lower than others that you have gotten in the past. We've talked about how television might be interfering with your study time. Until each teacher verifies that these grades have come up to at least a C or B, television will be limited to one hour a day. Then you can set up your own TV schedule again."

4. Punishment often makes the teenager pay again for past sins. "No you may not go over to Mark's. Last time you went over there, the two of you sneaked out."

Logical consequences focus on the present and future. "You may go over to Mark's tonight as long as you are willing to call and check with us if you want to go out somewhere."

5. Punishment is often carried out in an angry demeaning fashion. "I've never been so embarrassed in my whole life! There you were, talking throughout the whole service. I mean, the pastor had to call you down right from the pulpit! Don't ever ask me for anything until you get your act together."

Logical consequences are presented after both parties have cooled down. There remains a feeling of respect and good will. "Since you had trouble controlling yourself in church this morning, I'll want you to sit with us for the next four Sundays. Then you may try sitting with your friends again."

6. Punishment demands obedience. "You get to bed right now."

Logical consequences stimulate responsible decision-making. "Tomorrow is an early morning for you and you were up late last night. You can either go to bed early tonight or take a nap tomorrow afternoon."

The most advantageous discipline model may well be a blend between these two models. Teenagers need to be able to respond to authority figures and their own sense of responsibility at the same time.[47]

Teenagers Living in Single-Parent Families

Single-parent families have most of the dynamics and problems that two-parent families have, plus some. Most single-parent families have lost a parent either through divorce or death. Very few families originate with only one parent, though that situation does exist. The teenagers have to learn to relate with the parent authority, and also must adjust to the loss of one parent. If the parent died or left the household prior to the child entering adolescence, then the adjustment to the loss may have already been accomplished. When the loss occurs during the child's adolescence, that adjustment is added to the already complicated and difficult task of growing through the adolescent stage. Such experiences greatly threaten the security needs of the child and are likely to create strong anger and guilt. These feelings are typically directed toward the remaining parent who is struggling with his or her own pain, anger, guilt and insecurity.

Single parenting is probably one of the most demanding and personally challenging tasks that people in our society ever confront. If we accept the bias that marriage and a family structure are best for a fulfilling and meaningful life, then the single parent is having to operate without a major source of potential support. He or she has to work much harder and longer hours doing a wide variety of tasks because there is only one responsible adult present. This combination of increased workload and decreased support system creates stress for the parent.

Adolescents sometimes respond to this situation by taking advantage of the weakened parent. Other teenagers take hold of the opportunity to enhance their own feelings of competence by helping to parent the younger children. Some find a way to feel valued and appreciated because they feel more needed by the others if the family is going to succeed. Counselors who work with adolescents in single-parent families need to recognize whether or not the helpful support from the teenager represents a withdrawal from the necessary adolescent growing process.

Brothers and Sisters: A Social Laboratory

Socialization is the process through which people learn how to behave appropriately and successfully according to the rules and morals of society. This socialization process begins very early in childhood and continues through adulthood. Much of our socialization occurs within the home and the family becomes our laboratory for testing and learning how to live with others.

The particular family into which a person is born has had and continues to have a marked impact on who the adolescent person has become at that intermediate stage of development.

Though relationships between brothers and sisters are very important aspects of the family dynamic, children primarily learn the socialization process from the way their parents respond to them and to each other.

Jim and Sharon Caldwell initiated family therapy when the eldest of their four girls was experiencing serious problems in high school and developing a pattern of regular drug abuse. After a great deal of hard, painful growth both on the part of the daughter and her parents, the problems were worked through and therapy was terminated.

Several times over the next 10 years the Caldwells have returned to therapy during developmental crises with each of their daughters. Every situation was different, because the girls reacted according to their own unique personalities. Yet the situations were similar because the daughters responded to some of the same family dynamics.

Jim is a very conservative, rational man whose life is run by logic and reason. Sharon tends to be very much the same way. Both are committed to their Christian faith and seek for ways to make it a working part of their daily lives. Both have the capacity for deep, emotional love and caring. But its expression is seldom a pure, heartfelt, emotional release. They have expressed love to their daughters primarily by providing, teaching and protecting them. Jim has been an excellent provider and Sharon has periodically helped out by taking executive secretarial positions. They have made consistent and concerted efforts to provide their girls with Christian training and solid academic education.

Dad always seemed to be in total control, except during certain crises. And that is why the crises probably occurred. Donna, the eldest, started failing in her schoolwork and was heavily involved with drugs. Debbie, the next eldest, ran away from home at age 17 and got married. Joanie was arrested for shoplifting and also had a drug problem. And Jean, the youngest, became sexually promiscuous during her last two years of high school.

Each daughter at last, got a pure, emotional response from her mother and father. Each created a different situation where Dad no longer had control. Sadly, in each situation the girl's life was negatively affected.

The concept of family constellation helps us to understand why children can be born and raised in the same family and turn out to be so different. Psychologist Rudolph Dreikurs, who studied under Alfred Adler, helped to develop a theory that shed a great deal of light on the confusing diversity between siblings.[48] This concept of family constellation has been popularized by a number of authors.[49]

The central focus is the ordinal position or birth order of the child (oldest, middle, youngest). Parents tend to act differently to the children born in each ordinal position. Siblings also respond differently to each other based on their respective positions in the family.

First-born adolescents typically are high achievers. They are often very good students who conscientiously and consistently study hard in order to excel. They also tend to make good leaders and will be found running for school or youth group office (especially desiring to be president). But first-born teenagers also tend to carry a lot of tension within them and feel anxious about change. They are typically apprehensive about the ever-perceived possibility of failure. They believe that self-reliance is the surest road to success. "If you want a job to be done well, then do it yourself," is a common first-borns' motto. They shy away from free emotional expression, tend to be loners and are usually very rational, logical thinkers.

The dynamics that produce these characteristics within first-borns are primarily related to the way parents respond to their first child. The birth is given very special attention. First-time parents usually have high standards for the quality of their own parenting behaviors as well as high expectations for their child. They have somthing to prove to themselves, their parents, their friends, and their own brothers and sisters. They need to prove that they are good parents. And "the proof is in the pudding," or in this case, the first-born child.

While still in infancy, the child picks up on his or her parents' apprehension and high standards. As the child grows, he or she wants to be the very best in order to please Mom and Dad. A first-born child tends to walk, talk and toilet train sooner than other children. As younger siblings are born, the eldest is expected to be more mature. "Act your age" and "you have to set a good example" put on more pressure to be as near perfect as possible. As younger siblings begin growing older and becoming more capable, their competition pushes the eldest into even stronger efforts to be the best. These dynamics have been reinforced time and time again by the time the child reaches adolescence. It is no wonder that these patterns are deeply entrenched.

Parents of second-born children are pros. They have already been through it. They are usually less tense, less apprehensive and less demanding of their second child's performance. They trust their own parenting more and they also trust that their second child will naturally grow, learn and succeed because they have already seen their first child do quite well. In other words, the first child has "blazed the trail" for the second child and serves as a model. After watching an older brother or sister go through adolescent rebellion, the second child can figure out how to avoid some of the same hassles and confrontations.

Like all children, second-borns need to excel in something in order to feel securely valued. They are usually smart enough not to try to compete in the older sibling's field of expertise. They often choose something quite different to be "the best" at. Hence, the diversity between children that are next to each other in ordinal position. Second-born and middle children tend to be more relaxed, assertive, sociable, competitive and independent. Since birth, they have had to compete with formidable odds and find a way to do it successfully. They have discovered the value of flexibility and how to respond to both older and younger siblings.

The youngest child in the family is in a very special place. He or she has parents and older brothers and sisters to take care of things. Youngest children become very adept at getting others to do their bidding. They generally start to talk later than other children because they simply do not have to say as much in order to get their needs met. They get away with more and often become experts at setting up older siblings and friends to get into trouble.

As youngest children reach adolescence they are often very manipulative, socially outgoing, demanding of others and sometimes appear to be quite helpless. They tend to date first-born children or others who get their strokes by taking care of others.

The "only child" is a first-born child who never had to adjust to the changes that come with younger brothers and sisters. Only children develop many of the first-child characteristics because they are first children and are treated as such. But they are also last or youngest children and are sometimes treated in an overprotective, cautious manner.

They are usually expected to function in an adultlike manner too early. They learn how to be adultlike because much of their time is spent interacting with adults. They miss out on the day-to-day process of learning how to live with other children which usually makes their interpersonal adjustment to peers more difficult until they reach adulthood. Then, finally, their peers are the people that they have been dealing with all of their lives. Only children usually become quite conscientious and reliable adults. However, during adolescence they often feel defeated and worthless because they fail to reach the level of perfection they set for themselves.

There are a few special considerations that need to be looked at in order to more accurately understand these important family dynamics. First, the greatest degree of competition is felt between siblings who are next to each other in their ordinal positions. The further apart two siblings are, the less the competitive impact.

Second, there is greater competition between siblings who are separated by up to three years than there is when four or more years separate the two children. When six to eight years separate one child and the next born, there exists essentially two psychological families.

Third, greater competition exists when children who are next to each other in ordinal position are either both boys or both girls. If the first two children are both girls, or both boys, they will probably develop quite differently from each other. On the other hand, if one is a girl and the other is a boy, both might exhibit first-child characteristics (the first girl and the first boy).

The fourth special consideration is when a child either is born or becomes handicapped through accident or illness. Parents tend to treat such children with special care and spend more time and energy on them. The heaviest impact is on those brothers and sisters who are next to them in ordinal position. Often the next younger sibling of a handicapped child will take over his or her role. This reversal presents a very threatening situation for the handicapped child who will respond either by intensifying attempts to maintain his or her position or by giving up and settling for a more dependent role.

Our fifth consideration regards miscarriages and death of a sibling. When a woman has a miscarriage, the next child is usually treated as a very special gift from God. The relief and thankfulness the parent feels sometimes is poured out onto the child by spoiling, overprotecting and pampering. The death of a child obviously has a drastic impact on the whole family, but it also changes the family constellation. The deceased child's older and younger siblings are now adjacent to each other in ordinal position, which will alter their relationship dynamics.

The sixth special consideration is the specific way that the parents interact with the child. The way they were parented, their cultural background, education, age, desire to have the child, economic level, overall life situation and level of personal maturity will deeply impact the way they interact with their child.

Family Meetings

Many families schedule regular meetings as a way of trying to keep things together at home in the midst of a flurry of activities and busy schedules. For some homes, it becomes a weekly opportunity to be together that is valued so highly that most potential intrusions into the scheduled time slot are met with a resounding "no" by teenagers as well as by parents. But it does not happen this successfully overnight. They will protect that scheduled time only after the family members experience consistent value and worth from being involved. Three different kinds of family meetings will be presented here, each for a different purpose: the regularly scheduled family meeting, the problem-solving meeting and the contract problem-solving meeting.

All three formats yield excellent benefits. The one that is selected will depend on the purpose for which the meeting is needed and the form of leadership in the family structure. The family counseling session is a perfect place to teach how to use and benefit from a family meeting.

Regularly scheduled family meetings. Regularly scheduled family meetings work well in every style of family leadership except for the extremely authoritarian and excessively permissive styles. The authoritative and democratic families thrive on these kinds of meetings. Because they are held often and regularly (at one-week intervals), a wide variety of purposes can be accomplished: sharing the important activities, concerns and projects that are currently in each person's life; sharing devotions; praying for one another; expressing complaints and problems between family members; resolving conflicts and disagreements between family members; deciding how to distribute the chores; planning family fun times and vacations; and expressing encouraging and loving things to each other.

Unfortunately, many families report unsuccessful attempts to establish regular family meetings.[50] Such unsuccessful attempts reflect the difficulty in trying to establish a new direction in a pre-existing situation. Change is difficult, particularly change that is sometimes threatening. Other families have problems because their typical interpersonal relationship styles are not well-suited for family meetings. Some meetings are first tried during times of crisis when feelings are tense and angry. This makes it much more difficult to build positive momentum.

There are some guidelines that will help families have successful meetings:

1. Establish a specific time and place for the weekly meetings.

2. Select a chairperson and a secretary for each meeting. These positions should be rotated regularly so everyone gets a chance at them.

3. Establish and adhere to time limits. Always start on time, even if someone is absent and never go over the allotted ending time. Families with adults and teenagers usually meet for one hour, but one-half hour is usually better when younger children are involved.

4. Give everyone ample opportunity to voice his or her ideas.

5. Encourage everyone to bring up issues and concerns that he or she wants discussed. Have an agenda book available during the week so members can write down these items.

6. Prevent meetings from becoming only gripe sessions. When complaints are logged, make sure that positive attempts to resolve them are followed through.

7. Distribute chores fairly and rotate them on schedule.

8. Use part of the time for planning family events.

9. Use the family meeting as a time to help each other practice listening and communicating skills.

10. At the close of each meeting invite every member to share feelings. Any suggestions for improving meetings can be dealt with then or at the next meeting.

11. At each meeting discuss whether everything had been done that was agreed upon during the last meeting.[51]

The problem-solving meeting. The family problem-solving meeting format is an excellent tool for families when a conflict or problem comes up that affects two or more members.[52] Before a successful problem-solving meeting can be accomplished, the involved parties first should work through their emotional reactions so that they can work together. They must be willing to agree to work on a solution. Let's go through the eight steps of this type of meeting:

1. Determine the meeting time and place. Unlike the regularly scheduled family meeting, the problem-solving meeting concerns only

those family members who are involved in the problem and who are affected by it. The meeting time and place must be agreeable to all who are concerned.

2. Choose a recorder who will write down what happens during the meeting. Volunteers are best but if there are none, select someone with everyone's approval.

3. Define the problem or situation that needs to be addressed. What has happened? What is the existing situation? Why is it a problem? For whom is it a problem? Everyone needs to be heard during this step. If the problem is not adequately defined, then the solutions will never seem adequate.

4. Brainstorm every possible solution as a group. Encourage creativity from everyone and the recorder writes down every idea suggested, even if offered in jest. Assume that every idea offered by every member is worthy of consideration. Establish that absolutely no negative or disparaging comments are to be made about any idea given or about any member who makes any suggestion. Negativity spoils creativity.

5. Review the ideas offered during the brainstorming stage. The recorder reads each solution, one by one. If anyone rejects the solution after it has been discussed, the recorder draws a line through it and then introduces the next solution, and so on. When this reviewing process yields one or more unanimously acceptable solutions, proceed to the next step. If every solution is rejected, go back to step three and work again at defining the problem. If this process is gone through three times without producing one acceptable solution, schedule a contract problem-solving meeting (this will be discussed next).

6. As a group, discuss and decide which of the acceptable solutions will be employed. Depending on the situation, only one, several or all of the possible solutions might be used.

7. Decide who does what by when and where. The recorder must be careful to keep detailed records.

8. Just before adjourning, schedule another meeting between one and two weeks in the future to follow up on the progress that members are making on their assignments, get feedback on how everyone thinks the solutions are working and evaluate whether any new problems related to the originally defined problem need to be dealt with.

The contract problem-solving meeting. This meeting model is particularly helpful in situations where the regularly scheduled family meeting and the problem-solving meeting are unable to produce a solution. When two or three family members are upset with each other's behavior and want changes to occur, this is a powerful and effective model to employ.[53] In order for this contract method to work, three prerequisites must be met. Before the meeting is scheduled, each person must understand and agree to each of these: Everyone who comes to the meeting, parents as well as teenagers, must be willing to make some personal changes. Everyone must come with a spirit of good will and in good faith, hoping that the meeting will produce positive results. The participants must try not to hurt each other.

Now, let's look at each of the six steps in this model:

1. The meeting participants must decide on a meeting time and place. The location should be private and secure from disturbance from other family members.

2. Each participant makes a list of the behaviors that he or she wants the other to change. List only specific behaviors, not attitudes, beliefs or personality traits. The teenager lists the behaviors that he or she wants the parents to change. If both parents are present, then they work together to create a list of specific behaviors that they want their adolescent to change. Ten minutes are allowed to complete the lists. Then the participants prioritize three items they want to discuss during the contract meeting.

3. On another sheet of paper the participants list specific behaviors that they want the other person to keep. Ten minutes are allowed for this step. Participants then check three behaviors from this list that they want to discuss.

4. Next, the participants discuss the things that they want each other to change. This is the most difficult step in this model. It requires honesty as well as caring about not hurting each other. Flip a coin or use some other arbitrary means to select who goes first. Let us say that the teenager wins the coin toss so he or she starts.

The first item about the parents' behavior that is desired to be changed is read and explained. The parents repeat back what they heard their adolescent say to make sure that there is a common understanding. When the teenager agrees that they understand, the parents can ask to discuss the issue between themselves or with their child in the meeting. After the discussion, the parents state either that they will make the requested change, or they will not make the desired change or they counter with a compromise change. If the parents agree to their teenager's request, it is written down on a sheet of paper and signed by all parties. If a compromised solution is discussed and agreed upon, then it is recorded on a sheet of paper and signed by each participant. If the parents answer "no," the teenager accepts their answer.

It is now the parents' turn to read or explain their first request for change. This process is repeated, taking turns until parents and teenager have discussed and made decisions about all three of each of their requests.

This step is a very difficult and potentially volatile process. Several points need to be emphasized to insure a successful meeting: Each request should be made as specific as possible. Respond to each request as a separate issue. Exercise good will and good faith, trying to be as agreeable as you honestly can. Be careful to not agree to something that you do not want to or think you cannot live up to. Discuss no more than three behaviors at each contract meeting.

5. The most difficult and painful part of the meeting is over. Now it is time to try to regenerate mutually positive feelings. It helps to keep the relationships in a more accurate perspective. Flip the coin again to see who starts. Then begin taking turns discussing the behaviors that you like in the other person (step three). Do this until all three checked behaviors on each person's list have been discussed.

6. Schedule a follow-up meeting in one or two weeks. During this meeting the same participants will discuss how well they think the changes have been going and how they are feeling about them.

These three kinds of family meetings have value for different families in different kinds of situations. The perceptive counselor can evaluate which format best fits the family that he or she is working with and then lead them through the process during a counseling session.

Letting Go

The most dramatic experience in families with late adolescents is the rapidly accelerating movement toward the teenager's separation from the family. The ties that link the adolescent with the family are being loosened in two realms: First, the psychological world of the teenager's personality is changing and becoming less dependent. Second, the selection and quality of other relationships reveal movement away from the family.[54]

This process produces very difficult adaptation problems for families. Shaky marriages often do not survive the loss of children from the family structure.[55] Parents who have lived vicariously through their children or who have used their children for emotional support find letting them go an extremely difficult and painful process.[56] At the same time that the teenagers are shifting their loyalties away from home, their middle-aged parents are needing to deepen their interpersonal loyalties.[57] Seeing their late adolescents leaving home and feeling full of excitement and anticipation about their new lives causes some adults to question the meaning and value of the lives and relationships that they themselves have developed. Many adults in our contemporary "runaway culture" take the "cue" from their departing adolescents, and leave also.[58]

When parents are able to keep their marriage and family intact, while letting go of their late adolescent, they are supporting their maturing teenager's growth into young adulthood. This process of gradually shrinking the domain of parental responsibility while increasing the domain of the teenager's responsibility has been called "deparenting."[59]

The deparenting process actually begins shortly after the child is born. During early and mid-adolescence, the area of "negotiable responsibility" covers all of those decisions that parents and teenagers both can have input. Of course, the parenting model that is used in the family has a lot to do with this. The area of negotiable responsibility will be very small in authoritarian and permissive families, larger in authoritative families and largest in democratic families. As the teenager moves into late adolescence the range of negotiable responsibility diminishes. The teenager has become a young adult.

Notes

1. Charlotte Buhler, Patricia Keith-Spiegel, and Karla Thomas, "Developmental Psychology," in *Handbook of General Psychology*, ed. Benjamin Wolman (Englewood Cliffs, N. J.: Prentice-Hall, 1973), pp. 861-917.

2. L. J. Stone and J. Church, *Childhood and Adolescence*, 2nd ed. (New York: Random House, 1968).

3. Fritz Ridenour, *What Teenagers Wish Their Parents Knew About Kids* (Waco, Texas: Word Books, 1982).

4. Buhler, Keith-Spiegel, and Thomas, "Developmental Psychology."

5. Gene R. Medinnus and Ronald C. Johnson, *Child and Adolescent Psychology* (New York: John Wiley, 1969).

6. Derek Miller, *Adolescence: Psychology, Psychopathology, Psychotherapy* (New York: Jason Aronson, 1974).

7. A. M. Johnson, "Factors in the Psychology of Fixations and Symptom Choice," Psychoanalytic Quarterly 22 (1953):425-496.

8. Derek Miller, "Family Interaction in the Therapy of Hospitalized Adolescent Patients," Psychiatry 21 (1958):227-284.

9. James Anthony, "The Reactions of Adults to Adolescents and Their Behavior," in *Adolescence: Psychosocial Perspectives*, eds. G. Caplan and S. Lebovici (New

York: Basic Books, 1969).

10. Bruce Narramore, *Adolescence Is Not an Illness* (Old Tappan, N. J.: Fleming H. Revell, 1980).

11. Thomas D. Gnagey, *How to Put Up With Parents: A Guide for Teenagers* (Ottawa, Ill.: Facilitation House, 1975).

12. E. Douvan and J. Adelson, *The Adolescent Experience* (New York: John Wiley, 1966).

13. Bruce Narramore, *You Can Be a Better Parent* (Grand Rapids, Mich.: Zondervan, 1979).

14. Ridenour, *What Teenagers Wish Their Parents Knew About Kids.*

15. Ibid.

16. Bruce Narramore, *Parenting With Love and Limits* (Grand Rapids, Mich.: Zondervan, 1979).

17. Rudolph Dreikurs and Vicki Soltz, *Children: The Challenge* (New York: Hawthorn Press, 1964).

18. Peter Buntman and Eleanor Saris, *How to Live With Your Teenager* (Pasadena, Calif.: Birch Tree Press, 1979).

19. Narramore, *Parenting With Love and Limits.*

20. Ridenour, *What Teenagers Wish Their Parents Knew.*

21. Narramore, *Parenting With Love and Limits*, p. 34.

22. Miller, *Adolescence: Psychology, Psychopathology, Psychotherapy.*

23. Gnagey, *How to Put Up With Parents.*

24. Narramore, *Adolescence Is Not an Illness.*

25. Sidney M. Jourard, *The Transparent Self* (Princeton: Van Nostrand, 1964).

26. Narramore, *Adolescence Is Not an Illness.*

27. Sven Wahlroos, *Family Communication* (New York: Macmillan, 1974).

28. Ibid.

29. Eric Berne, *Games People Play* (New York: Grove Press, 1964).

30. Ridenour, *What Teenagers Wish Their Parents Knew.*

31. Paul Tournier, *To Understand Each Other* (Richmond, Va.: John Knox Press, 1972).

32. Buntman and Saris, *How to Live With Your Teenager.*

33. Haim G. Ginott, *Between Parent and Child* (New York: Avon Books, 1965).

34. Haim G. Ginott, *Between Parent and Teenager* (New York: Avon Books, 1969).

35. Thomas Gordon, *P.E.T.: Parent Effectiveness Training* (New York: Peter H. Wyden, 1970).

36. Don Dinkmeyer and Gary McKay, *Systematic Training for Effective Parenting of Teens: Parent's Guide* (Circle Pines, Minn.: American Guidance Service, 1983).

37. Buntman and Saris, *How to Live With Your Teenager.*

38. John Powell, S. J., *Why Am I Afraid to Tell You Who I Am?* (Chicago: Argus Communications, 1969).

39. Gordon, *P.E.T.: Parent Effectiveness Training.*

40. Ibid.

41. Buntman and Saris, *How to Live With Your Teenager.*

42. Dinkmeyer and McKay, *Systematic Training for Effective Parenting of Teens.*

43. Buntman and Saris, *How to Live With Your Teenager.*

44. Paul D. Meier, *Christian Child-Rearing and Personality Development* (Grand

Rapids, Mich.: Baker Book House, 1977).

45. Dreikurs and Soltz, *Children: The Challenge.*

46. Dinkmeyer and McKay, *Systematic Training for Effective Parenting of Teens.*

47. Ibid.

48. Dreikurs and Soltz, *Children: The Challenge.*

49. Kevin Leman, *Parenthood Without Hassles* (Irvine, Calif.: Harvest House, 1979).

50. Ridenour, *What Teenagers Wish Their Parents Knew.*

51. Dinkmeyer and McKay, *Systematic Training for Effective Parenting of Teens.*

52. Buntman and Saris, *How to Live With Your Teenager,* p. 29.

53. Ibid.

54. Carl P. Malmquist, *Handbook of Adolescence: Psychopathology, Antisocial Development, Psychotherapy* (New York: Jason Aronson, 1978).

55. Miller, *Adolescence: Psychology, Psychopathology, Psychotherapy.*

56. A. T. Jersild, *The Psychology of Adolescence,* 2nd ed. (London: Macmillan, 1963).

57. Helm Stierlin, *Separating Parents and Adolescents* (New York: Jason Aronson, 1981).

58. Ibid, p. 29.

59. Ridenour, *What Teenagers Wish Their Parents Knew.*

PART II

A Christian Approach to Counseling Teenagers

■ CHAPTER 4

Perspectives on Counseling

It would be the height of presumption to plot a course of action or establish a planned approach to any important task without first stopping to learn from those who have explored the intended territory before us. Solomon wrote, "Without counsel plans go wrong, but with many advisers they succeed" (Proverbs 15:22). Believing that all truth is from God, we will consult with psychotherapists and counselors who write both from a Christian context and from other viewpoints. Each orientation will be surveyed, evaluated and compared with the other approaches.

Learning From Our Teachers

It has been estimated that there are more than 250 psychotherapeutic methods in use.[1] Most of these methods can be grouped into major schools of thought or theoretical orientations. Then these theories can be grouped under broader classifications that share similarities. Grouping theories is a difficult project because the classifications are artificial and exist only for our understanding. Most therapy incorporates characteristics of more than one theoretical orientation. But, like any categorization, lines must be drawn, labels affixed and boxes filled.

The chart that appears next includes some of the most common forms of therapeutic interventions. These therapies have been grouped under four headings: psychodynamic, existential/experiential, cognitive and learning/behavioral. The theories within each category share many similar propositions regarding: the nature of humanity, the nature of dysfunctional behavior, the therapy goals, the counselor's role, the treatment techniques, the treatment components and the nature of psychological wellness.

Common Forms of Therapeutic Intervention

Psychodynamic Theories	Existential/ Experiential Theories	Cognitive Theories	Learning/Behavioral Theories
Psychoanalysis (Freud)	Client-Centered (Rogers)	Trait and Factor (Parsons, Williamson)	Reciprocal Inhibition (Wolpe)
Analytical Psychotherapy (Jung)	Gestalt (Perls)	Rational-Emotive (Ellis)	Reinforcement Counseling (Dollard and Miller)
Psychoanalytic Psychotherapy (Fromm, Reichmann)	Logotherapy (Frankl)	Individual Psychotherapy (Adler)	Biofeedback (Green)
Ego Analysis (Hartmann, Rapaport, Erikson)	Existential Analysis (May)	Reality Therapy (Glasser)	Behavioral Counseling (Krumboltz)
	Primal Scream (Janov)		Modeling Therapy (Bandura)
	Bioenergetic Analysis (Lowen)		
	Transactional Analysis (Berne, Harris)		
	Reparenting		

Illustration 6

A basic understanding of the various models is necessary in the choice of counseling approaches. The following chart presents a brief overview of the four main groupings: psychodynamic, existential/experiential, cognitive and learning/behavioral theories.[2]

Comparison of Counseling Models

CHARACTERISTIC	Psychodynamic Theories	Existential/Experiential Theories	Cognitive Theories	Learning Behavioral Theories
1. Nature of Humanity	People are both animalistic and human; capable of both destructive and constructive behavior. The psyche is constituted of id, ego and superego structures that operate by unconscious and conscious energy dynamics. Behavior is produced from biological drives, especially sexual and aggressive instincts, that are blocked by external restraints, developing into internal controls. All of this occurs largely in the unconscious.	People are primarily good, rational and trustworthy. They seek naturally for self-actualization, personal meaning, independence and autonomy in a manner that enhances the common good for society. The self-concept is central to behavioral motivation. Behavior is directed by positive pull from future goals more than driven by past experiences and instincts.	People are primarily rational beings, though they struggle against strong biological and social pressures. They seek to develop potentialities through emphasis on rational thinking and reliance on others' support.	People are primarily mechanistic creatures whose behavior is or is shaped showing lawful changes in relation to antecedent conditions and events immediately following the behavior. Behavior is a product of external events, not goal-directed, planful thought.
2. Nature of Dysfunctional Behavior	Dysfunctional behavior results from a breaking down of ego functions from excessive pressure from anxiety caused by: conflicts between id impulses, superego demands and ego defenses, early childhood trauma or other memories.	Dysfunctional behavior results when external force or internal tension, anxiety or frustration interferes with natural drives toward self-awareness, self-esteem, actualization of potential, sense of fulfillment and sense of meaning in life. It results from the threat of loss of personal identity and the threat of non-being.	Dysfunctional behavior is the result of irrational thinking and incomplete knowledge that leads to confusion, ineffective behavior and unhappy responses from the environment. This results in pain, anxiety, anticipation of catastrophe and further reinforcement of irrational thought patterns.	Dysfunctional behavior is maladjustive behavior that has been learned; behavioral reactions that have been reinforced, perhaps by immediate anxiety reduction, even though in the long run they are inappropriate to the situation.

Comparison of Counseling Models, continued

Comparison of Counseling Models

CHARACTERISTIC	Psychodynamic Theories	Existential/Experiential Theories	Cognitive Theories	Learning Behavioral Theories
3. Therapy	Partial or complete personality reorientation and reconstruction are accomplished through: bringing repressed memories and associated emotions, repressed conflicts and unconscious roots of current anxieties to consciousness; strengthening ego functions; releasing creative energy.	Increased self-awareness and self-acceptance leading to self-actualization; self-concept becoming congruent with personal experience; non-defensiveness, openness to experience; trust in one's perceptions, thinking and emotions so that the person can act, rather than be acted upon; awareness and acceptance of personal values; sense of meaning in life.	Alleviation of pain and anxiety by increasing awareness of reality and developing functional, rational thought patterns and beliefs that correspond with internal value systems.	Eliminate maladaptive behaviors and learn new adaptive behaviors; changes in perception, attitudes and feelings follow from changed behavior.
4. Counselor's Role	Assists counselee in bringing unconscious material into consciousness; helps counselee to understand associations between previously repressed material and current anxieties; supports the release of repressed emotionality; initial passivity becomes active in questioning and interpreting.	Creates safe, open environment for counselee to undertake risky self-exploration; helps in the process of clarifying thoughts, attitudes, values and beliefs; supports acceptance and expression of feelings; supports counselee's search for meaning; is an actively involved partner with the counselee's growth process.	Helps counselee become aware of beliefs, perceptions, attitudes and values; helps to correct irrational beliefs and translate new rational thinking into adaptive behavior; actively involved.	Helps counselee identify maladaptive behaviors; designs procedure for eliminating maladaptive behaviors; specifies more adaptive behavior patterns; designs procedure for strengthening constructive behavioral responses; is actively involved.

5. Treatment Techniques	Free association, catharsis, interpretation, dream analysis, analysis of resistance, analysis of transference.	Unconditional acceptance, empathy, congruence, reflection, self-disclosure, interpreting, free association, focus on here and now, focus on counselee-counselor relationship; some use a variety of non-verbal and physical methods.	Teaching, suggestion, persuasion, confrontation, altering environment, interpretation.	Reinforcement, extinction, desensitization, modeling, assertiveness training, aversion techniques, implosion methods, relaxation training, applied behavioral analysis, counterconditioning.
6. Treatment Components	Long-term, intense therapy; time focus during initial stages of treatment is on past, then moves toward present; diagnosis and prognosis are important; psychological tests, especially projective techniques, are often used; history is viewed as very important but not taken in a structured manner.	Short-term to long-term, intense therapy; past is understood as important but the primary focus is on the present moment; diagnosis and prognosis are contra-indicated by some and viewed as essential by others; psychological tests are used sparingly; history-taking is contraindicated by some and viewed as essential by others.	Short-term, non-intensive therapy; time focus is on the present; diagnosis and prognosis are important; psychological tests are used extensively in trait and factor counseling but seldom by others; history-taking is used in trait and factor counseling but seldom by others.	Short-term, non-intensive therapy; time focus is on the present; diagnosis and prognosis are important; psychological tests are used sparingly; structured history-taking is very important.
7. The Nature of Psychological Wellness	Strong ego functioning; existence of a mature, well-integrated personality structure that operates to a great extent according to conscious rather than unconscious energy dynamics; major intrapsychic conflicts are resolved and the ego is adequately functioning so that minimal anxiety is experienced from internal or external sources.	An ability and willingness to be and accept who we are; congruence between self-concept and experience; ongoing process of actualizing potentials; sense of meaning in being alive; taking responsibility for one's own life, becoming the person one wishes to be, and living in a socially constructive and meaningful style.	Adaptive and constructive behavioral patterns that emanate from correct, logical thought processes; beliefs that correspond with the internal value system and are functional in daily living.	Adaptive behavior patterns that meet the person's needs and at the same time are constructive to the social group.

Illustration 7

Psychodynamic orientation. The psychodynamic understanding of man, and to some degree every psychotherapeutic approach, originated in the work of Viennese neurologist, Sigmund Freud (1856-1939). Although he was not the first to suggest the existence of the unconscious, he probably was the first to describe its contents: a veritable cauldron of inherited sexual and aggressive instincts and repressed thoughts, attitudes and emotions that are so heavily laden with anxiety that they must be kept out of conscious awareness.[3] His structural theory of personality established the roles of id, superego and ego. His dynamic theory explained the psychic energy processes that occurred within and between these three structures.[4] His presentation of eros as the basic generative, constructive life force and thanatos, the central degenerative, destructive death force has also had lasting impact on the development of psychotherapeutic and counseling thought.

In addition to his own extensive writing, Freud impacts us today through the many students he trained and inspired. They have continued to alter, broaden and enrich Freud's theoretical propositions. Alfred Adler, the first to break away from Freud, developed his theoretical orientation which he labeled "individual psychology."[5] He rejected the sexual etiology of neurosis and suggested that feelings of inferiority and inadequacy were the central cause. He also stressed the impact of the social environment on the psyche and de-emphasized the force of biological instincts.

Carl Jung broke with Freud regarding the concept of libido. Freud viewed libido as total sexual expression of psychic energy. Jung thought that during early and possibly pre-human stages of human evolution, libido was primarily sexual but that it had become, through the process of evolution, a more undifferentiated or universal life drive.[6] Jung expanded the concept of heredity to include inheritance of not only biological attributes, but also of the experience of our ancestors.[7] Archetypal images are seen in patients' dreams, fantasies, drawings and associations, and are interpreted as a vital part of therapeutic process.[8]

Otto Rank began to experiment with short-term therapy and a more active role as therapist.[9] He emphasized the role of the person's will as the central and integrative force that moves the individual toward autonomy and independence. Birth trauma (separation from mother) became a more important theme in psychological disorders.

Harry Stack Sullivan placed an overwhelming balance of importance on the interpersonal realm of human existence, de-emphasizing the intrapsychic.[10] Indeed, his concept of becoming human meant becoming socialized. He, like Freud, presented stages of human development. But his stages were founded upon characteristic interpersonal patterns rather than the physical location of biological energy.

Erich Fromm's writings focus on the interrelationship between intrapsychic functioning and society.[11] A person's freedom is found as he or she chooses to unite with others in a mutual effort toward increasing self-fulfillment, productivity and an improved society.[12] When the possibility of freedom produces too much anxiety, the person chooses isolation or the bondage of an authoritarian relationship.

The ego analysts, including Heinz Hartmann, David Rapaport and Erik Erikson have not really developed a separate system of psychotherapy. Rather, they are viewed as having supplemented or extended Freud's theoretical system. They focused much of their study on people's normal or healthy behavior. The role of the ego is emphasized. Behavior is seen as a developmental process in relationship to the environment. Though humans are animals who are driven by instinctive urges, emphasis is placed on the strength of learned behavior.

Existential/experiential orientation. The writings of the neo- and non-Freudians voiced quite a lot of discontent about traditional Freudian psychoanalytic thought and technique. Europe had struggled through World War I, economic chaos, World War II and then found itself in the clutches of the Cold War. In Europe, a number of philosophers, psychologists and theologians (including Kierkegaard, Sartre, Camus, Heidegger, Laing, Husserl and Tillich) were at the forefront of reshaping thought about the nature of humanity, causes of abnormal behavior, how people become whole and meaning in life.

Rollo May, Viktor Frankl and Ludwig Binswanger have been involved in translating existential philosophy into the clinical practice of psychotherapy and counseling. Depersonalization, alienation, loss of direction and meaning, and the inability to make commitment are important treatment issues. Much of Frankl's logotherapy comes from what he experienced and learned while imprisoned in a German concentration camp during World War II.[13] He states that finding satisfactory values is central to the task of experiencing adequate meaning in life.[14] There are three kinds of values to be found: creative, experiential and attitudinal. Some of them can be (and must be) realized in every life situation in order for life to maintain its meaning. Rollo May's contribution to psychotherapy has been manifold, including sensitive and penetrating insights into the healing process of counseling.[15]

A vital role in the existential/experiential revolution has been played by Carl Rogers, whose writings have dramatically influenced not only the nature of psychotherapy, but virtually every area of our lives.[16] He was the first psychotherapist to invite the researchers and their tools into the inner sanctum of the therapist's confidential office.[17] For the first time studies could be made on what was actually done and said by both client and therapist.[18] Audiotapes, typescripts and later videotapes proved to be far more valid and reliable reporters on therapy than the therapists' and clients' report of what had happened. This revolutionary change opened the doors to the process of validating reports by therapists and theoreticians with research.

Roger's theory of counseling has progressed through three stages: the non-directive stage, the client-centered stage and the stage of active counselor involvement.[19]

The non-directive stage focused attention on the healing and growth-enhancing effects of the counselor's attentive listening and empathic reflective responses to the client's expression of emotion. The client-centered stage focused the same strong emphasis on the client's internal ability to heal and grow. The role of the counselor became less constrained to giving only reflective responses. During the last of the three stages, the counselor's role has expanded to be a very active one, giving self-disclosures, direct feedback, questions and interpretations. Yet nothing is taken away from the all-important role of the counselee in his or her own healing.

Essentially, Rogers believes that if the therapist possesses and adequately expresses three qualities, then the counselee will grow.[20] These three qualities are: genuineness or congruence; unconditional and non-possessive love, warmth and positive regard; and accurate empathic understanding.

A number of other theories can be grouped under the existential/experiential heading. Gestalt therapy, devised by Frederick (Fritz) Perls, sees human nature from a wholistic perspective.[21] As a person goes through life, parts of the self are lost and splits develop in the psyche. The active and directive nature of Gestalt therapy refocuses the patient on the "here and now" in order to restore the split-off parts of the person back into the whole. Powerful treatment experiences are a hallmark of Gestalt therapy. They include the empty-chair technique, split-self dialogue, and acting-out dreamwork.

Transactional analysis is a theoretical approach developed by Eric Berne.[22] It has gained tremendous popularity within the community of therapists and in the lay community, largely because of its systematic use of simple labels for complex psychological and interpersonal dynamics. Berne postulates that there are three ego states: child, parent and adult. There are also four possible "life positions" that a person can adapt that help to determine the kind of "script" or "life plan" that the individual will follow throughout his or her life.[23] These four life positions are: I am OK, you are OK; I am OK, you are not OK; I am not OK, you are OK; and I am not OK, you are not OK. Transactional analysis and structural analysis are designed to help counselees stop playing "games" and "rackets" and start moving toward a more self-directed, autonomous life pattern.

Bioenergetic analysis was founded by Alexander Lowen as a result of his studies, personal analysis and practice with Wilhelm Reich.[24] Bioenergetics, based upon Reichian analysis, emphasizes the interacting role of the body in the development of the psyche, the etiology of psychological dysfunction, and in the psychotherapeutic treatment of psychological disorders.[25] Importance is placed on the mind/body response to stress and conflict, which produces several different character structures. Each character structure exhibits different body and personality traits. The character structures that Lowen describes are the schizoid, oral, hysterical, psychopathic, masochistic and rigid character structures. Bioenergetic analysis combines verbal techniques with body work to unblock and release physical and psychological energies in order to help the individual to function again as a unified, whole person.

There are many other therapies that can be placed under this existential/experiential heading. Among them are primal scream therapy (Janov) and reparenting therapy. Often these can be described more as therapeutic techniques than therapeutic systems.

Cognitive orientation. Another type of therapeutic approach minimizes the importance of unconscious processes and de-emphasizes the need to work with the person's emotions. These theories place more emphasis on supplying needed information and correcting inaccurate perceptual and thought patterns. These therapies are more brief and cognitively oriented and owe their historical beginning to Alfred Adler. He believed that most psychological distress emanates from characteristic ways of perceiving the world and solving problems. This "life style" was usually marked by incorrect assumptions that lead to dysfunctional emotional and behavioral patterns. His therapy approach was to help the patient discover these incorrect assumptions, alter them, and to adjust his or her life style to fit more adequately with reality.

Trait and factor theories are other types of cognitive therapy.[26] Frank Parsons and E. Williamson present two examples of trait and factor approaches.[27] These are therapies designed to help the counselee understand his or her interests, aptitudes and traits in relation to the demands and requirements of the external worlds of work, school, relationships, etc.[28]

Rational-emotive therapy is a very active, directive type of short-term therapy developed by Albert Ellis.[29] Fundamental to this theory is the proposition that psychological dysfunction is created by the internalization of incorrect beliefs that lead to ineffective and self-defeating behavior. There are certain irrational statements that people often tell themselves (self-talk) that become intricately involved in distressed, unhealthy living. Ellis compiled a list of some common irrational statements.[30] For example: "If I am to be okay, everyone around me must love me and approve of me." "I must always be functioning perfectly, adequately and competently if I am to be good enough." "It is horrible, catastrophic and totally unacceptable if things don't turn out as I wish them to be." Rational-emotive therapy is designed to help counselees become aware of the irrational statements that they tell themselves, to help them understand how these irrational statements lead to dysfunctional behaviors and to help them change these incorrect assumptions into more accurate and functional ones.

Another short-term, active therapy is William Glasser's reality therapy.[31] People are believed to have made value decisions in their very early years that have great impact throughout their whole lives. These values generate behaviors that either enhance or disrupt the development of identity. The theory holds that one's identity can change if behavior changes. Therefore, therapy focuses upon altering the person's behavior to constructive and adaptive patterns, thus leading to a more constructive and adequate identity. The therapist helps the client accept full responsibility for his or her selection of values and behavioral responses. The therapist encourages and supports the counselee's decisions and commitments, accepting no excuses for lack of follow-through. But the approach is positive and encouraging, never punishing or negative when there is a lack of follow-through.

Learning/behavioral orientation. Clustered under the label learning/behavioral theories are a large selection of therapeutic procedures and orientations that are based on the belief that psychological disorders are manifested in dysfunctional behavior and that treatment is most efficiently accomplished by changing these into more adaptive behaviors.[32] These therapies can be divided into two groups, those that are based on operant conditioning techniques and those that are based on classical conditioning theory and procedure.

B.F. Skinner's early research during the 1930s and 1940s primarily included rats and pigeons in an experimental chamber that has become known as the Skinner box.[33] By providing certain positive (food) or negative (electric shock) stimuli immediately after the occurrence of a specific target behavior, Skinner was able to cause that behavior either to increase or decrease in frequency.[34] He then found that he could increase the probability of the occurrence of certain behaviors (positive reinforcement) and decrease the probability of other behaviors (negative reinforcement) in human subjects as well.[35]

John Dollard and Neal Miller's reinforcement counseling is one application of operant conditioning theory.[36] Their theory represents a collaborative effort between an experimental psychologist and a cultural anthropologist who formulated their theory from the psychoanalytic works of Freud, the learning theory of Hull, and the writings of several anthropologists.[37] They view learning, at its simplest level, to be a sequence of these conditions or events:

1. The presence of either an innate (hunger) or learned (money) drive.

2. Occurrence of an event (cue) that in the presence of the particular drive will elicit particular kinds of responses. Cues are often verbal statements like, "Dinner is ready" or "It's time to go to work."

3. An internal subjectively observable response (r) like hope, anticipation or disappointment occurs.

4. An external, objectively observable response (R) then occurs.

5. The intensity of the original drive is then reduced (reinforcement). In short-hand version, learning looks like: drive-cue-r-R-reinforcement.

The person's response must result in a lessening of the intensity of the original drive in the learning sequence. When that occurs (reinforcement), the probability of response occurring in the presence of the same drive and cue is increased. Therapy is essentially a two-part process: extinguishing undesirable behavior and reinforcing desired behaviors.

John Krumboltz is another major researcher in behavioral counseling.[38] His research and editorial efforts have done much to advance the psychotherapeutic use of reinforcement techniques.[39]

Operant conditioning based therapies have been very effective approaches with autistic children, stuttering problems, depression, inpatient schizophrenics, hyperactive behavior, aggressive behavior, procrastination, academic performance problems and fear of speaking in front of groups.

Psychotherapies that are based on classical conditioning theory have been just as effective. Pavlov's early experiments on dogs, sheep and goats formed the experimental basis for these theoretical developments.[40] In the classical conditioning model, a conditional stimulus (bell) is paired contiguously with an unconditional stimulus (meat). The dog normally salivates when presented with the meat (unconditional response) and after several such pairings, will salivate when hearing the bell only (conditioned response). In everyday living some dysfunctional responses are learned in the same way. A child who has been bitten by a dog may fear all dogs (or even all furry objects).

Andrew Salter believes that the cause of emotional illness is inhibition.[41] His therapeutic goal is to recondition his patients to become excited rather than inhibited. He helps them think less and act more spontaneously upon their emotions. He instructs and coaches his patients: to say what they feel; to express emotions through facial expression; to speak up when they disagree; to use the word "I" as deliberately and as often as possible; to express agreement when praised; and to live creatively in the here and now without planning.

Joseph Wolpe has been successful in treating phobic patients with his reciprocal inhibition psychotherapy.[42] He introduces an alternate response that opposes the anxiety response. If the alternate response replaces the anxiety response, then the latter is said to be either partially or completely inhibited. Assertive and relaxation responses are the most commonly used replacements.

Systematic desensitization is a particular form of reciprocal inhibition.[43] Phobic patients are taught to be more aware of their level of body tension. They are taught a method for systematically relaxing each muscle group in the body, usually starting with the head and moving down to the feet. Patients are taught to do deep-muscle relaxation whenever they feel tension in their bodies. Then, with the aid of their therapist, they create an anxiety hierarchy of events. These experiences are arranged in order from the least anxiety-producing to the most anxiety-producing. During the desensitization sessions the patient is relaxed to a deep level and is then helped to imagine the least anxiety-producing experience of his or her hierarchy. If the patient experiences any body tension, the therapist is signaled, usually by a raised index finger. At that point the patient is taken back to deep-muscle relaxation and the imagery is attempted again. When the patient is able to complete the imagined experience without feeling any muscular tension, the next experience in the hierarchy can be imagined, and so on, until the hierarchy is completed. This relaxation response, then, transfers to the counselee's real-life situations.

Implosive therapy has been used very successfully with anxiety neurotics and phobics. This therapy is based on the belief that the patient's problems originated with prior painful experiences. The therapist tries to recreate these experiences in the patient's imagination using vivid descriptions, films, slides, recordings, smells, etc., in order to cause the patient to experience again the intense anxiety associated with the original event. This is repeated several times in a safe, supportive therapeutic environment. Implosive therapy is based on the idea that since there is no pain or punishment to reinforce the anxiety response, it will become extinguished.

Another behavioral therapy based on classical conditioning theory is modeling therapy.[44] In both the experimental psychologist's laboratory and in the therapist's office, people learn from models who are often portrayed on film.[45] Children who have strong fear of dogs will approach them more closely after watching a film of other children petting and enjoying contact with dogs.[46] Albert Bandura also found that people who had phobic fears of snakes could be encouraged to sit still while a snake crawled around them after watching a person model fearless snake handling.[47]

There are endless variations of therapies that can be clustered within the four theoretical orientations presented in this chapter. To elaborate further would be beyond our scope and purpose. As we move on to examine a therapeutic approach that encompasses a healthy theology and adequately addresses our spiritual being, let us give appropriate appreciation to those who have discovered so much even though they may have been working within systems that are not specifically Christian in nature.

An Overview of Christian Approaches to Counseling

"Are you a Christian counselor?" "Do you counsel from the Bible?" "What makes your approach any different from secular therapy?" These important questions are often asked by people seeking help and by people who want referral information. These questions are important because they reflect the sincere concern that counseling be able to support the person's spiritual growth. The questions also reflect a fear that therapy will be detrimental to one's faith. Most of us have heard war stories (and some are true!) about how a psychologist turned his or her patient against the church or about a case of seduction by a psychiatrist. Christians have traditionaly been suspicious about therapy. In the summer of 1971, a speaker at a Christian youth workers conference exclaimed, "The study of psychology will very likely ruin your faith." Many distressed and hurting Christians have been told to not see a psychologist. "Just trust more in God." "You need more faith." Does this remind you of the infamous counsel that Job received from his friends?

Fortunately, since the 1960s there have been significant efforts from the Christian community to find out more about psychotherapy and counseling. Much credit for this recent direction toward integration is due to Dr. Clyde Narramore. His Narramore Christian Foundation, Rosemead Counseling Center and numerous publications have done much to unlock church doors to the positive offerings of psychological study. *The Psychology of Counseling* presents educational material on the counseling process, the nature of psychological problems and the use of scripture in counseling.[48]

Many efforts toward integration of psychological thought and Christian faith have come from a variety of sectors and in many different forms. Ministers and lay people have been reading both secular and Christian "pop" psychology. These attractively packaged, positively motivating and sometimes informative pieces have influenced Christians to think and talk in psychology-influenced patterns. Words and phrases like: "body language," "self-esteem," "self-concept," "positive mental attitude," "unconditional love," "body image," "motivation," "depression" and "anxiety attack" are just a few of the many examples of popular psychology that appear so frequently in our daily language.

Pastors preach a significant percentage of their sermons about psychological issues: how to overcome depression, winning the battle over fear, what the Bible has to say about sex, how to be a godly parent, how to make your marriage succeed. Innumerable sermons and books by pastors about these and other topics have flooded the Christian listening and reading market during the past two decades. They are Christian ministers' efforts toward integration of psychological findings and Christian beliefs.

Probably the most pronounced effort toward this integration has been coming from Christians who are professionally involved in providing mental health services. Individual Christian psychotherapists are integrating their faith and psychological training during every therapy session everyday. They are writing books and publishing research that increase our knowledge and understanding of the psychological perspectives on God's creation. Christians who share professional activities are joining together for fellowship and the advancement of this process. The Christian Association for Psychological Studies (CAPS) and the National Association for Christians in Social Work (NACSW) are two noteworthy examples. There is also a special division within the American Psychological Association (APA) that was established to study the integration between psychology and religion.

There are many educational institutions that are designed to teach undergraduate and graduate students to integrate psychological theory with theology. Fuller Theological Seminary in Pasadena, California and Rosemead School of Psychology, La Mirada, California are two exceptional examples. Two professional journals publish research and theoretical papers that focus on the relationship between psychology and theology: the Journal of Psychology and Christianity[49] and the Journal of Psychology and Theology.[50]

The following chart will give us a broad picture of the various ways that Christians formulate counseling. Some of the concepts that are presented found their genesis in earlier publications by Lawrence Crabb.[51] Other concepts were by Frank Minirth and Paul Meier.[52]

Approaches to Relating Christianity With Psychology

Compartmentalization	PSYCHOLOGICAL BASIS	THEOLOGICAL BASIS	Spiritual Reduction
Psychological theory and theological understanding deal with two different and distinct issues. Though they may interrelate in some instances, they are best dealt with separately. Psychology and theology are two different disciplines that require different methodologies. They need not be compatible with each other.	*Integration-Singular Theory*		All truth is revealed in the Bible. Psychology is in opposition to Christianity and all counseling philosophy and methods must be found in and based upon scriptures.
	A specific psychological theory is the basis for the counseling approach. Compatible scriptural principles are integrated.	Theological beliefs based on scripture provide the basis for counseling, which integrates compatible psychological theory.	
	Integration-Eclecticism		
	A variety of psychological theories and methods provide the basis for the counseling approach. Compatible scriptural principles are integrated.	Theological beliefs based on scripture provide the basis for counseling, which integrates compatible psychological principles and therapeutic approaches from a variety of theoretical approaches.	

Illustration 8

Compartmentalization. Some people approach humanity in a manner that essentially carves people into distinct parcels, each to be studied and treated by professionals who limit their work to a highly specialized field. Pastors preach, lead Bible studies, disciple and counsel only in the area of spiritual problems. Medical doctors only treat physical illnesses and symptoms. Financial advisors counsel only on financial planning issues. Tax advisers offer help only with tax-related issues.

When a problem occurs, decisions are made about the category that it fits best, who is best qualified to deal with that category and what should be done about it. Little consideration is given to understanding how problems in one area affect functioning in another area. There is also little concern about how helping with one problem might affect other aspects of the person's life. Let's look at a counseling example with a 15-year-old girl that demonstrates this issue.

Counselor: "You seem to be in a turmoil over something, Karla."

Karla: "I sure am. Boy, you don't know the half of it. My parents are so unreal. I think they're being mean or something."

Counselor: "So you think your parents are being pretty unfair."

Karla: "You got it. I'm so ticked. 'No single dating till you're 16,' they say. Can you believe that?"

Counselor: "You really are angry."

Karla: "Darn right I am. And I'm doing something about it. I'm not putting up with all that crap! I'm leaving. I've got it all planned out. I'll stay at a friend's awhile. I'll show them they can't stop me from dating."

Counselor (pastor/spiritual view): "Karla, I'm concerned about what this decision means spiritually for you. Aren't you really planning to violate the biblical principles of obeying, respecting and honoring your parents?"

Counselor (family therapist/relational view): "Sounds like you've just about given up on your parents, Karla. I'm wondering what happens in your relationship with them that makes resolving problems so difficult."

Counselor (psychologist/intrapsychic view): "There's a real conflict inside between wanting to please your parents on the one hand and wanting to do your own thing on the other. For now, wanting to do your own thing is winning."

The compartmentalist sees Karla's problem from his or her own perspective and approaches the situation from a singular point of view. In our example, all three orientations have strong value. But the compartmentalist counselor would counsel only from one of the three perspectives, believing that the other two fell outside of his or her domain.

Not only does the compartmentalist fail to address important issues with the counselee, but the exclusion of certain perspectives might be damaging. Let's go back to our example of Karla:

First, compartmentalized spiritual counsel would neglect a more comprehensive view of the family's relationship patterns that might clarify why Karla's choice was to leave instead of some other option. It also does not give proper attention to Karla's need to separate psychologically from her parents. Without understanding the total family relationship, Karla's behavior is not seen in context. Without knowing psychodynamic and developmental theories, the counselor remains ignorant of significant psychological meaning underlying her behavior. Ignoring family relationships and psychological dynamics makes spiritual counsel too narrow. Spiritual counsel alone might never reveal that Karla's father has an ongoing incestuous relationship with her. It also might make her feel unnecessarily guilty for her innate need to separate psychologically from her family.

Second, compartmentalized family relationship counseling would ignore the spiritual principles of honoring and respecting parents. The issue of Karla's relationship with God and the concept of finding strength and guidance from his presence would not be addressed. Ignoring the spiritual aspects of Karla's behavior might have serious ramifications in her future spiritual, psychological and conscience development.

Finally, individual psychological counseling is incomplete and insufficient without adequate consideration of spiritual issues and family relationship dynamics. Karla's psychological development involves her spiritual growth and the two need to be considered together. Her developmental pattern and psychodynamic process are intrinsically involved with the relationship process within her home. One cannot be adequately understood in isolation from the other.

Spiritual reductionism. "Materialistic reductionism" refers to a view of the world that reduces all of reality down to the material level. The materialistic reductionist believes that concepts like "mind," "thought," "emotion," "heart," "faith" and "spirit" can all be explained as having certain physical or material properties that can be observed, measured and experimentally manipulated.

On the other side of the reductionistic coin are the spiritual reductionists. Spiritual reductionism believes that all of reality is ultimately explained and caused by spiritual properties. We are somewhat familiar with the Christian Science view that physical illness is not an unhealthy condition within a physical body. Rather, it is an image or expression of unhealthy mind, spirit or faith.

Dr. Robert Schuller, pastor of the Crystal Cathedral in California, is an example of a spiritual reductionist. His publications *Move Ahead With Possibility Thinking*,[53] *You Can Become the Person You Want to Be*[54] and *Self-Love: The Dynamic Force of Success*[55] all focus on the power of thought and attitude on personal goals. Schuller states essentially that the combined power of positive thinking, positive attitudes, faith and prayer create much of our present and future reality.

Another expression of spiritual reductionism from Christian thought is the belief that all psychological problems are spiritual in their genesis. Psychological well-being is attained through applying spiritual cures. This essentially anti-psychology orientation is promoted by a number of professional clergy as well as some professionally trained psychologists.

Two persons who hold this position are Bill Gothard and Tim La-Haye. Neither of them have formal training in psychopathology or in treating mental disorders. But both express very strong opinions about the genesis, nature, and treatment of mental and emotional problems. In his seminars, Gothard talks about a wide variety of personal, relational, family and spiritual problems. Virtually everything that is said in the seminar and written in the accompanying notebook is backed by at least one scriptural reference. A basic premise to this approach is that all of truth is revealed by God in the Bible. He has left essentially nothing for us to discover outside of the pages of scripture. Skinner's materialistic reductionism is unacceptable because it denies people's ability to think creatively and even more because it denies the existence of spiritual reality. In similar fashion, Gothard's spiritual reductionism is unacceptable because it denies the importance of the mental, emotional and psychological aspects of humanity.[56] LaHaye starts with a physiologically based theory of behavior and finishes with spiritualistic answers for behavioral problems.[57]

The most comprehensively formulated approach to spiritual reductionistic counseling has been offered by Jay Adams. In *Competent to Counsel* he presents "nouthetic counseling."[58] This approach represents a strong negative reaction to the bulk of non-Christian psychotherapeutic work. But like so many reactions, Adams' nouthetic counseling seems to be an overreaction. His basis for truth is the Bible. All elements of counseling theory and practice must be completely supported by specific scriptural references. If there is no biblical reference that supports the use of a certain technique, then it is to be discarded as unbiblical and non-Christian. Consequently, he has opened himself to criticism regarding his interpretation of the Bible.

In both *Competent to Counsel* and *The Christian Counselor's Manual* he indicates that the most important training for effective counselors in theological rather than psychological.[59] If a person is spiritually healthy and theologically accurate then he is more competent to counsel than is a non-Christian psychologist or psychiatrist, even if the Christian lay person has no training in counseling.

Adams and other spiritual reductionists hold strongly to the belief that the narrowness of their epistemology is one of their greatest assets. It seems, however, to be one of their greatest vulnerabilities. Everything hinges on one thing and one thing alone: their interpretation and understanding of scripture.

A discussion of "biblical counseling" in a recent San Diego chapter meeting of CAPS illustrates this vulnerability. The presenter, a Christian college professor with a strong biblical counseling orientation, was using the illustration of Christ's interaction with a Samaritan woman as an example of how Christ counseled (John 4:4-43). His point was that we ought to counsel as Jesus did. The story is a remarkable account of how a brief contact with Jesus radically changed one promiscuous woman's life so profoundly that it resulted in many more being changed as well. The presenter proceeded to point out that it was the content of Christ's teaching and his confrontation of the woman's sin that caused her subsequent behavioral change, when a hand in the audience was raised. "Perhaps it was not only what Christ said," offered the responder, "maybe it was how he related with her. We don't know from scripture whether it was just what Christ said that changed her life. Possibly it was the fact of his unconditional positive regard (Carl Roger's term) and his own personal openness that enabled her to lower her defenses, see herself in a more honest light and believe that she could be different." The point was made that evening and it holds true. Scripture is our most solid basis for truth, but our interpretation, understanding and application are always subject to criticism, alteration and additional insight. Therefore when people limit their knowledge to only one source, even when that source is the Bible, they place themselves on a very precarious epistemological base.

Another difficulty with reductionistic approaches is their characteristic intolerance for the abstract and for "not knowing." In contrast to Rollo May, there is little or no art in their counseling.[60] It is a concrete

process of confrontation, exhortation, teaching and holding the counselee accountable. "Not knowing" and ambiguity are viewed as negative states that serve no positive purpose. A different view is presented
in a thought-stimulating book titled, *The Faith of the Counsellors:* "For
the Christian, 'faith' is a condition in which simultaneous affirmation of
doctrine and of everyday empirical reality is made possible by a surrender to a beatific vision in which the autonomies are fused in a state
of grace. Believing Mary was a virgin and believing that she couldn't
have been, and believing that Christ rose from the dead and believing
that he couldn't have, are affirmations which, though contradictory,
fuse in an elation of largeness of generosity. The contradictions
become complementary to produce an awareness in which 'the law of
the excluded middle' is no longer binding."[61]

Integration. Up to this point we have looked at counseling approaches
that are not directed toward integration. Compartmentalists do not
want integration of psychology and theology because they believe that
the two disciplines deal with totally different and separate areas of human functioning. Spiritual reductionists allude to psychologists, but usually in disparaging terms, viewing that discipline as having gone astray
from truth and a threat to spiritual well-being. Since the reductionists
believe all of the truth we need to know is in the Bible, they recommend only theologians and pastors who are intentionally ignorant of
psychology to counsel.

True integrationists express an honest valuing of both the psychological and theological perspectives of human behavior. Further, they perceive that these two disciplines are focused on areas of human functioning and are overlapping. They seek the truth that is discovered
from both approaches in order to enrich their understanding and to increase their counseling effectiveness.

We can look at integrationists on a continuum with those who place
the heaviest emphasis on psychological theory at one end and those
who place the greatest weight on theology at the other end. Though
some integrationists may be at the midpoint on this bipolar scale, the
majority will find themselves placed to the left or right of midpoint. We
can spot, then, four different types of counselors who seek integration
between psychology and theology: counselors who work primarily
from a psychological basis according to one theory; counselors who
work primarily from a theological basis according to one theory; counselors who work primarily from a psychological basis with an eclectic
system; and counselors who work primarily from a theological basis

with an eclectic system.

The thesis presented in this book is that the best counseling approach integrates psychological theory with theological understanding. Several factors will influence the specific manner in which an integrationist counselor approaches this difficult task.

First, the counselor's educational background will have an impact. Those who have had primary training in a psychological graduate school may emphasize the psychological base, while seminarians may focus more on the theological base. Students who have been well-trained in one specific orientation might tend to counsel within that particular therapeutic framework, while those who have been exposed to a variety of therapeutic models may lean toward eclecticism.

Second, the setting in which a person works also has an effect upon counseling style. Counselors who work on a church staff or in a church-affiliated counseling center may base their approach on theological considerations. Those who work in independent centers, medical settings, government agencies or private practices may focus on psychological orientations.

Third, the nature of a counselor's continuing education will affect his or her counseling approach. Books, seminars, workshops, professional organizations, and the journals we read reflect and impact our counseling orientation.

Fourth, both the style and the quality of the counselor's spiritual life will have an effect on his or her counseling orientation. The more a person is focused on God, the more his or her counseling will reflect it.

Fifth, the counselor's personality structure will have a profound impact on counseling style and orientation. Compulsive and authoritarian counselors might prefer singular theories and gravitate toward a stronger theological base.

A final determinant is whether or not the counselor has been through any significant personal therapy or counseling. If so, feelings about his or her therapist and therapeutic experience may influence the counselor to use or avoid the approach used by the therapist.

Let us look closely at each of the four approaches to integration:

1. *Primary focus on psychology: singular theory.* Counselors in this category have been trained primarily from a psychological orientation with little formal theological training. They have developed a strong thrust and appreciation for their psychological heritage and have become particularly adept in the counseling application of one particular theoretical position. They approach all of their counseling cases from

the same theoretical framework and typically refer counselees who require a different approach. They are concerned about the theological compatibility of their approach and are willing to alter their therapeutic formulations in order to integrate their theological beliefs.

Psychiatrist O. Quentin Hyder is an example of this type of integrationist. In his book *The Christian Handbook of Psychiatry* he demonstrates his preference for one theory (Christian doctrine) and his theoretical adaptations to gain compatibility with those doctrines. He writes, "As yet there is no one therapeutic technique or theory consistently better than all others. It is therefore my privilege to use in my practice, the methods and principles I deem best in my hands for the benefit of my patients. This I have done. My method is a form of reality therapy integrated with basic Christian doctrines, and my principles are to be found in the Old and New Testaments which I believe to be inspired by God."[62]

2. Primary focus on theology: singular theory. Counselors in this category often have a strong background in theological training and may or may not have done extensive work in psychology. It is very important that their theoretical structure fits comfortably with scripture and finds its genesis in scripture. Counselors from this orientation also require that their approach be consistent with a certain psychological orientation, whether it is from the psychodynamic, existential/experiential, cognitive or learning/behavioral orientation.

Lawrence Crabb emerges as an adequate example of an integrationist who strongly advocates a theoretical approach that is heavily based in scriptural understanding. He explains his approach in *Effective Biblical Counseling.* "Because I believe counseling includes a wide variety of behavior without one unifying behavioral strategy like confrontation, I do not want to convey that my model of counseling is a cut and dry, mechanical, 'ask this, then do that' approach. Far from it. Counseling is a relationship. Relationship interactions vary depending on the temperaments, problems, personalities of the people involved . . . even though counseling includes a diverse set of operations, still it is possible, I think, to abstract a basic game plan which a counselor, through all his varied behavior, can follow."[63]

His "game plan" for counseling involves seven stages: identify problem feelings; identify problem behavior; identify problem thinking; clarify biblical thinking; secure commitment; plan and carry out biblical behavior; and identify Spirit-controlled feelings.

His approach to counseling is clearly biblical. He is a singular theorist because he delineates seven specific stages through which effective counseling should progress. But then he sounds eclectic because of his encouragement to use a wide variety of specific counseling behaviors while proceeding through the seven stages.

3. *Primary focus on psychology: eclectic.* Counselors in this category tend to have strong psychological backgrounds. They may or may not have any formal theological training, and though they are interested in compatibility between their psychology and theological doctrines, the primary genesis of their counseling approach comes from studies in psychology. They have not been sufficiently impressed with any one therapeutic approach. Rather, their counseling approach is based on the particular elements in each individual case.

Ronald Koteskey, writing in the area of general rather than clinical or counseling psychology, is an example of this orientation. In the preface of *Psychology From a Christian Perspective* he explains how students of psychology can use his book. "By reading this book with their general psychology textbooks, they can place the various parts of psychology in a Christian world-view."[64]

He starts with a summary of psychological research and theory. His goal is to pull out the truth that has been discovered through the study of psychology and then redefine or reinterpret this truth from a Christian perspective. He defines healthy adjustment as "being like God" while maladjustment is "being unlike God."[65]

He draws from psychology and Christianity to find the various causes for maladjustment. Physical disorders, underlying conflict, sin, immaturity and demon possession are those that he emphasizes. His eclecticism is apparent particularly in his overview of methods that Christian counselors can use to help a person readjust, or become more like God. He discusses physical methods, behavior therapy, psychotherapy, salvation, discipleship and casting out demons as viable treatment processes.

Better known in the study of Christian counseling is Gary Collins. In *Christian Counseling: A Comprehensive Guide*, he displays his strong eclectic foundation in psychological training.[66] His book discusses a large number of problems and situations that are often the presenting problems of counselees who are seeking help. Concise, informative descriptions, along with counseling guidelines and goals are presented for each problem area. No singular theoretical framework unifies his methodology. His counseling goals and methods are specifically oriented to the problem for which the counselee requests assistance.

His approaches arise from his comprehensive understanding of the psychological struggles and inner conflicts that bring people to the counseling office. As one discovers Collins' direction and counseling approach, there is no hint of anything that is contraindicated by Christian principles. Though scripture is integrated comfortably in his presentation, there is no compulsive desire for "proof texting."

4. *Primary focus on theology: eclectic.* Counselors in this last variety are integrationists typically well-trained in theology and they feel the need to base their counseling approach in scripture. They formulate their ideas about psychological dysfunction, counseling goals and treatment methods primarily on Christian beliefs. They then draw from psychological research and theory to complete their system. Their eclecticism is evident in the breadth of treatments and the lack of a tightly structured theoretical system.

Frank Minirth and Paul Meier suggest a "Christian eclectic approach."[67] The eclectic nature and scriptural preeminance over psychology are emphasized in their approach: "We examine each case on an individual basis and carefully determine which of the methods will be of greatest use. We take the best from each of the major categories of psychotherapy. We employ, then, an eclectic approach. But underlying all our decisions in these matters is a burning concern to insure that the Bible is central to our counseling techniques. Not only is the word of God to be used in conjunction with the therapies of the secular schools, it is to be the overriding factor."[68]

The study of approaches to counseling and psychotherapy leads toward a more comprehensive understanding of human behavior. We must learn from others, even those with whom we disagree. The psychodynamic, existential/experiential, cognitive and behavioral theorists have made rich contributions to our knowledge of the psychological aspect of humanity. We are fortunate that fear and prejudice between psychology and Christianity have begun to (and are) eroding. Although we can learn from the compartmentalists and are challenged by the spiritual reductionists, we are greatly enriched by the integrationists who seek and find compatibility in the disciplines of both psychology and theology.

Notes

1. Frank Minirth and Paul Meier, *Counseling and the Nature of Man* (Grand Rapids, Mich.: Baker Book House, 1982).

2. The following sources were used in compiling the information for this chart:

James Coleman, *Psychology and Effective Behavior* (Glenview, Ill.: Scott, Foresman, 1969).

Bruce Shertzer and Shelly Stone, *Fundamentals of Counseling* (Boston: Houghton Mifflin, 1974).

Minirth and Meier, *Counseling and the Nature of Man.*

Gardner Lindzey, Calvin Hall, and R. Thompson, *Psychology* (New York: Worth Publishers, 1975).

Allen Ivey and L. Simek-Downing, *Counseling and Psychotherapy: Skills, Theories and Practice* (Englewood Cliffs, N. J.: Prentice-Hall, 1980).

Paul Meier, Frank Minirth, and Frank Wichern, *Introduction to Psychology and Counseling* (Grand Rapids, Mich.: Baker Book House, 1982).

C. H. Patterson, *Theories of Counseling and Psychotherapy* (New York: Harper and Row, 1966).

Robert Harper, *Psychoanalysis and Psychotherapy: 36 Systems* (New York: Jason Aronson, 1974).

Donald Ford and H. Urban, *Systems of Psychotherapy: A Comparative Study* (New York: John Wiley, 1967).

John Watkins, "Psychotherapeutic Methods," in *Handbook of Clinical Psychology*, ed. Benjamin Wolman (New York: McGraw-Hill, 1965).

3. Harper, *Psychoanalysis and Psychotherapy: 36 Systems.*

4. Sigmund Freud, *New Introductory Lectures on Psychoanalysis*, trans. J. H. Sprott (New York: Norton, 1933).

5. Alfred Adler, *The Practice and Theory of Individual Psychology* (New York: Harcourt Brace Jovanovich, 1927).

6. Joland Jacobi, *The Psychology of C. G. Jung* (New Haven, Conn.: Yale University Press, 1962).

7. Carl G. Jung, *Modern Man in Search of a Soul*, trans. W. S. Dell and Cary F. Baynes (New York: Harcourt Brace and World, 1933).

8. Carl G. Jung, *Man and His Symbols* (New York: Dell, 1968).

9. Otto Rank, *Will Therapy and Truth and Reality* (New York: Knopf, 1947).

10. Harry S. Sullivan, *The Interpersonal Theory of Psychiatry* (New York: Norton, 1953).

11. Erich Fromm, *Man for Himself: An Inquiry into the Psychology of Ethics* (Greenwich, Conn.: Fawcett Publications, 1947).

12. Erich Fromm, *Escape From Freedom* (New York: Avon Books, 1941).

13. Victor Frankl, *Man's Search for Meaning: An Introduction to Logotherapy* (Boston: Beacon, 1959).

14. Victor Frankl, *The Doctor and the Soul* (New York: Knopf, 1955).

15. Rollo May, *The Art of Counseling* (Nashville: Abingdon, 1967).

16. Carl R. Rogers, *Client-Centered Therapy* (Boston: Houghton Mifflin, 1951).

17. Carl R. Rogers, *On Becoming a Person* (Austin: University of Texas, 1958).

18. Carl R. Rogers, *On Becoming a Person: A Therapist's View of Psychotherapy* (Boston: Houghton Mifflin, 1961).

19. Eugene Gendlin, "A Short Summary and Some Long Predictions," in *New Directions in Client-Centered Therapy*, eds. J. Hart and T. Tomlinson (Boston: Houghton Mifflin, 1970).

20. Carl R. Rogers, "Facilitation of Personal Growth," The School Counselor 2, no.

1 (January 1955).

21. Fritz Perls, *Gestalt Therapy Verbatim* (Moab, Utah: Real People Press, 1969).

22. Eric Berne, *Games People Play* (New York: Grove Press, 1964).

23. Thomas Harris, *I'm OK—You're OK* (New York: Harper and Row, 1967).

24. Alexander Lowen, *Physical Dynamics of Character Structure* (New York: Grune and Stratton, 1958).

25. Alexander Lowen, *Bioenergetics* (New York: Penguin, 1975).

26. Frank Parsons, *Choosing a Vocation* (New York: Agathon, 1967).

27. E. Williamson, *Counseling Adolescents* (New York: McGraw-Hill, 1950).

28. E. Williamson, "Some Issues Underlying Counseling Theory and Practice," in *Counseling Points of View*, ed. Willis E. Dugan (Minneapolis: University of Minnesota Press, 1959).

29. Albert Ellis, "Rational Psychotherapy," Journal of General Psychology 59 (1958):35-39.

30. Albert Ellis, "Rational Psychotherapy and Individual Psychology," Journal of Individual Psychology 13 (1957):38-44.

31. William Glasser, *Reality Therapy* (New York: Harper and Row, 1964).

32. John Krumboltz and C. Thoresen, eds., *Behavioral Counseling: Cases and Techniques* (New York: Holt, Rinehart and Winston, 1969).

33. B.F. Skinner, *The Behavior of Organisms* (New York: Appleton-Century-Crofts, 1938).

34. B.F. Skinner, *Science and Human Behavior* (New York: Macmillan, 1953).

35. B.F. Skinner, *Verbal Behavior* (New York: Appleton-Century-Crofts, 1957).

36. John Dollard and Neal Miller, *Personality and Psychotherapy: An Analysis in Terms of Learning, Thinking and Culture* (New York: McGraw-Hill, 1950).

37. Ford and Urban, *Systems of Psychotherapy*.

38. John Krumboltz, ed., *Revolution in Counseling: Implications of Behavioral Science* (Boston: Houghton Mifflin, 1966).

39. Krumboltz and Thoresen, *Behavioral Counseling*.

40. I.P. Pavlov, *Conditioned Reflexes*, trans. G.V. Anrep (New York: Oxford University Press, 1927).

41. Andrew Salter, *Conditioned Reflex Therapy* (New York: Creative Age Press, 1949).

42. Joseph Wolpe, *Psychotherapy by Reciprocal Inhibition* (Stanford, Calif.: Stanford University Press, 1958).

43. Peter Lang, "Experimental Studies of Desensitization Psychotherapy," in *The Conditioning Therapies*, eds. Joseph Wolpe, A. Salter, and L. Reyna (New York: Holt, Rinehart and Winston, 1964).

44. Albert Bandura, "Influence of Models: Reinforcement Contingencies on the Acquisition of Imitative Responses," Journal of Personality and Social Psychology 1 (1965):589-595.

45. Peter Lang, "Experimental Studies of Desensitization Psychotherapy," in *The Conditioning Therapies*, eds. Joseph Wolpe, A. Salter, and L. Reyna (New York: Holt, Rinehart and Winston, 1964).

46. Ibid.

47. Bandura, "Influence of Models' Reinforcement."

48. Clyde Narramore, *The Psychology of Counseling* (Grand Rapids, Mich.: Zonder-

van, 1960).

49. Journal of Psychology and Christianity (Farmington Hills, Mich.: Christian Association for Psychological Studies).

50. Journal of Psychology and Theology (LaMirada, Calif.: Rosemead School of Psychology, Biola University).

51. Lawrence Crabb, *Effective Biblical Counseling: A Model for Helping Caring Christians Become Capable Counselors* (Grand Rapids, Mich.: Zondervan, 1977).

52. Minirth and Meier, *Counseling and the Nature of Man.*

53. Robert Schuller, *Move Ahead With Possibility Thinking* (New York: Doubleday, 1967).

54. Robert Schuller, *You Can Become the Person You Want to Be* (New York: Hawthorn Books, 1973).

55. Robert Schuller, *Self-Love: The Dynamic Force of Success* (New York: Hawthorn Books, 1969).

56. G. Keith Olson, "Strange Bedfellows," *Counselors Notebook* 2, no. 2 and 3 (Wheaton, Ill.: Youth for Christ, 1975).

57. Tim LaHaye, *The Spirit-Controlled Temperament* (Wheaton, Ill.: Tyndale, 1966).

58. Jay Adams, *Competent to Counsel* (Nutley, N. J.: Presbyterian and Reformed Publishing, 1970).

59. Jay Adams, *The Christian Counselor's Manual* (Grand Rapids, Mich.: Baker Book House, 1973).

60. May, *The Art of Counseling.*

61. Paul Halmos, *The Faith of the Counsellors* (New York: Schocken Books, 1966), pp. 164-165.

62. O. Quentin Hyder, *Christian's Handbook of Psychiatry* (Old Tappan, N. J.: Fleming H. Revell, 1971), p. 167.

63. Crabb, *Effective Biblical Counseling*, pp. 148-149.

64. Ronald Koteskey, *Psychology From a Christian Perspective* (Nashville: Abingdon, 1980), p. 9.

65. Ibid., p. 131.

66. Gary R. Collins, *Christian Counseling: A Comprehensive Guide* (Waco, Texas: Word Books, 1980).

67. Minirth and Meier, *Counseling and the Nature of Man.*

68. Meier, Minirth, and Wichern, *Introduction to Psychology and Counseling*, p. 57.

■ CHAPTER 5

A Counseling Approach You Can Use

Several phone messages on your answering machine await your return from lunch. One seems particularly urgent. It is from Mrs. Nickens, who called regarding her 14-year-old daughter, Paula. "We just found out that Paula has been shoplifting," she said. "She finally admitted to it when she realized we knew she wasn't innocent. She doesn't know that I'm telling you this, so handle it as you wish when you see her." You have met with Paula in three previous counseling sessions. She had some behavioral problems at the end of the last school year, got sexually involved with her boyfriend and has had some relationship struggles with her parents. But during the last two weeks, Paula and her parents indicated that things were going better. And now this new, disturbing information. What do you do? Do you change your counseling approach? Do you become more directive and confrontive? Or do you become even more loving and accepting?· How does this new information impact the goals, methods and process of your counseling with Paula?

Each counselor will respond to these questions differently according to his or her own counseling approach. As we discovered in the last chapter there is an impressive array of counseling theories, methodologies and dogma. It is the task of each counselor to develop an approach that feels comfortable, is effective with counselees, and is well-grounded in responsible psychological and theological positions.

Lay counselors, most pastors, youth workers and Sunday school teachers cannot expend anywhere near the amount of time, energy and expense as professionally trained psychiatrists do on developing their counseling skills and theoretical approach. A few books and perhaps a seminar or two on lay counseling usually sum up the training experience for non-professional counselors. Seminarians usually complete one or two classes that focus on pastoral counseling. Some churches have sponsored special training in peer counseling. Parents gain experience from counseling with their own children nearly every day.

The purpose of this chapter is to present a counseling approach that can be adapted and used by pastors, lay counselors, Sunday school teachers and parents as they work with teenagers. The type of counseling approach outlined in this chapter is often the general procedure used by experienced clinicians as well.

It is beyond the scope of this book to present a complex counseling theory. Such an effort would entail the presentation of a comprehensive philosophy of humanity, a thorough discussion of the nature of health, an equally exhaustive study of the development of disordered behavior, and a well-documented and researched presentation of therapeutic process. What *is* presented here is an approach that can be understood, learned, practiced and personalized by anyone seriously interested in counseling teenagers. A clarification is needed at this point: There is no substitute for the personal and professional stimulation that a solid graduate program can generate. But a lot of helping, supporting and counseling goes on each day within the church. This book is designed to help caring adults develop their God-given interpersonal talents into more effective counseling skills.

The Orientation

The last chapter presented a system for understanding counseling approaches in relation to their scriptural or Christian perspectives. Before describing the current suggested approach, let's look at its orientation in light of this same classification system.

This suggested approach is an integrative effort because it finds inherent value in both psychology and theology. It is not a compartmentalist view. Human behavior is viewed from a wholistic perspective. Although psychology and theology have their own domains, there is a very large sphere of overlap. The following diagram illustrates the concept that a person's spirit and psyche share common properties, mutually affect behavior and reciprocally impact each other.

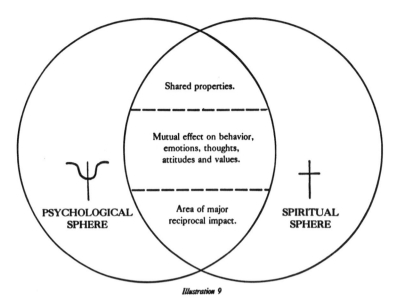

Illustration 9

This approach is not a spiritual reductionist view, since it believes that truth is both revealed and discovered. The Bible is recognized as truth revealed by God to humanity. "All scripture is inspired by God and profitable for teaching, for reproof, for correction and for training in righteousness, that the man of God may be complete, equipped for every good work" (2 Timothy 3:16-17).

The integrationist view holds that in addition to the truth that God has revealed in the Bible, God has made limitless knowledge and truth available for our discovery. Our discoveries are limited only by the limits of our scientific and aesthetic understanding, and by the limits of our technology. Paul writes, "For our knowledge is imperfect and our prophecy is imperfect; but when the perfect comes, the imperfect will pass away. For now we see in a mirror dimly, but then face to face. Now I know in part; then I shall understand fully, even as I have been fully understood" (1 Corinthians 13:9-10, 12).

Truth and knowledge are as limitless as the God who created them. The limitations in our knowledge do not mean that God is limited. Our limits are caused by: the limits that God imposed on his revelation; our limited capacity to perceive his revealed truth; limitations in our scientific and aesthetic approaches; limitations in our technology; and our state as finite beings created by an infinite God.

It is important to realize that the Bible is not a psychology textbook.[1] Neither is it a manual to teach people how to attain and maintain emotional balance and well-being. Nor is it a treatise on adolescent developmental processes. It does, however, contain propositions and guidelines for each of these areas. And since it is divine revelation, all other discovered truth and understanding must have compatibility with scripture. Yet even with the help of the Holy Spirit, our interpretations of the Bible are limited in their accuracy. Again we encounter the looming shadow of human imperfection. But this suggests the value of a tolerant attitude, a comprehensive wisdom and a diligent search for truth.

Our counseling approach is solidly integrationistic. Remember that there are four types of counseling approaches that are designed to meaningfully integrate psychology and theology: primary focus on psychology with a singular theory; primary focus on theology with a singular theory; primary focus on psychology with an eclectic approach; primary focus on theology with an eclectic approach.

The approach considered in this chapter is of the third variety. It's primary focus comes from the author's studies in psychology, his years of full-time clinical practice and a wide variety of other professional experiences. It also values the Bible as God's revealed word and accepts the absolute necessity for a harmony between psychological and theological perspectives. Central to this form of integration is the belief that a thought, insight or awareness can originate in various settings: a psychology journal, a discussion with a colleague, a counseling session, or even on a jog or in the shower. When the thought or insight registers in our consciousness, whatever the source, that is when integration begins. "Hey, that's interesting. I've never thought of it like that before. It seems to make sense." And our minds continue to search out the newly discovered apparent truth in order to test its limits. At what point does its logic break down? Does it conflict with other beliefs you hold to be true? If so, take a quick inventory of those standing beliefs. Check them out in light of your new idea. Are you sure that *they* are true? Does it have a scriptural basis? Look at the broader scriptural context.

What do you do if you cannot seem to bring your psychological insight and scriptural interpretations into compatible proximity? If you honestly think your insight seems true, can you allow the ambiguity to exist for a while?

As an example, let us look at a counseling issue regarding prayer. Jay Adams was heard on a Christian radio station saying, "If your counselor doesn't pray with you during your first session, then avoid him as you would avoid Satan himself." Perhaps there is another Christian view that is more appropriate. Some counselors select not to pray with a particular client because they see that the individual uses prayer unhealthily. Maybe they only pray about the issue at hand and avoid taking other necessary steps to resolve the problem. Perhaps prayer is used as a form of manipulating the other person. These are only two of the commonly seen unhealthy uses of prayer.

The Christian counselor may choose not to pray with the counselee as a part of the overall healing process. Immediately there is ambiguity! Why would a Christian refuse to pray with someone who is seeking help? Sometimes the tension from such ambiguity is the driving force that propels us into a deeper understanding of our being and of our faith.

Look again at the illustration presented earlier in this chapter. There are issues that are essentially spiritual (e.g., sin and salvation) and others that are specifically psychological (e.g., defense mechanisms and anxiety). But not even these issues are totally separate from the other sphere. This integration approach believes that an experience in any sphere of the human structure impacts the other spheres.

A more comprehensive conceptualization also includes the physical sphere of human structure, illustrated below. It has the same mutually interactive dynamics with the psychological and spiritual spheres.

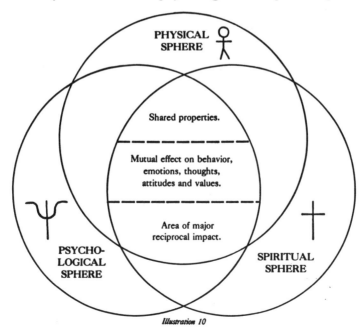

PHYSICAL SPHERE

Shared properties.

Mutual effect on behavior, emotions, thoughts, attitudes and values.

Area of major reciprocal impact.

PSYCHO-LOGICAL SPHERE

SPIRITUAL SPHERE

Illustration 10

In addition to its primary psychological base, our approach is eclectic rather than singular in its theoretical orientation. No one theory is conclusive enough to describe and explain the origin and nature of every psychological dysfunction. An eclectic approach recognizes and respects the rich diversity among personalities, interpersonal relating styles, past experiences and psychological defense systems. The eclectic approach believes that a wide variety of counseling skills best equips the counselor to work effectively with a wide variety of people with a broad spectrum of problems.

A General Plan for the Eclectic Counselor

This counseling plan applies directly to the work of lay counselors. It is adaptable and useful to the mother who is consoling her 17-year-old daughter whose boyfriend just broke off their steady relationship, for example. Yet the counseling plan is also appropriate and useful for the professional therapist working with a 15-year-old drug dealer who has a severe personality disorder.

The counseling approach has essentially six steps or stages. The counseling process usually follows the sequential order of these six stages, though they overlap each other and sometimes must be gone back to and repeated several times. The counselor will, of course, operate somewhat differently, depending on his or her relationship with the teenager, the setting, the individual young person involved and the problem that the teenager is presenting. The six counseling stages will be briefly presented and then discussed in more thorough detail. The stages are: establish and maintain the relationship with the counselee; explore and define the problems that the counselee needs to resolve; establish goals and structure the counseling process in ways that will accomplish those goals; help the counselee work toward attaining his or her goals; terminate the counseling relationship; follow up on the individual's progress after termination.

Establish and maintain the relationship with the counselee. It is necessary to establish a strong sense of mutual trust, openness and respect with counselees so that they feel comfortable talking with you, and also confident that you will help them.

In some situations this first step has already been accomplished before the counseling relationship is initiated. Ted, age 12 and a paper boy, thinks his boss is cheating him out of some of his money. Talking over problems with his dad in the past has usually been a good experience. Dad has provided the listening, understanding, encouragement and direction that has helped Ted work out some pretty complicated situations for himself. Ted already feels comfortable asking Dad for help. And he is pretty confident that he will get it. The counseling relationship is already established. If Dad responds positively to Ted's first queries for help in this situation, they will move quickly into the second stage.

Sylvia has known her Sunday school teacher for several years. Mrs. Turner is a friend of her family and has been involved at church for as long as Sylvia can remember. She is usually warm and friendly and Sylvia has always felt that Mrs. Turner liked her. So when things started getting pretty strained between Sylvia and her parents, Mrs. Turner was a natural to turn to. Sylvia needed to check out her feelings and perceptions with someone. After a few minutes of talking, she was glad she had asked Mrs. Turner for some time together.

It was more challenging for Pastor Dugan to establish rapport and trust with 17-year-old Ed. They knew each other. Ed had been active in their youth group for the past two years and during that time they had talked on quite a few occasions. But no really serious problems were brought up between them. So when Ed's girlfriend told him that she was pregnant, he felt really afraid, not knowing what to do. Out of desperation he called Pastor Dugan and set up a counseling appointment.

Rev. Dugan: "Well, Ed, it's good to see you. I was happy that you wanted to get together. Sounded on the phone like something was really upsetting you."

Ed: "Yeah, Pastor. I'm in kind of a jam. Wasn't sure what to do."

Rev. Dugan: "Well, sometimes it helps a lot just to talk things out with someone."

Ed: "Yeah, I guess so . . . (pause), but it's pretty tough to do."

Rev. Dugan: "Maybe you're not sure it's good for you to talk very freely with me."

Ed: "Nothing against you. It's just that I'm not sure what's going to happen, you know. We can talk, but it's my problem so I'm not sure what good it'll do. Besides, I'm not even sure that coming here was the right thing to do."

Rev. Dugan: "Ed, you might be having some of the same concerns that a lot of people have the first time they come in for counseling. People will often wonder what I might think of them if they share their problems with me. Others worry about somebody else finding out what was said. Do you think you can share with me your feelings and concerns that make it hard for you to be here?"

If Ed can adequately share his fears and hesitations and if Rev. Dugan can respond with sufficient openness, warmth and reassurance to help Ed feel more comfortable, then counseling can proceed to the second stage.

Unlike the professional therapy setting, most lay counselors know the counselees prior to the first session. However, establishing a positive initial experience is most important. The quality of the relationship will have tremendous impact on the effectiveness of the subsequent counseling stages.

Let us look more closely at the specific processes that occur during this initial stage of counseling. Therapists refer to the accomplishment of these initial tasks as the establishment of a "therapeutic alliance" with their counselee. In order for a positive alliance between counselor and counselee to develop, the following must occur:

1. The counselor must consistently express *warmth* in order to help the counselee feel genuinely liked by the counselor. "Just knowing that she likes me helps me feel better about myself." "Knowing that he likes me gives me enough courage to open up and be honest with him."

2. The counselee must *trust* the counselor to be genuine, congruent, confidential and to have the counselee's best interests in mind. "I know that my counselor isn't perfect, but she sure does care about me. I know that she really wants to help me."

3. There must exist a sense of *mutual respect* between the counselor and counselee. The counselee grows from experiencing the counselor's esteem and from experiencing and expressing respect for the counselor. "It helps me to trust myself more, just knowing that someone whom I respect so much also places faith in my judgment."

4. The counselee must develop *positive expectations* for receiving help from the counseling process. "I know there aren't any guarantees, but I really believe that this is going to help."

5. The counselor must *listen* attentively, focusing complete attention on the verbal and non-verbal expressions of the counselee. Attentive listening communicates respect to the counselee and helps the counselor learn vital information from the counselee. "When I'm in there talking to him, I've got his complete attention. That feels so good to me that even if I didn't get anything else from counseling, I'd leave each session feeling so much better."

6. The counselee usually needs to *ventilate feelings* that have been

held back, sometimes for many years. The counseling setting is often the only place that the counselees feel comfortable to release those feelings that they experience as frightening, sinful or unacceptable. Such ventilation and emotional release reduces internal tensions, strengthens the bond of trust with the counselor, and reinforces the value of the sessions for the counselee.

7. The counselor must gain *adequate knowledge* of the counselee's history and background information that is relevant to his or her problems. The style, extent and type of history-taking will depend largely on the counseling setting and theoretical orientation of the counselor. Professional therapists will usually be very concerned with adequate history-taking.[2] While psychodynamic psychotherapists will often seek a long and in-depth history, behavior therapists, short-term therapists and behavioral therapists tend to seek only historical information that directly and closely relates to the presenting problems.[3] Not only does adequate knowledge help the counselor to better understand the person seeking help, but it increases the counselee's feeling of being known and cared for.[4]

Explore and define the problems that the counselee needs to solve. This stage usually begins very early during counseling. As the counseling relationship deepens and greater trust develops, the counselee feels more freedom to express frightening or bothersome thoughts, feelings, impulses and behaviors. The individual is able to follow the counselor to lead him or her in an in-depth exploration of problems and defenses.

Experienced counselors know that the first problems the individual discloses are often not major or central ones. Counselees often volunteer safer, less threatening problems first. Then, after they gain confidence in the counselor's ability to help and willingness to accept them with their imperfections, counselees are more willing to share the most private and threatening problems.

A college sophomore (let's call him Karl) went into the counselor's office for the first time, feeling confused and frightened.

Counselor: "Well, Karl, what can I help you with?"

Karl (after a long pause of confused silence): "I need a car."

Counselor (showing interest and concern): "Maybe you could tell me a little more about your need for a car."

Karl (still feeling very confused, the thoughts coming out in almost random disorder): "I just need a car. I don't have enough money. Well, almost enough, but not quite enough. I have a job. I need to move away from home. I don't know how to do it. Things aren't very good at home. Thought I'd rent a room near campus."

Counselor (after Karl paused): "Sounds like you're concerned about several really important issues in your life, Karl. I'd like to hear more about them."

The counselor expresses interest in Karl and shows acceptance of his confused thinking and disjointed rambling. He continues to talk and as he does, his anxiety level is lowered, his thoughts become more logically connected and he gains a clearer picture of the problems and their solutions. The counselor's task is to accept, gently lead, and encourage as the counselee begins to understand and define his or her problems.

For the professional therapist, defining the problems usually involves formulating a provisional diagnostic impression. The psychologist relies on the diagnosis as a basic ingredient for formulating a treatment plan. The diagnosis helps to answer several important counseling questions: What are the events in this person's life that have lead to the development of these problems? What are the strengths and weaknesses within the counselee's personality structure? What is the exact nature of the problem (e.g., character disorder, adjustment reaction, anxiety disorder, affective disorder, pre-psychotic condition)? Which treatment plan will most likely provide the necessary help in the shortest amount of time and have the longest-lasting benefits?

Diagnosis is vital to the counselor because the same behavior or symptom can indicate more than one kind of problem. Sharon, a 15-year-old high school sophomore, was referred for counseling because of recent truancy, academic failure, running away from home and angry withdrawal from people. Her behavior could indicate a rather transitory adjustment disorder. Such behaviors could also represent masked depression or possibly the beginnings of a serious personality disorder.

The counselor uses a variety of tools to form a provisional diagnosis. Although acquiring the counselee's personal history is often a part of the initial relationship-building process, it also helps define the nature of the problem. While some therapists have their counselees fill in autobiographical questionnaires, others prefer to collect all of the historical data during the counseling sessions. While some counselors take notes during the sessions, others prefer to dictate or write their notations after the sessions. The latter approach ensures that taking notes does not dilute the quality of counselor-counselee contact.

A wide variety of psychological testing instruments are also employed by therapists to help them gain insight into the psychological functioning of their counselees.[5] The most accepted use of psychological tests is to give the counselee a "battery" or group of tests that produce information about several different areas of the counselee's psychological functioning.[6] The psychological test battery is usually administered very early during the counseling process.

The administering of these tests is restricted to those who have graduate level or other professional training in psychological testing and evaluation. However, an informal, valuable source of diagnostic information for all counselors to use is careful observation of the counselee's behavior during the interview or counseling session. How does the person respond to the counselor? Is there apparent nervousness, tension or anxiety? What about signs of depression, confusion or delusions? Does the counselee seem hyperactive or slow in speech and physical movements? What does the person talk about? What relevant topics are ignored? Careful observation of the counselee's verbal and nonverbal behavior yields a wealth of diagnostic data to the alert counselor.

A final source of diagnostic information is the feedback about the counselee that comes from other people. Parents, children, siblings, other relatives, employers, employees, fellow workers and neighbors can supply much-needed, valid information. When considering seeking this type of information, great care must be taken to insure that such action will in no way cause difficulty for the counselee. Ultimate caution must be taken to maintain the counselee's confidentiality. Ministers, physicians, attorneys, psychiatrists, psychologists and other therapists can be sources of valuable input. In most cases, information about the counselee is sought from other sources only with the counselee's permission. In formal settings that permisson should always be procured in written form.

The lay counselor usually will not engage in the formal psychodiagnostic process. But he or she still must gain a clear view of the counselee's problems in order to be of good help. Lawrence Crabb stresses the need to uncover the problem feelings, problem behavior and problem thinking that are creating difficulty for the counselee.[7] J. David Stone and Larry Keefauver suggest a four-step process of peer counseling.[8] The first two steps involve asking the counselee, "What do you want for you?" and "What are you feeling?" These first two steps aid in defining the counselee's problem behavior, thinking and feeling. The counselor gains valuable insight from answers to these questions.

The third step in Stone and Keefauver's model is to ask the question, "What are you doing to get what you want?" As both counselor and counselee gain a clearer picture of the problems that need to be resolved, counseling enters into the next stage.

Establish goals and structure in the counseling process in ways that will accomplish these goals. During the previous stage, the counselee learned why his or her earlier plan of action was not working. Major responsibility for life circumstances was accepted and now the counselee is ready to face the problem with new courage and hope. The third stage of counseling, using Stone and Keefauver's approach, addresses the question, "What do you need to do?" The counselor helps the counselee determine the necessary changes in action, thoughts and feelings.

It is important that these goals are realistic. If so, they need to be ordered so that the accomplishment of one goal leads to work on other goals. Neither the counselor nor the counselee are required to have complete listing of all of the necessary changes. Growth is an unfolding process. An overly compulsive plan is not advised. Instead, help the counselee to move in a general direction toward solving problems. The Christian counselor must develop an active trust in the Holy Spirit as a constant companion, guide and teacher for the counselee. "But the Counselor, the Holy Spirit, whom the Father will send in my name, he will teach you all things, and bring to your remembrance all that I have said to you" (John 14:26). Trust must also be developed in the counselee's God-given ability to grow and heal.

The counselee, encouraged and assisted by the counselor, begins to propose possible goals and changes. Feelings and attitudes about making these changes are called to the surface and expressed. "How do you feel as you think about doing that?" "That sounds like it might be pretty tough to pull off. Do you think you can really accomplish it?" "I wonder how the rest of your family might respond to your changed behavior." "Perhaps you can imagine how you would feel if you became more assertive."

The person is helped to anticipate and evaluate how family, friends and others might respond to the possible changes. As all of the counselee's personal and relational concerns about the counseling goals are discussed, certain ones emerge as more attractive. Discussion turns to the accomplishment of these objectives. Both the counselee's and counselor's roles are clarified. It is very important at this point that the counselee recognizes and accepts responsibility for accomplishing his or her goals. The counselor must secure some degree of commitment from the person to follow through and accomplish the goals.

The manner and level of commitment depends on the counselor's theoretical orientation. Learning/behavioral therapists often prepare written contracts that the counselee signs. Cognitive therapists also often require that their counselees commit themselves to formal contractual agreements. Psychodynamic and existential/experiential therapists generally view this commitment process as a more natural part of the counseling process and do not require formal contracts. Should your counselees experience difficulty following through with their decisions, it would be best to make some form of counseling commitment such as the formal contract. As counseling goals, treatment procedures and the appropriate level of commitment are established, the focus shifts to the next stage.

Help the counselee work toward attaining his or her goals. The "working toward the goals stage" is crucial in the counseling process. It is a critical point where failure in the counseling process could possibly occur. It is one thing to *decide* what needs to be done and quite another to *do* it. "The best laid plans of mice and men often go astray," goes the old saying. Unfortunately, this old cliche is too often true about the plans of counselor and counselee.

The counseling process is usually an anxiety-producing endeavor. Most people feel significant apprehension as they seek their first contact with a counselor. Anxiety is encountered again as the counselor churns up repressed memories and emotions within the counselee. But the most anxiety is produced by the necessary initiation of action that marks significant change on the part of the counselee.

It is at this critical stage that real counseling change either happens or fails. The counselor must be able to stimulate the counselee to act. Once he or she begins to act differently, then the new behavior can be reinforced by the counselor, by others in the counselee's life and by the person's own internal reinforcing mechanism. Lawrence Crabb writes, "Progress from merely 'assenting' to truth to deeply 'agreeing' with truth depends on behaving consistently with truth."[9]

In the Gospel of John we read, "Jesus then said to the Jews who had believed in him, 'If you continue in my word, you are truly my disciples, and you will know the truth, and the truth will make you free' " (John 8:31-32). Counselors can help people to know the truth in a manner that sets them free by helping them put the truth into action. Jesus said, "He who has my commandments and keeps them, he it is who loves me; and he who loves me will be loved by my Father, and I will love him and manifest myself to him. If a man loves me, he will keep my word, and my Father will love him, and we will come to him and make our home with him" (John 14:21, 23).

As the counselor helps the person put new thoughts, feelings and attitudes into action, healthy change and growth begins to take place. "So faith by itself, if it has no works is dead. You see that faith was active along with his works (Abraham), and faith was completed by works" (James 2:17, 22). The counseling process encourages and supports the person toward consistent positive action.

The specific way that the counselee is encouraged to implement the planned changes will depend upon the theoretical orientation of the counselor. Many counselors from a wide range of theoretical models find homework assignments to be useful tools for stimulating consistent behavioral change outside of the counseling room. Gary Collins lists five commonly used homework assignments for counselees:

1. Written assignments are given to the counselee to take home, complete and then return to the counselor. These include psychological tests, personal history questionnaires, personal logs or diaries, incomplete sentence forms and lists of options, interests, likes/dislikes, pros/cons, and so on. The completed assignments become the basis for further counseling discussion and work.

2. Discussion and study guides on a wide range of subjects are used to help stimulate interaction with family members or friends. These guides appear at the end of books or book chapters, are published as separate volumes, or are created by the counselors themselves. The counselee reports back to the counselor on what happened during the discussions.

3. Behavioral assignments are given in very specific terms in order to help the counselee change habit patterns and make difficult breakthroughs. "Meet five new people this week." "Eat only while sitting down at the dinner table or while at a restaurant." "Spend 15 minutes every day this week reading your Bible and an equal amount of time in daily prayer." The counselee reports his or her progress back to the counselor.

4. Reading assignments (bibliotherapy) are given to counselees to help them research ideas, concepts, values and activities that relate to his or her counseling process. It is very important that the counselor be familiar with the assigned book, article or excerpt.

5. Cassette tapes, disc recordings and videotapes can be assigned that deal with a wide variety of subjects. Some counselors maintain a lending library for their counselees to use. Useful recorded material includes music for relaxation and inspiration, speakers, instructional tapes and recorded stories, plays and programs that are relevant to the

counseling process.[10]

There are actually three different phases in this fourth stage of the counseling process. These three phases operate as a continuing cycle that recurs as many times as it takes to accomplish the counseling objectives. The three phases are:

1. Implementation. The counselee enacts the plan to reach a particular goal.

2. Evaluation. The counselee and the counselor evaluate the pace and direction of the changes taking place. Consideration is given to the impact of these changes on other people.

3. Reformulation. As a result of the evaluation, reformulated plans may be determined. If evaluation reveals that the goal has been accomplished sufficiently, a new counseling goal is established. If the evaluation reveals that the original plan is not working, an altered plan is suggested. This updated plan allows the counselee to reach the original goal in an altered fashion.

This implementation-evaluation-reformulation cycle can be diagrammed as follows:

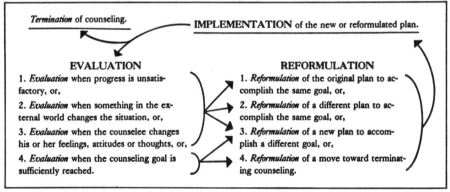

Illustration 11

The process continues until the determination is made to terminate counseling.

Terminate the counseling relationship. As the counselee successfully progresses through the implementation-evaluation-reformulation cycle, he or she should gain greater strength and self-confidence. Decision-making and problem-solving skills are learned and improved. The individual attempts to improve interpersonal relationships. The counselee is able to recognize both irrational guilt and real guilt and to deal with both effectively. Some internal conflicts are resolved. The person becomes better able to handle difficult situations with external reality. The counselee becomes less dependent on the counselor's support and encouragement.

As termination nears, it is helpful to review the person's progress. Affirm his or her increase in personal strength. Avoid any overprotective or dominating behaviors that might inhibit or sabotage further movement toward independence.

During this stage the counselee may express deep feelings of gratitude and appreciation for the help received from the counselor. It is important to receive these expressions with open acceptance without taking away from the counselee's responsibility for his or her own growth and progress.

Sometimes a counselee selects to terminate the counseling process before the problems are solved. There are many causes of premature terminations, some of which include:

1. A counselor-counselee relationship has failed to provide enough warmth, security and trust for a fully successful counseling experience.

2. Insufficient definition of problem areas has left the counselee with only vague ideas of what changes needed to be made.

3. The selection of inappropriate goals or plans of action left the counselee frustrated, disappointed and discouraged.

4. Ineffective translation of the counseling action plan into changed behavior prevented further growth or change.

5. Counselee resistance to therapeutic interventions by the counselor rendered the latter impotent as a change agent.

6. Unresolved transference and countertransference paralyzed the counseling process. In all terminations, whether premature or appropriate, the counselee should be invited to have further contact with the counselor. Counselees need to know that terminating the counseling does not close the door on the relationship.

7. Uncontrollable problems that were external to the counseling process stopped the sessions. For example, the counselor or the counselee moved out of state, excessive resistance from a family member, financial problems, etc.

8. Inadequate attention, focus, or follow through from the counselor at any point during the counseling process irreparably sabotaged further progress.

Follow up on the individual's progress after termination. What actually occurs outside the counseling room largely depends on the nature of the counseling relationship and the counseling setting. Counselees will often enjoy the opportunity to write or phone their counselor occasionally just to maintain contact or to let the counselor know how they are doing. Other people like to know that they can come back for periodic "checkup" visits simply to make sure that their progress is continuing in a positive manner.

Notes

1. Millard Sall, *Faith, Psychology and Christian Maturity* (Grand Rapids, Mich.: Zondervan, 1975).

2. O. Quentin Hyder, *The Christian's Handbook of Psychiatry* (Old Tappan, N.J.: Fleming H. Revell, 1971).

3. C. Eugene Walker et al., *Clinical Procedures for Behavior Therapy* (Englewood Cliffs, N. J.: Prentice-Hall, 1981).

4. Lewis Wolberg, *Handbook of Short-Term Psychotherapy* (New York: Thieme-Stratton, 1980).

5. Anne Anastasi, *Psychological Testing* (New York: Macmillan, 1961).

6. Lee J. Cronbach, *Essentials of Psychological Testing* (New York: Harper and Row, 1960).

7. Lawrence Crabb, *Effective Biblical Counseling: A Model for Helping Caring Christians Become Capable Counselors* (Grand Rapids, Mich.: Zondervan, 1977).

8. J. David Stone and Larry Keefauver, *Friend to Friend: How You Can Help a Friend Through a Problem* (Loveland, Colo.: Group Books, 1983).

9. Crabb, *Effective Biblical Counseling*, p. 157.

10. Gary R. Collins, *Christian Counseling* (Waco, Texas: Word Books, 1980).

■ CHAPTER 6
Counseling Techniques

The techniques of effective counseling are the actual skills employed to accomplish the tasks in the six counseling stages. Since this is an eclectic approach, the techniques that will be discussed here are applicable to a wide variety of counseling approaches. They are fundamental skills that counselors from a wide variety of theoretical orientations regularly employ. In-depth descriptions of highly specialized techniques like systematic desensitization and gestalt dream analysis are beyond the focus of this book. We will define, describe and give examples of the techniques that establish the foundation of successful counseling intervention in virtually every theoretical orientation.

The Immense Value of Listening

Without accurate listening the counselor is rendered totally ineffective. Listening is not so much a technique that the counselor uses or does as it is a required ingredient for all counseling. Therefore, listening will be presented separately from the other counseling skills.

The author of James gives us some excellent guidelines on this topic. "Know this, my beloved brethren. Let every man be quick to hear, slow to speak, slow to anger" (James 1:19). If anyone should be "quick to listen" it should be the counselor. Hurting people need to know that someone is interested, that someone cares. Effective counseling communicates, "I hear you and I'm here for you." And yet, it is in this basic listening process that counseling failure often has its roots. Listening does not come naturally or easily to most counselors.

Peter Buntman and Eleanor Saris, in their training manual for certified instructors of their parenting course, present seven aspects that affect the way an individual hears the messages that are received. Counselors need to be conscious of these personal characteristics that influence the way they hear and the way they interpret what their counselees tell them. The counselor's "seven veils of listening" are:

Age. People in different age groups tend to hear and react to things differently.

Sex. Men and women have been trained by the socialization process to hear and respond differently.

Education. A psychologist who has been well-trained in a Ph.D. program that specializes in the psychodynamic orientation will likely hear something differently from the pastor who graduated from an evangelical seminary.

Past experiences. The variety of experiences and relative degree of pain and difficulty that a counselor has lived through will impact his or her level of understanding and capacity for empathic response.

Perception of future expectations and goals. Counselors who tend to be either optimistic or pessimistic about their own future will usually reflect the same attitude toward their clients' expectations and goals.

Personal feelings about the counselee. Counselors are more attentive, open and positively responsive to counselees whom they like and tend to be less attentive, closed and negatively responsive to counselees whom they dislike.

Current emotional and physical feelings. The counselor who feels depressed or headachey will tend to hear more negative statements from the counselee, while the happy, energetic counselor may hear more positive statements.[1]

The counselor who is conscious of these personal factors can make adjustments in what he or she is hearing. We are told, "If one gives answers before he hears, it is his folly and shame" (Proverbs 18:13). Some of the most embarrassing moments that counselors can experience result from inadequate listening.

Charles: "I was driving my friend across town last night and we had a blowout. The front, left tire just all of a sudden exploded."

Counselor: "I'll bet that was scary. Who was driving?"

Charles: "I just said that I was."

Here is another example of inadequate listening:

Florence: "Mom's birthday was last Sunday. What a drag. Seemed like the whole family was there. They wouldn't even let me go into my room. I had to be out there around all of the adults."

Counselor: "How old was your dad on Sunday?"

Florence: "It wasn't my dad's birthday. It was my mom's. Besides, what difference does it make anyway how old they are?"

Such slips are not only embarrassing indicators that the counselor was not listening carefully, but they can also seriously hinder the counselee's trust in the counselor. There are quite a few things that can hinder a person's listening capacity. Let's look at some of the more common deterrents to effective listening in the counseling relationship and examine what the counselor can do about it.

Source of the Deterrent to Listening	*Counselor's Solution*
1. The counselor is physically exhausted or too sleepy.	Getting adequate rest and sleep, as well as proper nourishment are the most obvious solutions. Feeling tired and sleepy may also indicate lack of fulfillment or depression. These possibilities should be considered as well as evaluating the pattern of the symptoms. Do they occur with just certain counselees, on certain days, at certain times during the day or all the time? Sometimes adjusting schedules or changing work patterns is helpful.
2. The counselor is overworked.	Professional counselors can prevent "burnout" symptoms by restructuring their counseling schedule; taking more frequent, short vacations or long weekends; taking well-spaced, long vacations; varying their work activities (e.g., teaching, writing, learning and implementing new counseling methods) and reducing the number of hours in their work week. Lay counselors and pastors should reduce other work duties as their counseling load increases. Effective counseling is far more energy demanding than "just talking with people."
3. The counselor is dissatisfied with his or her job.	Professional and lay counselors can be unhappy with their jobs for a variety of reasons: unsatisfactory work setting; unhappy work relationships; displeasure with pay and/or advancement opportunities; desire to be somewhere else; wish to do something else; and a personality that does not fit well with the job descrip-

tion or job roles. Some type of personal growth or change, a change in the job description or a change in jobs is required.

4. The counselor's thoughts are focused on personal conflicts or problems in his or her own life.

Counselors certainly cannot be expected or required to be perfect. Some ask, "How can you help someone else if you have problems yourself?" Everyone, including the best of counselors, has problems. Effective listening requires that the counselor use adequate problem-solving, decision-making, and conflict-resolving strategies in his or her own life, so that adequate energy can be invested in listening to the counselee.

5. The counselor has unexpressed and repressed feelings of envy, aggression, competition, sexual arousal, intimidation, infatuation, love or other feelings that he or she views as reprehensible and unacceptable.

Counselors, yes even psychiatrists and psychologists, are human too. Even though their training teaches them how to handle personal feelings that they may develop toward counselees, these feelings may become intense. Lay and professional counselors need to respond directly to these feelings instead of denying or repressing them. They do not just go away. Sometimes it is appropriate to confront the counselee with the feelings. In other instances that course of action would be destructive to the counselee and the matter should be broached with a colleague or friend. Do not delay. Resolve the issue as soon as possible.

6. The counselor has developed countertransference feelings toward the counselee.

Countertransference occurs when a counselor projects onto the counselee his or her own unconscious or repressed feelings, conflicts or needs because the counselee or the counseling situation represents a person or situation in the counselor's past. It is incumbent upon the counselor to bring this material to a level of consciousness that allows for more complete resolution of these issues. The help of another counselor is usually necessary for this working-through process.

7. The counselor does not like the counselee.

God commands us to love others. "This is my commandment, that you love one another as I have loved you" (John 15:12). He even goes further. "But I say to you, love your enemies and pray for those who persecute you, so that you may be sons of your Father who is in heaven. For if you love those who love you, what reward have you? Do not even the tax collectors do the same?" (Matthew 5:44-46). These are very strong statements that must be heeded.

There is a difference between "loving" and "liking." A counselor can dislike a counselee. His or her own personality may be ill-suited to deal with that of the counselee. The counselor goes through some self-searching, seeks help from colleagues, finds no evidence of repressed feelings or countertransference, and still dislikes the counselee. The task, then, is to determine how to love this person who has sought help from the counselor. In some cases self-disclosing or confessing the feelings directly to the counselee will open the door to more positive relating. In other cases, the most loving thing for the counselor to do is to refer the counselee to another counselor.

8. The counselor believes that accurate listening is relatively unimportant to the counseling process and therefore deserves little attention.

Accurate listening is understood to be a fundamentally and vitally important part of the counseling process by practitioners from every therapeutic orientation. There is reason to seriously question whether or not a counselor, lay or professional, who disagrees with the foundational importance of listening should be involved in the practice of counseling at all.

Effective listening is an essential ingredient to the counselor's attending behavior.[2] The word "attending" can be defined as stretching out to; giving heed to; looking after; waiting for; going or staying with as a companion or servant; being present with; applying the mind or paying attention; and being ready for service. It is vital that the counselee feel "listened to." Eye contact, facial expressions, body posturing, gesturing and verbal expressions will corporately express one of two statements: either "I care about you enough to listen and attend to you" or "I am really not concerned enough about you to listen or attend to you." So important is effective listening to the counseling process, that psychiatrist Robert Langs has written a comprehensive volume on *The*

Listening Process.[3] Though written from a distinctively psychoanalytic position, it offers enriching insights to all of us who are involved in counseling.

Effective listening is important during each of the six counseling stages. It is essential to the process of building an open, supportive and trusting relationship with the counselee. The counselor must listen carefully if he or she is to help the counselee clarify problem areas, define counseling goals and establish a plan of action to accomplish the goals. Without effective listening during the implementation-evaluation-reformulation stage, whatever efforts are taken to reach the established goals will likely fail. Careful listening during the sensitive termination phase is essential in order to assist the counselee toward independence from the counselor. During follow-up contacts listening is important because it helps to assure the person that they are genuinely cared about even though formal counseling has been terminated.

The following bar graph depicts the immense importance of listening during all six stages of the counseling process:

The Value of Listening During the Six Stages of Counseling

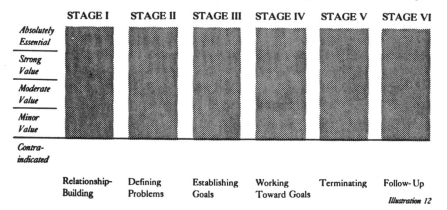

Illustration 12

Ten Important Counseling Techniques

The following 10 techniques are presented as having viable places in our eclectic counseling approach. Some of the techniques will be preferred and used more frequently by some counselors and the use of others will be shunned by other counselors. The techniques that each counselor most frequently uses will depend on his or her theoretical orientation, personality structure and the specific nature and problem of the counselee.

For purposes of conceptualization, the techniques are presented in a general order from authoritative and directive ones to least authoritative and directive ones. No "better than" or "worse than" evaluation is intended. Good eclectic counseling makes effective use of all 10 techniques. Whether the technique is "good" or "bad" depends upon how the counselor uses it, its appropriateness to both the counselor and counselee, and the timing of its use.

Teaching. Some counselors tend to broadly equate teaching with counseling. "Basically this is what counseling really is. The helpee is learning how to act, feel and think differently; the helper is fulfilling the role of a teacher."[4] We shall be using the term "teaching" in a more restrictive sense. Our usage refers to it as the imparting or giving of information or knowledge.

In this more restricted sense of the word, teaching still encompasses a variety of counseling behaviors. Giving advice, directions and instructions regarding decisions that need to be made, problems that need to be solved and conflicts that require resolution are forms of teaching responses. Christian counselors teach their counselees by leading them through Bible studies on certain passages that relate to their problems. When carried to an extreme, this type of counseling replicates Sunday school instruction, preaching, Bible study or discipling, only on a one-to-one basis. It is not so much a question of whether or not teaching is a useful counseling tool. It certainly is for the eclectic counselor. But when teaching becomes the overwhelmingly predominant technique, there exists a valid question of whether or not the counseling relationship has changed into an education process.

Central to the effective use of teaching as a counseling tool is the counselor's motivation for using it. The following guideline is suggested: When the counselor believes that the counselee needs new information and that it would be either very difficult or impossible for the counselee to procure this information, then the counselor can impart (teach) the information.

It is usually a good policy to check to see if the person already has or knows the information. "I'm wondering which are the ways of dealing with anger that you already know." "Sounds like you're pretty concerned about venereal disease. I wonder if you'd tell me what you know about it." "You're really struggling with the decision of whether or not to have premarital sex. Would you be willing to share with me your knowledge of what the Bible says about it?" In each instance the counselor respectfully invited the counselee to share and explore his or her own relevant knowledge first. This process helps the counselees explore the limits of their own knowledge and reason first, thus affirming their own awareness. It also avoids the demeaning and wasteful process of telling someone what they already know. Sometimes counselors, like parents, will do this anyway when they experience helplessness and frustration, just to feel useful. In such cases any possible teaching impact is lost. The only thing that is gained is a temporary reduction of the counselor's anxiety and guilt feelings.

Advice-giving is closely related to teaching, and unfortunately is one of the easiest, self-reinforcing and often-used techniques. There are a few instances when giving advice is acceptable counseling practice.[5] When the situation is over the counselee's head, when the person does not have the knowledge or tools that are necessary, and when the person is healthy enough to accept the advice, then it is okay to advise.

But giving advice is seldom that helpful. Most people receive an overabundance of advice from a myriad of sources: friends, parents, teachers, television, books and magazines to name several. When the counselor agrees to give advice, he or she risks stepping out of that unique role labeled "counselor" and becoming like everyone else to the counselee. If the person has not been able to respond positively to others' advice, he or she will not be able to profit from the counselor's advice either. Often, when persons request advice, they are really looking for reassurance that somebody cares, release from anxiety, freedom from confused uncertainty, and the hope that there really is a solution or answer for their problem. Most often, counseling responses other than advice will meet their needs more effectively.

Returning to the broader issue of teaching as a counseling technique, Quentin Hyder offers a valuable perspective. Speaking of traditional psychodynamically oriented therapy, he writes, "The therapist does not attempt to tell the patient what he or she should do. His theory is that once the patient understands why things have gone wrong he will change. Insight leads to improved behavior. A nice theory. The only trouble is that it usually does not work. There is a limit to how much I can learn by my mistakes. Yes, sometimes I can learn by them, but I will learn very much more quickly and just as thoroughly if I am taught the correct way by someone else who has the right answers."[6]

Teaching is an effective counseling tool as long as it is used carefully so as not to undermine the movement of the counselee toward greater strength and independence in his or her own decision-making and problem-solving behavior.

During the initial stage of counseling, teaching should play a very minor role. Other than imparting some brief information about the counselor, the counseling process and logistics (e.g., length of appointments, scheduling arrangements, etc.), teaching or information-giving is detrimental to the relationship-building process. During stages two through four, teaching has its greatest value as a counseling technique. While defining what is and what is not a problem, counselees often gain from learning more about the development of psychological well-being and the nature of psychological conflicts and dysfunctions. Just learning that "I'm not the only one who has this problem" can be of great help.

Many counselees must first be taught how to establish goals before they will be able to do it for themselves. People often initiate counseling with preconceived ideas of what will happen during the sessions. "I will finally be able to talk to someone who will tell me what to do to solve my problems." When the counselee's preconceptions do not match with the counselor's orientation, an adjustment needs to be made. One of the counselor's tasks is to teach the counselee how to work within the process. A great deal of unnecessary and non-productive frustration results from incomplete or ineffective teaching or clarifying about how counseling will proceed. During the "working" stage teaching can also play an important role as counselees learn new skills and approaches for dealing with threatening impulses, internal conflicts, difficult interpersonal situations and developmental tasks.

During the final two stages, termination and follow-up, the value of teaching is generally negated. The counselee is moving toward independence, and reliance on his or her own strengths and skills must be reinforced. The following graph shows the value of teaching as a counseling skill during the six stages of the counseling process:

The Value of Teaching During the Six Stages of Counseling

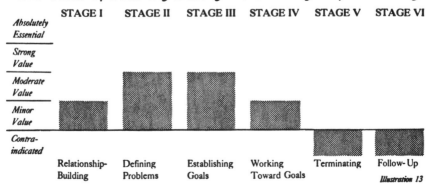

Illustration 13

Evaluating. When a counselor selects to express some form of judgment about a counselee's thought, attitude, feeling or behavior, an evaluating response is being given. An important assumption is made each time that an evaluation is given. The counselor is essentially saying, "This person is unable to adequately or accurately evaluate his or her own behavior and therefore needs me to do it." Counselors must be very sure that they are not sabotaging the counselee's growth toward greater maturity and independence. Judgments are sometimes given for the counselor's own self-assurance. "If I tell him how unwise his decision is, maybe he won't actually do it." "By my telling her what a good job she did, maybe she'll want to do it again." "I can't make her decisions for her, but I can sure let her know what I think of them." "I've lived longer and have experienced a lot more of this life than he has. I'd be negligent if I didn't tell him what was right and what was wrong about what he is doing." All of these statements share something in common. They all express the counselor's awareness that they cannot control their counselee's decisions. In addition to that sense of helplessness, the counselor's feelings of insecurity and lack of trust in the counselee's ability to make their own evaluations are expressed.

Before making such statements, the need for making evaluations must be weighed carefully and cautiously. Otherwise, the counselee might falsely learn that his or her own judgment is without value and is not to be trusted. Excessive dependency, discouragement, giving up and depression are all possible results.

Precautions about the use of evaluative statements have been registered, but do they have a place in an eclectic approach as a viable counseling tool? In order to answer that question, let us broaden our understanding about the types of evaluating statements. There are qualitative and comparative evaluations as well as positive and negative ones. By combining the above two parameters we have four combinations.

Qualitative statements evaluate feelings, attitudes and behavior with labels with good/bad, strong/weak, right/wrong, healthy/unhealthy, helpful/unhelpful, wise/unwise, mature/immature, Christian/un-Christian, and so on. Positive qualitative evaluations are statements of the counselor's positive judgment about the person's behavior. Examples of *positive qualitative judgments* are: "You did such a good job leading songs last night." "You showed a lot of strength last week by confronting your parents with your feelings." "I think you did the right thing by saying 'no' to your boyfriend." "I know you want to lose weight quickly, but if you go on a gradual diet you'll be making the healthy choice."

Examples of *negative qualitative judgments* are: "You have a very unhelpful attitude toward your mother." "I think it would be unwise of you to stay out to 2 a.m." "You're acting really immature with your anger." "It's very un-Christian the way you develop cliques at youth group."

Comparative evaluative statements make a judgment about some aspect of the counselee's functioning as it relates to something else. Comparisons are made to other people, external standards and the person's own previous behavior. Examples of *positive comparative evaluations* are: "You seem to be so much more responsible than other kids your age." "You're really keeping up well with your daily Bible reading and prayer time." "It seems like you're being a lot more thorough now than you used to with doing your chores around the house."

Examples of *negative comparative evaluations* are: "You're not witnessing as much as the other kids in the group." "It seems to me that you're not being obedient enough to your parents." "You're more closed off and withdrawn now than you were a few months ago."

The same general guideline that we discussed regarding the use of teaching as a counseling tool also applies for the use of evaluating. Share the counselor's evaluation only if the counselee is unable to make an adequate self-evaluation, and only if such an evaluation is eminently important for the counselee. Being evaluated, even positively, makes it more difficult for a counselee fully or unconditionally to feel accepted. They often think, "If I don't keep up this positive pattern, then they will be displeased with me."

Of the four types of evaluative responses, the positive qualitative ones are the most constructive. Positive comparative statements that compare the counselee's current behavior with past performance are also sometimes beneficial. Negative qualitative types are usually contraindicated.

Since it is so vital for the counselee to feel unconditionally accepted, during the relationship-building stage of counseling, evaluative responses are contraindicated. During stages two and three the counselor's expressed evaluations may play a minor role. It is during the "working" stage of counseling that evaluative response tends to be more useful, helping to encourage and direct the counselee. Even here, these kinds of responses will play a relatively minor role. The counselor's evaluations should play a decreasingly important role during the termination stage and should not be a part of follow-up contacts. The following graph depicts the relative importance of evaluative responses during the six stages of the counseling process:

The Value of Evaluation During the Six Stages of Counseling

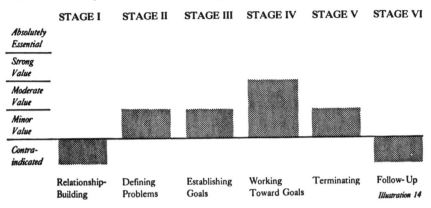

Illustration 14

Interpreting. Counselor's interpretive statements are intended to identify, conceptualize, and express meanings and patterns that underlie the counselee's statements and actions. This is a very powerful counseling technique because it makes direct contact with unconscious material, bypassing the counselee's defense mechanisms. Great care must be taken by the counselor not to interpret material that may be too threatening to the counselee.

Timing is a vital issue. Interpreting emotion-laden material too soon can cause excessive anxiety and a rejection of the interpretation, the counselor and the whole counseling process. Even though an interpretation is correct, if it is ill-timed, serious detrimental effects may result. For instance, early in the counseling relationship it would be inappropriate to interpret the connection between severe early-life traumas (e.g., death of a parent, sexual molestation, serious fire or accident, etc.) and current symptoms.

Psychologist Carl Rogers gives us some very helpful guidelines for effective use of interpretation:

1. Avoid interpreting when the counselor feels unsure or insecure.

2. Use the counselee's own terms and symbols as much as possible in the wording of the interpretation.

3. Interpret ideas and attitudes that have already been expressed.

4. Do not be argumentative or persuasive when the counselee disagrees or rejects an interpretation.

5. Counselees will spontaneously see applications of an interpretation to their lives when genuine insight has been gained.[7]

Since interpreting the meaning of an individual's behavior can be such a powerful tool, great care must be taken in its use. Interpretive statements are best given in a soft, sensitive, tentative or suggestive manner rather than in a dogmatic, directive manner. "I'm wondering if part of your anger at your boyfriend relates to how your father treated you." "Do you suppose there might be a connection between your wish to quit school and your fear of failure?" "Perhaps getting girls to have sex with you is one way of trying to feel powerful and in control." Both question and statement forms are appropriate. But the interpretation should be worded in a way that allows the counselee to either accept or comfortably reject its accuracy.

Though accurate interpretations are the most effective, even incorrect ones can be of good counseling value. An incorrect interpretation can stimulate the counselee to search elsewhere for the motivations and meanings that underlie his or her words and behavior.

Counselor: "Maybe taking drugs is a way that you have of telling your parents how angry you are at them."

Counselee: "It could be, but I don't think so."

Counselor: "Perhaps you have some ideas about why you use drugs."

Counselee: "I don't know."

Counselor: "Maybe it has something to do with being accepted by your friends."

Counselee: "Yeah, most of my friends do use drugs pretty regularly. I would hate to be left out of their parties. And they sure wouldn't invite me if I didn't smoke up with them."

Two other psychologists, Lawrence Brammer and Everett Shostrom, suggest six criteria for us to use as we evaluate the appropriateness and adequacy of an interpretation:

1. There should be sufficient evidence for the accuracy of the interpretation.

2. The depth of the interpretation should be appropriate to the level of counseling intervention.

3. Interpretations should make references to specific counselee behaviors whenever possible.

4. The intensity or strength of the interpreted behavioral trend should be evaluated.

5. The relative importance or centrality of the interpreted behavioral tendency to the counselee's personality structure should be estimated.

6. A distinction between the adaptive and maladaptive aspects of the interpreted pattern should be established.[8]

The use of interpretation can be a valuable tool for the eclectic counselor. During the relationship-building stage, fairly light level interpretations that relate to the counselee's feelings and attitudes about counseling are appropriate.[9] During stages two, three and four, interpretations can deepen and become more powerful. The counselor is getting to know and understand the counselee much more fully and the counselee is becoming less defensive and more trusting. The value of interpretation lessens as counseling progresses through terminating and into the follow-up stage. The following graph presents the value of interpreting through the course of counseling:

The Value of Interpreting During the Six Stages of Counseling

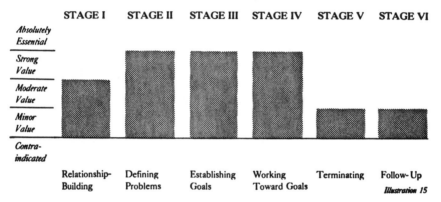

Illustration 15

Probing. Counselors make probing responses when they think that the counselee would benefit from further discussion about certain topics or issues. Probing responses assume that the counselor knows better than the counselee what should be talked about. Probing, like interpreting is most effectively done in a soft, relatively unobtrusive manner. It is important that the counselee retain as much responsibility for the content and direction of counseling as possible. Sometimes the counselor has a broader perspective and a more objective evaluation of the counselee's situation than the counselee does. Even when this is the case it is important for the counselor to avoid the "junior psychologist" syndrome. This is the "disease" that most beginning psychologists contract. Though the student really suffers no pain, those who know him or her usually experience a great deal of misery. The junior psychologist takes nothing at face value. There is a deeper meaning underlying everything.

Friend: "Hi, Stewart. How are you doing?"

Student: "Your question may indicate an underlying problem with excessive curiosity."

Friend: "No. I was just being friendly. You know. Just wondering how things were going for you."

Student: "Maybe you need to talk more about your wish to know about my personal life."

Friend: "Forget it." He walks off, shaking his head.

A counselee will usually initiate conversation about the important issues. But first, the counselee must build confidence and trust that the counselor will be able to understand and help. When the time and conditions are right, the counselee will usually bring the focus onto the pain, conflict, insecurity, helplessness or guilt that is central to the problem. But sometimes the counseling process is made more helpful by timely probing. Let's look at some examples of probing responses. "You said that you usually feel depressed on the weekends. Can you tell me more about that?" "Tell me how you feel about your older brother being so successful." "Why do you think it's so hard for you to say 'no' when a boy asks to have sex with you?"

Probing responses during the initial stage of counseling help the counselor to understand the counselee more fully. They also demonstrate to the counselee that the counselor is really interested. During the problem-defining and goal-establishing stages, probing is of particular importance. Fine tuning the definition of target problems and clarifying exactly how to accomplish specific goals takes some probing on the part of the counselor. It is also a valuable technique during the fourth stage because it helps the counselor to gain a very clear picture

The Value of Probing During the Six Stages of Counseling

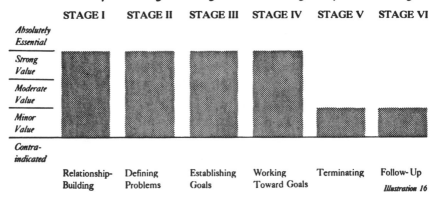

Illustration 16

of how the work toward accomplishing the counseling goals is progressing. As with other more directive counseling techniques, the usefulness and appropriateness of probing sharply drops off during the last two stages of counseling. Termination and follow-up are designed to help the individual become self-reliant and less dependent on the counselor. The preceding graph depicts the role of probing through the counseling process.

Questioning. Questioning may be the most frequently used counseling technique. It is one of the easiest techniques to use because asking questions is a very common experience in other relationships. "How are you doing?" "What's happening in your life?" "Do you know what time it is?" "How are things going with your parents?" Asking questions is the most common information-gathering process that people use.

Many fledgling counselors will overuse this technique because they feel comfortable with it. While much of the training of counselors discourages question asking, other counselors, like Jay Adams, actually encourage the use of questions. "Asking questions is a vital part of data gathering." "Since questioning is the principle means of data gathering . . . " are two quotations that suggest his heavy reliance on this directive technique.[10]

The eclectic counselor must know why he or she chooses to ask a particular question. The technique assures that the counselor knows better than the counselee what is important to discuss. Questioning places more responsibility on the counselor for the emotional tone and direction of the counseling session. The counselee can soon learn that counseling is a situation in which, "I wait for a question to be asked, I answer the question, and then I await the next query."

In order to prevent such a limited view of counseling, questions should be limited to two situations. First, when the counselor needs to know more data in order to maximally help the counselee. Second, when the counselee will gain from the experience an added awareness that will come from providing the answer. Counselors should be open to using more creative techniques to accomplish these two needs. Reduction in the use of questioning usually increases the counselee's sense of responsibility and active participation in the counseling process.

When questions are used, it is best to ask open-ended ones that allow the counselee the greatest latitude in self-expression and self-discovery. Instead of asking, "Are you sorry that you shoplifted?" try asking, "What kinds of feelings have you experienced since you shoplifted?" Or try asking, "What solutions have you considered to bring up your grades?" instead of, "Do you think you ought to quit your part-time job so you can study harder?"

It is very important that the counselor's questions do not carry an undertone of judgment, suspicion or accusation. Often voice tone, inflection, facial expression, verbal rate and gestures communicate these feelings even when the words alone do not. An unknown author once wrote that the question mark at the end of a sentence is a demand that "hooks" the other person into giving a certain kind of response. Careful wording can soften this hooking dynamic of questions. "Why did you lie to your sister?" will tend to raise more defensiveness than, "Can you share with me some of the pressures you were feeling that led up to the lie you told your sister?"

Asking questions has a place in all six stages of the counseling process. Questioning can also aid in the process of defining what problems need attention and what goals are important to work toward. Questions can also help to facilitate the process of working toward accomplishing the counseling goals. During the last two stages, questioning becomes less appropriate. The graph which appears below depicts the relative value of asking questions during the six stages of counseling:

The Value of Questioning During the Six Stages of Counseling

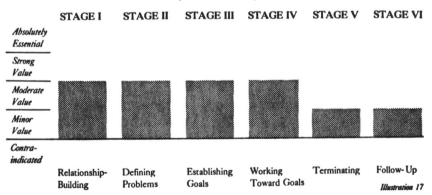

Illustration 17

Confronting. A dictionary definition of confronting reads, "to cause to meet" and "to bring face to face."[11] Sometimes counselees have defended themselves so well that even in a safe, nurturing and supportive counseling relationship, they strongly resist meeting face to face those facts they tried to hide. The counselor's empathic understanding, unconditional acceptance, and congruent self-expression have built an atmosphere of trust and openness to which the counselee responds well. Still, perhaps significant change in the problem behavior is lacking. The counselor needs to be more confrontive.

Christian psychologist Gary Collins reminds us that confrontation was often used by Jesus Christ to help people see their lack of understanding, hypocrisy and misplaced values.[12] We are reminded that confronting in a spirit of love is a gentle and patient process that respects the counselee as an equal. It is the counselee who decides his or her own actions and who is responsible for those actions. The counselor's responsibility is to confront with firmness and gentleness in a manner that facilitates the counselee's growth toward increasing self-responsibility. We are instructed and warned by Paul about this process, "Brethren, if a man is overtaken in any trespass, you who are spiritual should restore him in a spirit of gentleness. Look to yourself, lest you too be tempted" (Galatians 6:1). Our Lord cautions us about confronting from too lofty an elevation, "Judge not that you be not judged" (Matthew 7:1).

There are two different types of confrontations that counselors can use. The first type is confronting the counselee with *external reality* which suggests that a change is needed. Christian counselors will often confront their counselees with scripture that countermands their thoughts, attitudes, plans or actions. Lay counselors are often in a position to see the person interacting in social, family and church settings. These observations provide the counselor with valuable insights, observations and reports from others that can all be used as reality-testing material. "I hear you telling me that you're getting good grades but your history teacher tells me that you're failing." "At youth group you're almost always sitting way in the back by yourself." "Looked like you were really angry at your sister this morning. I heard you calling her some pretty strong names." Other forms of external reality that counselees sometimes need to be confronted with include traffic laws, school rules, church standards and family expectations regarding grooming, dress, language, etc.

The second type of confrontation utilizes the counselee's own *internal reality*. Of the two types this is the more powerful because the counselees are actually confronted with themselves. People can argue with external sources. "Well, it's stupid to have a stop sign there anyway." "I disagree with you. That's not what the Bible means." "If my parents had seen what my sister did first, then they wouldn't have gotten so upset at me for hitting her." It is much more difficult for counselees to argue against their own internal experience.

This form of confrontation causes counselees to see inconsistencies in their own functioning. Inconsistencies often emerge between a person's words and actions. "You're telling me that you are studying very hard and yet the whole evening has been spent talking with friends on the phone and watching television."

Other inconsistencies appear between plans and actions. "You're really wanting to make the first-string squad, but you're showing up late to practice about every day." Counselees sometimes evidence inconsistencies between their thoughts and their feelings. "I know that you really do think that church is important, yet you're feeling so turned off and cold when you're there." Another place where inconsistencies are found is between past history, or the person's track record, and plans for the future. "You're planning on becoming a premed major and going on to medical school, yet your worst grades are in the natural sciences."

These kinds of confrontations are powerful. They can provide the necessary nudge to help a counselee make a major breakthrough. Always remember the counselee's need for your unconditional acceptance and non-judgmental attitude. Receiving this kind of confrontation can be very threatening. If not handled supportively and with a great deal of reassurance and understanding, the counseling relationship easily could be ruined. Dr. Gary Collins reminds us that a counselee may not be able to respond positively to the confrontation right away. There may be an initial resistance or rejection. Teenagers may need time to think about the confrontation in order to identify with the changes, integrating them into their own personality structure. When the confrontation is handled positively and timed well, it can actually strengthen the counseling relationship.[13] It indicates genuine caring to the counselee when a counselor is willing to risk confrontation. And when the confrontation is accurate the counselee realizes how well the counselor really knows him or her.

Confrontation is generally not advised during the relationship-building stage of counseling because a secure relationship is an important undergirding support during the confronting process. During stages two, three and four, confrontation will find its most common use. Like other strong directive techniques, confrontation is used less during the termination and follow-up stages. The following graph illustrates the usefulness of confrontation through the counseling process:

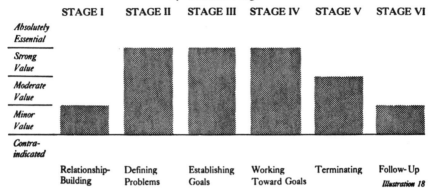

The Value of Confronting During the Six Stages of Counseling

Illustration 18

Self-disclosing. Self-disclosing is seen not only as a personal characteristic but also as a specific counseling tool. As stated in an earlier chapter, there are two kinds of self-disclosure responses. The first is when the counselor tells the counselee about something that he or she had experienced that is similar to what the counselee is currently experiencing. The goal is to help the counselee feel convinced that his or her counselor really does understand. Unfortunately, this "storytelling" type of self-disclosure seldom does much good. It draws the focus away seldom does much good. It draws the focus away from the counselee and places it where it does not belong, on the counselor.

The second type of self-disclosing response can be a very effective counseling technique. The counselor openly expresses relevant, current thoughts and feelings to the counselee. A psychologist named Johari has devised a graphic scheme on the issue of openness. It is called Johari's Window. Adapted to counseling, it looks like this:

	COUNSELEE SEES	COUNSELEE DOES NOT SEE
I (COUNSELOR) SEE	Public Self	Private Self
I (COUNSELOR) DO NOT SEE	Unconscious Self	God Only Knows

Illustration 19

The public self is that which the counselor is personally aware of and also allows the counselee to know. The private self is that which counselors know about themselves and choose to not share with their counselees. The unconscious self encompasses those aspects of the counselor that the counselee sees even though the counselor is not aware of them. And the God only knows segment contains those aspects of the counselor that neither the counselor nor the counselee knows about.

Sidney Jourard emphasized the importance of openness in all human relationships.[14] Another researcher found that when interviewers disclosed more about themselves their interviewees also shared more intimate material and greater amounts of information about themselves.[15] The self-disclosing counselor can be depicted by Johari's Window:

	COUNSELEE SEES	COUNSELEE DOES NOT SEE
I (COUNSELOR) SEE	Public Self	Private Self
I (COUNSELOR) DO NOT SEE	Unconscious Self	God Only Knows

Illustration 20

The counselor who is closed and reluctant to disclose personal information will tend to have more difficulty helping counselees be open.

	COUNSELEE SEES	COUNSELEE DOES NOT SEE
I (COUNSELOR) SEE	Public Self	Private Self
I (COUNSELOR) DO NOT SEE	Unconscious Self	God Only Knows

Illustration 21

When disclosing personal thoughts, feelings or attitudes it is important for the counselor to be able to answer the question, "How is this self-disclosure designed to help the counselee?" Share only that which is judged to be helpful to the counselee. An important point to remember is that openness does not equate with honesty. Honesty is commanded by God. Translated into counseling terminology it becomes congruent. Everything the counselor says should accurately reflect his or her true thoughts and feelings. But obviously complete openness to the counselee about all of the counselor's inner awareness would be totally inappropriate. The counselee need not know what the counselor had that morning for breakfast or what plans are scheduled for that evening. And the thoughts and feelings that are important for the counselee to hear must be expressed with the appropriate amount of openness. "I'm having a hard time plugging into today's session" and "I'm bored stiff" both express honestly the same internal experience. But in most counseling situations the former disclosure, though less open, is honest, congruent and far more appropriate.

Self-disclosures of the second variety (expressing relevant, current thoughts, feelings and attitudes) are very appropriate throughout the whole counseling process. When the counselor experiences a strong feeling, impulse, thought or attitude, it should be disclosed appropriately to the counselee. If it is withheld, internal tension builds and the counselee is likely to sense that something is going on. Often the counselee's guess will be worse and more harmful than if the counselor took the risk and self-disclosed. The following graph illustrates the need for counselor self-disclosure through the counseling process:

The Value of Self-Disclosing During the Six Stages of Counseling

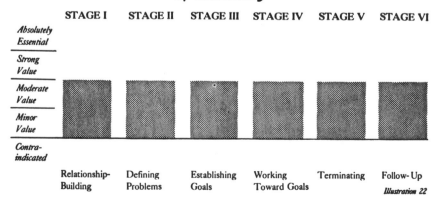

Illustration 22

Encouraging. As a counseling technique, encouraging encompasses a wide variety of responses that are geared to help the counselee feel understood, believed in and supported. In his letter to the Galatians Paul writes, "Bear one another's burdens, and so fulfill the law of Christ" (Galatians 6:2). One way that counselors carry others' burdens is by helping them to believe in and exercise their own strength more fully. Psychologist Don Dinkmeyer uses the term "encouragement" to refer to those procedures that help the counselee to experience and believe in his or her own personal worth.[16]

From initiating the first contact with the counselor to termination, counseling involves a great deal of risk, anxiety and pain for the counselee. Encouragement from the counselor, each step of the way can help insure a positive outcome for the counselee. It is very important, though, that the counselor never gives false reassurance. Statements like, "Everything will be just fine," "I'm sure everything will be okay" and "I know you'll win" come across as very glib, patronizing remarks that cause a loss of faith and trust in the counselor. Such responses suggest that the counselor is not emotionally in touch with the counselee, is minimizing the importance of the counselee's problems, or uncaring about the counselee's struggle.

Sometimes encouragement comes in the form of offering reassurance to a counselee who is feeling depressed, doubtful, helpless or anxious. One author suggests eight different types of reassurance that can be given to counselees:

1. The counselee might be reassured by knowing that his or her problem is really quite common.

2. Reassurance can be given that the problem has a known cause and that something can be done about it.

3. Reassurance can be given that though the symptoms are annoying, they are not dangerous.

4. Counselees can often be reassured that specific treatment methods are available.

5. Reassurance can be given that a cure or resolution of the problem is possible.

6. The counselee may need reassurance that he or she is not going insane.

7. Reassurance that relapses may be expected to occur and that their appearance does not imply that the condition is worsening, may be very helpful.

8. When appropriate, counselees should be reassured that their prob-

lems are not the result of sinful action.[17]

Christians often struggle more about whether it is okay for them to seek help, especially from a professional counselor, for their problems. "I should be able to handle life without needing this kind of help. A lot of people have had a lot harder life than I've had. Besides, if I had the faith in God that I should have, then I wouldn't be having these problems." Christians need to be reassured that the existence of problems invalidates neither the value of their person nor their faith. Christians can be reassured that counseling is a partial expression of James 5:16: "Therefore confess your sins to one another, and pray for one another, so that you may be healed."

Resistance and discouragement can be experienced during every stage. Honest encouragement given with integrity can be a valuable tool during each of the six counseling stages. The following graph illustrates the value of encouraging responses:

The Value of Encouraging During the Six Stages of Counseling

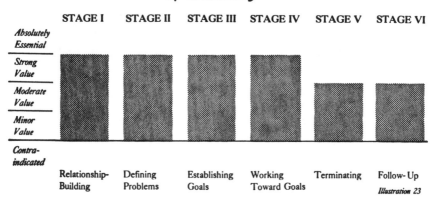

Illustration 23

Reflecting. Simply stated, reflecting is the process of expressing back to the counselee some component of what he or she has previously expressed. Carl Rogers defines it as an effort "to understand from the client's point of view and to communicate that understanding."[18] This technique has foundational importance to several theories of therapy. At the same time that it helps the counselee feel heard and understood, it helps the counselor to very accurately sense and comprehend the internal experience of the counselee. It gives the counselor a very sensitive and gentle way of checking out what he or she is hearing and communicating that back to the counselee.

Lawrence Brammer and Everett Shostrom have summarized the counseling value of reflection.[19] Here are some adaptations of their thoughts about what it does and why it works:

1. Reflection helps the counselee to feel deeply understood.

2. It helps to disrupt destructive, irrational and neurotic thought and communication patterns.

3. Reflection of emotions impresses upon counselees the understanding that their emotions form part of the causative base for their actions.

4. It helps counselees to become evaluative of their own behavior.

5. It helps counselees to experience a stronger feeling that they can make choices about their lives.

6. Reflection helps counselees to clarify their thinking so that they can more objectively see and evaluate their life situations.

7. It helps the counselor to communicate that he or she does not regard the counselee as being strange, weird, or one of a kind because of the problems that have been shared.

8. Reflection helps counselees self-examine their own motivations.

There are three different levels or types of materials that the counselor can reflect: First, counselors will reflect the counselee's *verbal content* as a way of checking out and communicating the counselor's understanding. Such reflections usually rephrase some of what has been said, though little attempt is made to interpret the material.

Counselee: "It's been a horrible week. My dog ran away, I flunked my history exam and I'm on restriction because I got home too late Saturday night."

Counselor: "Wow, a lot has gone wrong for you last week!"

Counselee: "Yeah. Something's got to change. (Pause.) I don't know what to do but I gotta do something different. Seems like I always get somethin' messed up."

Counselor: "You want to do something to make things better but you're not sure what will work."

Counselee: "You got it. Sure, some things I could change. Like I could study more and I guess I could have gotten home earlier last Saturday. But other stuff I can't do anything about. Like my dog running away. What could I do about that?"

Counselor: "You have learned what you can do to prevent some problems. You don't yet see a way that you could have prevented your dog from running away though."

Each of the counselor's responses were content reflections that were structured to let the counselee know that he had been heard. The reflections were also designed to help him experience increasing responsibility for his situation and to help him make better choices.

Second, reflection of counselees' *feelings and emotions that are nonverbally expressed* along with content helps them to recognize, accept and understand repressed material. There is an emotional component to virtually everything that counselees say. Gentle reflections of these emotions help the counselees gain awareness of their emotional world. Gradually these affective responses can be worked through during the counseling process so that the counselee can integrate them into conscious understanding. Such integration is vitally important because repressed and unaccepted emotions continue to motivate behavior that is often destructive and dysfunctional until the emotion is brought to conscious resolution.

Counselee: "I'm so mad at Bruce. He's such a creep. Two days before homecoming he backs out of our date. Just two days."

Counselor: "Melinda, you're really feeling upset."

Counselee: "Yeah, I really am. He shouldn't have done it. We've been going together for over a year. (She begins to cry.) And just like that, he calls and says that we're not going to homecoming together. (Blowing her nose and then making a fist and shaking her head.) What a jerk. (Crying harder and voice growing softer.) He just shouldn't have done it. It's not right."

Counselor: "Seems like there's even more hurt there than anger."

Counselee (still crying hard): "Yeah, I guess so. (Pause.) It does hurt. I feel so bad."

The counselor has helped Melinda to identify, express and accept the deep pain that her anger was masking. As she experiences the full force of her pain in the protected, supportive environment with her caring counselor, she will find that she survives and outlives the pain. The stage is now set for counseling to help her learn from this experience, to integrate it with other past experiences, and to make adjustments that are appropriate for present and future living.

The third type of reflection focuses on the *interaction* that occurs between the counselee and either the counselor or another person who plays an important role in the counselee's life. The reflection is focused at the transaction that is occurring. This process overlaps with interpretation in that it is telling the counselee what is being perceived in addition to the content of what the counselee is saying. An example will help to clarify our understanding of this type of reflection.

Nineteen-year-old Bret is talking with his counselor who is a woman:

Bret: "Nothing much has been happening. (Very little eye contact with the counselor except for brief expressionless glances.) Really, I don't know what to talk about." (Long pause.)

Counselor: "Bret, I get the feeling that you're pushing me away right now."

Bret (looks momentarily surprised): "Oh, I don't know. Not really. I mean, I don't know what you're talking about. There's just nothin' to say. (Long silence, eyes cast downward and jaw tightly set.) You just keep prying. You're never satisfied. (Now leans forward, looking straight at the counselor.) Just like my parents. No matter how much I tell you, you want to hear more. More, more, more, more!" (Leans back in his seat, eyes again fall to the floor, but he is less tense.)

Counselor: "It's hard to open up to me because you're afraid that, just like your parents, I'll never be satisfied with you."

This type of reflection can open up the blocked counseling process by bringing problem dynamics to the surface and allowing them to be resolved between the counselor and counselee.

Of all the basic counseling skills, reflecting emotions is the most difficult to learn. Reflecting content is easy but reflecting feelings in a natural, communicative style is hard. It is so different from typical social interaction. Bruce Shertzer and Shelly Stone have found that practicum and intern counselors "are more adept in responding to counselees who express negative feelings toward parents, teachers or rivals than in helping bring to conscious expression hostile feelings toward themselves or the counselor. In the latter situations, counselors are inclined to rise to the defense of the counselee because of sympathy or react defensively because their ability as a counselor is challenged."[20] It is easier for us to reflect counselee feelings that we identify with and most difficult to reflect those that we experience as personally threatening.

Good reflecting is a complex skill that heavily calls upon the counselor's personality makeup, defensive structure, observational capacities and interpersonal skills. Brammer and Shostrom suggest seven errors and problems that are encountered when counselors reflect:

1. Repeated use of a stereotyped introductory phrase like "You're feeling . . .."

2. When many feelings are being expressed by the counselee, significant emotions can be bypassed if the counselor waits for the counselee to stop talking before reflecting. It is sometimes good to interrupt with a reflective statement that focuses the counselee's attention on signifi-

cant material.

3. Inaccurate or unwise selection of counselee feelings that the counselor chooses to reflect.

4. Reflecting content using the counselee's same words, amounts to simply repeating content. It fails to lead the counselee more deeply into significant material.

5. Reflecting feelings at either too shallow or too deep a level.

6. Adding to or taking away from the meaning of the counselee's expression.

7. Use of inappropriate language or terminology that fails to adequately communicate with the counselee.[21]

Remember that reflection is not an end in itself. It is healing because it is a means to bring the counselee to self-confrontation. "Feelings are thought by the client to be subjective and not to be trusted. They tell him of danger when there is no danger, of presence of symptoms when he is tired and discouraged. The expression of feeling, therefore, is to make possible the discovery of the idea which underlies or is attached to the feelings. The client should be taught to trust the expression of his feelings."[22]

Reflection is a significant counseling technique. In its three forms, reflection can play a major role of the therapeutic process in all six stages of counseling. The following graph depicts this importance:

The Value of Reflecting During the Six Stages of Counseling

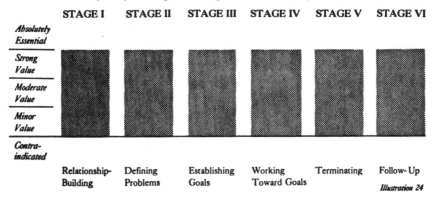

Illustration 24

Using silence. Using silence is another counseling technique which is difficult for new counselors to learn. Most of us associate silence in an interpersonal situation with feelings of awkwardness, disapproval, rejection or boredom. Since counseling is an interpersonal situation, the experience of pauses or silence is likely to give rise to such feelings within both counselee and counselor. Counselors who feel insecure, unsure of themselves or overly responsible for the success of the session will tend to have even greater difficulty comfortably handling silent pauses.

The counselor's task is to learn a new perception of silence. Novice counselors usually equate counseling "work" with talking. But it is often during the quick moments and long minutes of silence that counselees gain their most significant, life-changing insights. Dr. Clyde Narramore writes, "The insights gained in this setting usually have lasting value since they have been uncovered by the counselee himself. Because he has thought of them, he is more willing to accept them. Indeed, pauses (quiet times of patient thought and reflection) are not mere empty, vacant spaces, awkward and hard to endure. Rather, they are the golden moments when a counselee gains insights and when a counselor is working at his professional best!"[23]

There are times during the counseling process that the counselor's response is one of silence. R.H. Tindall and F.R. Robinson indicated three different types of these counselor pauses. The first type is *deliberate* pause which is created to add emphasis to what was just said or done. The second kind of pause is *organizational* and is used to facilitate transition from one issue to another. The third is a natural *termination*, which is used to bring a particular issue to an end.[24]

A very helpful categorization of different kinds of silence along with suggestions for counselor responses is presented by Shertzer and Stone. Their ideas are paraphrased here.[25]

The Counseling Situation in Which the Pause Occurs	*Appropriate Counselor Response*
1. During initial contacts, counselees often fear that they have "said too much" and become apprehensive about the impression of them that the counselor may have gained.	It is appropriate for the counselor to break the silence with reflection, light interpretation or other relationship-building response. "Sometimes it's scary to reveal ourselves, especially to someone we really don't know."
2. The counselee may pause in order to ponder or evaluate what he or she has just said.	The counselor needs to allow as much time as is needed for this potentially valuable process.

3. The counselor or counselee reaches the end of a train of thought and does not know where to proceed next.

Ending this silence fairly soon is appropriate for the counselor. "It seems that we've gone as far with that thought as we can."

4. Sometimes extended silence occurs at the beginning of sessions, following the exchange of initial greetings, while counselor and counselee are orienting themselves to the session that has just begun.

After a short pause, the counselor might reflect or interpret the silence that both are experiencing. "It seems a little difficult for us to get started today."

5. The counselee may be struggling with very painful or anxiety-producing feelings that, though he or she yearns to express, are very difficult to say in words.

Counselor expressions of understanding and encouragement may help. "Some feelings are so difficult to say out loud. Yet it often helps so much when we are able to do just that."

6. Some counselees perceive that it is their role to patiently wait for the counselor to ask questions, and then they will answer. Others are very shy and withdrawn and misperceive the counselor's silence as rejection and disapproval.

A reassuring and/or structuring response from the counselor is appropriate. "I'm interested to hear what thoughts and feelings you have been experiencing." "Perhaps you could share with me what is on your mind and then we can go from there." "Sometimes I'll remain silent for a little while so that you can think through some things. I'd really like to know what you've been thinking."

7. Sometime the counselee is needing reassurance, support or affirmation from the counselor that he or she is still acceptable or loveable.

A gentle interpretation or reflection, or encouraging response is needed. "After sharing as bravely as you have, it's important to know that I still like you."

8. The counselee has just finished expressing something, releasing a great load of heavy emotion.

Counselor's non-verbal expressions of acceptance and understanding are appropriate without verbalization.

A common mistake that young counselors often make is allowing the period of silence to continue too long. First, the counselor must determine if the pause is productive or unproductive. In other words, is the counselee working during the silent period? If not, then it is an unproductive silence and it should be ended. If, however, the counselee is thinking, pondering, increasing self-awareness, clarifying internal feelings or accomplishing some other task during the pause, the counselor should not interfere. Empathic understanding of the counselee and counseling experience help the counselor know how long to allow productive silences to continue. When effectively used as a counseling technique, silence can be used: to increase counselees' feeling of responsibility to talk about their problems; to slow down the pace of the interview; to help counselees gain insight and integrate emotion; and to increase the strength of counselees' emotional reactions.[26]

Silence can be an effectively used technique during all six of the counseling stages. Its successful use depends on accurate empathy and well-developed listening skills. During stage one, silences should be kept relatively short in order not to create anxiety too soon in the process. From that point on, the degree of usage of silence will depend on the orientation of the counselor and the style with which the counselee works. The following graph depicts the usage of silence during the counseling process:

The Value of Using Silence During the Six Stages of Counseling

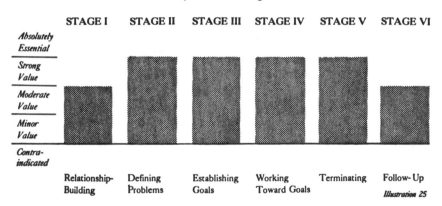

Illustration 25

Techniques Used in Each Stage of Counseling

In order to summarize this discussion of basic counseling techniques, it might be helpful to look at the flow of the counseling process through its six stages. The relative values of each of the techniques presented in this chapter during each counseling stage will provide the structure for our view of the counseling process.

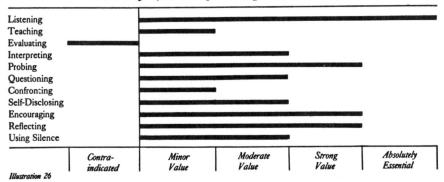

The Relative Values of the Basic Counseling Techniques During the First Stage of Counseling: Building the Relationship

	Contra-indicated	Minor Value	Moderate Value	Strong Value	Absolutely Essential

Listening
Teaching
Evaluating
Interpreting
Probing
Questioning
Confronting
Self-Disclosing
Encouraging
Reflecting
Using Silence

Illustration 26

The Relative Values of the Basic Counseling Techniques During the Second Stage of Counseling: Defining the Problem

	Contra-indicated	Minor Value	Moderate Value	Strong Value	Absolutely Essential

Listening
Teaching
Evaluating
Interpreting
Probing
Questioning
Confronting
Self-Disclosing
Encouraging
Reflecting
Using Silence

Illustration 27

The Relative Values of the Basic Counseling Techniques During the Third Stage of Counseling: Establishing Goals

	Contra-indicated	Minor Value	Moderate Value	Strong Value	Absolutely Essential

Listening
Teaching
Evaluating
Interpreting
Probing
Questioning
Confronting
Self-Disclosing
Encouraging
Reflecting
Using Silence

Illustration 28

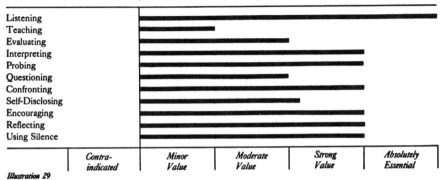

The Relative Values of the Basic Counseling Techniques During the
Fourth Stage of Counseling: **Working Toward the Goals**

Illustration 29

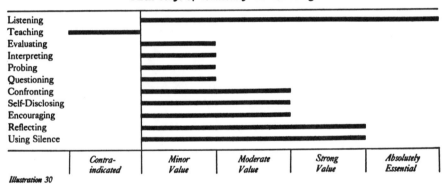

The Relative Values of the Basic Counseling Techniques During the
Fifth Stage of Counseling: **Terminating**

Illustration 30

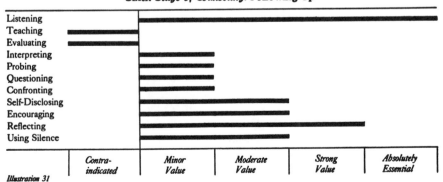

The Relative Values of the Basic Counseling Techniques During the
Sixth Stage of Counseling: **Following Up**

Illustration 31

It is important to note that this material was not created from empirical data. No methodical research was conducted to produce these relative values. They represent, instead, illustrations of an eclectic approach to counseling that is well-founded in psychological research, clinical theory, counseling practice, and is consistent with scriptural propositions.

A review of the use of the basic counseling techniques suggests some interesting insights into the process of counseling. Let's look at these insights in summary form:

1. If there is a backbone technique, it is listening. The use of listening runs through each stage as an absolutely essential part of the counselor's behavior.

2. The second, third and fourth stages of counseling bear a great deal of common resemblance. In fact, the second and third stages look the same as far as counselor behavior is concerned. In addition to listening, heavy emphasis is placed on interpreting, probing, confronting, encouraging, reflecting and using silence. These middle stages are marked by very active counselor involvement.

3. Stages five and six are characterized by a significant drop in the level of counselor activity. The attending responses of listening, reflecting and using silence are primarily used, followed by the use of self-disclosing and encouraging techniques.

Notes

1. Peter Buntman and Eleanor Saris, *How to Live With Your Teenager* (Pasadena, Calif.: Birch Tree Press, 1979).

2. Allen E. Ivey and L. Simek-Downing, *Counseling and Psychotherapy: Skills, Theories and Practice* (Englewood Cliffs, N. J.: Prentice-Hall, 1980).

3. Robert Langs, *The Listening Process* (New York: Jason Aronson, 1978).

4. Gary R. Collins, *How to Be a People Helper* (Ventura, Calif.: Vision House, 1976), pp. 50-51.

5. Bruce Shertzer and Shelly Stone, *Fundamentals of Counseling* (Boston: Houghton Mifflin, 1974).

6. O. Quentin Hyder, *The Christian's Handbook of Psychiatry* (Old Tappan, N. J.: Fleming H. Revell, 1971), p. 173.

7. Carl Rogers, *Counseling and Psychotherapy* (Boston: Houghton Mifflin, 1942).

8. Lawrence Brammer and Everett Shostrom, *Therapeutic Psychology*, 2nd ed. (Englewood Cliffs, N. J.: Prentice-Hall, 1968).

9. Shertzer and Stone, *Fundamentals of Counseling*.

10. Jay Adams, *The Christian Counselor's Manual* (Grand Rapids, Mich.: Baker Book House, 1973), p. 174 and p. 285.

11. *Webster's Seventh New Collegiate Dictionary* (Springfield, Mass.: G. and C. Merriam, 1963).

12. Collins, *How to Be a People Helper*.

13. Elizabeth Skoglund, *Can I Talk to You?* (Glendale, California: Regal Books, 1977).

14. Sidney M. Jourard, *The Transparent Self* (Princeton: Van Nostrand, 1964).

15. G. Keith Olson, "The Effects of Interviewer Self-Disclosing and Reinforcing Behavior Upon Subject Self-Disclosure" (Ph.D. dissertation, University of Arizona, 1972).

16. Don C. Dinkmeyer, "Use of the Encouragement Process in Adlerian Counseling," Personnel and Guidance Journal 51 (November 1972):177-181.

17. Frederick C. Thorne, *Principles of Personality Counseling* (Brandon, Vt.: Journal of Clinical Counseling, 1950).

18. Carl R. Rogers, *Client-Centered Therapy* (Boston: Houghton Mifflin, 1951), p. 452.

19. Brammer and Shostrom, *Therapeutic Psychology*.

20. Shertzer and Stone, *Fundamentals of Counseling*, p. 278.

21. Brammer and Shostrom, *Therapeutic Psychology*.

22. Ibid., p. 195.

23. Clyde M. Narramore, *The Psychology of Counseling* (Grand Rapids, Mich.: Zondervan, 1960), pp. 59-60.

24. R. H. Tindall and F. P. Robinson, "The Use of Silence as a Technique in Counseling," Journal of Clinical Psychology 3 (April 1947):136-141.

25. Shertzer and Stone, *Fundamentals of Counseling*.

26. Ibid.

■ CHAPTER 7

Special Considerations in Counseling

Our goal in this chapter is to examine several considerations that will help to insure your effectiveness as well as your sense of fulfillment as a counselor. The number and variety of considerations that could be covered are endless. Some of the most commonly encountered and important issues have been selected for our attention. They are: how to get started; you as a role model; discerning real problems; confession and repentance in counseling; physical contact during counseling; transference and countertransference; medications; ethics in counseling; when and how to refer. A more complete awareness and understanding of each of these issues will help to fill out your learning experience and better equip you in counseling work or ministry.

How to Get Started

The most important counseling contact that you will ever have with a counselee is the first one. It is during the initial session that counselees get their first impression of the counselor and of counseling. They learn the rules and begin comprehending what is expected of them. They also learn what to expect of the counselor and they learn from the counselor's attitude an either optimistic or pessimistic expectation about the outcome. Since the first counseling session is so fundamental to the future successful outcome of counseling, it is very important that the counselor have a well-developed and constructive plan for handling the first meeting with the counselee.

Counselors, psychologists and psychiatrists from different theoretical orientations have widely divergent perspectives on what should be accomplished during the initial interview. Some believe that the overwhelming task in the first session is to progress into a detailed history of the counselee so that a solid, provisional diagnosis and prognostic evaluation could be established. The diagnosis and prognosis then serve as a baseline for evaluating future counseling progress. Other counselors believe that the primary task of the initial session is to begin to develop the therapeutic alliance and to establish hope, or a positive expectation of improvement within the counselee.

The eclectic counselor feels most comfortable when capable of incorporating both goals within the scope of the initial interview. This position is clearly postulated in *The First Encounter*, a significant volume that is entirely devoted to examining the initial interview. "One must always evaluate everything that transpires in the interaction with a patient, and in the initial interview this can be accomplished only by active and searching questioning. Otherwise one can come to the end of the first interview and know a geat deal about the presenting symptoms, but next to nothing about who the patient really is: his background, his family, his developmental history, his education, his work and sexual relationships, his strengths and assets and creative potential, his accessibility to psychotherapeutic work, in other words, his past and his possible future. However, such active and searching questioning can only be meaningful and helpful if it takes place in the context of a relationship of trust and confidence, one that always respects the patients' anxieties and the various defenses that are called upon to deal with those anxieties."[1]

Leona Tyler outlines three goals for the initial counseling session: to establish an adequate foundation for the counselor-counselee relationship; to begin facilitating the counselee's opening-up process that will help him or her delve deeply into anxiety-producing, psychologically significant material; and to provide counselees with the basic structure of counseling that will help them gain the greatest benefit from their future counseling sessions.[2]

The eclectic approach values the process of establishing a provisional diagnostic impression and prognostic estimation which helps the counselor to evaluate therapeutic progress throughout the counseling process. But our approach places even heavier focus on the necessity of establishing a positive counselor-counselee relationship and developing within the counselee a hopeful anticipation of improving through the counseling process.

Reasons for seeking help. Some psychological researchers have found that significant counseling gains often come with the reasons why the counselee initiated counseling when he or she did.[3] Usually a person lives with a problem for quite some time before seeking help. There are often significant reasons why individuals take the initiative to enter counseling at the time they do. Focusing on these reasons appears to be productive of counseling success. Genuine confidence, optimism and enthusiasm from the counselor tend to inspire trust and faith within the counselee which, in turn, helps to produce energy for working through the difficult counseling process.[4]

Attitudes and expectations. Another issue that has a dramatic impact on the total counseling process is the attitudes and expectations that new counselees bring to the initial session. Counselors should begin each initial interview with several silent questions. "What has caused this person to initiate counseling at this time?" "How did this individual happen to set up an appointment with me?" "What are his or her expectations from counseling?" "What is this person expecting me to do?" "What does he or she think is going to happen during counseling?" Having these questions clearly in mind helps the counselor gain quick insight into the mindset of the new counselee.

The counselee's mindset. The counselee's mindset is influenced by several different factors. One of these is the method of referral that led the counselee to make an appointment with the particular counselor. Generally speaking, when a person voluntarily seeks counseling there exists a positive initial atmosphere. "I'm here because I want to be here" is a far more productive attitude than "I'm here because they are making me come." The former mindset says, "I'm ready to work," while the latter is essentially stating, "If you're going to get anything out of me, you're going to have to work for it."

The counselee's perception of the counselor is another central aspect of his or her mindset. The counselor's position and role identification strongly influence the counselee's expectations. When seeking counseling from a professional minister, people often expect to be told from the Bible what to do, to be judged and told to repent, to be forgiven graciously, to be prayed with, supported and encouraged. The specific expectations will be greatly influenced by the counselee's theological orientation, denominational affiliation and previous experience with members of the clergy.

When people seek counseling help from professional therapists, they often expect to be treated like a patient in the office of their family physician. Some anticipate that the "doctor" will be able to provide a rather instant cure. "I'll tell the therapist my problem and he will tell me what to do about it." What the individual has heard from relatives and friends, seen in the movies and on television, and read about professional therapists will affect what he or she anticipates from the experience. Some will expect to receive prescribed homework assignments, others direct advice, still others will anticipate going through psychological testing, and some have heard that the only thing psychotherapists do is sit there and occasionally say, "Uh-huh," "I see," "Yes, I understand," while the counselee does all the real work.

Richard Wallen suggests three common perceptions of therapists that counselees bring with them to the initial interview:

1. Psychiatrists and psychologists are especially often thought of as a *threat*. "If they think you're crazy, they can send you to the hospital and you may never get out." "Only crazy people go to a 'shrink,' and I'm not crazy!" "They can see right through you and know exactly what you're thinking."

2. Others view the counselor as the *miracle worker*. "If I can just make it to Tuesday when I talk to her, then I'll be okay." "You're my last hope. I know you'll be able to help me." Counselors who have particularly good reputations and those who have been highly recommended are particularly vulnerable to this false perception. Unfortunately, some counselors regularly reinforce this unhealthy bias as a way of buttressing their own faltering egos. People who have difficulty taking responsibility for their own lives are most likely to view counselors in this way, making the counselor the intended object for their dependency needs.

3. Other people hope to find in the counselor an *intercessor*. People who tend to be manipulative will expect the counselor to "get" others to act the way that they want them to. "If I go to a counselor, then that'll prove that I'm really serious about changing." "I sure hope that my counselor will be able to convince my parents to let me go to winter retreat." "When we get to the counselor, she'll tell you that I'm right."[5]

Christians who seek counseling help often struggle with additional expectations, apprehensions and conflicts. Many Christians have been taught, "The Lord is all that you need." That statement is certainly true in issues related to redemption, forgiveness and salvation, but is sometimes generalized to the point of absurdity. Many sincere and sensitive believers have been made to feel guilty and even to question the reality of their salvation, because they have sought the help of a counselor or therapist. It is no more a sign of insufficient reliance on faith to seek counseling help, than it is to seek medical help. God usually chooses healing to come about through the natural processes which he has instituted within us. He created us in his own image, designed self-restorative and healing mechanisms to be integral parts of our functioning, and typically relies on the integrity of his design to do its job. When there is physical injury, physical healing processes go into action. And when there are psychological or spiritual injuries, then the respective psychological and spiritual healing processes must be relied upon to do their job.

Though injury in any one sphere of the person's being (physical, spiritual or psychological) impacts the other two spheres, the primary healing must take place in the sphere where the majority of the injury was sustained. There are times when the injury is severe enough that we need the assistance of a trained specialist. Severe physical injury often requires the help of a medical doctor. Strong spiritual confusion or conflict can often be best worked out with the help of a trained minister. And serious emotional and behavioral problems are often best worked through with the help of qualified counselors. In none of these three situations is there any indication of lack of faith. Rather, they give us three different perspectives on the body of Christ, "from whom the whole body, joined and knit together by every joint and with which it is supplied, when each part is working properly, makes bodily growth and upbuilds itself in love" (Ephesians 4:16).

Christians sometimes labor under the misperception that psychologists are diametrically opposed to the Christian faith. With some exceptions, this is a fallacy. Like Christian counselors, secular therapists want to help all people live happy, productive and fulfilling lives. Their approach, though not always consistent with scripture, often helps their Christian counselees use their faith more effectively. Remember that non-Christians, too, can understand and operate by many of God's laws and created principles.

Fielding questions. The counselor is likely to receive a wide variety of questions from counselees during the initial interview. The insightful counselor listens carefully to these questions, responds with frank answers, avoids lengthy and detailed explanations, and recognizes these questions as behavior that is revealing of the counselee's mindset about counseling and reflecting his or her inner psychic structure.[6] Here are some examples of commonly asked questions: "What do you want me to tell you?" "Do you want me to lie down on your couch?" "Should I tell you about my dreams?" "I keep a daily diary that has a lot of information in it about me. I brought it with me. Do you want to read it?" "I have seen several doctors before. Do you want to call them and ask about their impressions of me?" "Do I have to tell my parents what we talk about?" "How many times will I have to come back?" "What kind of therapy do you do?" "Would you hypnotize me so we can get done faster?" "My friend who told me about you saw you last year for several sessions. She's a lot better. Will you be able to help me as much as you helped her?" "Do you do Christian counseling?" "What church do you attend?"

Counseling beginnings. Let's turn our attention specifically to look at why teenagers usually are seen in counseling by a youth sponsor, pastor or professional counselor. There are a wide variety of reasons. Here are some of them:

1. Youth leaders may initiate at least one session with a teenager who has recently made a major decision or commitment regarding his or her spiritual life.

2. Young people will sometimes initiate their own session with a youth group leader, pastor or counselor if they need help.

3. Counseling sometimes is initiated at the request of a parent, school teacher or administrator, probation officer, church staff member, friend or other concerned person.

4. The pastor or youth worker may initiate an interview to check out rumors that the young person is having particular problems (e.g., with parents, drugs, sex, school, etc.).

5. Counseling is sometimes initiated because of noticeable and fairly rapid changes in behavior. Examples include: becoming markedly more aggressive, withdrawn, silly, sullen, super-spiritual, etc.

6. Counseling can be initiated because of continuous annoying or irritating behavior. Examples include: attention-getting questions, smart remarks, arguing, boisterous behavior, loud talking, etc.

7. In other cases counseling attention is brought to a teenager who is consistently quiet and withdrawn.

8. An adolescent who craves incessant attention, wants always to be around the youth pastor, or who is overly eager to always be helping can often benefit from counseling contact.

Physical setting. An important but often overlooked aspect of successful counseling is the physical setting in which the helping process occurs. The counselor usually takes responsibility for determining where the meeting will take place. Professional ministers and therapists usually have an office that is designed to establish a conducive atmosphere for counseling. Lay youth leaders may have to be more innovative. Park benches, empty classrooms, church and school lawns, and a parked car all represent possible informal counseling sites.

Wherever the counseling takes place, there are several criteria that must be met. First, the environment must provide privacy. The counselee needs and deserves auditory and visual privacy from parents, teachers, friends, etc. It is the right of the counselee to keep private the fact that he or she is even seeing a counselor. Second, the counseling session should be made as safe from interruptions as possible. Office settings can be secured against interruptions by insulating the office against telephone and walk-in interruptions. Closed doors, "do not disturb" signs, a secretary on duty, and an answering service or telephone answering machine are all effective measures that help to protect against intrusion. Probably the most effective assurance though, is the counselor's own profound valuing of the privacy and uninterrupted quality of the counseling interview. The counselee will quickly sense this attitude and will greatly appreciate it. When privacy and uninterrupted time are assured it is far easier for the counselee to feel secure and experience the freedom to lower his or her resistances to sharing personal material.

Time and length of session. The time and length of the interview are also important aspects of the initial as well as following counseling sessions. Some noteworthy insights into this issue were presented by Clyde Narramore and are adapted here:

1. Establishing a definite beginning and ending time for the counseling session helps both parties to focus on the purpose of the meeting. The counselor does not have to wonder, "How long is the counselee expecting me to spend with him?" And the counselee need not worry, "I hope I'm not taking up too much of her time. Maybe I'd better hurry." Both can relax, concentrate and work hard together for the allotted time.

2. The counselee can feel a sense of security that this is his or her time that is guarded against interruption and already agreed upon.

3. When time limits are established ahead of time or at the beginning of the session, the counselee is less likely to feel rejected when the session comes to a close. It is beneficial when the counselor helps the

counselee to prepare for the end of the session. "We have about 10 minutes more together. I'm wondering what is most important to you for us to work before we have to stop."

4. The time of the session and the time allotted should be such that the counselor does not feel rushed or resentful that he or she is losing valuable time for other interests. It is very important that teachers, pastors and youth sponsors do not expend so much time doing counseling that their other tasks and families are neglected.

5. The timing of the session should be such that it does not place undue pressure on the counselee. Less will be accomplished if the counselee has sandwiched the session in between other items in a busy schedule.

6. Time limits usually vary between 30, 45, 50 and 90 minutes. Most professional therapists see counselees in 45- or 50-minute sessions. Thirty-minute sessions are used mostly for quick "checkup" contacts and for severely disturbed and exceedingly anxious counselees who cannot tolerate longer sessions. Sixty- and 90-minute sessions are often used for conjoint marital and family counseling.[7]

Focus on counseling issues. A very common error is to be *too timid* about focusing on counseling issues. Too much time can be spent discussing the weather, the office decor, and the latest major sporting events in the interest of making both the counselor and the counselee comfortable. A much more direct approach is preferred. It can show friendliness and warmth at the same time that it suggests the counselor's self-confidence and purposefulness. After the initial greetings and introductions are accomplished, the counselor can direct the focus to the issues that need to be examined. Here are a few suggested approaches: "I'm glad that we could meet together today. As we get started, I'm wondering if you have any questions that you would like to ask me?" "I'm very happy to meet you. Perhaps you would like to tell me why you wished to see me." "Often when people think of the word 'counseling,' they have a certain mental picture. I wonder if you could share with me what counseling means to you."

Since the pastor, youth minister or lay youth sponsor usually knows his or her counselees, a more informal initial approach is needed: "Hi, John. It's sure good to be able to have some one-to-one time with you. I'm interested to hear what you wanted to talk about." "Lisa, I'm sure happy that you felt that you could call on me. You sounded upset on the phone. Can you tell me what the problem is?"

Sometimes the counseling is at the request of the person who is doing the counseling: "Hi, Charlie. I sure was glad that you could come down to see me today. I've been concerned about you and felt the need to share those concerns directly with you." "Sue, I know that it must have been hard to come to see me. It took a lot of courage on your part because I think you know why I wanted to see you. Would you like to say something first or ask me anything? You're more than welcome."

All of these opening statements express warmth, caring and respect for the counselee. They also quickly help the counselee to focus on the purpose for the counseling session.

Respond to and gather new information. During the initial interview the counselor is receiving and internally responding to a great deal of new information. This is particularly true when the counselor and counselee have never before met. The skillful counselor is able to receive and process vast amounts of new data, respond to some right away and log the rest for future counseling attention. This is a demanding task that requires what Theodore Reik calls "moral courage" in his book *Listening With the Third Ear.*[8] The counselor is expected to be able to receive, accept and appropriately respond to whatever emotional reactions the counselee might have. Above all else, the counselee's greatest need is acceptance.

The actual amount of information that is gathered during the first session will vary widely. The counselee's need for emotional release, level of defensiveness, degree of trust in the counselor, and conscious awareness of the problem will affect his or her ability to divulge important material. Before the session ends the counselor will usually have fairly complete answers to the following questions: What is the current problem that brings the person into counseling? What are some of the other problems that are related to the presenting problem? What are the possibilities for the central or core problem? When were the current and core problems first noticed? What efforts to solve these problems have been attempted in the past? And, what were the results of these attempts to solve the problems?

Closing the initial session. Another crucial point during the initial counseling session occurs when the allotted time for the appointment nears the end. Part of the counselor's task is to insure that the counselee is composed sufficiently to leave at the end of the appointment. A quite direct statement of a counselor's concern might be expressed about 10 or even 15 minutes before the end of the session. "I know that you're feeling a great deal of pain. I just want you to know that we have about 10 more minutes together." Counselees generally appreciate such statements and receive them as expressions of caring and concern.

Similar "warnings" are appropriate even when the counselee is not emotionally upset. "We have about five more minutes. I'm wondering if there is anything else that you especially wanted to deal with today."

As the end of the initial session nears, it is important to determine such things as: Will further sessions be scheduled? Will it be left up to the counselee to call if he or she desires an additional appointment? Will a referral be made, or will some other plan of action be agreed upon and implemented? "I have enjoyed meeting and talking with you. Do you think that talking again might be of further help to you?" "Do you think that you can feel comfortable enough talking with me about these issues?"

The manner in which the initial session is closed determines whether or not the counselee will follow through with the agreement on the disposition. Does the counselee feel genuinely valued by the counselor? Does he or she feel a warm invitation to continue counseling? Does he or she feel the counselor's support and commitment to help him or her follow through with a frightening medical appointment? Effective follow-through is one very good reason why relationship-building is such an important aspect of the initial session.

The Counselor as a Role Model

This book was started with a very strong emphasis on the personal characteristics of the counselor. Certain qualities have been found by psychological researchers to be important ingredients of the counselor's personality, no matter which theoretical orientation forms the basis for his or her counseling. Counselees often model their behavior after the healthy and healing characteristics of their counselors.

"Perhaps regular physical exercise would lower your stress level and help you feel better both physically and emotionally." This statement from a counselor who exercises regularly and who is in good physical condition will have a stronger and more positive impact on the counselee's behavior than the same statement coming from an overweight, out of shape counselor.

"I'm wondering if you're really listening carefully when your mother talks to you." This query has its strongest impact when the counselee feels heard and listened to by the counselor. The same statement loses much of its force when the counselor repeatedly has interrupted what the counselee was saying.

This topic of role modeling is not new. The New Testament is replete with documentations of its importance. The third epistle of John suggests that we will imitate behavior and that it is up to us to try to initiate constructive behavior. "Beloved, do not imitate evil, but imitate good" (3 John 11). In several of his epistles, Paul enjoined his readers to model their behavior after his own. "What you have learned and received and heard and seen in me, do; and the God of peace will be with you" (Philippians 4:9).

Discerning the Real Problems

Serious problems have usually taken months and sometimes years to develop. It is unrealistic to expect that the counselee will always have a clear grasp of the problem and be able to openly disclose it in succinct terms to the counselor. This process of defining the problem often requires several sessions to accomplish. The counselor's patience, sensitivity, understanding, acceptance and knowledge of psychological mechanisms are all vital ingredients for success in this task.

Overcoming resistance. The counselee's resistance is a major roadblock to progress at this stage. Psychologists find two different levels of resistance that often operate together to impede the process of counseling. First, counselees defend against allowing anxiety-laden unconscious memories, feelings, impulses and thoughts to become conscious. Second, counselees defend against disclosing painful, frightening and embarrassing material to the counselor. Working through the resistance can be a slow process. It must take place at a pace that the counselee can tolerate. It must happen at the counselee's own pace.

Resistance is expressed in a variety of ways. One signal of resistance is when a counselee begins coming late to appointments or forgetting them altogether. This, like most expressions of resistance is often an unconscious process. The counselee may have no awareness that his or her lateness or "forgetting" is purposeful. One young woman had developed a consistent pattern of punctuality with her appointments until the counselor began focusing more on her experience of being sexually molested by her uncle when she was going through puberty. During a certain period of time, she called to cancel two or three sessions, she was late by as much as one-half hour to several others, and totally missed one without notifying the counselor ahead of time. It was not until a few appointments later that she could admit to herself and the counselor the hidden purpose behind this change in her pattern.

Resisting counselees will sometimes diminish the importance of conflict-laden material. They will suggest that talking about those issues would be silly, a waste of time or even inappropriate. "That happened so long ago. I think that it's stupid to keep talking about the past." "Sure my dad beat me up when I was a little kid. I was scared to death of him. But I'm just as big as he is now. I'm not afraid of him anymore. So, why talk about it?" "It's true. I did set several fires when I was in junior high. Some pretty big ones, too. But I've prayed about it. I've confessed it and I know God has forgiven me and I don't do it any more. So why not just forget about it? God has."

Some counselees will spend tremendous amounts of time dwelling on just one area of their life in order to avoid focusing on other more upsetting areas. An obsessive concern about a relatively unimportant issue sometimes suggests that the counselee needs that issue to remain in order not to have to work on more threatening material.

Other counselees become very confused and ramble from one topic to another. Their confusion and aimless rambling prevent a productive focus on any one topic. They unconsciously choose to be confused because it feels safer than risking direct contact with threatening issues.

Resistance is sometimes experienced by periods of silence and an almost complete inability to speak. When confronted with painful and distressing material, one counselee would fall completely silent and become glassy-eyed. She would stare straight ahead, see nothing and her facial muscles would become twisted with tension. It was as if her whole body and mind turned off and clamped down tightly in order to try to avoid the horribly painful and risky material upon which counseling was focusing.

Another expression of resistance occurs when the counselee doubts the counselor's training, qualifications or competence. Such doubts or attacks are projections of the counselee's own insecurities and fears. They are essentially saying, "I am so afraid and feel so overwhelmed by my problems that I fear it will take the absolute best help to have a chance of surviving." Lay counselors may be distrusted because they, after all, are not professionally trained and may not have even a bachelor's degree. Pastors might be rejected because they only know about spiritual problems. Marriage and family therapists and clinical social workers might not be acceptable either because they are not really psychologists. And, of course, psychologists are so steeped in worldly humanism that they can never be trusted. And what about psychiatrists? Well, everyone knows that they have so many problems themselves that they cannot help anyone. Resistance can make it very difficult for a counselee to accept help from anyone.

Maintaining confidentiality. In addition to the clinical manifestation of resistance that we have discussed already, there are other aspects of the counseling process that the counselee must first resolve before more fully confronting painful or threatening material. The counselee must become sure that the counselor will handle what is said with careful confidentiality. This issue is particularly troublesome when a person seeks help from a lay leader or pastor in their own church. The fact that the counselor already knows the counselee has an added advantage. But since they see each other in church and social settings with other people, the assurance of confidentiality is vital. Lay and pastoral counselors very soon develop reputations one way or the other.

A positive and accepting attitude. Counselees need to know that their confessions and disclosures of self-revealing material will be received and responded to with a positive and accepting attitude. Being a counselor automatically does not make a person loving and accepting of everyone. Each counselee gradually learns what kinds of attitudes to expect from his or her counselor. The degree of openness from the counselee will depend largely on the attitudes that the counselor evidences.

Facilitate initial conversation. Early in the counseling process, what looks like resistance might be that the counselee simply does not know how to begin. Teenagers, especially, will wait for the counselor to direct the process. They are used to having adults structure experiences for them and this expectation carries over into counseling.

Recognize resistance. When resistance occurs, it should be dealt with from a patient, understanding perspective. It should never be confronted head on. The counselee should never be accused of "being resistive." Instead well-timed, gentle interpretations that suggest to the counselee what is happening are best. Remember, resistance serves a purpose. It protects against fear, anxiety, hostility and embarrassment. When the counselee grows to recognize that the resistance is not needed, then it will be dropped.

Here are some examples of appropriate interpretive statements: The counselee missed the last appointment. "Sometimes we tend to forget things that are extremely unpleasant or threatening for us."

The counselee questions the counselor's competence. "Sounds like you fear that your problems might be too difficult for me to help you."

The counselee talks only about her weight problem and completely avoids speaking about her sexuality. "It's good that you can discuss your problem with weight with me. A related issue that seems a little more threatening is sexuality. I wonder how you would feel about focusing on that for a while today?"

The counselee is talking non-stop about many different issues without going into much depth with any of them. "We've covered a lot of ground during the last couple of sessions. Sometimes it's more difficult to stay focused on one problem. I wonder if you would try to select one of the problems that you have shared in order to see how much progress we might be able to make toward solving it."

Successful resolution of resistance strengthens the counselee-counselor relationship and opens the door to further counseling progress.

Confession and Repentance in Counseling

The issues of confession and repentance certainly have deep religious significance. We Christians believe that confession of our sins to God is an absolute prerequisite to receiving his forgiveness. "If we confess our sins, he is faithful and just and will forgive our sins and cleanse us from all unrighteousness" (1 John 1:9).

We believe that repentance is a part of and a follow-through from genuine confession. Repentance includes deep sorrow for one's sin, a humbled and broken heart that has lost all boastfulness of self, and an attitudinal and behavioral change from sin to righteousness. Peter is recorded as teaching, "Repent and be baptized every one of you in the name of Jesus Christ for the forgiveness of your sins" (Acts 2:38).

Confession and repentance, though usually called by other names, have also often played major roles in the psychotherapeutic process as well. Psychologists have used terms like catharsis, congruence, transparency and self-disclosure to carry much of the same meaning as the word *confession*.

In essence, all of these terms imply an honest expression of the self. They suggest that the external behavior correctly reflects or fits with the internal condition of the person. The same spiritual meaning and implications are not, of course, suggested by these terms that are used by psychologists. Several do, though, come interestingly close, and actually deepen and broaden our understanding of confession.

Sin. The concept of sin is obviously related to that of confession. Secular psychologists sometimes find great value in Christian language and concepts. O. Hobart Mowrer says, " 'Sickness' is a concept which generates pervasive pessimism and confusion in the domain of psychopathology; whereas 'sin,' for all its harshness, carries an implication of promise and hope, a vision of new potentialities. Just so long as we deny the reality of sin, we cut ourselves off, it seems, from the possibility of radical redemption (recovery)."

If one is tempted to believe that Mowrer has a grasp on the Christian view of sin, reading a little more will clarify it further. "Sin used to be, and in some quarters still is, defined as whatever one does that puts him or her in danger of going to hell. Here was an assumed cause-and-effect relationship that was completely metaphysical and empirically unverifiable; and it is small wonder that it has fallen into disrepute as the scientific outlook and method have steadily gained in acceptance and manifest power. But there is a very tangible and very present hell-on-this-earth which science has not yet helped us understand very well; and so I invite your attention to the neglected but very real possibility that it is this hell—the hell of neurosis and psychosis—to which sin and unexpiated guilt lead us and that it is hell that gives us one of the most, perhaps the most, realistic and basic criteria for defining sin and guilt. If it proves empirically true that certain forms of conduct characteristically lead human beings into emotional instability, what better or firmer basis would one wish for labeling such conduct as destructive, self-defeating, evil, sinful?"[9]

Like Mowrer, Karl Menninger advocates that we call sin just what it is, sin. In his widely accepted book *Whatever Became of Sin?* Menninger traces the historical metamorphosis in our culture of sin into crime, symptoms and collective irresponsibility. He calls upon the clergy, lawyers, judges, police officers, teachers, media personnel statesmen, politicians, doctors, counselors, and finally, every individual person to be a moral leader. "So there you are, you and I. If we believe in sin—as I do—we believe in our personal responsibility for trying to correct it, and thereby saving ourselves and our world. We diminish our long-drawn-out, indirect self-reproach which despairs, but repairs nothing."[10]

Benefits of confession. Confession is viewed as an integral part of the counseling process by many therapists. Existentialist Rollo May writes, "Contact having been made with the counselee, and rapport having been established, we now find ourselves in the central stage of the interview, the confession. This stage consists of the counselee's 'talking it out.' It is the 'piece de resistance' of both counseling and psychotherapy. So important, in fact, is the confession that counselors can well hold themselves to the practice initiated by the psychotherapists; namely, that of reserving at least two-thirds of every hour for talking on the part of the counselee."[11]

The benefits of confession include:

1. Forgiveness: "If we confess our sins, he is faithful and just and will forgive our sins and cleanse us from all unrighteousness" (1 John 1:9).

2. Healing: "Therefore confess your sins to one another, and pray for one another, that you may be healed" (James 5:16).

3. Mercy: "He who conceals his trangressions will not prosper, but he who confesses and forsakes them will obtain mercy" (Proverbs 28:13).

4. Reconciliation: The prodigal's confession is found in Luke 15:21. "And the son said to him, 'Father, I have sinned against heaven and before you; I am no longer worthy to be called your son.'" The loving father's response to his son's confession and repentance was apparently immediate. "But the father said to his servants, 'Bring quickly the best robe, and put it on him; and put a ring on his hand, and shoes on his fee; and bring the fatted calf and kill it, and let us eat and make merry; for this my son was dead and is alive again; he was lost, and is found.' And they began to make merry" (Luke 15:22-24).

5. Happiness: Psalm 32 traces an episode in David's life from confession, "I acknowledged my sin to thee and I did not hide my iniquity" (v. 5); to forgiveness, "I said, 'I will confess my transgressions to the Lord' then thou didst forgive the guilt of my sin" (v. 5); to happiness, "Blessed is he whose transgression is forgiven, whose sin is covered" (v. 1).

In *The Art of Understanding Yourself* Cecil Osborne states his belief that the "failure to accept forgiveness and feel forgiven constitutes the greatest single problem for most people."[12] Though his point may be overstated, the confession process does play a major healing role in counseling.

All true confessions seem to involve a great deal of pain. Whether confessing a sin amidst deep feelings of remorse or admitting to consciousness a long-repressed, anxiety-laden memory, the counselee struggles with very strong pain reactions. Part of this pain is often the result of strong, though possibly unconscious, self-rejection that surfaces along with the confessed material. Counselees feel guilt-ridden over past sins and perceived personal failures.

The confession emerges from the midst of inner tension between the need to withhold and conceal the self on the one hand, and the need to disclose the self on the other. The struggle is intensified because a true confession must be totally honest. No minimizing of the importance of the confessed material is allowed. Neither can a projection of blame onto circumstances or other people be a part of the confession process.

The role of the counselor. There is much that the counselor can do to help the counselee gain the maximum benefit from confession.[13] Cecil Osborne and Rollo May are particularly insightful about the role of the counselor in this process.[14] Here are some ideas:

1. The counselor must respond with an attitude of acceptance and caring. The fact that we are all sinners reminds us that there is no place for a judgmental or superior attitude in the counseling office. Neither should the counselor be shocked or offended by what the counselee confesses. Being shocked or feeling offense indicates that the counselor is either too naive, too immature or too personally involved in the person's life to counsel effectively.

2. The counselor can help lead the counselee through an important preparatory process prior to confessing. Neglecting this preparation is sometimes the cause for the failure of the person to actually accept forgiveness and to feel forgiven. A time of meditation and prayer can increase the level of the counselee's consciousness to a level at which his or her confession has maximum positive effect. Thinking about God, focusing on his love and forgiveness, and recalling memories of previous warm and loving contacts with him will provide encouragement to the counselee. Focusing on other experiences with confession that brought release of heaviness, healing and reconciliation to the counselee are also helpful.

3. The counselor must define his or her role as a facilitating one, being only as verbal as it is necessary to help the counselee accomplish his or her task. Part of the benefit of confession is the catharsis that takes place. Overinvolvement and interruptions disrupt and rob the counselee of the release that otherwise could have been gained.

4. Since the confessing process is usually very painful, the counselor often needs to sensitively lead the counselee toward feeling comfortable enough to confess his or her problem. Much of this focusing and opening occurs during the important preparation phase.

5. Confessing painful material that is associated with a deep sense of guilt or shame often brings an accompanying emotional release. This release can be valuable to the counselee and should be responded to with empathic caring and acceptance. It is important, though, that the emotional response does not redirect the focus away from the content of the confession. That would limit or destroy the success of the confession and would probably be the result of unconscious defensive strategy.

Counselors must understand that confessing is often a long process.

Some confessions come quite readily, but it requires weeks, months, and even years for people to move into the central areas of their psyche in order to know their core thoughts, attitudes and orientations toward life. Sins at this level are made conscious and confessed only after extensive counseling, psychotherapy or some life-changing traumatic event. So the counselor's task is to be patient, understanding, accepting and respecting of the counselee's pace of growth.

What About Physical Contact?

The issue of physical touch between counselor and counselee has been a source of thinking and rethinking within the therapeutic community. There certainly is no question about the value of touch. For many years we have known that adequate touching, stroking and cuddling of infants and very young children is vital for their healthy development. The mortality rate is far higher for infants who do not receive adequate physical contact than it is for infants who do receive adequate contact. But what about teenagers and adults?

Indications are that maturing and aging do not remove our need for touch. Have you ever ached inside just to be held by someone? Therapists often find that a counselee's symptoms worsen when they receive little or no physical contact. Rita is a 55-year-old Christian woman who has had some rather serious bouts with depression. As a little girl, she received little attention from her busy parents and was expected to take care of her younger sisters, a task which she did in exemplary manner. She was married to a man who was quite loving and affectionate, though his affection became intermittent and less dependable as his alcoholism became more severe. After 17 years of marriage he died of a heart attack, leaving her alone to raise three children.

Several years later she remarried. This time her husband turned out to be very egocentric, narcissistic and incapable of maintaining an adult-level, emotionally intimate relationship. At this point she entered therapy. Some months later she divorced him and has remained single. One of her most difficult tasks has been to learn how to cope with an overwhelming sense of loneliness. There were depressed times with suicidal thoughts and days of crippling agitation. Before she worked through the source of her difficulty, the only thing that would relieve her symptoms was to be held.

Studies on patients in intensive care units have revealed some startling results. Monitored vital signs of failing patients have shown significant improvement when a nurse or visitor touches or holds the patient's hand. This effect is strong even when the person remains silent, saying nothing to the patient.

Touch has been long considered to have healing properties. Picture the sick child with a temperature being soothed by his or her mother's gentle stroking touch. Consider the positive reassuring effect of the gentle strength in the examining physician's touch. And meditate for a moment on the New Testament's many accounts of the healing touch of Jesus Christ as he made people whole through laying his hands on them.

Clinical opinions on touch. With such an overwhelmingly positive case for the healing properties that are intrinsic to human touch, what is the recommended therapeutic or counseling position on physical contact between counselor and counselee? Unfortunately, we cannot state what the one clinical stance is because there are several opinions. The most traditional stance is that there is no place for physical contact between therapist and patient. The psychoanalyst is then a rather aloof and non-responsive person in the patient's life. This "distance" is purposefully created in order to allow the patient's personality dynamics to be expressed clearly in the way the patient relates to the analyst.

The late 1950s, 1960s and 1970s saw major departures from traditional psychoanalytic and psychodynamic therapy. Many of the existential/experiential therapies allowed and encouraged physical touch. This contact was intended to encourage the counselee's abreaction, or release of repressed and inhibited emotionality. The kind of physical contact was determined by the particular emotion that was desired to be released. For instance, holding and rocking the counselee might draw out feelings of sadness while shoving and pushing would likely release anger or rage reactions. Gestalt and primal scream are two therapies that freely use physical contact for such purposes. Another psychotherapeutic treatment, bioenergetic analysis, as well as rolfing involve "body work" or physical work with the counselee's body in order to help the counselee accomplish therapeutic gains. During this same time span a major popularization of group therapies was also extolling the benefits that physical touch has for mental and emotional well-being.

What, then, is the preferred stance of the Christian eclectic counselor with regard to counselor-counselee physical contact? The position must be ethically and morally Christian. It must also have the breadth of a true eclecticism. The decision to have or not to have physical contact must be decided by each counselor with regard to each counselee and the decision should be cautiously and carefully made.

Guidelines and precautions for the Christian eclectic counselor. Some guidelines and precautions might be helpful for further consideration:

1. The counselor needs to evaluate whose needs would be met through the physical contact, his or her own needs, or those of the counselee. Cautious self-examination will reveal any unconscious needs of the counselor that might be partially fulfilled through physical touch in the counseling session. In such cases, physical contact should definitely be avoided as it would cause injurious results for the counselee.

2. A careful evaluation of the psychological condition of the counselee should also precede any physical contact. How emotionally stable is the counselee? What are his or her emotional feelings toward the counselor? What are the issues that he or she is working on? How is the counselee likely to react to the contact? What is the counselee's history like when it comes to physical contact?

3. Closely related to the evaluation of the counselee is a careful evaluation of the nature of the current counseling process. In which stage of counseling is the person working? Are there unresolved transference issues? What is the level of trust that the counselee has in the counselor? How is physical contact likely to impact the ongoing counseling process?

4. The counselor needs to know that he or she is not being manipulated or seduced by the counselee into making the contact. Very often the counselee desires contact with the counselor and tries to set things up so that it will occur. Sexual seductions bring a tragic end to counseling as well as often wreak havok in the lives of those who are near to both parties. And there are other than sexual manipulations and seductions that can trip up relatively unaware counselors. Counselees who need to feel in control and those who are aggressive will sometimes try to manipulate counselors into making physical contact that relates with the counselee's unresolved internal conflict or need.

5. The counselor must be confident that he or she is not being sexually or romantically seductive with the counselee.

6. The possibility of manipulating or emotionally hurting the counselee through passive-aggressive ploys that involve physical touch needs to be examined.

7. Is the physical contact expressive of a need that the counselor might have to exercise control over the counselee?

Common types of physical contact. Hugs, touches, pats on the back and handshakes are common expressions of encouragement, acceptance and liking. These contacts usually occur at the close of the session. Similar contact at the beginning of the appointment usually suggests that the counselor is happy to see the counselee and is looking forward to the session. During the session many counselors will feel freedom to stroke, gently rest a hand on the leg or back of a deeply distaught counselee, or hold and even rock a counselee who is hurting.

J. David Stone and Larry Keefauver advocate closing a peer counseling session with some kind of physical touch. They differentiate five levels of touch: a slap on the back; a handshake; a slight hug; a "bear" hug; and a hug and a kiss.[15] Their approach assumes that counselor and counselee have a friendship that pre-exists their counseling relationship. They suggest that the parting physical contact should be the same level of touch that is customarily shared between them.

Watch for Transference and Countertransference

The complex dynamics of transference and countertransference have been the cause of more counseling failures than any other source. Unhappily, these two common and vital counseling issues characteristically receive little direct attention during graduate psychotherapy training. Effective handling of these issues can enhance counseling gains immensely.

Transference. Transference occurs when the counselee identifies the counselor as being similar to an important person in his or her past such as a parent, sibling or lover. Certain key aspects about the past important figure are projected onto the counselor's person and the counselee develops emotional reactions toward the counselor that are reminiscent of the feelings that he or she held for the earlier individual. The feelings that are attached to the counselee can be positive, negative, or most commonly, ambivalent. Positive transferences include feelings of love, admiration, affection and dependence toward the counselor. Negative transferences express hostile, mistrusting, fearful and envious feelings toward the counselor. Ambivalent transferences include both positive and negative feelings. The important person from the counselee's past is typically someone who was centrally related to an internal, emotional conflict which has not been resolved.[16] The unresolved nature of the emotions make them available for projection onto a current object (the counselor). A counselee might repond to the counselor as if he or she were the counselee's nurturing mother or domineering older sister. Another counselee might respond to the counselor in the same way that he or she felt toward a past unfaithful spouse, cruel father or an accepting grandparent. An example of ambivalent transference is when the counselee perceives the counselor as a person who protects and cares, but who punishes by selfishly withholding affection.[17]

But the counselee does not form these transferences in a vacuum. Effective counseling is a very intimate process, during which the counselee is exposed to the counselor's behavior, communication style, gestures, sense of humor, expressions of interest, caring, support and confrontational style. James Strachey believed that the personal characteristics of psychoanalysts are important factors in the patient's formulation of transference. He brought attention to the unconscious interaction between analyst and patient.[18]

Robert Langs has distinguished between two different kinds of transference. In classical transference, the primary dynamic is the patient's displacement from past important figures onto the therapist. In interactional transference, the primary dynamics relate to what is actually occurring in the analyst-patient relationship. The patient projects certain characteristics and emotional reactions onto the analyst and infers and personalizes certain reactions from the analyst. The reality of what is happening in the present shapes much of the content of the interactional transference material.[19]

The conceptualization and therapeutic use of transference has been most highly developed within the psychoanalytic framework. The analyst's behavior is specifically geared to facilitate the development of a strong transference reaction. This tranference helps the patient bring into consciousness feelings that were previously deeply conflicted and repressed.[20] The therapist is able then to analyze the transference and interpret it to the patient. The final stages of analysis are reached when the patient gains insight, resolves the transference relationship and is able to reestablish a normal doctor-patient relationship.

Counseling uses and treats transference in quite a different manner than does classical psychoanalysis. The counselor does not actively try to foster the development of a full transference.[21] However, when it does develop, it must be diagnosed and adequately responded to in order to facilitate healthy growth during counseling. Positive transference is often helpful in lowering the counselee's resistance. Counselors tend to deal with the counselee's positive and negative transference in much the same way that they do any other positive and negative attitudes and feelings. They are often interpreted and if they are problematic, steps toward resolving them are taken. The counselee gains insight into the origins of the feelings and is helped to reality test their appropriateness and healthfulness in the present situation. If behavioral or attitudinal adjustments are needed, the counselor helps the counselee to make those adjustments.

Countertransference. Counselors need to be very conscious and accepting of their humanness. Though they seek a rather objective, nonjudgmental stance in the counseling relationship, they cannot, nor should they, completely divorce themselves from the reality of their own emotions, attitudes, biases, prejudices, and patterns of perceiving and thinking that formulate much of their individuality. It is the counselor's own humanness that gives birth to countertransference dynamics.

In its broadest sense, countertransference has been used to describe all of the reactions that a therapist has to his or her patient. But this definition has been found to be too broad and generalized to be useful or meaningful.[22] The term has become more specified to refer to: positive and negative feelings toward a patient at a personal level because of perceived similarities between the patient and another significant person in the therapist's life; and the displacement of feelings and projection of unconscious unfulfilled needs and unresolved conflicts onto the patient.

Countertransference is destructive to therapy because it distorts the therapist's perception of the patient, makes a personal intrusion into the life and feelings of the patient, and can further exacerbate the same problems that brought the patient into treatment.

Positive countertransference includes strong liking, affectionate, sexual and protective feelings. Negative countertransference involves strong disliking, critical and judgmental feelings. The countertransference sometimes surfaces when the counselor tries to develop a relationship with the counselee that is inappropriate for the role of counselor and is based on the counselor's self-gratification. In other cases it is the impetus behind a treatment program that is not well-suited to the needs of the counselee.[23] Counselors' normal feelings of liking, warmth and anger are not considered to be countertransference unless they become extreme or intrusive in the counseling process.

What is true for the counselee is also true for the counselor. The countertransference is often formulated at least partially in response to the counselee's transference. The primary source of the countertransference can be either the counselor's own intrapsychic state, or the counselee's relational dynamics. There also exists a difference in the degree to which the counselor is conscious of his or her countertransference reaction. Robert Marshall defines and diagrams the countertransference issue:[24]

Types of Countertransference

	UNCONSCIOUS	CONSCIOUS
Therapist Induced	I	II
Patient Induced	III	IV

Illustration 32

This two-dimensional model yields four different types of countertransference. Type I countertransference is unconscious and is therapist induced. This is the classical countertransference, the type that is most sabotaging to the therapy process and most destructive to the counselee. It emanates from the counselor's internal psychic conflict and unconsciously distorts his or her perception of the counselee. Robert Marshall specifies that this type is usually resolved only by the counselor's own personal therapy, or by therapeutically oriented supervision.

Type II countertransference is also therapist induced but he or she is conscious of what is happening. The counselor is aware of the problem and is having difficulty correcting it. Close supervision will usually help to bring resolution.

Type III countertransference is patient induced and is unconscious. It is often stimulated by patient or counselee transference and because of its unconscious nature, it can seriously impede therapeutic progress. In time, an alert and insightful therapist will realize what is happening and regain control of the therapy process. Often this type of countertransference resolves into type IV countertransference. Supervision and discussion with colleagues is often helpful.

Type IV countertransference is patient induced and is conscious. The therapist is well aware of what is happening. His or her task is to maintain that clarity while helping the patient to resolve the transference or whatever other dynamics that are operative which induced the countertransference. Marshall suggests that this type of countertransference is not only unavoidable, but even necessary for successful therapy.

Disrupting the counseling process. Let's look at some clues that can alert us to the probability that countertransference is disrupting the counseling process with a teenager. These indicators are adapted from Marshall's chapter:[25]

1. Quickly yielding or giving in to the counselee's requests.

2. Gratifying the teenager with food, gifts, extra time or other "treats."

3. The occurrence of any strong feeling (e.g., anger, sexual attraction, envy, admiration), especially if guilt or anxiety feelings accompany the emotional experience.

4. Losing focus, feeling bored, daydreaming, or feeling sleepy or tired when the adolescent repetitiously focuses on certain topics.

5. Impulsive talk or action.

6. Physical contact that does not follow the precautions discussed previously.

7. Allowing parents to interrupt during the teenager's allotted time.

8. Consultation with parents, teachers, pastor or other person without the agreement or involvement of the teenager.

9. Strong unresolved feelings toward the teenager's parents.

10. Resistance or inability to effectively involve the adolescent's parents in the counseling process.

11. Preoccupation with the task of altering the teenager's behavior, especially when such changes are strongly desired by parent, teacher or pastor.

When a counselor becomes aware of countertransference, it is best to not disclose such to the counselee. Even when it is counselee induced, the feeling reactions belong to the counselor. It is his or her task to resolve them. Help should usually be requested from a supervisor or colleague, not from the counselee. Only in certain situations, when it would be predictably helpful to the counselee, should it be shared.

Even though much of the language in this section has referred to analysts, psychotherapists and patients, the same dynamics apply to counselors and counselees as well. Counselees of marriage and family therapists, clinical social workers, pastors and lay counselors often develop strong transference reactions to their counselors. And these therapists and counselors are often more susceptible to countertransference than psychiatrists and psychologists. Most psychiatrists and psychologists have received more training about these dynamics and have learned more about their own specific vulnerabilities through the personal psychotherapy that is required of most of them.

Some form of supervision or regular case consultation should be required of all therapists, pastors and lay people who are involved in providing counseling services to hurting people. Such experiences not only help us to continually update and sharpen our skills, they also help to protect us and our counselees from the potentially disastrous results of transference and countertransference.

An Overview of Psychotropic Medications

Psychotropic medications include all prescribed drugs that are designed to have specific effects on psychic functioning. Some are geared to change the person's affect or feelings. Some are used to help people who experience difficulty with their cognition or thinking. Still others reduce felt anxiety and help people with behavioral problems like sleeping, eating and impulse control difficulties.

Common attitudes. Many people, including a large percentage of Christians, have a strong bias against using drugs to help control and resolve problems with affect, thought and behavioral functioning. For some, their bias is based on their beliefs about physical health and nutrition. They believe that ingesting these chemical substances is likely to cause further mental or physiological complications because of their side effects, possible toxicity, negative physiological reactions, and possible addiction or dependency.

Others disagree with psychotropic drug therapy because they see "taking a pill" as an irresponsible way to deal with problems. "Problems need to be faced head on. The persons need to do something about it themselves. They shouldn't just let some pill do the work for them. They need to accept responsibility for their own feelings and actions and make whatever changes are necessary."

Christians very often ascribe to this latter viewpoint. In addition, they also mix into their argument some pretty powerful spiritual rationale. "Peace I (Christ) leave with you; my peace I give to you; not as the world gives do I give to you. Let not your hearts be troubled, neither let them be afraid" (John 14:27). Christ is also quoted as saying, "Hitherto you have asked nothing in my name; ask, and you will receive, that your joy may be full. I have said this to you, that in me you may have peace. In the world you have tribulation; but be of good cheer. I have overcome the world" (John 16:24, 33). And then we have Paul's absolutely astonishing personal testimony. "Not that I complain of want; for I have learned, in whatever state I am, to be content. I know how to be abased, and I know how to abound; in any and all circumstances I have learned the secret of facing plenty and hunger, abundance and want. I can do all things in him who strengthens me" (Philippians 4:11-13).

The well-meaning Christian will often draw from scriptures such as these the conclusion that people ought to rely upon Christ, not upon drugs. Taking psychotropic medication according to this view, is tantamount to testifying of a lack of faith in God's healing power.

One more often-voiced argument is that, "doctors just prescribe pills because they don't know what else to do." Some argue that psychiatrists get rich from keeping their patients "too doped up" to get any better. Some professional counselors, therapists and psychologists agree that certain psychiatrists rely too soon and too heavily upon medication, stating that they underestimate the value of psychotherapy and counseling.

A closer look at opinions and arguments against medication. Let's take another look at each of these arguments against the use of psychotropic medication, this time exposing ourselves to the respective counterargument.

1. "Taking drugs ingests alien chemicals into the body which create negative side effects, potential toxic reactions and addiction."

Certainly, no drug should be considered lightly. No medication should be taken without some degree of reasonable assurance that the anticipated benefits of the drug far outweigh the possible negative effects. Drugs should also be taken only if the symptoms are severe enough to cause the individual significant distress or behavioral dysfunctioning. Perhaps some reliance on the Food and Drug Administration's efforts to safeguard the American public from high-risk drugs is also warranted. A certain degree of trust in the physician who is prescribing the drugs is also required. The doctor should understand the drug, its side effects, its appropriate dosage, its effect when mixed with other drugs, and over what period of time the patient can safely take it. The physician should have thorough knowledge of the patient, current symptoms, history of the presenting problem, what has been done about the problem, medical history, family history, and the patient's feelings and attitudes about drugs.

And one more thing. We are ultimately responsible for what we ingest into our systems. Doctors can say what medications a patient should take, but the patient needs to accept personal responsibility for making a definitive decision about what he or she will actually do. "Okay, I'll take the medication" is one response. Others are: "Let me think about it for awhile." "I'd like to get a second medical opinion."

"No, I'd rather handle the situation without medication."

2. "Taking pills is an irresponsible way to deal with problems."

People who adopt this rationale are usually speaking from quite limited knowledge about what psychotropic medications really do, what they do not do and exactly why they are prescribed. The protest is valid if an individual is taking medication in the anticipation that it will "cure" all of his or her problems. But drugs are often a valuable adjunct to psychotherapy and counseling. Tranquilizers can take enough of the "edge" off a person's anxiety so that he or she can at least function at home and at work while working in therapy to resolve the source of the problem. Antidepressants can relieve some of the depression so that the person is less suicidal and more able to take care of himself or herself while working through the causes of his or her depression. Some depressions seem to be totally the result of biochemical imbalances that must be treated psychopharmacologically.

Pills do not give a person growth or maturity, but they may help the individual to be able to work more effectively toward those goals.

Many people, particularly Christians, respond to physically manifested dysfunction in a very different way than the manner in which they respond to psychologically or emotionally manifested dysfunction. For instance, do any of us really "blame" the severely crippled arthritic patient for his or her condition? We might understand that certain healthy practices, habits, or nutrition were missing and might have made the patient a more likely candidate for the illness. But isn't our reaction an overwhelmingly caring, accepting, and empathic one that seeks to bring encouragement and relief? Is any ill thought about such an ailing one who would take prescribed anti-inflammatory preparations or pain pills sometimes in order to lessen his or her suffering?

How differently we respond to people who are equally as crippled through severely restricted psychological freedom. An enthusiastic "Yes," to the arthritic taking anti-inflammatory drugs. A much more reluctant "If you must," to the depressed person taking antidepressants. An understanding "Certainly," to the arthritic taking pain medication. A head-shaking judgment "It's a cop-out," to the anxiety-ridden obsessive-compulsive for taking a tranquilizer.

God is certainly capable of healing injuries and illnesses of both physical and psychological types. Does medical assistance in either case really limit our belief in his power? Does the use of pharmacological intervention in our pain (physical or psychological) really limit our concept of his love and magnitude? Perhaps our use of such help in a responsible manner as a part of a comprehensive treatment program reflects the wisdom that God has created within us to develop.

3. "Psychiatrists are getting rich by keeping patients too drugged, partly because they do not know what else to do."

Such accusations are usually made as the result of a personal bias rather than coming from a reservoir of adequate knowledge about psychological dysfunction and psychopharmacology. The question, "Is this the best treatment program?" should be honestly and openly offered, with the intent to gain from the answer. It should not be merely a rhetorical challenge that is intended to bolster our own position.

When you have questions about medications, consult the *Physicians' Desk Reference*, your physician, or the physician who is medicating your counselee.[26]

The Ethics of Counseling

The counseling process plunges us deeply into the intricacies of human functioning and interpersonal relationships. The counselor often finds himself or herself in the midst of highly pressurized forces. These forces and pressures demand much from the counselor's system of values and ethics. Many difficult decisions have to be made. Choices between conflicting values continuously challenge the counselor's good judgment during the counseling process. Examples of the most commonly encountered values conflicts will be presented later in this section.

But first, what are we speaking of when we talk about ethics in counseling? One writer defines ethics as "the standards of what is right and wrong." He relates ethical conduct to "what the counselor (morally, philosophically and otherwise) personally expects or limits himself or herself to in his or her work with clients."[27]

Values play an integral part in any system of ethics. Ethical codes, both personal and organizational, are built upon value systems. Ethics cannot be established according to logic and rationality alone, though they certainly must be logical and make rational sense. This rational ethical system must be built upon and find its genesis in a well-articulated and thoroughly developed value system.

Ethical codes have been designed and adopted by several national professional organizations. Of particular significance are the ethical standards that have been adopted by the American Psychological Association and by the American Personnel and Guidance Association.

Purposes for ethical codes. John McGowan and Lyle Schmidt cited several important purposes for ethical codes.[28] They are summarized and adapted here for our benefit:

1. To provide standard behavioral guidelines to help each member of the profession to determine his or her conduct in difficult value-conflict work situations.

2. To help clarify the counselor's responsibilities to the counselee and to help protect the counselee from the counselor's violation of, or failure to fulfill those responsibilities.

3. To reassure other members of the profession that the conduct of each member will not be detrimental to their reputation, functions and purposes.

4. To give society some guarantee that the counselor's services will demonstrate adequate regard for the social codes and moral expectations of the community.

5. To provide the individual counselor a basis for safeguarding his or her own privacy, integrity and identity as counselor.

Professional counselors should become very familiar with the ethical standards that have been adopted by the professional organizations and associations in which they have membership. Lay counselors would also benefit from an awareness of these codes. They not only establish boundaries for responsible counseling behavior, but also stimulate valuable introspection on the part of the individual counselor into his or her own value system.

Gilbert Wrenn presented a very early version or precursor to today's various ethical standards. Part of his "personal creed for counselors" reads:

"I will respect the integrity of each individual with whom I deal. I will accord to him or her the same right to self-determination that I want for myself. I will respect as something sacred the personality rights of each person and will not attempt to manipulate him or her or meddle in his or her life.

"I will define my personal and ethical responsibility to my client as well as my legal and vocational responsibility to my organization and to society. I work for both the group to which I am responsible and for each individual that I serve as a client. This dual responsibility must be defined and understood by my employers and by myself."[29]

Christian counselors draw much of their value base from scripture. A thorough understanding of the Bible paired with an adequate knowledge of professional ethical standards well equips the professional or lay counselor.

Basic ethical principles. Now let's look at some basic ethical principles that are commonly adapted by counselors:[30]

1. The counselor's primary responsibility is to the counselee. The counselor must respect the counselee's integrity and guard his or her welfare throughout the counseling relationship.

2. All information which the counselee divulges during counseling sessions is to be held in strict confidence. The counselor must obtain the counselee's permission (preferably written) before communicating any of this information to a physician, social agency, school, employer, family or anyone else. There are three situations where the confidentiality rule is excepted: when there is clear and imminent danger to the counselee (suicide); when there is clear and imminent danger to another (homicide); and when there is any report of child abuse.

3. Examples taken from counseling interviews for use in books, articles or teaching should obscure the names and identities of the counselees very carefully.

4. Any audio or video recording of counseling sessions must be done with the counselee's prior written consent.

5. Counselor's notes and records should be kept in a safely locked file.

Alexander Schneiders suggests that confidentiality is more a matter of degree rather than absolute. He gives us seven general principles for evaluating each given situation with respect to the issue of confidentiality: "The obligation of confidentiality is relative rather than absolute since there are conditions which can alter it. Confidentiality depends on the nature of the material so that material which is already public or can easily become so is not bound by confidentiality in the same way as is the entrusted secret. Material that is harmless does not bind the counselor to confidentiality and the material that is necessary for a counselor or an agency to function effectively is often released from the bonds of confidentiality. Confidentiality is always conditioned by the intrinsic right of the counselee to his or her integrity and reputation, to the secret and to resist aggression. Such rights can be protected by the counselor even against the law. Confidentiality is limited by the rights of the counselor to preserve his or her own reputation and integrity, to resist harm or aggression and to preserve privileged communication. Confidentiality is determined and limited by the rights of an innocent third party and by the rights of the community."[31]

6. When the counselor's role is different from that of therapist and requires divulging interview material, the counselee must be made

aware of the counselor's intent and role function.

7. Psychological information, such as results of personality inventories or diagnostic evaluations should be revealed to the counselee at a time and in a manner that facilitates the counselee's acceptance of the information. This kind of feedback can be very threatening to receive and can have a powerful impact on self-concept and self-esteem. Therefore, the giving of such information must be integrated sensitively with the rest of the counseling process.

8. Counselors should be involved in an ongoing program of updating their knowledge and improving their skills. There is no excuse for a counselor not knowing vital skills and information that is central to helping people who are hurting.

9. When the counselee evidences symptoms or problems that are beyond the counselor's sphere of competence, a referral to the appropriate professional must be made. This issue will be examined more closely in the next section of this chapter.

10. Counselors carry the responsibility to be aware of the inadequacies and areas of weakness within their own personalities and interpersonal relationship patterns. Such awareness will help them to prevent a biased perception of the counselee and help limit the chances of distorting the relationship with the counselee. Counselors should not work with counselees that would place too much demand on their own personality structures.

11. When a counselee refuses a referral and wants to continue working with the counselor, the latter must evaluate the immediacy of the need for the referral. The nature of the refusal should also be understood. Is it manipulative or motivated by dependency? When need for referral is based on imminent danger, the counselor might refuse to see the counselee who does not accept the referral.

12. Counseling procedures like dynamic intervention, interpretation, encouraging, self-disclosure and administering psychological instruments are very powerful procedures. They should be utilized only in a professional setting or in serious counseling relationships.

13. Counselors should participate in regular supervision that affords them the opportunity for case consultation and improvement of counseling skills. Group supervision, regular meetings with a peer-level counselor, or formal supervision with a superior constitute valid supervision experiences.

14. Counselors should not talk about other therapists or counselors disparagingly. Such remarks are particularly inappropriate and often

damaging when made in the presence of a counselee who has previously sought help from the other therapist. These kinds of statements usually reflect competitive and insecure feelings within the counselor,
and ignorance about the negative impact that they can have on the
counselee.

15. Counselors should be very cautious about physical contact with
counselees. Anything beyond a cordial handshake can be potentially
destructive to the counselee and to the counseling process. The counselor must know that any such contact is not purposed to meet his or
her own needs, but the needs of the counselee. Thorough understanding of the counselee is also required in order to correctly anticipate how
the touch or hug will be received.

16. Though effective counseling can occur in many different loca-
tions, it should be professionally appropriate, affording convenience,
privacy, security, and comfortableness to both the counselor and the
counselee.

One must ask, "Why all of this emphasis on ethics in counseling?
Aren't most ethical choices simply common sense decisions anyway?"
Many of the situations that counselors find themselves facing are anything but ethically simplistic. There are characteristics in the external
environment as well as in the counselor's intrapsychic world that create
many an ethical dilemma.

Milton Schwebel differentiated between unethical behavior and unethical practice. He defines unethical practice as acts that do not fit
within ethical standards, but not necessarily imply anything unethical
about the counselor's motivation, intent or values. Unethical behavior
suggests that unethical motives, intent and values underly the unethical
practice. Schwebel suggests three causes for unethical behavior: self-
interest in the form of profit, self-enhancement, security, status and
other motives; unsound judgment due to inadequate training and/or inadequate supervision; ignorance of technical information and ignorance
of the counselor's values.[32]

Decision-making situations. Now let's expose ourselves to some of the
potentially uncomfortable decision-making situations that arise during
counseling. These kinds of situations press us back into our own value
systems for our response. Each counselor must arrive at what is the
"right" action for himself or herself. Harley Christiansen provides some
practical situations. [33] What would you do in each of these instances?

1. The youth pastor has, through his counseling experiences,
learned that several of his counselees in the church youth group are us-

ing drugs. The senior pastor wants to know any such names. Should the youth pastor divulge these names or hold them back?

2. A lay counselor discovers that her teenage counselee is planning to run away. Should she alert the parents or keep quiet?

3. A psychologist is told of plans to commit malicious mischief and burglary. Should he notify the authorities or maintain confidentiality?

4. A local church or school was recently vandalized and robbed. A counselor discovers who was involved. Should he report it, or work only with the counselee?

5. A senior pastor is told during a counseling session about a child abuse incident. What should he do?

6. The youth pastor has had four counseling sessions with a teenager in the youth group. The child's father calls and asks the youth pastor about what is surfacing in the sessions. What and how much should be shared with the father?

7. A counselor has been helping a high school senior with the decision to go or not to go to college. The parents have asked the counselor to influence their child to decide to go to college. How should the counselor respond?

8. A pastor referred a parishioner to a professional therapist and now after several sessions has called the therapist to ask about the counseling progress so he can be of better help. How should the therapist respond?

9. A counselee expresses, during a session, her desire to commit suicide.

10. At a party, people ask a counselor to show them how she gets people to open up and tell her about themselves. How should she respond?

11. A counselor has been working with a teenager for four months. The youth was just caught for auto theft and joy riding. To what degree is the counselor responsible?

12. A female counselee shares with her pastor that a man has threatened to beat her up. She has insisted that he tell no one, for fear of stirring up more problems. What should he do?

13. The police and probation department are asking the church youth sponsor about a teenager whom he has been counseling. Can he divulge any information without breaking the counselee's confidence?

14. The pastor sees indications of serious psychological problems in his adolescent counselee. He wants to refer the youth to a local Christian psychologist but the parents refuse. What is the pastor's role?

15. A professional therapist is approached by a social friend. "I've been having some personal problems for quite some time. Can I set up a time to come in to see you?" How should the counselor respond?

The foregoing 15 situations provide just a sampling of the many difficult experiences that confront the counselors with ethical binds.

Gilbert Wrenn writes: "A counselor to be ethical has to do more than observe a code of ethics. He must be great within himself because he relates himself to God and the greatness of the Infinite. I propose that our profession is not in want of a respect for evidence and scientific truth, or in want for a drive to serve individuals and to advance human welfare. We are aware of our technical and knowledge limitations and have a great discontent with the imperfectness of much that we do. If this profession is in want of anything, it is in neglect of the proposition that man is spiritual as well as intellectual in nature—it is a failure to recognize that man has a relationship to the Infinite as well as to other men. The profession has established a code of ethics but its application calls for decisions that will require great personal courage and depth of conviction. It is at this point that the counselor may have to have recourse to the great values and principles of the human race in order to resolve the ethical conflict. The counselor may truly have to think more of others than himself. Counselors need to strengthen their moral courage as well as their understandings and skills, for it is the constellation of all these qualities that provides true professional competence."[34]

Making Referrals

Sometimes the best counseling process is to facilitate a referral of the counselee to a source of help that is especially well-suited to meet the specific needs of the case. Just because someone comes to a counselor for help does not imply that that counselor is the best source of care for the particular counselee. It is important that the counselor not feel competitive, chagrined or self-condemning when he or she recognizes the need to refer. People who are caring individuals and who gain a sense of personal satisfaction from being able to help others are susceptible to the "messiah complex." This malady inflicts us with the false and unrealistic expectation that we ought to be able to help everyone. That somehow our stature is lessened when we are unable to cure, solve or help someone with his or her problems. We must recognize that people vary so widely in their differences from each other. And human problems are just as intricate, complex and widely variant as are their owners. It is totally unreasonable to expect that any one person could effectively meet all of these varieties of needs. Christian counselors must learn what their role and function is within Christ's body. They then can fulfill that role to the extent that their development of their God-given gifts allows. Remember too that each counselor's personality, personal history and training is well-suited for effective work with some counselees and not so well-suited for others.

Indications for referral. Now let's turn our attention to the situations that suggest the efficacy of making a referral. Common indications for referral are presented here:

1. The most common reason for referral is that the counselee requires specialized help that the counselor is not trained to offer. The implication here is not that the counselee's need is too serious or dangerous for the counselor to continue. Rather, a different or additional specialization is required to meet a specific need for which the counselor is not prepared to treat. Examples would include: referral of a sexually molested teenager to the police for police intervention; referral of a counselee who is being sued to an attorney for legal assistance; referral of a counselee who appears to be in poor health to a medical doctor; referral of a family having serious problems to a marriage and family therapist; referral of a significantly depressed or anxious counselee to a psychiatrist for evaluation for possible medication maintenance; and referral to a pastor for clarification of a scriptural or theological issue.

2. Another common reason for referral is when the counselor believes that he or she is dealing with therapeutic issues that present immediate and/or serious risks that are beyond his or her training or expertise. Whenever counselors believe that their counselee's well-being or safety is at risk, that they are unable to adequately address the problem, and that a more fully trained or better qualified person could fulfill the need, then the decision to refer should be made. Some examples are: referral to a psychiatrist of an adolescent counselee who has stated a desire to commit suicide; referral to a psychiatrist, psychologist, or other professional therapist of a severely depressed or anxious counselee; and referral to a psychiatrist, psychologist or other professional therapist who specializes in therapy with adolescents, of a teenager who evidences serious acting-out behavioral problems.

3. Sometimes counselees want to be treated by a specific technique or therapeutic orientation. They may have heard about a certain behavior modification technique or they might have a friend who was helped by a Gestalt therapist. People often want for themselves what

has worked for others whom they know. Here are some examples: referral to a behavioral modification specialist the counselee who has heard about it and is confident that it will help him with his shyness; and referral to a qualified hypnotherapist the client who is strongly interested in that form of therapy for her phobic reactions.

4. Though the phrase "personality conflict" is so amorphous that no one really knows what it means, sometimes a counselor and counselee have such negative reactions to each other that a referral is appropriate. Sometimes a counselee's negativity toward the counselor is evidence of a strong transference reaction. When that is the case, effective counseling can often result. At other times, though, the two people just do not get along well. Here are some instances where referral is appropriate: the counselor and counselee feel strongly competitive with each other; there develops a strong dislike between counselor and counselee; and there exists interfering racial, cultural, sexual or lifestyle prejudices between the two.

5. There sometimes occurs an inappropriate fit between counselor and counselee that interferes with the therapy or counseling process. In such instances, it is not because of the specific personalities involved. The problem arises from certain identifying characteristics about them or external issues. Here are some examples: referral to a female counselor of a male counselee who needs to resolve a long-standing conflict with his mother that impedes the development of healthy relationships with women; referral of a counselee who knows the counselor socially and desires more anonymity; and referral to a younger therapist of an adolescent counselee who has some difficulty relating with an older counselor.

6. Some referrals need to be made in order to make the counseling contacts more logistically accessible. Examples are: referral to a counselor whose office is closer to the counselee's residence, school or place of work; and referral to a counselor whose schedule permits adequate timing and frequency of appointments.

7. Referrals are also necessitated when either the counselor or counselee moves out-of-town and continuing counseling is indicated.

Professional therapists and their selection. A common hurdle that lay counselors, youth pastors and pastors face when they see the need to refer someone to a professional therapist is that of finding one. "Who should I refer to?" "What kind of therapist would be best?" "What's the difference between a psychologist and a psychiatrist?" "Do non-Christian therapists try to ruin your faith?" These and other questions will be answered in this section.

There are several kinds of professional therapists that are well qualified to provide excellent counseling and psychotherapeutic services. Psychiatrists are medical doctors who, following the attainment of the M.D. degree, complete a psychiatric residency in mental hospitals and psychiatric wards in general hospitals. Psychiatrists, in addition to doing psychotherapy, prescribe medication, admit patients and supervise them while in hospitals, and can prescribe electro shock and insulin shock therapy. They work in private practice settings as well as in psychiatric clinics and hospitals.

Clinical psychologists usually have a Ph.D. degree in psychology. They are well trained in doing psychotherapy and have specialized skills in psychological testing and psychodiagnostic evaluation. They work in private practice settings, mental health facilities and psychiatric hospitals. Some psychiatrists and clinical psychologists take specialized training in psychoanalytic theory and practice in order to become psychoanalysts.

Marriage and family therapists have received either a masters or doctoral level graduate training. They do counseling and therapy that is particularly focused upon marriage and family dynamics. Their work settings are usually private practice offices, mental health clinics, and less frequently, psychiatric hospitals.

Clinical social workers have earned a master's degree in social work and have been trained in doing psychotherapy as well. They, like marriage and family therapists, also work with individuals, couples and entire families.

The academic background and training that a clinician has received is one thing to look for when selecting a therapist for referral purposes. But there are fine counselors and therapists in each of the professional disciplines outlined above. Another criterion for selection might be their theoretical orientation. The referring pastor or counselor might wish to refer a particular counselee to a therapist of a certain orientation. Psychiatrists, psychologists, marriage and family therapists, and clinical social workers are all represented in the psychodynamic, existential/experiential, cognitive and learning/behavioral orientations. These different theoretical orientations have been discussed in a previous chapter.

Another factor that Christians often consider is whether the therapist is a Christian. A discussion of this issue requires that we ask two questions: "Is the therapist a skilled and effective clinician?" and "Is the ther-

apist a Christian?" Applying these questions to each in a group of therapists would probably yield a selection of four types. They are listed here in a descending order of desirability:
1. Good therapists who are Christians.
2. Good therapists who are not Christians.
3. Ineffective therapists who are Christians.
4. Ineffective therapists who are not Christians.

There is probably little if any dispute over the first and fourth classifications. But what about the allotted positions two and three? Why in that order? Isn't it more important that the clinician be a Christian than skilled? After all, don't most non-Christian therapists try to disrupt a Christian counselee's faith? Unfortunately, there are some therapists who use their counseling relationships as a battleground for their own internal conflicts regarding religion, especially Christianity. But there are some other therapists who unethically act-out their sexual, racial and other hang-ups onto their counselees, too.

Good therapists, effective clinicians, do not let their own religious, sexual, racial, political, or other biases and prejudices negatively impact their therapeutic relationships. Good non-Christian therapists are eager to help their Christian counselees relate to God and use their faith in healthy ways. The major drawback is in the secular therapist's lack of intimate understanding of how faith and interaction with the Holy Spirit really works. Therein lies his or her major limitation.

We are correctly reminded. "Be sober, be watchful. Your adversary the devil prowls around like a roaring lion, seeking someone to devour" (1 Peter 5:8). But we must not allow our caution to lead us into paranoia. When this happens, the roaring lion has quite cleverly won another victory.

But where can I find the names of therapists to whom I might possibly refer? Most communities have several available sources for locating qualified therapists. People tend to have the greatest confidence in therapists who are personally highly recommended to them. Their pastor, medical doctor and friends are all possible sources for such recommendations. When no personal recommendation surfaces, there are usually several agencies that can be contacted for referral services. State and county mental health centers and local professional associations for therapists often make good referral agents. Certain national organizations like the American Psychiatric Association, American Psychological Association and the American Association of Marriage and Family Therapists are willing to supply lists of their membership in the person's general locality. One last general source of names is the yellow pages to the phone directory. Look up psychiatrists (under physicians), psychologists, and marriage and family therapists.

If a Christian therapist is specifically desired, local pastors and Christian physicians are often excellent sources for names. Local seminaries, Christian colleges and private Christian schools also are able to provide referrals. Many communities have Christian business and professional directories that list only therapists who profess to be Christians. Referrals to Christian therapists may also be obtained from the Narramore Christian Foundation in Pasadena, California; Fuller Theological Seminary and Graduate School of Psychology in Pasadena, California; the Christian Association for Psychological Studies and the Christian Medical Society.

The referral process. Now let's turn our attention to the actual process of facilitating the referral. The counselor has decided that a counselee needs the services of a professional therapist. The names of two or three eligible therapists have been located. Now what? Let's go through the referral process, step by step:

1. The counselor should be familiar with the referrals. Knowledge of their location, directions for getting there, procedures for scheduling appointments, financial policies, length of interview sessions, and something about their therapeutic procedure should be known by the referring counselor.

2. The counselor needs to discuss the possibility of referral with the counselee. The nature of this discussion is important because the way that it is handled will have significant bearing on the outcome of the attempt to refer.[35] Discussions that are handled in a candid and caring manner tend to produce the best results. "Wanda, I think that we've reached a point in our counseling where you might gain a lot from talking with a professionally trained counselor, someone who does this sort of thing for a living who can bring a lot more expertise to these difficult areas with which you're working. What do you think?" Whenever possible, the interaction should be relaxed and easy, not urgently approached as if in a grave emergency. The counselor best discusses these issues in a reassuring manner, born from a respect and confidence in the counselee's ability to continue to grow and to develop increasing personal strength.

Though referrals are best made to sources of help in which the counselor has confidence, the counselee should not be led to expect miracles or any specific therapeutic procedure. "The kind of referral most desirable from the counselor's point of view is one that does not commit him or her in advance to any one particular plan of action."[36] The referring counselor should also focus on the counselee's need for the referral and not on why the counselor is not able to effectively provide those services.[37]

3. The next step requires a decision on the part of the counselee to accept or reject the referral. It is best when the counselee can fully decide and own the decision as his or her own. In some cases, referral is urgently needed, so the counselor confronts quite directly. "I'm very concerned about your deepening depression and suicidal thoughts. In situations like this, talking to a professional therapist seems to be a necessary step. Are you willing to trust me in this decision and go along with it?" A very different, more relaxed approach is best in situations where the counselee is not in an emergency. "The idea about talking some of these things out with a professional therapist might be an interesting one for you to consider. Think it over and then let's talk about it when we get together the next time."

When working with teenagers, it is almost always necessary to involve the parents in this decision.[38] It should usually be discussed first with the youth and then, with his or her knowledge and consent (if possible), it can be presented to the parents for their consideration.

4. Once the decision has been made to accept the referral, then the next step begins. The counselor facilitates the follow-through, helping the counselee to do what is necessary to establish a meaningful working relationship. The counselor's involvement here also depends in part upon the referral source's preferred procedures. The counselor's task is to provide support and facilitative assistance as needed by the counselee in order to insure the best possible transition. Placing an initial phone call to the referral source, finding the new office on a map together, and even accompanying the counselee to the first session or two can communicate reassurance and security to an unsure counselee.

5. In some instances it is not only appropriate, but very important for the referring counselor to maintain contact with the counselee. This decision should be made between the counselee, counselor and the referral source, prior to the time that the referral decision is finalized.

The counselee's response. When a counselee refuses to follow through with a referral, the counselor should gain a clear understanding of the reasons for the rejection. Was the counselor's timing off? Was the explanation not clear enough? Did the counselee feel rejected by the counselor? Is the counselee feeling excessively dependent on the counselor? Are there any external issues like finances or negative reactions from family or friends that sabotaged the referral? Is the counselee manipulating the counselor into maintaining the relationship?

As the counselor gains a clearer picture of the counselee's motives for rejecting the referral, he or she can reinitiate the referral process to the original source or a different one; continue the counseling relationship with the counselee; or the counselor may terminate the counseling.

Another issue relating to counselees' responses to the referral process, is how they select the therapist that they wish to see. Elizabeth Skoglund handles this issue with interesting insight. Too often counselees feel that they "should" or "have to" like and agree to work with the particular therapist to whom they were referred. This places them in an emotional bind that can be limiting and even damaging to their counseling progress and personal growth.[39] Counselees often feel that they have to go along with the referral in order to please their counselor and gain his or her favor. Here are some suggestions that might help the counselee maintain his or her own sense of self-respect, self-valuing and personal sense of responsibility for what they do:

1. Suggest the names of two or three possible referral sources to the counselee with the assurance that any selection within those choices would be fine. Encourage counselees to exercise their responsibility for their own lives by assisting self-reliance in their own decision-making process.

2. Encourage counselees to talk on the phone with the therapists before making the final decision. Help them formulate questions that will clarify their preference between their options. Following a brief description of their problems, the counselee might want to ask, "Do you work effectively with people like me who are having this sort of problem?" Other questions might provide further help in the counselee's selection process. "What is your basic approach to therapy?" "Can you describe your academic and professional experience background?" "How do you deal with spiritual issues in therapy?"

3. When the selection of a therapist is made, try to stay with that therapist, even if at first things do not seem to be working out very well. It takes time for the counseling relationship to develop. Too often, counselees terminate counseling prematurely. They run into their own resistance sometimes just before making big breakthroughs. How important it is to not terminate at those crucial points. Commit to stay with the therapy for at least 10 sessions in order to give it an adequate opportunity to work.

4. When counselees are feeling uncomfortable about something that is happening in the counseling process, they should express their discomfort or dissatisfaction to the therapist. Then both have the opportunity to seek understanding and resolution together.

5. Counselees also need the personal freedom to terminate a therapeutic process that is not working for them. Just because the therapist is somewhat of an authority figure does not mean that the counselee loses his or her right to decide whether or not to be there. If, after full discussion of the situation, resolution seems untenable, then termination might be the most appropriate solution. Neither counselee nor therapist should feel the burden of failure. They can gain understanding about why it did not work out better, part comfortably, and each move on in his or her own directions.

At this point counselees have three options: to seek a referral from the therapist; to seek another referral from the original counselor; or to take a break from counseling in order to gain some clarity for themselves before reinitiating another therapeutic relationship.

Notes

1. William A. Console, R. Simons, and M. Rubinstein, *The First Encounter* (New York: Jason Aronson, n. d.), p. 14.

2. Leona E. Tyler, *The Work of the Counselor* (New York: Appleton-Century-Crofts, 1969).

3. M. R. Harris, M. Kalis, and E. Freeman, "An Approach to Short-Term Psychotherapy," Mind 2 (1964):198-207.

4. Lewis R. Wolberg, *Handbook of Short-Term Psychotherapy* (New York: Thieme-Stratton, 1980).

5. Richard W. Wallen, *Clinical Psychology: The Study of Persons* (New York: McGraw-Hill, 1956).

6. Jergen Ruesch, *Therapeutic Communication* (New York: Norton, 1961).

7. Clyde M. Narramore, *The Psychology of Counseling* (Grand Rapids, Mich.: Zondervan, 1960).

8. Theodor Reik, *Listening With the Third Ear* (New York: Farrar, Straus and Cudaky, 1949).

9. O. Hobart Mowrer, "Some Constructive Features of the Concept of Sin," in *Counseling and Psychotherapy*, ed. Ben N. Ard Jr. (Palo Alto, Calif.: Science and Behavior Books, 1966), pp. 217-222.

10. Karl Menninger, *Whatever Became of Sin?* (New York: Hawthorn Books, 1973).

11. Rollo May, *The Art of Counseling* (Nashville: Abingdon, 1967), p. 131.

12. Cecil Osborne, *The Art of Understanding Yourself* (Grand Rapids, Mich.: Zondervan, 1967), p. 71.

13. Ibid.

14. May, *The Art of Counseling.*

15. J. David Stone and Larry Keefauver, *Friend to Friend: How You Can Help a Friend Through a Problem* (Loveland, Colo.: Group Books, 1983).

16. Philip G. Zimbardo and F. Ruch, *Psychology and Life*, 9th ed. (Glenview, Ill.: Scott, Foresman, 1975).

17. Ephraim Rosen et al., *Abnormal Psychology* (Philadelphia: W. B. Saunders, 1965).

18. J. Strachey, "The Nature of the Therapeutic Action of Psychoanalysis," International Journal of Psychoanalysis 15 (1934):127-159.

19. Robert Langs, *Technique in Transition* (New York: Jason Aronson, 1978).

20. Clifford T. Morgan and R. King, *Introduction to Psychology*, 5th ed. (New York: McGraw-Hill, 1975).

21. Bruce Shertzer and Shelly Stone, *Fundamentals of Counseling* (Boston: Houghton Mifflin, 1974).

22. A. Reich, "Further Remarks on Countertransference," International Journal of Psychoanalysis 41 (1960):389-395.

23. Lawrence Sank and M. Prout, "Critical Issues for the Fledgling Therapist," Professional Psychology (November 1978):638-645.

24. Robert J. Marshall, "Countertransference With Children and Adolescents," in *Countertransference*, eds. Lawrence Epstein and A. Feiner (New York: Jason Aronson, 1979), pp. 407-444.

25. Ibid.

26. *Physicians' Desk Reference*, 37th ed. (Oradell, N. J.: Medical Economics, 1983).

27. Lyle D. Schmidt, "Some Ethical, Professional and Legal Considerations for School Counselors," Personnel and Guidance Journal 44 (December 1965):377.

28. John F. McGowan and L. Schmidt, *Counseling: Readings in Theory and Practice* (New York: Holt, Rinehart and Winston, 1962).

29. C. Gilbert Wrenn, "Trends and Predictions in Vocational Guidance," Occupations (May 1947):503-515.

30. The following sources were used in compiling the information for this chart:
C. Gilbert Wrenn, "The Ethics of Counseling," in *Counseling and Psychotherapy.*
Allen E. Ivey and L. Simek-Downing, *Counseling and Psychotherapy: Skills, Theories and Practice* (Englewood Cliffs, N. J.: Prentice-Hall, 1980).
Shertzer and Stone, *Fundamentals of Counseling.*
Narramore, *The Psychology of Counseling.*

31. Alexander A. Schneiders, "The Limits of Confidentiality," Personnel and Guidance Journal 42 (November 1963):252-253.

32. Milton Schwebel, "Why Unethical Practice?" Journal of Counseling Psychology 2 (Summer 1955):122-128.

33. Harley D. Christiansen, *Ethics in Counseling: Problem Situations* (Tucson: The University of Arizona Press, 1972).

34. Wrenn, "The Ethics of Counseling," pp. 184-185.

35. Tyler, *The Work of the Counselor.*

36. Ibid., p. 54.

37. Shertzer and Stone, *Fundamentals of Counseling*, p. 331.

38. Ibid.

39. Elizabeth Skoglund, *Can I Talk to You?* (Glendale, Calif.: Regal Books, 1977).

■ CHAPTER 8

Special Counseling Situations

The three most commonly encountered special counseling situations that are faced by people who work with teenagers are: family counseling; group counseling; and crisis intervention counseling.

Each of these types of counseling presents very different logistic, theoretical and therapeutic problems that need to be addressed by the counselor. Some professional psychotherapists spend years gaining specialized expertise in only one of these three types of counseling. Our task is not to be so thorough. Rather, the goal of this chapter is to provide the reader with a very basic understanding of the relevant dynamics inherent in each situation, and to outline the beginnings of a working approach to these three counseling situations.

Family Counseling

When working with adolescents who are struggling with psychological, emotional or interpersonal problems, it becomes evident that there often exist related difficulties in the teenagers' homes. This relatedness between the family problems and the youths' difficulties is usually functional and often causative. A growing number of counselors are experiencing better success through working with the whole family than when working only with the person who is identified as having a problem.[1] And that is the essence of family counseling. Though there is a wide variety of styles, methodologies and theories, they all focus on the family as a functioning whole that operates according to some kind of a system.

Certain family systems are viewed as functional. These usually produce and retroactively are produced by healthily functioning people. Dysfunctional family systems, conversely, tend to produce dysfunctional behavior in their members. Family counselors seek positive changes within the system, anticipating that these alternatives will be conducive to healthier functioning on the part of each of its participants.

Nathan Ackerman is credited as an originator of family counseling. "None of us live our lives utterly alone. Those who try are doomed to a miserable existence. It can be said fairly that some aspects of life experience are more individual than social, and others more social than individual. Nevertheless, principally we live with others, and in early years almost exclusively with members of our own family."[2]

Four types of family therapies. J. C. Wynn identifies four different types of family therapies: problem-oriented therapists; psychodynamic therapists; intergenerational theorists; and behavioral therapists.[3] Problem-oriented therapists' primary focus is on helping people solve family relationship problems. A major focus in their work is on improving the family's communication process.

Virginia Satir writes about five modes of communication that occur during stress in family relationships. *Placating* is the act of passively going along with whatever is said or done while inside feeling resentful and hostile. *Blaming* is the process of accusing the other person of being at fault and showing who is in charge. *Being super reasonable* is a way of denying or being out of touch with one's emotionality. It is a way of denying the importance of the other person's feelings as well as one's own by rising to the heights of intellectualization in order to avoid real human contact. *Being irrelevant* amounts to a total denial of reality. This style is being out of touch not only with the self and the other person, but also with external reality. The fifth communication style, *being congruent*, is by far the healthiest. During congruent communication the individual is in touch with his or her own feelings, the other person's feelings and with the external reality.[4] A major emphasis in problem-oriented family therapy is to help the family members to interact with each other as consistently as possible in a congruent manner.

Family therapists who operate from the psychodynamic tradition bring strong applications from psychoanalytic theory to their family treatment, relying heavily upon insight-oriented methodology.

The intergenerational theorists place a great deal of emphasis on tracing family problems back through the mother and father to their respective families of origin. These therapists have the parents literally go back to their mothers and fathers to resolve unsettled conflicts.

Behavior therapists who treat families work with the family as a tremendously powerful reinforcing system that has great impact on its members' behavior. They use behavioral counseling methods within the structure of the family system.

Is family counseling the answer? How does a counselor know when switching from working with the adolescent individually to a family group approach is recommended? Some family therapists assert that family counseling is always superior to individual therapy. But that position seems to be a bit too extreme and rigid. Here are some indicators that suggest that family counseling might be the preferred mode:

1. The teenager requests a conjoint session with all or part of the family together.

2. The teenager's parents or siblings request a session with all or part of the family to meet together with the counselee.

3. A major problem that the adolescent is facing seems to be a relationship difficulty between the counselee and one or more other family members.

4. There is evidence that a family problem or dysfunctional system is either at the root of the teenager's problem or is exacerbating it.

5. When there appears to be a strong level of family love and support that could be effectively marshalled to undergird and encourage the teenager as he or she works toward accomplishing the counseling goals.

In each of these instances, if individual counseling has already begun with the teenager, his or her permission must first be obtained before scheduling a family session. It is very important to help the teenager express and resolve his or her apprehensions, suspicions, anger and other feelings about the conjoint session prior to the session itself.

There seem to be some situations in counseling that would contraindicate the employment of a family counseling approach.[5] These would include: situations when a central member of the family unit would not, because of schedule, distance, etc., be able to regularly participate in the sessions; those times during the counseling process when the focus is primarily on an individual rather than family issue; and the lack of availability of a counselor who is flexible and active enough as well as adequately trained to do effective family counseling.

Ackerman has suggested other guidelines that would suggest family counseling is not recommended. His indicators are summarized here:

1. A destructive, seemingly irreversible trend toward the fragmentation and breakup of the family has made the system totally unresponsive to helpful measures.

2. An exceedingly strong destructive motivation within the family group that is consistently predominant over all other motivations.

3. One parent who is consistently and comprehensively paranoid, unchangeably psychopathically destructive, or who continues in an active pattern of criminal or perverted behavior.

4. A central member (especially a parent) of the family who is consistently dishonest and deceitful.

5. The existence of an apparently valid family secret which prevents the occurrence of therapeutic disclosures.

6. The existence within one or more family members of a strong and rigidly defended cultural, religious or economic prejudice against this type of counseling intervention.

7. The existence in one or more family members of rigid or brittle psychological defenses which, if broken, might result in a psychotic reaction, a psychosomatic crisis or violent acting-out.

8. The presence of a disabling disease or handicapping injury that precludes one or more central family members from attending the counseling sessions.[6]

Dysfunctions. Assuming that none of the above referenced contraindications are present, let's look at some of the dysfunctions that the family counselor often treats. Dysfunctional families are often isolated from their sociocultural environment, confused regarding their generational boundaries, struggling with the "letting go" process, and often involve parents who are still anxious about their relationships with their own parents. Wynn categorizes the types of family problems that are often dealt with in family counseling. They are summarized here:

1. Problems incurred during the adjustment phase to the marriage relationship: including relationships with in-laws, lifestyle adjustment, infidelity, separation and divorce.

2. Difficulties that arise with the job of parenting: including the establishment of generational boundaries, developing self-discipline and discipline of children, improving communication, and other adjustments that must be made during each person's ongoing growth and change.

3. The varieties of problems that relate to the stages through which

families develop: such as adjusting to the caring for small children, dealing with children's adolescent process, coping with parents' middle-age crises, "letting go" of children growing into young adulthood, handling crises of family members who sometimes need radical personal changes, meeting the needs of aging parents and accepting the fact of aging in friends, spouse and self.

4. Adjustment problems relating to the addition of people into the family: through birth, adoption, people moving back home after having left, etc., and crises confronted with the loss of family members through death, hospitalization, imprisonment, joining the military, moving away to school, getting married and so on.

5. Particular crises or emergencies: such as violent acting-out, runaway, alcohol and other drug abuse, loss of job, economic reversal, physical injury or illness, emotional or mental breakdown.

6. Difficulties that relate to the issue of sexuality: such as struggles with sexual identification, sexual impulse control difficulties, incest, sexual immorality, problems with homosexuality and bisexuality and various sexual dysfunctions.[7]

When dysfunctional families encounter crisis situations, they are ill-prepared to resolve them and to grow from that process. Gerald Caplan has isolated four phases that unhealthy families go through during crisis: First, they try to resolve the crisis in the ways that have worked for them to at least some degree before. Second, tension within the family increases when their problem-solving attempts prove to be ineffective. Third, more drastic measures are attempted in efforts to resolve the rising tension. And finally, disruption and possible disintegration of the family occurs if the problem remains unresolved and if sufficient tension prevails for a long enough period of time.[8]

Goals of family counseling. The goals of family counseling have been stated in a variety of ways. Isabel Stamm presents the understanding that the goals can broadly be defined in terms of: changing the total family unity; changing subgroups within the family; changing individuals in the family; or changing the way the family relates with a part of the sociocultural world in which it exists (e.g., the school system, a financial advisor, bank, etc.). She goes on to state that personal growth within the individual family members along with improved family interaction patterns are both necessary in order to gain stable positive changes in family functioning.[9]

Wynn more specifically outlines goals for family counseling:

1. To treat the presenting problem that caused the family to enter in-

to counseling.

2. To significantly change dysfunctional behavior so that family members can better cope and even enjoy living together.

3. To relieve enough pain and tension so that the family members feel motivated to continue working toward the resolution of other family problems.

4. To help each member of the family become more assertive and honest about saying "yes" and "no," and more openly owning his or her thoughts and feelings.

5. To functionally relate the presenting problem to their family system as a way of increasing awareness of both the strengths and the weaknesses of their system of operating together.

6. To help the family members work their way toward termination as they gain greater trust in their collective ability to handle life's challenges.

7. To help the family members feel welcomed back for checkup sessions whenever they feel the need for some additional help or encouragement.[10]

Virginia Satir's research isolates four major aspects of effective family living. They are presented here in summary fashion as goals of family counseling:

1. To increase family productivity, or the ability to resolve disagreements and plan things together. Functional families gain a good balance between meeting work or task needs, and personal emotional needs.

2. To experience a fluid leadership pattern where various family members maintain leadership roles in different situations. Movement away from strong autocratic matriarchy or patriarchy, or inept attempts to be equalitarian, toward non-defensive sharing of the leadership role in different situations is functional for building healthy, adaptive families.

3. To be able to adequately express differences between family members, and deal with and resolve those differences without excessive conflict being generated through the process. Maladaptive families are marked with either a great absence of conflict or entirely too much conflict.

4. To increase the clarity and effectiveness of family communications.[11]

The family counselor strives to help families meet these goals because of a deep belief in the reciprocal value that exists for families and individuals. Family counseling is geared to help reinforce both the individual's importance to the family and the family's importance to the individual.[12]

The counselor's role. Andrew Ferber and J. Ranz have described four different models that help to define the counselor's role during family sessions. Each counselor can determine which role or combination of roles seems most appropriate for working with each family. Here is a brief description of the four models:

1. The counselor/mediator helps family members come together from their divergent positions in order to find solutions that are workable for all. The task is to help each faction understand more fully the thinking and feelings of the other side. Mediators suggest compromises and help the family members come to solutions in such a manner that neither side has to feel defeated. Mediated resolutions usually fall short of what each person ideally hoped for, but contain enough of what each wanted in order to make them acceptable. Mediating counselors seek to help family members learn the art and advantages of working together for the common good, being willing to sacrifice some of their own desires in order to enjoy a closer family experience.

2. The counselor/diplomat highly respects each family member's right and ability to assert his or her wishes and goals. The diplomat helps to translate each person's words, feelings and thoughts into language that is more readily understood by the other members. Perhaps the most difficult and yet most important task is to help the family participants build a mutual sense of trust.

3. The counselor/director takes a very active role in the family sessions in very much the same way that a director structures the scene of a stage play. In this case, the actors are the family members, the play is the story of the family's experience, the scene is the current interaction that is the counseling focus, the choreography consists of the actors' movements, and the script is comprised of the statements that the members make to each other. Initially, the director asks the actors to play out the scene using the script that is typical for them. As the play progresses the director begins to rewrite the scene, suggesting new lines and restructuring the choreography. Through this active process, families experience and learn new interaction patterns that they can continue to use at home.

4. The counselor/Lone Ranger enters the ongoing family process, makes a diagnosis of the dysfunctional elements in the system, intervenes with some immediate problem-solving techniques, and helps

them to establish some immediate and long-term goals. As soon as these interventions have been accomplished, the counselor sends the family on its way to adopt the procedures which have been learned.[13]

Whichever model is used, the counselor must remain objective and unbiased, not thinking in terms of who is at fault and who is innocent. Recognize that each family member plays his or her own part in the family dynamics, each contributes both positive and negative elements to the overall family system.

Youth pastors and lay counselors who are not married or who do not yet have adolescent children sometimes feel reticent to counsel parents with their children. No apologies are needed. But the young counselor must also recognize that in most cases the parents have been doing far more right than they have been doing wrong.

John Bell, a leading figure in the field of family therapy, outlines the way that the family counselor acts as a change agent. His five propositions will be quoted here: "In all social groups, and particularly the family, the communication and interaction is structured within certain operational limits that produce stereotyped patterns of reactions between family members and a restriction on the permissible ranges of individual behavior." "Most older children and their parents have available to them potential patterns of behavior beyond those they use in the family." "The therapist is a community figure in relation to whom the individual family member may show behavior that extends beyond what he or she normally reveals in the family." "In response to the new patterns revealed, the rest of the family members must revise their stereotypes about the family member, must reevaluate him or her, and must respond with new attitudes and new accommodations of their own behavior." "Having developed new modes of interacting, supported by mutual commitment that they are better and should be continued, the family consolidates these new patterns."[14]

The six stages of family counseling. Family, as well as individual counseling, can be perceived according to the six-stage model of counseling presented in chapter 5. Let's expand that model to apply to family counseling:

1. Building a relationship. In order for effective family counseling to take place, a meaningful relationship must be established between the counselor and each family member. There must also develop a working relationship between the counselor and the total family unit. The "purists" among family counselors schedule the initial session as a united family session as well as all of the succeeding sessions. Others

prefer to start with individual appointments or sessions with family sub-groups (e.g., younger children, adolescent children and parents). When adequate contact has been developed, the counselor then adjusts to family group sessions.

During the initial stage of counseling the techniques of listening, probing, encouraging and reflecting are heavily used. These techniques particularly are helpful in getting the family members to let themselves be known more fully not only by the counselor, but also by each other.

2. Defining the problem. This stage actually begins while the first stage is in progress. The observant counselor sees how the family members interact with each other, how they enter the office, their pattern of eye contact with each other, who speaks to whom, how the members talk with each other, where they sit in proximity with each other and so on. By carefully observing these interpersonal behaviors, the counselor begins to gain insight into the family's problem areas.

By the time a family reaches the counselor's office, each member usually has already figured out what the problem is, who is at fault and what needs to be done to change things. Often each person believes that he or she is in the right and that justice will prevail if the counselor will support his or her cause and put pressure on the others to change. These kinds of "surface" attitudes and perceptions are invaluable because they hint at underlying family dysfunctions.

Family members are encouraged to talk, to share their perceptions and to explain their side of the story. During this second, or problem-defining stage, the counseling techniques of listening, probing, questioning, confronting and reflecting can be powerful tools. Interpretation is not used during this stage of family counseling as much as during the same stage of individual counseling. The family counselor uses the interaction between family members to define the problem areas.

3. Establishing counseling goals and formulating a plan of action. Each family member needs to know that his or her stated needs and goals are respected by the counselor. The formulated counseling goals need, in some way, to incorporate the needs and wishes of each family member so that all of the participants can anticipate gaining something from the counseling process.

A family quite often enters counseling with the belief that it is there to help one of its members, the identified client, to work out his or her problems. One of the counselor's tasks is to help the family to again accept and treat the identified client as a whole person and not simply as a "sick one" or "bad person."[15] Everyone begins to recognize that the identified client's behavior has, in some ways, expressed the total family dynamic. This recognition helps each family member to accept some responsibility and focus on needed changes in the family dynamics, not change in only one person's behavior.

During this third stage, the counseling techniques of listening, probing, questioning, confronting, encouraging and reflecting are particularly useful.

4. Implementing the counseling plan of action. This, as in individual counseling, is the main goal when counseling families. The family sets goals and works to achieve them. If the goal is achieved, the family works on another or terminates counseling. If the goal is not achieved, the family needs to evaluate what went wrong and set a new goal or new plan of action. This active process is more frequent and lively in family counseling than in individual counseling because of the increased number of people involved in counseling.

Family counselors are generally characterized by the freedom to use a wide variety of methods and techniques. Well-known family therapist Jay Haley writes: "The more experienced family therapist tends to feel that any set procedure is a handicap; each family is a special problem which might require any one of several different approaches. Instead of fitting the family to a method, he or she tries to devise a way of working which varies with each particular problem."[16] Listening, teaching, evaluating, interpreting, probing, questioning, confronting, encouraging and reflecting are all useful counseling techniques during this working stage of family counseling. This stage employs various combinations of methods for the unique problems of each family.

Some common counseling techniques are used somewhat differently in family sessions. For example, interpretation is useful in both individual and family counseling. In the former, the technique is used to help bring unconscious motivations, impulses, thoughts, feelings and memories into conscious awareness. This awareness helps the counselee gain a greater conscious control in his or her day-to-day life. In family counseling, interpretations fulfill a translating function. The counselor helps one family member understand more clearly the message that another participant has sent. "I'm wondering if you heard anger in your father's voice as he was telling his side about what happened?" "Mom, it sounds like Cynthia really does care about your feelings. Did you sense her concern?"

Haley suggests that the counselor should design interpretations to help family members find the positive aspects of the other person's words and actions.[17] For example, 16-year-old Millie is very upset about her father's limits on who she can go out with and on when she has to be back home. "Millie," begins the counselor, "I know that you're very upset about your father's restrictions that he places on your dating activities. I'm wondering what you think are his motivations? Can you sense any caring in your dad's restrictions that he places on you?"

Family members often try to talk only to the counselor as the family sessions get underway. They will often seek to use the counselor as an intermediate communications link rather than talking directly to each other. The counselor will often tell the family members to address each other directly. "I want you to look at your father and talk directly to him."

Counselors are also concerned that each person be involved actively in the communicating process during the session. "Sally, we haven't heard much from you today. I'm really interested in knowing what you think about what has been going on."

Some family counselors have found very powerful counseling aids in tape recorders and video systems. They give their family a decision-making or problem-solving assignment, leave the room and record (video and/or audio) the family's process as it works on the assignment. The tape is then played back to the family with the counselor present. This powerful immediate feedback can have great effect in helping people change their dysfunctional behavior. "I had no idea that I sounded so demanding and grouchy. No wonder you don't like to talk with me." Listening and seeing ourselves as others perceive us are very powerful motivators for changing our own undesirable behavior patterns.

Role playing is another effective tool in the family counselor's repertoire. Role reversal is the technique of having two or more people play each other's roles. Mom role plays her 12-year-old son who, in turn role plays his mother. They are assigned the task of determining chores, which was one of the presenting problems. Role reversals help us to experience what it's like to be in the other person's position as well as to see how the other person views our behavior.

A role play of two or more family members can also be done by other participants. "Dad, you and Bill have been observing how Mom and Connie have been interacting. I'd like you two to role play what you have been seeing. It might help Mom and Connie see what's happening between them." Role plays can be very powerful, heavy, and even forceful stimulators of change. They can also be sources of humorous tension release.

Sculpting is a fascinating counseling tool that the skilled helper who is willing to become actively involved can use to unlock deeply entrenched family dynamics. The counselor places the family members in physical postures and moves them into positions relative to each other that match the verbal and psychological interactions and roles that are being lived out with each other.

For example, during one family session, Mom is very angry and is demanding compliance from Dad and 15-year-old Bart to be of more help in the yard and around the house. Dad and son sit quietly, listening, acquiescing, and trying to placate Mom into settling down. Twelve-year-old Kari is delighted that her brother is getting the heat and not her. The counselor decides to sculpt this family scene. She jumps up and pulls Mom to her feet, helping her to adopt a demanding position. Dad and son are directed to a kneeling position on the floor, and are helped to take on a begging, cowering posture in front of Mom. And sis? She is pushed to the side of the room and told to laugh gleefully, pointing at the two weak and beaten figures on the floor. The participants are instructed to continue their dialogues as before, in these physical positions.

Then the counselor begins to sculpt in desired changes. She brings Dad and Bart to their feet and positions them into strong, firm postures. Mom's posture is altered to one that suggests a humble, requesting attitude. And Kari is brought to center stage and positioned into a posture that would suggest wanting to be involved in helping her mother. They are instructed to continue talking with each other and as they do, their communications gradually change to match their newly sculpted roles.

A wide variety of structural communication games are utilized to help break up dysfunctional patterns while teaching more healthy communication patterns. One example is the instruction that family members exchange a series of "I messages" using no other kinds of verbalizations.

Modeling open, direct communication teaches the same to blocked, repressed families. The counselors become what Harry Stack Sullivan calls "participant observers."[18] They actively intervene in the counseling process, and actually become a temporary member of the family system. From this powerful position, the counselor impacts the family system from within, causing it to adjust to his or her healthful presence, thereby altering the system itself.

Counselors also teach families how to run their own family meetings by leading them through meetings during the counseling sessions. Problem-solving and contract problem-solving meetings along with regularly scheduled family meetings, were discussed earlier in chapter 3. The two problem-solving meeting formats were also presented by Peter Buntman and Eleanor Saris in their helpful book for parents, *How to Live With Your Teenager.*[19]

J.C. Wynn gives us some precautions about counseling methods that are of little or limited usefulness in family counseling: "It does no lasting good for the family therapist to work out solutions, no matter how wise, on behalf of families; too much time spent on diagnosis can be time ill-spent in family therapy; counselees' insight is of limited value in family therapy because it lacks the power to change behaviors; interpretation by a therapist is an overrated form of intervention in family practice; promoting or even allowing family conflicts and hassles during therapy interviews is of little worth, indeed it is often a detriment to treatment; conducting family therapy by the 'bits-and-pieces' method is undisciplined, and can be destructive to the outcome."[20]

5. Terminating counseling. The fifth stage, terminating, is begun as the family becomes increasingly able to maintain a more functional system of relating to each other. The counselor becomes less actively involved and sessions are scheduled on a less frequent basis. Listening, encouragement and reflecting are the most useful counseling techniques during this disengagement process.

6. Following up with the counselee. Some families benefit from periodic checkup sessions. They feel more secure knowing that the counselor is there if needed during a crisis or emergency. Also, just knowing that a session is already scheduled for a month, three months or even farther off, can provide a healthy reminder to continue doing what has been learned in counseling. Listening, encouraging and reflecting are the most valued techniques during these follow-up sessions.

Family counselors need to practice the same freedom to refer exceptionally difficult cases as do counselors of individuals. Certain families will present dynamics that make ongoing treatment by the particular counselor contraindicated. The family counselor can follow the guidelines set down in the previous chapter regarding the referral process.

Group Counseling
History and philosophy. Probably the earliest use of a group counseling

or therapy approach was in 1905.[21] Joseph H. Pratt, a Boston internist organized his tubercular patients into groups of up to 25 patients. People suffering with tuberculosis during that time were apt to become depressed and discouraged not only because of the devastating physical effects of the disease, but also because tuberculosis was thought of as a social disease with some associated judgment falling upon its victims. His patient groups met weekly, with each person keeping a personal progress chart. During the meetings, Pratt lectured, encouraged and stimulated his patients to support each other. His group members realized that they were not the only ones in their condition, and developed a sense of comradery that strengthened their own battles. Pratt's development of his groups represented a synthesis of his own background in religion and psychology as well as medicine.

One of the first uses of the group approach for psychological treatment was in 1909. L. Cody Marsh, a minister who later became a psychiatrist, worked with psychoneurotics using the group mode.[22] In 1910, J.L. Moreno originated the technique of psychodrama which is a highly specialized version of the group approach to therapy. He did not coin the phrase "psychodrama" until 1931. Another psychologist, Kurt Lewin, used groups to train community leaders during the 1940s to work more effectively with racial tensions.[23] Lewin's approach placed a heavy emphasis on observing the group process. The participants simultaneously learned about group process and about their own functioning. His approach eventually led to the development of the National Training Laboratories, now called the NTL Institute for Applied Behavioral Sciences, and to the development of T-group (for training) or sensitivity training groups.

A major cause for the rapid increase in popularity during the 1960s and 1970s of group approaches to training, therapy and counseling lies in the sociocultural atmosphere of the time. Carl Rogers writes: "In our affluent society, the individual's survival needs are satisfied. For the first time, he is freed to become aware of his isolation, aware of his alienation, aware of the fact that he is, during most of his life, a role interacting with other roles, a mask meeting other masks. And for the first time he is aware that this is not a necessary tragedy of life, that he does not have to live out his days in this fashion. So he is seeking, with great determination and inventiveness, ways of modifying this existential loneliness. The intensive group experience, perhaps the most significant social invention of this century, is an important one of these ways."[24]

Today's interest in group counseling. Some of the specific social and cultural phenomena that have increased our sense of alienation, isolation and emotions include a lack of intimacy in social relationships, lack of community closeness, geographic and occupational mobility, family instability, greater distances separating extended families, the anonymity and impersonality implicit in mass education, mass communication, mass transportation and mass housing complexes. In addition to the broader sociocultural influences, many people suffer a great deal of shame, guilt, anger and anxiety from painful past relationships.[25] Their struggle often involves one or more of the following patterns:

1. They wall themselves off from others because they are convinced that others will disapprove of them because of some perceived unacceptable aspect of themselves.

2. They recognize that this personal aspect is inescapable, though they try to oppose and reject it.

3. They believe that no one will love them as long as that despicable part is within them.

4. They realize that even if they are loved, they cannot accept it because of their fear that the love will turn into rejection.

5. As they hold themselves back from others, they become their own internal enemy, acting out the role of the disapproving parent.

6. They project their own internal self-judgments onto those around them, resulting in the belief that others are being rejecting of them.

The counseling group provides a specially structured setting that provides contrived intimacy that enables the participant to begin to overcome some of his or her blockages to a meaningful relationship. The group environment resembles society more closely than individual counseling does. The counselee can respond much as he or she does in everyday life, letting the counselor and other participants represent significant people in their real world.[26] Group counseling affords anxious counselees the opportunity to find out that they are not the only ones feeling as they do, and gives them the opportunity to receive feedback from other people.

Nathan Hurvitz has suggested three additional reasons for the increased interest in group counseling (especially the interest in groups with minimized involvement of the professional counselor) the limitations of conventional one-to-one psychodynamic psychotherapy; the popularization of psychological thinking that has brought the assumption for many that help for hurting people will have to emanate from a psychological source; and the American ideals of democracy and pragmatism have fostered concepts of self-help and peer-help.[27]

Group counseling from a Christian perspective. The rising interest in group counseling and other helping approaches that involved group activity fostered a cry of alarm from some Christians. Great concern was voiced about the erosion of morality reportedly being caused by the sensitivity training groups. Protests were voiced against the alleged brainwashing, manipulating and immorality that seemed implicit in many of their techniques. Caution was urged not only from the Christian community, but also from professional psychologists.

That some have misused group dynamics does not mean that group process is bad. Nor does it mean that the powerful forces of group interaction cannot be harnessed to produce positive results. In fact, one of the finest examples of a leader with a small group is Jesus working with his twelve apostles. Paul Meier, Frank Minirth and Frank Wichern draw our attention to John 13:34-35 to help us understand the core that unifies a group.[28] Christ announced to his disciples, "A new commandment I give to you, that you love one another; even as I have loved you, that you also love one another. By this all men will know that you are my disciples, if you have love for one another."

It is certainly not the case that group process unified and empowered the disciples. It was Jesus Christ himself who empowered them. It was Jesus who unified. And one method that he utilized to accomplish his great task was the employment of group dynamics. Just prior to his arrest, Jesus prayed: "I do not pray for these only, but also those who believe in me through their word, that they may all be one; even as thou, Father, art in me, and I in thee, that they also may be in us, so that the world may believe that thou hast sent me. The glory that thou hast given me I have given to them, that they may be one even as we are one, I in them and thou in me, that they may become perfectly one, so that the world may know that thou hast sent me and hast loved them even as thou hast loved me" (John 17:20-24). The unity that Christ came to give is imparted to us through his love.

Christ's unifying power is reflected in his disciples' actions following his crucifixion. "On the evening of that day, the first day of the week, the doors being shut where the disciples were, for fear of the Jews, Jesus came and stood among them and said to them, 'Peace be with you!' " (John 20:19). Only Thomas was absent from this meeting of their group. And some days later, just after witnessing the ascension of Christ, we have the following record. "Then they returned to Jerusalem from the mount called Olivet, which is near Jerusalem, a Sabbath day's journey away; and when they had entered, they went up to the upper room, where they were staying, Peter and John and James and Andrew, Philip and Thomas, Bartholomew and Matthew, James the son of Alphaeus and Simon the Zealot and Judas the son of James. All these with one accord devoted themselves to prayer, together with the women and Mary the mother of Jesus, and with his brothers" (Acts 1:12-14). Again, the group joins together spiritually for prayer and mutual comfort, support, encouragement and strength.

The same values in group involvement are available for us today. O. Hobart Mowrer is cited by Nathan Hurvitz that the practice of open confession of sins in small groups was common practice among Christians until 375.[29] By the 12th century confession had become a completely private matter, made secretly to a priest. Protestant confession is usually without human contact, being made directly to God through Christ. The issue here is not the spiritual/theological aspects of confession. Rather, the current focus is upon the psychological/emotional aspects of confession. Something is sorely missed when we bypass the directive given to us by James. "Therefore, confess your sins to one another, and pray for one another, that you may be healed. The prayer of a righteous man has great power in its effects" (James 5:16).

Confession directly from the believer to God certainly brings forgiveness. But it misses the intrapsychic and interpersonal healing which Mowrer stressed. Mowrer states that when people sin, that is, break the rules of their community that they have incorporated as their conscience, they feel guilt. These guilt feelings estrange them from their community and arouse other unpleasant feelings that dispose them to learn behavior defined as inappropriate or deviant and to manifest symptoms. The individual can overcome his or her alienation from the community, unpleasant feelings, inappropriate or deviant behaviors, and distressing or disabling symptoms by confessing his or her sins to "significant others" in the community and where appropriate, by making restitution to them. He or she is thereby reunited with the community and exemplifies the original meaning of religion, which comes from the Latin "ligare." "Religion literally means a reconnection that can be achieved by confession and restitution. Through reconnection with his community one learns appropriate behavior and is encouraged to live it."[30]

John Drakeford (a Christian psychologist) provides more insights about the small group experience in the Christian community in his book, *Farewell to the Lonely Crowd*.[31] Much of what Sidney Jourard writes about self-disclosure and transparency in his book *The Transparent Self* can also be applied to our use of group process in Christian settings.[32] The author of Hebrews urged us forward in our group process, "Not neglecting to meet together, as is the habit of some, but encouraging one another, and all the more as you see the Day drawing near" (Hebrews 10:25).

Similarities and differences with respect to individual counseling. When evaluating the use of group counseling, it is important to examine its similarities and differences with respect to individual counseling. Bruce Shertzer and Shelly Stone offer some useful insights on the similarities:

1. The overall objectives in group and individual counseling are frequently similar. Both seek to help the counselee achieve self-direction, integration and self-responsibility. In both approaches counselees are helped toward self-acceptance and understanding of their motivations.

2. In both individual and group counseling an accepting, permissive climate must be provided if the participants' need to maintain their defenses is to be reduced. In both, individuals feel free to examine their feelings and experiences because respect has been accorded them. Both approaches strive to engender confidence in the counselee's ability to be responsible for his or her own choices.

3. In both individual and group counseling the counselor's techniques are important: clarification of feeling, reflection of feeling, restatement of content, structuring and acceptance. The counselor's skills are used to draw out counselees so that they are aware of their feelings and attitudes and can examine and clarify them.

4. The recipients of individual and group counseling are individuals who experience normal developmental problems. Both approaches deal with the common needs, interests, concerns and experiences of the generality of individuals.

5. For both approaches, individuals need privacy and a confidential relationship in order to develop and to make use of their personal resources.

The differences between individual and group counseling are:

1. The group situation provides immediate opportunities to try out ways of relating to individuals and is an excellent way of providing the experience of intimacy with others. The physical proximity of the members to one another brings emotional satisfactions. A counselee may get his or her peers' reactions and suggestions concerning alternate ways of interaction. An immediate, first-hand opportunity is present to test others' perceptions of oneself in relation to other people.

2. In group counseling, the counselees not only receive help but also help others. The more stable and cohesive the group, the more the mutual assistance. The cooperative sharing relationship helps the members feel closer to others, to understand and accept them. The interaction nurtures members, influences behavior, facilitates mutual expression of feelings, and aids in interpretation of meanings.

3. The counselor's task is more complicated in group counseling. The counselor not only has to understand the speaker's feelings and help him or her become aware of them but also must observe how the speaker's comments influence other group members. The counselor must be aware of the discussion and interplay of relationships among the members.[33]

Types of groups. Attempts to clarify groups into different types has become a very confusing task. Categories can be set up based upon a variety of parameters including leadership style, primary activity, theoretical orientation, purpose and combinations of the above. Another way to classify groups is to differentiate between those that are designed to treat counselees with maladaptive behavior patterns from those that help "normal," healthy participants to develop self-understanding, improve relationships and increase personal effectiveness.[34] Another classification system essentially adds a third category.[35] These groups are established for the purpose of helping their participants to learn more about how groups function and how they impact the lives of the participants.

Morris Parloff has come up with another dichotemized classification of groups.[36] He differentiates between process-centered and individual-centered groups. The former place the emphasis upon the study of what happens as groups of people meet together. The latter focus on the growth, behavior change, and interpersonal activities of the group members as individuals.

A final classification system devised by Jack Gibb looks at theoretical orientation and the practices that are used in various group processes.[37] He has arrived at 10 theory and practice clusters:

1. Sensitivity experiences. These groups help their participants become more sensitive to social reality, using role playing and other such methods to accomplish their goals.

2. Authenticity experiences. These experiences emphasize openness, authenticity, congruence, transparency, and confrontation on the part of the members. These are essentially basic encounter groups.

3. Creativity release experiences. A wide variety of methods like

body movement, sensory awareness, finger painting, free verse, interpretive dance, meditation, fight training, Zen, contextual maps, induced aggression, and non-verbal encounters are used to reduce inhibitions and fears, increase spontaneity and increase communication.

4. Programmed experiences. Groups are led according to a fully structured format that is designed to bring about a specified kind of learning or behavior change.

5. Imbedded experiences. Leaders and facilitators work in the actual social environment in which the participant is embedded. The family at home, work team, management group, athletic team, clubs and community committees are all possible settings for this approach.

6. Religious experiences. A wide variety of experiences that are transcendent, mystical or spiritual are often related to the individual's relationship with God.

7. Motivation shift experiences. The use of group experiences to increase or redirect participant's motivation to accomplish occupational or educational goals.

8. Cognitive shift experiences. The goal is behavior change through changing the participant's assumptions about people, the world and themselves.

9. Depth therapy experiences. The focus is on individual therapy in the group setting.

10. Emergent or interdependent experiences. These groups begin without structure and without leadership so that the group must initiate its own experience, make its own decisions and decide on its own activities, in order to emerge with its own identity built upon the members' interdependence.

Now let's take a brief look at several of the better known approaches to group process: sensitivity training or T-groups ("T" stands for "training") were formulated in 1947 by the Basic Skills Training Group of the National Training Laboratory. They typically consist of 10 to 12 members whose group forms an actual learning laboratory in which the participants learn how to learn.[38] The process is focused on "here-and-now" experiencing of thoughts, feelings, impulses and behavior. They work toward expanding consciousness and increasing the participants' perception of available choices and options. Authenticity in interpersonal relationships is stressed, helping people to increase self-awareness and self-expression. These groups are usually presented as training, rather than therapy experiences, though personal changes associated with therapy are sought and often gained.

Encounter or personal growth groups are comprised of patients or counselors who are working toward changing dysfunctional behavior, or normal healthy people who are seeking to improve their interpersonal effectiveness and enhancing their own personal growth and development. Focus is placed on the participants and their interaction styles. Group size ranges usually between six to 12 members.

A very powerful style of therapeutic intervention called psychodrama was introduced by Moreno who in 1921 founded the theater of spontaneity in Vienna. Though psychodrama is often used as one therapeutic tool among several in group therapy, it was originally intended by Moreno to stand alone as a comprehensive therapeutic approach itself. Moreno presents five instruments to be used in his psychodrama: the stage; the patient or participant; the director; the staff of therapy aids or auxiliary egos; and the audience.[39]

Marathon groups are time-extended encounter experiences that involve 12, 18, 24, 36 or even 48 hours of group process interrupted only by short sleep periods in the longer sessions. Intensive psychological contact, physical exhaustion, intense interpersonal involvement and confrontation are all geared to break down psychological defenses as quickly as possible.[40]

Goals of group counseling. The decision to engage in a group counseling venture, either as leader or as participant, must assume a basic understanding of what group process can accomplish. In other words, what are its goals? What can we expect group process to do for our young people? for ourselves? As we have already discovered, there are quite a few different types of group experiences available. But even with this variety, many of the same goals are shared by most of them. It will be helpful for us to examine and articulate what we can expect to gain from involving ourselves and our teenagers in group process. Psychologist Hobart Thomas stimulates our thinking both as Christians and as counselors. "To me, the encounter group is essentially an experiment with freedom. I believe we are putting to the test the assumption that in a climate where people are free to be whatever they are, they will move in growth-enhancing directions. We are also testing the assumption that at his deepest levels the individual is capable of knowing what is right for him."[41]

The above quote should draw from you a well-articulated theological response that integrates naturally with an equally well-articulated psychological reply. This response should lead you toward understanding the kind of group process for you to participate in and lead. A look at more specific goals of the group process will be helpful. Morris Parloff suggests three categories of counseling goals:[42] enhanced organizational efficiency, enhanced interpersonal skills and enhanced personal sense of well-being. Our focus, as counselors of teenagers, is in the last two categories, interpersonal skills development and increased sense of well-being. The goals of adolescent group counseling concentrate on interpersonal skills development and improving self-image. A summary of the research results is in the following list of goals:

1. To develop a stronger sense of identity, which implies becoming open to knowing one's thoughts, feelings, perceptions and values.

2. To grow in self-acceptance and self-worth.

3. To resolve feelings of alienation, depersonalization and meaninglessness.

4. To resolve sources of inner conflict, emotional problems and to provide a vehicle for bringing repressed material into consciousness.

5. To increase the level of self-determination, acceptance of personal responsibility; to make and keep commitments.

6. To improve and expand decision-making and problem-solving skills.

7. To increase a basic level of trust in the self as a thinking, feeling, perceiving and valuing being; trust in other people as being safe enough to interact with; and trust in the world as an okay place in which to work and live.

8. To develop a comfortable level of interpersonal interdependence so that one can live and work with others.

9. To develop and expand interpersonal skills.

10. To increase sensitive awareness and accurate empathic understanding of others.

11. To deepen the level of openness and congruent expression of the self toward others.[43]

Other authors have specified counseling goals for adolescents who work in groups. The following 20 goals are particularly relevent for teenagers who are in group counseling. While some of these goals are included in the list of more general group counseling objectives, some of these are uniquely adolescent in nature:

1. To reach a clearer definition of one's identity, including awareness of interests, abilities and aptitudes.

2. To increase the level of self-acceptance and feelings of self-worth.

3. To develop an increased appreciation of one's personal creative

energy.

4. To improve confidence in skills necessary for clear thinking, problem-solving, decision-making and goal-setting.

5. To increase ability and willingness to practice self-control by placing and maintaining limits on behavior.

6. To be able to alter behavior patterns that are destructive, dysfunctional or that cause feelings of guilt.

7. To realize through open discussion that they are not the only ones who have their particular problem.

8. To develop new and more effective communication skills.

9. To understand the impact that their behavior has on others and to develop new and more positive social skills.

10. To practice independence-oriented behavior in order to stimulate growth toward independent autonomy.

11. To learn how to better cope with and relate with authority figures.

12. To understand and cope with their physiological changes associated with puberty and adolescent maturation.

13. To learn how to adapt to the behavioral roles and guidelines associated with adolescence.

14. To fulfill part of the need to belong by being valued as an equal member within the group.

15. To fulfill the needs to give and receive love and care during the group process.

16. To increase the level of social interest and stimulate the presence of unselfish feelings.

17. To promote the congruent expression of the self to others.

18. To work out solutions to problems with family members, friends and others.

19. To develop sensitivity to others' needs.

20. To gain information about the future and about choices that are available.[44]

When considering group counseling for teenagers, it is important to think of the differences between younger adolescents (14-17 years old) and older adolescents (17-20 years old).[45] Younger adolescents' major developmental tasks are to work at separation from parents and to establish a relatively autonomous identity. Their psychological defense mechanisms are still in their formative stage. Group involvement provides the younger adolescent an external focus which relieves some of the intense anxiety produced by the common internal changes and conflicts during that age. Group interaction also tends to be less anxious than the more intimate one-to-one contact. Some even view the activity of grouping as the major defense mechanism of young adolescents.[46]

Older adolescents typically have established more of their own identity structure and therefore have less need for the group as a place of safety and as a point of identification. Their primary task is to validate the identity and roles that they have begun to establish. Because of these differences it is usually best to separate younger and older adolescents into different groups.

Processes that make groups work. Group counselors have discovered a variety of processes that are unique to this kind of group interaction. These processes must occur if the healing and growth-stimulating effects are to be experienced by the participants.

Groups are usually initiated with a minimum of structure. The facilitator seeks to help create in the group sessions an atmosphere in which the participants feel free to express their thoughts, attitudes, values and feelings. During the initial sessions, the members try to present certain images of themselves. These facades represent the pictures that they want other people to have of them. As the group proceeds, these facades are gradually let down and broken through and a deeper level of honesty is reached. Chances are taken with risky self-expression to the other group members. Immediate feedback is available to help participants learn how others view them and react to their behavior.

The emotions that are produced earlier in the process are often angry and hurt feelings that have been stockpiled over the days, weeks, months and years preceding the group involvement. But as these feelings are expressed, accepted and responded to by the group, the relationships between group members become more special and valued. Positive feelings of warmth, caring, acceptance and love are genuinely given and received. Self-respect and self-esteem are stimulated and increased, and the members develop their sense of identity more fully. The group's leader is fully involved in every aspect of group movement, but not in the traditional counselor or therapist role, nor as teacher. Rather, the leader's role is to facilitate the occurrence and progress of the group dynamics as they unfold.

Clarence Mahler has given us a set of principles that serve as guidelines or rules that are helpful to those of us who work with groups. They are summarized and adapted here for our reference:

1. People have a right to their own feelings.

2. Each person must decide for himself or herself what to work on.

3. Individuals are to work on themselves and not on others.

4. How people feel about a situation is more important than the situation itself.

5. There are many advantages to being open with others.

6. Effective group process helps us to better understand our own behavior.

7. We are responsible for our own behavior.

8. Some type of action is necessary to change behavior.

9. We can develop alternate solutions for difficult situations.

10. A commitment to change is necessary for growth to be accomplished.

11. What is learned in the group can be applied to our daily lives.

12. As we become more accepting of ourselves, we become less defensive.[47]

With the forgoing principles in mind, let's examine the specific interaction processes that make group counseling beneficial for the participants.[48]

1. The group that is more attractive to its members has a greater influence on them. Attractiveness of a group is determined by its values, helpfulness, prestige and similarities to the individual.

2. When the person feels genuinely accepted by the group, the need for belonging is partially fulfilled. A sense of security, confidentiality, and trust with both the leader and other members is involved in feeling accepted.

3. Members must accept personal responsibility for their own change and feel committed to helping other members to accomplish their desired changes.

4. Members need to discuss their situations and behaviors with the group. From this process individuals can discover that they are not the only ones with their problems.

5. Active focus on here-and-now interaction and feelings makes for a more profitable group experience.

6. Groups and members who have clear expectations of what they hope to gain are more likely to accomplish their goals.

7. Feedback that is descriptive rather than evaluative or judgmental is the most helpful.

8. Group process that stimulates thinking and cognitive understanding along with emotional release and ventilation produces the best climate for accomplishing desired behavior changes.

9. An atmosphere of controlled and gradually increasing emotional intimacy promotes healthy growth within the group. This gradual deepening of intimacy is described in Berzon's six stages of personalization as cited by Clarence Mahler: In the first stage no personally relevant material is discussed. Discussion centers on preferences in automobiles, who won the ball game, what one likes to eat, etc. In the second stage there is an aloof, superficial manner in presenting facts about public aspects of themselves. Problems may be mentioned, but they are not recognized as such. Stage three contains an "inward reference" to material, but the discussion does not move toward exploring the significance or meaning of the material. This is the typical "playing the patient" or "being the psychology student" role. In stage four there is increased emotional involvement on the part of group members in their own contributions. Individuals want to know more about themselves. When they discuss problems they speak of their own reactions. Stage five involves a tentative probing and effort toward self-exploring and an inward search for discovery of new feelings. And in the final stage members are actively exploring their feelings, their values, perceptions of others, fears and decisions with emotional proximity to the material.[49]

10. A high level of empathic understanding between group members is necessary for healthy group functioning.

11. A productive level of tension during group sessions helps to stimulate growth and change.

12. Some type of action in response to and in expression of new thoughts, feelings and values in order to accomplish desired changes.

13. An adequate level of hope to draw the individual ahead through the sometimes difficult and threatening process of counseling.

Group leadership. One of the major determinants of how well the group process will fulfill the needs of its participants is the group leader. The style, personal characteristics and particular functions that the leader fulfills, shapes the type of group interaction and progress that the group and its members make.

Clarence Mahler delineates four different methods of leadership. The "leader-dominated" group has most of its functions directed by its authoritarian-styled leader. The "planless, catch-as-catch-can or non-leadership method" seems to be an overreaction to the authoritarian approach that goes too far in the opposite direction. Counselors who are very passive, unassertive or who lack self-confidence, lead with this style. "Subtle or invisible leader control" is exhibited by group leaders who try to make their indirect efforts to focus the group's attention away from issues that feel too risky or who try to direct group process without the participants' awareness of their efforts. The method in which the leader provides encouragement and direction has a major effect in the amount of interdependence and personal autonomy fostered within the group.[50]

A six-category system of classifying group leader types is proposed by Morton Lieberman[51] and by Lieberman, Irvin Yalom and Matthew Miles:[52]

Type A leaders are energizers. They tend to challenge and heavily confront group members, causing them to release emotionality and disclose their values, attitudes and thoughts. They are active in directing group process and exhibit high levels of caring.

Type B leaders are providers. They express high levels of loving to the members as well as giving information, ideas and concepts on how they can accomplish their goals. They are moderately active in challenging and confronting as well as directing the process of the group.

Type C leaders are social engineers. These leaders focus more on group interaction dynamics. Though they tend to express moderately high levels of caring, their primary concern is with making sure that the interpersonal dynamics within the group are functioning productively.

Type D leaders are impersonals. They are more emotionally distant and unexpressive of caring to the group members. They are quite aggressive, confrontive and demanding in their group interactions, heavily focused on breaking down defense mechanisms.

Type E leaders are laissez-faires. These leaders tend to be relatively uninvolved with group members. Their responses are general rather than personal. They are primarily interested in helping participants learn how people grow and change behavior rather than actually helping them grow and change their behavior.

Type F leaders are managers. These leaders are extremely controlling of how group members interact with each other and about the content of discussions. They often use structured exercises and limit spontaneity in group members' self-expressions.

These different types of leaders were found, through an elaborate research project, to fulfill quite different roles within their groups. They exhibited different leadership skills and interacted quite differently with their group members. In order to develop adequately a healthy and well-rounded leadership style, one must first be aware of the wide variety of leader functions that are important in facilitating group counseling process.

Effective group leaders are able to be a valuable and accessible resource for their participants. They can provide interpretations, explanations, clarifications and concepts that help group members to better understand their own behavior. They are, in a sense, interpreters of reality.

Group leaders establish a climate of psychological and emotional safety where risks can be taken, new behaviors can be tried out and frightening questions can be asked.

They provide an environment that stimulates the group members' emotional expressions. Cathartic reactions and ventilation are often encouraged in order to help participants move beyond emotional blocks and dysfunctional inhibitions.

Caring responses that are adequately expressed by the leader are very important to the success of the group process. They have a direct healing effect on the members as well as provide positive role modeling and encouragement for similar expressions between the members.

Group leaders also fulfill a wide variety of functions that are more executive or administrative in nature. They set limits, establish rules and guidelines, help to determine goals and directions. They also intercede in the process, ask questions, elicit responses and facilitate decision-making.

Leaders serve as interpersonal interpreters, helping the participants understand the transactions that are occurring between them. They look for patterns of interpersonal behavior and assess the group's progress. Mahler suggests four ways that the accuracy of the counselor's assessment is important: the readiness of each member to share; the readiness of each member to lower his or her defenses; the readiness of members to confront unconscious material that relates to surface behavior; and the readiness to admit and discuss socially disapproved behavior.[53]

Don Dinkmeyer and James Muro have listed eight characteristics of the effective group counselor:

1. The effective group counselor is one who is perceived by group members as their advocate.

2. Group counselors are able to operate within the emotional and developmental phases of the group.

3. Group counselors are positive individuals.

4. Effective group counselors are able to affix a status role to group members.

5. Successful group counselors are an integrated blend of artistic sensitivity and scientific understanding.

6. The effective group counselor is conscious of the total interaction pattern within the group.

7. The effective group counselor allows autonomy among group members.

8. All group counselors are more effective when they are matched with the personality styles and work levels of the group members.[54]

Group participants. Group leaders are not the only ones who play vital roles in the group process. The group participants directly control the destiny of the group. It is the quality of their interaction that determines the quality of the group dynamics and the value of each member's eventual gain. Each counselee in the group has the responsibility to be committed to active involvement and participation in the counseling process. The form and type of involvement that each member has depends largely upon the personality and defense mechanisms that are characteristic of the individual.

Walter Lifton has carefully expanded a broad range of roles that counselees play during group process. He lists these group roles into three different categories: group task roles, group growing and vitalizing roles, and antigroup roles.[55]

Group task roles is one category of counselees whose jobs include facilitation and coordination of group problem-solving activities. Specific titles that fall under this category are:

1. Initiator contributor. Offers new ways to view the group problem or goal. Suggests solutions on how to handle group difficulties. Suggests new procedure for group or new organization for group.

2. Information seeker. Seeks clarification of suggestions in terms of factual adequacy, authoritative information and pertinent facts.

3. Opinion seeker. Seeks clarification of values pertinent to what the group is undertaking or values involved in suggestions made.

4. Information giver. Offers facts or generalizations that are "authoritative" or appropriately relates his or her own experience to group problem.

5. Opinion giver. Appropriately states personal belief or opinion to suggestions. Emphasis on his or her proposal of what should become group's views of pertinent values.

6. Elaborator. Gives examples or develops meaning, offers rationale for suggestions made before, and tries to deduce how ideas might work out.

7. Coordinator. Clarifies relationships among ideas and suggestions, pulls ideas and suggestions together, or tries to coordinate activities of members of subgroups.

8. Orientor. Defines position of group with respect to goals. Summarizes. Shows departures from agreed-upon directions or goals. Questions direction of discussion.

9. Evaluator. Subjects accomplishment of group to "standards" of group functioning. May evaluate or question "practicability," "logic," "facts" or "procedure" of a suggestion of some unit group discussion.

10. Energizer. Prods group to action or decision. Tries to stimulate the group to greater or higher quality activity.

11. Procedural technicians. Performs routine tasks or manipulates objects for group (distributes materials, rearranges chairs, etc.).

12. Recorder. Writes down suggestions, group decisions or products of discussion. Group memory.

A second major category of counselees includes those with group growing and vitalizing roles. Those that build group-centered attitudes and orientation. Specific titles that fall under this category are:

1. Encourager. Praises, agrees with and accepts others' ideas. Indicates warmth and solidarity in his or her attitude toward members.

2. Harmonizer. Mediates intragroup scraps. Relieves tensions.

3. Compromiser. Operates from within a conflict in which his or her idea or position is involved. May yield status, admit error, discipline himself or herself, come halfway.

4. Gatekeeper and expediter. Encourages and facilitates participation of others. "Let's hear about . . ." Why not limit the length of contributions so we all can react to the problem?"

5. Standard setter or ego ideal. Expresses standards for group to attempt to achieve in its functioning or applies standards in evaluating the quality of group processes.

6. Group observer and commentator. Keeps records of group processes and contributes this data with proposed interpretations into group's evaluation of its own procedures.

7. Follower. Goes along somewhat passively. Is friendly audience.

A third category of counselee jobs is titled antigroup roles. These counselees try to meet personal needs at the expense of group health rather than through cooperation. Specific titles that fall under this category are:

1. Aggressor. Deflates status of others. Expresses disapproval of values, acts or feelings of others. Attacks group or problem. Jokes aggres-

sively, shows envy by trying to take credit for other's idea.

2. Blocker. Negativistic. Stubbornly and unreasoningly resistant. Tries to bring back an issue group intentionally rejected or bypassed.

3. Recognition seeker. Tries to call attention to himself or herself. May boast, report on personal achievements, and in unusual ways struggle to prevent being placed in "inferior" position, etc.

4. Self-confessor. Uses group to express personal, non-group-oriented "feeling," "insight," "ideology," etc.

5. Playboy. Displays lack of involvement in group's work. Actions may take the form of cynicism, horseplay or other "out-of-field behavior."

6. Dominator. Tries to assert authority in manipulating group or some individuals in group. May use flattery, assertion of superior status or right to attention, giving of directions authoritatively, interrupting contributions of others, etc.

7. Help seeker. Tries to get "sympathy" response from others through expressions of insecurity, personal confusion, or self-depreciation beyond "reason."

8. Special interest pleader. Is verbally for the small-business man, grass roots community, housewife, labor, etc. Actually cloaking own prejudices or biases on stereotypes that best fit his or her needs.

Group members are usually playing more than just one role at a time. For example, an individual might fulfill the roles of "harmonizer" and "elaborator" at the same time. Another member might simultaneously play out the roles of "recognition seeker" and "compromiser."

Group counseling stages. Group counseling, like individual counseling, can be broken down into a series of developmental stages. Most researchers have conceptualized four stages in the group counseling process.

During stage one, members familiarize themselves with the group and find out how they can best relate with the leaders and other members. Facades are up and little if any real interpersonal contact is made.

During stage two the group members are beginning to express feelings. Most of these feelings, are negative as they jockey for position with each other, often feeling competitive and apprehensive. Defenses are still strong, though there are some attempts to open up.

Stage three ushers in productive group work. Group members are developing more trust in each other. They are being helped through the group process and are feeling more positive about their experience together. More of a sense of belonging is felt by the members and group pride is felt. Phrases like "my group" are heard more often.

These positive functional aspects carry on into stage four. Members who have previously remained resistive often enter the group process, knowing that the available time to accomplish their goals is limited. Participants go through the process of bringing the group to a close, saying "goodbye" and transitioning gains from the group into their everyday lives.

Carl Rogers, however, has specified eight developmental stages that occur as a counseling group progresses from beginning to end: milling around; resistance to personal expression or exploration; description of negative feelings; expression and exploration of personally meaningful material; expression of immediate interpersonal feelings in the group; development of a healing capacity in the group and the beginning of change; dropping of facades, confrontations and feedback; and expression of positive feelings and behavior change.[56]

Benefit and risks of group counseling. This discussion about group counseling might stimulate some questions about its usefulness and appropriateness. "Does group counseling really accomplish anything?" "Why should I counsel teenagers in groups rather than individually?" "Do the hazards of group counseling outweigh the benefits?" Let's take a look at both the potential dangers and the results of group counseling.

In their extensive research, Morton Lieberman, Irvin Yalom and Matthew Miles studied the participants in 17 groups.[57] They found that at the termination of their groups slightly over 60 percent of the participants felt that they had benefited from their experience. Six months later between 10 and 20 percent of the original 60 percent felt less positive about their gains. The greatest type of positve change that was found in the study was in the area of interpersonal openness. Participants felt that they were more open and honest in their self-disclosures, more able to confront and generally more direct in their self-expression. They indicated increased self-esteem and sense of self-worth. There was an accompanying greater respect and tolerance for other persons' behavior, habits, opinions and mistakes. Another gain was improvement in their coping strategies. When faced with problems, instead of avoiding, denying or fleeing, they more frequently confronted the problem. A final change was a significant shift in values toward greater concern for others.

Another researcher (J.R. Gibb) evaluated the results of several studies on group counseling. He found that group members significantly increased in sensitivity to their own experience as well as to the feelings and perceptions of others. There was a tentative increase in the group participants' ability to manage their feelings. He found indications that group members became more self-determining and self-directing. Significant gains in self-esteem and self-acceptance, and decrease in the difference between real-self and ideal-self ratings were also discovered and explored.[58]

Lieberman, Yalom and Miles found that the individual leader had a great impact upon group members' outcomes after their group experience. The most positive effects were gained by leaders who were very loving, caring and supportive, and who were able to give insights and understanding about how to solve problems, make decisions, and establish productive relationships.[59]

Unfortunately, there are also certain risks involved in group process. The expression of aggressive, hostile and other negative feelings is sometimes very frightening. As facades are broken down, defenses against anxiety are also weakened, sometimes leaving the individual too vulnerable to anxiety arising from both inner conflict and external pressures. Parloff reports that emotional and psychological reactions have resulted from group therapy, including psychosis.[60]

Another type of difficulty is sometimes faced during the reentry process. Group participants commonly find that the real world does not operate by the same rules and allowances regarding openness to emotional expression and confrontation that the group accepted. Teenagers soon discover that they cannot respond to their parents in the same way that they related to their group leader.

Of the Lieberman, Yalom and Miles study's 206 group participants, 7.6 percent suffered significant psychological injury attributed to their group experience. The greatest number, 10, suffered reactions after verbal and psychological attacks from the group leader. Feeling rejected by the leader or group figured in the symptoms of six of the group casualties. Four participants experienced negative reactions because they failed to achieve personal unrealistic goals through the group process. Two of the group members felt psychological symptoms as a result of being unable to meet the leader's or group's demands or expectations. Finally, several participants seemed to suffer injury from a traumatizing overstimulation or emotional input overload.[61]

These group casualties occurred predominantly in groups in which leaders were aggressive, confrontive and demanding. The leaders focused more on individuals rather than on group process. These results underline the need for group counselors to be relatively non-demanding, very caring, respectful and supportive. Leaders should not apply excessive pressure on any individuals within the group.

Details to consider when planning a counseling group. There are a number of logistic and operational details to consider when starting a counseling group. Careful planning can greatly increase the chances of developing a group that both the leader and participants can benefit from and enjoy.

1. Member selection. When selecting members to participate in an adolescent counseling group, several characteristics should be considered. It is recommended that groups consist of only certain *age ranges*. Early adolescents, from about 13 to 15 years old, are primarily involved with the task of separating from parents and joining with their peer group. Mid-adolescents, 15 to 17 years old, are actively establishing their identities, exploring relationships with the opposite sex, handling responsibilities relating to money and driving, and considering decisions about careers and college. Late adolescents, from about 18 to 20 and older, will vary according to the setting (e.g., military, camp, college, factory), but will be dealing with the transition into young adulthood, establishing definite career direction and movement into a heterosexual relationship.

Whether groups consist of one or both *sexes* depends largely on the purpose of the counseling. Particularly during late and mid-adolescence, there is much to be gained from mixed groups. Regardless of the sex makeup of the group, there is good value in having male and female co-counselors leading the group.

There can be a wide spectrum along the *intellectual abilities* continuum in the same group. The level of verbal fluency is just as important to consider as is the level of intellectual functioning.

Though there should be more than one person in the group with a specific problem, a fairly *wide spectrum of problems* can be represented in the same group. One researcher has outlined the advantages and disadvantages of both homogeneous and heterogeneous groupings along the lines of psychological dysfunctions.[62] He cites the advantages of homogeneous groups: rapid formation of group identification; rapid expression of transferences; quick development of insight; faster disclosure of psychodynamics; shorter treatment duration; more regular attendance; lessened negative impact from interferences and resistances; less formation of cliques; and more rapid recovery from symptoms. Disadvantages of homogeneous groupings include: difficulty in forming such groups; possible decreased level of interaction; less impact on character structure; less reality testing.

Advantages in heterogeneous groups are: deeper levels of therapy; greater impact on character structure and symptom formation; more adequate and thorough reality testing; richer variety of transference formations; and groups are more easily assembled. The disadvantages to heterogeneous groups include: slower recovery of counselees; magnified tensions; slower group identification; delayed therapist transference; slow insight acquisition; and irregular attendance.

When screening counselees it is helpful to classify them in order to establish a preliminary "psychological picture" of the new group. Eric Berne offers us such a classification scheme. His categories are: unsophisticated counselees; sophisticated counselees; skeptical counselees; receptive counselees; referred counselees; reluctant counselees; unready counselees; group-shy counselees; and ineligible counselees.[63]

2. Setting. The counseling room should be relatively small, though not uncomfortable. The atmosphere should be informal and relaxed with seating provided in either soft chairs or on cushions on the floor. It should offer visual and auditory privacy and confidentiality.

3. Group size. Counseling groups operate optimally with between six to 10 participants. Fewer than six members often limits the variety and richness of interaction between members. More than 10 members is often unwieldy and individuals have less time to work on their personal issues during group sessions.

4. Frequency of meetings. Most counseling groups are scheduled to meet once per week at a regularly scheduled time and place.

5. Length of sessions. Adolescent group counseling sessions should last 60 to 90 minutes. Groups for early adolescents should last about one hour and groups for late adolescents should last about 90 minutes. Sessions should start and end promptly so that members will become more responsible for their use of the time.

6. Duration of the group. The minimum number of sessions should be 10. Fewer sessions prevent adequate development of group dynamics. Often the length depends on other logistics. For example, a counseling group could be established to run according to a church's 13-week quarter.

7. Open versus closed format. Closed groups start with a specified number of members and finish with that same membership. New group members are not allowed to join. Open groups allow new members to join during the course of the meeting. Groups that are meeting for a rather short duration and those that are for adolescents with

strongly dysfunctional behavior are usually closed groups. Open groups cause members to deal with the process of losing and gaining members throughout the sessions. And open groups often limit the maximum number of members allowed to join.

8. Attendance. Regular and prompt attendance of every member is important to the smooth functioning and continuity of the group process. Absence and lateness are often indicators of resistance and should be confronted.

9. Outside meetings of members. Group members should not meet together during the week between group sessions. Of course, this stipulation must be adjusted when group members have youth group, school or other activities that they share. But even in these cases, there should be a solid commitment that no group business should be dealt with between members outside of the group sessions.

10. Individual counseling during group treatment. A teenager may be seen individually or in family counseling while he or she is in group counseling. In these cases it is important that group business is not handled in those auxiliary counseling settings.

11. Beginning group counseling. During the first session, with some repetition and clarification in the next few sessions, the leader's task is to: clarify the general purposes of the group; explain the facilitator's role; discuss each member's responsibility to the group; outline the rules, guidelines and expectations for group functioning. During these initial sessions the leader is also modeling good communication skills, empathy and encouragement, while beginning to discuss feelings, problems and behavior.

12. Ending a group. The process of terminating a group involves helping each member: to wrap up therapeutic work; to summarize his or her counseling gains; to establish goals and procedures for transferring counseling gains into benefits for everyday living; and to say "goodbye" to other group members.

"Do's and don'ts" for the group counselor. George Bach has listed some helpful "do's and don'ts" for the group counselor that have been adapted for our use. In order to end on a positive note, we will look at his "don'ts" first:

1. Do not underestimate your own unconscious drives and motives.

2. Do not behave spontaneously in a counseling group as you would in an ordinary social discussion group.

3. Do not encourage or reinforce the counselees' natural tendency to cure themselves by and through authority.

4. Do not get discouraged by the complex and intense emotions of the counseling group.

5. Do not let your concern with helping to create and maintain a level of cohesiveness in the group trick you into overzealous tendencies to suppress realities.

6. Do not allow yourself to be pushed into the role of guardian of the communication.

7. Do not forget the counselees after the completion of counseling.

8. Do not think that you have to be a father or a mother to your group.

9. Do not forget that, inevitably, you help your own psychological growth. In a sense, you are a counselee in your own group.

Now, on to Bach's "do's" for group counselors:

1. Do try to be an accurate reflector of the experiences of the counselees.

2. Do remember that you are a service-training member of the group.

3. Do think of a group of counselees as a basically constructive force, a manifestation of the capacity for mutual aid in humanity that can and will grow.

4. Do recognize your responsibility for counseling leadership, since the counselor is both promise and threat to the group.

5. Do contribute to the group, through your helpfulness and democratic leadership, rather than through lecturing about all that you understand.

6. Do share what you can of your personal knowledge, feelings, experiences and values with the group when such sharing can serve as a useful stimulus.

7. Do help group members to increase their tolerance for individual differences.

8. Do always attempt to gauge correctly and reflect the majority group consensus concerning any topic.

9. Do learn to distinguish pressures on individuals among the group.

10. Do acknowledge being puzzled, if appropriate.

11. Do always keep in mind that the goal of counseling is the well-being of each individual counselee.

12. Do at all times reflect and reinforce the group's own natural, but usually latent, interest in becoming aware of all the factors involved in problems.

13. Do learn to see and respect the constructive wisdom in the counselees.

14. Do accept your role as a guardian of a beneficial milieu for counseling in which the creative as well as the non-creative aspects of the counselees can find explicit, shared communications.

15. Do clearly formulate the counseling objectives you wish to attain and the means for accomplishing them.

16. Do continue to improve pre-counseling screening, diagnosis and prognosis of every counselee who might benefit from group counseling.

17. Do recognize the principles of the social interdependence of human personalities.

18. Do engage in research. Keep records. Exchange ideas with colleagues.[64]

19. Do trust in God, that his will is being done. Do look to God for strength and guidance.

Crisis Intervention Counseling

This is the type of counseling that in one form or another is done by more people than any other kind of counseling contact. If you are someone's pastor, youth leader, teacher, relative or friend, then you have periodic opportunities to lend some type of counseling intervention during or immediately following a crisis. This section is designed to be an introduction of crisis intervention work to these lay counseling positions.

Crisis definitions and types of response. There are times in each of our lives when an event occurs or when the cumulative effects of stress reach such a level that our coping mechanisms can no longer adequately handle the emerging anxieties. These are crisis situations. Richard Lazarus writes, "Crisis seems to imply a limited period in which an individual or group is exposed to . . . demands that are at or near the limits of their resources to cope. In crisis, the focus is on a period of the person's or group's life in which major threats and frustrations that tax adaptation are prominent."[65] During some crises our coping mechanisms continue to function well on our behalf. At other times, however, they weaken and we need supportive help.

Carl Malmquist cites two types of crises that are common to teenagers: situational and developmental. Situational (or accidental) crises are external events that heavily impact the individual's life. Examples of this type of crisis include the birth of a sibling, the death of a loved one, separation or divorce of parents, loss of a friend, moving out of state, being hospitalized, being seriously ill or injured, moving to another school or town, a family member becoming emotionally disturbed, becoming unexpectedly pregnant and experiencing serious financial problems. Developmental crises for adolescents include the onset of puberty, increased need for social involvement with peers, entering high school, taking "gang" showers in gym class, and dating.[66]

Aaron Lazare and his associates conducted a survey of the types of patients who visited a psychiatric walk-in clinic. They were able to isolate 14 different categories that represent the wide variety of types of counselees who need crisis intervention work. Their categories appear here in an adapted form:

1. Counselees who want a strong person to protect and control them. "Please take over for me."

2. Those who need someone who will help them maintain contact with reality. "Help me know that I am real."

3. Those who feel exceedingly empty and need loving. "Care for 'me."

4. Those who need a counselor to be available for a feeling of security. "Always be there."

5. Those ridden with obsessive guilts who seek to confess. "Take away my guilt."

6. Those who urgently need to talk things out. "Let me get it off my chest."

7. Those who desire advice on pressing issues. "Tell me what to do."

8. Those who seek to sort out their conflicting ideas. "Help me to put things into perspective."

9. Those who truly have a desire for self-understanding and insight into their problems. "I want counseling."

10. Those who see their discomfort as a medical problem that needs the ministrations of a physician. "I need a doctor."

11. Those who seek some practical help like economic assistance or a place to stay. "I need some specific assistance."

12. Those who credit their difficulty to ongoing current relationships and want the counselor to intercede. "Do it for me."

13. Those who want information as to where to get help to satisfy various needs, actually seeking some community resource. "Tell me where I can get what I need."

14. Non-motivated or psychotic persons who are brought to the

counselor against their own will. "I want nothing."⁶⁷

The above list also represents several different kinds of responses to crisis. A person's response to a crisis depends on several issues, including the individual's personality, the current state of his or her defense mechanisms, the nature of the crisis and the intensity of the upsetting aspects of the crisis. Mark 14:46-51 yields the account of a crisis experience and several persons' different responses to the experience. "And they laid hands on him and seized him. But one of those who stood by drew his sword, and struck the slave of the high priest and cut off his ear. And Jesus said to them, 'Have you come out as against a robber with swords and clubs to capture me? Day after day I was with you in the temple teaching, and you did not seize me. But let the scriptures be fulfilled.' And they all forsook him and fled.

"And a young man followed him, with nothing but a linen cloth about his body; and they seized him, but he left the linen cloth and ran away naked."

We find four different responses to the crisis of Christ's arrest. One in verse 47 was impulsive, aggressive and impotent. Another in verse 50 was the classic flight reaction. Another in verses 51 and 52 was ambivalent and uncertain. And Christ's own response in verses 48 and 49 was centered and goal-directed.

Feelings of confusion, guilt, anxiety, self-judgment, hopelessness and helplessness are often experienced by people within a crisis. In the midst of this disruptive process, the person's defenses are often weakened, leaving the individual more vulnerable to these feelings. But it is this same increased vulnerability that often causes the person to be more willing to change and open to participate in counseling.

When the counselor seeks to help a teenager who is either currently going through a crisis or who recently has gone through one, he or she is advised to carefully evaluate four variables: the symptoms; the nature of the precipitating crisis; the family system's effect on the counselee; and the psychologically significant aspects of the counselee's background. Careful evaluation of these four variables will help to determine what kind of help is most appropriate for the adolescent.⁶⁸

The counselor should be aware of various alternatives for crisis intervention assistance. Walk-in crisis clinics provide both psychological and medical help, usually at a low cost and without requiring an appointment. The hospital emergency room is available in acute situations of severe agitation, depression and suicide-risk cases. Most communities have several "hot lines" that are available for teenagers and others who require immediate attention. Some of these 24-hour telephone lines are staffed with counselors who are specially trained to work with drug abuse, suicide attempts, child abuse, alcoholism, poison control information and other areas of specialization.

The lay counselor and crisis intervention counseling. Let's turn our attention now to crisis intervention counseling as it can be done by the pastor, teacher, youth leader and qualified lay counselor. The counseling process is viewed as short-term, lasting typically between one and six sessions.[69] Christian psychologist Gary Collins emphasizes the importance of contact with the counselee as soon as possible after the need for help has been made known.[70] The sessions are often held quite closely together. Crisis events unfold very rapidly and individuals who are under high levels of stress can fluctuate markedly in their sense of emotional balance. Counselors usually make themselves available to their crisis counselees' telephone calls until the acute stage is passed. Simply knowing that the counselor's phone is available is often most reassuring to the counselee.

Crisis intervention counseling sessions are typically quite structured by the counselor. A rather quick evaluation of the nature and intensity of the counselee's symptoms is paired with an initial impression of his or her current personality functioning. What are the apparent personality strengths and weaknesses? What is the status of the coping mechanisms? How depleted is the counselee's energy reserve? How much of what kinds of external supports are going to be needed? All of these factors will help form a provisional diagnosis of the counselee's problem. An initial prognosis of how well the counselee is expected to do should also be determined very early during the counseling process. This assessment of the counselee's psychological functioning is necessary in order to select the most appropriate counseling approach.

During crisis counseling, the focus should be kept on concrete behaviors, thoughts and feelings and not on abstract generalizations. What exactly is the counselee feeling now? What did he or she think when the crisis event occurred? What specific actions did the counselee take and how did they work out?

Help the counselee to move toward accepting the reality of what has actually happened. Confront denial and other defense mechanisms that block the counselee from knowing. When the individual accepts reality, then he or she can be more effective in doing something about it. Hearing the counselee verbalize his or her feelings and impulses can be quite discomforting, especially for the novice counselor. But such verbalization is very important to helping the counselee accept reality.

Immediate reduction in anxiety, depression, and any other strong symptoms is a major goal of crisis intervention. Do what is necessary to help the individual to gain normal, healthy functioning. Encouraging the teenager to take action is a major anxiety-reducing and healing function in the counseling process. It helps to focus the counselee's attention on the question, "What can I do about the situation?" Activity releases tension and anxiety. And successful or productive activity increases the counselee's feeling that, "I really can do something about this situation."

The counselor can also be involved in obtaining other forms of real, tangible help. Temporary lodging, money, food, babysitting, a job and transportation are just some of the kinds of help that people often need during crisis experiences.

In some cases, a referral to a psychologist or psychiatrist is highly recommended. Indications for such a referral include the occurrence of any of the following: physiological symptoms; an apparent mental illness in a person who may be dangerous to himself or herself or others; the need for medication; the presence of a suicide attempt or threat in the counselee's personal history; and a special request to see a psychologist or psychiatrist.[71]

Because of the very active, time-limited nature of crisis intervention, the counselor's style will be quite different from the more traditional eclectic style that was presented earlier in this book. The counseling techniques of listening, encouraging, teaching, probing, questioning and confronting are highly useful. Evaluating, interpreting, self-disclosing, reflecting and using silence are less valuable in crisis intervention. The table on the following page clarifies the relative values of the counseling techniques during crisis intervention:

Practical issues. Let's look at Lewis Wolberg's 16-point summary of practical issues relating to crisis intervention counseling. They are adapted and listed below:

1. See the counselee within 24 hours of the time that the call for help was made.

2. At the initial interview alert yourself to counselees who may be high suicide risks.

3. Immediately work on any depression in suicide-risk counselees.

4. Evaluate the stress situation.

5. Evaluate the counselee's existing support systems.

6. Estimate the counselee's personality strengths.

Counseling Techniques During Crisis Intervention

	Contra-indicated	Minor Value	Moderate Value	Strong Value	Absolutely Essential
Listening					
Teaching					
Evaluating					
Interpreting					
Probing					
Questioning					
Confronting					
Self-disclosing					
Encouraging					
Reflecting					
Using silence					

Illustration 33

7. Help the counselee toward an awareness of the factors involved in his or her reaction to the crisis.

8. Provide empathic listening and supportive reassurance.

9. Suggest tranquilizers only when anxiety is so great that the counselee cannot make decisions. (This point applies only to psychiatrists.)

10. Deal with the immediate present and avoid probing of the past.

11. Avoid exploring for psychodynamic factors.

12. Aim for increasing self-reliance and finding alternative constructive solutions for problems.

13. Involve the family or significant others in the treatment plan.

14. Group counseling can also be helpful.

15. Terminate counseling within six sessions if possible and in extreme circumstances no later than three months.

16. When the counselee needs further help for purposes of greater personality development after the pre-crisis equilibrium has been restored, engage in that type of counseling or refer to another counselor.[72]

Notes

1. Charles H. Kramer, *Becoming a Family Therapist* (n. p.: Human Sciences Press, 1980).

2. Nathaniel Ackerman, "The Family as a Social and Emotional Unit," *Bulletin* (n. p.: Kansas Mental Hygiene Society, 1937).

3. J. C. Wynn, *Family Therapy in Pastoral Ministry* (San Francisco: Harper and Row, 1982).

4. Virginia Satir, J. Stachowiak, and H. Taschman, *Helping Families to Change* (New York: Jason Aronson, 1975).

5. Group for the Advancement of Psychiatry, The Committee on the Family, *Treatment of Families in Conflict: the Clinical Study of Family Process* (New York: Science House, 1970).

6. Nathaniel Ackerman, *Treating the Troubled Family* (New York: Basic Books, 1966).

7. Wynn, *Family Therapy in Pastoral Ministry.*

8. Gerald Caplan, *Principles of Preventive Psychiatry* (New York: Basic Books, 1964).

9. Isabel Stamm, "Family Therapy," in *Casework: A Psychosocial Therapy*, ed. Florence Hollis, 2nd ed. (New York: Random House, 1972).

10. Wynn, *Family Therapy in Pastoral Ministry.*

11. Satir, Stachowiak, and Taschman, *Helping Families to Change.*

12. Stamm, "Family Therapy."

13. Andrew Ferber and J. Ranz, "How to Succeed in Family Therapy: Set Reachable Goals—Give Workable Tasks," in *Progress in Groups and Family Therapy*, eds. Clifford Sager and S. Kaplan (New York: Brunner/Mazel, 1972).

14. John E. Bell, "A Theoretical Position for Family Group Therapy," in *Creative Developments in Psychotherapy*, eds. Alvin R. Mahrer and L. Pearson (Cleveland: The Press of Case Western Reserve University, 1971).

15. Wynn, *Family Therapy in Pastoral Ministry.*

16. Jay Haley, "Family Therapy," in *Progress in Group and Family Therapy*, eds. Sager and Kaplan.

17. Ibid.

18. Harry Stack Sullivan, *The Interpersonal Theory of Psychiatry* (New York: Norton, 1953).

19. Peter H. Buntman and Eleanor Saris, *How to Live With Your Teenager* (Pasadena, Calif.: Birch Tree Press, 1979).

20. Wynn, *Family Therapy in Pastory Ministry*, pp. 113-114.

21. Max Rosenbaum, "Group Psychotherapy and Psychodrama," in *Handbook of Clinical Psychology*, ed. Benjamin B. Wolman (New York: McGraw-Hill, 1965).

22. Robert A. Harper, *Psychoanalysis and Psychotherapy: 36 Systems* (New York: Jason Aronson, 1974).

23. Leonard D. Goodstein and R. Lanyon, *Adjustment Behavior and Personality* (Reading, Mass.: Addison-Wesley, 1975).

24. Carl R. Rogers, "Interpersonal Relationships: U.S.A. 2000," Journal of Applied Behavioral Science 4 (1968):265-280.

25. Bertram R. Forer, "Therapeutic Relationships in Groups," in *Encounter: The Theory and Practice of Encounter Groups*, ed. Arthur Burton (San Francisco: Jossey-Bass, 1969).

26. Clifford T. Morgan and R. A. King, *Introduction to Psychology*, 5th ed. (New York: McGraw-Hill, 1975).

27. Nathan Hurvitz, "Peer Self-Help Psychotherapy Groups: Psychotherapy Without Psychotherapists," in *The Sociology of Psychotherapy*, eds. Paul M. Roman and H. Trice (New York: Jason Aronson, 1974).

28. Paul D. Meier, Frank Minirth, and Frank Wichern, *Introduction to Psychology and Counseling: Christian Perspective and Applications* (Grand Rapids, Mich.: Baker Book House, 1982).

29. Hurvitz, "Peer Self-Help Psychotherapy Groups."

30. Ibid, pp. 96-97.

31. John W. Drakeford, *Farewell to the Lonely Crowd* (Waco, Texas: Word Books, 1969).

32. Sidney M. Jourard, *The Transparent Self* (Princeton: Van Nostrand, 1964).

33. Bruce Shertzer and Shelly Stone, *Fundamentals of Counseling*, 2nd ed. (Boston: Houghton Mifflin, 1974).

34. James C. Coleman and C. Hammen, *Contemporary Psychology and Effective Behavior* (Glenview, Ill.: Scott, Foresman, 1974).

35. Philip G. Zimbardo and F. Ruch, *Psychology and Life*, 9th ed. (Glenview, Ill.: Scott, Foresman, 1975).

36. Morris B. Parloff, "Group Therapy and the Small Group Field: An Encounter," in *Progress in Group and Family Therapy*, eds. Sager and Kaplan.

37. Jack R. Gibb, "Meaning of the Small Group Experience," in *New Perspective on Encounter Groups*, eds. Lawrence N. Solomon and B. Berzon (San Francisco: Jossey-Bass, 1972).

38. Robert T. Golembiewski and A. Blumberg, eds., *Sensitivity Training and the Laboratory Approach* (Itasca, Ill.: F. E. Peacock, 1970).

39. J. L. Moreno, "Psychodrama and Group Psychotherapy." Sociometry 9 (1946):249-253.

40. Morton Lieberman, Irvin Yalom, and Matthew Miles, *Encounter Groups: First Facts* (New York: Basic Books, 1973).

41. Hobart F. Thomas, "Encounter—The Game of No Game," in *Encounter*, ed. Burton.

42. Parloff, "Group Therapy and the Small Group."

43. The following sources were used in compiling the information for this chart:

Solomon and Berzon, eds., *New Perspectives on Encounter Groups*.

Don Dinkmeyer and James Muro, *Group Counseling: Theory and Practice* (Itasca, Ill.: F. E. Peacock, 1971).

Clarence A. Mahler, *Group Counseling in the Schools* (Boston: Houghton Mifflin, 1969).

44. The following sources were used in compiling the information for this chart:

Irving H. Berkovitz, ed., *Adolescents Grow in Groups: Experiences in Adolescent Group Psychotherapy* (New York: Brunner/Mazel, 1972).

Elizabeth Skoglund, *Can I Talk to You?* (Glendale, Calif.: Regal Books, 1977).

Shertzer and Stone, *Fundamentals of Counseling*.

Dinkmeyer and Muro, *Group Counseling: Theory and Practice*.

Elizabeth Mintz, *Marathon Groups: Reality and Symbol* (New York: Appleton-Century-Crofts, 1971).

Merle M. Ohlsen, *Group Counseling* (New York: Holt, Rinehart and Winston, 1970).

45. Barry Sherman, "Marathons for Adolescents," in *Marathon Groups: Reality and Symbol*, ed. Mintz.

46. P. Blos, *On Adolescence* (New York: Free Press, 1962).

47. Clarence A. Mahler, *Group Counseling in the Schools* (Boston: Houghton Mifflin, 1969).

48. The following sources were used in compiling the information for this note:

Irvin D. Yalom, *The Theory and Practice of Group Psychotherapy* (New York: Basic Books, 1970).

Dinkmeyer and Muro, *Group Counseling: Theory and Practice.*

Burton, ed., *Encounter*

Mintz, *Marathon Groups: Reality and Symbol.*

Lieberman, Yalom, and Miles, *Encounter Groups: First Facts.*

Ohlsen, *Group Counseling.*

Mahler, *Group Counseling in the Schools.*

49. Mahler, *Group Counseling in the Schools*, pp. 83-84.

50. Ibid.

51. Morton A. Lieberman, "Behavior and Impact of Leaders," in *New Perspectives on Encounter Groups*, eds. Solomon and Berzon.

52. Lieberman, Yalom, and Miles, *Encounter Groups: First Facts.*

53. Mahler, *Group Counseling in the Schools.*

54. Dinkmeyer and Muro, *Group Counseling: Theory and Practice.*

55. Walter M. Lifton, *Working With Groups*, 2nd ed. (New York: John Wiley, 1966), pp. 20-21.

56. Carl R. Rogers, *Carl Rogers on Encounter Groups* (New York: Harper and Row, 1970).

57. Lieberman, Yalom, and Miles, *Encounter Groups: First Facts.*

58. J. R. Gibb, "The Effects of Human Relations Training," in *Handbook of Psychotherapy and Behavior Change: An Empirical Analysis*, eds. A. E. Bergin and S. L. Garfield (New York: John Wiley, 1971).

59. Lieberman, Yalom, and Miles, *Encounter Groups: First Facts.*

60. Parloff, "Group Therapy and the Small Group."

61. Lieberman, Yalom, and Miles, *Encounter Groups: First Facts.*

62. W. Furst, "Homogeneous Versus Heterogeneous Groups," International Journal of Group Psychotherapy 3 (1953):59-66.

63. Eric Berne, *Principles of Group Treatment* (New York: Oxford University Press, 1966).

64. George R. Bach, *Intensive Group Therapy* (New York: Ronald Press, 1954).

65. Richard S. Lazarus, *Psychological Stress and the Coping Process* (New York: McGraw-Hill, 1966), pp. 407-408.

66. Carl P. Malmquist, *Handbook of Adolescence: Psychopathology, Antisocial Development, Psychotherapy* (New York: Jason Aronson, 1978).

67. Aaron Lazare, F. Cohen, O. Jacobsen et al., "The Walk-in Patient as a 'Customer': A Key Dimension in Evaluation and Treatment," American Journal of Orthopsychiatry 42 (1972):872-883.

68. Lewis R. Wolberg, "Psychiatric Techniques in Crisis Therapy," New York State Journal of Medicine 72 (1972):1266-1269.

69. Ibid.

70. Gary R. Collins, *How to Be a People Helper* (Ventura, Calif.: Vision House, 1976).

71. Lewis R. Wolberg, *Handbook of Short Term Psychotherapy* (New York: Thieme-Stratton, 1980).

72. Ibid.

PART III

Special Issues in Counseling Teenagers

■ CHAPTER 9

Defense Mechanisms

Each one of us must face stress on a daily basis. Stress is inevitable. Whether stress invades us from our external world or results from our inner conflicts, we all must adapt to it simply to keep our sanity. There are several healthy, normal responses to stress that most of us use every day. But when stress becomes too severe, or lasts for too long, less healthy ways of adapting are often used. These less healthy ways of handling stress and conflict are defense mechanisms. And although we all need them to some degree, their overuse is certain to cause problems. This chapter looks at the various healthy (adaptive) and unhealthy (less adaptive) reactions to stress and offers guidelines for leading teenagers away from inappropriate uses of defense mechanisms.

Reactions to Stress and Anxiety

Task-oriented reactions. James Coleman calls the more adaptive styles of responding to stressful situations "task-oriented" reactions.[1] They are essentially, realistic responses that deal directly with the stress situation. They are employed by individuals who have enough self-confidence to assess the situation objectively, determine a course of rational action and confidently carry out the planned solution. There are three types of task-oriented reactions: attack reactions, withdrawal reactions and compromise reactions.

1. The task-oriented *attack reactions* are characterized by an assess-

ment of the stress situation followed by an effort to meet the need of the situation with direct action. Most task-oriented attack reactions involve the ability to focus the majority of one's personal resources, thoughts and energies onto the stress situation. The person is able to inhibit and suppress fears and emotions so that they do not become disruptive. Attack reactions are flexible in the approach to the crisis situation. The person develops new resources and skills that would be helpful and affiliates with a group if collective action is needed.

Aggression is typically a component of the task-oriented attack response. The aggressive response is a direct approach to try to change a situation or its outcome. For example, 17-year-old Stuart desperately wanted a job at a nearby auto dealership. When the owner turned him down because he was not yet 18 years old, Stuart went back to the dealership to try to persuade the owner to hire him anyway.

The attack response often involves making a choice between alternatives. When Stuart spoke again with the owner, he was given the choice of working there until his birthday at a below-minimum wage or trying to get a better-paying job elsewhere.

When the stress situation places pressure on the individual, resistance to the pressure is the task-oriented attack response. The owner of the auto dealership tried to talk Stuart into the low-paying job. Stuart resisted this pressure, holding to his decision to not work for less than minimum wage.

2. Task-oriented *withdrawal reactions* amount to a withdrawal or avoidance of stress situations that we prefer to not meet. Escape and avoidance are often positive, adaptive ways to deal with stress. Connie is a 15-year-old high school sophomore who has been dating a 19-year-old college freshman. He has been pressuring her to develop a sexual relationship with him. She can escape the stress by telling him that she is breaking up with him because of the sexual pressure that she has been receiving. She might also avoid the pressure by agreeing to go out with him on double dates or group dates. In these situations he is less likely to be as sexually demanding.

Withdrawal reactions like escape and avoidance acknowledge that the stress situation is either too difficult or that there is not enough to be gained by continuing to deal more directly with it. Withdrawal reactions attempt to leave a stressful situation and establish a new direction toward a more rewarding and appropriate goal.

3. The last type of attack-oriented reactions is *compromise reactions*. These are the most common and they involve elements of attack and

withdrawal reactions. Compromise reactions accept substitute goals and substitute means to accomplish those goals.

One form of compromise is the substitution of an unattainable goal with a more realistic one. Accommodation (another form of compromise) involves accepting or settling for only part of what is ideally desired. Twelve-year-old Harold has his heart set on a fully equipped bicycle. His parents have agreed to pay one-half of the cost, but Harold is still about $50 short. One of his options is to substitute a less expensive model that he could afford. Another compromise solution would be to buy his favorite bicycle without some of the deluxe options.

Defense-oriented reactions. When a person's task-oriented behavior fails to deal adequately with stressful situations, anxiety becomes an increasingly predominant life experience. Anxiety further complicates a person's life. In addition to dealing effectively with the stress situation, one must protect the self from anxiety overload and psychological disorganization. Coleman outlines three types of defense-oriented mechanisms that are designed to help the individual prevent or lessen emotional pain and anxiety: certain "wired-in" reparative mechanisms, learned ego defense mechanisms, and the use of substances (such as alcohol and other drugs) to alleviate felt discomfort and distress.[2] The first category of defense-oriented mechanisms will be discussed, followed by a detailed breakdown of ego defense mechanisms. The third type, drug abuse, is discussed in chapter 15.

The *"wired-in" reparative mechanisms* are defensive because they usually have no direct effect upon the stress situation itself. Rather, their purpose is to help repair psychological damage and to aid in regaining psychological equilibrium. These operations occur usually with full consciousness, though their appearance may be quite spontaneous and to some degree outside of the person's control. The most common examples of this type of mechanism are crying, talking it out (catharsis, ventilation), laughing it off, thinking it through and leaning on others.

These first-line defense reactions will often accomplish their goals. They should be encouraged as normal, healthy behaviors that all of us need to use when appropriate.

Unfortunately, there are times in our lives when we are unable to deal with life's stresses with the use of these first-line defensive operations. In such cases, strong anxiety becomes a very real threat. And the effects of strong anxiety can be psychologically devastating. Lewis Wolberg describes anxiety in this way: "It is characterized by a violent biochemical and neurophysiological reaction that disrupts the physical, intellectual, emotional and behavioral functions of the individual. Anxiety is indicative of a collapse of a person's habitual security structure and his (or her) successful means of adaptation. So uncontrollable are its effects that the individual attempts to escape from it through various maneuvers. These are usually self-defeating because those very maneuvers are often regressive in nature, that is, they revive outmoded, childish ways of dealing with discomfort. They only further interfere with assertive and productive coordinations."[3]

It is often this type of anxiety experience that causes an individual to seek counseling. Hans Selye describes the "exhaustion reaction" of the body's organs and systems after prolonged exposure to stress. The physiological and psychological reactions to prolonged and intense stress interact to create the symptoms of severe anxiety reactions. The anxiety can come either from external danger or internal conflict. The person may be aware or totally unaware of the source of the stress. And it is the *meaning* that the threat or conflict holds for the individual more than the event itself that determines how stressful the experience will be for a given person.[4]

Lewis Wolberg graphically pictures the physiological and psychological manifestations of extreme anxiety: "First, there is a vast undifferentiated, explosive discharge of tension which disorganizes the physiological rhythm of every organ and tissue in the body. Long-continued excitations may produce psychosomatic disorders and ultimately even irreversible organic changes. Thus, what starts out as a gastric disorder may turn into a stomach ulcer; bowel irritability may become a colitis; hypertension may result in cardiac illness and so on.

"Second, there is a precipitation of catastrophic feelings of helplessness, insecurity and devalued self-esteem. The victim often voices fears of fatal physical illness, like cancer or heart disease or brain tumor, as interpretations of the peculiar somatic sensations or symptoms that are being released by anxiety.

"Third, there is a wearing down of repressions to the point where they become thin in certain areas. Consequently, a breakthrough of repudiated thoughts, feelings and impulses, ordinarily controllable, now may occur at random. These outbursts further undermine security and produce fear of being out of control, of not knowing what to expect.

"Fourth, various defenses are mobilized, their variety and adaptiveness depending upon the flexibility and maturity of the individual. If these strategies fail to control or dissipate the sense of terror, then a further set of maneuvers is initiated."[5]

Severe stress. Anxiety's effect on the physiological systems has been described by Selye's theory of the general-adaptation syndrome. The body, according to Selye, reacts to sustained severe stress in three major phases: an alarm reaction, a stage of resistance and a stage of exhaustion. A person's psychological state under stress follows a similar pattern as physiological breakdown.[6]

1. During the *alarm reaction* stage, the person's coping mechanisms are mobilized. Emotions are aroused, tension levels are increased, sensitivity and alertness are heightened, and efforts to maintain self-control are strengthened. Task-oriented and/or defense-oriented reactions are mobilized. If these measures do not adequately handle the stress situation, certain symptoms of maladjustment may develop, such as feelings of anxiety, increased muscular tension, gastric upset and so on.

2. Through the use of task-oriented reactions, people can usually attain a level of *resistance* to the stress where psychological equilibrium is restored. However, if the stress continues, then more defense-oriented reactions are mobilized. These measures are used to exaggerated extent in order to try to control against the mounting threat of anxiety. The defenses become more rigidly entrenched, self-insight is lost, and the flexibility for trying different, more adaptive coping measures is lost.

3. Individuals finally reach an *exhaustion stage* if severe stress levels continue. Dysfunctional defense mechanisms are used and seriously distort the individual's contact with reality, sometimes to psychotic proportions. These measures represent a significant restructuring of reality as last ditch efforts to maintain some level of psychological integrity.

Another model suggests that there are four levels of defense to long-term stress: conscious efforts at maintaining control by manipulation of the external environment; interpersonal relationships; repressive defenses that alter internal reality and change intrapsychic dynamics; and regressive defenses that regulate physiological mechanisms. As stress is relieved or intensified and as the personality structure strengthens and weakens, the lines of defense alter between these four levels accordingly.[7]

Ego Defense Mechanisms

"But the Lord God called to the man, and said to him, 'Where are you?' And he said, 'I heard the sound of thee in the garden, and I was afraid, because I was naked; so I hid myself' " (Genesis 3:9-10). So

Adam and Eve donned their fig leaf aprons and hid themselves in the bushes. Since that time hiding the self has been considered the natural state of humanity. When a person succeeds too well at hiding from others, he or she tends to lose touch with his or her real self and this loss contributes to many forms of psychological and physical disorders.[8]

Far more sophisticated ways of hiding ourselves have been developed since those earliest years of human existence. The psychological defense mechanisms are some of the most complex, most sophisticated and most effective. However, they are also some of the most potentially hazardous mechanisms that we employ. And at least a moderate level of understanding of the psychological defense mechanisms is a vital asset to counselors. Much of the behavior that brings people in to see a counselor relates directly to their use of particular defense mechanisms. And these same defenses are operative at often intensified levels in the counselor's office.

Just what are these defense mechanisms? Essentially, they are learned ways of protecting the self from harmful levels of stress, anxiety and conflict. Starting in early childhood, we experience a wide variety of pressures from external sources such as parents, teachers, other authority figures, schedule demands and so on. Difficult situations arise that throw us into value conflicts. We engage in actions that later we regret. Our interpersonal interactions bring us into contact with anger, hostility, envy, caring, love and compassion. And within most there are feelings of remorse and guilt about personal failures.

All of these situations are anxiety-producing events. We have already looked at the destructive effects of anxiety. We have also surveyed the various task-oriented reactions to stress. When these efforts fail and the stress continues, defense-oriented reactions are needed to protect the integrity of the self.

Their usefulness is their neutralizing impact on anxiety-producing events. Unfortunately, they also distort the person's perception of reality. All defense mechanisms operate either fully or partially subconsciously. They are often activated without our even knowing it.

Defense mechanisms are learned as a normal part of the socialization process. They become a part of our self-controlling behaviors that prove to ourselves and society that we can be a functioning, productive part of our social milieu. When stresses reach temporary high peaks of intensity, ego defenses are most helpful in maintaining psychological and emotional equilibrium.

But there are also some problems inherent with the use of these defenses. Since they operate through the distortion of one's perception of reality, their function involves a certain degree of self-deception. In most cases we would be better off to deal directly with the source of the stress itself. When our perception of the stress is blocked or distorted, we are actually less able to do something directly to ameliorate the actual stress itself. Instead, we adapt to the stress by distorting our perception of it, thereby actually leaving ourselves open to even longer periods of stress.

A survey of common defense mechanisms is presented below. Some of these are the classic defenses described by Anna Freud (Sigmund Freud's daughter).[9] Others, such as compulsions and hallucinations, serve as symptoms as well. Still others, such as controlling and self-aggression are included even though they are not in the strictest sense defense mechanisms since they are used sometimes unconsciously in defense of the self. The ego defense mechanisms are listed in alphabetical order:

Acting out. Anxiety and tension are reduced behaviorally, expressing previously rejected thoughts, attitudes and impulses. Examples: vandalism at school; sexual promiscuity; joy riding.

Blocking. Anxieties from unconscious conflicts or impulses interrupt the flow of thought and communication. Words, thoughts, phrases, names, etc., are suddenly "lost" or "forgotten." Example: Fifteen-year-old Ron starts to tell his parents about an experience at school that involved a female classmate. He suddenly "forgets" what happened and experiences confusion. He has had sexual fantasies about the girl and unconscious anxiety blocked his memory.

Compartmentalization. Attitudes, thoughts and feelings are experienced as separate, unrelated issues in order to protect the person from anxiety arising from internal conflicts. Example: Joyce is a Christian, and she is running for junior class president at her school. As part of her campaign, she is spreading derogatory stories about her opponent. She sees her Christianity and her campaign behavior as two separate, unrelated matters.

Compensation. Perceived inferiority is compensated by strengthening or emphasizing a strong desirable trait. This is a "mask" or "makeup" for a weak or undesirable characteristic. Another compensation for frustration in one area is to overindulge in another. Example: Fourteen-year-old Joe is cut from the freshmen football squad and then compensates by lettering all four years on the tennis team. *Overcompensation* is an attempt to cope with a perceived inadequacy by striving for superior performance in that same area. Example: Claudia, who believes that she is unattractive and klutzy overcompensates by going to modeling school, dressing extravagantly and spending hours doing her hair, nails, makeup, etc.

Compulsion. Behaviors that are often repetitive must be done, usually in a very precise manner, or they must be redone "until they are done right," then the whole pattern is repeated. The behavior appears to not make sense, but it controls against anxiety with force. Example: Nineteen-year-old Stan continuously retraces where he has just driven to make sure that he didn't hit someone with his car; a behavioral measure to try to control his hostile impulses.

Controlling. The attempt to determine and control others' thoughts, feelings and actions in an attempt to make up for one's own feelings of inadequacy, insecurity or powerlessness. Examples: "I know just how you feel." "This is how you ought to do it." "Don't even worry about it because I'll take care of everything."

Conversion reaction. The loss of a motor or sensory function in a part of the body that protects the person from an anxiety-producing thought, impulse or experience. There are no physiological reasons for the dysfunction and under hypnotic suggestion, the malfunction is alleviated. Example: Bob feels a lot of pressure from his parents to play the piano with perfection. Just before a major recital he experienced numbness and partial paralysis in his hands, which prevented him from performing.

Delusions. False beliefs that run contrary to logical and objective reality, either in fragment form or in well-developed belief systems. (Delusions of grandeur or persecution.) Example: Sixteen-year-old Elaine consistently receives poor grades and she thinks that her teachers are involved in a CIA plot to keep her from becoming president.

Denial of reality. A refusal to accept into consciousness the reality of unpleasant or threatening thoughts, feelings, experiences or memories. Example: Young Tony got into a physical fight with his father. When asked about it a week later he remembers only a verbal shouting match, feeling positive that there was no physical fight.

Displacement. The emotion (usually anger) is aroused toward one object and is transferred onto another object that is less threatening or dangerous to express the feeling toward. Example: Thirteen-year-old Nancy has just been scolded by her mother for something she did not do. Her anger, which is too threatening to express to her mother, is unconsciously redirected at her little sister.

Dissociation. A segment of the individual's behavior is detached from consciousness in order to allow expression of repressed impulses or actions that are very threatening or repulsive to the person. Emotion is detached from the behavior and it is improbable that it will be remembered. Examples: sleepwalking, fugues, psychogenic amnesia and multiple personalities.

Emotional insulation. The degree of emotional involvement in a situation is reduced in order to protect the individual from potential pain, disappointment or other emotional damage. Example: Theresa feels no sense of excitement, happiness or anticipation even though she has been asked to the prom by the boy she has wanted to date all year.

Emotional isolation. An event is experienced, a thought is made conscious or a memory is recalled without the expected accompanying emotion. The emotion has been split off because of the anxiety that accompanies it. Example: Terry witnessed a terrible car accident while driving to school one morning, and watched helplessly as a woman died in flames. At school later that day he told the counselor about the incident in vivid details, but was unable to feel any fear, repulsion, horror, sadness or other emotion as he talked.

Fantasy. A way of temporarily gratifying or escaping frustrated desires and other unpleasant reality through creating a more pleasant "imagined reality." Two common themes are the "conquering hero" and the "suffering hero." Example: Steve is 13 years old and deeply resents his parents' insistence that he accompany them on their Sunday afternoon drives. He spends the time slouched in the corner of the back seat daydreaming about athletic, sexual and even academic conquests.

Hallucinations. The occurrence of a sensory experience without any stimulation to create the sensation. Such disordered perception usually indicates severe psychological problems. Example: Margie, who was admitted to the psychiatric hospital because of irrational and bizarre behavior, said that she could feel the fluid in her "eyeballs drying up" because her parents made her work over the hot stove cooking meals.

Hypochondriasis. A conviction that there is a real illness or an exaggeration of an illness, in either case causing a focusing of major time, energy and attention upon perceived physical symptoms, which helps the person to avoid something more threatening. Example: On the day of final exams Joan wakes up feeling nervous. She has no appetite and has some diarrhea. The unconscious connection is made between feeling sick and missing exams. She becomes convinced that she has the flu, she becomes nauseated, develops muscular aches and feels abdominal cramps.

Ideas of reference. The belief that unrelated external events, like people talking, laughing or joking, are meaningfully connected to the person. Example: Fourteen-year-old Jim has not yet reached puberty and is embarrassed by "gang" showers in gym class. He sees a group of boys on the other side of the shower area talking quietly and laughing. Jim is sure that they are laughing at his relatively underdeveloped body.

Identification. Because of feelings of inadequacy, inferiority, or powerlessness, people adopt the values, attitudes and behaviors of esteemed people, groups or institutions, hoping that by becoming more like them, then they will feel better about themselves. Example: Pauline is feeling very insecure on her first job. She is a receptionist in a medical clinic and finds that she feels much more confident when she models her behavior after that of the clinic's business manager.

Inhibition. Some individuals, because of their fears about not being able to accomplish their desires, either give up their true wishes and accept lesser goals, or experience an inability to make themselves respond in a way that might accomplish their desires. Example: Craig had high aspirations to become an airline pilot but feared that he could never make it that far. He talked himself out of his goal ("it's too dangerous") and took another job.

Intellectualization. This process, similar to emotional isolation, avoids threat from unconscious conflict or external pressure by excessive talking, philosophical discussion and theoretical interpretations, in order to avoid dealing with uncomfortable or threatening emotions. Example: "How are you feeling since your boyfriend broke up with you last night?" asks the counselor. Her client responds, "It's really great knowing that God is in charge. I just praise him for everything and I understand that God is teaching me to deal with loss in my life so that I can be a stronger person."

Introjection. Perhaps an extreme form of identification; the person incorporates into his or her own ego structure the values, attitudes and standards of another person, group or institution. Example: Twelve-year-old Charles is deeply discouraged and believes that he can never be really successful. He admires his youth pastor and unconsciously seeks to become "just like him" in every way, incorporating his characteristics into his own personality structure.

Magical thinking. A form of overcompensation in which the individual believes that he or she has very subtle, magical or spiritual powers to make supernatural changes in the external environment. Example: A young man who was experiencing the stress of separation from his wife believed that he could make people sneeze and yawn by his subtle thoughts and words.

Obsession. Repetitive words, thoughts or daydreams that symbolically release energy from repressed impulses and conflicts. Unfortunately, obsessions sometimes increase anxiety because of their destructive content. Example: Frank is exceedingly frustrated by his inability as an athlete, his poor academic performance and his inability to please his parents. His aggressive response to his strong frustration unconsciously motivates his obsessive ruminations about killing and fighting.

Phobia. Fear or panic about a repressed inner drive or impulse is projected on to an external object or situation in order to relieve rising anxiety levels. Example: Laurel feels panicky whenever she touches, holds, or even is near a sharp knife. A few months ago, during an angry fight with her mother while they were in the kitchen, Laurel saw a sharp knife and thought of stabbing her mother with it. The thought horrified her. She felt guilty and afraid and she repressed it as quickly and as thoroughly as she could.

Projection. Includes blaming others for one's own problems. In a fuller sense, it is attributing to another person one's own impulses, thoughts, feelings, attitudes and/or values that are felt to be too negative or threatening to accept into consciousness as aspects of the self. Example: Lance is sure that Robert, a classmate of his, is a homosexual. He feels very condemning and repulsed by Robert. Lance has transferred his anger (which he in reality feels toward himself) for feeling sexually attracted to Robert.

Rationalization. This common "excuse making" response provides logical, rational explanations for one's behavior, which was probably motivated by unconscious and therefore irrational impulses and drives. The goal is to feel more comfortable with one's own self. Example: "I didn't complete my assignment on time because I felt that it was more important to spend time over the weekend being with my family."

Reaction formation. Feelings or impulses from consciousness that are perceived as dangerous, unacceptable or repulsive are blockaded by exhibiting exaggerated behavioral expressions of exactly the opposite feeling or impulse. This intense behavior prevents the individual from being aware of (let alone expressing) the forbidden impulse. Example: Jenny is so sweet and loving to her little brother that it seems unreal. It is unreal. Actually, she feels hatred toward him, but unconsciously tries to control that impulse with the opposite behavior. "Heaping fiery coals on an enemy's head" can also be a reaction formation.

Regression. The retreat from a difficult, current reality back to an earlier developmental period that was less demanding, less complex, and less stressful. The problem-solving and defensive behaviors of that age level are used, even though they are no longer appropriate or helpful. Example: Nineteen-year-old Karen is renting an apartment while going to college. Whenever any small problem occurs (a faucet breaks, neighbors get too noisy, etc.) she calls for the landlord to take care of it for her rather than assuming that responsibility herself. She has made the landlord her surrogate "father."

Repression. This defense mechanism involves forcing anxiety-producing thoughts, feelings, attitudes, impulses and memories into the unconscious. Repression prevents the person from becoming aware of what is there. This process can seriously distort the perception, learning, memory, emotion and behavior of the individual. Example: Dennis, 15, has repressed all of his sexual thoughts and impulses because of an earlier incestual experience initiated by his mother that created a great sense of guilt, shame and repulsion.

Self-aggression. Hostile impulses that are felt toward others are repressed and then are directed at the self, often resulting in depression, accident proneness, self-mutilation and suicide. Example: Jack is 17 years old and for the first time has developed a long-term dating relationship with a girl. Though the relationship provides a generally positive experience, he has episodes of anger toward her. Because of his fear that she might break up their relationship and reject him if she saw his anger, he represses it. The energy from those repressed hostilities is then redirected onto himself and he feels depressed and self-critical.

Somatization. Repressed impulses, feelings and conflicts create great internal pressures on the body's organs and systems, sometimes causing physiological problems. These are often called psychosomatic disorders. Example: Susan is a high school senior and feels a great deal of pressure to excel academically in order to gain admission to graduate school. Yet she is in conflict because when she does so well her friends tease her and distance themselves from her. Her conflicted feelings become repressed because there is seemingly no good solution. As her level of body tension increases, her gastrointestinal system undergoes alterations and she develops a pre-ulcer condition. If her conflict is not dealt with more effectively at a conscious level, a bad ulcer will develop.

Sublimation. The transformation of psychic energy associated with unacceptable impulses or desires into behaviors that are personally and socially acceptable. Example: Ken has never felt accepted or liked by his peers. He feels misunderstood and very angry about this rejection but sees no way to express his hostile impulses directly. Instead, he takes up karate lessons, investing tremendous amounts of energy into its practice and perfection.

Substitution. Replacing a highly desired but unacceptable object with one that is less valued but available and psychologically acceptable. Example: Marla wants very much to become a professional dancer and work in a Broadway troupe. However, some of her religious family and friends strongly oppose this plan so she goes to work for a local Christian theater group where she has at least some limited opportunities to dance.

Suppression. The conscious or semi-conscious decision to put something that produces anxiety "out of mind" or to postpone dealing with it. Example: Lorna, a 16-year-old girl, is two months pregnant. She is unmarried and is deciding between keeping the child, adoption or abortion. The decision process raises strong anxiety from her own internal conflict as well as heavy pressures from her boyfriend, parents and friends. She suppresses the anxiety by putting off the decision. "I'll wait until the weekend when I'll have more time to think about it."

Undoing. Saying or doing something that is unconsciously designed to negate or take back words, thoughts or feelings in order to push away the anxiety caused by them. Examples: "I'm sorry." "I didn't mean it." "You misunderstood me." Also, some Christians use prayer and confession in this way to relieve themselves of personal blame.

Withdrawal. Either a physical or psychological movement out of or away from an extreme anxiety-producing situation. Example: Though Milton is quite an excellent debater, speech meets create strong anxiety responses within him. These responses are based on fear of conflict with others. He wants to quit the debate team.

Grouping Defense Mechanisms

Learning and understanding all of these defensive processes can be an imposing task without some meaningful categorization system. There are several different types of systems that can be used to group the ego defenses.

One method is to group the defense mechanisms according to their *psychological developmental sophistication.* In other words, how primitive or sophisticated are they? Robert White discusses this issue: "Clearly, there is something about repression that differentiates it from the other defense mechanisms. It is more fundamental, more drastic, more primitive than the rest . . . repression, therefore, is to be conceived as a direct manifestation of what we have discerned to be the basic protective device: defensive inhibition. For this reason we shall classify repression along with denial, as a primary defensive process. Other mechanisms will take their place as secondary processes serving to fortify the primary defense and adjust the person to its consequences."[10] White's *primary defensive process* includes the defense mechanisms of denial and repression. The *secondary defensive process* includes projection, reaction formation, displacement, intellectualization, rationalization, emotional isolation and undoing.

In similar fashion, Peter Nathan and S. Harris differentiate between defense mechanisms according to their more *primitive* or *mature* characteristics.[11] They see that repression and suppression are the most basic defense mechanisms. Primitive defenses are those that are most commonly used by infants, children and psychotic patients, though normal or healthy people also use them to some degree. They include the defenses of identification, introjection, projection, displacement and denial. They indicate that the more mature defensive techniques are usually used by normal and healthy people. These mechanisms include reaction formation, undoing, emotional isolation, sublimation, regression, rationalization, substitution and dissociation.

Perry London says that different kinds of defenses are *learned at different stages of development*: "A child threatened much at an early age will master the defenses appropriate to it and keep relying on them as he grows. If he was not threatened much in early life, he will rely more on defenses that he learns later. Either way, as he gets older and smarter, he pools the different mechanisms and, in most adult encounters, combines and uses several at once.

"The main difference between the earlier level and the later level defenses is that the former are more primitive. They are more action-oriented and less verbal, more massive and less subtle. The more primitive defenses, in other words, tend to be regressive, and the more mature ones repressive." His full classification system looks like this:

1. Regressive defenses: withdrawal, fantasy and acting-out.
2. Repressive defenses: repression and denial.
3. Verbal defenses: emotional insulation, emotional isolation, rationalization and intellectualization.
4. Ritual defenses: obsessions, compulsions and reaction formations.
5. Displacement and sublimation.

6. Growth defenses: identification, projection, delusions.[12]

Determining the principle defense mechanisms that a counselee uses is one indicator of his or her level of psychological functioning. There are also typical defenses that are used to defend against different types of stress and anxiety. Coleman suggests the following pairings:[13]

Stress relating to:	Usual ego-defense mechanisms:
Failure	Rationalization, projection, compensation.
Guilt	Rationalization, projection, undoing.
Hostility	Fantasy, displacement, repression, reaction formation.
Inferiority feelings	Identification, compensation, fantasy.
Disappointment in love	Emotional insulation, rationalization, fantasy.
Personal limitations	Denial of reality, fantasy, compensation.
Forbidden sexual desires or behavior	Rationalization, projection, repression.

Illustration 34

Counseling Perspectives

How should the Christian counselor perceive and work with defense mechanisms? What should our approach be toward a counselee whose psychological functioning is heavily impacted by the use of defense mechanisms? Let's look first at the approaches to defense mechanisms from various perspectives in counseling.

The *compartmentalist counselor* treats his or her counselees' behavior, including their defense mechanisms totally from a psychological perspective, assuming that spiritual ramifications have no bearing on the counseling.

The *theologically based integrationist counselor*, while recognizing the psychological implications of defense mechanisms, strongly orients his or her approach from a biblical *interpretation* of defenses. For example, one biblical interpretation is to view defense mechanisms as "smokescreens" for sins: "Defense mechanisms are automatic reactions to frustration and conflict. Our human brains automatically deceive us into viewing everyday conflicts and frustrations in a somewhat prejudiced way so that we can defend our false pride and put the blame for these conflicts on anyone other than ourselves. Defense mechanisms are unconscious or beyond the awareness of the persons using them, since such persons decide themselves about their real desires and goals. Defense mechanisms are sinful because all forms of deceit, including self-deceit, are sin. The purpose of these automatic, unconscious, self-deceiving defense mechanisms is to maintain a false sense of self-esteem and to avoid anxiety. It is true that these mechanisms frequently do prevent or delay insanity because the reality about our depraved desires and motives is extremely painful. An alternative is new birth in Christ followed by progressive sanctification as we meditate on scripture and gradually accept more and more of the truth about ourselves."[14]

The *psychologically based integrationist counselor* does not discount the inherent dishonesty in defense mechanisms. Defense mechanisms do distort reality and deceive the counselee. Jeremiah understood the ways of fooling ourselves: "The heart is deceitful above all things, and desperately corrupt; who can understand it?" (Jeremiah 17:9). Proverbs 21:2 also points out our inherent resistance to the truth about ourselves: "Every way of a man is right in his own eyes, but the Lord weighs the heart."

The Christian counselor should understand the inherent fallenness of humanity. But he or she should also understand the psychological aspects of defense mechanisms. Instead of simply branding them as sinful, we should attempt to understand and deal with each counselee's *overuse* of them. Do not try to ignore or downplay defense mechanisms, since they tend to cover up the person's real problems.

Counseling Guidelines

The first task for the counselor is to determine the teenager's levels of maturity, security and support systems. Is the home environment supportive and secure? Does the teenager have trustworthy friends? If the teenager belongs to a youth group, is he or she acccepted and cared for in it? Is he or she on the fringe? a new kid? Does the young person belong anywhere at school, such as in the band, athletics, clubs, etc.? The answers to these questions will help answer the most important question regarding the teenager's defense mechanisms. How well does he or she handle stress and anxiety in life?

The second task of the counselor is to determine the particular defense mechanisms that the teenager is using. This needs to be accurate. Look through the list of defense mechanisms explained earlier in this chapter. It is most likely that the teenager uses several of them. Discern the more commonly used ones.

The third task for the Christian counselor is to determine an appropriate plan of action for helping the adolescent understand and deal with the defense mechanisms. This plan should be based on the findings of the first two tasks. Chances are high that you will find the teenager is either "stronger" or "less strong" in terms of personality, maturity and insight.

For a "stronger" adolescent, more confrontive and interpretive techniques should be helpful in counseling. This teenager, for example, might have things pretty well together but is experiencing problems with grades, problems at home, etc. You can confront the person by saying something like, "Hey, it seems to me that you're saying you want to go to college, but by the amount of time you study, the way you relate to teachers and the way you resist your parents, you appear to have no intent on going to college. What's happening here?" If the teenager can see the difference between his or her words and actions, you can help the person deal with the real problem. In this case, the real problem is fear and anxiety of the future.

For a "less strong" adolescent, more gentle and supportive responses are needed to help him or her deal with defense mechanisms. This teenager generally has had more difficulty in life. Perhaps he or she has a life history of family problems, academic struggles, short attention or hyperactivity. Try to understand, encourage and nourish these young people. Unlike the "stronger" adolescent, this young person often does not have a strong peer group, a sense of belonging or other support systems for dealing with problems. For example, a therapist working with a 13-year-old found the teenager relying heavily on rationalization. His life history was essentially a shambles. His parents divorced when he was 3 years old. He lived with his mother, who moved to several states within a decade. His mother became addicted to alcohol and other drugs. She had several relationships with men, none of them resulting in marriage. She provided little structure and support for the boy. His only rule was that he had to be home by 6 p.m.

After the boy turned 13 years old, the mother committed suicide. The father, who had since remarried and become a Christian, invited the son to live with them. His father and stepmother had two daughters, ages 4 and 6. The father had seen his son very rarely after the divorce so there was really no bond between them.

The new home environment was very stressful for all the members of the newly altered family. The son had to adapt from a loosely structured home to a very structured one. The stepmother tended to be very compulsive. She wanted a lot of order and predictability in life. All of a sudden her life was thrown into turmoil by a rather uncontrolled adolescent boy. She needed to work through her angry feelings of not wanting an adolescent boy to raise. As a result the boy regressed in psychological age. He competed for attention with the little girls. He desperately wanted to belong in a somewhat hostile and uninviting environment. There was talk that if the situation did not work out, he would be transferred to the home of his grandparents, which would mean yet another high-anxiety change in his life.

When confronted gently by the therapist about his behavior, he would either deny or rationalize it. He had to find a way to explain that his inappropriate behavior was really okay. Otherwise he would feel guilty. It all revolved around, "I'm not good enough," which resulted from a deeper guilt, "If I were a better kid, my mother wouldn't have killed herself." He had to deal with that guilt. In order to do that he had to see the ways he was defending himself against it. Even though the counselor saw right through the denial and rationalization, the young man first needed a secure and supportive counseling relationship. The young man gradually became strong and secure enough to face the guilt over his mother's suicide and the reality of adjusting to a new home.

The key in dealing with defense mechanisms is to provide a setting in which basic needs for belonging are met. When basic needs are met, behavior will generally improve. Too often, youth leaders will be pressured from senior pastors, parents and others to get the kids "shaped up." They're pressured into making sure the kids are not using drugs, not having sex and are not bombing at school. If youth leaders respond to that pressure by "shaping up" the kids, they will lose the position of counselor. Our goal should be to help young people to feel secure, to gain a sense of belonging and to feel cared for. When these positive conditions are experienced in some way by young people, there will be a gradual growth in their lives. The positive growth mechanisms that God has planted in teenagers will develop. They will deal more directly with their real problems and less often rely on the negative overuse of defense mechanisms.

Notes

1. James C. Coleman, *Psychology and Effective Behavior* (Glenview, Ill.: Scott, Foresman, 1969).

2. Ibid.

3. Lewis R. Wolberg, *Handbook of Short-Term Psychotherapy* (New York: Thieme-Stratton, 1980), p. 92.

4. Hans Selye, *The Physiology and Pathology of Exposure to Stress* (Montreal: Acta, 1950).

5. Wolberg, Handbook of Short-Term Psychotherapy, p. 93.

6. Hans Selye, *The Stress of Life* (New York: McGraw-Hill, 1956).

7. Wolberg, *Handbook of Short-Term Psychotherapy*.

8. Sidney M. Jourard, *The Transparent Self* (Princeton: Van Nostrand, 1964).

9. Anna Freud, *The Ego and the Mechanisms of Defense* (London: Hogarth, 1937).

10. Robert W. White, *The Abnormal Personality*, 3rd ed. (New York: Ronald Press, 1964), pp. 212-213.

11. Peter E. Nathan and S. Harris, *Psychopathology and Society* (New York: McGraw-Hill, 1975).

12. Perry London, *Beginning Psychology* (Homewood, Ill.: Dorsey Press, 1975), pp. 383-384.

13. Coleman, *Psychology and Effective Behavior*, p. 227.

■ CHAPTER 10

Difficult Emotions and Related Problems

Extreme mood swings and some degree of emotional instability are characteristic of adolescence. These normal erratic fluctuations create significant disruption and confusion for both the young people and the adults who work with them. When these patterns reach dysfunctional or pathological proportions, very serious consequences often result. Lay counselors, teachers, pastors and counselors are often requested by teenagers or their parents for counseling assistance even during the course of normal adolescent development. When unhealthy emotional responses are evident the assistance of a professional counselor, psychotherapist or well-trained pastor is essential.

This chapter contains sections that focus on these often volatile and potentially problematic emotions and accompanying problems: anger, guilt, anxiety and fear.

Anger

Anger is a very commonly experienced and displayed emotion during adolescence. Sometimes its occurrence is understandable and predictable, at other times it comes as a surprise and shock to everyone including the angry individuals themselves. Anger is an emotion that is common to each of us. But what is anger? How does it get started? What causes some people to be more angry than others?

In order to more fully understand anger, we must start with a knowledge of aggression which is a more basic, core element. We most often think of aggression as a destructive, malignant intent to inflict some sort of evil or injury upon another person or other object in external reality. But aggression in another broader sense refers to forceful action. Something is described as being aggressive if it is marked by a driving forceful energy or noteworthy initiative. "Ro   sure ran an aggressive campaign. No one deserved to be elected more than him." "Terri really surprised us. She was the most aggressive alesperson that we had. She sold more tickets to the carnival than nyone else."

Aggressive behavior is absolutely essential to heal   functioning. Without it, successful functioning with the external environment is doomed to failure.[1] Its presence is essential for the physiological and psychological preparation of the person to tackle tough decisions, complete difficult assignments and take on scary challenges. Teenagers need a certain degree of aggression to successfully meet the challenges that the adolescent stage of development brings. Because of the energy charge associated with aggression, and its characteristics, the subjective experience of anger is often associated with aggression. The two become natural and comfortable partners. One theorist writes that at the roots of every aggressive response is an attempt to cope with some externally provoked experience that is potentially damaging or unpleasant.[2]

The anger response is elicited in quite a wide variety of ways and emanates from several different sources, most often in response to some external event or situation. Let's review some of the most common sources of anger with particular reference to teenagers.

Frustration. Adolescence is a very active, energized, expansive and expressive stage in human development. Frustration represents particular significance during this phase because of the vast amounts of psychological and physical energy that can be blocked from adequate expression. And that is what frustration is: the blocking of one's progress toward or attainment of a goal. The energetic movement toward a goal is either stopped or appreciably slowed down. The individual feels frustrated and also usually angry. Paul is 12 years old and enjoys nothing more than playing with his group of buddies. One afternoon they swarm into his driveway on their bicycles and call for him to join them. Excitedly running to the garage for his bike he suddenly stops at the sight of his flat front tire.

Maria is a high school senior and desperately wants to go to her homecoming game and dance. But she is on restriction!

In both examples, the accomplishment of a desired goal or objective has been frustrated by an external intervention. For Paul, the block came from an inanimate object, a flattened tire. Maria's frustration came from a human source, her parents.

Gary Collins suggests that the frustration level increases as: the goal becomes more important; the obstacle becomes greater; and the frustration lasts for a longer duration. Though the level of anger does not automatically increase proportionately with the level of frustration, the potential for it does.[3]

Injustice. Adolescents tend to be strongly idealistic and firmly hold to their value system, imposing that system onto others. They are particularly sensitive to any violations of their ethical code or value system because such violations symbolically represent encroachments on their developing autonomy. They are particularly sensitive to perceived injustices that are perpetrated by parents, teachers, political leaders, pastors or other authority figures because of the immediate implications to their own movement toward independence.

Anger is likely to ensue whether the injustice is done to them personally, a member of their peer group or a stranger, though the more close or personal the tie with the victim, a greater probability of a stronger angry response. Anger is also a greater probability when the victim is in a helpless condition. The injustice then seems far more unfair and outrageous.

During the 1960s and early 1970s the adolescent conscience was far more easily angered and outraged against incidents of perceived injustice than in the 1980s. The adolescent conscience of the 1960s was definitely a social conscience. That of the 1970s was more of a self-conscience. The adolescent conscience of the current decade appears somewhat disillusional, unsure and searching. So the angry response to injustice is less intense, less collective and less cohesive a factor in the 1980s adolescent mentality.

Alienation. During early adolescence, peer group acceptance and involvement is vitally important for healthy adjustment to occur. As the teenager reaches mid-adolescence, the process of developing a "best friend" and special friends of the opposite sex emerges as the predominant social need. The deepening quest for intimacy, especially with the opposite sex, continues to predominate. Teenagers are extremely sensitive to any indication of rejection or isolation from their group or from their special friends. Such isolation brings not only feelings of loneliness, but deeply felt and grave questions about one's own identity, basic okayness and ultimate value as a human being.

Peer relationships are the primary arena for identity development during the teenage years. Alienation threatens the very process of identity formation. Feelings of alienation elicit a core-level anxiety response which typically gives rise to an angry reaction that one's deepest needs are not being met. In the 1960s and 1970s, some of the more traditional high school and college campus social structures broke down, leaving students in greater danger of experiencing role diffusion as the identity formation process faltered. Many of them joined other less traditional groups like SDS and the Children of God.[4] During the middle and late 1970s, the movement appeared to be toward both traditional and non-traditional religious groups. Teenagers during the 1980s are very much a part of the groundswell that is making physical fitness so popular.

But the threat of alienation always has and always will haunt the adolescent. It is part of the normal developmental struggle. It goes with the turf. And when alienation is deeply felt by a teenager, anger reactions are normally expected. They can be outwardly expressed or they can be internally directed in self-destructive, risk-taking substance abuse and even suicide.

Injury and the threat of injury. An aggressive or angry response when injured or when injury is threatened is part of our physiological survival mechanism that mobilizes the person to either fight or flee in the face of danger. The greater the experienced hurt that coincides with the injury, the stronger the anger response. The hurt which produces anger can be either physical or psychological in nature. The anger is usually directed toward the perceived cause of the injury and pain. For example, a glancing blow to the thumb by a carpenter's hammer that just misses the nail usually brings not only intense pain, but a rush of anger at one's self for being so "careless," "stupid" or "clumsy." But should someone else dare call us those same derogatory names, where is the anger directed? Right. We are angry at our unsupportive and non-sympathetic "friend" as well as at ourselves.

Early and mid-adolescents are quite insecure about their changing bodies, their sometimes faltering coordination, their emerging sexuality, and their fluctuating interpersonal behavior. Being made fun of, teased, called names, ostracized or otherwise hurt will invariably stimulate a strong anger reaction. And like all anger, it will be directed either outwardly toward the perceived tormenter, inwardly toward the self or some combination of the two.

Learning. We hear much about the effects of portrayed violence and sex in the mass media presentations to the public. There seems to be a general agreement that role models, especially when presented in an attractive, powerful or prestigious fashion embody a strong modeling power. Children and adolescents are apt to alter their behavior, value systems and ethical codes to incorporate the modeled behavior. Well-known research psychologist Albert Bandura has written a book on the subject titled *Aggression: A Social Learning Analysis*.[5] In this volume he examines both individual and group aggression in light of social learning theory. He also discusses the role of modeling in trying to reduce aggressive behavior.

The family environment is the most powerful social learning laboratory in existence. And parents are the most powerful models. By the time a child reaches adolescence, the 10-12 most powerful learning years have already been experienced. They have been instructed over and over again on how to handle anger. They have already learned that it should be repressed, denied, lied about, verbalized, expressed physically or used to get even.

Anger is a normal human response. When handled appropriately, it can become a constructive part of human behavior. But when mishandled, it can take any one of several dysfunctional and destructive forms.[6] Rage is anger that is so intense that it is beyond the person's control. Hostility is anger that is felt for a longer period of time and involves the wish or impulse to inflict pain or harm to the object of the anger. Hate or hatred is a more complex form of hostility that is deeply intense and malevolent in nature, wishing for the demise of the hated object. Resentment is another destructive form of anger that develops when a hurt or transgression is not confronted, forgiven.

A biblical perspective on anger. The subject of anger has particular interest and significance for Christians. Anger is often presented as being the opposite of love. The implication is that if people are angry at others, then they do not love them. The incorrect conclusion from these beliefs is that anger is intrinsically sinful.

A biblical perspective, however, does not support that conclusion. Anger is an attribute of God's character. He is angry at sin and was repeatedly angry with the Israelites when they were unfaithful. Jesus was angry at the religious leaders of that day because of their lack of love, lack of perspective and perverted worship. While healing a man with a "shriveled hand" on the Sabbath in the synagogue, Jesus asked, " 'Is it lawful on the Sabbath to do good or to do harm, to save life or to kill?' But they were silent. And he looked around at them with anger, grieved at their hardness of heart, and said to the man, 'Stretch out your hand' " (Mark 3:4-5).

What then about Christ's injunction to "love your enemies" (Matthew 5:44)? Some would say that either Christ is being inconsistent or that scripture is in error. Neither is the case. We must watch carefully for two common sources of error as we seek to understand the Bible and apply it to our lives: interpreting scripture out of context; and incorrect or incomplete understanding of the content of the scripture that we are studying.

Let's look at a little more than "love your enemies" in Matthew 5. Starting with verse 43, "You have heard that it was said, 'You shall love your neighbor and hate your enemy.' But I say to you, love your enemies and pray for those who persecute you, so that you may be sons of your Father who is in heaven; for he makes his sun rise on the evil and on the good, and sends rain on the just and the unjust" (Matthew 5:43-45). It is clear that Christ is instructing us to not have hate, resentment or vengeance. But what about anger? How do we know that scripture does not consider it to be sin as well?

In his epistle to the Ephesian church, Paul wrote: "Therefore, put away falsehood, let everyone speak the truth with his neighbor, for we are members one of another. Be angry but do not sin, do not let the sun go down on your anger, and give no opportunity to the devil. Let no evil talk come out of your mouths, but only such as is good for edifying, as fits the occasion, that it may impart grace to those who hear" (Ephesians 4:25-27, 29). The message takes on increasing clarity. We are to deal with our anger openly, honestly and readily so that it can have a constructive impact on the people who are involved.

Paul continues, "Let all bitterness and wrath and anger and clamor and slander be put away from you, with all malice, and be kind to one another, tenderhearted, forgiving one another, as God in Christ forgave you" (Ephesians 4:31-32). Anger that is not dealt with soon in a straightforward manner can become a destructive force.

Myths and maladaptive responses. One reason why teenagers and adults develop problems with handling their anger is that they have incorrect beliefs about it. In their Christian self-help book, William Backus and M. Chapian list five common misbeliefs about anger:

1. Anger is bad and if I'm a good Christian, I will never get angry.

2. Anger always means to yell and throw things or do whatever else it takes to "drain off" the emotion.

3. If I do get angry, it's always better for me to swallow the anger

than express it.

4. I have every right to be angry when another person does not live up to my expectations. I have no choice but to stay angry as long as things don't change.'

5. It is outrageous and insufferable when others do things I don't like or if they fail to treat me as well as I ought to be treated.[7]

These incorrect beliefs about anger represent both bad theology and bad psychology. And they typically result in very unhappy and unfortunate consequences for all involved. Adolescents very often experience problems handling their anger in a constructive mode. Many have been taught to believe one or more of the above listed myths about anger and have developed dysfunctional ways of dealing with their emotion. Counselors need to be able to spot maladjustive styles that their young counselees are utilizing with their anger in order to help them to discover and learn more functional approaches.

Here are some of the maladaptive responses to anger:

1. Feeling guilt and self-rejection. "I should never be angry. As a Christian, with the help of the Holy Spirit, I ought to be able to squelch that feeling and always respond in a nice way." We have already discussed the incorrect beliefs that lead to this reaction. It is not bad to feel angry. It may feel bad, but it is not evil. Anger is a fact of our existence. It is what we do with our anger that is either righteous or unrighteous, constructive or destructive, good or bad.

2. Denial. The atmosphere in a family counseling session was filled with tension. Dad, with clenched fists, white knuckles, beet red face and jaws clamped shut declares, "I'm not angry." Unconscious denial prevents persons from being aware of what they really do feel inside. Without that awareness, nothing constructive can be done about the feeling because there is no admission that it even exists. Conscious denial of one's anger to another person is of course deliberate deceit. There is possibly nothing more damaging to the individual or to his or her relationships than making the decision to be dishonest and misrepresent the self.

3. Silence. It has been said that there is no more powerful or unmovable position than that of silence. A silent, glaring stare can cut more deeply and convey more hatred than any words or most actions. And how can an effective response be given to such angry silence? The angry person using silence in this way has given up on trying to work out the problem. He or she is only trying to win. But no one wins in that kind of situation.

4. Avoidance. Avoidance of angry feelings is essentially a confession that, "My anger is too frightening and too powerful for me to risk dealing with." Perhaps some have seen the destructive force of uncontrolled anger in their parents. They may still feel painful remorse over their own previous destructive angry reactions and fear its reoccurrence. No sooner is the first hint of anger experienced within themselves than they immediately react in some way to avoid it. They may physically turn around and walk out of the room. They might go into hiding behind a book or newspaper, or find refuge in a tunnel-visioned focus on the television. Homework, church work, work around the house and yard and jobs are equally effective ways to withdraw from angry feelings.

5. Acting-out. When a person expresses the energy from his or her emotion in relatively uncontrolled and destructive overt physical behavior, psychologists label it as acting-out behavior. Poor impulse control is suggested by such behavioral reactions that usually suggests some immaturity in personality development. Four types of angry acting-out behavior can be differentiated: verbal aggression toward the target of the anger; non-verbal aggression toward the target of the anger; verbal aggression toward a displaced target; and non-verbal aggression toward a displaced target.

Yelling, screaming, stomping feet, vigorous arm and hand movements, name calling, swearing and hurling accusations are all too familiar expressions of verbally acted-out aggression. The use of language in the expression of anger and aggression has particular importance for adolescents.[8]

"Language, as an attempt to reinforce feelings of separateness and autonomy may also be used to show defiance. Mixing rebellion with independence, employing language similarly to clothes and hair styles, adolescents attempt to demonstrate the gap between themselves and the world of adults. Since language, like all fashions, seems to be taken over by adults, adolescents then have to devise new techniques of communication."[9] Not only do teenagers use language as a way of distancing themselves from adults, but from each other as well. Ethnic groups, social and economic class groups, and interest groups reinforce their own cohesiveness while excluding others through the use of language.

Swearing is one of the most common expressions of verbal aggression. The particular words that are used for swearing in a particular society are words or phrases that arouse special anxiety because they refer to topics that are commonly associated with conscious or unconscious conflict.[10] Most swearing relates to sex, religion, motherhood, bowel and urinary functions and homosexuality. As different issues within the society become more sensitive, swearing focuses on phrases and words that touch on those internal conflicts.

How shall the adult world respond to adolescent swearing? Psychiatrist Derek Miller gives us some valuable guidance:

"Adolescents have a need for aggressive defiance of the openly stated forms of adult society. To accept bad language is to deny adolescents a whole area of potential defiance that is relatively safe. If bad language between parents and children is totally forbidden, the probability is that young people will conform as they do in main areas of interfamily functioning.[11] Other outlets for aggression will then have to be found. If bad language is disapproved of but implicitly condoned from time to time, it will be used when adolescents wish to show aggressive defiance."[12]

As Christians, we certainly cannot condone swearing from our adolescents. But we can respond differentially to their behaviors depending on how serious or destructive they really are. Paul teaches, "Fathers, do not provoke your children to anger, but bring them up in the discipline and instruction of the Lord" (Ephesians 6:4). One form of exasperating teenage children is by being overly oppressive of all of their expressions of independence. The result will be either giving up their efforts to develop their own identity, or resorting to more aggressive forms of acting-out behavior. Physically aggressive behavior involves an attempt to damage or hurt objects, animals, other people or the self. Attacks on objects are usually symbolic expressions of anger at certain people. Breakage of household items usually is a symbolic attack on the parents.[13]

Bullying is probably the most frequent expression of aggressive acting-out in teenagers. They often bully others who are weaker for three reasons: they are not yet able to control their frustration when frustrated; they do not think the bullying is wrong because the victim is dehumanized; and the victims are scapegoats who, though they are really weak, are perceived to be strong.[14]

There are several reasons why certain teenagers tend to bully others: they feel bullied by their parents; they are experiencing emotional disturbance because of some upsetting event like the birth of a younger sibling, parents getting a divorce, etc.; they come from an ethnic group or socioeconomic class where physical aggression is more acceptable;

they feel little or no support or caring from the adults in their immediate environment; they have serious doubts about their own self-perceived weakness, symbolically attacking it by lashing out at others' weaknesses; and they strongly envy others who have what they do not possess.[15]

Counseling goals and guidelines for dealing with anger. When counseling with an adolescent who struggles with some aspect of his or her angry behavior, there are a variety of different goals that can be established:

1. Help the counselee to admit how he or she really feels. Gradually breaking down denial and other defenses that prevent the counselee from self-admission of the anger is often the first goal.

2. Provide an environment in the counseling setting that is accepting of some catharsis or ventilation of anger. Counselees need to know that anger is not bad and the counselor's acceptance of some cathartic release is helpful in communicating that fact. After some release is gained, the counselee will be better able to focus on other counseling tasks.

3. Help the counselee differentiate between anger feelings and various reactions to the anger. Then they can be helped to differentiate between constructive and destructive expressions of their anger and confess any sinful responses to God. This goal should be accomplished with a great deal of care and support, being sure that no messages of condemnation, disapproval or judgment are being conveyed. Adolescent counselees need to know that everyone mishandles anger.

4. When appropriate, help the counselee to communicate his or her anger to the person toward whom the anger is felt. This is the most effective way of teaching the value of "be angry but do not sin" (Ephesians 4:26). Formulating expressions of anger in non-accusative, non-blaming and non-hostile statements will boost the counselees' self-confidence that they can handle their strong angry impulses. Teach them how to formulate "I" messages (e.g., "I am feeling angry with you"). Help them to own their anger, taking full responsibility for feeling as they do. Suggest that expressing their feelings of anger to the other person is really a horizontal confession. It is being open and honest in an attempt to build a bridge or rebuild one that has been destroyed.

5. Help teenagers to accept and understand their impulses and feelings. Impulses that feel dangerous, frightening and threatening, lose some of their threat when we understand that there is a good reason why we feel them. Counselors should know that all behavior is purposeful. There is a reason, a cause, for every emotion. Causes are not

excuses, they are valid reasons for valid feelings. As counselees begin to realize that there are good reasons for feeling as they do, they are more free to determine what to do about them.

6. Help the counselee to slow down his or her response to the anger. Slowing down the response gives the teenager time to think through which response would be most appropriate in the situation. John Powell suggests that we experience our emotions fully, carefully think through the situation, determine which action is most appropriate, and then carry out that response.[16] James warns us, "Let every man be quick to hear, slow to speak, slow to anger, for the anger of man does not work for the righteousness of God" (James 1:19-20).

7. Encourage the giving and accepting of forgiveness in young counselees. Help them to feel the courage to ask for forgiveness if they have been destructive or sinful with their anger. And when forgiveness is extended, support their acceptance of it so they do not continue feeling guilt needlessly. And when another genuinely asks for their forgiveness, encourage them to offer it. Much of our anger is resolved in the process of forgiveness and the reconciliation that follows.

8. Help counselees understand how they may create difficult, intense and angry situations. Deep feelings of resentment, feelings of inadequacy and just plain never having learned how to interact with others, are often the causes of teenagers developing a habitual pattern of aggressive encounters.

Some young people seem to draw a lot more aggression than others. Derek Miller identifies the adolescent whose defenses are rigid but weak, who is distressed, who is apt to overreact to being teased, as being a particularly prime target for being bullied by others. "They are ready-made victims for those adolescents who fear loss of control themselves and who can reassure themselves that they would behave differently."[17] But teenagers need to realize that everyone from time to time will have people angry with them.

William Backus and M. Chapian have listed seven helps for dealing with these situations when others are angry at us. Counselors can use these guidelines as they work with angry adolescents:

1. Knowing that we can deal with other people's anger at us, we need not become upset every time someone gets angry.

2. We should be ourselves, not trying to shape our behavior into what we think will keep others from being angry with us.

3. We should not reward others' angry outbursts with the same type of behavior in return.

4. We need not be intimidated. We can respond assertively, even in the face of another's anger.

5. Responding in a kind and loving manner may help the other person to get better control over his or her angry outburst.

6. When there is truth in an accusation that is levied against us, we need to acknowledge it, confess it and ask for forgiveness.

7. We need to recognize and admit to ourselves that others will at times be angry with us, and that that is okay.[18]

Teenagers usually resist telling an adult in the case of being bullied. Asking for adult help amounts to breaking the adolescent peer group faithfulness code. When an adolescent boy asks for adult help there is also the possibility that the young person is seriously questioning his own masculinity. "When adolescents complain that they are being bullied, the usual, initial adult response is inactivity with appropriate empathy."[19] The response is usually best when it offers caring understanding of the counselee's pain along with encouraging belief in the individual's ability to personally handle the problem.

Guilt

Guilt is an inescapable fact of human existence. Unfortunately it is a very painful, disruptive fact that plays a significant part in many of our psychological, emotional and physical disorders. Christian psychiatrist Quentin Hyder described the complex phenomenon of guilt in this way: "It is partly the unpleasant knowledge that something wrong has been done. It is partly fear of punishment. It is shame, regret or remorse. It is resentment and hostility toward the authority figure against whom the wrong has been done. It is a feeling of low self-worth or inferiority. It leads to alienation, not only from others but also from oneself, because of the discrepancy between what one really is and what one would like to be. This leads to loneliness and isolation. Guilt, therefore, is partly depression and partly anxiety."[20]

Guilt has been called by one psychologist, "potentially the most dangerous and destructive" of the many psychological reactions.[21] Its pain is so intense both because of its strength and because of the variety of attacks upon the personality that it brings. Central to the issue of guilt and its destructive impact upon the person is the concept of conscience. Two Christian psychiatrists write that the Old Testament contains no reference to the concept of conscience, but that there are 32 references in the New Testament. They state that the New Testament reference is in the form of the Greek word "sunerdesis" which they report means "to know together with."[22] Conscience lets us know when we are doing something wrong. It seems to possess an inherent wisdom that understands when we are considering action or are engaged in an activity that is damaging the self or another person.

Christians often have an even more difficult time coping with guilt. Those who tend to be more legalistic in their theology struggle with the guilt at not being perfect. They falsely believe that with the help of the Holy Spirit they should be able to live sinless lives. Therefore, as they repeatedly have to reapproach God with confession and true desires to repent, they heap upon themselves more guilt. But this is the reason why Christ came. We are helpless to live perfect lives, even with the Holy Spirit in our lives because the old nature is still a part of our being. The New Testament speaks clearly to our continuing need for forgiveness. "If we say we have no sin, we decieve ourselves, and the truth is not in us. If we confess our sins, he is faithful and just and will forgive our sins and cleanse us from all unrighteousness. If we say we have not sinned, we make him a liar, and his word is not in us" (1 John 1:8-10). These words were penned to people who had already received Christ, people who had already been forgiven but who needed continuing forgiveness for new sins.

Objective and subjective guilt. Several schemes for differentiating between types of guilt have been presented. The one that seems to be most accurate and functional is by Gary Collins. He differentiates between objective guilt and subjective guilt:

Objective guilt is the existence of the fact of guilt. A law has been broken. A transgression has been committed. Whether or not the person experiences a feeling of guilt, the fact of guilt remains. Collins differentiates between four different types of objective guilt:

1. Legal guilt exists when a person breaks a law of society.

2. Social guilt is present when an individual violates an unwritten code of social ethics like failing to keep an appointment or gossiping about a friend.

3. Personal guilt exists when an individual does something that goes against his or her own internal urgings, even though there exists no violations against society, other people or God. Examples of personal guilt include earning poorer grades in school than what individuals expect of themselves, and failing to maintain a consistent daily Bible reading program that had been planned.

4. Theological guilt is present when God's laws have been broken.

Subjective guilt, as defined by Collins, involves the internal response of the person that is typically defined as guilt feelings. Subjective guilt includes feelings of remorse, self-condemnation, regret, shame, discouragement, anxiety, fear and alienation.[23] Paul Tournier defines this type of guilt as "functional guilt."[24] Hyder refers to it as "false guilt."[25] Dr. Bruce Narramore, in one of his several works on the topic of guilt, differentiates three categories of subjective guilt feelings: fear of punishment; loss in self-esteem; and feelings of loneliness, rejection and isolation.[26]

Subjective guilt feelings are sometimes the normal ones that result from objective guilt. However, these subjective feelings of guilt can become so strong and problematic that they create a "pathological" guilt. Pathological guilt feelings seem to never be able to be released. They "usually reflect immature, rigid and unrealistic moral standards that no human being could possibly follow, with such an unrealistic but implacable conscience, the individual is foredoomed to perpetual failure and devaluation."[27]

Categories of defenses. When guilt feelings become too painful or threatening, the individual resorts to psychological defense mechanisms to protect the integrity of the self. Dr. William Justice outlines 37 ways not to deal with guilt in his provocative book, *Guilt: The Source and the Solution.* "Since the feelings of guilt come as an attack upon the inner sense of well-being, almost always inflicting pain, we feel it necessary to defend ourselves."[28] Since the counselor works daily with people who are struggling with subjective guilt, it is important to be able to identify the mechanisms of defense that counselees often use. Justice outlines four broad categories of defenses: offensive; surrender; escape; and evasion. Offensive defenses are the more assertive or aggressive efforts to defend against the pain of guilt. Some examples of this are:

1. Repetition. By repeating guilt-producing behavior over and over, the impact of the associated negative feelings is gradually lessened.

2. Balancing. This compensatory action seeks to draw personal attention away from guilt-producing behavior by exaggerating the value of one's positive behavior.

3. Confession. Disclosing one's sin to another in order to relieve the subjective experience of pain is really nothing more than a defense mechanism.

Surrender defenses are tactics that a person uses to give in temporarily to the pressures of subjective guilt. Some examples of this type of defense mechanism are:

1. "That's just the way I am." The person does not deny the behavior, but the responsibility for the behavior is denied.

2. Passage of time. This is a passive waiting for the pain of the guilt to gradually numb.

3. Self-recriminations. Self-recriminations are designed to draw expressions of pity and reassurance from others in order to make the individual feel better.

4. "Everybody's doing it." This form of rationalization is geared to help the individual feel less guilt without doing anything about it.

Escape defenses are used to try to get away from the painful effects of guilt. Examples are:

1. Suppression. This is a conscious decision to push away thoughts and other evidences of guilt feelings.

2. Repression. This is a fully unconscious process of pushing extremely painful thoughts, feelings and memories out of the conscious awareness.

3. Knowledge. It usually helps to know that we are not the only ones experiencing difficulty.

4. Distractions. People will often invite certain distractions to aid in their attempts at suppression. Examples of distractions include sleep, sexual intercourse, masturbation, criminal activity, intellectual challenges, forced mental activity like memorizing Bible verses, work and play.

5. Isolation. This defense detaches the person's consciousness from the emotional pain.

6. Masking. People suffering from subjective guilt often try not to be really seen by others as well as by themselves.

7. Fantasy. Daydreaming is an easy and pleasant, temporary escape from the anxiety produced by subjective guilt.

8. Opiates. Drugs numb the sensation of both psychological and physical pain.

9. Insanity. Craziness is a drastic resort which reflects on the potentially devastating consequences of guilt.

Evasion defenses are used by the person who is trying to elude the sense of guilt. Examples of this type of defense mechanism are:

1. Sublimation. The individual tries to fulfill a guilt-laden urge by engaging in some alternate activity which is not forbidden.

2. Overreaction. This is actually reaction-formation, a mechanism of reacting publicly in an exaggerated manner that is just the opposite of the internal impulse.

3. Denial of standards. All standards are seen as relative and flexible

and therefore no guilt should be felt.

4. Willy Lomanism. This is the process of always trying to please others and never taking responsibility for one's own behavior, thereby evading guilt.

5. Regression. This is a retreat to an earlier life stage where living was a simpler, less painful process.

6. Denial. Some people refuse to admit personal culpability for their sin, sometimes as a conscious, and other times as an unconscious process.

7. Ignorance. "Ignorance is bliss," or so the saying goes. It becomes an excuse for not accepting responsibility.

8. Perfectionism. The state of being perfect and the striving for perfection are dodges to the reality of the present.

9. Rigid rightness. The unbelievable claim that, "I am always right; I never make mistakes," is an airtight defense against anxiety and guilt.

10. Defensive aggression. Should anyone remind the individual of his or her guilt, a counterattack is immediately levied in order to funnel off awareness of one's own guilt.

11. Hate the harmed. Turning hatred and contempt onto the one harmed tends to dehumanize the victim and justify the sin which, if not defended against, would likely stimulate strong guilt feelings.

12. Scapegoating. One's own guilt is projected onto another along with feelings of anger and indignation which are also projections of one's own self-hatred.

13. Substitution. People find it easier and less threatening to give things rather than giving themselves.

14. Undoing. Some people seek to right their wrong by saying things like, "I didn't mean it."

15. Displacement. A person might feel guilty for a lesser transgression in order to not focus on the guilt of a greater sin that he or she has committed.

16. Rationalization. By selecting and developing an explanation for why they did what they did, the guilt feelings are talked out of having any rational basis.

17. Justification. This is really a form of rationalization that is designed to justify the person's actions.

18. Identification. Some people will see themselves as very admired or esteemed in order to aid the painful reality of what they really are like.

19. Chance. The belief that their actions probably did not do any real harm. "It probably would have happened anyway, sooner or later."

20. Dilution. Individuals will experience less subjective guilt if they lessen their personal culpability by seeing that their sin was just one little part of a larger group action.

21. Approval. Trying to get the approval of a respected authority for one's action is another way to evade guilt feelings.[29]

Counseling goals and guidelines for dealing with guilt. Severe guilt most often plays a major role in serious depressive reactions. Unfortunately, none of the defensive maneuvers described previously deal effectively with either objective or subjective guilt.

Counselors need to be able to help their adolescent counselees resolve guilt in more than a Band-Aid fashion. First, the differentiation needs to be made between objective and subjective guilt. When the presence of objective guilt is established, the counselee can be helped to deal with it in an appropriate manner. Two well-known writers in the field of psychology and psychiatry are O. Hobart Mowrer and Karl Menninger. Neither of these men write from a Christian perspective, yet they have both emphasized the need for individuals to accept responsibility for their own behavior, make sincere confession of their sins, and make constructive alterations in their patterns of behavior if they are to be freed from the guilt of their sin.[30] Counselors can help their young counselees through the confession-repentance-forgiveness process that is appropriate to their sin and to their life situation.[31]

Helping counselees with their subjective guilt is even more complex. Here are some suggested goals and procedures which might be helpful:

1. Teenagers who are suffering from subjective guilt are usually very sensitive to the possibility of being condemned or judged by others. In fact, they often expect it. It takes a great deal of courage for them to disclose their feelings of guilt. Nothing encourages this delicate process more than for the counselor to be genuinely understanding, accepting and non-judgmental. This attitude reassures, "I am not interested in evaluating your behavior or judging your morality. I am interested in helping you to establish and accomplish your own goals."

2. The particular manner that adolescents experience subjective guilt and attempt to deal with it is largely determined by their past history. Help them to recall important incidents, people and general awarenesses from their earlier childhood. As this material is recalled and expressed, then help the young person to a more full understanding of how he or she developed his or her particular behavioral patterns and styles of dealing with subjective guilt.

Collins lists several questions that both the counselor and the counselee should gain specific knowledge about in order to help the counselee gain the greatest benefit from the counseling process: "What were parental expectations of right and wrong? Were standards so high that the child could never succeed? What happened when there was failure? What is the counselee's experience with forgiveness? Were blame, criticism and punishment frequent? What did the church teach about right and wrong? Was there biblical basis for these teachings? Was the counselee made to feel guilty? What makes the counselee specifically feel guilty today? Does the counselee show any of the defensive reactions, self-condemnation, social reactions or physical reactions that indicate the presence of subjective quilt?"[32]

As insight is gained, then a clearer understanding between past causes, influences and current patterns is gained.

3. The counselee can be helped to unlearn false beliefs about guilt. To accomplish this, the counselor can participate as a teacher and even as a disciple, helping the counselee to gain an accurate, objective perspective of his or her perceived guilt. The new beliefs are reinforced by the counselor, who encourages action based on the new beliefs.

4. The counselor evaluates the conscience and superego development in the counselee. Is there overdevelopment, too much demanding rigidity, too harsh self-judgment? Or is there underdevelopment in the conscience and superego? Is there too little openness to experience subjective guilt? Evaluate any marked presence of manipulative tendencies without any apparent guilt responses. In cases where this pattern exists, there may be the development of rather serious personality disorder problems. If this is suspected, a consultation with a professional therapist is suggested.

5. Determine the current status of the counselee's personal strengths. Are there strong feelings of inferiority? To what extent is the counselee engaged in self-condemning attitudes and behavior? What is the current level of self-esteem? How does the individual describe himself or herself? The answers to these and similar questions will help the counselor to assess the personal strength that can be relied upon and built up during the counseling process.

6. In light of information gained from investigating the issues under the previous point, evaluate the counselee's current self-expectations. What demands are being placed on the self? How perfectionistic are those self-demands? Does there seem to be an allowance for falling short of personal goals? Do the counselee's personal goals emanate more from within the individual or more from the external pressures of

others' expectations? Counseling may be able to help the counselee to establish reasonable goals that will have the effect of pulling the person forward in his or her personal growth rather than creating discouragement, disillusionment and stronger guilt arising out of a sense of failure.

7. The counselor can help counselees learn and adopt new and accurate beliefs about guilt, confession, repentance and forgiveness. New actions that are formulated on the basis of these beliefs can be reinforced. The counseling relationship itself can offer a powerful experience for teenagers to learn and adopt new attitudes and new behaviors.

Anxiety and Fear

Along with anger and guilt, anxiety and fear are major players in the lives of many teenagers who seek counseling help. The dynamics of anxiety are often closely intertwined with a person's anger, subjective guilt and depression, though there are instances where the person's symptoms are more purely anxiety and fear. Strong anxiety feelings, because they are so disruptive and debilitating to one's life, are often the force that prompts a person to initiate a counseling relationship.

Anxiety can be defined as the experience of unrest, apprehension, dread or agitated worry. It has been described as a fear in the absence of real danger, or a fear of something that is not clearly understood. Fear is typically related to a specific object, experience, person or definite future possibility. A related experience, worry, is a form of fear and anxiety that is related to a possible future event about which the individual feels helpless and hopeless. No positive outcomes are foreseen and the person is given to compulsive fretting about the anticipated situation.

Anxiety, fear and worry form a complex system of emotions that make clear differentiation between them quite difficult. They tend to overestimate the negative or threatening aspects of a situation while drawing attention away from the positive or reassuring aspects. The person is left feeling uneasy, concerned, restless, irritable and fidgety.

Positive and negative aspects. Two writers, Backus and Chapian, have suggested that there are two major misbeliefs that underlie anxiety: "1. If the thing I worry about were to happen, it would be terrible. 2. Even though the likelihood of the terrible happening to me is utterly remote, I believe it is actually inevitable."[33] By believing things that are untrue, we often place ourselves in situations where it is impossible to feel successful or good. Feeding ourselves untruthful, self-entrapping statements greatly increases our feelings of helplessness, hopelessness and generalized anxiety. Many adolescents who come for counseling believe one or more of the following false beliefs:

1. It is essential that I am loved or approved by virtually everyone in my community.

2. I must be perfectly competent, adequate and achieving in order to consider myself worthwhile.

3. It is a terrible catastrophe when things are not as I want them to be.

4. Unhappiness is caused by outside circumstances, and I have no control over it.

5. Dangerous or fearsome things are causes for great concern, and I must continually dwell upon their possibility.

6. It is easier to avoid certain difficulties and self-responsibilities than to face them.

7. I should be dependent on others and I must have someone stronger on whom I can rely.

8. My past experiences and events are the determiners of my present behavior, I cannot eradicate or alter the influence of my past.

9. I should be quite upset over other people's problems and disturbances.

10. There is always a right or perfect solution to every problem, and I must always find it or the results will be catastrophic.[34]

So far in our discussion, anxiety has been considered totally in negative terms. But there are some very positive aspects to both fear and anxiety. In mild to moderate degrees, anxiety can help motivate the person to optimal performance. Some anxiety helps the student to study for an exam, motivates the athlete to train more rigorously, and can stimulate the employee to become more creative and industrious. It can push the vacillating individual into making decisions and constructive action. Fear sometimes protects the teenager from doing something that is excessively dangerous even though dared or called a "wimp," "chicken" or "pansy." Mild levels of anxiety even stimulate imagination and creativity. And feeling some anxiety of an existential nature helps the adolescent to search for values, goals and beliefs which will help them to experience meaning and fulfillment in his or her life.[35]

One writer is quoted as stating, "Thus anxiety is a Janus-headed creature that can impel man to self-improvement, achievement and competence, or can distort and impoverish his existence and that of his fellows."[36]

However, at high or strong levels of intensity, anxiety is quite destructive. It sometimes is acute, with a sudden onset, high level of intensity and short duration. Barbara wakes up at 7 a.m. with the sudden realization that she has forgotten to study for her English midterm exam scheduled for that day. Her heart is pounding and her body is filled with tension. "Oh no!" she gasps, suddenly struck with the awareness that it is really too late to do anything about it. However, she soon is able to think about other ways to protect her grade in English. There are other tests, papers, classroom work and even extra credit assignments that she can focus on to bring her grade back up. As she considers these solutions, her feelings of anxiety and dread subside.

Some anxiety is chronic, or long term. Chronic anxiety often begins gradually, slowly building in intensity and lasting without resolution for weeks, months and even years. During the course of chronic anxiety, the levels of intensity fluctuate relative to changes in the anxiety-producing stimulus, the person's overall condition, and other factors in the person's life.

Causative factors. The experience of anxiety is aroused by a wide array of causative factors. Eight categories of these factors will be discussed here:

1. External situations. Certain aspects of the external world create feelings of anxiety. Novelty in a social situation can be particularly anxiety producing for a teenager because of the importance of peer relationships and self-consciousness that is experienced in public settings. Poverty or severe financial pressures within the family, moving to a new school or community, and many different types of objects and situations (e.g., snakes, mice, bridges, heights, crowds, etc.) can cause anxiety.

2. Physical well-being. Experiences that hinder or disrupt a person's sense of physical health and well-being tend to produce anxiety. Undiagnosed pain causes apprehensive reactions. Injury and illness often bring unconscious anxiety about disfigurement, disablement and death into consciousness. Since teenagers are quite concerned about themselves, anxieties centering around their bodies are particularly prevalent.

3. Learning. Some anxieties that adolescents experience revolve around their abilities to learn and function well in the school setting. Competence in academics is to the adolescent what competence on the job and in parenting is to adults. Some anxieties are also learned through the processes of modeling and identification. They model

themselves after their heroes' characteristics, identify with, and try to become like them. When they see anxiety portrayed in their heroes behavior, they will tend to replicate the anxiety response in their own behavior. As parents become more anxious about finances, their children are likely to be also. If teachers are seen to be anxious about the political situation, their students are likely to model that response.

4. Conflict. There is a wide variety in the types of conflict that people experience. Each type is likely to arouse anxiety. For many years psychologists have identified three different types of conflict-producing situations:

Approach-approach conflicts exist when the person has two attractive or positive alternatives but must choose only one of them. Charles is a senior in high school and is strongly attracted to two classmates. He obviously can ask only one to go to the prom with him, so he must choose between the two.

Approach-avoidance conflicts are present when an impending decision carries both positive and negative aspects. Athletics are very important to Dale. But practicing after school everyday means that he can not keep his part-time job too, because he cannot do both and keep his grades up. Without his job, he cannot buy a car or have much spending money. Dale has an approach-avoidance conflict.

Avoidance-avoidance conflicts present the person with two negative options, one of which must be selected. While on a date last night, Lon scratched the fender of his father's car. He can either take it into the shop and pay for the repair today or tell his father. If he does it himself, his dad probably will not find out about it, but Lon will be out about $250. On the other hand, his father's insurance will cover it, but Lon will have to face his father's anger.

5. Identity. Identity formation is such a major part of adolescent development that it is not surprising that it is also central to much of the anxiety that teenagers experience. Psychologist Eric Erikson stipulated that the adolescent who fails to establish an adequate personal identity will suffer what he called "role diffusion."[37] They do not possess a core sense that proclaims, "This is me. This is who I am. I am an individual; somewhat different from everyone else." Instead, they are left with a very ill-formed, fuzzy concept of themselves that is essentially the sum of the roles that they fulfill, like student, son or daughter, friend, brother or sister, cheerleader, church youth group member, clarinet player and so on. Young people in this position struggle with severe anxiety reactions because there is the feeling of no substance or unify-

ing structure at their center. Hence, they feel at a loss to develop any consistency in the way that they interact with others, in their interests, activities, or their academic and vocational aspirations.

6. Loss. Adolescents experience the subjective feeling of loss from a wide variety of sources. Early adolescents experience loss when they stop sleeping with a stuffed animal and give up other objects and behaviors that have been treasured aspects of their childhood. When older brothers and sisters move out of the house, though they may gain a private bedroom, they lose regular contact with a person who has been important in their lives. Psychological loss is experienced each time their school team loses in athletic competition, whenever a friend decides to not be so close, when semester grades are lower than anticipated, when a dating request is met with "no," and whenever parents set limits on what the young person wants to do. Extreme loss is felt when there is a breakup with a long-term boyfriend or girlfriend, when a relative or friend dies, when a close friend moves out of town, and when teenagers are dropped from the speech team or athletic squad because they aren't "good enough."

Loss is very painful at any age, but particularly so during adolescence. Feelings of insecurity, helplessness, anger, and self-doubt are likely to soar until the adolescent is helped to accept and resolve his or her difficult emotional responses.

7. Existential issues. Part of the adolescent task is to move from a strongly egocentric base of narcissism to an ability to reach beyond the self and to be able to form associative links with other valuable people, objects, ideas, values and experiences in the world.

Existential anxiety is experienced when the teenager falters in his or her efforts to transcend egocentricity. When meaning, value and purpose are elusive, anxiety is incumbent. And when ideals and goals are grasped at only to find them disappointingly empty or false, disillusionment reigns.

8. Perceived threat. When a person anticipates that any of the above anxiety-producing situations will arise, a future threat is perceived. Such experiences are usually met with what psychologists call "anticipatory anxiety." Very often, the anticipatory anxiety is worse than the feared experience itself. Unfortunately, the anxiety partially blocks the person's functioning and renders him or her less capable to deal well with the feared event. For instance, when going to the doctor for an injection, which is worse? The feelings of anxiety, worry and dread ahead of time, or the shot itself? For many, it is the minutes, hours and days

of mounting anticipatory anxiety that finds release only after the injection is administered.

Most psychologists agree that the experience of anxiety is at the core of most psychological disorders. The avoidance of anxiety is the purpose and driving force behind the psychological defense mechanisms. They function to help protect the individual from the destructive impact of severe and prolonged anxiety. And yet it is the overuse or particular types of usage of these defense mechanisms that disrupts the person's accurate contact or effective coping with reality.

Anxiety-related disorders. Up until the 1980 publication of the third edition of the **Diagnostic and Statistics Manual** (DSM-III) by the American Psychiatric Association, many of the psychological disorders that result from anxiety were classified as various types of neuroses. However, the DSM-III no longer uses that diagnostic nomenaclature.

Pastors and lay counselors will often have periodic counseling contacts with teenagers who are in psychotherapeutic treatment with a professional therapist. It may be helpful to have a cursory understanding of the variety of anxiety related disorders that adolescents in such contacts might have.

Anxiety disorders of adolescence that have as their primary symptom the experience of anxiety itself include:

1. Separation anxiety disorder. This is evidenced when the youth has excessive worry or anxiety about being separated from the parent or major attachment figure.

2. Avoidant disorder of adolescence. This is when the teenager desires warm, close and affectionate relationships with family members but strongly avoids making contact with strangers. Peer friendships are also significantly disrupted by the avoidance tendencies.

3. Overanxious disorder. This type is characterized by a predominant generalized worry that is aroused by a variety of conditions.

Eating disorders of adolescence are usually centered in some anxiety dynamic. Some of these disorders include:

1. Anorexia nervosa. This is evidenced by an intense fear of becoming obese, a disturbed body image of "feeling fat" while in reality that is not the case, a weight loss of 25 percent of original body weight, and a refusal to maintain adequate body weight.

2. Bulimia. This disorder is characterized by recurrent binge eating which is often followed immediately with self-induced vomiting as a weight-control technique.

3. Pica. This is a much more rare disorder which is evidenced by a

repeated eating of a nonnutritive substance which continues for at least one month.

Stereotyped movement disorders are usually anxiety-related. Some examples of these are:

1. Transient tic disorders. These are tics that last for at least one month but not more than one year.

2. Chronic motor tic disorder. This involves involuntary repetitive motor movements (tics) that continue for at least one year.

3. Tourette's disorder. Essentially this is a chronic motor tic disorder that involves several muscle groups.

4. Atypical tic disorder. The title refers to tics that do not adequately fit within any of the other categories.

Other anxiety-related disorders with physical manifestations are ones that fit the category title and do not comfortably fit anywhere else, such as: stuttering; sleepwalking; and sleep terror disorder that is marked by repeated awakening from sleep with intense feelings of anxiety that last from one to 10 minutes.

The general category of anxiety disorders includes several types of disorders that have anxiety as the central component in their symptom complex. Counselees who are diagnosed with one of these anxiety disorders are experiencing strong anxiety feelings because their psychological defenses are weakening, allowing excessive amounts of anxiety to flood into the counselee's consciousness. Adolescent counselees are sometimes diagnosed with the following anxiety disorders.

Phobic disorders occur when the individuals experience excessive, intense and unrealistic fear when thinking about or confronted with certain objects or situations. Their anxieties become associated with the object so that the original cause of the anxiety remains unconscious and therefore usually unresolved unless the help of psychotherapy or in-depth counseling is sought. There is an indefinite number of possible phobias since phobic reactions can occur to virtually any object or situation. A popular medical dictionary lists 368 different phobias.[38]

1. Agoraphobia is often a particularly incapacitating phobic reaction to open or public places, particularly where there are crowds of people. Some agoraphobics have panic attacks associated with their phobia while others do not.

2. Social phobias occur when individuals experience a persistent and irrational fear of certain social situations centering around the person's fear of being humiliated or embarrassed.

3. Simple phobias are intense irrational fears and needs to avoid

things and situations other than open spaces and certain social situations.

Anxiety states contain various conditions of extreme anxiety symptoms, such as:

1. Panic disorder occurs when the individual experiences a series of specific episodes of intense and irrational apprehension and fear that are not precipitated by exposure to a phobic stimulus, physical problem or agoraphobia.

2. Generalized anxiety disorder occurs during late adolescence and older. It is indicated when an anxious mood continues for over a month.

3. Obsessive-compulsive disorder is indicated by the significant presence of obsessions and/or compulsions.

4. Post-traumatic stress disorder is indicated by the reexperiencing of a trauma that has been previously encountered. There are both acute and chronic or delayed forms of disorder.

5. Atypical anxiety disorder includes anxiety disorders that don't meet the criteria for the above specified conditions.

Adjustment disorders occur when there is no specific mental disorder per se, but rather a maladaptive reaction to a specific psychological stressor. Examples of this type of disorder are:

1. Adjustment disorder with anxious mood includes maladaptive adjustment responses where anxiety is the prominent symptom.

2. Adjustment disorder with mixed emotional features includes responses where anxiety symptoms are mixed with other emotional reactions like depression.

3. Adjustment disorder with mixed disturbance of emotions and conduct includes a mixture of anxiety and other emotional symptoms along with specific behavior reactions, like truancy, vandalism, fighting and so forth.

The Bible appears to differentiate between two types of anxiety.[39] The first is a genuine concern about a real problem or issue that is worthy of some anxious attention.[40] The apostle Paul writes, "But God has also adjusted the body, giving the greater honor to the inferior parts that there may be no discord in the body, but that the members may have the same care for one another" (1 Corinthians 12:24-25). In this passage, "care" suggests an active concern that is mutual and helpful. It is productive of good results.

In his second epistle to the Corinthian church, Paul describes his many sufferings after which he expresses his concern, "And apart from other things, there is the daily pressure upon me of my anxiety for all the churches. Who is weak, and I am not weak? Who is made to fall, and I am not indignant?" (2 Corinthians 11:28-29). It is most significant that immediately after sharing his own suffering, Paul expresses anxiety or pressured concern not about himself, but about the churches, especially those individuals who are spiritually weak and those who are "made to fall."

The Bible refers to a second type of anxiety. As the Lord interprets the parable of the sower he explains, "And as for what fell among thorns, they are those who hear, but as they go on their way they are choked by the cares and riches and pleasures of life, and their fruit does not mature" (Luke 8:14). The destructive aspects of ineffective anxiety that is focused on issues of lesser value is certainly implied. The Bible also suggests some remedies for this type of anxiety including the recognition of God's nearby presence, and prayerful petition to God. "The Lord is at hand. Have no anxiety about anything, but in everything by prayer and supplication with thanksgiving let your requests be made known to God. And the peace of God, which passes all understanding, will keep your hearts and your minds in Christ Jesus" (Philippians 4:5-7).

It is this latter type of anxiety that is likely to result in psychological symptoms that require counseling. It presents a very difficult task even for the well-seasoned therapist.

Counseling goals and guidelines for dealing with anxiety and fear. Let's look at some of the personal requirements, tasks and goals that are involved in successfully counseling with individuals who are experiencing serious anxiety dysfunctions:

People who are experiencing strong anxiety symptoms tend to elicit anxiety arousal reactions in those who are around them. It seems almost contagious. Therefore, the counselors must be aware of their own anxiety level and understand how they typically defend against and cope with anxiety. A related issue is the great need for counselors to be patient with their counselees' often slow and inconsistent progress. All too often there are significant anxiety-producing aspects of counselees' environment that sabotage and interfere with therapeutic progress. When reversals are experienced counselees are likely to become discouraged, feel hopeless and want to terminate counseling.

Seldom is adequate communication of the counselor's empathic understanding more important than with these counselees. Anxious counselees must feel safely accepted and cared about by their counselors or they won't continue in counseling. Also in these cases, the counselee must be able to develop an adequate trust in the counselor's level of competence, in his or her dependability and consistency, and in his or her desire and ability to help. Developing trust is a difficulty that appears to be intrinsic to anxiety reactions. The importance of the first stage of counseling, developing the relationship, is obvious.

After gaining a clear and comprehensive picture of the counselee's symptoms, it is important that the counselor help the counselee gain insight into the unconscious and background causes for his or her reactions. Just understanding that there is a specific reason for why they feel as they do can help relieve anxiety that counselees feel about their symptoms. This kind of understanding is a step toward defining and resolving the problems that are creating the symptom complex.

From the earliest stages of the counseling process with anxiety-ridden individuals, efforts directed toward the buildup of their self-esteem is vital. Anxiety and the inability to successfully deal with it creates a drain on one's self-esteem. Continuous encouragement is required, helping the counselees to believe that they will come out on top in their battle with anxiety.

Another aspect of successful counseling is the channeling of the counselee's energy into productive problem-solving behavior and preventative actions. Anxiety blocks these functions and reopening their effective working is a major focus in the counseling process.

Anxiety, like depression, tends to narrow and rigidify the counselee's perception of reality. Often only the negative is seen and there is fear that the symptoms will never subside. A major counseling goal is to help the counselee to gain a broader, clearer and more accurate picture of reality. Counselees need help differentiating between anxiety that is warranted and anxiety that is irrational. They need to be helped to take things one day at a time rather than trying to solve the whole problem at once.

Central to the helping process is the ability of the counselor to encourage counselee openness. They often feel embarrassed and easily humiliated when admitting the intensity and nature of their fears. Openness, unconditional acceptance and non-judgmental responses help encourage counselees to discover and disclose these threatening aspects about their functioning. Continued unfolding and articulation of their fears helps the counselees toward increasing self-acceptance.

One valuable reality-testing tool that counselees can learn is to ask themselves in a given situation, "What is the worst thing that could happen to me?" And then, "Would that really be so terrible? Would I be able to survive it? What are the chances of that actually happening?" And finally, "Is worrying about that possibility being helpful enough to me to counterbalance all of the negative aspects of the anxiety that it is causing me?"

A related issue is that of procrastination. Helping counselees to reverse their tendency to procrastinate helps them feel more productive, industrious and more capable of initiating their own action. As more control is felt over one's life, there is usually less anxiety felt.

Another goal that is related to the counselees' perception of reality, is helping them to divert attention and energy away from that which appears impossible and hopeless. Encourage them to see the positive as well as the negative. Reorienting energies into positive and productive work and other activity is also helpful. It draws them out of a totally inward focus on that which is negative. Understanding that, "I'm not the only one" is often very helpful. Many people who suffer from excessive anxiety are also helped by daily meditative experiences focusing on positive scriptures that affirm God's love and compassionate presence that is continuously with his children.

One of the strong temptations of people who struggle with high levels of anxiety is to withdraw from people as another way of avoiding having to deal with those anxieties. The counselor encourages the counselees to talk through their problems, reducing the level of stress that they carry within themselves.

Anxiety symptoms are often intensified when the counselee is in weakened physical condition. Counselors need to be aware of the interplay between physical health and the person's ability to handle anxiety adequately. Encouraging sufficient sleep, regular and adequate nourishment, and healthful cardiovascular and pulmonary exercise can be a great asset to the counselee's improvement. Occasional breaks during the school week, active fun recreation, and periodic vacations tend to replenish and refresh the person, helping him or her get a fresh look at problems and their solutions.

Learning specific relaxation methods like systematic muscle relaxation, visual imagery, and deep breathing can greatly strengthen the individual's ability to deal effectively with stress. A book that presents a wide variety of self-learning methods of dealing with stress is *The Relaxation and Stress Reduction Workbook* by Martha Davis et al.[41] Another good resource is *Learn to Relax* by C. Eugene Walker.[42]

Involvement with a positive group of people on a regular basis is also advisable. Groups at school and at church provide a good balance for teenagers. Regular contact with groups supports the counselee's reality-testing efforts. It can encourage action and help the individuals see positions in themselves and in the world around them. Involvement with Christian groups can encourage the young person to exercise his or her faith by praying with the group. Such action can also encourage a sense of rejoicing and worship.

Counseling sessions with counselees who are becoming less anxious and less self-critical can teach them the value of periodic self-evaluations. Doing this too early in the counseling process can revert the counselee back into withdrawn, self-critical introversion. Timing is important. Make sure reality testing is quite accurate before trying to focus on self-evaluative responses.

Notes

1. K. Lorenz, *On Aggression* (London: Methuen, 1966).

2. J. P. Scott, *Aggression* (Chicago: University of Chicago Press, 1958).

3. Gary R. Collins, *Christian Counseling: A Comprehensive Guide* (Waco, Texas: Word Books, 1980).

4. Derek Miller, *Adolescence: Psychology, Psychopathology and Psychotherapy* (New York: Jason Aronson, 1974).

5. Albert Bandura, *Aggression: A Social Learning Analysis* (Englewood Cliffs, N. J.: Prentice-Hall, 1973).

6. James C. Coleman, *Psychology and Effective Behavior* (Glenview, Ill.: Scott, Foresman, 1969).

7. William Backus and M. Chapian, *Telling Yourself the Truth* (Minneapolis: Bethany House, 1980).

8. Miller, *Adolescence: Psychology, Psychopathology and Psychotherapy.*

9. Ibid., p. 231.

10. M. F. A. Montague, "On the Physiology and Psychology of Swearing," Psychiatry 5 (1961):189-201.

11. E. E. Macoby, R. S. Mathews, and A. S. Morton, "Youth and Political Change," Public Opinion Quarterly 18 (1954):23-29.

12. Miller, *Adolescence: Psychology, Psychopathology and Psychotherapy*, p. 238.

13. Derek Miller, "Family Interaction and Adolescent Therapy," in *The Predicament of the Family*, ed. P. Lomas (London: Hogarth Press, 1967).

14. N. Cohn, *Warrant for Genocide* (London: Eyre and Spotliswood, 1967).

15. Miller, *Adolescence: Psychology, Psychopathology and Psychotherapy.*

16. John Powell, S. J., *Why Am I Afraid to Tell You Who I Am?* (Chicago: Argus Communications, 1969).

17. Miller, *Adolescence: Psychology, Psychopathology and Psychotherapy*, p. 248.

18. Backus and Chapian, *Telling Yourself the Truth.*

19. Miller, *Adolescence: Psychology, Psychopathology and Psychotherapy*, p. 256.

20. O. Quentin Hyder, *The Christian's Handbook of Psychiatry* (Old Tappan, N. J.: Fleming H. Revell, 1971), p. 113.

21. George W. Kisker, *The Disorganized Personality* (New York: McGraw-Hill, 1964), p. 142.

22. Frank B. Minirth and Paul Meier, *Counseling and the Nature of Man* (Grand Rapids, Mich.: Baker Book House, 1982).

23. Collins, *Christian Counseling*.

24. Paul Tournier, *Guilt and Grace* (New York: Harper and Row, 1962).

25. Hyder, *The Christian's Handbook of Psychiatry*.

26. Bruce Narramore, "Guilt: Where Theology and Psychology Meet," Journal of Psychology and Theology 2 (1974):18-25.

27. Coleman, *Psychology and Effective Behavior*, p. 411.

28. William G. Justice, *Guilt: The Source and the Solution* (Wheaton, Ill.: Tyndale, 1981), p. 42.

29. Ibid.

30. O. Hobart Mowrer, *The Crisis in Psychiatry and Religion* (Princeton: Van Nostrand, 1961).

31. Karl Menninger, *Whatever Became of Sin?* (New York: Hawthorn Books, 1973).

32. Collins, *Christian Counseling*, p. 124.

33. Backus and Chapian, *Telling Yourself the Truth*, p. 72.

34. Albert Ellis and R. Harper, *A Guide to Rational Living* (Hollywood, Calif.: Wilshire, 1974).

35. Coleman, *Psychology and Effective Behavior*.

36. E. E. Levitt, *The Psychology of Anxiety* (Indianapolis: Bobbs-Merrill, 1967), p. 200.

37. Erik H. Erikson, "Identity and the Life Cycle," Psychological Issues 1 (1959).

38. Arthur Osol, ed., *Blakiston's Gould Medical Dictionary*, 3rd ed. (New York: McGraw-Hill, 1972).

39. Collins, *Christian Counseling*.

40. Minirth and Meier, *Counseling and the Nature of Man*.

41. Martha Davis, E. Eshelman, and M. McKay, *The Relaxation and Stress Reduction Workbook* (Richmond, Calif.: New Harbinger Publications, 1980).

42. Eugene Walker, *Learn to Relax* (Englewood Cliffs, N. J.: Prentice-Hall, 1975).

■ CHAPTER 11

Depression

The experience of depression in some form is common to all people. Nearly everyone from time to time feels "blue," which is a normal experience of depression. More serious forms of depression result in moderate to severe handicapping of the individual's subjective sense of well-being and effective academic, occupational, physical and interpersonal functioning. Depression is often a progressive complex of symptoms which, if not treated, will have devastating effects on the individual's life. Christian psychiatrist O. Quentin Hyder describes the degenerative signs of depression:

"The early signs of depression are sadness of facial expression, loss of interest in work or leisure-time activities, restlessness and agitation with easy irritability, and expressions of low self-esteem, worthlessness, failure, hopelessness, shame, self-reproach and guilt. Physical effects include generalized lethargy, loss of sexual interest, inability to get to sleep or stay asleep, early morning waking, physical fatigue after little effort, multiple complaints of aches or pains, constipation and poor appetite leading to weight loss. As the depression gets worse, there will be a severe slowing of thought processes, withdrawal first from social contacts and then even from close family members, total preoccupation with the self as revealed in speech, marked diminution of all physical activity, and eventually loss of all communication and responsiveness."[1]

Depression Symptoms
Depression is probably the most common psychological disorder.

Under depression's large "umbrella" is everything from mild "blues" to catastrophic psychic states. Depression sometimes is very clearly evident, leaving no doubt to the sufferer or to those nearby what the problem is; sometimes it is mixed with other problems. At other times the central depressive reaction is "masked" by other symptoms.

In his very helpful and easily understood volume on depression, Dean Schuyler lists 12 symptoms that are characteristic of most of the varieties of psychological depression: eating disorder, weight loss or gain, sleep disorder, frequent crying spells, feelings of guilt or inadequacy, suicidal thoughts or behavior, fatigue or listlessness, inability to concentrate, decreased mental productivity, decreased sexual libido, inability to enjoy usual pleasures and aggravation of any existing physical pathology.[2]

Because depression is so common and presents such a major problem for teenagers as well as adults, it will be worth our efforts to look more closely at the types of depression symptoms. We will examine them in the following symptom categories: affect, cognition, physical, behavior and interpersonal.

Affect. Careful reading of the preceding chapter on anger, guilt and anxiety will provide a partial understanding of the depressed person's affect. In addition to anger, guilt and anxiety, depressed people experience feelings of depersonalization, sadness, discouragement, desolation, despair, loss of sexual desire, low feelings of self-confidence and self-esteem, agitation, anticipatory anxiety, fears of being alone and of death, hopelessness, boredom and irritability. Not all of these symptoms will occur in each depressed counselee, but several of them will play a prominent role in his or her symptom picture. Also, these symptoms may come and go and rise and fall in their intensity during the course of the depression. There is commonly a diurnal variation (a predictable patterned fluctuation during the course of the day) in mood.

Depressed people usually look sad. A common expression speaks of people "wearing their feelings on their sleeves." In depression, people wear their feelings on their faces and in their posture. Facial features are often marked with a wrinkled forehead, drooped mouth, vacant or teary eyes and a generally glum expression. Posture is often slumped as if carrying the "weight of the world" was taking its toll.

Cognition. All of the thinking processes are grouped under the term "cognition." Though most people think of the affective changes that are caused by depression, the individual's cognition is also greatly impacted. Negativity is the hallmark of depressed thinking. Aaron T.

Beck has articulated what he calls the "cognitive triad" in depression: a negative view of the self, or low self-esteem; negative view of the world; and negative expectations of the future, or pessimism.[3]

Depressed individuals typically are very self-blaming when anything goes wrong. They are self-critical, self-demanding. Their self-preoccupation is filled with ruminations about their past failures and feelings of worthlessness. They worry excessively about their body functions, physical health and expectations of rejection from others. Feeling helpless and hopeless gives way to wishing that they had never been born. wishing to die and active suicidal thoughts. Personal motivation is lost and blame for what is wrong is sometimes projected onto others. They long for magical solutions, believing that it would take some omnipotent force to even help them to feel better and solve their problems.

People suffering from severe depression are likely to experience delusional thinking. Leonard Cammer defines delusional thinking in very straightforward, understandable terms: "Simply stated, a delusional thought is a fixed, false belief. The person cannot be talked out of it; that is why it is called 'fixed.' Also, it does not conform with reality and is therefore considered 'false.' "[4] The most common forms of delusional thoughts are delusions of persecution (e.g., "the CIA and the KGB have joined forces to kill me") and delusions of grandeur ("I am the literal bride of Christ"). Other delusional thought patterns center on religion, the body, guilt and unworthiness, poverty and nihilism.

Roger MacKinnon and Robert Michels remind us that the topics that never enter the depressed person's mind are just as important as those that are at the focus of preoccupation.[5] The lack of positive memories, appreciation for the self and hope for the future are as significant as the presence of negativity.

The same authors widen our understanding of depressed cognition even more: "Not only is the thought content of the depressed patient disturbed, but his cognitive processes are distorted as well. His thoughts are diminished in quantity, and although he may be responsive, he shows little initiative or spontaneity. He answers questions, but does not offer new data or topics, and his mental life has little variety. He understands what is said, and replies appropriately, although his thinking is slowed and his speech may be halting or uncertain."[6] Depressed people tend to be indecisive, experience decision-making problems and use poor judgment. Their concentration is usually lacking, they have difficulty remembering and experience inhibition in using their will.

Physical. In addition to changes in affect and in cognition, depression involves changes in body functioning. The changes occur in every body function that is under the nervous system's control.[7] Just as there is a cognitive triad in depression, so is there a "somatic triad," which includes insomnia, anorexia and constipation.[8] There are two types of sleep disturbance in depression: hypersomnia (excessive sleep) and insomnia (reduction in sleep). There are three insomnia patterns: initial insomnia (difficulty falling asleep), middle insomnia (waking after a few hours of sleep) and terminal insomnia (early morning waking). Anorexia simply refers to the loss of or reduction in appetite and is to be distinguished from anorexia nervosa which is a separate clinical condition. In some cases, depressed people have been noted to have excessive appetites. Constipation is the most common form of bowel disturbance in depressed counselees, though in earlier stages of depression, diarrhea sometimes occurs.

Other physical changes and symptoms that commonly occur during depression include aches and pains in the bones and joints, nausea, dizziness, stomachache, pressure in the head, lowered metabolic rate, dry mouth, fatigue, lowered sex drive, headache, backache, unpleasant taste in the mouth, rapid heart beat and heart palpitations. Women sometimes experience irregularities in their menstrual cycle, occasionally having complete cessation of menses for several months.

These physical changes are often functional. For instance, they may keep the teenager from going to school where he or she feels panicky about facing his or her peers. This is not to suggest that the symptoms are not real. They are real but their origin is understood more in the benefit that the person gains from them rather than in any organic cause. Depressed people often develop a hypochondriacal fixation on their symptoms, which often focuses their attention onto their physical well-being rather than focusing on their depression and its causes.[9]

Behavior. The behavioral changes in depressed counselees are for the most part caused by the depression-induced affective, cognitive and physiological alterations. Most common among the behavioral symptoms are crying, withdrawal, slowed-down movement, agitation and hallucinations. In one research sample, 83 percent of the severely depressed patients reported crying more often than usual. Some wanted to cry, felt like crying, but could not make their tears come.[10] Crying appears to have a tension-releasing effect for the depressed counselee, especially if a caring person is at hand to hear, understand and accept the person. Sometimes a hug or other expression of emotional support is also therapeutic.

The depressed counselee tends to withdraw from contact with the outside world. Meaningful contact requires an investment of energy but the depressed counselee is characteristically short on energy. Withdrawal is also associated with the slowing down process that is common in very depressed people. They tend to talk and walk slowly. They sometimes appear rigid in their body movements. This slowing down, especially when in significant degrees, is called psychomotor retardation. Its purpose seems to be both for energy conservation and withdrawal from excessive stimulation.[11]

In some severe depressions a very agitated state exists which prevents any effective or well-directed behavior from occurring. Agitated persons pace, wring their hands, appear driven but are incapable of any sustained, productive activity. Hallucinations are also common among severely depressed counselees. Hallucinations are essentially the occurrence of a sensory experience without any stimulation of the senses. In other words, the individual sees, hears, feels, smells or tastes something even though nothing is there. Hallucinatory experiences are usually indicators of psychotic depressions. The delusions which were discussed earlier often represent the individuals' attempts to make sense of these "crazy" sensory experiences. For instance, psychotic depressed patients might hear voices talking to them (auditory hallucination). In order to explain this phenomenon they may "understand" that it is the evil spirits or messengers from outer space talking to them.

Related to both withdrawal and slowing down is the tendency toward self-neglect. Moderate to severe depression is usually indicated when a person shows a downward shift in his or her personal grooming, hygiene and dress. Withdrawal and slowing down will tend to produce a deterioration in teenagers' academic, athletic and other performances.

Behavioral acting-out is another variety of indicators of depression. Acting-out is particularly common among depressed teenagers because their normal defenses are depleted. They are prone to exaggerated mood swings, feelings of rage, extreme self-depreciation and frustration.[12] The presence of these conditions sets the stage for easily triggered acting-out of a violent or destructive behavioral impulse.

Sexual acting-out in depressed adolescents is usually designed to help relieve the depressed feeling.[13] They seek close contact with another human being in the best way they know how: through sexual intercourse. The result is usually the return of empty feelings plus guilt and more depression, which may lead the individual into more promiscuous sexual activity, thus continuing the cycle.

Alcoholism seems to have a similar effect on depression.[14] Some researchers have found that alcohol acts as an antidepressant both for depressed patients and for alcoholics.[15] Their theory is that the alcoholic is depressed, that the consumption of alcohol lessens the depression, but that increasing quantities of alcohol lead to more depression.

Interpersonal. The depressed person withdraws from people. During the early stages of depression, people often increase their level of social activity, trying to relieve the pain of their depression through interpersonal contact. While they crave love, affection and esteem from others, they seem incapable of responding to others in such a way that encourages those reactions. Their obsessive self-preoccupation with their own needs, fears and insecurities sabotages their efforts to meet those same needs.

Mildly depressed counselees repress feelings of envy and anger, fearing that others will notice them and respond with rejection.[16] This continuing repression usually results in the anger being turned in on the self, which deepens their sense of despair. As the depression deepens, the counselees finally give up on interpersonal fulfillment and withdraw from social interaction. The counselee anticipates that only rejection would come from social contact. His or her interpersonal behavior tends to turn others off, which simply reinforces his or her false belief about being unlikable, unworthy and unlovable.

Types of Depression

Depression has become a major focus of psychological and psychiatric research during the past two to three decades. As a result, quite a variety of ways of looking at depression have been developed, each having its own value. A review of these perspectives will give us a richer understanding of depression.

One way of differentiating between types of depression is to compare those of short duration with those of longer duration.[17] Acute depressive reactions usually have a sudden onset, are marked by intense symptoms, have rather short duration, and often are relieved spontaneously without treatment. Chronic depressions typically develop more gradually, have symptoms of widely varying intensity, may last many years and are resistive to recovery even with psychotherapeutic and chemical treatment.

Another perspective differentiates between "pure" depressions and depressions that occur in some combination with manic symptoms.[18] Unipolar depression refers to the occurrence of episodes of depression without evidence of mania. Bipolar depressions are those with recurrent episodes of depression along with at least one manic episode. The manic phases in bipolar disorders are often seen as one way that the counselee's subconscious seeks relief from the painful symptoms of depression. It is as if a rush of energy temporarily releases the person from the imprisonment of the depressive illness.

The difference between primary and secondary depression is fairly self-evident. Primary depression is identified as a depressive episode that occurs without the presence of any other psychological illness. Secondary depression occurs in an individual who has some other pre-existing psychological disorder like schizophrenia, compulsive personality disorder or cocaine abuse.

The least severe and most normal, healthy form of depression is the "blues." Virtually everyone has experienced the blues. One author suggests that they are cyclical, occurring in regular cycles in some people, and in cycles of varying length in others.[19] The blues last from a few hours to a few days in length. The primary symptoms include sadness, apathy, some degree of anorexia, withdrawal and insomnia or hypersomnia. The blues are sometimes stimulated by experiences like moving, holidays, and the period immediately following anticipated exciting events like vacations, childbirth and visits from loved ones.

Depression immediately following the death of a loved one is termed as grieving. Grieving is a normal and healthy response to such an important loss. Grieving is not considered dysfunctional or pathological. Rather, it is an important process for working through or resolving death and loss.[20] The normal grief process typically lasts between a few weeks to about six months. If grieving continues for much more than that amount of time, if the individual's symptoms become disproportionately intense, or if the person experiences excessive guilt or feelings of personal inadequacy, grieving has given way to a depressive reaction.

Reactive depression refers to a dysfunctional reaction to an event that occurs in external reality. The counselee is pathologically depressed but from the counselor's perspective, the reaction makes sense. "If that had happened to me I might be depressed, too."

Depressions are common reactions to losses (of loved ones, jobs, business opportunities, homes and friendships), separations (moves, graduation, divorce), serious physical illness or injury and new responsibilities (a new job, promotion, marriage, and a new home and larger mortgage). Though other factors like the counselee's general physical and psychological health and available support system are involved, there should be some correlation between the intensity of the precipitating event and the severity of the depressive reaction. Reactive depressions usually last for a period of several weeks to several months and are responsive to counseling and some prescribed drugs.

Psychotic (or endogenous) depressions are the most serious and difficult to treat of the depressive reactions. They are depressions for which no identifiable precipitating external cause can be found. They essentially come from within the individual and are often thought to have a biological cause. They are marked by the following symptom picture: psychomotor retardation, severely depressed affect, lack of responsiveness to environmental events, loss of interest in life and physical symptoms. Anorexia, insomnia, guilt feelings and suicidal behavior are additional symptoms. The presence of hallucinations or delusions is a sure indicator of psychotic depression when they occur with other major depressive symptoms like intense despair and strong self-destructive attitudes.

One final type of depression is masked depression. Psychiatrist Stanley Lesse has written a book that focuses on depressions that are hidden by other symptoms. For instance, some adolescent depressions are shielded or masked by delinquent behavior, substance abuse, sexual acting-out, physical illness and family problems.[21]

Why Do People Get Depressed?

We have looked at the symptoms of depression and have examined the major types of depressive reaction. But why do people get depressed? What causes some people to struggle with depressions throughout most of their lives, while others rarely even feel blue? Researchers have isolated several different possible causes: biological, life history, life stresses, anger, learning and thinking.

Biological. The biological factors that have been linked as causes of depression include physical injury, illness and genetics. In addition to the reactive depression that typically follows severe illness or injury, there are certain physical problems that more directly bring about depression. Minor problems like loss of sleep and inadequate diet as well as more severe problems like cerebral tumors, low blood sugar and glandular disorders are common causes of depression. Though it is not believed that people inherit depression, there are significant suggestions from genetic research that people can inherit a biochemical propensity or predisposition to depression. Some studies have found that when one twin is depressed there is a higher occurrence of depression in the other twin when the twins are monozygotic (identical) as compared to dizygotic (fraternal or non-identical) pairs.[22]

Life history. A variety of background life experiences have been found to be predisposing events that tend to make the individual more prone to later depression. We have already discussed the experience of loss and separation as two such events. Perceiving one's own personal failure, rejection from others and experiencing helplessness and powerlessness are also important historical causative factors.

Life stress. When a person encounters stressful events in life that feel overpowering or threatening, one possible reaction is depression. The Social Readjustment Rating Scale was produced to help measure the amount of stress that a person is experiencing from external sources.[23] Any change (positive or negative) produces stress because it requires the individual to adjust or adapt in some way to it. When the person's adaptive mechanisms fail, depression is likely to occur.

Anger. Much of the depression that counselees experience is believed to be caused by or exacerbated by repressed or otherwise unresolved anger. Many children grow up in homes where it is taught that all anger is bad. Many parents are very threatened by anger and do not know how to deal with it. The child then learns to feel guilty about feeling angry as well as feeling fearful about being angry if he or she has been punished for his or her feelings. Gary Collins has developed a flow chart (adapted in this work) that helps us to trace the development of angry feelings into destructive responses.[24]

Illustration 35

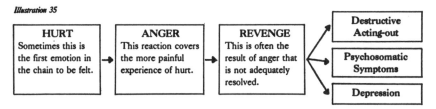

Learning. Unfortunately, many children are taught that anger is bad and to repress it. This often results in depression. Parents sometimes teach their children to be depressed. The child "learns" that anger is bad. The parents probably "model" repression of angry feelings. Some children even "identify" with the depressive behaviors that their parents model and others learn that depression becomes a powerful way of manipulating other people.[25] Depression for some becomes a way of gaining attention and special favors. For others, depression is a way of punishing others by making their lives miserable too. For some it is self-punishment that tends to relieve a sense of guilt.

Thinking. Which comes first? Negative thinking or depression? Negative thinking is probably both cause and effect of depression. Aaron Beck has listed five errors in thinking that depressed people tend to make: arbitrary interpretations, selective abstractions, exaggerations, incorrect labeling and overgeneralizations. He proposed a model to explain the downward spiral of worsening depression. He suggested that the depressed counselee's awareness of his or her dysfunctional thinking, feelings and behavior reinforces his or her negative expectations and lowered self-esteem.[26]

Teenagers and Depression

Let's turn our discussion toward the topic of depression in adolescents. Since teenagers are in transition between childhood and adulthood, it is not surprising that their depressions also share characteristics of the depressions of childhood and adulthood. Many adolescents' depressions relate to developmental struggles. They often feel a sense of loss and longing for earlier childhood when life was less demanding and solutions were far less complex.[27] Adolescents are often confronted with loss experiences and are involved primarily with the tasks of formulating their own identity and separating from their parents. Perceived rejection from peers, failure to achieve academic, athletic and social goals are typically very painful during adolescence and can severely strike the psychological underpinnings of the adolescent psyche. Adolescent vulnerability to self-questioning and insecurity easily gives way to disconcerting thoughts like, "My parents don't love me anymore." "I'll never be able to succeed at anything." "No one will ever want to marry me." "My body looks ugly and stupid."[28]

Some depression in adolescence is quite normal, probably more normal during this developmental stage than at any other (except perhaps old age). These normal adolescent depressions are essentially the blues that have already been described. Our primary attention, however, is geared to understanding and helping teenagers who are suffering with more severe depression than the blues.

Dean Schuyler differentiates between acute depression and chronic depression during adolescence. Acute depressive episodes will often occur in young people who are quite well-adjusted. Acutely depressed teenagers will evidence sad affect, withdrawal, feelings of helplessness, insomnia or hypersomnia, anorexia or bulimia, psychomotor retardation and sometimes suicidal thoughts. These depressions are usually reactive to an identifiable external event.

Chronic depressions are most likely to occur in teenagers who have a more marginal social adjustment and who have had repeated separations from significant adults. These depressions are more endogenous in nature, lacking a clearly evident precipitating event and are less responsive to psychotherapeutic treatment.[29]

Leonard Cammer differentiates between withdrawal patterns and hostility patterns in early adolescent depressive symptoms. In the withdrawal pattern, the primary symptom, in addition to sad affect, is social withdrawal. They pull away from friends and adults and become preoccupied with introspection about their problems. Passive resistance is often the characteristic of their responses to anyone who reaches out to make contact with them. It amounts to a test to see "if you really do love me."

The hostility pattern signifies a somewhat stronger psyche. Anger is closer to the surface and is released in quite destructive ways. Adolescent rebellion is magnified and released without the constraint of normal personality controls. Sometimes the goal is specifically to hurt (either directly or symbolically) people whom they perceive have hurt them. Sometimes the overt hostility masks the underlying depression, making accurate diagnosis difficult.[30]

There has also been a differentiation between depressions experienced in early and later adolescence. Depressions during early adolescence reflect the inconsistent patterns indicative of the age: boredom and restlessness, alternations between total lack of interest to intense preoccupation with activities and events; fatigue and preoccupation with body features and function; extreme mood swings; concentration problems; acting-out and withdrawal from people. Depressions in later adolescence closely resemble the clinical manifestations of adult depressions.[31]

The final forms of depressive reactions that occur in adolescence are the masked depressions. They appear on the surface to be something other than depression. Hyperactivity, aggressiveness, psychosomatic illness, hypochondriasis and delinquency are all common masks for adolescent depression. Children from severely disturbed families are more frequent sufferers of masked depression.

Christians, unfortunately, have a particular vulnerability to depression. Because we have been taught and do believe that "Christ is the answer," we are puzzled when a "good Christian" struggles with depression, especially when the symptoms are severe and prolonged. Paul wrote to the Galatians, "But the fruit of the Spirit is love, joy, peace, patience, kindness, goodness, faithfulness, gentleness and self-control; against such there is no law" (Galatians 5:22). And to the church at Colossae he wrote, "And let the peace of Christ rule in your hearts, to which indeed you were called in the one body. And be thankful" (Colossians 3:15). It is easy to infer incorrectly from these verses that every Christian should always have a perfect or at least a near-perfect sense of psychological peace. The incorrect assumption is that anxiety and depression are experienced by a Christian only if there is some kind of serious sin yet unforgiven in the individual's life. The account of Job should help us to understand that that is not always the case.

Surely depression can be the result of guilt and wrong behavior. In his letter to the Galatians Paul writes, "Do not be deceived; God is not mocked for whatever a man sows that he will also reap. For he who sows to his own flesh will from the flesh reap corruption; but he who sows to the Spirit, will from the Spirit reap eternal life" (Galatians 6:7-8). "Corruption" in the above reference clearly refers to an eternal ruin because of its juxtaposition against "eternal life." But may we not infer that the reaping of eternal living and the reaping of corruption or destruction begins here in this temporal life? Experiencing the natural and logical consequences of our actions is one of the most powerful influences that helps us to live responsible lives. It is being accountable. Depression is sometimes caused by guilt and internal conflict that arises when we pursue an action that we know is a sin against ourselves, God and others. But to assume that guilt is the only cause of depression has been clearly demonstrated to be a much too narrow and limiting explanation for this widespread disorder.

For many, the knowledge of God's forgiveness and cleansing, purifying action in their lives has brought release from guilt-induced depression. One Christian psychiatrist writes, "Hope is the antidote to depression: hope in this life that things will be better tomorrow and hope for the future in everlasting life."[32] Christian hope implies a trust that God really does care and that he is involved. This hope serves to countermand the feelings of alienation reactions in the depressed individual, helping him or her to know at least that God is there.

For some, hope in God is misunderstood. Their hope is not in God's presence so much as it is that God will make their circumstances better for them. Depressed Christians are particularly vulnerable to feeling (falsely) that God has abandoned them when he does not choose to alter painful external circumstances. Depression can be so painful and the feelings of hopelessness and helplessness so deep, that the counselee thinks the only possible solution would be a magical one or the intervention of some omnipotent force.[33] Depressed Christians are apt to use prayer as a way of acting-out this sort of magical wish. The real danger when this happens is that the person is likely to become more depressed if God does not give the direct answer that was requested.

Counseling Guidelines

Working with depressed individuals presents some very demanding challenges for counselors. There are a number of common traps and pitfalls during the counseling process with depressed individuals. Because of the counselee's feelings of helplessness, he or she will probably place on the counselor unrealistic expectations to catalyze a magical cure.[34] Sometimes direct advice is requested but usually more passive maneuvers leave no doubt about the counselees' state of helplessness. The display of inadequacy, dependency and need are partially motivated by conscious or unconscious wishes for the counselor to take care of them.

Sometimes the problems are stated followed by a silence that seems to say, "And I just don't have any idea of what to do." At other times, tributes to the counselor's wisdom, strength and experience are suggested. The counselee might proclaim, "I don't know what to decide about going to college. I sure wish I had your experience and knowledge. I'll bet you know what I should do." The counselee's dependency on the counselor and accompanying efforts to try to get the counselor to take more responsibility for his or her life presents a very complex and potentially hazardous situation in the counseling process.

Closely associated to the counselee's dependency is his or her anger. Intense dependency carries with it anger at the self for not being strong and competent enough to take care of the self. The anger is then projected onto the very person whose help is needed as a way of escaping the pain of self-inflicted anger. Both counselee and counselor are caught in a complex trap.

The counselee feels strong dependency on the counselor. The more this dependency is felt and expressed, the more self-directed anger is felt by the counselee. This experience is so painful that the anger is projected onto the counselor. But the counselee fears that he or she would be rejected if the counselor knew of the anger, so it is repressed, which tends to deepen the depression.

The counselor's dilemma is equally as complex. When help, compassion, understanding, and advice or suggestions are offered, the counselee's dependency is likely to be reinforced and deepened. If the counselee's demands or requests are withheld, then anger is likely to be incurred. However, anger will be expressed by the counselee from time to time no matter what the counselor does. Anger is used by the counselee to become more independent from the counselor. Anger is the common reaction when the counselor is found not to be omnipotent, perfect or godlike. The counselor is disappointingly human. Anger will likely be a response whenever the counselor says "no" to a request. And anger will probably follow when a counselor's advice or suggestion does not solve the counselee's problem as it was expected. These dynamics are greatly intensified with adolescent counselees because of their normal developmental process of separating from their parents or parent figures. Their ambivalent and often extreme feelings toward parents and other authority figures are often also directed toward the counselor, a process of transference that must be understood by the counselor if the counseling is to have successful results.

These complex dynamics often leave the counselor feeling that there is no way to win. It is easy to get frustrated. And yet, as MacKinnon and Michels emphasize, "Perhaps one of the most critical aspects of treating the depressed patient is to respond to such experiences with understanding rather than irritation."[35] This is a particularly difficult task when the counselees pull out the "heavy artillery," like suggesting suicidal impulses. Telling the counselor about their habit of carrying razor blades, their stash of sleeping pills or their desire to jump from a bridge accomplishes several subtle purposes: a genuine plea for help, a manipulation of the counselor's attention, an attempt to punish the counselor (perhaps for not doing something that the counselee demanded), an angry threat, an angry demonstration of how impotent the counselor really is to save the counselee's life. The uncomfortable truth is that suicidal outpatient counselees can kill themselves if they are determined.

Vacations, holidays and even weekends provide difficult times for counselees who have strong transference reactions to their counselors. They may feel angry or envious that their counselor is able to have such a "good time." They often feel left out and even rejected by the counselor. "If she really cared about me she couldn't just take off like that." There is often jealousy which is directed at the counselor's spouse, children, friends or family in general. The depressed counselee is likely to recognize the irrational aspects of his or her thinking, but this insight does not make the feelings go away. They get more angry at themselves for feeling as strongly toward the counselor as they do.

The counselor needs to spot signs of transference as early in the counseling process as possible and help the counselees to talk openly about their feelings. They need to be reassured that their feelings are completely normal and non-offensive to the counselor. "It seems to me that your feelings are very normal and understandable. It's natural to develop strong affection for someone that you talk with so personally about yourself. It's important that we're able to talk openly about these feelings so that they don't interfere with your progress." Counselors need to anticipate events like vacations and holidays that are apt to stimulate difficult transference-related reactions.

There are also several kinds of counselor responses to depressed counselees that can cause major problems. One very common response while working with depressed counselees is to feel a drop in one's energy and a somewhat lowered affect. When these reactions are mild, it is not a countertransference. Rather it is the sensitive counselor's empathic response to the counselee's depression. Such a response should be recognized as completely normal and healthy and perhaps discussed with a colleague.

There are several countertransference reactions that are commonly elicited by depressed counselees.[36] The paternalistic, overprotective or omnipotent countertransference is elicited by the counselee's complementary dependency transference reaction. Some counselors gain more secure feelings about their own worth and significance by feeling responsible for and in control of other people's lives. The result is usually to sabotage the counselee's growth toward independence.

Another countertransference reaction centers on the counselor's feelings of guilt and anger. We have already discussed the depressed counselee's propensity for eliciting these responses. When counselors struggle with unresolved feelings of guilt and anger, they are quite vulnerable to such counselees' maneuvers. One older teenage girl seemed to break down into deep sobbing near the end of every counseling session. The counselor felt trapped between his guilt and angry feelings. He felt guilty about closing the session when she was crying so heavily. But he also felt angry because he was feeling manipulated to give extra time and attention to her.

Still another countertransference reaction is boredom and impatience. Counselors often need their counselees to "get better." If their own feelings of security about their competence rest too heavily on how well their counselees are doing, then they are likely to feel angry at depressed counselees because of their very slow progress. Since such anger is unacceptable it is often quickly repressed. Feelings of boredom and impatience serve as part of the defense against this repressed anger.

The counselor who seeks to be entertained by his or her counselees will also soon show signs of boredom when working with depressed individuals. The counseling room is not where the counselor's personal needs should be fulfilled. Counselors who seek personal gratification from their counselees will sooner or later become disappointed and then angry or impatient. They may even subtly try to force the counselee out of counseling. Such action creates feelings of rejection within the counselee, reinforcing the depression and feelings of worthlessness and hopelessness.

This discussion is leading us to the proposition that some counselors are far better equipped to work with depressed adolescents than other counselors. MacKinnon and Michels write: "Depressed people want to be cared for, but a central aspect of their pathology is that they drive away the very thing they crave. If the counselor recognizes the inevitability of this pattern, he is less likely to overreact to the patient's needs and also less likely to reject the patient for having them."[37]

The counselors who work effectively with depressed teenagers embody to some significant degree the following characteristics:

1. They have a very strong capacity for developing immediately warm and empathic contacts with depressed youth.

2. They are dependable and consistent in their responses.

3. They control themselves and the counseling setting through an intelligent use of their authority that in no way demeans or devalues the adolescent counselee.

4. Their presentation of themselves presents a positive picture for the formation of an ego ideal for the counselee.

5. They are able to tolerate being mistrusted without feeling angrily defensive or self-doubting.

6. They can comfortably develop relationships with their teenage counselees that are marked with narcissistic self-absorption on the part of their counselees.

7. They are able to be very encouraging and supportive of their

counselees' movements toward independence.

8. They are able to tolerate their counselees' hostile, angry attacks without reacting with anger, defensiveness or self-doubt.

9. They should be counselors who, because of their appearance, personality, counseling style and overall presentation, are generally accepted and well-received by teenagers.

The actual counseling process with depressed teenagers should be characterized by certain goals and procedures. The following list can be used as general guidelines for developing a counseling approach:

1. The counselor is generally more actively involved, more assertive, more directive and more interactive when working with depressed counselees. These individuals lack much of the energy and motivation for change that many other counselees bring with them to the counseling setting. Therefore, the counselor must work that much harder to initiate and continue counseling gains. One psychiatrist describes it as the use of "gentle bullying."[38] Often the counselor will provide more structure in the sessions to help make sure that the important issues are covered. Depressed adolescents will often seek to hide certain feelings or events from the counselor. In many cases the depressed counselee is struggling because his or her defensive structure is ineffective. In these cases the counselor seeks to enhance the functioning of various defense mechanisms. Giving suggestions and advice is sometimes appropriate, but it should be clarified that such activity on the part of the counselor is temporary, while the counselee is in crisis. Another example of directive intervention is helping counselees to set up a workable daily schedule.[39] Even though a more directive approach is recommended with depressed adolescents, we are warned against confronting, probing questioning, and demanding action because these techniques, especially near the beginning of counseling, may do more harm than good.[40]

2. The process of developing a positive therapeutic alliance is often very difficult with depressed teenagers. As soon as possible, it is important to overcome resistance, establish a sense of hope, expect growth and make a commitment to counseling. One researcher has found that consistently approaching the young person as though "one were responding to a plea for help" has been an effective way to make contact with teenagers in counseling.[41]

3. The presence of emotional support and reassurance from the counselor is vital when working with depressed adolescents. Complete acceptance of the counselee is one of the best ways to communicate

support. The counselor's realistic optimism that there is "light at the end of the dark tunnel of depression" is often very encouraging to a counselee who feels absolutely hopeless. And when the depressed teenager shows some gains or makes some movement, compliments and statements of encouragement are in order. The counselee's subjective guilt about being depressed can be relieved by helping him or her understand the reasons underlying the depression. Depression is destructive and miserable, and it helps at least a little to understand that there is a reason for being depressed. "At least it's not just because I'm lazy, or bad or something." Comparing themselves to others, depressed individuals typically feel very self-critical and self-condemning. "A lot of people are far worse off than I am and they seem to be doing okay. I don't know why I can't handle things any better. Maybe I just don't deserve to be happy." For many counselees, just knowing that they have an appointment scheduled, or knowing that they can call their counselor on the phone is immensely reassuring.

The counselor shows acceptance by not becoming impatient with the timing and pace of the depressed counselee. The counselee's tears are accepted as expressions of pain, sorrow and sometimes frustration. A reflective response to the emotion underlying the tears helps the counselee to feel deeply understood and accepted. "You're feeling so very sad right now." An encouragement that crying is okay is very freeing. "Tears are such a valuable release for our painful feelings." "It's so good to have a place where we feel comfortable enough to cry openly."

Depressed counselees require a great deal of support. But remember that they are also typically rejecting of what they want and need. They become uncomfortable if the counselor becomes overly supportive or expressive of warmth. They may feel unworthy of this much help. They may feel smothered by it or too controlled by the counselor, therefore needing to push away in order to feel more control over their own lives.[42] When a counselee pulls back from the counseling relationship, the novice counselor is likely to try even harder to express caring. This only exacerbates the counselee's struggle to maintain contact both with the helping person and with his or her own sense of self-control.

4. One of the counselor's primary goals is to help relieve the counselee's acute depression, to alleviate his or her immediate suffering. An aim here is to help the counselee strengthen his or her weakened psychological defense mechanisms so that the depression can be lifted more easily.

5. Another immediate goal is the protection of the counselee from

his or her own self-destructive tendencies. Anticipating and questioning about any thoughts or plans for suicide is important to do when working with depressed adolescents.[43] Many depressed teenagers also need to be protected from self-mutilating acts like cutting themselves with razor blades or pouring acid on their skin. These acts are not suicidal. They are meant to cause pain or disfigurement. Depressed counselees will also tend to make major decisions, hoping that they will alleviate their misery. They should be cautioned against making such decisions while depressed because they may not wish to live with the consequences of these choices after they recover from their depression.

6. Fairly early in the treatment of adolescent depression, the counselee needs to be able to ventilate or in some way release his or her feelings of anger, guilt and self-doubt. These repressed feelings will block all other efforts at movement out of depression until they are given up. Release or catharsis is a form of confession of the inner self. Releasing threatening thoughts, impulses, and fantasies along with their strong feelings and emotions in the counseling sessions helps to build stronger trust in the counselor, which deepens the therapeutic power in the relationship. The counselor's task is to encourage such expression, accept it and work toward helping the counselee channel this released energy into constructive directions.

7. Hopelessness is a powerful dynamic in depression. One of the counseling tasks is to turn this devastating sense of hopelessness into a sense of hope and anticipation of growth and happier days in the future.

8. After the counselee's acute depression is relieved, then insight-oriented approaches can be used to help complete the recovery process and stimulate further personality development so that depressive tendencies can be lessened. Effective use of insight techniques promotes a deeper understanding of the origins of depression, gives clues for needed change, and enables the gradual lessening of depressive defenses. Asking questions, suggesting insights, giving explanations and reflecting emotions are all effective insight-stimulating tools. They help counselees to better understand how they got depressed, why their symptoms do not change easily, how to use thought patterns that are less likely to lead into depression, and how to see new choices and options more clearly. Both supportive and insight-oriented techniques are important.

9. The importance of peer group involvement, especially for the early adolescent, has been established earlier. Withdrawal from this important arena of social contact is one of the signals of adolescent de-

pression, and the reversal of this process is an important counseling goal.

10. Depressions are often at least partially in response to loss experiences. This is particularly true in adolescents. Supportive counseling can help to facilitate the young person's mourning process.

11. There are also occasions when the counselor can help to restructure parts of the counselee's environment in order to make them more supportive and encouraging. With the counselee's awareness and permission, educative contacts with parents, pastors, teachers and friends can alert them to new ways to helping the young person as well as providing more background information for the counselor. It is absolutely imperative, though, that in such contacts the counselor never divulge confidential information from the counselee.

12. In most counseling situations the use of silence can be a most powerful therapeutic tool. However, with depressed counselees silence should be used quite sparingly because they are likely to misinterpret silence as an expression of the counselor's disinterest, disapproval or frustration. There is typically not enough ego strength to tolerate the silent space. They need more direct contact with the counselor, not reflective silence, especially during the earlier stages of counseling.

13. In seriously depressed counselees, especially where chronic depression, abrupt and intense symptom changes, or suicidal thoughts are present, medical treatment is indicated. The counselee should be referred to a psychiatrist. The psychiatrist may initiate a course of antidepressant medication and, in very severe cases, a relatively short hospitalization.

Notes

1. O. Quentin Hyder, *The Christian's Handbook of Psychiatry* (Old Tappan, N. J.: Fleming H. Revell, 1971), pp. 77-78.

2. Dean Schuyler, *The Depressive Spectrum* (New York: Jason Aronson, 1974), p. 38.

3. Aaron T. Beck, "The Core Problem in Depression: The Cognitive Triad," Science and Psychoanalysis 17 (1970):47.

4. Leonard Cammer, *Up From Depression* (New York: Pocket Books, 1969).

5. Roger A. MacKinnon and Robert Michels, *The Psychiatric Interview in Clinical Practice* (Philadelphia: W. B. Saunders, 1971).

6. Ibid., pp. 177-178.

7. Ibid.

8. Schuyler, *The Depressive Spectrum.*

9. Stanley Lesse, ed., *Masked Depression* (New York: Jason Aronson, 1974).

10. Aaron T. Beck, *Depression: Clinical, Experimental and Theoretical Aspects* (New York: Harper and Row, 1967).

11. G. L. Engel, "Anxiety and Depression-Withdrawal: The Primary Affects of Unpleasure," International Journal of Psychoanalysis 43 (1962):89.

12. Carl P. Malmquist, *Handbook of Adolescence* (New York: Jason Aronson, 1978).

13. James M. Toolan, "Masked Depression in Children and Adolescents," in *Masked Depression*, ed. Stanley Lesse.

14. Max Hayman, "The Relationship of Depression to Alcoholism," in *Masked Depression*, ed. Stanley Lesse.

15. W. McCord and J. McCord, *Origins of Alcoholism* (Stanford, Calif.: Stanford University Press, 1960).

16. MacKinnon and Michels, *The Psychiatric Interview in Clinical Practice*.

17. Gary R. Collins, *Christian Counseling: A Comprehensive Guide* (Waco, Texas: Word Books, 1980).

18. Schuyler, *The Depressive Spectrum*.

19. Hyder, *The Christian's Handbook of Psychiatry*.

20. E. Lindemann, "Symptomatology and Management of Acute Grief," American Journal of Psychiatry 101 (1944):141.

21. Lesse, *Masked Depression*.

22. Paul Meier, Frank Minirth, and Frank Wichern, *Introduction to Psychology and Counseling* (Grand Rapids, Mich.: Baker Book House, 1982).

23. F. H. Holmes and R. Rahe, "Social Readjustment Rating Scale," Journal of Psychosomatic Research 2 (1967):213-218.

24. Collins, *Christian Counseling*.

25. Meier, Minirth, and Wichern, *Introduction to Psychology and Counseling*.

26. Aaron T. Beck, "Affective Disorders," in *American Handbook of Psychiatry*, ed. Arieti, 2nd ed. (New York: Basic Books, 1974).

27. Sherman C. Feinstein, "Adolescent Depression," in *Depression and Human Existence*, eds. E. James Anthony and T. Benedek (Boston: Little, Brown, 1975).

28. Irving B. Wiener, *Psychological Disturbance in Adolescence* (New York: John Wiley, 1970).

29. Schuyler, *The Depressive Spectrum*.

30. Cammer, *Up From Depression*.

31. Benjamin Kleinmuntz, *Essentials of Abnormal Psychology* (New York: Harper and Row, 1974).

32. Hyder, *The Christian's Handbook of Psychiatry*.

33. MacKinnon and Michels, *The Psychiatric Interview in Clinical Practice*.

34. Ibid.

35. Ibid., p. 224.

36. Ibid.

37. Ibid., p. 228.

38. Hyder, *The Christian's Handbook of Psychiatry*, p. 80.

39. Beck, *Depression: Clinical, Experimental and Theoretical*.

40. Collins, *Christian Counseling*.

41. Feinstein, "Adolescent Depression," p. 332.

42. MacKinnon and Michels, *The Psychiatric Interview in Clinical Practice*.

43. P. F. Regan, "Brief Psychotherapy of Depression," American Journal of Psychiatry 122 (1965):28.

■ CHAPTER 12

Suicide

Mrs. Kramer, an attractive, well-dressed woman in her mid-40s, had initiated counseling upon the referral of her pastor. He had known the Kramer family quite well for the past four years that he had been a pastor in their congregation. Their family of five was about as near to a "model family" as one could realistically hope to become. Their three children, two boys and a girl, were healthy, bright, good achievers and seemed to be progressing through their teenage years quite successfully. There had been some marriage difficulties about 10 years earlier but Mr. and Mrs. Kramer were able to resolve their problems and advance with a happy, full marriage and family life. That is until one Friday evening about six months prior to Mrs. Kramer's initial counseling session.

Their eldest son, 17-year-old Kevin, was a solid performer on his high school football team, achieved adequate grades and was a leader in their church youth group. He was reasonably popular with his peers. His one area of personal struggle seemed to be in his relationships with girls. As a senior, most of his buddies were doing quite a lot of dating. But Kevin seemed to be a "late bloomer" in this area of his life.

Then he began dating a girl who lived in their neighborhood. Millie was a freshman and was at first flattered that a senior boy would want to be with her. She gladly accepted Kevin's first few requests for dates but soon began feeling pressure from him. But as their dates continued, Millie was beginning to feel smothered. She was still only 14, had not really dated before, and was allowed to go out with Kevin only because her parents knew him from the neighborhood. But they were becoming concerned about the amount of their daughter's time that Kevin was monopolizing and began pressuring her into slowing things down with Kevin. Relieved that they felt as they did, Millie felt strong enough to begin telling Kevin, "no." She explained that her parents wanted things to slow down and tried to get him to understand her need to be with her girlfriends, to spend more time on her schoolwork and to just have more free time with which to decide what she wanted to do.

Kevin was crushed. He felt rejected, thinking that her parents did not think he was good enough for her. He was angry and confused. She said that she liked him a lot and yet did not want to spend so much time with him. That didn't make sense! All he wanted to do was to spend time with her. Early one evening after one such confrontation Kevin felt especially defeated. Dismayed and bewildered, he walked home and past his family. They were gathering at the kitchen table for the evening meal. Without recognizing their presence he proceeded to the den, got his father's shotgun and one shell, and then went into his bedroom. A few moments later his family was startled by the sound of an explosion. Kevin had gone into his bedroom, sat on his bed, loaded the gun, held it between his knees, rested the end of the barrel against his forehead, and pulled the trigger.

Seventeen years of parenting, hoping, loving and praying suddenly ended in the blast of a shotgun. Six months later Mrs. Kramer had not recovered from her feelings of anger, regret, guilt and deep grief. The tragedy had also struck the fatal blow to their marriage because there was not enough history of love, commitment and effective communication to hold them together as they struggled to adjust to their loss.

What Is Suicide?

We can define suicide as any deliberate self-damaging act from which the chance of surviving is uncertain. In order to better understand suicide we need to realize the varieties of behaviors that are classed as suicidal. The task of differentiating between these behaviors has been approached differently by different researchers.

Karl Menninger describes a three-way divison of suicidal behavior: chronic suicide, which includes asceticism, alcohol and drug addiction, antisocial acting-out and psychosis; focal suicide, which includes self-mutilations and intentional accidents; and organic suicide, which relates to psychosomatic illnesses.[1] As another researcher notes, this scheme is so broad that it includes virtually all self-destructive behavior, whether it is potentially fatal or not.[2]

Two other researchers found four different classifications of the degree of intent in suicidal acts: suicide gesture; ambivalent suicide attempt; serious suicide attempt and completed suicide.[3]

G. Raines classifies suicidal behaviors that do not result in death: suicidal thoughts or ideas, suicidal preoccupation and ruminations, suicidal gestures and suicidal attempts.[4] Alex Pokorny suggests the following three-way classifications: completed suicide, suicide attempts and suicide ideas.[5]

As we can see, the process of understanding suicidal behavior is more difficult than at first it would seem. There are more successful suicides each year that are counted as other forms of death because of lack of knowledge of the victim's intent or motivation. A significant percentage of one-car accidents are actual suicides rather than accidents caused by "loss of control." Some people who are medically ill die only because they stopped taking their medication. And others "flirt with death" by their involvement in high-risk occupations and sports (e.g., sky diving, undersea exploration and mountain climbing) and life-endangering habits (e.g., smoking, heavy drinking and drug abuse).[6] And finally, Marvin E. Wolfgang has studied a form of suicide that is mainly peculiar to adolescents and young adults. "Victim-precipitatal homicide" occurs when one person provokes or sets up another person to kill him or her.[7] Depressed, antisocial adolescents will sometimes threaten police officers in such a way that the latter are forced to shoot to kill.

People who have successfully committed suicide have sometimes completed a pattern of behavior that may last from just a few days to many years. At first they may have just a few fleeting thoughts about dying. These may develop into stronger wishes to die, which become intense obsessions. Finally, the person formulates and carries out a specific plan for killing the self.

Other issues relating to suicide include lethality, intent, mitigating circumstances and the method of self-injury. Lethality relates to the deadliness inherent in the method. For instance, rat poison is far more lethal than cough syrup. Intent refers to the degree of sincerity that the individual had in the attempt to die. Mitigating circumstances include a wide variety of variables that would affect the individual's likelihood of attempting suicide. Hallucinogenic drugs will sometimes "cause" a person to attempt suicide when he or she otherwise would not. The method of injury often carries symbolic meaning about the individual's personality, values, type of pain and suffering and level of anger.

Estimates indicate that suicide is the 10th leading cause of death in the United States; about one-half million people commit suicide each year worldwide. Between 10 and 20 percent of the people who make a suicide gesture eventually do kill themselves. More men than women kill themselves, although far more women make suicidal gestures. Divorced, widowed and single people are more apt to kill themselves than are married people. Suicidal deaths are also more common in urban areas than they are in rural settings. Suicidal deaths occur at the highest rates during adolescence and during the later years. Rates are particularly high among college students.

The suicide rate is between 25 and 35 times higher among depressed patients than the national rate and substantially higher than the rates for any other mental illness patient group.[8] Approximately one-third of suicides are completed by individuals who are emotionally or mentally disturbed.[9] Many of these people suffer from severe feelings of guilt, hopelessness, despair or helplessness. They are often confused and are not completely in touch with reality.

Teenagers who commit suicide have often recently experienced events such as moving to a new residence, changing schools, separation or divorce of parents, death in the family, or they have experienced other behavioral problems.[10]

Reasons for Suicide

We are beginning to see that the phenomenon of suicide is quite complex. Various types of people attempt to kill themselves in quite a few different ways. And they seek death for a wide variety of reasons. A periodic review of the following list of reasons and motivations for suicide attempts will help us to spot possible suicide victims among the youth with whom we work.

Escape (surcease). Many people long for death as the only way that they can find to escape an intolerable situation. They feel hopeless about any other solution really working and they feel helpless about their own abilities to do something about it. Sometimes the conflicts are internal, creating unbearable anxiety, agitation or depression. The person who suicides as an escape is unable to see other options.

Escape (sleep). The wish to make all the pain go away is sometimes expressed by the suicidal wish to die in the form of sleep. People who use sleep and sleeping medications to avoid psychological discomfort as well as those who "escape" through sleep are especially at risk here.

People who attempt suicide by taking sleeping pills may equate death with prolonged sleep.[11]

Physical illness. Seriously ill or injured people often experience depression as a result of lost mobility, activity and general potency. Ensuing depression sometimes causes the person to give in and give up. For some who are terminally ill, life has lost all meaning and purpose. The thought of sitting around while waiting to die of their disease is unbearable. So they choose to speed up the inevitable, hoping to avoid excessive pain and discomfort.

Death and loss. For some, the death of a parent, close friend or loved one seems too painful to bear. Perhaps too much of the meaning and security of one's existence was wrapped up in the dead person's life. Without the relationship and identification with the dead person, there is not enough internal strength to keep going. When a person depends too much on external reality, the loss of that reality is overwhelming. When death removes the external support, the individual must very quickly build internal support structures or face serious consequences.

Avoiding being a burden. Suicide notes left by elderly or ill individuals often indicate that the thought of being a burden or an imposition on loved ones was too threatening to risk. For some it is the fear of not really being loved and only tolerated that is unbearable. For others it is the feeling of being an intrusion into a loved one's life. The tragedy in both instances is that the suicide makes the decision for the other individual, taking away the opportunity to express love, care and compassion. Both people are robbed by the terminal decision of the one.

Revenge. People, often young people, feel so overwhelmed by being hurt by another, that their wish to hurt back overrides their wish to live. The suicide of revenge is usually directed toward a lover, parent or parent figure. Some psychologists believe that whenever revenge is the motive for suicide, it is a symbolic acting-out of the early need to hurt parents back for pain or humiliation resulting from them. These suicides grossly underestimate the cost of the maneuver to hurt the other individual—the victim's life.

Guilt. Suicide is often the individual's own attempt to take control of punishment for sins or other misdeeds of which he or she feels guilty. When no punishment has been received from society, friends or family, the individual chooses to be the victim of his or her own self-punishment. Too often suicide becomes the ultimate punishment.

Attention. A suicide attempt is very often a "cry for help." The person is pleading, "Please someone help me. I'm hurting so badly that I don't think I can keep on going. I desperately need help." The severity of this cry for help suggests the intensity of the need for help. And the real tragedy is when the gesture is too convincing and the plea really becomes an accidental suicidal death.

Manipulation. Manipulative suicidal gestures, like attention-getting maneuvers, reflect the extreme need that underlies and drives them. There is almost always a significant component of anger involved in the manipulation, and a distrust in the person being manipulated. But again, the cost is too high.

Impulse or whim. Particularly during adolescence, suicide can be accomplished as an impulsive act. The teenage years are known for their volatile reactions and wide-ranging emotional swings. It is also a phase of life when fantasy can play a major role in the individual's thought life. This tendency toward fantasy and idealism blended with impulsiveness creates dangerous propensity for suicidal acts.

Reunion with a deceased loved one. This motivation for suicide is often the reason why people kill themselves shortly after a loved relative or particularly beloved friend dies. It is one of the oldest known motivations for suicide and has even become a culturally sanctioned tradition in some societies. The frequency of this type of suicide is highest in the elderly but also occurs in the young. In his comprehensive and helpful book on suicide, Bill Blackburn writes, "Careful attention needs to be paid to a child's or adolescent's view of death lest he innocently or impulsively attempts suicide following the death of someone he loves."[12]

Delusions. For some, fears and suspicions reach such an intensity that there is a marked departure from reality both in their content and in their strength. Some people fear imminent financial ruin even though they have a steady job and money in the bank. Others feel utterly hopeless about the possibility of someone ever wanting to marry them, even though they are attractive, bright, have a pleasing personality and enjoy a moderately active dating life. Their fears are related to internal insecurities, apprehensions and anxieties more than to their real situation. People are often shocked to hear that a particular individual committed suicide because the death was more related to internal conflicts than to external reality.

Mastery over fate. For many who commit suicide, the act comes after years of feeling out of control. Life for many people becomes a long string of events that overwhelms and subdues the drive toward maturity, independent action and identity development. Discouragement, disillusionment and feelings of hopelessness are likely to ensue, reducing the person's options to either giving up or active rebellion. In these cases, suicide is perceived as the only way to feel control over their own fate.

Expression of love. Though all suicides are tragic, these are certainly among the most heart-rending. Loving emotions in adolescents and young adults are often extremely intense and loyal. The breakup of a romantic relationship, a divorce and the death of a loved one deal the rejected or surviving individuals a shattering blow. Their emotions are numbed, their perceptions distorted and their hopes for the future destroyed. Their total focus is on the object of their lost love. Their last self-expression is a twisted proclamation of their love—the ultimate sacrifice of their lives.

Teenagers and Suicide

There is a significant rise in the suicide rate among adolescents. Blackburn lists seven influential factors that contribute to this alarming increase: changing moral climate, society's high mobility, high divorce rate, frequent alcohol and other drug abuse, popularization and glorification of violence in the mass media, easy availability of guns and the already high suicide rate.[13]

Teenagers who commit suicide are often reacting to a recent distressing event or problem. The problem is most often a conflict within their family. Some feel that they have failed to live up to parental expectations. Others intensely fear parental pressure. Others were failing to establish or had lost a close interpersonal relationship. Feelings of loneliness are common among teenage suicides. Those who kill themselves are more apt to be isolated rather than simply withdrawn.[14] Utter hopelessness, helplessness and loss of self-esteem are common ingredients in the psychological picture of the adolescent suicide.

Blackburn presents a simplified but helpful view of how a faltering external support system in a teenager's life can lead to suicidal behavior: "The sources of support become shaky foundations. When the foundations become shaky, some young people turn to alcohol and other drugs for solace. These agents, when mixed with a teenager's romantic notions of death, a society that glorifies violence and easy access to the means of suicide, combine into a powerfully lethal mixture that spells death for more and more adolescents. Finally, suicide begets suicide. Suicide attempted or completed plants the idea of self-generated death in the minds of others. Also, suicide in the family especially pulls other family members closer to that option."[15]

Predicting Suicides

As counselors of teenagers we can be helpful in two ways. First, we should be aware of the "signs" of a suicidal teenager. Second, we need to counsel high-risk individuals and those who have survived attempts.

The first helping action is to predict possible suicide attempts before they endanger their lives. Many suicides can be prevented when counselors, pastors, teachers, family members and friends are familiar with signals that an individual might attempt suicide. The following are common signals of suicide:

Previous suicide attempt. This is probably the strongest predictor, including those cases where the attempt was more of a gesture or cry for help. Of completed suicides, about 45 percent have had previous attempts.[16] However, only about 10 percent of those who have attempted suicide actually do complete suicide.

A threat to commit suicide. People who talk intentionally about killing themselves (threaten) are more apt to carry out the act than those who do not let somebody know of this intent.

A plan. The presence of a plan to carry out the suicide threat is a very strong indicator of risk. Each "yes" answer to the following questions increases the risk factors: Is the plan feasible? Has there been a time, date or place set for the attempt? Does the person have in his or her possession what is necessary to implement the plan? Has the person begun to implement the plan?

Stress. Sudden, unexpected, severe and prolonged stress can overwhelm the person's defenses, making him or her a likely candidate for a suicide attempt.

Loss and rejection. Experiencing loss of any kind or rejection from people who are cared about often leads to a questioning of the value of living.

Loneliness. Feelings of alienation and loneliness, especially when the person is in a relatively isolated or withdrawn situation, make it very difficult to maintain adequate ego strength and personal controls.

Mental illness. The presence of mental illness, especially depression, is a high-risk factor.

Sudden behavior change. Any marked and sudden behavior change is worthy of concerned attention. Something is causing the alternation. For example, a sudden mood change or release from depression might follow a decision to escape through suicide.

Negative emotions. The presence of hostile, masochistic, hopeless, guilty, worthless and helpless feelings sometimes indicates propensity toward suicide.

Impulsiveness. The lack of adequate impulse controls, especially in combination with depressive symptoms is a danger signal.

Dependency combined with dissatisfaction. The dependent individual who is dissatisfied with life usually combines personal inadequacy and anger. This combination often results in intense, self-directed hostility.

Physical illness. Physical illness weakens the psychological as well as organic defenses. Degenerative, life-threatening illnesses are often responded to with suicidal wishes.

Success. Ironically, the attainment of success can be associated with suicidal acts. Success can bring new responsibilities that can feel overwhelming. It often marks the culmination of a long and hard effort, after which a void may be experienced.

Preparing to die. It is fairly common for people who are planning suicide to "get their affairs in order" by organizing insurance papers and legal documents, paying off bills, writing letters, etc., prior to the suicide attempt.

Suicide note. A written (or recorded) suicide note is often found after the attempt. When found prior to a warned attempt it should be taken very seriously.

Prediction of suicide attempts by adolescents is usually very difficult. Since their emotions, thoughts and attitudes change so quickly, suicidal ideas can come and go quite readily. However, several attempts have been made to collect together a group of reliable suicide predictors for adolescents. Irving B. Weiner proposes the following five predictive cues: depressed mood, recent significant breakdown in previously effective communication channels, previous suicide attempts or accident proneness, high degree of lethality in previous suicide attempts, and the presence of conscious wishes to die coupled with attempts that occur in isolation from others.[17]

Blackburn compiles a somewhat different list of indicators of adolescent suicide: history of personal problems, recent traumatic event, communication problems, significant behavior changes, moodiness, withdrawal, violent acting-out, abuse of alcohol and other drugs, feeling rejected and unwanted, and the presence of general physical complaints.[18]

Efforts to prevent suicide attempts more effectively have led to the development of several suicide prevention scales. Their use helps the counselor to find what the most valid indicators of suicide are. The counselor can use them to estimate more accurately whether a particular counselee will attempt suicide.

One easily used questionnaire was developed by A.G. Devries in order to make a quick evaluation from the counselee's self-ratings.[19] Here is an adaptation of Devries' scale:

Illustration 36

	YES	NO
1. My future happiness looks promising.	___	___
2. I have recently had difficulty sleeping.	___	___
3. I think that I am to blame for almost all of my troubles.	___	___
4. When I am ill, the doctor frequently prescribes sedatives for me.	___	___
5. My future looks secure.	___	___
6. Sometimes I am really very much afraid.	___	___
7. I sometimes fear that I will lose control over myself.	___	___
8. I have not lately felt like participating in my usual activities.	___	___
9. I go on occasional drinking sprees.	___	___
10. Within the last few years I have moved at least twice.	___	___
11. I have someone whose welfare I care about very much.	___	___
12. I generally feel that I am completely worthless.	___	___
13. I frequently have a drink in the morning.	___	___

Suicidal counselees will tend to produce the following pattern of responses:

1. No	4. Yes	6. Yes	9. Yes	11. No
2. Yes	5. No	7. Yes	10. Yes	12. Yes
3. Yes		8. Yes		13. Yes

Devries' questionnaire provides good indicators for suicide potential. Its weakness (which may also be its strength) is its heavy reliance on the counselor's subjective evaluation. A significant advance in rating the prediction of suicide behavior is William Zung's "Index of Potential Suicide" (IPS). His questionnaire is designed to produce a numerical rating that allows for objective as well as subjective evaluation of suicide risk.[20]

Index of Potential Suicide (IPS) Interviewer Form

Illustration 37

Item	Interview Guide	Severity of Observed or Reported Responses				
		None	Min	Mild	Mod	Sev
1. Depressed mood	Do you ever feel sad or depressed?	0	1	2	3	4
2. Diurnal variation: worst in a.m.	Is there any part of the day when you feel worst? best?	0	1	2	3	4

Item	Interview Guide	Severity of Observed or Reported Responses				
		None	Min	Mild	Mod	Sev
3. Crying spells	Do you have crying spells or feel like it?	0	1	2	3	4
4. Sleep disturbance	How have you been sleeping?	0	1	2	3	4
5. Decreased appetite	How is your appetite?	0	1	2	3	4
6. Decreased libido	How about your interest in the opposite sex?	0	1	2	3	4
7. Weight loss	Have you lost any weight?	0	1	2	3	4
8. Constipation	Do you have trouble with constipation?	0	1	2	3	4
9. Tachycardia	Have you had times when your heart was beating faster than usual?	0	1	2	3	4
10. Fatigue	How easily do you get tired?	0	1	2	3	4
11. Confusion	Do you ever feel confused and have trouble thinking?	0	1	2	3	4
12. Psychomotor retardation	Do you feel slowed down in doing the things you usually do?	0	1	2	3	4
13. Psychomotor agitation	Do you find yourself restless and can't sit still?	0	1	2	3	4
14. Hopelessness	How hopeful do you feel about the future?	0	1	2	3	4
15. Irritability	How easily do you get irritated?	0	1	2	3	4
16. Indecisiveness	How are you at making decisions?	0	1	2	3	4
17. Personal devaluation	Do you ever feel useless and not wanted?	0	1	2	3	4
18. Emptiness	Do you feel life is empty for you?	0	1	2	3	4
19. Suicidal ruminations	Have you had thoughts about doing away with yourself?	0	1	2	3	4
20. Dissatisfaction	Do you still enjoy the things you used to?	0	1	2	3	4
21. Anxiousness	Do you ever feel anxious?	0	1	2	3	4
22. Fear	Have you ever felt afraid for no reason?	0	1	2	3	4
23. Panic	How easily do you get upset?	0	1	2	3	4
24. Mental disintegration	Do you ever feel like you're falling apart? going to pieces?	0	1	2	3	4

Item	Interview Guide	Severity of Observed or Reported Responses				
		None	Min	Mild	Mod	Sev
25. Apprehension	Have you ever felt that something terrible was going to happen?	0	1	2	3	4
26. Alcoholism: pattern	Do you ever take a drink in the morning?	0	1	2	3	4
27. Alcoholism: quantity	Do people ever tell you that you drink more than you should?	0	1	2	3	4
28. Professional help: (M.D., Ph.D., R.N., minister, lawyer, social worker, etc.)	Have you seen anybody professional within the last 3 months because you have been worried about yourself or your health? Who?	0	1	2	3	4
29. Somatic complaints	Do you ever have aches and pains where nothing seems to help?	0	1	2	3	4
30. Physical health	Do you feel that you are in as good a shape physically as you've ever been?	0	1	2	3	4
31. Drug abuse	Do you take sleeping pills on your own?	0	1	2	3	4
32. Lack of support	Do you feel that there is somebody who cares for and understands you?	0	1	2	3	4
33. Lack of alternatives	Do you feel that there is a way out of your present situation?	0	1	2	3	4
34. Hopelessness	Do you feel that, in time, things are going to get better?	0	1	2	3	4
35. Self-blame	Do you blame yourself for everything that goes wrong?	0	1	2	3	4
36. Guilt	Do you have guilt feelings about your past?	0	1	2	3	4
37. Punishment	Do you ever feel that you deserve to be punished?	0	1	2	3	4
38. Available support	Do you feel that when things seem to be at their end, there is someone you can turn to?	0	1	2	3	4
39. Self-control: aggression	Do you ever have fits of anger or lose your temper?	0	1	2	3	4
40. Aggression	Do you ever get into physical fights?	0	1	2	3	4

Item	Interview Guide	Severity of Observed or Reported Responses				
		None	*Min*	*Mild*	*Mod*	*Sev*
41. Self-control	Do you take chances when driving a car?	0	1	2	3	4
42. Personal appearance	Does it matter to you how you look in public?	0	1	2	3	4
43. Suicide: projection, idea	How often do you think other people think about suicide?	0	1	2	3	4
44. Suicide: projection, action	How often do you think people who think about suicide actually kill themselves?	0	1	2	3	4
45. Personal responsibility	Is there someone who depends upon you?	0	1	2	3	4
46. Suicide: rumination	Have you had recent thoughts about dying?	0	1	2	3	4
47. Suicide: method	Have you been thinking of ways to kill yourself?	0	1	2	3	4
48. Suicide: prior threat	Have you ever said to someone that you wanted to kill yourself?	0	1	2	3	4
49. Suicide: prior attempt	Have you ever tried to do away with yourself? How?	0	1	2	3	4
50. Suicide: other person	Have you ever known anyone who committed suicide? Who?	0 = NO				YES = 4

Zung found in his research that people who evidenced no suicide behavior produced a mean score of 43.2, while a mean score of 72.8 was registered by suicide attempters.

The following guidelines are suggested for effective use of Zung's IPS:

A. Each item should be independently rated without reference to any other item.

B. Each item's rating should be the average of the counselee's range of responses, not the extreme range.

C. The items are rated in terms of intensity, duration and frequency on a five-point scale:

   0 = none, not present or insignificant.

   1 = minimal intensity or duration, present only a little of time in frequency.

2 = mild intensity or duration, present some of the time.

3 = moderate intensity or duration, present a good part of the time.

4 = severe intensity or duration, present most or all of the time in frequency.

The severity of the condition can be better established by asking the following questions:

Intensity: "How bad was it?"

Duration: "How long did it last?"

Frequency: "How often, or how much of the time?"

D. Score items positive and present when:

1. the behavior is observed.

2. the counselee described the behavior as having occurred.

3. the counselee admits that the symptom is still a problem.

E. Score items negative and not present (zero) when:

1. the symptom has not occurred and is not a problem.

2. the counselee gives no information relevant to the item.

3. the counselee's response is ambiguous even after clarifying questions have been asked.

Counselors are encouraged to use the IPS or other instruments in order to help them predict suicides more accurately.

Counseling Guidelines

Once it has been assessed that a teenage counselee is a potential suicide risk, definitive counseling intervention is a must. The stakes are high because a person's life is at risk. Recognition of this fact brings a sober determination to the counselor. The first counseling task is to help the counselee stay alive and move out of his or her endangered psychological position. The second task is to help the individual gain insight into how he or she became suicidal and to make the changes that are necessary to insure that it will not happen again. Conventional counseling methods seem to be the best approach because they help the counselees alter behavior so that they can more adequately cope with life situations. Let's look at the specific counseling procedures that are recommended for work with adolescent counselees who are suicidal risks.

The first step in all but the most imminent emergency counseling sessions is the relationship-building phase. Since suicidal counselees tend to be alienated from meaningful relationships, this initial relationship-building phase is particularly vital. The teenager is likely to resist any closeness and will fear developing any dependency upon the counselor. He or she has probably been hurt or rejected in past relationships and is disillusioned about the potential value of friendship and any interpersonal helping relationship. The more effective the interpersonal contact is at this point, the more helpful will be the overall counseling process.

There are few more powerful healing forces than the positive impact of caring, acceptance and genuine concern. Effective counseling absolutely requires generous expressions of total acceptance and warm caring. The only way that the adolescent's defenses can be softened is through the counselor's consistent and genuine caring.

Suspecting that a young person might be suicidal, counselors often hesitate saying something about it for fear of giving him or her the idea. This is an unwarranted fear. Do not wait to ask if the person has been having suicidal thoughts. If he or she has, then there is an opportunity to get the thoughts out into the open where they can be discussed and worked through. Just talking about the suicidal thoughts releases energy that might otherwise be used to motivate the act. If the person was not preoccupied with suicidal ideas, then no harm is done. Certainly the counselor's mention of suicide will not make the counselee want to accomplish it.

Bring the counseling focus to bear directly upon the immediate problems precipitating the suicidal impulses. What are the particular stresses and conflicts that create such anxiety or feel so overwhelming that suicide seems like such an attractive solution? By understanding the nature of the problems that the counselee is failing to cope with, we understand more about his or her personality strengths and weaknesses. Carefully defining the problems also leads to effective solutions later in the counseling process.

Explore the counselee's motivations that drive the suicidal impulses. Find out through sensitive questioning and attentive listening what it is that suicide represents to the counselee. The counselor can then help the teenager to understand why suicide seems appropriate. This understanding will form the basis for making more constructive decisions.

Confront the counselee about his or her beliefs about death. Adolescents often have very unrealistic beliefs and highly romanticized illusions about death. Many have never seen death firsthand. They have not yet been exposed to its pain, destructiveness or finality. They may dwell on the attention that it might bring to them without thinking of the fact that they would not be able to enjoy it. They may think of that would be left behind them. Helping them to gain a more realistic view of death may help them to test their suicidal plans against reality.

Discuss the method by which the individual is planning to commit suicide. The method usually has a symbolic meaning for the individual. Get the person to talk about it, delineating the details of the plan. Listen carefully for clues regarding the seriousness of the person and the intensity of the death wish. Search for indications that might lead to treatment and effective intervention.

Soon after the problems are classified, establish the available resources that the counselee can use to work through the problems. Many problems are due to the teenager's lack of knowledge of available resources and how to use them. Often there are friends, family members, teachers or pastors who would happily give support, encouragement and suggestions for dealing with difficult stress situations. Part of the value of counseling is helping the individual to maximize his or her opportunities and to draw strength and help from his or her support system. As counselees find that there is more support available to them, they begin to experience success in their coping efforts. Consequently, they gradually increase their feelings of trust in their ability to cope effectively with life.

A plan for action needs to be established quite soon in this type of counseling. The plan should take into account what has been learned in regard to the preceding counseling guidelines. The plan should relate first to reducing the risk of a completed suicide. Second, the plan should include realistic goals that go beyond simply keeping the individual from committing suicide. Adolescents who are struggling with suicide impulses need to have something concrete to do. They need some assignment or specific plan of action in order to feel a sense of security and assurance that they can really do something about their painful situation.

One of the greatest fears when working with suicidal teenagers is that they may not follow through with the plan for positive action. Since they are especially impulsive and are given to sudden and extreme mood swings, the possible lack of follow-through is especially present. Counselors who establish firm verbal contracts with their suicidal counselees can have a greater assurance that the counseling plan will be carried out. Maintaining direct eye contact, demanding direct verbal statements (and even a handshake) firm up the contract and increase the probabilities that the counselee will abide by it. Particularly important are contractual statements like: "I will call you if I get more depressed." "I will call you tonight at 8 p.m. to let you know that I am okay." "I will make arrangements with one of my friends to spend the night so I won't be alone."

The contract tightens the counselor-counselee relationship. It is another way of communicating active caring that helps the insecure counselee feel that he or she can really depend upon the counselor's commitment to be there for him or her.

Whenever a counselee talks about suicide as an option, he or she should be referred to a professional therapist, psychologist or psychiatrist. Lay counselors, teachers, pastors and youth sponsors can continue providing very meaningful support for the troubled adolescent after the referral is accomplished. But for both legal and clinical reasons such a referral in these cases is necessary. Familiarity with local crisis centers, "hot lines" and therapists will help to facilitate a comfortable natural referral when it is needed.

Following the referral, be sure to continue warm, supportive contact with the counselee, even if counseling is suspended. Often it is inadvisable to continue counseling sessions when psychotherapy has been initiated through referral. Continued supportive contact is important, however, so the young person does not feel that the referral was made out of disinterest or a desire not to see the counselee.

Notes

1. Karl Menninger, *Man Against Himself* (New York: Harcourt, Brace, 1938).

2. Alex D. Pokorny, "A Scheme for Classifying Suicidal Behaviors," in *The Prediction of Suicide*, eds. Aaron T. Beck, H. Resnik, and D. Lettieri (Bowie, Md.: The Charles Press, 1974).

3. T. Dorpat and J. Boswell, "An Evaluation of Suicidal Intent in Suicide Attempts," Comprehensive Psychiatry 4 (1963):117-125.

4. G. Raines, "Suicide: Some Basic Considerations," Digest of Neurology and Psychiatry 18 (1965):97-107.

5. Pokorny, "A Scheme for Classifying Suicidal Behaviors," in *The Prediction of Suicide*, eds. Beck, Resnick, and Lettiere.

6. Dean Schuyler, *The Depressive Spectrum* (New York: Jason Aronson, 1974).

7. Marvin E. Wolfgang, "Suicide by Means of Victim-Precipitated Homicide," in *Suicidal Behavior*, ed. H. L. Resnik (Boston: Little, Brown, 1968).

8. Alex D. Pokorny, "Suicide Rates in Various Psychiatric Disorders," Journals of Nervous and Mental Diseases 139 (1964):499-506.

9. Gary R. Collins, *Fractured Personalities* (Carol Stream, Ill.: Creation House, 1972).

10. Peter E. Nathan and S. Harris, *Psychopathology and Society* (New York: McGraw-Hill, 1975).

11. Roger A. MacKinnon and Robert Michels, *The Psychiatric Interview in Clinical Practice* (Philadelphia: W. B. Saunders, 1971).

12. Bill Blackburn, *What You Should Know About Suicide* (Waco, Texas: Word Books, 1982), p. 24.

13. Ibid.

14. Derek Miller, *Adolescence: Psychology, Psychopathology and Psychotherapy* (New York: Jason Aronson, 1974).

15. Blackburn, *What You Should Know About Suicide*, p. 31.

16. Ibid.

17. Irving B. Wiener, *Psychological Disturbance in Adolescence* (New York: John Wiley, 1970).

18. Blackburn, *What You Should Know About Suicide*.

19. A. C. Devries, "A Potential Suicide Personality Inventory," Psychological Reports 18 (1966):731-738.

20. William Zung, "Index of Potential Suicide (IPS): A Rating Scale for Suicide Prevention," in *The Prediction of Suicide*, eds. Beck, Resnik, and Lettiere.

■ CHAPTER 13
Identity Problems

Successful identity formation is a necessary prerequisite for developing healthy, intimate relationships, making adequate career choices, and for movement into successful young adult living. But the development of a healthy identity is an extremely complex process. It is subject to a variety of sabotaging intrusions that can cause many different types of psychological and behavioral reactions.

Identity Formation
Three phrases in identity formation. As we move on with this discussion, the definitions of three phrases will be important to understand:

1. Identity crisis. This has been defined as a "period of transition marked by confusion, experimentation and emotionality; it comes about when one's former view of himself or herself is no longer appropriate to a changing life setting, as in adolescence or in middle age."[1] Identity crises are normal during adolescence and middle age.

2. Identity diffusion. This occurs when the individual fails to accomplish an adequate adjustment. The person is either unwilling or is incapable of adapting to society's expectations and demands. He or she is also unable to develop and maintain his or her self-perception and related response style. An *acute* identity diffusion is a temporary but quite intense breakdown of the individual's identity formation in response to death as being rest and refuge without thinking of the pain and sorrow

significant stress. The level of adjustment both prior to and following the breakdown is generally quite successful. *Chronic* identity confusion refers to an individual's inability to make the necessary identity adjustments such that his or her continuing psychological development is seriously affected.

3. Identification. Though this is a psychological defense mechanism, it is also a critically important part of the socialization process. As you will recall, identification is a process by which a person believes himself or herself to be very much like another individual. The role model with whom the person identifies then has a strong influence on the individual's personality, attitudes, values, morals, beliefs and behavior. During earlier childhood the parents are the most often modeled adults. But during adolescence, teachers, pastors, counselors and parents of friends are also identified within addition to the parent figures. Parents who are aware of this process seek to expose their teenage children to other role models who will reinforce similar values and lifestyles to their own. Thus the local church becomes a major socializing influence on the teenagers who regularly attend and take part in its activities. Many teenagers identify with their youth pastors, unconsciously hoping to have their perceived power, prestige, popularity and independence. This postive type of identification is blocked or prevented in the absence of such positive role models. It can also be hampered by excessive external stress, strong internal conflicts, extremes in adolescent rebelliousness, and very weak ego strength that prevents any consistent identification.

Reactions to developmental conflict. Depression is a very common reaction to developmental conflict.[2] Much of adolescent depression is *reactive depression*. Reactive depression occurs in individuals who are fairly well-adjusted. When overwhelmed by external stress, the temporary depression actually indicates that the person is able to tolerate developmental conflict.

A far less adaptive response to these adolescent stresses is *withdrawal* from life involvements that stimulate the developmental crisis.[3] Contact with the opposite sex, movement toward developing occupational choices, and trying to separate from parents are three normal adolescent tasks. The passive teenager lacks the internal strength that is required to confront these developmental challenges successfully.

Roger Ballard, a high school junior, is an example of this unhappy failure to meet these developmental requirements. He is the youngest of three children. His two older sisters and mother made a practice of anticipating and meeting his needs throughout his childhood and protecting him from conflicts with neighborhood children and schoolmates. At home Roger essentially had a free ride. Discipline was minimal and responsibilities were non-existent. He found himself totally unprepared to meet the demands of adolescent adjustment. He felt, and to a large extent was, inadequate to accomplish and cope with the normal adolescent tasks.

The prospects of initiating and developing relationships with girls brought such strong anxiety that he could tolerate only friendships or "buddy" relationships with them. He had only had two dates, and both of them were initiated by the girls. As far as developing occupational goals, he had no idea of even how to go about planning for an occupational or professional future. And the thought of moving away from home and living in an apartment in the next few years was very threatening to him. He felt dependent on his parents and hated feeling incompetent and inadequate. He felt an increasingly widening gap between himself and his peers. He felt more comfortable with younger adolescents, junior high kids and freshmen. He withdrew from his peers and family. Even though he had some passing moments of horrible anxiety, for the most part he could screen out both the anxiety and the reality of his situation.

Symptoms of identity diffusion. Developmental psychologist Erik Erikson specified intimacy, time perception, and industry as three areas that bring to the surface the symptoms of identity diffusion.[4] Often, when teenagers are struggling with developing intimacy they move in the direction of pseudo-intimacy which gives them reassurance (though it is false security) that they really are developing meaningful relationships. These pseudo-intimate ventures into relationship-building occur with members of the same and opposite sex, and most often occur in group settings. Groups afford a sense of security and protection from the demands of deepening relationships on a one-to-one basis.

When a genuine effort is made to become intimate with someone, pre-existing weaknesses and internal conflicts become consciously evident. In the above-cited example, Roger became anxious, clumsy and awkward when faced with the possibility of a dating relationship. Therefore, he never asked any girl for a date, but was able at least to accept a dating request from two different girls. Roger's identity was so vague and weak in its form, that he could not tolerate anything that approximated an intimate relationship. Instead of attempting to be himself, he could only try to anticipate what would be acceptable to the other person and then seek to present that facade as a rather spurious picture of himself. Distance is the opposite of intimacy. Many teenagers *push others away* through the use of their judgmental attitudes, self-righteous posturing, and passive ignoring of those who present a threat of genuine intimacy. The defenses are necessary in order to prevent further personality breakdown under the pressures of deepening intimate contact.

Another symptom of identity diffusion is *disturbed time perspectives* (similar to those experienced by depressed adults). During acute identity diffusions the symptoms are quite mild, but in chronic diffusion time can seem very dissociated.[6] Adolescents sometimes feel simultaneously very young and regressed, and extremely aged. For some the focus is primarily on the future while for others it is overwhelmingly on the past. The time perception dysfunctions are both direct and symbolic representations of the intrapsychic conflict that is occurring.

Anxiety resulting from identify diffusion severely impedes the teenager's ability to concentrate. This *concentration difficulty*, in turn, becomes disruptive to the individual's school work, athletic performance, on-the-job work, and ability to function optimally in any competitive environment. Relief from this anxiety is often found in *compulsive behavior*, such as excessive reading and preoccupation with any one hobby or task. These behaviors focus the individual's attention on pursuits that are perhaps productive but usually less important than school, work or family matters. Junior high and high school students whose grades suddenly begin to drop may be suffering from identity diffusion which is adversely impacting their industry.

A striking feature of severe or chronic identity diffusion is the phenomenon of selecting a *negative identity*.[7] In the struggle for identity the teenager will become polarized against traditional or peer-accepted values. Sex-role standards may be the targeted trait. Adolescent boys may develop stylized feminine traits while teenage girls may take on more masculine effects. Taking on a negative identity explains part of the reason why some adolescents identify with clothing, hair, music, beliefs, attitudes and behavioral styles that are unacceptable to their parents, church or society as a whole. The negative reactions that the teenagers get from others reinforce their attachment to the negative identity.

The tragedy of negative identity is that it becomes both externally reinforced and internally self-reinforcing as well. Plastic surgeon Maxwell Maltz is well-known for his work on the self-fulfilling prophecies that emanate from the self-image.[8] The teenager's behavior continues to express more and more the negative identity which has been adopted. This in turn draws even stronger reaction from others, still more strongly associating the youth with the identity.

Another response that is common in adolescents suffering from chronic identity diffusion is withdrawal to a distant, emotionally isolated *position of spectator*.[9] Ronald G. Poland says the spectating teenager becomes an observer of life rather than a participant: "To be continually a spectator has its risks. The person may sometimes feel he is on the outside edge of life, looking in. He can evolve to seeing himself as a stranger, a trespasser on territory that always belongs to someone else, an alien, unwanted and unloved within his own family and sometimes even unwelcome in the gang of friends he once thoroughly belonged to."[10] Spectatoring as a defensive process is particularly conducive to producing further alienation in the struggling adolescent.

When teenagers who are suffering from chronic identity diffusion are seen by professional therapists, they are frequently diagnosed as having an identity disorder. Both Erikson and Carl Malmquist believe that this diagnosis not only misses the mark as far as accuracy is concerned, but they also believe that this diagnosis can reinforce the processes of negative identity formation.

Causes of identity diffusion. Let's now turn our attention to the causes of identity diffusion. Since identity development is a normal adolescent task, why do some teenagers struggle with such difficulty? Why do some so utterly fail at the task while others proceed through it with good success and relative ease?

Some researchers say that many teenagers struggle so much with their process of identity formation because society offers *unclear guidelines* to direct the young person in this complex task.[11] Another writer proposes that identity formulation is often difficult when parents maintain *tight controls* over their teenagers' behavior until it is time for them to move out on their own.[12] A very sharp demarcation is created between dependent childhood and responsible young adulthood which creates a seemingly wide chasm between the two. Movement from dependency to autonomy is far more easily attained when taken in small steps of natural progression.

Malmquist suggests three environmental contributions to teenager's disillusionment and identity diffusion: the oversell of education; burnout; and over-responsiveness to environmental changes.[13] *Extreme emphasis is placed on education* as teenagers' path to happiness, personal fulfillment and wealth. "Without an education, you'll never amount to anything. With a good education, the sky's the limit." Quite a contrast between that statement and the well-worn line, "Your Ph.D. and a quarter will buy you a cup of coffee almost anywhere." (Understand that inflation has raised the quarter to about a dollar, but the meaning remains the same: education alone does not assure one that they will have a full and enriching life.) And some children, by the time they reach early adolescence, are already suffering from *burnout*. They have had so many different experiences and have had to adjust to so many different changes that they have given up on believing that life has any real or consistent meaning. And other teenagers are disillusioned from their repeated attempts to identify with a person, commit to a cause, or belong to a group, only to have the identification, commitment or belonging spoiled by some change or disappointment in the external environment.

Background studies have indicated several common factors in the families that produce adolescents who experience severe identity diffusion.[14] The mothers of these teenagers tend to be very conscious of social status. They are *social climbers*, extremely aware of appearance and invested in presenting a facade that boasts, "We are among the social elite and we are perfectly comfortable and natural being this way." It is not so much their actual social status as it is their *value of appearances* that leaves the inner life experience more hollow. Their sensitive children are drawn into the pretense. Under their mother's influence, their dress, grooming, personal behavior, selection of friends, hobbies, interests and activities are all carefully choreographed to produce the desired effect. At the time that the young teenager is searching the answer to, "Who am I?," such forced focus on external issues can be devastating.

Another characteristic of the mothers of these disturbed adolescents is their *desperate, intense loving* that tends to repel the child. Erikson labels this quality a "penetrating omnipresence" that would intrude upon and seek control over virtually every aspect of the child's person. These mothers are quite insecure, jealous, out of control and often play the role of martyr in an attempt to regain a sense of control over their lives. To individuate from such a mother is healthy but usually means experiencing a great deal of imposed guilt. Failure to individuate means failure to develop an adequate sense of identity.

Fathers of these troubled adolescents usually tend to be quite *successful* in their occupations or professions, while rather *passive* and *dependent* with their marriage partners. They become quite *assertive* in their careers but *fear rejection* from their wives and opt for a more passive, compliant stance with her in order to prevent having to be confronted with her anger. The father is also more *passive with his children* and encourages them to not "upset your mother" as a further means of keeping the peace at home.

The early childhood and pre-adolescent experience for most of these teenagers is usually quite normal. Some other cases are marked by a pre-adolescent trauma, often dealing with separation (or the threat of separation) from parents or sexual abuse. These earlier life experiences appear to have negatively impacted the teenagers' sense of internal security and personal integrity, which retards their movement toward identity development.

One critically important aspect of identity is the individual's *body image*. Body image is the person's perception of, concept of, and feeling about his or her own body. It includes the person's fantasies, fears and attitudes about the body. And the problems that teenagers have with their body images often have their origins in childhood. Scenes of teasing and rejection based on physical features are all too common between younger children. Parents, teachers and other adults sometimes also tease or ignore children with physical weaknesses, handicaps or some defects.

Children develop several different types of reactions. While some become defensive and angry, others join the attack and ridicule themselves. Still others withdraw not only from others but from themselves as well. They avoid looking at themselves in mirrors, try to conceal their defects under clothing and makeup and retreat into fantasy and denial. During adolescence, all of these mechanisms become intensified in order to protect the individual from the more intense feelings of anxiety, hostility and pain.

These pre-adolescent concerns are compounded with the radical physiological changes that occur as a result of puberty. Early and mid-adolescents are narcissistically focused upon the appearance, shape, strength and functioning of their own bodies. So focused is their concern on their bodies that anxieties arising from other life issues are often mistakenly associated with their physical well-being. Teenagers tend to be very competitive and this, along with their need to be liked by their peers, arouses significant anxieties for early developers as well as late bloomers. Boys who reach puberty later than usual are apt to question their virility and masculinity. Girls who reach puberty late or who develop slowly (particularly with small breasts) are likely to lose self-esteem because of their questions about their sexual attractiveness. Early maturing boys and girls are viewed with more respect and esteem, though these girls sometimes feel discomfort and confusion from being different from their peers, from heightened competitiveness from their peers and from sexual interest from boys.

While boys are concerned about being too short, girls are worried about excessive height. Both sexes worry some about being too heavy, though girls are especially conscious about their weight. Teenagers in general are concerned about facial complexion, body odor, irregular teeth, wearing glasses (contact lenses are a great help here), shape of face and nose, etc. Boys want to develop muscular physiques while girls want slim shapely physiques. Girls judge the physical maturity of boys by the appearance of their beard and the status of their voice change, while boys judge girls by their figure, especially their breast development.[15]

Not only are early and mid-adolescents adjusting to new changes in their bodies, but some are mourning the loss of their pre-adolescent bodies.[16] The happy, simple and relatively carefree pre-puberty years are gone and in the midst of all of the anxiety-producing changes that come with puberty, the passing of those earlier years are often mourned. A major task for adolescents is to accept their bodies. Young people who continue feeling rejecting and judgmental toward their bodies will struggle also with negative impacts from this conflict on their overall developing self-esteem.

Counseling Guidelines

Most teenagers who are struggling with their identity formation can be significantly helped from counseling with pastors, teachers or other lay counselors. Only when severe acute diffusion or serious, long-term identity diffusion is present does the teenager need professional psychotherapy. The greatest challenge to counseling with these identity-confused teenagers is also the key to their successful psychological re-integration. The first step in any counseling process is *developing an effective relationship* with the counselee. But relationship development is probably the most difficult and threatening task that these young people can take on. They have tremendous difficulty making emotional attachments.[17]

The counselor's caring and acceptance of the teenager will likely be tested and retested in an effort to determine whether or not he or she can really be trusted. Self-destructive behaviors, including getting poor grades, becoming obese, being destructive of the counselor's property and exhibiting antisocial behavior are common methods for testing the genuineness of the counselor's caring. "Is the counselor powerful enough to control my aggression?" If the counselor knows just how hostile and aggressive I really feel, will I then be rejected?" These answers must be known with some degree of certainty before the adolescent can develop adequate trust in the counselor. There are few counselees with whom relationship-building is a more difficult or tenuous process than with these teenagers whose identities are so threatened. Yet, when this stage has been successfully accomplished much of the healing is well on its way.

Unconditional acceptance, caring responses, patience, congruence, dependability, and a respectful attitude are all vital ingredients in the counselor's efforts to win the counselee's trust. This relationship becomes a vital link in the teenager's movement toward developing stronger self-love and self-acceptance. The adolescent internalizes and then identifies with the image of the loving or caring counselor as intermediate steps leading to developing his or her own more mature self-love.

Defining the problem entails developing an understanding about the causes of the person's identity confusion. Does the teenager's relationship with his or her mother and father predispose the young person to have such a reaction during adolescence? Were there any early childhood psychological disorders, such as infantile autism? Was there a pre-adolescent trauma like separation from parents or sexual molestation? If any of these questions draw forth positive responses, the counseling task is a bigger one because the identity diffusion is likely to be more serious. If there are no significant predisposing events, then the counselor is probably treating an adolescent who has fairly well-developed ego strength despite the identity crisis.

The *plan of action* for the teenager needs to contain elements that directly clarify the confusion and reaffirm the areas of insecurity and doubt that the person has about himself or herself. A counseling plan of action might include several of the following elements:

1. Make a list of characteristics that describe the real self and ideal self, and then compare the two lists.

2. Deepen the intimacy in at least one relationship each with a same-sex and an opposite-sex friend.

3. Establish at least one new friendship with a member of each sex.

4. Determine the teenager's role models.

5. Identify and alter any self-destructive behavior patterns into more adaptive styles of responding.

6. Identify any dysfunctional family relationship patterns and support the adolescent's positive ways of dealing with them.

7. Help the counselee to develop some tentative ideas about possible future career goals.

8. Improve the individual's body image through encouraging the person to get better acquainted with his or her body, exercise regularly, enjoy and develop physical talents and abilities, and improve his or her dress and grooming.[18]

The *termination process* with these counselees is almost as sensitive an issue as in the relationship-building stage.[19] Resistance should not be given to teenagers who wish to terminate in order to try out their new identities. However, if counseling is stopped prematurely, then the identity confusion symptoms are most likely to return. It is often difficult to discern whether the effort to terminate is motivated by a desire to test the strength of a newly developed personality structure or attitude, or a test of the counselor's caring, saying essentially, "If you loved me you would not let me go so easily." The decision to terminate must be completely talked through and understood by both counselor and counselee. The open invitation is extended to return to counseling whenever the teenager believes that it might be helpful.

Some type of *follow-up* after termination of counseling is also advised. A phone call or a short note in the mail to the counselee says that his or her relationship is still there, even though there may not be any actual continuing counseling contact.

The Special Identity Crisis of Anorexia Nervosa

A special kind of identity crisis encountered in adolescence and young adulthood is anorexia nervosa. It is one of several eating disorders related to identity and self-concept. (Two others are bulimia and pica.) This disorder is characterized by an obsessive aversion to food and the compulsive practice of losing weight.

Almost all of the reported cases of anorexia nervosa are among girls (about 95 percent). Our society puts so much pressure upon girls and women to look thin and trim. Being slender is culturally associated with being acceptable, lovable, attractive, and being a person of value and worth.

Symptoms of anorexia nervosa. One symptom is an intense and unrealistic fear of becoming obese. The person may be a little heavy and decide she wants to lose about five pounds (or some other target weight). Maybe the girl weighs 115 pounds, and she wants to weigh 110. In her mind, she expects that she will feel physically perfect at 110 pounds. So she loses weight and gets down to 110. Then she looks in the mirror and she still sees herself as fat. She still sees a roll here or there. "I'm not thin enough, so I better get down to 105," she says to herself. Of course, when she reaches 105, she's not satisfied because she is still not perfect. Her unconscious attitude is, "Unless I am perfect, then I'm unacceptable and unlovable." The person can never reach that ideal weight. Even though she may lose weight, it doesn't diminish the feeling of being fat.

A second symptom of anorexia nervosa is an extreme disturbance of the body image, feeling obese when the person is very thin. The girl may be excessively thin yet look in the mirror and actually perceive herself as grossly overweight. For example, a counselor once worked with a 19-year-old adolescent who wore long sleeves and pants in any type of weather or situation because she did not want people to see her "fat" legs and arms. Yet she was 5 feet 8 inches tall and weighed 97 pounds.

The third symptom of anorexia nervosa, which is a technical one, is a 25 percent loss of the normal body weight. For example, if a girl whose normal weight is 125 weighs 95, she is medically an anorexic and needs help.

The fourth symptom is an absolute refusal to maintain a body weight that is over the minimal body weight for her age and height.

The fifth symptom is the absence of any physical cause that would account for the weight loss. If there are no metabolic problems, no thyroid problems, no glandular problems or illnesses that would indicate the weight loss, the cause is psychological.

Causes of anorexia nervosa. There are several factors that cause a girl to become anorexic. One of the factors is a very low self-esteem. Most anorexic girls have a very low image of their intellectual, social and physical abilities and appearances. They have low self-confidence and do not believe they are going to amount to anything. They also perceive themselves as having little control over their environment. The family may move. They are transferred from one school to another. They may feel little or no control over their grades. They probably feel very little control over their relationships.

One very common characteristic of anorexics is that they are often very intelligent girls but tend to be overly perfectionistic. They are usually over-achievers. A girl tries so hard to be good enough and yet cannot ever feel that she is good enough. They also tend to think in all-or-none patterns. Something is good or it is bad. Something is strong or it is weak. Their emotions will often go in the same pattern. They're either tremendously happy or terribly depressed. They're either having a good time or having an absolutely horrible time. There are few in-betweens for the anorexic.

Most anorexics come from middle-class and upper-class families. The girl has learned perfectionistic and over-achieving dynamics from her parents. One of the anorexic's major issues is the relationship with her mother. The anorexic usually is very close to her mother. They often have a symbiotic relationship, meaning that they're very emotionally bound to each other so that what the mother does and what the daughter does has a profound impact on the other. Often the mother is perceived by the daughter as being invasive or smothering. This is an issue of *control*. The daughter's aversion to eating is a symbolic expression of the need for control, even if it is control only over her own body. Often the mothers themselves are perfectionistic. They have a lot of goals for their daughters: to be successful, articulate, the most popular girl.

The fathers of these girls are often very successful in their occupations. They are professional men, but they tend to be somewhat aloof. They tend to be emotionally detached from their girls. They are usually proud to have attractive and intelligent daughters yet do not invest much time or energy in them. The girl therefore receives mixed messages that her dad loves her but doesn't feel very loved. He's proud of her but doesn't talk with her much. The relationship is confusing.

The patterns of anorexia nervosa. We need to differentiate the various kinds of anorexics.[20] First there is the *true anorexic*. This girl has virtually no contact with food, will not eat unless forced and then eats very little. The *bulimic* is a person who eats compulsively, in "binges." The person absolutely gorges herself but then experiences a tremendously deep sense of guilt that she has lost control. The *mixed anorexic* is a combination of the true anorexic and the bulimic. The person will go on an eating binge and then feel very guilty. She will then purge herself. One of the most common ways of purging is vomiting. The binge eater will often rush into the bathroom, stick her finger down her throat and vomit out all the contents of her stomach. Another way of purging is compulsive exercise after a binge. She will exercise compulsively in order to purge her body of the food. The full feeling of eating the food is a constant reminder of her loss of personal control. The bulimic will binge and then purge and binge again. The cycle may take a day to a week to complete. The mixed anorexic will binge, then purge and then fast, but will sooner or later binge again. The fasting is an attempt to regain control. The mixed anorexic is probably the most common of the three.

Counseling guidelines. When youth pastors, pastors, parents or anyone else suspects that a teenage girl or young adult woman is anorexic, they should look for the symptoms mentioned earlier. If they sense that the girl is compulsive about dieting, is never satisfied with herself, is obviously getting very thin and yet perceives herself as fat and has lost more than 20 percent of her normal weight, then there is a real possibility that she is anorexic. Some people die of anorexia. They die of problems indirectly and directly related to starvation. This is a very serious life-threatening problem. The further anorexia nervosa goes, the harder it is to turn around. There are other problems that arise from severe anorexia, too, including chronic sexual problems, gynecological problems and endocrine disturbances. It's a severe medical problem as well as a psychological one.

The lay counselor's task is not to treat nor to counsel an anorexic with the idea that he or she is going to cure her. She very often requires hospitalization in order to be cured. But youth leaders can be of tremendous help by being aware of possible anorexics. They are often better able to spot the problem than even the girl's parents. Her parents may not notice the change because they see her every day.

If a girl is expected of being anorexic, the counselor needs to talk with her and find out how she feels about herself, how she feels about eating and how often she eats. She may be very manipulative and hide the fact that she doesn't eat. A talk with the parents is very much in order. What patterns have they seen? Have they talked to her about it? Is there a physical problem? Recommend strongly that the girl be taken to a professional psychologist or the family physician. The physician can determine if there is a case of anorexia nervosa.

The lay counselor can play a very important role in encouraging the girl. Sometimes the girl will need to be hospitalized in a unit for eating disorders. These units provide individual and group therapy, nutrition classes and family counseling. In order to change the eating behavior effectively, hospitalization usually requires several weeks. Unfortunately, what often happens is that the patient leaves the hospital and returns to the same family dynamics that caused anorexia nervosa. It's at this point that the counselor can help the anorexic and her family. The counselor might talk with the staff at the hospital and understand her unique case. The counselor can talk with the girl's parents in order to help them understand more fully the dynamics between the daughter and mother and between the father and daughter. Maybe the mother needs to back off a little bit more, to give the daughter more freedom to be her own person, to exert less pressure as far as her appearance and academics. The father may need to spend more time with his daughter, take her places, do things with her and express his love for her in both word and deed.

Notes

1. Philip G. Zimbardo and F. Ruch, *Psychology and Life*, 9th ed. (Glenview, Ill.: Scott, Foresman, 1975), p. 709.

2. Carl P. Malmquist, *Handbook of Adolescence* (New York: Jason Aronson, 1978).

3. Ibid.

4. Erik H. Erikson, *Identity: Youth and Crisis* (New York: Norton, 1968).

5. Ibid.

6. Ibid.

7. Ibid.

8. Maxwell Maltz, *Psycho-Cybernetics* (Hollywood: Wilshire, 1960).

9. Ronal G. Poland, *Human Experience: A Psychology of Growth* (St. Louis: C. V. Mosby, 1974).

10. Ibid., pp. 76-77.

11. E. Z. Friedenberg, *The Vanishing Adolescent* (Boston: Beacon Press, 1959).

12. Poland, *Human Experience*.

13. Malmquist, *Handbook of Adolescence*.

14. Erikson, *Identity: Youth and Crisis*.

15. D. Rogers, *The Psychology of Adolescence* (New York: Appleton-Century-Crofts, 1962).

16. Malmquist, *Handbook of Adolescence*.

17. Derek Miller, *Adolescence: Psychology, Psychopathology and Psychotherapy* (New York: Jason Aronson, 1974).

18. G. Keith Olson, "How's Your Body Image?," Group (December 1981/January 1982):26-29.

19. Miller, *Adolescence: Psychology, Psychopathology and Psychotherapy*.

20. Randy Northrup, "Anorexia Nervosa and Bulimia" (Lecture: The San Diego Chapter of Christian Association for Psychological Studies, 1983).

■ CHAPTER 14

Sexuality Issues

In the first chapter of this book the tremendous importance of the teenager's emerging sexuality was discussed. Puberty brings alterations in hormonal secretions. These stimulate major changes in the body and in the person's psychological functioning. These alterations result in behavioral implications that are sure to create significant stress in the young person's psyche, in relationships with the opposite sex, and in relationships with parents, church and other authority figures and institutions.

Interpersonal relationships are increasingly accented with sexual attitudes. Direct sexual behavior becomes more common as the increasing frequency and intensity of sexual arousal, sexual impulses and sexual thoughts grow.

Parental and societal reaction to this marked increase in sexuality is a major contributor to the adolescent development of the sexual being. Early childhood sexuality is diffuse and generalized. Its modes of gratification are many and non-specific, including cuddling and snuggling, romping and wrestling, smooching and kissing, as well as playing with one's own genitals. Childhood homosexual play and looking at opposite-sex bodies are normal means of learning and exploring pre-puberty sexuality.

But as the child reaches puberty, sexuality becomes more specific with sexual sensations becoming localized in the genitals. This genital focusing of pleasure occurs much more rapidly in males than females.

Girls continue much longer wanting to be held, caressed and cuddled more than genital stimulation. Puberty creates the need for new learning about sexual feelings, sexual behavior and sexual gratification. Parental and societal responses greatly determine whether this new learning will promote healthy psychosexual development or unhealthy development. Robert White, professor of clinical psychology at Harvard University, gives us an important warning: "When sexual fear is suppressed and denied because it implies something shameful and dirty, or when it is even more completely repressed because it awakens anxiety, the chances of its participating in new learning at puberty are sharply reduced. The consequences may be a general inhibition of sexual interest and behavior."[1]

There are several reasons why the adult community responds in repressive ways to emerging adolescent sexual expression. First, its spontaneity and intensity often stimulate anxious reactions in adults because of their unresolved feelings about their own current or past sexuality. Second, adults are concerned about the morality of adolescent sexual behavior. Third, adults fear how far teenagers' sexual expressions will develop before they have the maturity to control and cope with them. Fourth, adults fear that sex will dominate teenagers' lives so much that other areas like academics, sports, family and friends will be ignored. Finally, adults fear pregnancy and sexually communicated diseases.

Permissiveness is as damaging to adolescent sexual development as is repressiveness. The teenager is not psychologically mature enough to handle active genital sexuality without suffering very painful results from such freedoms. As Christians, we are also concerned about the moral and spiritual ramifications of such behavior. But it is not only Christians who see dangers for teenagers in sexual permissiveness.

We arrive then at a position somewhere between repression and complete permission. This position allows for growth, learning, and experimentation within limits that are established and maintained through loving and firm support.

In this chapter we will examine normal adolescent sexual adjustment issues and then we will survey different forms of deviant sexual behavior. White's definition of deviant sexual behavior as "developmental abnormality" will be used here.[2] Normal adolescent sexual development is disrupted, causing the full energy of genital sexuality to be expressed in some earlier childhood pattern that is inappropriate at this later life stage. Maladjustment in adolescent sexual expression, if not adequately treated, may prevent the individual from developing into a healthy adult.

Non-Deviant Sexual Adjustment Issues

Let us first approach the more common adolescent sexual issues. Familiarity and understanding of these issues will help the counselor to be better able to assist teenagers who have questions or concerns in one or more of these areas. Specifically, the following issues will be examined: puberty-related problems, masturbation, handling sexual temptations and illegitimate pregnancy.

Puberty-related problems. Puberty is viewed as both a physiological and a psychosocial phenomenon. Certain physiological changes that involve the central nervous system, glands and endocrine secretions must occur before adequate psychological and interpersonal adjustments to adolescence can be enacted.

Precocious puberty occurs when the onset of puberty is early. The guidelines for this determination are: for girls, signs of sexual maturity before their sixth birthday or menarche before their eighth birthday; and for boys, signs of sexual maturity prior to their eighth birthday. Girls with this condition need support and information about what is happening in their bodies. With proper support and reassurance that everything that is happening is normal, they usually don't experience any serious adjustment problems. Though they do have to learn how to respond to older boys' and men's sexual reactions to them while still very young, with adequate support and opportunity to discuss their feelings with parents and other trusted adults, their adjustment is usually quite successful. Research indicates that sexual activity, including masturbation, sex play, sexual curiosity and sexual intercourse, in these girls followed the normal pace and course of development when compared with girls who reached puberty in the median age range.[3]

Precocious puberty occurs less frequently in boys than it does in girls.[4] For boys, early puberty onset can be a status symbol. The appearance of phallic and armpit hair, beard growth, increased size of penis, increased muscular strength, growth spurt and masturbation with ejaculation are all valued signals of acquiring masculinity. Same-sex peers show respect and often respond to these boys as leaders while girls may tend to see them as more mature and interesting than other boys. These boys are only moderately accelerated in their psychosexual development.[5] Erotic fantasies and masturbation with emission occur significantly earlier than median-age pubertal boys, but their fantasies usually reflect very immature content that discloses ignorance about sexuality which is quite age-appropriate.

Some counseling may be in order to help these boys understand their new and typically strong sexual urges as normal and healthy. They need to know that though fantasies are expected and normal, they need to be learning self-control regarding their thought patterns. They need also to understand masturbation and ejaculation, and their relationship to heterosexual sexual intercourse. Imparting this information in the context of Christian ethics and principles will help the youth toward a happy and fulfilling adolescent growth process that will lead him on toward maturity.

Delayed puberty probably occurs with equal frequency between the sexes, and is diagnosed when puberty onset occurs between two and three years past the median age.[6] Girls seem to have very few problems with delayed puberty as compared with boys. When, at age 15 or 16, boys have not yet reached puberty, they experience a variety of disadvantages. Late-puberty boys are commonly thought of as still being "little kids" and are often ridiculed, made fun of, and excluded from desirable groupings. They make poor athletes and are usually retarded in their acquisition of social and dating skills. Some research studies indicate that delayed puberty can also have long-lasting negative results in the boy's life.[7] Significantly delayed puberty onset can cause a delay in the youth's later career development as well as delaying his ability to enter into a healthy marriage relationship.[8]

These teenage boys can benefit greatly from supportive counseling. Psychotherapy is usually not necessary, since what they need primarily is the opportunity to voice their concerns and their pain to someone who can listen, accept and support their okayness. Counseling focuses on reassurance and support rather than insight.

Masturbation. Though the focus of much unneeded controversy, masturbation is a very normal part of human sexual functioning. It is normal from several different perspectives: statistical, physiological, psychological. From a statistical perspective, Alfred Kinsey found that 93 percent of American males and 62 percent of females admitted to having masturbated.[9] It has been jokingly said that, "Ninety-nine percent of teenage boys admit that they masturbate. The other one percent are liars." Certainly, just because an act is common does not mean that it is okay, normal, moral or healthy. But if a behavior is common to the vast majority of people, Christians as well as non-Christians, it does give us a place to start.

From physiological and psychological perspectives masturbation is also normal. From very early childhood, both boys and girls experience pleasure from fondling their genitals. Pre-puberty genital pleasure is not so intensely gratifying as is post-pubertal pleasure, but it does feel good to the child.

With onset of puberty the adolescent male is able to ejaculate and masturbation from this point on is usually done in order to reach orgasm. Nocturnal emissions and masturbation are the two most common ways that adolescent boys release their rapidly building sexual tensions since heterosexual genital intercourse is not a sanctioned release.

There have been many threats to young males and females about the physical and psychological damages of masturbation. It has been claimed to be the cause of not only acne, loss of hair, physical weakness and too much stress on the heart, but also inability to function in a sexually normal way in marriage, insanity, mental retardation and even syphilis. The medical and psychological communities find no evidence that masturbation causes these or any other such difficulties.

Masturbation has been much more of an issue for adolescent males than it has been for girls for two primary reasons. First, early and mid-adolescent girls typically do not have a strong need for genital sexual release. Their sexual arousal is satisfied for a longer period of time through being held and cuddled.[10] Their stronger sensations of genital arousal begin occurring with more intense petting and foreplay, and especially with genital penetration. A second reason for masturbation being less of an issue for adolescent girls is that their sanctions against masturbation have been much stronger. Until quite recently masturbation in females was thought to be abnormal.

Psychologically, masturbation gives boys a feeling of control over their rapidly increasing sexual urges. It takes little or no external stimulation for spontaneous erections to occur, often at inopportune and very embarrassing times. The slightest fantasy fragment, visual contact with a pretty girl, or external physical stimulation (like wearing tight-fitting jeans) can cause a strong erection to occur anywhere—in class, at Bible study or riding in the car. Releasing sexual tension through masturbation gives some sense of control. It also provides young people opportunity to learn more about their own sexual arousal.It helps them to feel reassured that they function normally.

There is no scriptural reference to masturbation. However, one reference has often been misunderstood and misused by well-meaning Christians to try to dissuade young people from masturbating. The reference, Genesis 38:6-10, relates the story of Onan's sin:

"And Judah took a wife for Er his first-born, and her name was Tamar. But Er, Judah's first-born, was wicked in the sight of the Lord; and the Lord slew him. Then Judah said to Onan, 'Go in to your brother's wife and perform the duty of a brother-in-law to her and raise up offspring for your brother.' But Onan knew that the offspring would not be his; so when he went in to his brother's wife he spilled the semen on the ground, lest he should give offspring to his brother. And what he did was displeasing in the sight of the Lord, so he slew him also."

Onan's sin was not masturbation. It was, rather, a method of birth control called coitus interruptus, a method which is not terribly effective because it requires strong self-control on the part of the male to withdraw his penis from the vagina just prior to ejaculation. This text should not be misinterpreted to mean that God is against birth control, either. Onan's sin was his refusal to provide children to his deceased brother's name. He refused to obey Jewish custom and law.

There appear to be three potential problems related to masturbation that counselors often see in adolescent boys:

1. Because it is so intensely pleasurable during a life stage that is typically fraught with discord, turmoil and uncertainty, masturbation can become compulsive. It is autoerotic and self-centered. Boys who tend to withdraw from threatening interpersonal situations, who feel alienated and isolated, and who feel insecure and lonely, are likely to develop a compulsive pattern of masturbating. The pleasure from the act, along with the accompanying fantasies of being with an attractive girl tend to give temporary relief to their psychic pain. It is the compulsiveness, not the masturbation itself, which is the problem that needs primary counseling focus.

2. The strong feelings of guilt and anxiety that often accompany masturbation create problems for many teenagers. Some have been misled to think of the act as sinful. Others, because of strongly repressive parental attitudes about sex in general, believe that it is a dirty or nasty habit. And some boys, hearing other adolescents making snide remarks about it, think of themselves as being perverted or immature because they masturbate. The problem here is not with masturbation itself, but with the boy's emotional reaction to it and what he thinks about it. Counseling is usually very helpful to these young people. It can help them gain needed information about masturbation, give them

an opportunity to express their fears and concerns, and reinforce the normality and healthiness of their developing sexuality.

3. Though masturbation is itself not a sin, the lustful thoughts that usually accompany the act may be. Spontaneous sexual thoughts, fantasy fragments, and sudden erotic impulses are exceedingly common especially for adolescent and young adult males. These are natural occurrences that are normal byproducts of healthy psychosexual development. But when these feelings and thoughts become the focus of attention, they then take the form of lustful fantasies which are sinful. Christ said, "You have heard that it was said, 'You shall not commit adultery.' But I say to you that everyone who looks at a woman lustfully has already committed adultery with her in his heart" (Matthew 5:27-28). Since the cognitive process of fantasy is an important aspect of adolescent intellectual development, it is no wonder that some of these fantasies actively incorporate the strong sexual urges that are also normal for the age. Exactly at what point these fantasies associated with masturbation become sinful no one really knows. And for most people masturbation without fantasy loses much of its appeal. This issue needs to be handled on an individual subjective level. Christians can help their adolescent counselees honestly confront their own behavior in light of scripture and Christian morality and then provide support and reinforcement as the young person seeks to follow through with his or her decision and plan of action.

Handling sexual temptation. Strong sexual temptation, it must be understood, is a normal stress during adolescence. The strong and rapid increase in the intensity of sexual impulses during the teenage years has already been documented. As youth progress into mid- and late adolescence, they move from valuing peer group involvement as being primary to seeking out individuals, especially of the opposite sex. As they pair off heterosexually and spend increasing amounts of time together, they naturally seek further sensual and sexual exploration as well. The goal and task of the counselor and other adults who work with teenagers is to help them to develop individually and relationally in sexually healthy ways. Part of this task is accomplished by helping young people to progress gradually in their sexual maturing. Some Christians have advocated almost complete abstinence from any heterosexual activity (not even kissing) until engagement or marriage. This seems very ill-advised since it seriously retards the youth's psychosexual development and assumes that on the wedding night several years of growth can be accomplished. This type of thinking denies all that we know about the developmental principles of growth that God built within his children.

Permissiveness, at the other end of the spectrum, is no better answer. Teenagers have not yet developed the personality strength or level of integration that allows them to make consistently wise decisions and handle the intensity of psychological conflict that excessive sexual activity brings.

Instead, teenagers need to learn self-control while they are enjoying the gradually increasing sexual pleasure that God has created for them. Petting is a major part of this process. One author aptly defines petting as "tender exploration of one another by two people who do not intend to have intercourse."[11] Petting is very much like foreplay only the latter is more specifically for emotional and physical preparation for sexual intercourse. When appropriately controlled, petting progresses to a level of intensity that corresponds with the level of emotional intensity and commitment in the relationship. The difficulty is that because sexual pleasuring feels so good, people want to continuously push further in order to intensify their pleasure. Problems arise when the couple moves sexually too fast too far so that their relationship falls out of balance. When their relationships become primarily sexual or sensual, teenagers feel torn between enjoying their intense pleasure on the one hand, and feeling like they are using each other on the other hand. They often experience anxiety and guilt, sometimes without fully understanding why. Teenagers find themselves having to deal with peak-level sexual drives at the same time they are learning how to control them.

Some adolescents feel no sense of guilt at all. They are "out after all that they can get" and do not really care about the other person's feelings. These young people are often openly seductive or manipulative in order to get what they want. This pattern of sexual exploitation is not only indicative of a serious spiritual problem, but also suggests the possible presence of significant personality disorder. Counseling with these teenagers requires much intense therapeutic intervention in order to alter these unhealthy personality developments.

Counseling with normally developing teenagers can follow a much more supportive format. Our first task is helping teenagers understand what is happening to them. Listening carefully to their voiced concerns helps them to feel not so alone. Help young people to feel the courage and self-confidence that is required to set their own standards and limits. Avoid the temptation to structure limits for them. The more they can decide for themselves the more their character strength develops and the more adequately they are able to direct and control their dating experiences. Help them understand that sexual desires are normal but that we need to be able to control them.

Pornography is attractive to adolescents since they are curious about the opposite sex. Pornographic media offer food (albeit junk food) for this curiosity. Again, control is the key. If the young person will confess and talk openly with the counselor about this activity, he or she will gain that much more control over the desire to look at pornography. When a person talks about behavior and feelings, then much of the energy that would be used in the inappropriate activity is directed into positive action. Simply talking about the desires and conflicts in a non-judgmental setting will reduce the chances of sexual acting-out. After this initial confession, the young person will be much more able to set some goals for controlling this (and other) sexual activity. Perhaps the teenager will realize that overstimulation is hard to control.

Another very common issue is the situation in which a young person develops a "crush" on an adult youth minister or volunteer sponsor. This is essentially a transference issue: A young person transfers feelings that are more appropriate for a boyfriend or girlfriend onto the adult youth worker. The youth worker need not become frightened or feel guilty. Do some quick evaluation. Youth workers should ask themselves if they did anything to stimulate the young person's feelings. Then gently confront the young person and gradually let him or her know that such feelings are normal. Help the young person understand why he or she feels that way. Are there feelings of dependency? Sometimes the youth minister is perceived as very righteous, powerful and near-perfect. While that may be flattering, youth workers should help the young person explore the possibilities of hero worship. Sometimes the feelings are related to parent replacement. Maybe the young person is a 15-year-old girl whose relationship with her father is very empty or lacking. Regardless of the dynamics, youth workers should talk with the young person (perhaps with another adult the same sex as the young person) before the situation gets out of hand.

When teenagers do develop a full sexual relationship they need to be encouraged to express how they feel about what has happened. Confront only when necessary and avoid reiterating familiar scriptures. When there is resistance to admitting to wrongdoing, patiently search out the source of these feelings. They may originate in the adolescent's need to rebel or form a competitive relationship with overly restrictive parents. Counseling responses that seek resolution of these internal conflicts will be far more helpful than pushing for immediate confession of wrongdoing or penitent attitude. Unless there is a deeper psychological problem, these positive responses will be forthcoming if an adequate counseling relationship of trust has been established and if internal conflicts have been sufficiently resolved. When that point is reached the counselee will be able to drop his or her defenses and own responsibility for the action.

A deeper understanding about how the incident occurred, what actions led up to it and what decisions could have prevented it can all be discussed within an atmosphere of caring and support. The counseling focus shifts to the future. What now? How can future problems be prevented? What decisions need to be made now that will enable the couple to better control their sexual relating? Here too, most of the ideas should come from the counselee, encouraged and guided by the counselor. Young people need to know that serious mistakes are often made yet there is always in Christ's forgiveness a chance for a new beginning. Counselors can play major roles in being agents that facilitate those new beginnings.

It is a matter of true confession, true repentance, talking it through with the sexual partner and deciding to move away from that pattern with that person. Help them to understand that it would be very difficult to go backward in the relationship, away from sexual involvement. If they have had a strong dating relationship and had sex, it would probably be very difficult for them to maintain a strong relationship without continuing to have sex. Part of the recovery process and a measure of true repentance is that they pull away from that relationship, trusting that if God does want them together at a later time, he probably will reunite them. They need to accept responsibility for it and not blame their partner for seducing them. This all needs to be done in an atmosphere of a non-judgmental counseling situation in which there is forgiveness balanced with confrontation of the behavior.

Illegitimate pregnancy. This discussion of illegitimate pregnancy in adolescent girls will be confined to dealing with the relevant psychological aspects, the alternatives that are available to her and counseling guidelines for helpful intervention.

Psychiatrist Derek Miller offers some valuable insights into the psychological motivations that sometimes either consciously or unconsciously lead an unmarried adolescent girl to become pregnant.[12] The point is validly made that since contraceptive measures are so readily available and are so commonly used, that becoming pregnant is usually quite purposeful, though the motivation may not be readily apparent even to the girl who has recently conceived. Some girls become pregnant because of intellectual inadequacy, an inability to say "no" to a boyfriend's need to prove his potency and sometimes because of an ill-founded belief that God would not let it happen. Some pregnancies are planned to force a boyfriend into marriage, or to coerce reluctant parents into allowing a teenage wedding. Some teenage girls have a fantasy that marriage and homemaking will bring them happiness and stability in an otherwise confusing and demanding world. Still other girls have an almost magical notion that they could not become pregnant while others give their boyfriends the complete responsibility by naively believing their assurances that they will take whatever precautions are necessary.

Pregnancy in adolescent girls often represents an attempt to feel whole and valuable as a woman.[13] When counseling teenage girls who have discovered that they are pregnant, it is important to gain a deepening understanding of the underlying motivations and to help the girl to understand and admit them to her consciousness as well. Often pregnancy brings to the attention of adults that the boy and girl have been having sex. It usually is not a big surprise to their friends because adolescents have a pretty good idea who is sexually active. At this point, the counseling focus must be directed to helping the girl examine her options and decide what she will do about her pregnancy. Essentially, there are four options open to her:

First, she might marry her boyfriend. The benefits are significant if they are fairly mature and deeply love each other. Married adolescents sometimes live with one of their families though it is usually preferred for them to be able to have an apartment on their own, even if they require some temporary financial support. This gives them the privacy required for successfully transitioning from being single teenagers to being a young married couple. The major problems with this choice revolve around their relative immaturity, need to finish school, and the severe impact upon their peer relationships. These negative impacts become greater with younger teenagers.

Second, she might decide to give birth to her baby and keep it without getting married. Often she lives at home and the child is raised by her with her parents' and siblings' help. The benefits are that the child has an established home, the girl does not have to enter unwisely or prematurely into an undesirable marriage and she can more easily carry on her schooling and peer relationship activities in a more normal fashion. She also has the benefit of the readily available emotional, financial, and learning support from her parents provided that they have maintained a positive relationship. The drawbacks revolve around possible relationship difficulties that can arise between the girl and her parents, particularly her mother. Instead of being only an adolescent daughter, she also has become a mother who will desire to parent her own child to some degree in her own way. Conflicts over child-rearing practices with her mother are certain to occur.

Another difficulty is that teenage girls often have very naive views about what being a mother of an infant or toddler is really all about. Their concept may be a very regressed and unrealistic one that is more akin to playing dolls or playing house. In these cases the girl's immaturity will prevent her from doing any effective parenting and the major responsibility of raising the child may fall back onto the girl's mother. Depending on the mother's goals in life, this arrangement may or may not work out very well.

Third, the girl might decide to give birth to the child and then adopt it out to another family. One advantage to this decision is that it allows the girl to be responsible to her unborn baby without locking herself, her boyfriend or her parents into an 18-year commitment (or longer) just because she got pregnant. Adoptions can be arranged through an adoption agency, the girl's gynecologist or independently through friends or relatives. These measures help the girl to feel assured that her baby will be well cared for and raised in a strong home environment. For some girls, adopting out their child after carrying it for nine months and giving it birth into life is their last gift of love to their baby.

But adopting out a child is a very difficult process. It marks the end of what is probably the most intimate of all human relationships. Girls need to grieve at such a time because they are losing a relationship. When they do not adequately mourn their loss, they tend to feel empty and incomplete inside, which often leads to another pregnancy.[14]

Jeanne Lindsay has written a very sensitive and helpful book titled *Pregnant Too Soon*.[15] Her subtitle is "Adoption Is an Option." In her book she strongly recommends that girls should have some contact in the hospital with their babies before the adopting parents take them home. Seeing their baby makes it all seem more real and, though painful, facilitates the mourning process. For some, just seeing the infant through the nursery window is sufficient. Others should be allowed to hold and cuddle their baby and for others, even breastfeeding is advisable while in the hospital. Saying goodbye is an individual matter and should be handled flexibly in order to best meet the needs of the young mother.

Fourth, the most efficient and convenient option is abortion. The benefits of abortion are also related to its drawbacks. Because of its efficiency and the emotionally as well as clinically sterile procedure, the girl can go through the whole process with little psychological involvement in what is really happening. Not only her child, but her sense of responsibility is aborted as well. The responsibility for choosing to have sexual intimacy with someone and the responsibility for conceiving a new life is seriously lessened through this procedure. Abortion is essentially an escape from these responsibilities and prevents girls from going through a difficult though very valuable learning experience by dealing with the consequences of their decisions and actions. Derek Miller states: "There are no psychological indications for abortion; there are only psychosocial justifications."[16] He states that abortion is a "magical" solution and that when magic is available, counseling is felt to be not only useless, but also tedious. If a girl is to have an abortion, the counseling relationship should be well-established before the surgical procedure is performed.

When adults encourage a girl to get an abortion, she may interpret this as an indication that the adults do not respect her as a woman. After an abortion, especially if the girl had felt the baby move within her, she is likely to feel murderous and need counseling to help her resolve these feelings. Some girls annually remember the date of their abortion with renewed guilt, remorse and grieving.

Christian counselors need to help girls deal effectively with the spiritual aspects of abortion. They need to work sensitively, fully accepting her and communicating no sense of judgment toward her while, at the same time, confronting her with the reality of what abortion really is. Intensive counseling may be required to help her to resolve the spiritual, mental and emotional aftermath of abortion.

Sexually Deviant Behaviors

Adolescent sexuality is a period of transition from childhood sexual expression to adult sexuality. Teenagers, then, will exhibit both childhood and adult forms of sexual behavior. As the young person grows from early adolescence, through mid-adolescence, and into late adolescence, their sexuality should be taking on increasingly adult characteristics.

The wide variety of sexually deviant behaviors are expressions of sexual energy that are significantly divergent from what is normally expected of individuals of a particular age from a specific ethnic and sociocultural environment. Normal sexual behavior varies within four different continuums: the intensity and the frequency of its gratification, the mode of gratification, the object for sexual gratification, and the context within which the sexual drive is aroused and gratified. Sexually deviant behaviors will be grouped under these four headings. Though any one deviant behavior may be considered abnormal in more than one dimension, it will be grouped in the category that identifies the greatest deviation. For instance, homosexual sadism/masochism is deviant both with regard to the sexual object (homosexuality) and to the mode (inflicting pain). The following table presents the groupings of the sexually deviant behaviors that involve teenagers:

Deviant Intensity and Frequency	Deviant Mode	Deviant Object	Deviant Context
Promiscuity Nymphomania Satyriasis	Transvestism Transsexuality Sadism Masochism Frottage Exhibitionism Voyeurism Obscene communication	Homosexuality Bisexuality Incest Pedophilia Bestiality (or Zoophilia) Fetishism	Prostitution Rape

Illustration 38

Deviant Intensity and Frequency

The three sexual patterns considered here are promiscuity, nymphomania and satyriasis. They imply no abnormality as to mode or object of sexual gratification, though there is at times also a contextual deviance.

Promiscuity. This is relatively indiscriminate, loveless sexual intercourse, which is experienced with a variety of partners. The sexual contact is said to be indiscriminate because the choice of the sex partner is often based on availability more than on any other criteria. "Who will do it with me?" Whoever can be seduced, whoever is interested, curious or vulnerable enough will do. Physical appearance, social status, age and material possessions are more important than emotional involvement, level of maturity, similarity in values or sense of commitment to a relationship. In fact, there is often virtually no relationship, only a brief sexual encounter.

Promiscuity is always a sign of serious psychological disorder in the adolescent.[17] Young people who feel rejected by their parents, who feel lonely, empty and isolated are particularly apt to develop loveless sexual relationships. Not having their needs met for love, they tend to regress, demand attention and are very seductive in order to get it. Mid-adolescent girls are particularly vulnerable. They need to be held and cuddled and some willingly pay the price of intercourse. Boys also need physical contact and particularly enjoy the intense pleasure of genital release without caring very much about the girl who is willing to provide that pleasurable experience.

Promiscuous sexual behavior is more a relationship with a part of someone's body (penis, vagina, breasts, etc.) than it is a relationship with a person. Derek Miller claims that the regressed teenage girl is apt to accept the boy's penis into her vagina in much the same way that a baby sucks its thumb.[18] Promiscuous sex tends to devalue the personhood of both people. It sometimes involves hostile expression and a wish to hurt back at parents and life in general for not meeting their needs.

Parents of promiscuous children realize painfully that they cannot control the sexual behavior of their children. Such teenagers, particularly teenage girls, need inpatient treatment in order to redirect their sexual behavior and resolve their underlying psychological pain.

Parents of early and mid-adolescents walk a thin line between being overly oppressive and overly permissive. They need to provide sufficient guidelines and structure to bolster the youth's incomplete defensive structure. And they need to allow enough freedom for the teenager to develop his or her own maturity. A hypersexualized society and strong peer group social pressure to be sexually active do not help. Sexually curious girls and boys are especially vulnerable at unsupervised parties where drugs or alcohol are present. Ingestion of these chemicals tends to lower individuals' resistance and make them far more vulnerable to personal impulses and social pressure. Most early and mid-adolescents are not mature enough to be able to handle that kind of pressure. They need the structuring presence of adult chaperones at their parties. Caution should be used in allowing younger adolescents to attend parties where late adolescents will also be involved.

Nymphomania. The following excerpts are from an account of a sexual encounter by a late adolescent male with a girl who evidenced many characteristics of nymphomania: "Her name was Norma and she was perfect. Polite. Well-dressed. Virtuous-looking. The kind of girl we used to call 'clean cut.' What she gave me that day was an unforgettable sense of freedom. For once nothing had to be hidden or hinted at. 'I love to ask for it,' she said. Afterwards she kept saying, 'Thank you, thank you, thank you.' "[19]

The girl in this excerpt, like most nymphomaniacs, has made sexual intercourse practically her sole means of having interpersonal contact. Without sexual contact she cannot feel loved or cared about. This extreme sexual appetite is usually related to other psychological disorders and is a symptomatic expression of those problems.

Satyriasis. This is the analogous disorder in men that nymphomania is in women. Satyriasis is relatively unheard of because masturbation has been a far more acceptable means of sexual release for adolescent boys. But highly promiscuous boys who "notch their bedpost" with each "score" would fall into this category, especially if their behavior extends for a long period of time. Boys with this pattern are usually looking for reassurance of their masculinity, wanting to feel loved and valued, or are rebelling against parental control.

Deviant Mode

The category of the mode or type of behavior that is used to bring sexual gratification includes a wide variety of deviant patterns that appear in adolescent sexual behaviors. The deviant modes that will be described here are: transvestism, transsexuality, sadism, masochism, frottage, exhibitionism, voyeurism and obscene communication.

Transvestism. Transvestism literally means cross-dressing. Transvestite behavior occurs in a wide variety of contexts, ranging from wearing the opposite sex's clothes at Halloween parties to an inability to achieve sexual arousal and orgasm without dressing in clothing of the opposite sex. Some researchers report that the latter extreme has been recorded only among men.[20]

Though the cause of this gender identity disorder is unclear, the origin probably lies in eary childhood. Some people who cross-dress adopt a name and personality that correspond with the clothes they are wearing.[21] The adolescent boy, for example, may take on feminine attitudes, vocal characteristics, posturing and movements while dressed as a woman. He then reverts back to his masculine personality when he changes back into boys' clothing. Carl Malmquist writes that a variety of transvestite behaviors occur during adolescence: innocent fun at parties, theatrical roles, efforts to attract potential homosexual partners and sexual gratification.[22]

Some, but not all, transvestites wish they were the opposite sex.

Most feel an added sense of security while cross-dressing. Boys tend to feel loved and comforted while girls tend to feel powerful.[23] It represents an attempt to convince the self that no one else is necessary, that the person is capable of satisfying his or her own needs.[24]

Teenage transvestite boys often are found out because they are caught stealing women's clothing. When they enter into a counseling relationship, the goal is twofold: to reduce the frequency and intensity of the cross-dressing behavior and to support the adolescent's emerging identity. Counseling for this problem is best accomplished with younger teenagers. Complete remission is not likely if the transvestite is in late adolescence.

Transsexuality. The term transsexual means going from one sex to another. Though many children and adolescents have isolated transsexual thoughts or dreams, patterned transsexual behavior and feelings are far more rare. True transsexuals actually believe that they are of the opposite sex. As very young children they believed that they were of the opposite sex, began behaving with cross-sex mannerisms and believed that they would grow up to become the opposite sex. Their anxiety level is greatly increased when puberty brings the secondary sex characteristics that confirm their real gender. Some adolescents react to the increased disparity between their real gender and identified gender by becoming depressed and suicidal.[25]

The cause of transsexualism is unclear, though several hypotheses have been offered:

1. Biological isomorphism (genital structure that has both male and female characteristics) compounded by cross-sex reinforcement in the environment.

2. Covert genetic tendencies that contribute toward masculine or feminine characteristics.

3. Childhood raising practices that are ambiguous or neutral relating to sexual identity, so that at puberty the occurrence of cross-sex identity is possible.

4. A family atmosphere in which the child is forced into adopting the behaviors of the opposite sex.

5. An alteration in their internal or external sex organs that causes greater confusion in sexual identity.[26]

Mothers of transsexuals are often unhappy in their marriages, dissatisfied with their sex lives, and are unsure about their femininity.[27] They are often depressed and plagued with feelings of emptiness and incompleteness. Fathers of these children are absent physically from the family much of the time, and are withdrawn and uncommunicative when they are at home.

The cause of transsexuality is both hereditary and environmental with the latter playing the more major role. Intensive counseling or psychotherapy during early and mid-adolescence is especially important for the developing transsexual. The emotional, psychological and social turmoil of the early adolescent allows for new self-perceptions, new attitudes and new behaviors to be learned. It is probably the initial time for counseling intervention if a significant change is to occur.

Counseling should involve initially very warm and accepting responses from the counselor. Quite early in the counseling process direct measures should be taken in order to help the young person to establish a strong and appropriate sexual identity with fitting behavioral expressions.

Sadism. When an individual gains or intensifies his or her level of sexual gratification from inflicting pain on the sexual partner, he or she is said to be sadistic. Males in our culture are more often sadistic than females because greater aggression is traditionally allotted to them. Sadism can be in verbal or physical forms. Verbal sadism includes abusive teasing and demeaning and threatening language. Mild physical sadism includes pinching, scratching and biting along with sexual intercourse. More severe sadistic behaviors include kicking, whipping, hard biting and slapping the sex object before, during or after sexual intercourse. Some sadists fantasize inflicting pain on a sex partner while masturbating. In the most serious cases (the person is psychotic), sexual gratification is achieved only with the death of the sex object.

Psychologists see the link between aggressive and sexual impulses. Some believe the sadistic behavior is based on the individual's need for absolute control over the other person as a compensation for his or her self-perception as a relatively powerless and ineffective person.

Rebellion and anger are necessary and healthy feelings within adolescents as they seek to individuate from parents, family and other authority. It is very easy for aggressive impulses and the need for power to become associated with the teenager's very strong sexual impulses. Sadistic themes appear to some degree for most teenagers in their sexual fantasies. Problems arise when these sadistic fantasies become obsessive and when they are acted out in the young person's behavior. These problems usually denote deeper psychological problems that should be treated psychotherapeutically. Such therapeutic intervention can be backed up by supportive, affirming counseling from a teacher, youth pastor or sponsor.

Masochism. In this form of deviant sexual behavior the individual derives sexual pleasure from being punished, humiliated or having pain inflicted on one's body as a part of the sexual experience. Masochism is more prevalent among women than men in our culture, probably because of the traditional emphasis placed on submission and compliance as a part of the female role.

One theory about the cause of masochism is early childhood teachings about sex being bad or dirty. Some case histories indicate a combination of pain and sexual stimulation while being punished during childhood as a causative factor. Older sisters, baby sitters and even mothers have been known to stimulate little boys' genitals while spanking them, an act that can create a very confusing and destructive link between sexual pleasure and pain.

Most people who are masochistic also have components of sadism and vice versa. When both behaviors are present within the same person, the descriptive term, sadomasochism, is used. N. Cameron explains: "Sadistic and reciprocal masochistic attitudes of abnormal intensity are usually present in the same person—that is, if a person fantasizes sadistic acts, he also fantasizes the masochistic experiences which they would arouse, and vice versa. Even when sadism appears alone, the sadistic person seems to identify strongly with his victim; and where it is masochism that prevails, the masochist seems to experience pleasure in fantasizing about what sadists do."[28]

Mild masochistic fantasies are not unusual in adolescents, especially teenage girls. But when fantasies become obsessions or when they become regular themes associated with masturbation, serious problems may develop. Masochistic behavior is always an indication for referral to psychotherapy. Masochism is sometimes the expression of sadistic impulses which are rejected or frustrated and turned inward onto the self. The impulses sometimes result in self-inflicted pain and too often physical injury and even death as either accidental or intended suicide.

Frottage. This seldom-heard term refers to a fairly common occurrence among adolescents. It is actually a normal aspect of adolescent sexual learning about themselves and about the opposite sex. Frottage is gaining sexual pleasure by rubbing against another's body. Much of petting, dancing closely, and even sitting close to another so that sexually arousing physical contact is made is considered frottage. Growth into adult sexuality normally makes this means of gratification less pleasurable as the maturing person desires more direct genital pleasure and release.

Problems arise when a psychologically immature adolescent, or a teenager who has very poorly developed impulse controls touches, rubs or feels someone's body without invitation. Immature individuals seek to rub against and feel pre-puberty children as a way of gaining sexual gratification. Ongoing compulsive frottage behavior indicates severe sexual frustration and retarded psychosexual development. These young people need very supportive counseling intervention along with psychotherapeutic focus into the underlying causes of their failure to develop to greater psychosexual maturity.

Exhibitionism. Displaying one's naked body or genitals publicly may be classified according to several different motivations:

1. True exhibitionism occurs when the exhibitionistic act itself brings satisfaction for the sexual drive.

2. Exhibitionism is sometimes an instrumental act to try to excite or entice a female into having sexual intercourse.

3. Some impotent males gain reassurance that they still have some sexual power by observing females' reactions to their exhibitionism.

4. Exhibitionistic acts are sometimes a direct reaction to external stress or conflict as a way of releasing tension, hurting back or making a definite statement about one's independence.

5. Some exhibitionists have impaired intellectual or cognitive functioning that has the effect of lowering impulse control and restricting options for gratification.

6. Sometimes exhibitionism plays a part during the initiation of sexual activity in adolescence.[29]

Although exhibitionism, broadly defined as seductive display of the body, occurs both in males and females, the more specific definition of displaying the genitals for sexual gratification occurs almost totally in males. It is one of the most frequent sexual deviations and has high incidence among both adolescent and young adult males.[30] It most often occurs in males who are in conflict with a female, usually both fearing women and holding them in contempt.[31]

The exhibitionist gains sexual gratification at a safe distance from the sexual object, without any real contact with her at all. The aggressive component in exhibitionism is reflected in the perpetrator's desire to shock the victim, thereby exaggerating the level of sexual arousal. Exhibitionism also is designed to excite voyeuristic tendencies in others.

Voyeurism. In its non-clinical sense voyeurism plays a normal part in sexual behavior. For males, viewing the nude or scantily clad female body is sexually exciting, and is often a part of the arousal experience prior to sexual intercourse. Clinical voyeurism represents an extension of these normal tendencies. The true voyeur gains optimal sexual gratification from observing rather than from actual sexual intercourse.

Although most voyeurs prefer to spy on women or girls that they do not know, adolescents sometimes will look at their sisters, mother or girls that they know. "Peeping Tom" behavior seems gratifying only when the female thinks that she is private.[32] Peeking is usually done alone, though adolescent boys will sometimes do it in groups. It is almost always a secretive act and the goal is to visually catch a girl or woman outside of her awareness. Malmquist writes: "The impulse appears satisfied by the sight of forbidden aspects of the female, such as her breasts or genitals, to see her undressing or excreting, the prize catch appears to be that of coitus."[33]

Most voyeurs pose no real threat of physical violence.[34] Only a few voyeurs progress toward more physically violent acts. Those who enter homes or draw attention to themselves are more likely to become rapists.[35] Aggression toward women is expressed passively by spying on them. Sometimes the voyeur is able to interact with the woman he has previously spied upon, thereby holding a secret that gives him a hostile type of superiority over her.[36]

Voyeurs typically feel very ashamed about their compulsive behavior, largely because of its passivity. Effective counseling requires a great deal of acceptance and support which is designed to build the adolescent's sense of identity and self-confidence. As insecurity is overcome and self-doubts are answered, the young person is able to begin establishing more adequate relationships with girls. Psychotherapy or intensive counseling is often required in order for voyeurs to resolve underlying hostilities or conflicts regarding their mothers or other females.

Obscene communication. In the more extreme instances obscene communicators can be classed as clinical sexual deviants. These are individuals who gain sexual gratification through communicating sexual messages to others. Phone calls often start with pre-adolescence and written messages (like graffiti on lavatory walls) and drawings begin appearing during adolescence. Girls often outnumber boys as obscene phone callers, while boys (especially during mid- and late adolescence) predominate as graffiti artists.

Messages are sometimes sent directly to one particular person (e.g., phone calls to a disliked, widowed female teacher) and at other times directed to the public in general (e.g., obscene painting on the side of a building). Obscene communications provide another distant, relatively safe outlet for sexual and aggressive expression. The perpetrators usually exhibit low self-esteem, strong need for reassurance and a lack of feeling personal power.[37]

These individuals can usually be helped through effective counseling that understands the aggression, low self-esteem, feelings of powerlessness, and unmet needs for love and reassurance that underlie their behavior.

Deviant Object

The behavioral patterns that are considered to be deviant because of the object of sexual gratification may be completely normal as far as the intensity of the sex drive and context. Often the mode of sexual gratification is also deviant because of the object choice. The deviant sexual behaviors discussed here include: homosexuality, bisexuality, incest, pedophilia, bestiality (zoophilia) and fetishism.

Homosexuality. Few issues cause more intense emotional reaction than the subject of homosexuality. Fear, rage, repulsion and pity are among the most common reactions that people experience to this increasing phenomenon in our society. The intensity of our reactions results from several sources, including our relative ignorance about homosexuality, the far-reaching and often destructive effects that homosexuality has on a person's life, our own unconscious sexual impulses and anxieties about these urges, concerns about our children's sexual development and spiritual issues relating to sexuality.

Simply defined, homosexuality is a condition in which the individual requires or very strongly prefers involvement with members of the same sex in order to obtain full sexual gratification. Beyond this overly simplified definition, the picture becomes far more complicated. First, most people are not either totally heterosexual or totally homosexual in their psychosexual orientation. This is easier to understand if we look at psychosexual development. The infant's sexuality is generalized, is not genital and evidences neither homosexual nor heterosexual preference. The pre-puberty child's sexuality shows signs of being shaped through socialization forces and the process of identification. Onset of puberty brings sexual energy and the focus of sexual pleasure directly to the genitals. However, psychosexual maturity has not yet been accomplished, so there is often observed a blend of pre- and post-puberty behavior. Mutual sexual exploration, sometimes with masturbation, is common between members of the same sex, especially boys. The difference after puberty is that masturbation now produces an immensely pleasurable orgastic release along with the ejaculation of semen. As adolescent development progresses, there is a normal movement away from such homosexual exploration toward building heterosexual relationships that gradually increase in their level of sexual intimacy.

A key issue in this discussion is the difference between homosexual thoughts and feelings, homosexual behaviors and homosexual people. Virtually everyone has at one time or another experienced a homosexual thought or feeling. A spontaneous attraction, fleeting fantasy, or a passing homosexual thought as an isolated experience is common to many. But there is no pattern to their occurrence and there is no behavioral enactment of the thought or feeling. These experiences certainly do not make a person a homosexual. They are, instead, spontaneous expressions of what psychologists understand to be the latent homosexual aspect of our personalities. These experiences sometimes create a homosexual panic reaction which is an acute anxiety attack brought on by the fear that one is a homosexual. Adolescents, because their sexuality is still in a developing stage, are particularly subject to these types of reactions.

Homosexual behaviors occur when a choice is made to enact the thoughts, feelings or fantasy, or when it is forced upon the individual. The mere occurrence of one or more homosexual acts also does not make a person a homosexual.[38] Some homosexual behaviors are considered homosexual acts by necessity, accidental, pseudo-homosexual or circumstantial homosexual acts.[39] These terms are used to describe those homosexual acts that occur in unusual situations, such as prison, the military, or in a relationship with an older relative or admired person of the same sex who pressures or manipulates the individual into homosexual behavior.[40] These kinds of homosexual behaviors, though overt homosexual acts, do not justify the label, homosexual person. A person is homosexual for whom, over a long period of time, the objects of sexual fantasies and feelings are members of the same sex.

There is a wide variety of homosexual expressions. When a teenager has been identified or identifies himself or herself as a homosexual, not nearly enough is known about the person to come to hasty conclusions. What kind of person is this? What type of personality is present? What is the sexual history? How strong or varied is the sexual orientation? How sexually active has this person been, and with whom? How does the individual feel about his or her sexuality? What are his or her thoughts about it? Does the person want to change? Does he or she think it is possible to change? As these questions are answered, then it will be more possible to provide appropriate and effective counseling help.

Much female homosexuality is maintained on the psychological level without overt sexual expression.[41] And among overt female homosexuals, only a small proportion fit the characterization of the "dykes" or "butches" who prefer the more aggressive masculine sex role.[42] Others, "fems," still prefer the more traditional feminine, submissive sexual role, only with another female rather than with a male. The same variation in role preference is true for male homosexuals, some preferring the traditional masculine aggressive role while others adopt a more passive and submissive role. It is important to note here that heterosexual males and females also vary widely in the behavioral sex roles that they prefer.

A major study of homosexual males conducted by Evelyn Hooker began in 1954 and was published in 1965.[43] She found that many lived with the same homosexual partner for quite a few years though very few were monogamous. Most of her subjects thought of themselves as being masculine. They enjoyed both the active or aggressive and the passive sexual roles during sexual activity. On the average, homosexuals are more promiscuous and short-term in their sexual relationships than those of their heterosexual counterparts.

One major issue for psychotherapists and counselors who work with homosexuals is whether homosexuality is a mental disorder. One popularly used textbook presents this confusing issue: "On December 14, 1973, homosexuals were mentally ill sexual deviants. On December 15, 1973, homosexuals were no longer psychiatric deviants.

"This turnabout was not achieved by mass therapy, but by a vote of the trustees of the American Psychiatric Association. They declared homosexuality to be a 'sexual orientation disorder' not requiring treatment unless an individual desires it."[44]

The 1980 guidelines for psychiatrists and psychologists suggest that therapeutic intervention with homosexuals specifically for their homosexuality, should be done only when the individuals have experienced a long-term anxiety, discomfort or rejection of their homosexuality, and when they have had a consistent desire to become more heterosexual in their orientation. Some of the impetus for the direction of this movement comes as an overreaction to the previously held assumption that all homosexuals were mentally ill or somehow mentally defective. Hooker conducted another study in which she found no difference between a group of 10 homosexual males and 30 heterosexual males in terms of clinical symptoms of mental illness.[45] A more recent study found similarly that a group of 127 male and 84 female homosexuals did not differ significantly from heterosexuals in terms of defensiveness, personal adjustment, self-confidence and self-evaluation.[46] These types of research findings and the APA decisions to not treat homosexuality as a diagnosed sexual deviancy imply that that is the conclusion of all psychotherapists. However, many clinically trained and experienced therapists continue to believe that homosexuals are living with the results of multi-variant psychological or psychobiological disorders.

In his scholarly book, *Homosexuals in the Christian Fellowship*, David Atkinson summarized the predisposing conditions that can interact to cause a homosexual orientation: a faulty or impaired gender-identity, a fear of intimate or sexual contact with members of the opposite sex and opportunities for sexual gratification with members of the same sex.[47]

A more detailed look at the causes of homosexuality will help the counselor to understand and counsel a particular homosexual adolescent with whom he or she is working. Any one person's homosexuality has a combination of two, three or more of the following factors as its etiological base:

1. Genetic inheritance. Contemporary researchers and theorists do not believe that homosexuality is inherited. Some of them believe, however, that certain people inherit a propensity toward same-sex or bisexual traits and preferences. One researcher suggests that certain genetically inherited patterns might cause the individual to be more vulnerable than others to developing a homosexual psychosexual identity, given certain external or environmental circumstances.[48]

2. Glandular functioning. Similar to genetic vulnerability, some researchers believe that prenatal hormonal problems "may influence sexual pathways in the central nervous system to remain sexually undifferentiated or potentially bisexual."[49] But it seems that glandular and hormonal changes impact the intensity of the sex drive only, and do not relate to the individual's choice of sex object.

3. Early learning. It is not at all rare for counselees in intensive counseling or psychotherapy to be able to recall early experiences, fantasies, and dreams that led them to prefer certain sexual partners and

practices while causing them to choose against other partners and practices. The learning and conditioning principles of association, reinforcement, avoidance conditioning, and imprinting are sufficient to explain a great variety of heterosexual and homosexual practices and preferences. In simplified form, positive conditioning toward the opposite sex and aversive conditioning of the sexual response to the same sex will produce an inclination toward heterosexuality. Conversely, aversive conditioning of the sexual response toward the opposite sex and positive conditioning toward the same sex will tend to produce a homosexual orientation.[50]

4. Arrested development. The developmental perspective recognizes that traumatic experience, severe deprivation, and oversatiation can cause an individual to stop at a certain level of development. Later, under severe stress, the person is apt to regress to the fixated level of development in order to reduce the rising level of anxiety. It is quite possible that some homosexual patterns have been established in this manner. Many homosexuals are so narcissistic that they are relatively incapable of loving another person. Their choice of same gender sex objects reflects this preoccupation with the self. It is suggested that fixation in very early childhood could help explain the intense oral and anal pleasure that some homosexuals derive from oro- and ano-genital contact.[51]

5. Family dynamics. The primary family dynamics that have been factors in homosexuality are certain aspects of parenting. Fathers who are absent, detached, aloof, distant, hostile, cold, cruel, weak, passive or ineffective are most apt to produce children who develop homosexual orientations. The same results are most likely with mothers who are smothering, overbearing, overcontrolling, aggressive, dominant, possessive, indulgent and devaluing toward their children.

These types of fathers provide very ineffective role models and are often perceived by their children as being rejecting, such that both their sons and daughters relate better with their mother. Boys may lose respect not only for their father, but for their own sex as well. Daughters, similarly, may learn to disrespect men in general and never learn to trust a male. Sons of particularly hostile or cruel fathers often become fearful of competing with men and long for acceptance from males that may be adequately felt only through physical/sexual contact. Homosexual contact is far less threatening because heterosexual dating would place him in a competitive position with other males. Daughters of hostile fathers will often identify with their abused mothers and vow to never let the same thing happen to them. Homosexual patterns become a way of never having to deal with the fear and anger that they feel toward their fathers and men in general.

Boys will sometimes identify with their mother whom they over-idealize. In other cases boys will protect themselves psychologically from an aggressive mother by adopting the defense of identifying with the aggressor. The unconscious statement is, "If I become like her, then she won't dislike me." These mothers are likely to stifle or devalue their son's self-trust and masculinity, teaching them to avoid close contact with all women and to devalue their own masculinity. The overindulgent mother fosters such dependency in her son that she psychologically seduces him into thinking that he cannot handle life without her. With such strong dependency comes self-hatred and rage toward the intrusive, domineering mother. These aggressions are intolerable at a conscious level so they are repressed and are projected onto women in general, making close, intimate and sexual contact with them unthinkable.

6. Seduction. Certainly, not every child who experiences homosexual seduction will develop into a homosexual. There are more factors than seduction involved, but such experiences do seem to have played a major role in a significant number of homosexuals' lives.

To the degree that sexual choice is still relatively undifferentiated during these early years, then such seduction could have a profound effect. The intense genital pleasure becomes a strong reinforcer to the homosexual orientation for sexual release. The child is not old enough or experienced enough to adequately understand what is happening and personally cope with it. Yet the child's sense of anxiety and guilt about the experience, even when it is not at all his or her fault, often causes the child to say nothing to parents, teachers or others. Some seduced young people develop strongly reinforced homosexual habits before they have adequate opportunity to develop heterosexual habits.

7. Heterosexual segregation. Homosexual acts are reportedly common occurrences in boarding schools, jails, prisons and other environments where the sexes are segregated for long periods of time. Some writers indicate that confirmed heterosexuals may participate in these homosexual acts for their temporary sexual release without even becoming homosexuals in their preference or orientation.[52] The situation might be more impacting on the sexual orientation of early and mid-adolescents than on adults because of the greater power of early learning experiences.

Promoting the healthy psychosexual development of our young people is an important priority for parents, pastors, teachers, counselors and others who have regular contact with adolescent youth. It is important to recognize behavioral aspects that indicate the direction of the adolescent's psychosexual development:

1. The emergence and continuation of homosexual behavior, especially when it occurs with little anxiety or guilt.

2. The absence or delayed onset of masturbation, especially without fantasies, suggests internal conflict or excessive sexual inhibition.

3. The presence of fantasies where the fantasizer is beaten, tortured or injured, and where someone is forced to be cruel to another.

4. Boys who maintain strong feminine identifications through adolescence, especially when the mother is domineering and the father is either weak or absent.

5. Fears about heterosexual involvement during adolescence that cause such repression that little or no desire for sexual experience is felt at the conscious level.

6. A deep and persistent attachment to an older person of the same sex that takes on the characteristics of exclusiveness that is typically found in love relationships.

7. A sincere, conscious, and firm conviction from the adolescent that he or she is a homosexual.[53]

Teenagers who present any of these danger signals should be gently approached by a caring adult who can elicit conversation about this vital issue.

There have been some voices within the Christian community that suggest that homosexuality is purely a spiritual problem. They suggest that if the person struggles for an extended period of time against homosexuality without release, then the person really is not a Christian, he or she is lacking in faith, or he or she has personal unconfessed sins. It is an unanswered question why homosexuality is singled out for this "understanding" unless all psychological and particularly all psychosexual problems are viewed as totally spiritual problems. The suggestion is that salvation, confession and repentance, or some other spiritual remedy is all that is required to change one's homosexual orientation into a heterosexual one. Too many who have struggled with their homosexual orientation for many years suggest that although homosexuality definitely has spiritual consideration, purely spiritual measures are usually not enough. Just as appendicitis is usually cured with more than faith and prayer, homosexuality requires more than prayer and faith to overcome. Understanding the fuller scope of God's creation leads us to know more of the natural laws which he created for us to live by. Both physical and psychological healing usually take place according to these natural laws which God installed.

Although the purpose of this volume is not specifically to present a theological understanding or a scriptural defense for labeling a certain behavior as deviant, some such statement needs to be registered regarding homosexuality. Many voices rising with the "gay liberation movement" are proclaiming that there is no illness, no disorder and no sin inherent in homosexuality. One such voice is that of the Gay Christian Movement. Their statement of conviction reads: "It is the conviction of the members of the Gay Christian Movement that human sexuality in all its richness is a gift of God gladly to be accepted, enjoyed and honoured as a way of both expressing and growing in love, in accordance with the life and teaching of Jesus Christ: Therefore it is their conviction that it is entirely compatible with the Christian faith not only to love another person of the same sex but also to express that love fully in a personal sexual relationship."[54]

The message is essentially that though homosexuality is not usual, it is natural and condoned by God. They see their greatest problem to be the heterosexual community's ignorance, prejudice and rejection of them. It is in their opinion, then, an external problem that they confront, not an internal one. They deny that homosexuality is a psychological problem and they deny that homosexual behaviors are sin.

The psychological aspects of homosexuality have been our primary focus. Let us turn our attention briefly to the scriptural position. There are both Old Testament and New Testament references that denounce homosexual practices as sinful. Genesis 19:1-11, Leviticus 18:22 and 20:13, and Judges 19:22-25 are the Old Testament references. The New Testament references to homosexuality are Romans 1:25-27, 1 Corinthians 6:9-10, and 1 Timothy 1:8-10. Though God does not seem to judge homosexual acts as being "worse" than other sins, he does clearly judge them as sins.

Early in this section on homosexuality, the differentiation was made between: homosexual thoughts and feelings; homosexual behaviors; and homosexual people. There is no judgment for fleeting spontaneous thoughts or feelings of a homosexual nature, any more than there is for heterosexual urges. But when the individual focuses on these thoughts and builds them into fantasies whether of homosexual or heterosexual content, there exists sin. However, there is no sin in simply being subject to temptation, even when the struggle is difficult and long. The content of the temptation (heterosexual or homosexual) is not the issue. The issue is how the person struggles both from spiritual and psychological perspectives.

Homosexual acts are considered sin, as is heterosexual intercourse outside of the marriage relationship. But the person who commits homosexual sin is to be treated as any other person who commits any sin. We are reminded of the well-worn and true saying, "Christ hates the sin, but loves the sinner." And what of our response? Paul writes: "Blessed be the God and Father of our Lord Jesus Christ, the Father of mercies and God of all comfort, who comforts us in all our affliction, so that we may be able to comfort those who are in all our affliction, with the comfort with which we ourselves are comforted by God. For as we share abundantly in Christ's sufferings, so through Christ we share abundantly in comfort too" (2 Corinthians 1:3-5). Ours is not a seat of judgment. Rather, it is a relationship through which love, acceptance, support, understanding and help from Christ can flow. Remember that love is both confrontive and accepting.

We are all responsible for what we do with what we have and who we are. Sexual self-control is important, regardless the orientation. It must also be stated that strong self-control is much more difficult when in a largely unsupportive, hostile and rejecting environment. Our churches should not provide that type of environment for anyone. Unfortunately, the church is not supportive of the homosexual brother or sister in Christ. Consequently, it further adds to the difficulty of his or her struggle.

Most homosexuals suffer from tremendous psychic pain, both from internal conflict and external sources. When adolescents discover homosexual feelings within themselves, the feelings are usually accompanied with intense anxiety and fears. If the feelings persist, the young person is sometimes flooded with feelings of terror, that at times give way to deep depression. They feel out of control because they cannot feel heterosexual attractions, nor can they make the homosexual feelings cease. Self-questioning leads to self-doubting and then to self-depreciating thoughts. A deep sense of guilt may ensue.

Accompanying and exacerbating the internal conflicts is the psychic pain that is felt as the homosexual tries to relate to the outside world, most of which is structured for the "straight" community and is quite rejecting of the homosexual. The gay person often lives much of his or her life with a chronic feeling of emptiness with an aching sense of social alienation. Feeling that homosexuals never fit in, they seldom can relax and be who they are with any assurance that they will be welcomed and accepted. Homosexuals who have not "come out" live in continual fear of being detected, being exposed and then being rejected.

The desire for meaningful and lasting interpersonal relationships is largely unsatisfied for most homosexuals. Friendships with same-sex "straights" is either unsatisfying or tension-producing because of the fears about being "found out." And though some relationships between homosexual mates do last for many years, the overwhelming majority last for only a few days, weeks or months. The homosexual, so often chronically hungry to be fed through relationships, searches in vain among others who are equally starving and too empty to give. A major area of interpersonal pain for the homosexual is on the job. Many job settings force hiding homosexuals into close and prolonged contact with others. This setting challenges their defenses and causes them to determine to not get too close, lest someone suspect their gayness.

Let's turn the focus of our attention now to the task of counseling homosexual teenagers. Understand that this is often a very deeply established behavioral, emotional, cognitive and lifestyle pattern that has taken sometimes many years to build. It is an issue that involves every aspect of the person's life and therefore requires counseling that also impacts each area of the individual's life. This type of therapeutic change often comes very slowly and with very great effort.

The most needed ingredient in this type of counseling is the counselee's motivation. He or she requires a strong desire to change and to accomplish the counseling goals.

Who the counselor is, his or her personality style, personal background history, attitudes, beliefs, emotional responsiveness, and especially his or her feelings and attitudes about homosexuality will have far-reaching impact on the success or failure of the counseling process. Some counselors may be very effective with many different types of people. Still, they should carefully consider the issues before agreeing to counsel with homosexuals. People who have strong fear, anxiety, or angry reactions to homosexuals or to the subject of homosexuality should not counsel with homosexuals. In these cases, referral to another counselor is required.

One counseling approach that seems to have particularly good promise is the use of a male-female counseling team.[55] The initial sessions are held only with the same-sex counselor meeting with the counselee.

After background history is collected and the initial relationship is established during the first few sessions, the counselee then starts meeting with the male-female counseling team. The team approach enables the counselee to interact with a male and female role model. This helps the counselee work through pain and anger from past interactions with both sexes, including mother and father. The presence of counselors of both sexes also helps the counselee to learn how to interact with both men and women. This is a very powerful counseling approach with teenagers who are naturally learning sexual differentiation and identification.

Unconditional acceptance of the homosexual and high regard for his or her personhood conveys much needed respect for their personal dignity. Counseling is not the place for judgment, but acceptance of the person. This is a powerful dynamic for alienated, isolated people who hunger for relationships. A more positive self-concept is vital for personal growth and movement from one lifestyle to another. The counselor's warmth and caring is an invaluable support as the homosexual grieves over the loss of the gay friends that have been given up while making the transition to heterosexual friends.

Establishing a meaningful relationship is an initial step in any counseling, but so absolutely vital when working with a homosexual. Gays typically push very hard against the very thing they crave: a genuine, caring, non-usury, intimate relationship. Often it is within the structure of the counseling setting that they can venture further into intimacy where there is no manipulation, usury or sexual exploitation.

Quite early in the counseling process, the counseling goals should be discussed and agreed upon. Homosexuals seek counseling for a variety of reasons: to become more comfortable with their gay lifestyle; for relationship counseling with their gay partner; to make the transition from homosexuality to heterosexuality; to learn more about homosexuality; and to learn what the Bible has to say about homosexuality.

Depending on the counselor's ethics, he or she may choose to not work toward some goals that a homosexual might request help with, such as becoming more comfortable with the gay lifestyle. Establishing agreed-upon goals is important so that counselor and counselee are working in the same direction, blending their efforts in unified teamwork. Having well-articulated goals also enables the counselor and counselee to assess their progress periodically and serves as a check for staying on track.

A realistic sense of hope is beneficial for both the counselor and the homosexual counselee. Hopes for reaching goals that are unrealistically high can produce frustration and discouragement. To the other extreme, counselors or counselees who are afraid to hope for meaningful counseling gains may sabotage their efforts.

When it is appropriate, blending spiritual counseling into the overall approach will strengthen the effectiveness of the sessions. The Christian counselee has the added strength of the Holy Spirit's presence and the additional resources of prayer and relationship with God.

Effective counseling that challenges unconscious fears, impulses and decisions will increase the counselee's use of unconscious defense mechanisms. These defenses will be automatically triggered into action to protect the psyche from excessive anxiety or change. Periodic review of the psychological defense mechanisms, which were described in chapter 9, will keep these fresh in the counselor's mind. Counselees' verbal attacks, threats, withdrawals and other discomforting behaviors are part of their aroused defenses.

Homosexuals who seek counseling have probably repressed many fears, anxieties, hostilities, and painful memories because they felt unsafe to share with anyone and were too unbearable to handle consciously alone. As soon as a relationship of trust has been adequately established, the counselee will need to release this material in order to lower internal tensions and allow the counselor to delve more deeply into unconscious material. Talking out issues and emotional releases through crying, yelling and other reactions are important.

Early childhood experiences that produced pain, anxiety, anger and other difficult emotional reactions need to be brought back into the counselee's conscious memory, talked about and released. As these earlier life experiences are fully discussed, insights can be gained that help the counselee to understand how he or she developed a homosexual orientation. Mere understanding of the problem does not solve the problem. But it can relieve a deep sense of personal guilt. And with the guilt gone, a roadblock to change has been removed.

Teaching is one counseling response that is often quite helpful to homosexuals. They may, for instance, be laboring under the misinformation that homosexuality is always an irreversible condition. Or they may have been taught that it is a mental illness. Or perhaps they have believed that it is the unpardonable sin. Others might have been misled that God accepts homosexual behavior as he does heterosexuality. Teaching correct information when appropriate can provide a strong basis for building healthy and accurate attitudes. Christ said, "You will know the truth, and the truth will make you free" (John 8:32).

Confrontation as a powerful counseling tool should be used only after a strong trusting relationship has been established. Homosexuals live with the expectation of being rejected if they are discovered. Self-disclosure is a very threatening and dangerous process and homosexuals need a great deal of acceptance and reassurance before they can tolerate therapeutic confrontation. When confrontation is used, remember that its most effective forms are those which help the counselee toward self-discovery.

Part of the genesis of counselees' homosexual patterns is a long history of reinforced homosexual responses paired with punished or non-reinforced heterosexual responses. The counseling process can provide the opposite pattern by reinforcing heterosexual responses (e.g., talking with opposite-sex students between classes) and punishing or non-reinforcing homosexual responses (e.g., dating same-sex partners). Verbal reinforcers (e.g., "That's great." "Good for you." "What an accomplishment!") and non-verbal punishers (e.g., frowns, breaking eye contact, shaking head) are useful as long as the counselee knows that the counselor's acceptance of him or her is not at risk.

Behavior changes must be accomplished if the counselee is going to accomplish his or her goals. Internal emotional, attitudinal, and cognitive changes are actualized and more firmly established by making related behavioral changes. The counselee's new belief that God can be a powerful supportive help is made useful by regular worship, study, meditation and fellowship with other believers. Changes probably need to be made in virtually every aspect of the counselee's life including family, friends, school, work, worship, exercise, recreation and rest.[56] These changes should help the counselee find more pleasure and satisfaction in other than sexual areas of life. Success in these changes can reinforce within counselees the belief that they can also make significant changes regarding their sexuality.

Strengthening the home environment in which the homosexual lives will be a major help to maximizing the gains that are made during the sessions. Reversing some of the unhealthy family dynamics, though a very difficult process, can be well worth the effort. Family counseling is usually necessary in order to accomplish these kinds of changes. It is most successful when both parents are willing participants.

Pastors, teachers, and youth workers can be a significant support system to an adolescent who needs counseling regarding his or her sexual orientation. However, it must also be realized that adolescence is a critical time in the person's psychosexual development. Lay counselors as well as professional psychotherapists should deliberately decide whether they should counsel with adolescent homosexuals. Building a working relationship with a local professional therapist is advisable for two reasons. First, the therapist can be a valuable consultant. Second, the therapist can be more readily available for referrals if a relationship has been established.

Bisexuality. The bisexual person has a history of sexual activity with both sexes, either separately or at the same time as in a threesome or larger group. An individual could also be considered bisexual even if he or she had not actively engaged in such activities but had experienced overt imagery of doing so.[57]

Bisexuals usually have a preference for either homosexual or heterosexual partners and find themselves more easily aroused by one or the other. Assessing the ratio of heterosexual to homosexual involvement is helpful in understanding more about the psychosexual development of a particular counselee. The "50/50" bisexual shows little or no psychosexual differentiation. This situation would be more serious the older the person becomes because it suggests serious problems in the normal development of sexual identity. Similarly a heavy homosexually weighted ratio of say "20/80" would suggest serious cross-sex identification which might develop more completely as a homosexual lifestyle pattern. A heterosexually weighted ratio of "80/20" would present a more positive prognosis of future full heterosexual adjustment.

Another issue that is crucial to better understanding a particular counselee's bisexuality is having adequate information about the context within which both the homosexual and heterosexual contacts were made. Compare the two categories according to: active pursuit on the part of the counselee; victimization of the counselee; unusual circumstances like sex-segregated boarding schools or prisons; peer group pressure; and the degree of emotional involvement with partners. Some bisexuals will marry and establish reasonably happy and stable family relationships but feel stronger "in love" and erotic feelings toward other same-sex people. With these people, the issue of morality is not the gender content of their impulses, but the fidelity issue of commitment to their spouse, which is much the same as that for normal heterosexuals tempted by extramarital affairs.

The causative factors in bisexuality are, as far as we know, essentially the same as in homosexuality. As with homosexuality, the majority opinion of professional psychiatrists and psychologists is that bisexuality is not a disorder. However, many professional psychotherapists do view this condition as a treatable gender identity disorder. Counseling guidelines for working with bisexuals parallels those for working with homosexuals. The counselor of adolescents needs to remember that especially in early adolescence the sexual identification process is far from complete. Therefore, bisexual feelings, fantasies, and behavior at that age level do not denote the pathology which is suggested by the same indicators during late adolescence.

Incest. The definition of incest is difficult to determine. At its most basic level it refers to sexual intercourse between two people who are too closely related by blood to be married. Legal stipulations vary from state to state and even more from nation to nation regarding relational proximity and marriageability. What about cousins? adopted children? step-siblings? The legal definition of incest often specifies that there must be penetration in order to conclude that incest has occurred. But psychological perspectives do not require that the condition of penetration be met in order to conclude that a case of incest is at hand. Although expressions of physical affection need to be encouraged as frequent forms of family communication, those expressions that are strongly covertly or overtly sexual in nature are incestuous.

Of the wide variety of incestuous relationship patterns, the father-daughter pattern is most common. The overwhelming majority of fathers experience some degree of sexual attraction to their daughters, especially as their girls progress through puberty and into adolescence. Their girls' young attractive bodies, lively energy, and physical affection easily and naturally arouse erotic interest. When fathers can accept these internal responses as being natural without feeling threatened, no negative results are experienced by either father or daughter.

But several possible avenues for difficulty arise. The father's regressive tendencies may be elicited to such a degree that his behavior may take on an adolescent irresponsibility. His dependency needs may also be elicited, causing him to have an excessive need to be with his daughter and have her do things for him (e.g., haircuts, polish shoes, accompany him on errands, etc.). He may strongly desire her for a companion in a wide variety of ways, especially if he is divorced, widowed or unsatisfied in his marriage. The daughter at first responds positively and affectionately to this added attention because her needs to belong, to feel valued, to be found attractive and to be loved are partially met through his interest. But typically she soon begins to react against his possessiveness and jealousy when she wants to date boyfriends, be with girlfriends, spend time with her mother or just be alone.

Sexual play and then intercourse is introduced by the father and is usually not actively resisted at first by the daughter, particularly if she is pre-adolescent. She finds his attention pleasurable and responds to his touch with widely mixed reactions including sexual arousal, fear, guilt, pleasure and anger. Since children are raised to obey and trust their parents, they are typically quite vulnerable to incestuous seduction from them and should never be blamed for "going along with it." Their own typically harsh self-blaming and self-condemning attitude, which usually follows them for years after, is damaging enough. This is true even when the adolescent and sometimes pre-pubertal girl acts seductively toward her father. She is simply learning about her sexuality and cannot be expected to handle this new and powerful dynamic within her with full adult responsibility. The transition from pre-pubertal cuddling, squeezing, caressing, holding and other affectionate physical expressions to post-pubertal physical affection can be difficult for father and daughter. Sexual meanings have to be dealt with, erotic arousal must be recognized and resolved, and physical expressions of affection continued without overt or covert sexual ploys.

The mothers of daughters who have an incestuous relationship with their fathers usually play a significant role, too. They typically have some knowledge or at least suspicion of the incest but quickly deny its occurrence. This denial mechanism enables the family secret to be kept . . . and continued. It is as if there is a triangular collusion between father, daughter and mother to make everything look okay on the outside as a way of maintaining the status quo and keeping things from blowing apart.[58] The mothers are often depressed and feel constrained in their sexual relationships with their husbands. In the midst of their own felt-inadequacy, they essentially abrogate their position as lover and primary female in the household to their daughter. Often, incestuously involved girls find themselves fulfilling many of the household chores that their mothers used to do.

Some people would state that the only problems with incest are the anxieties caused by social and legal injunctions against it. One author proclaims, "The grotesque notion that it is everyone's business what two people do with their bodies in the privacy of their homes results in countless tragedies, incalculable suffering . . . society is damaged—as innumerable individuals are damaged—by anti-sexual measures taken against persons whose behavior is innocuous."[59]

But there is much clinical evidence that incest psychologically affects the youngster. These effects seem to be more severe when the incest occurs after puberty than when the occurrence is during pre-pubertal childhood.[60] In response to the deep sense of being betrayed by both parents (one for the sexual behavior, the other for not being there to help and protect), the daughter usually experiences strong rage reactions that are sometimes felt with murderous strength along with fantasies of killing the father. Aggressive acting-out in the form of petty theft, truancy from school, malicious mischief, running away from home and incorrigibility are common.[61] Promiscuous activity, which is both self-destructive and designed to satisfy her aroused sexual urges, is very common. The continuing destructive stress within the adolescent often shows up in physical forms such as anorexia, abdominal pain, nausea, vomiting, dizziness and fainting. Other girls experience episodes of hysteria, anxiety attacks and less common reactions such as recurrent urinary retention.

Sibling incest between brother and sister is probably the second most common intrafamily sexual pattern. Though such relationships are sometimes by mutual desire and consent, often it is an older brother who threatens his younger sister into having sex with him. This activity often indicates pathological development on the part of the adolescent boy. In cases where it continues for some time without detection, it also suggests unhealthy or inadequate parenting as well. One interesting study suggests that male/female siblings who restrained from pre-pubertal sex play will be more likely to engage in incestuous behavior as adolescents.[62] When daughters finally do report the incest to parents, they are all too often disbelieved and ridiculed rather than responded to and supported.

Mother-son incest is a pattern about which little is known. Typically, though, the mother is unsatisfied with her marital sexual relationship and often because of death or divorce the father is totally absent. These relationships are often consummated only through deceit or emotional blackmail of the son, e.g., "You might become a homosexual unless I teach you about sex with a woman."[63]

Homosexual incestuous relationships also occur. Brother-brother incest is usually exploratory in nature and fleeting. Great concern should be had about this pattern only if it occurs in mid- or late adolescence, if it occurs over a significant length of time, or if there appears to be retarded social or heterosexual development on the part of one or the other boys. Homosexual incest between sisters may be more indicative of pathological development because younger girls usually have less need for stimulation to orgasm than do their age-peer boys.

Both father-son and mother-daughter incest are likely to produce strong rage reactions in the children. These, especially in boys, are sometimes acted out in direct aggressive attacks on the parent. In other cases the attacks are displaced onto other less threatening objects (vandalism) or people (teachers). And sometimes the aggression is acted out in self-destructive ways through promiscuity, dangerous use of alcohol and other drugs, self-inflicted wounds, reckless driving and sometimes suicide.

Counseling with adolescent incest victims (the word "victims" is used deliberately) requires strong empathy and support. The story will probably be divulged very slowly, only as a deep sense of trust and liking is developed between the teenager and the counselor. The incest experience will probably not be the stated reason for seeking counseling. It will be brought to the surface only if an adequately trusting counselee-counselor relationship develops.

A lot is at stake for young people who disclose an incestuous relationship. Their fears often come true. Disclosures often result in their rejection by the rest of family, the breakup of their parents' marriage, hospitalization or incarceration of the perpetrating parent, the counselor's disbelief or mishandling of the situation, and intense and pervasive feelings of guilt, shame and humiliation.

The counseling task is made more complex by the legal requirement in some states to report any suspected child abuse (including incest) to the local authorities. Even in states where this is not a legal requirement, lay counselors should report any incest relationships to a professionally trained therapist or legal authority. Not doing so takes on too great a responsibility in a situation that is highly charged with tension and potentially far reaching in its possible negative impact on the youth and on the whole family.

Professionally trained therapists and pastors find their best success when they are able to counsel with the whole family as well as separately with the individuals who are directly involved in the incest. Intensive therapy is often required for both parents and the adolescent before family sessions can be of help. In many communities there are peer support groups for family members. Incestuous parents, spouses of incestuous parents, and the children often find great support and understanding from others who have "already been through it" who "know what it is like." The group experience also affords them the opportunity in time to be of help to others, which is therapeutic for them as well.

Pedophilia. Pedophilia occurs when an adult or adolescent (usually a male) uses a child (usually pre-pubertal) as a sexual object. Adolescents who engage in pedophilic behaviors can be grouped into three different categories:

1. Intellectually or cognitively impaired adolescents who have some cerebral dysfunction or intellectual retardation often evidence poor impulse controls. The impaired intellectual or cognitive development in combination with normally intense adolescent sexual urges, especially in boys, sometimes creates a situation in which sexual release is sought with less threatening pre-puberty children.

2. Some adolescent pedophilic behaviors result from internal conflict or either transient or persistent personality disorders. Many adolescents feel sexually inadequate and some find it self-reassuring to involve younger and naive children in sexual play, exploration and intercourse. Sexual contact with an age-peer or older person of the opposite sex may feel too threatening, such that the adolescent feels comfortable performing only with a younger child. Often this type of youth will engage in quite regressed forms of sex-play like playing doctor, undressing games, and non-genital sexual activities though they sometimes do consummate the activity in genital intercourse.

3. Adolescents with severe and deeply ingrained personality disorders are often hedonistic, narcissistic and given to impulsive expression. Their pedophilic episodes result only because the child sex object was available. Any other object would have been just as satisfactory, an age-peer girl or older woman, but none was available for use. These youths experience no guilt or remorse because of their pathologically retarded conscience development.[64]

When counseling with adolescent pedophiles, determine early which type of pedophilic behavior was used. Counseling goals, counseling approaches and decisions relating to referral will largely be determined by this categorization. Intellectually impaired or retarded pedophiles will require a great deal of structuring in their lives. Progress is expected to be very slow and difficult and insight-oriented techniques virtually useless except over very long-term counseling. Supportive, insight-producing counseling can bring significant results when working with internally conflicted youths. More directive approaches will be necessary when working with teenagers who have severe personality disorders.

In addition to the psychological nature of the adolescent, there are other factors that will help the counselor to better understand the underlying dynamics of the incident(s) and of the teenager:

1. The degree to which the youth used physical force or threats of force may indicate the level of rage or aggression that is in his or her personality structure. Some pedophilic episodes end with the murder of the victim which may result from the youth's fear of being discovered, arrested and punished.[65]

2. The sex of the child will suggest the development of either a homosexual or heterosexual orientation in the adolescent.

3. When the child is a relative or the child of very close family friends, a pattern similar to that of sibling incest is very possible.

4. Whether the behavior is a single occurrence, infrequently episodic or repetitive at close intervals, suggests the severity of the pattern, level of regression, intensity of possible fixation, and the overall level of psychosexual dysfunction.[66]

Counselors sometimes discover that an adolescent with whom they are working was on one or several occasions the victim in a pedophilic episode. What are the possible negative results from such experiences? Sometimes quite serious psychological damage, particularly disruption of the child's psychosexual development, results.[67] Some children, particularly those who feel deprived of adequate physical affection, may thoroughly enjoy being held, fondled and caressed.

Some children feel extremely helpless during the pedophilic experience, which can impose that type of self-identification as the child develops his or her self-concept.[68] As the child submits to the sexual experiences, he or she is apt to identify with the aggressor in order to feel less threatened. Unfortunately, this process often entails the introjection of the aggressor's feelings, often including guilt, shame or fear of detection. These feelings can be generalized and later attached to other sexual activities during adolescence that are completely normal and healthy. Being a victim as a child of a pedophilic experience could be at the root of adolescent guilt, anxiety and fear which is irrationally felt relative to normal sexual development and experimentation. The child will often feel anger about being used as a sex object. If not resolved, this anger could also intrude upon normal psychosexual development.

One of the few studies of the long-term effects of pedophilic experiences on the victims was conducted in Germany. Four conclusions from this study were proposed: Children from supportive environments and strong families suffered less negative impact. Children from lower socioeconomic levels are typically left unattended more often and are therefore more vulnerable to sexual assault. Repeated sexual offenses that recur during extended periods of time are more likely to result in more enduring psychological injury. The age of the victim at the time of the attack had no significant effect on the severity of the psychological impact.[69]

Teenagers who have been victims of pedophilic attacks may have extreme difficulty talking about their experiences. They may try to pass it off as nothing. "No big deal. I'd completely forgotten about it until you brought it up." Without forcing the issue, it would be important for them to talk about it. But be sensitive to their timing.

Bestiality (zoophilia). Obtaining sexual gratification with animals as sex objects is called bestiality or zoophilia. They are synonymous terms that refer to sexual experiences with animals which when transitory are fairly frequent among adolescents, especially boys who live in rural areas. Except for very few instances, these experiences are purely experimental and are no reason for concern about the youth's psychosexual development. The behaviors are usually masturbatory in effect, consisting of what constitutes mutual masturbation. Sometimes oral and/or anal penetration occurs between male animals and boys, and at other times boys will perform coitus with female animals. Much less frequent is the occurrence of girls submitting to sexual intercourse with male animals. Usually girls settle for general body contact with animals rather than more explicit sex.[70]

Counseling with teenagers who admit to having had sexual contact with animals must be handled in a non-judgmental and non-alarming manner. The most important task is to encourage the youth to talk about his or her motivations and feelings during and after the experience. In addition to mere exploratory motivations, some of these young people might be quite insecure and unsure of their sexuality. Addressing these fears and insecurities in a supportive, encouraging counseling relationship will probably insure that repeated incidents will not occur.

Fetishism. Fetishism is almost always a male deviation. It occurs when the person seeks and gains sexual arousal and gratification from inanimate objects like women's hats, shoes, bras and panties, or nonsexual body parts like hair, ears, hands and feet. In some cases, body deformities have become fetishes.[71] When an inanimate object is selected as a fetish it usually belongs to a woman or women in general.

When a female body part that is more popularly related to sexual arousal becomes all that is necessary to arouse the individual to orgasm, then that body part has become the fetish. Some boys and men need only to fantasize about, look at or touch a woman's shoulder, neck, breasts, buttocks, waist or thighs in order to gain sexual release.

Fetishes become even more of a problem when adolescents and young adult males steal the objects that give them such pleasure. Voyeurism is also a way for some fetishists to gain visual contact with certain body parts of women.

Fetishes are quite common among adolescent males, but they are mostly of the transitory variety and are not predictive of pathological adult fetishes, where the person prefers sexual release with the fetish more than genital coitus with a heterosexual partner.

Benjamin Kleinmuntz succinctly describes the psychodynamic origins of fetishes: "The fetishist is afraid of being rejected by the person to whom he is attracted for he knows that it would be humiliating to him. Therefore he fixates on an article of clothing or on a portion of the body because this fixation does not involve approaching the real person and remains under his complete control."[72]

Most psychologists believe that the particular fetish object takes on its sexually stimulating properties through the process of classical conditioning.[73] The object is present during one or repeated sexually arousing experiences and thereby takes on sexually arousing properties of its own.

Fetishist adolescents sometimes come to the attention of a counselor after being caught attempting to steal. When the problem reaches the intensity that theft is involved, the youth requires therapeutic attention. As with other sexual deviations, successful counseling requires adequate warmth, support, acceptance and a non-judgmental attitude. Insight-oriented techniques are useful to help the youth understand the meaning of his behavior. Then he can be encouraged to begin making more direct, responsible contact with girls whom he finds attractive. As he builds his self-confidence, starts to know girls as whole people (rather than simply as fragmented sex objects) and develops more satisfying heterosexual relationships, the fears of rejection recede as do his fetish symptoms.

Deviant Context

The sexual patterns discussed in this category are deviant usually only in the context that is required for adequate arousal in order to reach orgasm. There is not necessarily any abnormality in the intensity of the individual's sex drive, nor is there deviance in either the mode or the object of gratification. Two deviant patterns will be discussed: rape and prostitution.

Rape. The most frightening and destructive of the sexual deviations is rape. This is because the act of rape is just as much and sometimes more an act of violence as it is a sexual act. Rape always involves the imposition of one person's will and body upon another person's will and body. Privacy and control over one's body are both violated.

Rape is defined as gaining genital penetration of a woman without her consent by using force, fear or deceit. Historically only boys and men could rape. But homosexual rape can also be perpetrated by women using dildos or other objects of penetration. It is also conceivable that a woman or group of women could rape a male by forcing his erection and penetration of them. These are interesting expansions in our definitional concept of rape but for our purposes, two main topics will serve as our focus: the male adolescent rapist, and the female adolescent rape victim.

First, let's take a look at the rape perpetrators. Most rapists are either adolescent or young adult males, usually under 25 years old.[74] One study placed the highest concentration of both offenders and victims between the ages of 15 and 19.[75] Rapists personal histories are often marked by emotional deprivation, lack of parental loving, extreme sibling jealousy, chaotic and unstable childhood environment, rigidly repressive religious training, ignorance about sex, fears about women and being sexually abused as children.[76]

Rapists are usually quite immature, have a distorted view of sexuality, struggle with low self-esteem and often fail to accept responsibility for their own behavior. These personal characteristics are often exacerbated by the use of alcohol and to a much less frequent extent, by the use of other drugs. One researcher studied 77 convicted rapists, finding the following results about their use of alcohol and other drugs: 50 percent of the rapists were drinking at the time of the attack; 42 percent were drinking heavily (the equivalent of 10 or more beers) at the time of the rape; 35 percent were chronic alcoholics; 12 percent were using another type of drug with or without alcohol at the time of the rape; and three percent of the rapists were using another drug without alcohol at the time of the rape. The results of this study indicate that for a significant number of rapists, alcohol lowers their inhibitions and increases their level of aggressiveness.[77]

Psychological researchers have also found that different males rape for different reasons. There are different motivational forces that operate to produce rape behaviors. One group of researchers isolated five different types of rape perpetrators:

1. Assaultive rapists need physical violence or the threat of violence in order to achieve sexual release. Hostility is a major part of their interpersonal lives and violence often will bring orgasm without intercourse. In fact, many of these rapists are impotent. They usually attack women who are unknown to them and sometimes use a weapon.

2. Amoral delinquent rapists are grossly egocentric, hedonistic, and as such use women only as objects to satisfy their sexual desires. Force is used only to gain sexual access to the female if necessary.

3. Drunken rapists sometimes rape only when they have been drinking. They tend to have many internal conflicts and repressed hostilities that are apt to be released when the person has been drinking. Sometimes the release is in the form of rape.

4. Sudden, unexpected, explosively hostile rapes are often committed by youths from whom no one would expect such behavior. They are usually somewhat withdrawn, quiet, and very law-abiding young men who without warning commit a violent, brutal rape. These individuals are often schizoid and experience a regressive psychotic episode at the time of the rape.

5. Double-standard males tend to rape only "bad" girls or women who are provocative or seductive in their appearance or manner. This pattern is common among adolescent gangs who rape female hitchhikers and pickups.[78]

Another (and somewhat similar) classification of rapists according to their motivations delineates four categories:

1. Rapists who are hostile toward the women in their lives sometimes act out their aggression by raping other women. The victims are often older than the perpetrators and are usually unknown to them. The rape is often precipitated by an upsetting event with a woman who is important in the rapist's life. The motivation in this type of rape is the desire to hurt back. It is a perfect example of displaced aggression.

2. The sex-motivated rapist commits much more of a sexual than a violent act. He rapes because he wants sexual release and will often escape rather than use force to subdue a victim who fights back. This type of rapist selects his target, follows her, learns about her, fantasizes about her and finally consummates his fantasy by raping her.

3. The sexually sadistic rapist tries to get his victim to struggle

against him. The more she struggles, the more excited he becomes, and hence, the more sadistic also. Fortunately, these rapes constitute a rare minority of all the rapes committed. The adolescents who commit these rapes have a fusion between sexuality and aggression, so that they are always experienced together.[79] In extreme cases these attacks lead to rape-murders or lust-murders and rape-mutilations.

4. The impulsive opportunist rapes while committing another crime, simply because the opportunity is there. He may be burglarizing a home and if he finds a woman there, he rapes her before leaving. It is neither strongly sex-motivated nor violence-motivated. It represents simply taking something else that is available.

Counseling intervention with adolescent rapists, whatever the type of rape that was committed, is a must. Acting-out in such sexual and violent ways is always suggestive of very deep-seated, severe psychological problems. Psychotherapy with a well-trained adolescent specialist who is familiar with the psychology of criminal deviance is highly recommended. Pastoral and lay counselors can play both a supportive and a reality-testing role with rape perpetrators. They should request and receive permission from the counselee to talk with the psychotherapist in order to insure that their counseling efforts are complementary to the direction that psychotherapy is going. Often, the therapist is eager to involve a pastoral or lay counselor as a part of the therapeutic "team."

Christian counselors can bring the much-needed spiritual focus to the rapist as long as they are sensitive to their timing, manner and appropriateness of such an intervention. Some rapist counselees will be able to respond positively to the gifts that only Christ can offer: the expectation of behavioral responsibility and unconditional, complete forgiveness and cleansing of all sins.

Our second task in this section on rape is to gain a deeper understanding of the rape victim, what she goes through, how she may respond, and what counseling help would be beneficial to her.

The emotional response that a girl or woman has to a rape experience depends in part on the intent of the rapist. If the rapist used her primarily as an object to release his sexual tension, she will probably feel used and angry. If the primary intent was to vent hostility, strong fear reactions and defenseless vulnerable feelings predominate. And when rape is essentially a political maneuver, an attempt to overpower and subjugate the woman, she will have especially strong feelings of humiliation, self-devaluation and guilt at being defeated.

Her reactions will also depend on who raped her. Was the rapist a stranger? a friend? a lover? a relative? Or was she gang raped? Another consideration is what the rapist actually did. Did he threaten her with death or injury? Did he brandish a weapon? Did he purposefully cause her physical pain? Did he verbally berate her? Did he accuse her of wanting it? Did he unexpectedly betray her trust? The victim's reactions both during and after the rape will reflect what actually happened.

Rape is a traumatic experience that severely stresses a person's coping mechanisms. Most women fear during the rape that they will be killed.[80] Virtually all women report the experience as frightening, degrading and stressful. As soon as the woman becomes aware that she is in potential danger, she usually feels panicky, looks for a way out, tries to dissuade her potential attacker, tries to escape, starts fighting and screaming or is paralyzed by fear.

A variety of coping mechanisms are used by different women during the rape experience itself. Some comply readily with the rapist's demands thinking that it is better to be raped than killed. Others continue to fight, hoping to avoid penetration and trying to discourage their attacker from continuing the rape. Others just try to stay calm and maintain personal control while praying for help. Some mentally block out what is happening, as if their consciousness leaves their body until the ordeal is over. And still others experience involuntary physical reactions like vomiting, gagging, urinating, defecating, hyperventilating, passing out and getting nosebleeds.[81] Some women have coped by showing concern and compassion for the rapist, a response that sometimes lessens the aggressiveness within the rapist.[82]

The victim's emotional battle does not end after she has survived the rape attack. Her emotional reactions will last for months after the attack and psychological scars may affect her for the rest of her life. Particularly for the young and mid-adolescent girl, her psychosexual developmental pattern may be seriously disturbed.[83] Some such victims become quite promiscuous. Some totally withdraw from boys and men, not being able to tolerate any closeness at all. And others develop relatively normal relationships, marry, but are essentially non-orgasmic.

Immediately after the rape incident is over, most women experience a great sense of relief, being glad that they are alive. But they also are likely to feel angry, humiliated, embarrassed, guilty and very confused. Lingering fears, nightmares, fear of public places and intense feelings of vulnerability are common. Some victims also suffer from protracted physical symptoms such as hyperventilation, body soreness, uncontrollable shaking, gagging sensations and nausea. Clinical levels of anxiety as well as depression are frequently seen during the post-rape months.

What rape victims need more than anything is someone to listen to them and give them support. They need the freedom to sob, to voice their anger, to express their sense of guilt and to proclaim their self-condemning feelings in a relationship of friendly support, trust and caring. They do not need to be corrected (e.g., "No. You're wrong. You're not a bad person"). They certainly do not need to be taught how the whole thing could have been prevented (e.g., "If only you hadn't tried to walk home alone").

The victim needs to express all of her feelings. They will not be good feelings. Let her get it out. Encourage her to get it out, all of it. Several times it will have to be expressed.

Often referral to a rape crisis center is useful. Other women, usually previous rape victims themselves, are able to provide the counseling help that she needs. Short-term rape counseling has two primary goals: to help her gain control over her stressful and painful memories by encouraging her to talk about it, getting her to say the words that bring so much terror and revulsion when she hears herself saying them; and to help her to begin feeling acceptable, guiltless and clean again.[84]

After an experience with rape it is also advisable for the woman to do something to help her feel more prepared for possible future rape attacks. Assertiveness classes and self-defense classes will help restore her self-confidence while giving her skills that will be useful in preventing any recurrent episodes.[85]

Prostitution. The scope of our concern with prostitution is on the adolescent prostitute herself. What is her background? What are her motivations? What psychological impact does her prostitution have on her and how does she cope?

Many prostitutes get started in "the life" as teenage runaways. Studies report that about 65 percent of prostitutes got started as runaways and that about 80 percent were victims of incest, sexual or other physical abuse, or rape before they began prostitution.[86] Typically, they were from a single-parent home and often that parent was relatively disinterested in their well-being. Adolescent pregnancies and marriages were common but the marriages were typically short-lived and often violent.

This "typical" picture is often quite different from many of the higher-class independent call girls. Though they also may have begun prostitution during adolescence, they also often have a bachelor's degree or at least some college education. Their entry into the life was usually more deliberate and planned than that of the runaway who sees prostitution as "the only way to make it." They also often follow through with their plans to retire in their mid-30s. A key element in understanding why some girls get into prostitution and others do not is that those who have contacts in the life (a pimp or another prostitute) often gain entry into prostitution. Those without such contacts generally never take up prostitution.

Adolescent prostitutes represent a wide range of personality types. Often, because of their deprivation of love and affection, they sought emotional warmth through sexual contacts with boys, sometimes in promiscuous patterns, but not always. They often had been labelled "bad" or "immoral" and were rejected to some degree by their peers and families. This rejection often leads the girl to identify with some other rejected or deviant role model. Differential-identification theory suggests that developing this inner image of deviancy precedes and paces the way for the girl to enter prostitution.[87]

Stigmatization theory suggests that this derogatory image is then internalized by the girl.[88] She accepts the negative self-image that others have of her. By accepting the image and acting it out she hopes to receive approval from others, which of course is not forthcoming. The result is stronger feelings of alienation, possible depression, development of psychopathology (especially in the realm of personality disorders) and entrance into a systematized deviant lifestyle like prostitution.

When asked why they originally got involved in prostitution and why they continue, several answers are common: for the adventure and excitement of fast living; to have contact with relatively wealthier and higher status men; hoping for marriage; for the adventure of being on the streets alone; to be paid for their attractiveness and sexual pleasuring; to wear beautiful clothes; to choose their own working hours; to do easy work that sometimes is enjoyable; for the experience of power that comes from men enjoying them so much that they are willing to pay them; and because they enjoy playing the role of a professional.[89]

Being ostracized from most of society, guarding themselves against venereal diseases, evading police detection and arrest, and dealing with continuous intimate proximity without allowing themselves intimacy all combine to create a potentially very stressful lifestyle for prostitutes. They handle these stresses through a variety of coping mechanisms:

1. They deny their occupation to others, dressing conservatively

while not working, using their real name rather than their erotic professional name.

2. Some work in the prostitute's world but live in a totally separate middle-class world, going to school, attending church, avoiding swearing and sexual talk and being involved in family gatherings.

3. Many rationalize that their prostitution is necessary for supporting their children; that they provide a public service by relieving men's sexual tensions and thereby lowering their level of loneliness, desire to rape and fears about sexual inadequacy; and that they provide valuable entertainment.

4. Many set limits on the services that they provide, such as some prostitutes who will provide masturbation and fellatio but not genital or anal intercourse. By setting limits they develop their own personal value system within which they can maintain positive feelings about themselves.

5. Instead of believing that they are making money by selling their sex, some displace the responsibility onto their pimp, perceiving that what they are doing is an expression of love for him.

6. Many prostitutes depersonalize the sexual interaction itself, detaching themselves emotionally and even sexually to protect them from experiencing any erotic arousal or emotional involvement with their clients.

7. Often, in order to reinforce their own self-esteem, they think critically of their customers as being hypocritical, pretending to be respectable and for having to pay for sex.

8. Some turn to each other for support, understanding and for a feeling of community, becoming homosexually involved with each other.[90]

While these coping mechanisms do help the prostitute to maintain her psychological equilibrium while pursuing her deviant occupation, she often pays a high price for their long-term use. Feelings of alienation from the mainstream of society are intensified. Emotional isolation is increased as her psychic pain intensifies. Schizoid withdrawal and depersonalization symptoms deepen. Personality disorders often solidify into impulse-ridden or rebellious patterns with psychopathic overtones and hysterical reactions.[91] Some prostitutes resort to staying high on drugs throughout their sexual experiences in order to maintain control.

Adolescents who have been involved in prostitution, particularly for an extended period of time, need professional psychotherapeutic attention. Their defensive coping measures have seriously intensified any underlying personality disorders so that they will be quite resistant to change. Lay counselors can give valuable support, reinforcing the counselee's tentative moves back into the mainstream of social and interpersonal interaction. Christian counselors can help the adolescent who is turning away from prostitution to find release from guilt and added strength in her difficult struggle to change lifestyle patterns in a new commitment to Christ. Reassurance, reinforcement, and full acceptance in a relationship where there is no judgment or condemnation can be an invaluable aid during her crucial time of rebuilding. She will need help as she allows herself to begin experiencing intimacy with boys or young men in wholesome relationships.

Notes

1. Robert W. White, *The Abnormal Personality* (New York: Ronald Press, 1964), p. 121.

2. Ibid., p. 377.

3. J. Money and P. Walker, "Psychosexual Development, Maternalism, Non-Promiscuity, and Body Image in Fifteen Females With Precocious Puberty," Archives of Sexual Behavior 1 (1971):45-60.

4. F.L. Heino Meyer-Bahlburg, "Sexuality in Early Adolescence," in *Handbook of Human Sexuality*, eds. Benjamin Wolman and J. Money (Englewood Cliffs, N. J.: Prentice Hall, 1980).

5. J. Money and D. Alexander, "Psychosexual Development and Absence of Homosexuality in Males With Precocious Puberty," Journal of Nervous and Mental Disorders 148 (1969):111-123.

6. Meyer-Bahlburg, "Sexuality in Early Adolescence."

7. R. Ames, "Physical Maturing Among Boys as Related to Adult Social Behavior," California Journal of Educational Research 8 (1957):69-75.

8. K. E. Kierman, "Age at Puberty in Relation to Age at Marriage and Parenthood: A National Longitudinal Study," Annals of Human Biology 4 (1977):301-308.

9. Alfred Kinsey and P. Sebhard, *Sexual Behavior in the Human Female* (Philadelphia: Saunders, 1953).

10. Derek Miller, *Adolescence: Psychology, Psychopathology and Psychotherapy* (New York: Jason Aronson, 1974).

11. Gary Collins, *Christian Counseling* (Waco, Texas: Word Books, 1980), p. 294.

12. Miller, *Adolescence: Psychology, Psychopathology and Psychotherapy.*

13. H. P. David, "Abortion in Psychological Perspective," American Journal of Orthopsychiatry 42 (1972):61-68.

14. Miller, *Adolescence: Psychology, Psychopathology and Psychotherapy.*

15. Jeanne W. Lindsay, *Pregnant Too Soon* (St. Paul: EMC, 1980).

16. Miller, *Adolescence: Psychology, Psychopathology and Psychotherapy*, p. 300.

17. Ibid.

18. Ibid.

19. Monte Shertler and A. Palca, *The Couple* (New York: Coward, McCann and Geoghegan, 1971), pp. 43-44.

20. John Money and C. Wiedeking, "Gender Identity Role: Normal Differentiation and Its Transpositions," in *Handbook of Human Sexuality*, eds. Wolman and Money.

21. Ibid.

22. Carl Malmquist, *Handbook of Adolescence* (New York: Jason Aronson, 1978).

23. Ibid.

24. Miller, *Adolescence: Psychology, Psychopathology and Psychotherapy.*

25. Malmquist, *Handbook of Adolescence.*

26. Ibid.

27. R. J. Stoller, "Male Childhood Transsexualism," Journal of the American Academy of Child Psychiatry 7 (1968):193-209.

28. N. Cameron, *Personality Development and Psychopathology: A Dynamic Approach* (Boston: Houghton Mifflin, 1963), p. 671.

29. W. H. East and W. H. Hubert DeB., *The Psychological Treatment of Crime* (London: H. M. Stationery Office, 1939).

30. Ephraim Rosen et al., *Abnormal Psychology* (Philadelphia: W. B. Saunders, 1965).

31. H. Christoffel, "Male Genital Exhibitionism," *Perversions, Psychodynamics and Therapy*, eds. S. Lorand and M. Boliut (New York: Random House, 1956).

32. I. D. Yalom, "Aggression and Forbiddenness in Voyeurism," Archives of Genetic Psychiatry 3 (1960):305-319.

33. Malmquist, *Handbook of Adolescence*, p. 318.

34. A. K. Gigeroff, J. Mohr, and R. Turner, "Sex Offenders on Probation: The Exhibitionist," Federal Probation 32 (1968):18-26.

35. Malmquist, *Handbook of Adolescence.*

36. Rosen et al., *Abnormal Psychology.*

37. R. P. Nadler, "Approach to Psychodynamics of Obscene Telephone Calls," The New York State Journal of Medicine 68 (1968):521-526.

38. Peter Nathan and S. Harris, *Psychopathology and Society* (New York: McGraw Hill, 1975).

39. Rosen et al., *Abnormal Psychology.*

40. Collins, *Christian Counseling.*

41. A. Stoir, *Sexual Deviation* (Middlesex, England: Penguin, 1964).

42. Simone DeBeauvoir, *The Second Sex* (New York: Bantam Books, 1952).

43. Evelyn Hooker, "An Empirical Study of Some Relations Between Sexual Patterns and Gender Identity in Male Homosexuals," in *Sex Research: New Developments*, ed. J. Money (New York: Holt, Rinehart and Winston, 1965).

44. Philip Zimbardo and Floyd Ruch, *Psychology and Life*, 9th ed. (Glenview, Ill.: Scott, Foresman, 1975), p. 361.

45. Evelyn Hooker, "Male Homosexuality in the Rorschach," Journal of Projective Techniques 22 (1958):33-54.

46. N. L. Thompson, B. McCandless, and B. Strickland, "Personal Adjustment of Male and Female Homosexuals and Heterosexuals," Journal of Abnormal Psychology 78 (1971):237-240.

47. David Atkinson, *Homosexuals in the Christian Fellowship* (Grand Rapids, Mich.: Eerdmans, 1979).

48. John Money, "Sexual Dimorphism and Homosexual Gender Identity," Psychological Bulletin 74 (December 1970):435-444.

49. Money and Wiedeking, "Gender Identity Role," p. 281.

50. Perry London, *Beginning Psychology* (Homewood, Ill.: Dorsey, 1975).

51. Malmquist, *Handbook of Adolescence.*

52. Gardner Lindzey, C. Hall, and R. Thompson, *Psychology* (New York: Worth, 1975).

53. C. W. Socarides, *The Overt Homosexual* (New York: Grune and Stratton, 1968).

54. Atkinson, *Homosexuals in the Christian Fellowship*, pp. 23-24.

55. John E. Powell, "Understanding Male Homosexuality: Developmental Recapitulation in a Christian Perspective," Journal of Psychology and Theology 2 (Summer 1974):163-173.

56. Collins, *Christian Counseling.*

57. Money and Wiedeking, "Gender Identity Role."

58. Thomas G. Guthiel and N. Avery, "Multiple Overt Incest as Family Defense Against Loss," Family Process 16, no. 1 (March 1977):105-116.

59. R. E. L. Masters, *Patterns of Incest* (New York: Julian Press, 1963), p. 328.

60. P. Sloane and E. Kapinski, "Effects of Incest on the Participants," American Journal of Orthopsychiatry 12 (1942):666-673.

61. Malmquist, *Handbook of Adolescence.*

62. J. R. Fox, "Sibling Incest," British Journal of Sociology 13 (1962):128-150.

63. C. W. Wahl, "The Psychodynamics of Consummated Maternal Incest," Archives of Genetic Psychiatry 3 (1960):188-193.

64. Malmquist, *Handbook of Adolescence.*

65. Benjamin Kleinmuntz, *Essentials of Abnormal Psychology* (New York: Harper and Row, 1974).

66. Malmquist, *Handbook of Adolescence.*

67. Nathan and Harris, *Psychopathology and Society.*

68. S. Ferenczi, "Confusion of Tongues Between Adults and the Child," *Final Contributions to the Problems and Methods of Psychoanalysis* (London: Hogarth Press, 1955).

69. H. Brunhold, "Observations After Sexual Traumata Suffered in Childhood," Excerpta Criminologica 4 (1964):5-8.

70. Rosen et al., *Abnormal Psychology.*

71. Stoir, *Sexual Deviation.*

72. Kleinmuntz, *Essentials of Abnormal Psychology*, p. 324.

73. S. Rachman, "Sexual Fetishism: An Experimental Analogue," Psychological Record 16 (1966):293-306.

74. Menachem Amir, *Patterns in Forcible Rape* (Chicago: University of Chicago Press, 1971).

75. Menachem Amir, "Forcible Rape," Federal Probation 31 (1967):51-58.

76. Bart Delin, *The Sex Offender* (Boston: Beacon Press, 1978).

77. Richard Rada, "Alcoholism and Forcible Rape," American Journal of Psychiatry 132, no. 4 (April 1975):444-446.

78. P. H. Gebhard et al., *Sex Offenders* (New York: Harper, 1965).

79. Malmquist, *Handbook of Adolescence.*

80. Gilbert D. Nass, R. Libby, and M. Fisher, *Sexual Choices* (Monterey, Calif.: Wadsworth Health Sciences Division, 1981).

81. Ann W. Burgess and L. Holstrom, "Coping Behavior of the Rape Victim," American Journal of Psychiatry 133, no. 4 (April 1976):413-418.

82. Nass, Libby, and Fisher, *Sexual Choices.*

83. Miller, *Adolescence: Psychology, Psychopathology and Psychotherapy.*

84. Nass, Libby, and Fisher, *Sexual Choices.*

85. Burgess and Holstrom, "Coping Behavior of the Rape Victim."

86. Nass, Libby, and Fisher, *Sexual Choices.*

87. D. Glaser, "Criminality Theories and Behavioral Images," American Journal of Sociology 61 (1956):433-444.

88. S. Shoham and G. Rahaw, "Social Stigma and Prostitution," Annals of International Criminology 6 (1967):479-513.

89. Jennifer James, "Women as Sexual Criminals and Victims," in *Sexual Scripts,* eds. Judith L. Laws and P. Schwartz (Hinsdale, Ill.: Dryden Press, 1977).

90. Nass, Libbey, and Fisher, *Sexual Choices.*

91. Malmquist, *Handbook of Adolescence.*

■ CHAPTER 15
Delinquent Behavior

Some of the more difficult counseling situations are with angry resistive teenagers. Many times these young people are brought to the pastor, youth minister or therapist only after they have created delinquency problems for family members, neighbors, school personnel or community, sometimes attracting police involvement. Just about the last place they want to be is with a counselor. And they often let that be known in very certain messages. They have usually been brought. They were not asked, "How would you like to go?" They were told, "You're going." Threats of punishment have been levied against the youth simply to make sure that he or she gets to the counselor's office. Obviously, none of these pre-counseling circumstances instill desires within the young counselee to talk over his or her feelings and behavior with an adult.

In this chapter we will examine some of the different types of delinquent behavior, origins of juvenile delinquency and counseling guidelines that are effective with these young people. Before going further, let's agree on the definitions of some centrally important terms:[1]

1. Juvenile deviants. Children who exhibit deviant or odd behavior, whether or not antisocial in a legal sense.

2. Legal delinquents. All juvenile deviants who commit antisocial acts as specified by law.

3. Detected delinquents. Juveniles who are apprehended for committing antisocial acts.

4. Juvenile criminals. Juveniles who are waived to an adult criminal court to be tried for committing a criminal offense according to adult criminal law. If found guilty, sentencing also follows according to adult criminal court procedures.

5. Antisocial behavior. Acts that are directed against other people. Therapists understand that these types of behaviors are unconsciously designed to relieve internal conflicts within people who have developed certain personality disorders.

Origins of Juvenile Delinquency

The origins and causes of delinquent patterns of behavior in adolescence has been studied from several different perspectives. Effective counseling with a teenager who has developed a delinquent behavior pattern necessitates an understanding of how the behavior got started and what feelings it is expressing. Counselors first must grasp what meaning the behavior symbolizes. Then they may be able to successfully intervene. We will examine four types of causes of delinquent behavior: sociological, family dynamics, group influences and personality issues.

Sociological causes. In the 1920s and 1930s a group of Chicago researchers began sociological evaluations to help determine social causes of delinquency. One of the researchers, Clifford Shaw, evaluated delinquency rates for different population areas.[2] Inner city areas, particularly those sections characterized by physical deterioration and population decline, had the highest incidence of delinquency. The occurrence of delinquency paralleled the occurrence of poverty, vice, broken homes and foreign-born population. It was discovered that intellectual level and specific ethnic origin were not significant indications of delinquency rates. The lowest incidence was found in outlying residential areas that were populated primarily by native-born business and professional people.

Two sociologists, Emile Durkheim and Robert K. Merton, have applied the anomie theory as a cause of delinquent behavior.[3] The term "anomie" refers to the breakdown of the old norms and controls on behavior without the development of newer effective and acceptable behaviors.[4] As the socioeconomic conditions within certain urban areas have broken down, fewer legitimate means have remained for residents of those areas to attain their goals and aspirations. With the breakdown of socially structured opportunities, antisocial frustrations and behavior increase.

Shaw and his associates found that the rate of delinquent behavior in these urban areas was primarily determined by the degree of social disorganization prevalent at the time.[5] The greater the degree of disorganization, the more delinquency was found. Their populations are quite mobile; ethnic concentrations and language usage patterns are always changing. Neighbors are replaced by strangers and diverse cultural standards and ethnic identities exist side-by-side with little interaction. The families exist quite separate from each other, losing the mutually reinforcing influence on the social structuring of the teenagers' behavior. Peer group relationships, often in the form of street-corner groups, flourish in the relative absence of any sense of community. Delinquent associates and peer commitment within these groups have proven to be more predictive of delinquent behavior than social class.[6]

Another contributory aspect of social disorganization is the breakdown of clearly defined social roles.[7] Under these circumstances delinquent subcultures develop their own requirements for status. Status often comes from age, sex, race, class or attaining certain accomplishments. Roles are the prescribed behavioral patterns that are accepted as appropriate for people of various status positions. Members of these subcultures play out their roles in an effort to reinforce their sense of belonging and status. Stealing is often an example of role-playing behavior, especially among boys. Within the context of the delinquent subculture, stealing enhances the boy's masculinity. Girls also steal, but usually for different reasons. She predominantly steals objects such as clothing, jewelry and perfume that enhance her femininity. For the boy, the *act* of stealing enhances his role. For the girl, the *objects* that are stolen enhance her role.[8]

Psychiatrist Derek Miller uses the term "situational delinquency," referring to delinquent behavior that is predisposed and precipitated primarily by the social conditions surrounding the youth and his or her behavior.[9] A number of factors have been found to cause situational delinquency:[10]

1. Delinquent subcultures reinforce the occurrence of delinquent behaviors because those activities conform to the mores of that social system.

2. The breakdown of the extended family adds to the alienation between adolescents and authority figures and adults in general.

3. Rapid social change and abandoning emotional prejudices create the need for new patterns of dealing with aggressive impulses.

4. Drug dependence is perhaps the greatest cause of adolescent ur-

ban crime, largely because of the need to finance the dependency.

Six focal factors of lower-class culture have been isolated that affect the genesis of adolescent delinquent behavior.[11] It is not that these issues are concerns only of lower-class individuals. However, they do explain the causes of juvenile delinquency.

1. Trouble. To practice law-abiding behavior or law-violating behavior is a dominant concern in lower-class culture. Breaking the law or getting into trouble is often associated with status, strength, masculinity and leadership.

2. Toughness. Physical prowess, skills, masculinity, fearlessness, bravery and daring are all associated with the high value on being tough. Weakness, ineptitude, timidity, cowardice and caution are all scorned and people who exhibit these traits are devalued. The characteristics that indicate toughness are also, unfortunately, often related with antisocial behavior.

3. Smartness. Being smart in lower-class culture is very different from being smart in middle-class culture. Lower-class people are smart when they are interpersonally smart. They are able to outsmart, dupe, "con," gain money by their "wits," be shrewd and always have a comeback. The person who is not smart is gullible, "con-able," earns money by hard work, is mentally slow, dull-witted, and usually cannot muster a good comeback. Being smart, then, lends itself to certain sociopathic tendencies.

4. Excitement. Thrills, risks, danger, change and activity are sought after as relief from and avoidance of boredom, "deadness," safeness, sameness and passivity. Delinquent behaviors are often the source of the valued excitement.

5. Fate. Personal responsibility is often shunned in favor of a belief in fate. One is either "lucky" and has good fortune, or is "unlucky" and has had a bad omen. Considering the consequences of one's behavior as some externalized luck or fate lessens the sense of personal control over one's life.

6. Autonomy. Being free from external constraints, being free from authority, and being independent are highly valued. The presence of external constraints, the presence of strong authority, dependency, and being "cared for" are all signs of weakness and softness as opposed to toughness. The need for autonomy poses rather obviously anticipated problems associated with delinquent acting-out.

The motivational pattern of delinquent behavior within the middle-class culture is quite different from that of lower-class culture. The middle-class adolescent world is very peer-oriented, non-intellectual, and heavily focused on having fun and experiencing good times.[12] Their peer groups tend to establish norms, values and behavioral guidelines that are generally acceptable to their parents. Adults are often integrally involved in their activities such as is seen in student body government, high school athletics and community service projects.

Conformity and competition are foundational to successful middle-class peer group functioning. Dress, hair style, taste in music and cars, attractions to the opposite sex, are required to be in fairly tight conformity. But no matter how tight the conformity, there always seems to be room for competition. And it is through competition between group members that the leaders evolve.

Delinquency within the middle-class youth culture is found in young people who are actively involved in the "social scene" as well as in those who are not involved. The majority of middle-class delinquency is of a non-violent nature. Drinking alcohol, using and dealing in drugs, skipping school, speeding, obtaining liquor and becoming sexually intimate are common middle-class delinquent activities. They often express the teenager's social needs and quite highly socialized self-concept and normal developmental patterns.

Family dynamics. The overall most potent agent for socialization is the family. Socialization has been described by one psychologist as, "the outcome of a bargain that is struck between parents and child. The child's part of the bargain is to give up the privileges and unrestraint of a young child in favor of the responsibilities of an older one. The parents' part of the bargain is to set models of considerate and socialized behavior and to make it worth the child's while, in the coin of affection and praise, to undertake the required sacrifices."[13] To make this socialization process work, the parents must carefully assess their children's level of tolerance and frustration. They must balance demands and expectations with adequate encouragement and emotional support. When it works, the young person learns to feel good about himself or herself as a successfully functioning person. When the process breaks down, teenage delinquent behavior is often one result.

When there are almost no demands, expectations or restraints, the result is quite often a passive, dependent and irresponsible attitude, but seldom an adolescent pattern of delinquent behavior.[14] Making strong demands and setting high standards while giving very little encouragement and reinforcement creates a different result. The child makes sacrifices but because he or she receives nothing in return, the socialization process is thwarted. The youth's submissions become less and less frequent, frustration and anger increase, aggressive and rebellious impulses and behaviors are more common and delinquent patterns emerge.

Two other researchers found that active aggression, hostility or hating of the parents was central to developing serious delinquent patterns of behavior.[15] They found that this pattern became self-perpetuating. These teenagers fear dependence, mistrust signals of love and esteem, and thwart positive relationships with aggressive reactions. The results showed that these delinquent youths were ill-prepared for healthy relationships with peers as well as with adults.

Cohesiveness of the family and consistency of discipline have also been found to be important factors in preventing the development of delinquent patterns.[15] Higher delinquency rates were found in adolescents who were from families that were described as quarrelsome, neglectful and lacking in discipline. Punitive, erratic discipline and ineffective loving seemed most predictive of future delinquent behavior.

The relationship between the family structure and the surrounding society is also a major concern. When the family members are well integrated into the various social structures that, in turn, reinforce the value and traditional function of the family unit, socialization is reassured.[17] Schools, churches, community athletic programs, etc., help to integrate the family unit within the social structure while reinforcing the value of the family unit. A breakdown, whether in the family or in society, can lead to frustrations, disillusionment, hostility, aggression and overt delinquent behavior.

Increasing affluence has also been spotted as a determining factor for delinquent behavior.[18] Affluence is reported to have brought two impacts to family life that are conducive to the development of increasing delinquency: increased rates of separation and divorce because of added economic pressures and more families with two working parents; and greater mobility that has broken down contacts and interactions with extended family members. There are no close neighbors, aunts and uncles, or grandparents to serve as role models or to give adequate affection and support when the child's parents have serious problems or get a divorce. Thus the teenage subculture becomes increasingly important as a shaper of behavior and role definer. In the urban areas of affluent industrialized nations, this teenage subculture is often heavily oriented toward delinquency.

Another delinquency-producing association between families and society is reported by Robert K. Merton.[19] Lower occupational level parents sometimes project their own frustrated career goals onto their children. Unfortunately, these young people usually have no better opportunities for reaching these goals than their parents did. They deal not only with their own frustrations, but also with their parents' disappointments.

In some families, parental collusion has been found to be reinforcing of the teenager's delinquent acting-out. Some parents respond to hearing their child's delinquent behavior by reminiscing about their own adolescent rebelliousness.[20] The parents' unconscious needs may be partially satisfied by their teenagers' behavior. Parents may indirectly reinforce the misbehavior by neglecting to notice new acquisitions (clothes, stereo, TV) that their children have stolen. Reinforcement is implied when parents do not discipline their adolescents for misbehaviors that come to their attention.

Group influences. Peer influences and peer group involvement is important to all types of teenagers, but even more vital to delinquent youth.[21] Since the home lives of many delinquent adolescents is seriously disrupted, the gang becomes a new emotional home. It is in the peer group or gang that the young person finds both belonging and status needs met.[22] The greater the level of social disorganization in the residential area and the more dysfunctional the family unit, the more important the peer group involvement becomes.

Youth pastors often try to involve these young people in their church youth groups, which is a noble and sometimes beneficial effort. When a delinquent youth is able to overcome his or her insecurities, distrust and hostility enough to become involved in a Christian group, the sense of belonging, recognition, and status can be transferred to this potentially much more wholesome group involvement. But it is extremely difficult for the Christian youth group to match the excitement of the youth gang. The exciting and lawless character of gang activities helps the teenager to drown out thoughts and memories about his or her painful home life.[23] The rebellious nature of gang activities reinforces the same impulses within its individual members. Effective group functioning in gangs requires that several members that have similar adjustment problems group together.[24] When this happens, they are then able to develop a new set of cultural norms that will reinforce their behavioral patterns.

When groups of delinquent youths reject society's standards and adopt a new set of norms, a delinquent subculture has been formed.

Carl Malmquist lists six characteristics of these subcultures:[25]

1. Non-utilitarianism. Much of the group's activities are done just for the fun or excitement in it rather than to accomplish any particular goal. For example, many thefts are done for the challenge or excitement rather than to gain certain desired objects or money.

2. Maliciousness. Destructive, hostile acts are perpetrated against perceived oppressors. School facilities, police, police cars and businesses are common targets, as well as the members and property of rival gangs.

3. Negativism. Group members resist evaluating themselves by the middle-class norms that they find at school and work. A negativistic attitude tends to neutralize the anxiety and alienation that these youth feel from middle-class expectations.

4. Versatility. A wide variety of antisocial acts are acceptable expressions of delinquent adolescent frustration and pain.

5. Group autonomy. Only self-imposed decisions are acceptable. There is a very low tolerance for externally imposed restraints or regulations.

6. Hedonistic activities. Academic and career pursuits become frustrating, progressively unrewarding, and increasingly productive of status anxiety and feelings of inferiority. Most delinquent activities are marked by impulsiveness and quick gratifications.

Delinquent subcultures take a variety of forms and are marked by different types of sanctioned behaviors. Delinquent subcultures include the following types: criminal subcultures, conflict subcultures, retreatist subcultures, racket subcultures and theft subcultures.[26,27]

1. The criminal subculture. This type includes offenders of virtually all age levels in order to facilitate the learning and continuance of criminal behavior. Criminal role models promote the socialization of younger criminals through the dynamic of identification. Values are taught and integrated within the subculture and social controls are maintained over its membership. Participation in this subculture enhances the delinquent's opportunities for advancement in his or her criminal career.

2. The conflict subculture. This type usually develops in areas where transiency and instability contribute to a strong degree of social disorganization. Legitimate means to accomplish success are not available. Neither is there a well-established criminal pattern in the neighborhood. The primary release of frustrations and hostilities is through conflict-producing activities. Gang fighting and brawling are primary activities of these subcultures. Because of serious limitations in both conven-

tional and criminal opportunities, violence seems to be their only resort.

3. The retreatist subculture. This category is composed of delinquents who fail to reach culturally approved goals by legitimate means, and who blame themselves for their failure. They blame their own inadequacies and weaknesses for not being able to accomplish middle-class goals. The retreatist subculture reinforces giving up the struggle for success. Habitual use of drugs is a common means for dulling the intense anxiety and guilt that these delinquents feel because of their lack of success.

4. The racket subculture. This includes a variety of highly specialized and well-organized criminal activities. Many juvenile delinquents start as an apprentice in a particular racket subculture and then gradually work their way up toward the top. Numbers, loansharking and narcotics are examples of racket subcultures.

5. The theft subculture. This is differentiated according to the type of theft involved. Car theft, apartment burglary and stickup of stores are examples. Each subculture provides training and encouragement for its particular type of theft.

Personality issues. We have briefly surveyed the sociological, family and group dynamics of juvenile delinquency. Now let's shift our focus onto the individual personality issues that figure into the etiology of adolescent delinquent behaviors. Psychiatrist Derek Miller summarizes three different psychological syndromes that are likely to develop delinquent behavioral patterns:[28]

1. Teenagers sometimes fail to develop an adequate conscience so that they abstain only for short periods of time from delinquent activities only because they fear apprehension and punitive consequences.

2. Some adolescents with transient, or temporary, psychological disturbances find themselves lacking the personality strength to successfully withstand current external pressures. An example of this is insecure boys who impulsively steal cars as a proof of their masculinity.

3. Other teenagers turn to delinquent reactions as the result of feelings of profound deprivation of love and affection, as is commonly true with girls who become sexually promiscuous.

A much earlier study revealed six personal meanings that delinquent activities can have for adolescents:[29]

1. Escape or flight from a tense situation, as in truancy and running away from home.

2. Intense excitement and the thrill of running risks during delin-

quent adventures helps some young people cover over feelings of unhappiness, bitterness and remorse.

3. Achievement of recognition, status and respect from peers
through group delinquency.

4. Delinquent behavior shows proof that one is courageous and masculine, and serves to deny feelings of dependence, inferiority and
weakness.

5. Direct or symbolic expressions of revenge against parents.

6. The paradoxical meaning of seeking punishment in order to alleviate a conscious or unconscious sense of guilt.

One survey of sociological causes of delinquency revealed a variety
of social conditions and problems that predispose teenagers to become
involved with delinquent acting-out. Merton has studied five different
ways that people adapt to these social conditions, some are more conducive than others to generating delinquent trends.[30] The following
table summarizes his findings:[31]

Types of Individual Adaptation

Modes of Adaptation	Culture's Goals and Values	Institutionalized Means for Gaining Goals
1. Conformity	Accept	Accept
2. Innovation	Accept	Reject
3. Ritualism	Reject	Accept
4. Retreatism	Reject	Reject
5. Rebellion	Reject prevailing goals and values and substitute new goals and values	Reject prevailing means, substitute new means

Illustration 39

When widespread conformity is present, then society continues un-
disturbed. Conformity in this sense produces no delinquency.

Societies such as our own place high value upon success but limit the
number of practical, appropriate and acceptable ways of achieving
these goals. Innovation as an adaptive style produces both delinquent
and non-delinquent responses to frustration. While some teenagers become innovative within the limits of the law, others resort to delinquent solutions.

Other teenagers react to frustration by rejecting the values and goals
of society, but behave in very safe or traditional ways. They have been
disillusioned with society's values but do not feel freedom to become
innovative. Instead, they attach meaning to the ritualism of rigidly repeating institutionally approved behavior. This pattern seldom pro-

duces delinquency.

The least common form of adaptation is retreatism. The most discouraged and disillusioned are able to accept neither society's goals nor its sanctioned methods for attaining them. Teenagers who appear to have "dropped out" belong to this category. They often resort to alcohol or drug abuse which also constitutes delinquent behaviors. Withdrawal from interpersonal contact and fantasy are two non-delinquent examples of retreatism.

Rebellion is the adaptive style that is most common of delinquent behavior. Society's goals as well as the sanctioned means for reaching these goals are rejected, but attempts are made to substitute new goals in place of the old.

Impulsiveness and lack of self-control are characteristic of adolescent delinquents. These are indications that the socialization process has not adequately progressed. There are also indications that defects in thought processes may sometimes be associated with delinquent behavior.[32] Teenagers who cannot adequately discriminate may fail to discern the difference between praise and correction. They may react to both messages as if they were punishment. One important study of 910 teenagers found that delinquents less frequently interpreted positive events as being positive for themselves, and also tended to interpret positive events as more negative for themselves.[33] The importance of giving encouragement and other forms of positive feedback to teenagers has been stressed. But if the young person cannot correctly identify the positive message, then no benefit is derived. For instance, "You played real well today," might be heard as, "You did okay but you can do better." "You played the clarinet flawlessly tonight," could be heard as, "We expect perfection from you always."

Young people with these cognitive defects are almost sure to suffer from low self-esteem. No matter what is said to them, they draw out some negative message. And this low self-esteem is apt to lower their level of functioning in school, sports, spiritual development and in relationships with family, friends and members of the opposite sex.

Another aspect of delinquent process is the person's moral development which seems often to have been arrested at a pre-puberty level. They perceive most adult role models and authority figures operating from primarily selfish or power motives.[34]

Psychologist Leon Festinger's theory of cognitive dissonance has also been applied to the psychology of delinquency.[35] After a young person begins to commit antisocial acts, there is an initial discomfort because these behaviors result in a dissonance between the actions themselves and the behaviors that are expected, valued and rewarded. This dissonance will result in feelings of self-devaluation and self-rejection unless something is done. Youths will quite often begin to see their behavior as worthy or desirable in order to reduce the dissonance between their actual behavior and the expectations of others.

Another effort to understand delinquent behavior patterns is the trait-factor approach, which seeks to locate clusters of factors that tend to occur together. One early research project of this type identified three clusters of types of teenage delinquent behavioral problems:[36]

1. The unsocialized aggressive type who is prone to assaultive behavior, fighting, cruelty, defiance toward authority, malicious mischief and inadequate guilt.

2. The socialized delinquent who may be involved with group stealing, truancy, high absenteeism, breaking curfew and keeping undesirable company.

3. The overinhibited youth is likely to be withdrawn, seclusive, shy, apathetic, sensitive, compliant and worrying.

Delinquency is often the result of conflict in the youth's psychological history. William Healy's classic study, *The Individual Delinquent*, indicated that broken homes, inadequate parental control, undesirable companions, and unhealthy mental interests are common antecedents of delinquency.[37] Both external conflicts and intrapsychic conflict can be overwhelming to the adolescent's psychological development. Behavioral controls become weakened, decision-making and problem-solving processes are disrupted, and conscience development stunted when too much conflict is present during the formative years of childhood and adolescence. In most cases antisocial tendencies fade as growth continues through adolescence. Only in the more severely pathological cases does the delinquent pattern become entrenched and continue on into adulthood as a full criminal syndrome. This point spotlights the crucial timing of effective counseling intervention for teenagers who are developing delinquent behavioral patterns.

In some cases the delinquent behavior represents an inadequate and misdirected effort to deal with intense feelings of guilt. Freud isolated three character types, all partially related to reactions to guilt feelings, that hold strong potential for developing antisocial behavior patterns:[38]

1. The narcissistic and passive-aggressive personalities are typically seen in people who believe that they have somehow been mistreated and therefore deserve special treatment and attention. They tend to be

resentful, pouty, passively resistive, stubborn and demanding of immediate impulse gratification.

2. Another group that Freud isolated are those who cannot tolerate
success. For these youths, achievement activates a strong guilt reaction that is handled by behaviors that essentially undo the success. Receiving A's in school one semester may be followed by truancy and
poor academic performance during the following term. Self-destructive
behaviors like gambling, sexual promiscuity, risk-taking and daredevil
activities are common expressions of this pattern. Fear of success
sometimes becomes phobic in proportions so that the individuals do
everything that they can in order to avoid being successful.

3. The third type of guilt-motivated delinquent is the individual who
transgresses the law specifically to be punished. Seeking punishment
relieves guilt that arises from repressed impulses, thoughts and feelings. They commit an external act in order to experience judgment and
punishment from an external source so that they can avoid their own
self-judgment and self-punishment in reaction to their internal self. Until the underlying guilt-avoidance mechanism is worked through in
counseling, the delinquent acts will be repeated.

Several psychological researchers and theorists have linked self-destructive behaviors to aggressive impulses that are turned inward.[39,40]
This inwardly thrusted aggression is a common component of depression. Denial is a common defense mechanism of adolescents that often
leads to acting-out behavior, often of delinquent proportions.[41]

These young people suffer from profound psychological emptiness
and deeply inadequate identity development. Their delinquent behavior is arousal-seeking and guilt-satisfying in nature which helps them to
avoid their feelings of depression.[42] J.M. Toolan reports on his therapy
with a 16-year-old boy that illustrates the use of delinquent behavior to
mask depression: "As therapy progressed, it was readily apparent that
Richard was a frightened, anxious, chronically depressed boy. He recalled how unhappy he had been before he joined the gang, how inferior he had felt in comparison with other boys, how scared he had been
in the presence of girls, how stupid he had appeared at school, how
worried that he would never amount to anything.

"After he joined the gang, and by means of vicarious identification
with the other members' supposed strength, he had felt different. 'For
the first time in my life I felt alive. I was a different person. I no longer
worried, wasn't afraid of anyone.' He began to go out with girls and felt
equal to the social challenge.

"As therapy continued, a crucial period came when he became aware of the significance of the gang in relieving his previous depression. He wanted to quit the gang but was afraid that he might become depressed again. He finally quit the gang, but when he became depressed again, it could be properly handled."[43]

Psychological research indicates that delinquent adolescents evidence higher rates of depression than non-delinquent adolescents. One study concluded that delinquent teenagers are more rather than less depressed, delinquent girls are more depressed than delinquent boys, older delinquents tend to be more depressed than younger delinquents, and there is no correlation between ethnicity and degree of depression.[44]

In another publication the same researcher suggests that depression is especially related to the onset of delinquent activity.[45] In some cases, adolescents appear to stave off psychotic episodes with delinquent acting-out. For some, depression increases to a certain level of intensity and then is decreased by delinquent activity. But the depression is never fully resolved so it repeatedly increases, causing a repeated cycle to occur.

Striving for power is another source of delinquent patterns of behavior.[46] Adolescents often experience feelings of powerlessness. They may feel oppressed and at another's mercy. These experiences militate against their need for independence and autonomy. When the approved mechanisms for regaining self-esteem through academic performance, athletic prowess, or other means are either blocked or unavailable, delinquent acting-out of aggression may result. The aggression is often directed against the perceived oppressor, a symbolic representative of the oppressor, or displaced onto a less threatening object. Vandalism and theft often symbolize powerfulness over the oppressing adult world.[47]

An often overlooked motivation for delinquent behavior is the adolescent's desperate need for a relationship with an adult. It is a form of crying out for help, for contact. Being caught after delinquent activity is a way of insuring some kind of relationship with an adult. When the identity formation process is seriously faltering, a stable relationship with an adult figure can be vitally important to the youth's further maturing. The phenomenon of counselees suddenly developing new or worse symptoms in order to insure the continuation of their counseling relationship is familiar to experienced counselors. Renewed delinquent behavior sometimes serves the same purpose for troubled adolescents.

Derek Miller suggests that stealing is often done by teenagers who experience significant deprivation: "The feeling of chronic deprivation associated with chronic illness may be relieved by objects. The same applies to those who suffer from emotional deprivation due to isolation from other children or parental absence or loss."[48] Though theft sometimes is aggressive or an expression of power, it is sometimes an ineffective attempt to fill a chronic, emotional void with things.

Most teenagers have periodic urges to behave in antisocial ways. These behaviors are defined as delinquent only when the adolescent is caught. It is also only after the youth has been found out that he or she comes to the attention of a counselor.

Theft is a major antisocial behavior committed by adolescents.[49] Though rule-breaking among teenagers is common, theft represents more serious behavioral signals. Shoplifting is a form of theft that is often done in groups, sometimes in response to a dare, as evidence of one's masculinity and power.

Running away from home is another typical adolescent reaction, indicating a struggle with dependence/independence issues.[50] This reaction can express either frustration, manipulative maneuvering or an honest solution to a perplexing situation.

Drug Abuse

The most common form of delinquent behavior among adolescents is the illegal use and abuse of tobacco, alcohol, marijuana and other substances.[51] As we approach this subject, a humorous and at the same time thought-provoking quote is appropriate. At a drug symposium, the opening address began: "Welcome to those of you who use coffee, tea or tobacco, cough syrup, or who have an occasional martini before dinner. Welcome drug users. To those of you who have on occasion lent a tranquilizer to a friend or offered your sleeping pills to your neighbor, welcome drug abusers and transgressors against the law. If any of you have been so brave as to smoke pot, shoot "H" or pop a cap of acid, well, welcome drug abusers and committers of felonies. I guess that includes all of us because drug use is universal amongst human beings."[52]

Drug abuse has been defined as repeated, careless, non-medical use of drugs that has a potential for inflicting physical or psychological damage to the user and others.[53] Levels of drug abuse can be differentiated between three different levels:[54]

1. Drug experimentation during early and mid-adolescence is likely to involve taking the drug up to four or five times in order to gain a feeling of mastery over its effects.

2. Regular drug usage involves the regular taking of a drug (tobacco,

alcohol, barbiturates, marijuana, or any hallucinogenic or mood-altering substance) for its sedative or intoxicant effect.

3. Progressive drug usage usually involves a pattern of moving from "softer" (like tobacco or alcohol) to "harder" (cocaine or heroin) drugs. More pathology is indicated in level three than level two, and at level two than level one.

Drug dependence. With increased pathology is greater ego regression and denial of personal responsibility. As users progress in drug involvement, they often move from injesting and sniffing the substances to injecting them either intravenously or subcutaneously. Drug dependence (a state of physical or psychological dependence) has a higher probability of occurring as usage becomes more frequent and as the drug is used over a longer period of time.

Physical dependence is characterized by tolerance and withdrawal. Tolerance is the body's ability to adapt to the drug. Unfortunately, the body's tolerance for psychoactive drugs means that the person has to take steadily increasing amounts of the toxic substance in order to experience its subjective effects. Withdrawal illness occurs when a physical need for some drugs has developed through continued usage. In these situations, symptoms develop when the drug is absent from the user's system. Anticipating withdrawal symptoms increases the user's motivation for taking the drug.

Psychological dependence is indicated by the individual's repeated need for the subjective effects of the drug. The need can range from a relatively mild but persistent need to an uncontrollable, compulsive craving. Though often underestimated, psychological dependence can be sometimes even more compelling and enduring than physical dependence.

Reasons for drug abuse. For many years adolescents have used tobacco and alcohol, especially beer, as a part of their delinquent activities. Though there was some concern over these infractions, many adults looked on these activities with tongue-in-cheek, remembering their own experimental and rebellious use of tobacco and beer when they were teenagers.

Why have so many young people turned to drugs? What are their motivations? What kinds of teenagers are most likely to use illicit drugs? Personality testing has revealed some differences between drug-using and non-drug-using adolescents.[55] Non-drug users tend to have more poise, are more self-centered, more organized under stress, more flexible in their thinking and are more inclined toward aesthetic and social values. Drug users tend to score lower on scales that measure well-being and self-satisfaction. They are less conforming, less achievement-oriented through conforming, less secure, less optimistic about vocational futures and are less oriented toward economic, political and religious values.

Richard Blum and his associates note that the reason a person starts using drugs may not be the same reason he or she continues using.[56] It has been said that drug usage during early adolescence is often an attempt to imitate adult behavior, while use during mid-adolescence is an act of defiance against adults.[57] Younger teenagers usually hide their drug abuse from parents and society while older teenagers may flaunt it. Earlier usage often involves drugs that parents use, such as tobacco and beer. This involvement is often a part of the "initiation rites" into adolescence. Later on, drugs that are disapproved of by parents become more popular with mid-adolescents. Derek Miller says, "Socioculturally, drugs may be used as part of a phony war against adults. Adolescents who group together to use drugs often appear to believe that they are a group of non-conformists fighting a corrupt and conformist adult society that wishes to attack them. It is ironic that the adolescent who is least sure of his or her capacity to be independent is most likely to take drugs and become dependent upon them.[58]

Teenagers who are struggling against identity diffusion, along with becoming sexually promiscuous, experiencing academic failure and engaging in other forms of delinquency, will also often abuse drugs.[59] Conflicts relating to sexuality also can play a motivational role in the adolescent's drug abuse. Some substitute drugs for sex because drugs are easier to procure with less hassle. Others use drugs instead of sex or in conjunction with sex to lessen their fears about impotence. Still others use drugs to heighten the satisfaction that they receive from masturbation.

Tragically, when drugs are taken in relationship to sexual problems or identity formation disturbances, the problems usually worsen. The drug only temporarily masks the real disturbance and the teenager is likely to regress further and compound his or her problems.

The avoidance of anxiety is why many young people, like their parents, turn to the regular and often frequent abuse of drugs.[60] Drug usage may be initiated or increased following the loss of a girlfriend or boyfriend, death or divorce of parents or after a move to another geographical location. Illegitimate drugs are sometimes taken like adults take prescribed tranquilizers.

Depression is particularly prevalent in drug users. One well-conceived research study found the following results:[61]

1. Delinquents are more depressed than non-delinquents.

2. The more serious the delinquency, the deeper the depression.

3. Drug users manifest more depression than non-drug users.

4. Drug-using delinquents are more depressed than non-drug-using delinquents.

5. Non-delinquent non-drug users show relatively little depression.

6. Adolescents who frequently use alcohol evidence more depression than non-users of alcohol.

7. Adolescents who frequently use marijuana appear to be more depressed than non-users of marijuana.

Types of drugs. Let's turn our attention now to the types of drugs that are most commonly abused by teenagers. They can be grouped into five different categories: opiates, stimulants, depressants, hallucinogens and volatile substances. The term "narcotic" refers to any drug that relieves pain by dulling central nervous system activity. Adolescents use narcotics because they can produce a state of tranquility, elation, dullness or sleep. Overdoses can be extremely dangerous, producing systemic poisoning, delirium, paralysis or death. Most commonly defined as narcotics are the opiates, though United States narcotics laws include all drugs that cause either physical or psychological addiction, such as marijuana, amphetamines and LSD.[62]

1. Opiates. The opiates are opium and its derivatives, which include morphine, heroin, codeine and methadone. Morphine is often called "M," white stuff, junk, fix, paper, poison or cap; while heroin is frequently called "H," horse, harry, medicine, shot, stuff, junk, white stuff or flea powder. Both heroin and morphine are white crystalline powders. Morphine is about 10 times more powerful than opium, heroin is about three times more potent than morphine, and all are quite addictive.[63]

In the initial stages of use, morphine and heroin are often taken orally, though heroin is commonly sniffed as well. As the person builds tolerance for the drug, either greater quantities or more direct applications are required in order to get the desired effects. Injection is the fastest way of introducing the substance into the system. Some users open a blood vessel with a pin or razor blade and then insert the drug into the opening with a medicine dropper. Subcutaneous injecting (which is called skin popping) is often the first injection procedure that is used and can be the preferred procedure for many years of the drug use. Intravenous injections (mainlining) involve the injection of the substance directly into the blood stream. Mainlining is often the addict's preferred method since it produces the strongest results with the least amount of drug.

So much of the user's life revolves around the procuring and using of drugs that he or she typically becomes alienated from family members, non-drug-using friends and society. They are apt to become secretive, evasive and fearful of being "found out." In addition to alienation, people injecting drugs are subject to skin infections, abscesses, and hepatitis from using unsterilized needles, pins, razor blades, medicine droppers and syringes. Mainliners face the dangers of damaged and scarred blood vessels and vascular breakdown. Mainliners and skin poppers try to avoid detection by trying injection spots that are not readily visible. Favorite spots include between fingers and toes, the neck above the hairline and inside the mouth.

Adolescents who use opiates do so to experience a subjective sense of well-being, serenity, and relief from fear and apprehension. "A few seconds after the injection of a narcotic, the user's face flushes, his pupils constrict and he feels a tingling sensation, particularly in his abdomen. The tingling soon gives way to a feeling of elatedness (the "fix"), which lasts about 30 minutes. He later drifts into a somnolence ("going on the nod"), waking up, drifting again, all the while indulging in daydreams. During this phase, understandably, he has no interest in anything and spends most of his time in bed. He is easily wakened and answers questions accurately, but readily goes back on the nod. The drug effects wear off within about three to four hours, sometimes a little longer."[64]

Tolerance and withdrawal phenomena are characteristic of opiate use. Withdrawal illness lasts for two to three days and may be followed by a general feeling of discomfort for several months.

2. Stimulants. Drugs that stimulate central nervous system activity, typically called amphetamines, include Benzidrine, Dexedrine and Methedrine. They are also known by a variety of slang terms: bennies, pep pills, speed, crystal, meth, uppers, eye-openers, dex, dominoes and minstrels. Their common side effects include appetite reduction or loss, insomnia, agitation, irritability and fast-paced talking. Adolescents usually take stimulants for the subjective experiences that are commonly associated with their use. Feelings of elation, self-confidence, heightened alertness and initiative, and increased feelings of competence and power are the temporary benefits.

Most amphetamine users start out by taking the drugs orally. Some progress on to intravenously injecting in order to increase the psychoactive effects. Such injections produce a sudden "rush" or "flash" which is strongly pleasurable. Some youths adopt the very dangerous practice of taking several excessive and intoxicating doses in a relatively short period of time. As soon as the effect of the first injection begins to wear off, a second injection is made and so on. Acute amphetamine intoxication can follow in which the person experiences agitation, restlessness, sleeplessness, profuse perspiration, distractibility and impaired cognitive functioning. Physical damage, such as liver failure, heart damage, and nervous system dysfunction can also occur.

Amphetamine dependence is promoted by the combined effects of tolerance and the occurrence of fatigue and depression that often follow the amphetamine "high." Overdoses typically lead to paranoid delusions and sometimes psychosis.[65]

Cocaine, also called coke, gold dust, flake and snow, is a potent stimulant that has gained widespread popularity since the mid-1970s. Its unique popularity is not only with the adolescent population, but with adults as well. It is a frequently used drug in professional circles as well as non-professional. Many people sniff or "snort" cocaine, though repeated use in this way is destructive of the tender mucous membranes in the nostrils. Previous "snorters" often are found to be injecting the drug, which is a more serious form of involvement.

3. Depressants. Depressants include alcohol, barbiturates and hypnotics. Common barbiturates are Nembutol, Seconal and phenobarbital. Hypnotics include methaqualone (quaaludes) and librium. Slang terms for depressants are goof balls, yellow jackets, ludes, pink ladies, red birds, barbs and downers. Though all of these drugs depress central nervous system activity, adolescents do not take them for their sedation effect. At stronger toxic dosages, they tend to produce a state of overactivity and excitement just before the central nervous system activity is suppressed.[66] Alcohol, barbiturates and hypnotics tend to produce this euphoria, excitement and feeling of liberation. Alcohol increases the intensity of these drugs' psychoactive effects, and is often taken along with them for that purpose.

Barbiturates, in particular, can be very dangerous. The body builds tolerance to them very quickly so that larger and larger doses are required to produce the desired effects. But continued use at toxic levels produces undesirable and dangerous side effects. Muscle uncoordination, speech difficulties, confusion, disrupted thought processes and breakdown in emotional control are common. In severe cases, a toxic psychosis develops in which hallucinations and delusions of persecution are present as prominent symptoms.

4. Hallucinogens. The drugs that produce hallucinations are called hallucinogenic drugs. Hallucinations are sensory experiences without an appropriate stimulus. Seeing the image of a person and hearing the sound of a human voice when no person is there are examples respectively of visual and auditory hallucinations. Among the hallucinogens are marijuana, LSD, psilocybin, mescaline and phencyclidine.

The mildest of this group of drugs that we will review is also probably the one that has received the greatest notoriety. Marijuana is derived from the hemp plant, cannabis indica or cannabis for short. It is also known as love weed, Indian hay, joy smoke, locoweed, laughing grass, reefer, hashish, hash, weed or pot. Technically, marijuana is prepared from the flowers and leaves of the plant, while hashish or hash is taken from the plant resin. Hash is far more potent than grass. When eaten, marijuana has a much longer-lasting effect (about five to 12 hours) than when it is smoked. A cigarette, or joint, produces an effect that lasts about two to four hours. The principally active ingredient is tetrahydrocannabinol (THC).

Marijuana use causes just a few short-term physiological side effects: increased pulse rate, reddening of the eyes, and dryness of the mouth and throat. The short-term psychological effects are more varied. The first phase of intoxication is typically a 10- to 30-minute period of heightened anxiety. Teenagers who experience generalized anxiety sometimes take marijuana to give them a reality-based reason for their anxiety symptoms.[67] Intellectual and motor performance are both impaired, especially with more complex functions.[68] Alterations in time and space perception, impaired immediate memory, euphoria, altered sense of identity, exaggerated laughter, increased suggestibility and a feeling of well-being are common subjective effects of intoxication. Some users report dizziness, lightheadedness, nausea and hunger.

Higher dosages usually bring more intense and more varied symptoms. Very high dosages will typically cause thought distortions such as disturbed body image, depersonalization, paranoid thoughts and hallucinations.

The individual user's expectations about the drug's effects have an impact on the resulting subjective experience. Anticipating an exhilarating effect tends to facilitate that kind of experience, while fear, apprehension or guilt about using the drug will often lead to a much less positive and even negative experience. The person's level of personality integration and sense of psychological well-being also influences the subjective experience from marijuana intoxication. Both the person's positive and less desirable personality traits are amplified. Adolescents who have previously exhibited psychopathology are more likely to evidence hallucinations and other psychotic reactions from taking the drug.

The long-term effects of marijuana use are difficult to determine because it is hard to differentiate whether the drug or other dynamics like dysfunctional family patterns, genetic inheritance, or environmental influences are creating these suspected results of long-term marijuana usage. However, there are several behavioral symptoms that appear to be associated with extended heavy marijuana use. Several studies indicate that "heavy, chronic marijuana use causes an amotivational syndrome, or a loss of ordinary goal orientation and social indifference."[69] Two other studies associated the drug's protracted use with a form of social maladjustment that is characterized by loss of motivation to work, to face challenges, to keep personal grooming and to be involved in social interactions.[70, 71]

LSD or acid (lysergic acid diethylamide-25) is one of the most potent mind-affecting substances. It is a tasteless, odorless, white powder that comes from a fungus growth. It can also be synthetically produced. Timothy Leary's work at Harvard on LSD suggested its "mind expanding" or "consciousness expanding" properties. Terms like "psychedelic," "turned on," "tripping," "tripping out" and "bad trip" became common.

The experiences and symptoms that mark an LSD trip are widely varied and quite dramatic: visual hallucinations; acute sight and hearing; distortions of touch, taste and smell; anxiety; emotional instability; inappropriate affect; changes in body image, cognition, orientation and motor coordination. Physiological changes include: increased pulse and heart rate; elevated blood pressure; dilated pupils; raised body temperature; flushing of the skin; shivering and chills; appetite loss; nausea; vomiting; dizziness; headache; loss of muscular coordination and muscular tremors.

The LSD trip results from swallowing, inhaling or injecting a very small quantity of the drug. The trip begins about 30 minutes later and lasts eight to 10 hours, depending on the strength of the dosage and the physiological and psychological condition of the user.

Most LSD trips can be divided into four overlapping stages.[72] The first stage lasts from the time the drug is taken until the full effects are felt, which takes about 40 minutes. The second stage begins when the full physiological and subjective effects of the drug are felt and lasts until these symptoms begin to decline. This phase usually lasts between four and five hours. The third stage is essentially the recovery period, the time when the effects of the drug are diminishing. Altering waves of normal feelings and LSD symptoms are experienced up until about seven to nine hours after the drug is taken. The fourth stage, the aftermath, is marked by feelings of fatigue and tension. This last stage may last for several hours.

Flashbacks (recurrences of hallucinations) and other psychotic symptoms of the trip may occur up to several years after the trip. They are not as intense as the original trip experience, but they sometimes produce strong anxiety.

Psilocybin is similar to LSD.[73] It produces visual hallucinations, "visions," in florid color. It comes from a Mexican mushroom and is likely to produce a chronic toxic psychosis.

Mescaline is also known as peyote. It was used in the religious rituals of Central and South American Indians because of the often pleasurable perceptual changes caused by the drug. Hallucinations are common effects.

Phencyclidine has been wrongly called THC.[74] It is actually an animal tranquilizer and its growing popularity centers upon the often experienced warm and cozy feeling that is gained through its use.

5. Volatile substances. Airplane glue, turpentine, paint thinner, gasoline and other volatile substances present opportunities for cheap but dangerous highs. Teenagers saturate a rag with the substance and then sniff the fumes. These chemicals are central nervous system depressants. Like alchohol and barbiturates, they produce an initial feeling of exihilaration and release. Tolerance builds very rapidly so that a much larger amount must be used by regular inhalers in order to obtain a strong high.

The subjective high lasts up to an hour and is marked by nonsensical talking, slurred speech and loss of balance. After about an hour the user exhibits impaired judgment, nausea, vomiting and sometimes loss of consciousness. Habitual users of these substances often experience intense and frightening visual and auditory hallucinations. Physiological damage, including lesions to the liver, kidney, heart and brain have been reported.

Counseling Guidelines

We need to be reminded that rebellion is a very normal and healthy aspect of adolescent development, that anger is a normal and healthy component of the teenager's emotional life. Adolescent anger and rebellion usually make parents and other authority figures feel somewhat threatened and uncomfortable. For the adolescent, rebellion is a process of pushing away, creating independence from parents and other authority figures. That's a very important process because it allows teenagers to begin viewing themselves as separate, unique and somewhat self-sufficient. In younger teenage years, the rebellion is almost totally against adults and other authority figures. They bind themselves to a peer group that is largely held together because of similarities and mutual identification. In mid- and late adolescence, the rebellion takes place at a peer level as well as with adults. They tend to push away from peer groups. They are more capable of individuating, not only from parents, but also from peer groups. They are more capable of developing their own style, thoughts and identity.

When we see teenagers who are acting out in an aggressive, destructive way (perhaps through vandalism, property destruction, theft, drug abuse, sexual promiscuity) we are usually seeing young people who have partly failed in earlier developmental paths. They perhaps have been raised in a home environment that has been overly restrictive, which has blocked the necessary developmental processes, keeping the young person in childhood patterns. Perhaps the rebellion is an understandable reaction in these cases. Teenagers raised in overly permissive homes, however, may be just as rebellious as those from restrictive homes, although usually for different reasons. Youth from overly permissive homes may rebel against the lack of codes and expectations. In both home environments, there has probably been a years-long pattern of discouragement, lack of affirmation and direction from family and much self-criticism. By the time these children enter adolescence, they usually have very serious questions about their sense of worth, value and whether they belong.

By the time young people become overtly hostile, they have probably given up on a possibility of belonging in a group through positive behavior. The more normal behavior is to push away. Yet the adolescent still craves meaningful contact with adults because acceptance and approval from them is still very important. The teenagers, even though they are pushing away, are still looking to their parents and other adults for positive modeling behavior. But when an adolescent begins to act out in a seriously aggressive way, they usually have reached the point of discouragement that there is really no hope of maintaining any kind of meaningful contact with the adult world.

There are also young people who typically are very discouraged about belonging to their peer group. They often feel very rejected by their peers and have very little hope of having meaningful relationships with them. They identify with the hostility they see in other discouraged kids; they find support for their own anger and aggression. This is part of the reason why we find kids doing vandalism most often as a group rather than alone.

Counseling with an aggressive, hostile, angry, resentful teenager is one of the most difficult tasks that a counselor can face. The counselor faces complete rejection. A teenager is often brought to counseling against his or her will. A young person may say, "Hey, I don't want to be here." The teenager may cuss the counselor out during the first time they meet; the second or third time he or she may proclaim, "I'm only here because I have to be here. You're wasting my and your time, so we might as well stop now." One of the tasks that counselors need to face when working with a young person like this is to shield themselves from those kinds of verbal abuse. If counselors get trapped into defending themselves, justifying that they really are good people and that they can help if given a chance, then they have lost already. The teenager has gained control and has the counselor in a vulnerable position.

Though they may recognize their need for help, rebellious teenagers may strongly resist receiving any. Too much seems at stake. Feelings of failure, fear of humiliation and not wanting to compromise their developing identity block their free access to help. To receive aid from a counselor is often contaminated with the feeling that they are giving in to the adult authority and consequently betraying their peers, their cause and their own identity. Therefore, relationship-building (the first stage in counseling) is often a very difficult but extremely important task in working with delinquent counselees. Without a relationship, nothing is going to happen. And a relationship will help this kind of young person more than anything else.

The counselor's attitude must be correct if the relationship is going to work. Counselors must assert themselves as strong adults. A fast way to destroy the counseling relationship is to act like, to talk like or to relate like a teenager. These kids respect adult strength and want to see it in the counselor. It is also important to refrain from judging the counselee's developing identity. Help the person understand the meaning of rebellious behavior instead of judging its rightness or wrongness.

Try to help the counselee see that counseling will be worth his or her effort. Many delinquent youth have a latent belief in the omnipotence of authority figures.[75] They will continue to attack this perceived omnipotence as they continue their struggle for identity. Rebellious counselees will repeatedly set up situations that test the counselor's willingness and ability to forgive, to care unconditionally and to help. Only after repeated tests are they able to trust that the counselor, who is seen in the role of an adult authority figure, can really maintain a positive and non-compromising attitude.

Derek Miller gives us some wise advice for our counseling with delinquent youths:[76]

1. Counselors need to guard against being manipulated by the counselee into compromising situations. The counselee, for example, may tell the counselor of some recent or anticipated delinquent activity in a manner that tempts the counselor to insist that the activity be stopped. If the counselor is manipulated into a position of collusion, then his or her ability to help has been seriously hampered.

2. Adolescents sometimes tell counselors partial truths in order to prevent further probing into their aggressive activity. When this tactic succeeds and the counselor accepts what has been revealed as the whole truth, the teenager is likely to feel increased contempt for the counselor and all adults. The acting-out behavior will probably increase.

3. Delinquent adolescents typically communicate more effectively with their actions than with their words. They may wear expensive stolen clothing or jewelry or dress and act in sexually provocative ways in counseling sessions. These messages must be perceived, comprehended and appropriately responded to in order for the teenager to feel heard and understood.

4. Counselors need to understand and accept adolescent narcissism and egocentricity. There is no place for prejudice or stereotyping in the counseling relationship.

5. Counselors should not fixate on the issue of whether the counselee is telling the truth. All communications are valued as having significance. Whether it is truth or lie, the message carries interpretive meaning. Counselors need to search out these meanings instead of worrying so much about the "truth."

When a delinquent adolescent is brought to a lay, pastoral or professional counselor for treatment, the first temptation is to focus exclusively on the delinquent behavior. The parents usually expect that of the counselor. The teenager usually is braced in anticipation of that focus. And even the counselor who should know better will be tempted to skip over building a relationship in order to focus on the behavioral problem. Granted, a counseling relationship with a person who continues breaking the law is a sham. If using the leverage of the police, school officials or probation department will stop the destructive behavior, then use that leverage.

It is true that the delinquent behavior must be controlled. But if that is where the counseling effort stops, it falls far too short. Effective counseling searches out the psychological, spiritual, interpersonal and physical causes that underlie the behavior. Stages two and three of the counseling process (chapter 5) must address these causative issues if the counseling is to be successful. The counselor and the counselee work together to define these causative problems and establish counseling goals that impact those issues.

Many teenagers begin evidencing delinquent patterns of behavior during or shortly after experiencing excessive stress or depression. Their parents may be going through a divorce, their best friend moved out of town or they may have been rejected by their boy- or girlfriend. Resolution of the underlying stress reaction will often result in a reduction or termination of the delinquent behavior. If the behavioral pattern is more long-term, the effects of the behavior itself become compounded with the original motivations. The result is a deeply embedded problem that negatively affects personality development. These cases require more intensive counseling.

A plea for help is a common motivation for delinquent behavior. This should be considered, especially when the youth is easily found out and apprehended. Guilt-ridden teenagers may steal or vandalize in order to be caught and punished. The punishment temporarily relieves or reduces their sense of guilt and being caught provides the possibility of being rescued from internal psychological conflicts that they cannot resolve on their own.

Counseling sometimes provides a much-needed relationship with an adult authority figure. In some cases, the youthful counselee will resume delinquent activity when he or she senses that counseling is about to be terminated. One of the counseling goals should be to help the young person establish meaningful supportive relationships with other adults so that there is less of a vacuum when counseling is terminated.

A point that has been previously hinted at needs further development. Counseling with delinquent teenagers has two main goals: to control and contain the behavioral symptoms; and to resolve the causes of the delinquency. When delinquent behavior continues, it becomes socially reinforced by the peer group. It is also emotionally reinforcing because of its tension-releasing and other intrapsychic effects. The longer the behavior continues the more the adolescent will identify himself or herself as delinquent. Peer reinforcement and self-reinforcement operating together make longer-term delinquent behavioral patterns difficult to control and change.

Another complicating factor that counselors face is the intense short-term gratification that teenagers derive from sex, drugs and other delinquent activities.[77] Counseling represents a threat to the pleasure, escape, excitement and comraderie with delinquent peers that are gained from behaviors that need to be changed. Counseling does not offer magical or easy solutions. These counselees are not easily enamored with concepts of personal responsibility, self-control and cooperation with adult authority figures. They need to be convinced that following these concepts will be to their ultimate good. Their feelings of hopelessness and helplessness must be replaced by feelings of hope, personal strength and initiative.

Counselors should be aware that counseling rebellious and delinquent youth is a very difficult, slow and often frustrating task. The sessions may show little progress. The young person will not generally soften up simply because the counselor is a caring person. The teenager has probably built over the past several years some reinforced defense mechanisms and will use them when he or she perceives that somebody is starting to get close enough to be a psychological threat. Yet that is what counseling is all about: being close enough to help change the person's psychological structure and behavioral patterns. Counselors can help the teenager reach the point where he or she can change the patterns. The strong defenses are going to be brought against the counselor. Counselors need to understand that they cannot go on their own timetable. They have to be very patient and open to the possibility that therapy may take a long time. Success might be marginal at best. Counselors will do well to keep an active prayer and fellowship life. Constant contact with God will empower and guide counselors as they work with these special teenagers.

Notes

1. Carl P. Malmquist, *Handbook of Adolescence* (New York: Jason Aronson, 1978).

2. Clifford R. Shaw, *Delinquency Areas* (Chicago: University of Chicago Press, 1929).

3. Emile Durkheim, *Suicide*, trans. J. A. Spaulding and G. Simpson (Glencoe, Ill.: Free Press, 1951).

4. Robert K. Merton, *Social Theory and Social Structure* (Glencoe, Ill.: Free Press, 1951).

5. Clifford R. Shaw and H. D. McKay, *Report on the Causes of Crime* (National Commission of Law Observance and Enforcement, 1931).

6. Maynard L. Erickson and L. T. Empey, "Class, Position, Peers and Delinquency," in *Delinquency, Crime and Social Process*, eds. Donald Cressey and D. Ward (New York: Harper and Row, 1969).

7. Malmquist, *Handbook of Adolescence.*

8. S. M. Robinson, *Juvenile Delinquency—Its Nature and Control* (New York: Holt, Rinehart and Winston, 1960).

9. Derek Miller, *Adolescence: Psychology, Psychopathology and Psychotherapy* (New York: Jason Aronson, 1974).

10. E. H. Sutherland and R. Cressey, *Principles of Criminology* (Philadelphia: Lippincott, 1955).

11. Walter B. Miller, "Lower-Class Culture as a Generating Milieu of Gang Delinquency," in *Delinquency, Crime and Social Process*, eds. Cressey and Ward.

12. Edmund W. Vaz, "Juvenile Delinquency in the Middle-Class Youth Culture," in *Delinquency, Crime and Social Process*, eds. Cressey and Ward.

13. Robert W. White, *The Abnormal Personality*, 3rd ed. (New York: Ronald Press, 1964), p. 363.

14. D. M. Levy, *Maternal Overprotection* (New York: Columbia University Press, 1959).

15. Albert Bandura and R. H. Walters, *Adolescent Aggression* (New York: Columbia University Press, 1959).

16. W. McCord, J. McCord, and I. K. Zola, *Origins of Crime* (New York: Columbia University Press, 1959).

17. Malmquist, *Handbook of Adolescence.*

18. Jackson Toby, "Affluence and Adolescent Crime," in *Delinquency, Crime and Social Process*, eds. Cressey and Ward.

19. Robert K. Merton, "Social Structure and Anomie," in *Delinquency, Crime and Social Process*, eds. Cressey and Ward.

20. S. Szurek, "Genesis of Psychopathic Personality Traits," Psychiatry 5 (1942):1-15.

21. A. K. Cohen, *Delinquent Boys: The Culture of the Gang* (New York: Free Press, 1955).

22. Miller, "Lower-Class Culture."

23. White, *The Abnormal Personality.*

24. Cohen, *Delinquent Boys.*

25. Malmquist, *Handbook of Adolescence*, pp. 507-508.

26. Richard A. Cloward and L. E. Ohlin, *Delinquency and Opportunity: A Theory of Delinquent Gangs* (New York: Macmillan, 1960).

27. Irving Spergel, "Patterns of Delinquent Subcultural Behavior," in *Delinquency, Crime and Social Process*, eds. Cressey and Ward.

28. Miller, *Adolescence: Psychology, Psychopathology and Psychotherapy.*

29. W. Healy and A. F. Bronner, *New Light on Delinquency and Its Treatment* (New Haven: Yale University Press, 1936).

30. Merton, "Social Structure and Anomie."

31. Ibid., p. 263.

32. Malmquist, *Handbook of Adolescence.*

33. J. McDavid and H. M. Schroeder, "The Interpretation of Approval and Disapproval by Delinquent and Non-Delinquent Adolescents," Journal of Personality 25 (1957):539-549.

34. Lawrence Kohlberg, "Development of Moral Character and Moral Ideology," in *Review of Child Development Research* 1 (New York: Russel Sage Foundation, 1964), pp. 383-431.

35. Leon Festinger, *A Theory of Cognitive Dissonance* (Evanston: Row and Peterson, 1957).

36. L. E. Hewitt and R. L. Jenkins, *Fundamental Patterns of Maladjustment: The Dynamics of Their Origin* (Springfield: State of Illinois, 1946).

37. William Healy, *The Individual Delinquent* (Boston: Little Brown, 1915).

38. Sigmund Freud, "Some Character-Types Met With in Psycho-Analytic Work," Standard Edition 14 (1916):309-333.

39. S. Jones, "The Origin and Structure of the Super-Ego," International Journal of Psycho-Analysis 7 (1926):303-311.

40. W. Reich, "The Need for Punishment and the Neurotic Process," International Journal of Psycho-Analysis 9 (1928):227-246.

41. I. Kaufman and L. Heims, "The Body Image of the Juvenile Delinquent," American Journal of Orthopsychiatry 28 (1958):146-159.

42. H. L. Burks and S. L. Harrison, "Aggressive Behavior as a Means of Avoiding Depression," American Journal of Orthopsychiatry 32 (1962):416-422.

43. J. M. Toolan, "Masked Depression in Children and Adolescents," in *Masked Depression*, ed. Stanley Lesse (New York: Jason Aronson, 1974), p. 151.

44. J. Chwast, "Depressive Reactions as Manifested Among Adolescent Delinquents," American Journal of Psychotherapy 21 (1967):575.

45. J. Chwast, "Delinquency and Criminal Behavior as Depressive Equivalents in Adolescents," in *Masked Depression*, ed. Lesse.

46. Malmquist, *Handbook of Adolescence.*

47. O. Fenichel, "Trophy and Triumph," *The Collected Papers of Otto Fenichel*, 2nd series (New York: Norton, 1954), pp. 141-162.

48. Miller, *Adolescence: Psychology, Psychopathology and Psychotherapy*, pp. 518-519.

49. D. Offer, *The Psychological World of the Teenager* (New York: Basic Books, 1969).

50. Miller, *Adolescence: Psychology, Psychopathology and Psychotherapy.*

51. Ibid.

52. K. D. Gaber, "Today's Drug Problem: What's Happening," in *Drug Abuse: Data and Debate*, ed. P. H. Blachly (Springfield, Ill.: C.C. Thomas, 1980).

53. R. H. Blum, *Horatio Alger's Children: The Role of the Family in the Origin and Prevention of Drug Risk* (San Francisco: Jossey-Bass, 1972).

54. Miller, *Adolescence: Psychology, Psychopathology and Psychotherapy.*

55. Benjamin Kleinmuntz, *Essentials of Abnormal Psychology* (New York: Harper and Row, 1974).

56. R. H. Blum and Associates, *Society and Drugs* (San Francisco: Jossey-Bass, 1972).

57. Miller, *Adolescence: Psychology, Psychopathology and Psychotherapy.*

58. Ibid., p. 449.

59. Erik Erikson, *Identity: Youth and Crisis* (New York: Norton, 1968).

60. Miller, *Adolescence: Psychology, Psychopathology and Psychotherapy.*

61. Chwast, "Delinquency and Criminal Behavior."

62. C. L. Barnhart and R. K. Barnhart, eds., *The World Book Dictionary*, vol. 2 (Chicago: World Book, 1983).

63. Kleinmuntz, *Essentials of Abnormal Psychology.*

64. Ibid., p. 413.

65. Miller, *Adolescence: Psychology, Psychopathology and Psychotherapy.*

66. Kleinmuntz, *Essentials of Abnormal Psychology.*

67. Miller, *Adolescence: Psychology, Psychopathology and Psychotherapy.*

68. L. D. Clark, R. Hughes, and E. Nakashima, "Behavioral Effects of Marijuana: Experimental Studies," Archives of General Psychiatry 23 (1970):193-198.

69. Kleinmuntz, *Essentials of Abnormal Psychology*, p. 422.

70. S. M. Mirin et al., "Casual Versus Heavy Use of Marijuana: A Redefinition of the Marijuana Problem," (San Francisco: Paper presented at the 123rd annual meeting of the American Psychiatric Association, 1970).

71. D. E. Smith, "Acute and Chronic Toxicity of Marijuana," Journal of Psychedelic Drugs 2 (1968):37-41.

72. Kleinmuntz, *Essentials of Abnormal Psychology.*

73. Miller, *Adolescence: Psychology, Psychopathology and Psychotherapy.*

74. Ibid.

75. K. R. Eissler, "Ego-Psychological Implications of the Psychoanalytic Treatment of Delinquents," *Psychoanalytic Study of the Child* (New York: International Universities Press, 1952).

76. Miller, *Adolescence: Psychology, Psychopathology and Psychotherapy.*

77. Ibid.

■ CHAPTER 16

Experiences With Loss

Adolescence as a life stage is characterized by crisis. Teenagers are growing through many transitions. They are changing. Their bodies are developing sexually, their mental functions are maturing and their relationships are radically changing. In the midst of all of this change, teenagers are extremely vulnerable to the psychological impacts of crises.

Loss is one of the most difficult, painful and psychologically disruptive experiences that everyone will encounter. The death of a loved one is the most common loss. It is also one of the most difficult losses to cope with. This chapter will focus on teenagers' responses to death and other types of loss, especially divorce of parents.

Grief

A young minister once counseled the family of a deacon in his church who had recently died. "Death is a normal part of life. It's something that we all have to face," he told them. "As Christians we know that heaven awaits us on the other side of death. Therefore, it's not God's will for us to grieve or mourn. We should, instead, rejoice and praise God in all things. You show lack of faith in God and disobedience if you become overwhelmed with your emotion."

This well-meaning pastor was partially correct. Death is a normal part of life. Since the fall of humanity, death has been a part of the life process. It is a transition event that lies between temporal and eternal existence. Ecclesiastes 3:1-8 reads: "For everything there is a season and a time for every matter under heaven: a time to be born, and a time to die; a time to plant, and a time to pluck up what is planted; a time to kill, and a time to heal; a time to break down, and a time to build up; a time to weep, and a time to laugh; a time to mourn, and a time to dance; a time to cast away stones, and a time to gather stones together; a time to embrace, and a time to refrain from embracing; a time to seek, and a time to lose; a time to keep, and a time to cast away; a time to rend, and a time to sew; a time to keep silence, and a time to speak; a time to love, and a time to hate; a time for war, and a time for peace."

Death and loss must take their places in the natural process of life's cycles. They are ordained by God and operate within the realm of his presence.

The pastor was also correct that death is an issue that we must all face. Though our culture all too effectively insulates us from death, its reality must still be confronted. When a pet dies, when we hear that a distant relative finally succumbed to a long-term illness, when a friend is killed in a car accident, or when we contract a life-threatening illness, death must be faced.

The pastor was also correct that death is but a corridor from temporal existence that leads each soul to eternal reality. Heaven does await the Christian at the other end of the corridor. But he mistakenly concluded that we should not grieve or mourn the loss of a loved one, or friend or even a pet. To feel a deep sense of grief, to be overwhelmed with pain, to be in utter despair in response to such a loss is completely normal, healthy, and in line with God's plan and creation.

Mourning and grief are not only normal and healthy; they are psychological necessities. The traditions surrounding death in many cultures reveal the importance given to mourning. Jewish tradition "requires prompt burial, acceptance of the reality and open expression of sorrow. The tradition expects three days of deep grief, seven days of mourning, 30 days of gradual readjustment, and 11 months of remembrance and healing."[1] The actual duration of mourning depends on the individual's progress through grief work. Erich Lindemann, a leading researcher in grief and bereavement, states that there are three significant components to grief work: accepting the painful emotions that arise; actively remembering and reviewing a variety of experiences that were shared with the lost person; and gradually trying out new behaviors, activities and relationship roles that may help the individual to adapt to living following the loss of the deceased.[2]

Long before Lindemann published his research, Sigmund Freud described four major characteristics of mourning: profoundly painful feelings of dejection; loss of interest in the outside world; restricted capacity to love and an inhibition of general activity.[3]

Those who work with grieving people will see a wide range of symptoms. In order to help them, counselors need to recognize normal, healthy grief symptoms from unhealthy or pathological grief. They need to realize that grieving is expressed in physical, cognitive, emotional and behavioral symptoms. The more significant the deceased person was to the bereaved, the more disruption occurs in the latter's life.

Physical symptoms. Erich Lindemann describes three grief-related types of physical symptoms: laborious respiration marked by sighing and tightness in the throat; feelings of physical exhaustion and lack of physical strength and endurance; and digestive symptoms, including altered sense of taste, loss of appetite, insufficient salivary production and hollow feeling in stomach.[4] Colin Parkes found that those who suffer from the greatest deterioration in physical health following bereavement are those who have not been allowed to talk openly or freely about their feelings regarding the death.[5]

Cognitive symptoms. These include the alterations in thinking patterns caused by the loss. Denial is a very common defensive reaction among children, adolescents and adults when confronted with the death of a close friend or relative. Adolescents, in particular, are not yet ready to face their own mortality and will often protect their fledgling identity formation through the defense mechanism of denial.[6] To realize too soon the fact of the other person's death would present the threatening thought that "I also might die." The fact of death is not all that is denied. Teenagers often deny the conscious experience of their emotional reactions to death.[7] The fear of being overwhelmed by their anguish through breaking down and weeping reinforces the denial reaction.

Another cognitive symptom of grief is a preoccupation with the image of the deceased.[8] Obsession about the person, recalling shared experiences, staring at photographs of the deceased and endless chatter about him or her are often important aspects of the reparative grieving process.

An altered sense of time is another common experience during bereavement. Fixation on the past with an inability to look to the future is quite common. It is as though thoughts of the future without the dead person are too painful to bear. The present may be equally as disruptive because of the intense emotions in the grieving process.

Grieving may also present the bereaved with the need to change roles. Teenagers who lose a parent through either death or divorce often take over part of the missing parent's duties, jobs and privileges. When a brother or sister dies or moves away from home, the surviving siblings may assume part of the other's chores and responsibilities. Younger siblings may move into the bedroom of the one who is gone. In extreme cases teenagers sometimes overly identify with the absent person, adopting some of their personality and behavioral characteristics.

A final cognitive reaction to loss is the question, "Why?" Sometimes we ask the question because we really seek an answer. We believe that if we understand a reason, then somehow the pain will be easier to live with. At other times, however, our question is more rhetorical. It yells out an angry protest that wants nothing but to be heard. Pastors and lay counselors, as well as many professional counselors, typically feel the need to give an answer to the grief-stricken question, "Why?" A better counseling technique is to focus on the future instead of answering the unanswerable. A helpful response might be, "How are you going to deal with this loss and go forward in your life?"

Emotional symptoms. A wide variety of feelings are experienced by different people going through bereavement. Colin Parkes found that these symptoms are displayed in three different patterns, each person fitting most closely with one of the three:

1. Prompt emotionality is felt with great intensity during the first week of bereavement and remains through the first month and part of the second month. Following this intensity is rapid resolution, which lessens the emotional symptoms to the point that there are only mild emotional disturbances during the third month and thereafter.

2. Second-week emotionality is characterized by moderate reactions in the first week of bereavement, severe disturbances in the second week and rapid recovery thereafter.

3. Delayed emotionality is the most dysfunctional pattern of emotions following loss. In this pattern, the person experiences very little emotional disturbance during the first one to three weeks following the death. By the fourth week, moderate levels of emotional reactions are seen that increase to severe levels of disturbance at about three months after the loved one is lost. Following this reaction there is good improvement, but the bereaved can be expected to have an intense emotional relapse around the first anniversary of the death. These individuals tend to have had psychological problems prior to the loss, are of-

ten fairly young and adjust less effectively to the death than people who follow the first and second patterns.[9]

By carefully observing the initial emotional reactions of the bereaved adolescent, the alert counselor can anticipate and more effectively help the young counselee through his or her grief process.

Let us look now at the several common emotions experienced during the grieving process:

1. Anger is one of the normal emotional reactions following the loss of a close friend or family member. Anger is felt toward the deceased for leaving or abandoning the bereaved. Teenagers may feel angry at the available adults because they did not prevent the death from occurring. Doctors, hospital staff, and the person who may have caused a fatal accident are common targets of such anger. The anger could also be directed toward God for allowing such a thing to happen.

2. Many bereaved individuals experience a deep sense of guilt. Some feel guilty about past experiences or lack of contact with the deceased. "I should have been more patient and tolerant with her before she died." "I used to argue with him over everything. I feel so terrible." "I always wanted to do my own thing. I didn't spend enough time with him. He probably didn't even think that I loved him." Others feel guilty for not being able to prevent the death. Some even blame themselves for the death. "If I had only gotten her to the hospital sooner." "I should have known he wasn't feeling well." "If I hadn't always been causing problems in the house, I'll bet he never would have had a heart attack."

Most of these guilt reactions represent an attempt to again feel in control of life after it has dealt such a painful and shaking blow. The unconscious statement is something like: "If I can see myself as responsible for the death, then I can become more responsible and therefore prevent anything this painful from shaking my world again."

Adolescents are particularly prone to strong guilt reactions when the loss is experienced during a time when the relationship with the deceased is strained, hostile or in some other way dysfunctional. Teenagers' relationships with parents, brothers, sisters, friends, boyfriends and girlfriends usually run in cycles. They are sometimes marked with negativity and discord. A very heavy burden of guilt must be worked through when the death occurs during one of these episodes.

Elisabeth Kubler-Ross reminds us that sometimes the guilt is deserved.[10] Not all guilt is neurotic or irrational. In rushing in to relieve the guilt feelings of the bereaved, the counselor should listen empathically and sensitively to the counselee's venting of guilt feelings. Then, after adequate ventilation has occurred, help the young person to differentiate between his or her guilt feelings and actual guilt. This process can bring great release and open the door to recovery. False or irrational guilt may arise from the person's anger at the deceased. Guilt is often felt because of an interest in and anticipation of an inheritance. Others feel guilty because they feel, along with their sadness, a relief that a long, painful and stressful illness is finally ended. Real guilt exists when the person has done wrong or behaved destructively. The individual may have been negligent. He or she may have, in some way, contributed to the demise of the deceased. He or she perhaps was behaving in unloving, uncaring or destructive ways.

3. Closely related to guilt reactions are feelings of helplessness. Nothing is so irreversible as death and those who are left behind are utterly helpless to do anything about it. One of the most unacceptable experiences for an adolescent is to feel helpless.[11] To fight against this threatening feeling, the teenager often tries to take on a sense of responsibility for what has happened. In this way, guilt is often selected over helplessness.

4. Fear and anxiety are common reactions during the grieving process. They are often experienced when the death of a loved one is anticipated, such as during a long, life-threatening illness. There are fears about what will happen as the illness progresses. Many suffer great anxiety about not knowing how they will respond when their friend or loved one dies. Anxieties about the future without the deceased reflect the person's dependency and insecurity. Fears about one's own mortality must also be confronted during the bereavement period. These fears, along with the other emotions, must be freely expressed, talked out and worked through.

5. A deep feeling of having been abandoned leads to an intense sense of loneliness. To be alone by choice is one thing. To be forced by external events with aloneness is quite another. The latter is much more conducive to lonely feelings. While some adolescents react to grief with anger, others withdraw into themselves. Karl Menninger asserts that teenagers who withdraw and become more isolated are in worse condition than those who act out their anger aggressively.[12] The situation becomes even more dangerous because the withdrawn adolescent appears to many adults to be handling grief quite well. Counselors must not be fooled by what at first appears to be quiet and calm composure. Beneath that exterior may lie great intensities of pain, fear, rage and desperation.

Passive withdrawal and compliant attitude must be transitioned into contact with his or her genuine feelings. Sooner or later the feelings must be recognized and expressed. If that expression does not occur and if the emotional contact with a supportive and caring human being is not made, the results can be devastating. The teenager might lose the desire to live and become a cold, unemotional and unloving person who has little desire or ability to establish meaningful and fulfilling relationships with others.

Girls are more likely to withdraw into loneliness than boys.[13] They may still be able to function in relationships, but primarily without emotional content. As this trend continues, they time and again experience strong needs for emotional and physical contact. Promiscuity can become a resulting behavior pattern since sexual intercourse is often the price of being held and cuddled.

6. Depression is a common aspect of recovery from bereavement. It often intensifies a teenager's withdrawal from contact. Mild reactive depression (the "blues") is normal. The counselor should encourage the adolescent to talk, to respond to external events and people and to release the very feelings that can worsen the depression.

7. A sense of relief is sometimes felt by the bereaved. Relief may occur after a long-term illness is over. It may relate to the individual's concern over the mounting medical and hospital bills that had been seriously threatening the family finances. The inevitable has finally happened. The waiting is over. The rest of life can soon return to a more normal pace and pattern. When negative distrustful or hostile feelings were associated with the deceased, relief is also often felt at his or her death. The negative or painful realities of the relationship no longer must be encountered. The death of an alcoholic mother, a harsh and demanding father, an excessively jealous sibling or a hostile and competitive neighbor may leave a feeling of relief. Counselors need to help their counselees to accept and understand these feelings of relief as being normal.

Behavioral symptoms. The bereaved soon discovers how much his or her daily activities related to the life and activities of the deceased. These activities tend to be less pleasureful than before. This is especially true of social interactions such as going to parties, taking meals together and going to church.

Another behavioral change is the appearance of the dead person's traits in the behavior of the bereaved.[14] Speech, gait, mannerisms, interaction styles, hobbies and interests can all be altered unconsciously to incorporate aspects of the behavior of the deceased. This identification with the lost person represents a difficulty with letting go and admitting that the loved one has really died.

Another type of behavioral change in some bereaved adolescents is an increase in delinquent activities in the weeks or months following the death.[15] Some teenagers are likely to withdraw from meaningful contact with others. Without opportunities to ventilate their feelings, they are likely to act out their suppressed conflicts, emotions and anxieties through aggressive behavior. It is crucial that the counselor recognize the source of the antisocial behavior lies within the dysfunctional grief process. Once the connection is understood, the youth can be assisted to resolve his or her pain and anger relating to the loss.

Stages of grief. We have just reviewed the most common physical, cognitive, emotional and behavioral symptoms of grieving. Though not all of them are found in every grieving person, most bereaved individuals do exhibit several of these symptoms in many different combinations. But the occurrence of these symptoms is not randomly determined. Elisabeth Kubler-Ross and Colin Parkes both suggest that the grieving process takes the bereaved through a series of stages that amounts to "grief work." Grief work refers to the psychological adaptation to and recovery from the loss of the deceased. The stages in the grieving process generally occur in a certain order, though each stage follows quite naturally from the preceding stage and flows into the next one. These stages can also be skipped or repeated several times during the process of bereavement.

Parkes outlines seven stages of bereavement:

1. A period of realization during which the person moves from denial and avoidance to acceptance of the loss.

2. An alarm reaction marked by fear and anxiety.

3. Searching for the dead person in some form or symbolic representation.

4. Anger directed at people, circumstances, and other external objects and events.

5. Guilt about the self, past experiences and feelings.

6. Feelings of internal loss in reaction to the loss of the loved one.

7. Identification with the deceased.[16]

Kubler-Ross first studied the adjustment stages that people go same stages as do the dying.[17] These writers discovered a process from their psychological research and clinical practice that is also referred to in the Bible.

These writers discovered a process from their psychological research and clinical practice that is also referred to in the Bible.

John Claypool, a Baptist minister, wrote a short but very helpful and sensitive book titled *Tracks of a Fellow Struggler.*[18] The book contains four sermons that he preached relating to the illness and death of his 10-year-old daughter. The second of these sermons was presented shortly after she had her first relapse of acute leukemia and second remission. His text reads in part: "Have you not known? Have you not heard? The Lord is the everlasting God, the Creator of the ends of the earth. He does not faint or grow weary, his understanding is unsearchable. He gives power to the faint and to him who has no might he increases strength. Even youths shall faint and be weary, and young men shall fall exhausted; but they who wait for the Lord shall renew their strength, they shall mount up with wings like eagles, they shall run and not be weary, they shall walk and not faint" (Isaiah 40:28-31).

Applied to the grieving process, the bereaved people must accept that at first they may only be able to walk, struggling to not faint. Later on, they will be able to run without being overcome with weariness. Finally, they will be able to fly. And God is present during all three stages. He strengthens and enables people to recover from loss.

Claypool's last sermon in his book was preached one month after his daughter's death. He chose the story of Job. He traces the stages of Job's psychological and spiritual journey following his tragedies. Claypool finds rich parallels between Job's experience, his own, and others who suffer extreme loss and grief. Briefly, his five stages are: numbed shock that protects the sufferer from the full emotional impact of the tragedy that has occurred; utter despair and hopelessness; absorption in fond memories of the past; anger and resentment, with a tendency to blame people, God or events for the death; and a new understanding of the past and a fresh hope for the future.

Counselors who work with teenagers should realize that they mourn the loss of a loved one in a similar manner as do adults. The maturity and effectiveness of the adolescent's grieving will, of course, depend greatly upon his or her own level of maturity.

Pathological grief. Because of the tumultuous nature of the grieving process, it is sometimes difficult to differentiate between normal and pathological grieving. In many counseling situations the intensity of the symptoms indicates the severity of the psychological disorder. But not so with bereavement. Normal grieving typically involves explosive emotionality. Quick rage, intense anguish and gripping fear are normal.

Counselors need to know how to identify pathological grieving. Only after an accurate diagnosis is made can an appropriate counseling plan be determined. Two psychiatrists have isolated three intrapsychic processes that underlie pathological mourning: splitting, internalization and externalization.[19]

1. Splitting may allow the individual to survive psychic trauma without severe breakdown. It supports the mechanism of denial so that the individual can know that the death has occurred yet still function adequately. This process becomes pathological when the teenager gives intellectual assent to the death while responding emotionally and behaviorally as if nothing has happened. In more serious cases the individual's perception and judgment are also disturbed. For instance, while observing the corpse in the casket, the mourner may be sure that he or she saw perspiration or movement, which causes lasting questioning about whether the person has really died. This irrational belief allows the bereaved to avoid the mourning process, preventing adequate recovery and resolution.

2. Internalization is another defensive strategy that sometimes leads to pathological mourning. To avoid the painful awareness of their loss, some seek to preserve their relationship with the deceased by taking in the lost person and focusing on his or her internal presence.[20] In cases of pathological mourning the teenager fails to release the internalized person. There is a refusal to let go of the deceased as the bereaved rejects external reality in favor of internal reality.

3. Other people may develop a pathological use of externalization in order to avoid the pain of grieving. The individual fixates on an external object that is associated with the deceased. It may be a photograph, clothing, furniture, an automobile or any other object that serves as a bridge from the mourner's internal pain to the loved one who is gone. Keeping the object is an attempt to control grieving. The result is a pathological postponement of the inevitable need to admit the person is gone and to mourn the loss.

Types of Loss. One factor that determines how an adolescent responds to bereavement is the nature of the relationship that was shared with the deceased. Grieving the loss of a parent is predictably different from grieving the loss of a friend.

When an adolescent loses a parent, the first reaction is likely to be denial in order to protect the self from the other intensely frightening and threatening feelings.[21] The exact nature of the denied feelings depends upon the quality of relationship that the teenager had with his or her deceased parent. When a close and loving relationship existed, the reaction usually includes intense pain and anger at being left alone. The young person may believe that the parent was bad for leaving and feels guilty in turn for making that judgment. Anger is felt not only toward the deceased parent for leaving, but also toward the surviving parent for not preventing the death.[22]

The death of a brother or sister can create very disruptive reactions because of the mixed and intense feelings that siblings usually have for each other. Intense jealousy, fear, abandonment and guilt are all common.[23] When a sibling dies, the family interaction dynamics change. The child's grieving will be influenced by the grief reactions of the parents. And the parents' reactions to the surviving child often are altered by the death. In some instances the parents' anger about the death is projected onto the remaining children. In other families the parents become overly protective and suffocating with the surviving children. These teenagers need supportive counseling to help them resist the heavy pressures that these altered family dynamics exert upon them. Family counseling is also helpful for enabling each family member and the family group as a whole to make the most adequate adjustment to the grieving process.

When an adolescent loses a friend of the same age, strong anxiety reactions are likely to be a significant part of the grief reaction.[24] Teenagers know that adults die, particularly older ones. But the death of a peer is shocking. They are immediately confronted with their own mortality at an age when they are ill-prepared to handle the stress. Teenagers find the thought of death extremely threatening.

Another type of loss that teenagers are unfortunately having to deal with is the separation or divorce of their parents. When parents divorce or separate, the adolescent loses a sense of security and confidence in the future because of the radical changes that occur within the home and family. The amount of contact with one parent is usually markedly reduced. And the emotional reaction of the teenager is more difficult to resolve because the parent leaves voluntarily. The anger tends to be stronger and last longer because leaving was a choice rather than the result of unpreventable death. The adolescents' guilt also tends to be stronger and more difficult to resolve. They tend to blame themselves for causing too much stress in the home or in some other way contributing to the breakup of their parents' marriage.

Continuing healthy emotional growth necessitates a feeling of being loved and valued by their parents. It is difficult for teenagers to reconcile their feelings of abandonment with the reassurances from the parent that they are loved even though he or she is leaving them. The parent's choice suggests to the child that he or she is secondary.

Another teenage struggle with loss occurs when a parent, sibling or friend suffers with a chronic debilitating illness.[25] When severe pain or physical deterioration occurs in someone close to them, fears about their own vulnerability is usually aroused. Their anxieties, repulsion and confusion make it very difficult for them to respond in a consistently caring and considerate manner. They will sometimes withdraw from such situations. They feel guilty because they are not responding as they "should" or as others would wish of them.

If the person's illness ends in death, then the teenagers' situation is in some ways worse. Feelings of guilt are intensified. Irrational beliefs that if they had been more caring and loving the death would not have occurred are common. In such cases, counseling is essential if the young person is to adequately resolve these terribly complex and destructive intrapsychic stresses.

When a friend moves to another neighborhood or to a different city or state, rejection is not involved, but the pain created by the lost contact can feel just as intense. A similar loss is sometimes experienced when a sibling moves out of the family home.

Pets that get lost or die present teenagers with another type of painful loss. Dogs and other pets become safe objects for the investment of love and affection. Teenagers who feel threatened about developing intimacy with other people experience even greater pain when a loved pet is either lost or dies. The resulting loneliness can be troublesome.

Changing schools means leaving certain people behind. Schools are changed because of residential moves, graduations from one level to another and academic or disciplinary problems. Such moves are usually accompanied with the loss of teachers, administrators and friends that can impede the transition to the new school.

An emotional void is created when a friend moves, a pet is lost, school is changed or some other geographic relocation. This emotional void is as painful as the void when a death occurs, and the counseling process is similar.

Counseling Guidelines

Counselors who work with grieving teenagers allow themselves to be confronted with additional stress. There are several specific counseling guidelines and approaches that are helpful. But first let's examine some personal characteristics that counselors should possess in order to deal effectively with grief counseling without sustaining personal psychological trauma.

Characteristics. Counseling with the dying and with the bereaved causes counselors to confront their own attitudes about death. Have we accepted our own mortality? What are our own emotional reactions to the possibilities that we could become seriously ill or suffer a fatal accident? How would we handle the loss of a loved one? What is our spiritual, psychological and physiological understanding about death? Unresolved feelings within the counselor toward death will probably cause countertransference problems in the counseling relationship.

Counselors should examine their past experiences with death in order to anticipate and understand their reactions. Has a parent, sibling, other relative or friend of the counselor died? If so, how long ago? How did the counselor respond at that time? And how has he or she worked through those feelings? What are the counselor's reactions to that experience with death?

Counselors must have strong capacities for empathic sensing and skills for communicating their empathy to counselees who are dying or who are bereaved. Do we as counselors live our lives as though we are deliberately ignoring the inevitability of our own death? Successful death-related counseling requires counselors to be mindful of their own finitude.

Effective counseling with bereaved teenagers is a difficult but rewarding task. The need for personally working through one's own feelings about death has already been stressed. A thorough understanding of the psychological stages of dying and of bereavement is also necessary. The best way to grasp these processes is to have contact with people who are dying and with bereaved people.

The counselor's task. The counselor's task is essentially to share the teenager's grief work.[25] Counseling is designed to help adolescents release their attachment to the deceased and to support their movements toward the future.

An essential ingredient in successful grief counseling is an open acceptance of the feelings, thoughts and emotional releases expressed by the bereaved. Many are shocked by the intense rage and fathomless anguish that pours forth from the grieving. There is no room for judgmental platitudes such as: "You've cried enough now. It's time to pull yourself together." "You shouldn't be angry at God like that. It hurts him for you to feel that way." "You don't have to be so worried. I am sure that everything will be okay." These types of remarks are usually designed to try to make the bereaved act in a manner that makes the counselor feel more comfortable. They are most likely to do more damage than good for the counselee, especially with teenagers who tend to hold back their feelings. Instead, the counseling environment needs to be warm and supportive. Bereaved teenagers need not to be invaded or smothered by loving care but they do need to be surrounded by it.

When hostility is an initial grief reaction, it should always be handled with acceptance and understanding. The intense pain and anguish will more easily be released. To judge any such feelings as inappropriate, wrong or immature is destructive to the counselee's grief process. Feelings need to be ventilated before they can be controlled. Judgments tend to create a greater feeling of guilt, which in turn further restricts ventilation of feelings.

During the grieving process the teenagers will usually need to ventilate their feelings several times. They will need to talk out their memories of the deceased, their thoughts about how life might have been if the loved one had not died and the various good and negative characteristics of the one who has died. At these important times the counselees do not need advice, correction, judgment or even profound psychodynamic interpretation. Their need is for someone to listen totally to them. The act of talking is an act of release. Attentive caring and compassionate listening are the most effective healing activity counselors can provide.

Empathic understanding, one of the most healing dynamics in any counseling relationship, is particularly important when counseling with the bereaved. There are few moments in a person's life that are as vulnerable and fragile as when the death of a loved relative or close friend occurs. The need for safety in a secure relationship is strongest during such times. And empathic expressions of understanding, caring and support have significant healing impact.

The authors of *Getting Well Again* stress the difference between giving support and rescuing.[27] Though their comments are directed to the relatives of a cancer patient, much of their advice can be applied to counselors who work with the bereaved. The rescuing role is assumed when counselors believe that bereaved people are helpless and unable to recover from their grief. Rescuers fancy themselves as necessary to the counselee's growth. Rescuers think that without their help, the bereaved would never be able to readjust to normal healthy life. Counselors who adopt this rescuing role foster excessive dependency from counselees. This is a very destructive process in which the counselees question the accuracy of their own perceptions, feelings and thoughts. Instead of growing toward independence, counselees attempt to please the counselor.

Support encourages the counselee's growth. It reinforces movement toward independence while, at the same time, remaining fully accepting of the counselee's dependence when that need is also expressed. Support suggests to grieving teenagers that they can move fully into their pain, anger and sadness, emerging from the experience as a more mature whole person. Supportive counseling helps the bereaved to establish new relationships and to move forward into the rest of their lives, leaving their attachment to the deceased largely behind them.

The grieving adolescent usually needs to be encouraged to talk about the deceased. To talk about the dead parent, sibling or friend helps the young person to confront the fact of death. Counselors often hesitate to focus on painful material. However, teenagers often need the counselor's questions in order to feel the courage to speak about their lost loved one.

Well-meaning and caring counselors are sometimes also tempted to try to soften the adolescent's pain by shading the truth. Though the pain might be lessened for a brief moment, the risk of far greater damage prohibits this approach. Shielding from the truth is a rescuing behavior. It essentially says, "Knowing the truth would be too much for the mourner to bear. Therefore, I will protect him or her from the truth as I know it." But counselees will probably find out whatever was withheld. When this happens a sense of distrust is likely to develop. They are also likely to lose confidence in their ability to work successfully through the grief process.

Pastors and youth ministers are in a particularly strategic place to prepare teenagers with a healthy attitude, orientation and knowledge about death. Adequate education can help young people to respond healthfully and adjust to the death of a loved one when it occurs. Help them to see death as a natural stage in life that connects the temporal and the eternal.

The teenagers' sense of control over their own lives is seriously shaken when a close relative or friend dies. Death usually surprises them, even when they anticipate that death will come to someone they know who has been ill. Adolescents struggle to regain a sense of control in their lives. They want life to be more predictable. No more cruel surprises. Into this insecure setting, the counselor's warmth and caring presents the teenager with another potential crisis: "What if he or she leaves me too?" The question may be a conscious thought or remain as an unconscious fear. Sometimes this anxiety-producing possibility is too much to handle. The counselee may attempt to avoid "desertion" by rejecting the counselor. This is a way to keep control over the situation. Counselors do well to anticipate the possibility of being pushed away, walled out or in some way rejected by grieving teenagers. Patience, understanding and consistent caring will gradually help the teenager to take the chance on a relationship with another important adult.

Because adolescence is a life stage that is so marked with turmoil and transition, whenever a teenager loses a loved relative or close friend, counseling is advised. Symptoms may or may not be present. Remember, however, that symptom severity is not always a valid indication of the need for counseling intervention. In just a few sessions a counselor can assist bereaved teenagers through their grief process. The counselor can play a crucial role by listening, supporting and empathically caring as the adolescent mourner readjusts and adapts to a future without the presence of the deceased.

Counseling guidelines for teenagers of divorced parents. The primary focus of this chapter has been on teenagers' loss through death of loved ones. With the dramatic increase of divorce and single-parent families, teenagers are more and more confronted with the "half-loss" of a parent through divorce. The death of a parent is a definite, final loss. However, a divorce is an incomplete loss, which tends to confuse and distress teenaged children.

Most children, whether pre-adolescent or adolescent, tend to blame themselves at least partially for the divorce. This guilt expresses a desire to control the situation. The children feel helpless. They often think that if they were somehow better, more disciplined or did not cause problems, then their parents would not have divorced. Of course, then, they feel guilty as they try to take responsibility for their parents' actions.

Counselors must deal right away with that guilt. A young person may deny it at first but later on will usually focus on it. The counselor should also attempt to ask both parents to reassure their children several times (not simply once) that they love them, that the act of the marriage break does not mean that the parent-child relationship will also break. The counselor will need to help teenagers adjust to the new situation caused by the divorce.

Teenagers will usually feel that one parent is more at fault than the other for the divorce. If the counselor can encourage adolescents to talk out those feelings, then they will be able to deal with them instead of feeling guilt for harboring them. Help teenagers to accept (but not approve) the parent's actions, to forgive the parent and to move on in the new relationship. As in any crisis, teenagers' time perception might be disturbed. Ask them to imagine themselves at age 25 or 30. Will they want their children to have a relationship with both grandparents? If so, what will need to be done now to ensure those relationships?

Part of the new relationship will be limited contact with the parent who has left. Encourage teenagers to interact with their separated parents in as normal fashion as possible. That is hard to do, especially if the parent lives out of state or visits only one weekend per month. Some parents will feel the need to provide a "Disneyland" experience and some children will expect this experience from the parent. The counselor should help the teenagers develop realistic expectations for these visits.

When a divorced parent begins dating and getting serious with someone, the teenage children typically will react one of two ways. One reaction is intense jealousy. A lot of times a pattern of camaraderie develops between adolescents and the parent with whom they are living. The adolescents often take on more responsibilities and privileges at home. The parent and adolescents often must agree on limits such as spending money and care of younger children. Some adolescents become co-parents in a sense. When the parent dates someone, adolescents often feel threatened. Most teenagers feel that it is okay for their mother or father to remarry, but it still hurts. They fear yet another impending disruption in the family. They will often fight unconsciously against the parent's dating relationship. It is usually not a conscious process for them. All they know is that they are angry or upset, that they do not like the parent's friend or that they feel rebellious.

This situation is compounded if the parent marries a person who also is a parent with children at home. Most of these parents hope for "one, big happy family." That often simply does not happen, especially if the children are adolescents. When the teenagers move in together, they are much more apt to relate as cousins or as friends at best. They will usually keep their own last names. If the parents pressure them to act as a happy family, the children will rebel, resulting in a sort of "clan war" between siblings.

The counselor of teenagers in these situations should provide unconditional acceptance of their angry feelings. Teenagers feel angry because the situation is out of their control. They did not choose their living arrangement. It is up to the counselor to help the teenagers accept
their feelings toward the situation as okay. Once the feelings are ventilated, counselors can help adolescents handle them in constructive
ways. A session with all of the siblings may be very helpful. If they can
talk it out, they will come to realize that they all feel much the same
about the situation. With that in common, they can agree to make the
best of it without feeling they must like the situation.

Perhaps one or more of the adolescent children will want to move in
with the other parent who is not getting remarried. They may say
something like, "I don't want this family. I don't like this situation. I
shouldn't be made to live here." Depending on the situation in the
other home, the teenager's desires should be considered a potential
solution.

Another aspect of single-parent homes is the loss of a parental role
model for the children. Parents should never attempt to be both parents. Doing so may present a confused role pattern for the children.
Counselors can help adolescents by linking them to opportunities for
role identification with adults in various settings. Perhaps there are
adults in church or the community who lead youth groups, provide
part-time employment or direct worthy volunteer organizations. These
adults can provide adolescents with healthy, supportive and caring relationships.

Notes

1. R. S. Dunlop, *Helping the Bereaved* (Bowie, Md.: Charles Press, 1978), p. 56.

2. Erich Lindemann, *Beyond Grief* (New York: Jason Aronson, 1979).

3. L. Siggins, "Mourning: A Critical Review of the Literature," International Journal
of Psychoanalysis 47 (1966):14.

4. Lindemann, *Beyond Grief.*

5. Colin Parkes, *Bereavement: Studies of Grief in Adult Life* (New York: International Universities Press, 1972).

6. Derek Miller, *Adolescence: Psychology, Psychopathology and Psychotherapy*
(New York: Jason Aronson, 1974).

7. A. Bonnard, "Truancy and Pilfering Associated With Bereavement," in *Adolescents, Psychoanalytic Approach to Problems and Therapy*, eds. S. Lorand and H.
Schneer (New York: Paul Hoeber, 1962).

8. E. Lindemann, "Symptomatology and Management of Acute Grief," American
Journal of Psychiatry 101 (1944):141.

9. Parkes, *Bereavement: Studies of Grief.*

10. Elisabeth Kubler-Ross, *On Death and Dying* (New York: MacMillan, 1970).

11. Miller, *Adolescence: Psychology, Psychopathology and Psychotherapy.*

12. Karl A. Menninger, *The Vital Balance* (New York: Viking Press, 1963).

13. Miller, *Adolescence: Psychology, Psychopathology and Psychotherapy.*

14. Lindemann, *Beyond Grief.*

15. Miller, *Adolescence: Psychology, Psychopathology and Psychotherapy.*

16. Parkes, *Bereavement: Studies of Grief.*

17. Kubler-Ross, *On Death and Dying.*

18. John Claypool, *Tracks of a Fellow Struggler* (Waco, Texas: Word Books, 1974).

19. V. D. Volkan and D. Josephthal, "The Treatment of Established Pathological Mourners," in *Specialized Techniques in Individual Psychotherapy*, eds. T. B. Karasu and L. Bellak (New York: Brunner/Mazel, 1980).

20. O. Fenichel, *The Psychoanalytic Theory of Neurosis* (New York: Norton, 1945).

21. Bonnard, "Truancy and Pilfering."

22. Miller, *Adolescence: Psychology, Psychopathology and Psychotherapy.*

23. J. Gyulsay, "The Forgotten Grievers," American Journal of Nursing 75 (1975):1476.

24. Miller, *Adolescence: Psychology, Psychopathology and Psychotherapy.*

25. Ibid.

■ CHAPTER 17

Spiritual Problems

Difficulties in spiritual living are common to us all. Christians are precariously perched with one foot here in temporal earthly existence and the other in eternity. Juggling concerns about this present life with curious thoughts about the eternal is a perplexing task. It is no surprise that problems often arise regarding the spiritual life. Remember that the spiritual, physical and psychological aspects of our created human nature are interrelated parts of a whole. We have been fashioned as a working unit.

Spiritual problems can be defined as dysfunctions in: the person's relationship with God; personal spiritual development; unity with other believers; and interaction as a spiritual representative in the world.

Some spiritual problems arise directly from dysfunction within the spiritual realm. A poor relationship with God and incorrect perceptions of God are common problem sources within the spiritual sphere. Spiritual distress can also result from physical and psychological dysfunctions. Hypothyroidism often produces depressive symptoms such as energy loss, severe fatigue and a feeling of hopelessness. Paranoid thought patterns, generalized feelings of insecurity and learned distrust also make it very difficult for people to develop an attitude of faith in an unseen God.

Faith Development

Spiritual living is a developmental or growth process. Paul wrote to the Corinthian church, "I fed you with milk, not solid food; for you were not ready for it; and even yet you are not ready" (1 Corinthians

3:2). And the writer to the Hebrews asserts, "For though by this time you ought to be teachers, you need some one to teach you again the first principles of God's word. You need milk, not solid food; for every one who lives on milk is unskilled in the word of righteousness, for he is a child. But solid food is for the mature, for those who have their faculties trained by practice to distinguish good from evil" (Hebrews 5:12-14).

In order to understand healthy and disordered spirituality in teenagers, we must view spiritual living from a developmental perspective. To understand what is abnormal requires knowledge of normal adolescent spirituality. Teenagers' spiritual responses and behavior should be different from that of younger children and adults. Their capacity for spirituality is influenced by their level of emotional, intellectual and social development.

In a fascinating volume, *Stages of Faith*, James Fowler builds upon the work of Jean Piaget, Erik Erikson, and Lawrence Kohlberg in order to define six stages in the development of faith.[1] He specifies that infancy is characterized by "undifferentiated faith." This is really a pre-stage that contains the seeds of trust, courage, hope and love that will later become integral parts of faith.

Stage one is "intuitive-projective faith." This stage is typical for children who are three to seven years old. Fantasy plays a large role in their thinking. They are highly imitative and can be strongly influenced by the examples and stories of adults' faith. These children especially enjoy hearing Bible stories that tell accounts of heroic faith.

Stage two is "mythical-literal faith," which is typical of children who are about 10 years old. Beliefs, attitudes and rules are interpreted literally. Faith takes on the qualities of concrete thinking common among school children. The concepts of reciprocal justice and mutual fairness are important. Children in this stage are both reflective and able to understand others' perspectives. They take great pleasure in telling stories about their experiences.

Stage three is "synthetic-conventional faith," which is the most common structure of faith found in adolescents. The young teenager's world begins expanding far beyond the limits of the family. Friends, school, work, church youth group, athletic teams and the media all demand attention. Adolescents' faith must provide coherence and meaning to their many new experiences. Stage three is an interpersonally oriented faith that is geared to bring a sense of unity. It is conformist in nature in that it is highly aware of the opinions, expectations and judgments of significant others. Adolescents do not yet have a sufficiently formulated identity to have autonomous beliefs, evaluations and perceptions. They have fairly consistent patterns of values and beliefs but are largely unable to evaluate them. Though synthetic-conventional faith is most typical of adolescents, some adults never develop beyond it. This stage continues as the primary structure of faith for many adults.

Stage four is "individuative-reflective faith." It ideally emerges during young adulthood, though in many people it is not seen until the 30s and 40s. Sometimes stage four never emerges. Development into this stage requires an acceptance of personal responsibility for one's own beliefs, actions, attitudes and values. Identity is developed and differentiated from the perceptions and value systems of others. A more critical self-evaluation is accomplished and decisions and judgments are made that sometimes conflict with the surrounding environment.

Stage five is "conjunctive faith," which seldom appears prior to midlife. During this stage the individual consciously recognizes thoughts, impulses, feelings and memories that had been previously suppressed. There is an uncovering and working through of one's past. Conjunctive faith requires an honest recognition of the parental, social, ethnic and religious influences that have provided significant input into the development of the self. While stage four establishes boundaries that help to identify the self as separate from the world, stage five helps these boundaries to become less rigid and solid. Absolutes are seen as being more relative. Larger amounts of grey are experienced as the realms of black and white diminish. Ironies and paradoxes are allowed in the person's concept of truth and reality.

Stage six is "universalizing faith." It is rarely seen, but when it does occur, a significant impact is felt in the lives and society that is touched by stage-six persons. They are absolutely committed to the principle and task of universalizing the concepts of unconditional love and absolute justice. They are undaunted by threats to themselves or their loved ones. Their focus is broad. Nothing short of the ultimate good for all of humanity satisfies the longing heart and mind of stage-six individuals. These people are often viewed as potentially dangerous and subversive to the existing political and religious structures. Fowler includes Gandhi, Martin Luther King, Jr., and Mother Teresa of Calcutta as people who have evidenced universalizing faith.[2] But the person who epitomizes this ultimate level of development is Jesus Christ. His total purpose for being on earth, his manner of life, his way of interacting with people, the principles which he both taught and lived and the purpose and manner of his death, resurrection and ascension were all explicitly committed to the principles of unconditional love and absolute justice.

Steps in Spiritual Growth

The Bible presents us with a variety of perspectives on spiritual life and maturity. By synthesizing these views, we gain a more comprehensive picture of the scriptural presentation of spiritual growth. We can discern four different phases of growth that occur in patterned sequence. The four steps are: presenting and offering the self to God; establishing and equipping the self with spiritual strength and qualities; evidencing attitudes, feelings, thoughts and actions that express strong spiritual influence; and developing a strong interpersonal orientation that is centered in the value of service.

These steps toward spiritual growth occur at virtually all ages. The particular quality of faith that is viewed at each step is dependent upon the developmental stage of the person at that particular time. Let us look closer at these four steps toward spiritual growth.

Presenting and offering the self to God. This is the initiation of spiritual life and the starting of the process that opens the door to spiritual service. The Christians in Rome received this message: "I appeal to you therefore, brethren, by the mercies of God, to present your bodies as a living sacrifice, holy and acceptable to God, which is your spiritual worship. Do not be conformed to this world but be transformed by the renewal of your mind, that you may prove what is the will of God, what is good and acceptable and perfect" (Romans 12:1-2).

Presenting the self to God is an act of the will that recognizes God's reality and humanity as God's creation. The act, in essence, is an admission that fulfilled meaningful spiritual life cannot occur outside of a committed relationship with God. It expresses faith that God will participate actively in the person's life.

Establishing and equipping the self with spiritual strength and qualities. The individual walks daily with openness and vulnerability toward God's influence. A conscious intent to learn from God opens the seeker to personal spiritual changes that will alter his or her whole life.

Paul exhorted the Ephesians, "Finally, be strong in the Lord and in the strength of his might. Put on the whole armor of God, that you may be able to stand against the wiles of the devil. For we are not contending against flesh and blood, but against the principalities, against the powers, against the world rulers of this present darkness, against the spiritual hosts of wickedness in the heavenly places. Therefore take the whole armor of God, that you may be able to withstand in the evil day, and having done all, to stand.

"Stand therefore, having girded your loins with truth, and having put on the breastplate of righteousness, and having shod your feet with the equipment of the gospel of peace; above all taking the shield of faith, with which you can quench all the flaming darts of the evil one. And take the helmet of salvation, and the sword of the Spirit, which is the word of God.

"Pray at all times in the Spirit, with all prayer and supplication. To that end keep alert with all perseverance, making supplication for all the saints" (Ephesians 6:10-18).

Strength, truthfulness, righteousness, readiness, peace, faith, salvation and prayer are some important characteristics of the effectively equipped Christian. This equipping step is really never-ending. It is a process that ideally continues throughout the person's life, preparing the individual for the events that lie ahead.

Evidencing attitudes, feelings, thoughts and actions that express strong spiritual influence. The quality of our spirituality will be expressed in virtually every aspect of our behavior. Just as each person in the body of Christ is affected by other persons, so it is with our own selves. Each aspect of our being has an impact on every other part. A higher quality of spiritual functioning becomes evident in a variety of ways. Paul wrote to the Galatian Christians: "But the fruit of the Spirit is love, joy, peace, patience, kindness, goodness, faithfulness, gentleness, self-control; against such there is no law. And those who belong to Christ Jesus have crucified the flesh with its passions and desires.

"If we live by the Spirit, let us also walk by the Spirit. Let us have no self-conceit, no provoking of one another, no envy of one another" (Galatians 5:22-26). Opening one's self to God's word and his Spirit opens the way for spiritually motivated personal change.

Developing a strong interpersonal orientation that is centered in the value of service. Spiritual growth is not an entirely personal matter. It also depends on the giving of oneself to others. In his epistle, James writes, "What does it profit, my brethren, if a man says he has faith but has not works? Can his faith save him? If a brother or sister is ill-clad and in lack of daily food, and one of you says to them, 'Go in peace, be warmed and filled,' without giving them the things needed for the body, what does it profit? So faith by itself, if it has no works, is dead.

"But someone will say, 'You have faith and I have works.' Show me your faith apart from your works, and I by my works will show you my faith. You believe that God is one; you do well. Even the demons believe—and shudder.

"Do you want to be shown, you foolish fellow, that faith apart from works is barren? Was not Abraham our father justified by works, when he offered his son Isaac upon the altar? You see that faith was active along with his works, and faith was completed by works, and the scripture was fulfilled which says, 'Abraham believed God, and it was reckoned to him as righteousness'; and he was called the friend of God. You see that a man is justified by works and not by faith alone. And in the same way was not also Rahab the harlot justified by works when she received the messengers and sent them out another way? For as the body apart from the spirit is dead, so faith apart from works is dead" (James 2:14-26).

The message is clear. Our own personal spiritual growth is of little or no value until it expresses itself in our relationships with others. Our behavior expresses or confesses who we are on the inside. Our attitude toward both Christians and non-Christians reveals the character and quality of our inner spiritual life.

Adolescent Spiritual Problems

Now that we have looked at some theoretical and theological perspectives on spiritual problems, let us turn our attention to specific problems. Pastors, youth workers and other church-related helpers are regularly confronted with teenagers who are struggling with particular spiritual problems. The remaining pages of this chapter will examine the characteristics of these problems and suggest some counseling guidelines for each dysfunction.

Spiritual problems in relationship with God. Leaders and counselors who work with teenagers need to listen carefully to the conversations and comments of their young people. What do they say about God? How do they feel toward him? In what ways do they see God operating in the world? Blatantly incorrect concepts of God are plentiful in most youth groups. They must be discovered and corrected in order to prevent their development into more serious spiritual problems.

1. "God is so compassionate and loving that he would never allow a real tragedy to strike a faithful follower." "He is very demanding of perfection and is accepting of nothing but absolute obedience." "God is in control of everything. Everything that happens is under his direct con-

trol and determination." "God created the world and us in it. Now he's going to relax and see what we do with it."

Each of these statements represents a misperception of God. As with most faulty concepts of God, they contain some truth. But the truth is incomplete and far out of balance with the rest of the reality of his nature. J.B. Phillips, in a simple yet masterful way, describes a variety of identities that we ascribe to God.[3] Each of these identities is essentially a box into which we place God, thereby limiting our access to his full nature and power.

Although misinformation probably plays a role in the formation of an inadequate or incorrect perception of God, the sensitive counselor will probe more deeply for other possible causes. Listening attentively to teenagers will uncover the unconscious needs that influence their perception of God. Young Jared needs a sense of security. Therefore Jared "creates" God as a consistent and firm father figure who expects obedience. Fifteen-year-old Diana finds love and warmth by relating most to God's unconditional acceptance and daily forgiveness. The young person's concept of God reveals important aspects about his or her personality and gives a picture of what needs are (and are not) being met.

Counseling with adolescents who possess incorrect or dysfunctional images of God is most effective when it occurs on two different levels. The first level of incorrect images of God is a simple lack of knowledge. In this case, quality Bible studies and other creative learning experiences will help clarify the adolescent's image of God. The second level of incorrect images of God is usually associated with other psychological problems. Intensive counseling should first deal with identity problems, defense mechanisms and relationship patterns.

2. "I know that in the past I have had a personal relationship with Christ. But sometimes I even doubt that God is real. And at other times I think he's real but he seems to be so far away. When I doubt or have these scary questions I feel so guilty."

Often a young person experiences an emotional rush or psychological high during the days, weeks or even months following a new spiritual commitment. But after this energy charge dissipates, a mild to moderate depression occurs during which doubts and questions arise. These reactions usually cause significant anxiety, confusion and guilt feelings.

The counselor needs to be especially sensitive and encouraging. Remember that faith is a very difficult and abstract venture. It is a very difficult task to establish consistent Christian faith during adolescence.

In adolescence, significant psychic energy is utilized in efforts to push away from tradition and authorities. Identity is incompletely formed and continuously changing. Distrust of power, authority and convention are important components of normal adolescent rebellion. To establish and develop faith in an unseen, traditional authority figure (God) is a confusing and difficult task for the adolescent. The counselor's faithful and consistent caring and acceptance of the teenager may be the most effective way to support the young person's faith. Consistently offer reassurance that honest doubts and questions are not offensive to God. Support the teenager's transition from asking questions to finding answers. Emphasize reassuring scripture selections such as 1 John 1:9 and 1 John 5:11-13. Help the young person to recognize God's Word as the foundation of faith, not the individual's subjective emotional responses. Reassure adolescents that the reality of God's presence in their lives is not dependent upon their feelings of sureness. Parents' divorce or separation, death of a loved one and child abuse are examples of life experiences that teach young people not to trust. Help them understand that faith in God is at first far more difficult when life has already taught them not to trust.

3. "If God's so loving, why does he let me hurt so much? When my parents got a divorce, my life really got screwed up. That's just not fair. I didn't do anything to deserve that."

Very young children typically have a concrete way of thinking about morality. They are rigid in their beliefs about justice, fairness and equality. A major part of justice is viewed as everyone being treated equally. The slightest indication of someone being treated with either undue favor or disfavor is likely to be met with the shout, "That's not fair!" Elements of this concrete thinking continue on into adolescent mental functioning. Their anger at God for his supposed unequal treatment is often actually displaced aggression felt toward a parent, teacher or employer. Since direct confrontation with the authority figure may be so stressful, the angry energy is sometimes transferred to a less immediately threatening object. God often becomes this object.

Counseling teenagers with anger toward God can follow the guidelines for dealing with anger that were suggested in chapter 10. Reassure adolescents that their anger is not bad or unacceptable. Encourage full awareness of their own feelings and then support their honest direct expression of their emotions to God. This is confession. "God, I'm really angry at you. I'm sure that there is a lot that I don't understand or even see. But from where I stand, things don't seem fair. They don't seem right. And right now I'm mad about it."

God can handle our anger. He won't be shaken by it. He is secure enough that he can hear our pain and fear that hides beneath our rage. An angry confession of the self often turns into tears of openness and vulnerability as we make contact with our loving Lord. It is the counselor's own acceptance of the young counselee's anger that might give enough courage to confess openly such feelings to God. One counseling task is to help the teenager to move beyond simple cathartic self-release. Help the counselee to set some realistic goals for starting and maintaining a spiritual life.

Spiritual problems in personal growth. Another central counseling issue involves the definition of the terms "spiritual" and "spirituality." In their efforts to please, to make the spiritual grade, teenagers will often measure their own level of spirituality by how many days in a row they pray and read the Bible, how much time they spend in prayer, how many people they tell about Christ or some other behavioral measure.

1. "I'm on a spiritual plateau. I can't seem to get off it. I feel dry and dead, like I'm not growing any more."

Pastors, youth workers, counselors and teenagers are all unfortunately well-acquainted with the spiritual "roller coaster" and the spiritual plateau. It is often very reassuring to young people who are struggling to let them know something of your own battles. Self-disclose a little. Let them know that they are not the only ones who sometimes cannot seem to rise above a "low" in spiritual life.

There are several causes for this experience. One is the nature of growth itself. Growth does not lead us up a steady incline toward greater maturity. There are times of positive movement followed by plateaus and even regressions. The level planes are for integration of new learning into the personality. We all need times to rest, to meditate, to let what has been gained sift deeper within us. Sometimes spiritual life feels dry because we are not currently involved in some exciting activity, program or group of other believers. At other times the dryness comes as a lack of meditative experience, the loss of which leads to a starvation of the spirit. This sense of deadness can also result from chronic unconfessed sin and the resulting defenses against guilt and anxiety. It can also follow when other life issues force attention away from spiritual involvement, leaving an inner void or emptiness.

A very important phase of the counseling process for this problem is the second stage, that of defining the problem. Assisting the counselee to discover the causes for his or her plateau will be crucial before effective counseling can proceed. Accurate definition of the problem will lead to establishing specific counseling goals and plans of action for attaining those goals.

2. "I get so angry with myself. I know what I should do. I should read my Bible every day, pray every day, witness each day. I keep promising God that I'll be faithful and every time I fail."

Even though adolescence is an age of rebellion, teenagers still typically want to please others. Adolescence is also an age of idealism, which can cause teenagers to set their goals and aspirations unrealistically high. The result is perceived failure, frustration, self-recrimination, guilt feelings and a vow to try again. The results can be disastrous. The personal sense of failure and guilt can become a subjective wedge that widens the gap between the teenager and God.

One important task for the counselor is to help the adolescent assess his or her behavioral goals. Do they demand a reasonable or an unrealistic amount of time? Can they be scheduled in a way that makes sense with the other demands and interests? Do they represent a balance between spiritual activities and other areas of involvement?

Studying the Bible, praying, witnessing and fellowship are important. But their value is not totally related to the amount of time consumed in doing them. Indeed, rituals have no depth if the relationship with God has a lower priority. Their value emerges as they facilitate a growing relationship between the teenager and God.

3. "I seem different from most of the other Christian kids. They always seem to be really up, full of energy and happy. Sometimes it seems like I don't really belong. I feel so different that I've even wondered if I am a Christian."

Pastors, counselors, teachers and others who work with teenagers need to keep in mind the adolescent's needs for belonging and fitting in. Conformity to the peer group is the primary source of reassurance during early and mid-adolescence. Teenagers are very sensitive to the perceived differences between themselves and others. They will often judge themselves negatively on the basis of these differences.

Many churches unintentionally compound this problem by sanctioning certain social activities, styles of dress, music, political positions and other issues as Christian and desirable. Other types of self-expression are deemed substandard, non-Christian and undesirable, although there may be no real negative spiritual implications in them. The adolescent confronts in the church what is encountered in any group. Like every group, each church sets standards for evaluating present and potential members.

Teenagers struggling with these issues need to be assured that diversity is not only acceptable but actually desirable in the church. Counselors need to value and accept each teenager as a worthy individual. Draw out adolescents' feelings and attitudes about themselves. Help them to assess the amount of reality in their self-perceptions. Focus on their strengths and affirm their unique gifts. Several scriptures are very helpful for this process, such as 1 Corinthians 12:12-17.

Another helpful process is to explore the meaning of unity in the body of Christ. Dan Baumann notes that unity among believers is widely misunderstood.[4] He suggests that problems arise when we confuse unity with other similar yet significantly different terms. Unity means dedication to a singular purpose and goal. We experience problems when we mistakenly strive for unanimity (everyone in complete agreement), uniformity (everyone conforming to the same styles, behavior, etc.) or union (everyone belonging to the same group or organization). Teenagers are especially vulnerable to expectations of unanimity, uniformity and union because of their need for belonging, acceptance and identity. Help them to see that they can be united with other Christians without needing to be exactly like anyone else.

4. "I want my life to really count for Christ. I guess I probably ought to go to a Christian college. Besides, if I'm serious about tryng to really help the world, I'd better plan on being a pastor or missionary."

Adolescence is an age of idealism and lofty goals. It is a time for high ideals, strong values and intense energy. Tenderness and sensitivity increase teenagers' vulnerability to both encouraging and negative input from peers and adults. Much damage is done in some youth functions, church services and camp meetings that work too hard to extract lifetime commitments to ministry-related occupations. Such commitments should never be manipulated through emotional hype, group pressure or guilt-producing maneuvers.

Encourage the desire to serve God. Reinforce the wish to serve humanity. Support the positive values and ideals that are voiced in the youthful commitment. Suggest that the voiced commitment is still under construction, especially for early and mid-adolescents. Encourage young people to hold on to their desire to serve, while suggesting that their vocational and ministry goals and directions will probably go through changes as well. Help them to stay out of a guilt-laden corner where they feel like failures if they become an engineer rather than a missionary. Our task is to encourage their efforts to discover their own uniqueness, their own strengths, gifts and talents.

Adolescents often seek to gain approval by selecting career or ministry objectives that they think will please the important adults in their
lives. Counseling should direct them to their own likes and dislikes,
their own dreams and their own career objectives.

Spiritual problems in relationship with the church. Adolescents often attach their own high ideals to the church's lofty claims. They can become very disappointed, however, when they realize that the church is
often fraught with problems, bickering and seeming hypocrisy. Teenagers will need assistance as they reconcile their expectations of the
church with its reality.

1. "I thought Christians were supposed to be different from other
people. They're no better than anybody else. Just a bunch of hypo-
crites! Boy, did I get sucked in. I'm never coming back to church or
youth group. They're just a bunch of phonies!"

Because teenagers are so strongly idealistic, they are also easily disillusioned and disappointed. Church members also have to accept some
of the responsibility because they often present themselves, their fellowship and their church in a manner that is virtually impossible to live
up to. "The Friendly Church," for example, is an identifying phrase
that has been attached to more than one congregation. What does that
label suggest? That everyone in the church is friendly. That this congregation is friendly to everyone who might visit. That friendliness is
its major characteristic. That this congregation is friendlier than any
other in town. Some or all of these meanings might be communicated
by "The Friendly Church." But can any church adequately fulfill any of
these meanings? And what happens to an early adolescent who encounters unfriendliness within the congregation or youth group?

Proper counseling will affirm the disappointed adolescent's individuality, identity, thoughts and feelings. His or her negative reactions
should be gently explored and probed with an intent to help the teenager to accept ownership of his or her feelings and responses. Judgments and evaluations are typically not required from the counselor.
They hinder the teenager's own sense of accountability.

The adolescent needs to gain a clearer picture of why he or she is reacting so strongly. Does the problem touch a sensitive area? Does it remind him or her of some past event that is painful or depressing? As
awareness and understanding grow and as personal responsibility and
self-acceptance are deepened, counselors can help young people to
sort through positive options for dealing with the feelings. The ability

to control anger, hurt and disappointment will greatly aid their progress toward maturity.

2. "I don't see why there are so many denominations. They all think and act differently. It seems to me that since the Bible is God's word, it can be interpreted in only one way. Only one denomination is right and the others must be wrong."

Many teenagers struggle with competitive feelings with young people who attend churches from different denominations. They think concretely in terms of "right" and "wrong" about issues that are far too complex for such simplified formulations. Their prejudice and competition often marks deep insecurities about whether or not they are right. Rejection of somewhat differing views are attempts to reinforce their own sense of security. Differences, even in peripheral issues, become threatening to them and must be proved "stupid" or "satanic" in order not to create anxiety.

Counseling needs to assess the maturity level of the teenager, the home environment and the other factors that would tend either to strengthen or weaken the individual's sense of personal security. A major step in these cases occurs when the young person can allow differences to exist without negatively judging other groups. Counselors can help teenagers to learn that differences between denominations and worship styles are important in order to meet the needs of Christians who exist in widely varying cultures, family histories, lifestyles and personalities. Their concept of God can grow and expand to accommodate a much broader picture of the Bible's limitless God.

Spiritual problems in relationship with the world. Dealing effectively with temptation is one of the most perplexing, challenging and important aspects of the Christian's relationship with the world. It comes in so many forms, from so many directions and varied levels of intensity. Adolescents are especially impacted by temptation. Their identities are not yet well-established. Their defense mechanisms and self-control are not well-formulated. Moral and intellectual abilities are still developing. Physiological alterations and changes in interpersonal orientations produce opportunities for intense sexual arousal as well as strong emotional reactions like anger, jealousy and guilt.

1. "It seems like it's always something. If I'm not fantasizing about having sex, I'm wanting to cheat on an exam, or pick a fight with my brother, or gossip about our youth group president, or swear, or something. It seems like I'm always being tempted to do something. Doesn't it ever stop?"

All Christians struggle with two different natures: the physical and the spiritual. Our inconsistent and disturbing behaviors are often the products of this internal struggle. In his letter to the Christians at Rome, Paul described this inner conflict: "We know that the law is spiritual; but I am carnal, sold under sin. I do not understand my own actions. For I do not do what I want, but I do the very thing I hate. Wretched man that I am! Who will deliver me from this body of death? Thanks be to God through Jesus Christ our Lord!" (Romans 7:14-15, 24-25).

When teenagers break God's law and principles, the spiritual solution is rather clear. Confession and repentance are needed to renew openness with God. Guilt feelings often result not only from transgressions, but also after incidental thoughts, feelings and impulses. The spontaneous reaction may be immediately rejected and even confessed, but still the guilt feeling lingers. This overreaction to guilt sometimes comes from incorrect interpretations of specific scriptures. One of the more commonly misunderstood verses is 2 Corinthians 5:17: "Therefore, if any one is in Christ, he is a new creation; the old one has passed away, behold, the new one has come." Teenagers who believe that the old nature is completely eradicated at the moment of salvation believe that there is no understandable cause for a Christian to sin. A more realistic approach is in Romans 7, which clearly states that while the reign of the old nature is over, it unfortunately is not totally removed.

Counseling with teenagers who have yielded to temptation requires the stamp, "Special Handling Needed." Remember the idealism of the age. High ideals and lofty goals are common. Just as intense lows and discouragements are also common. Conviction from the Holy Spirit is often confused with and turned into self-condemnation. The self-punitive, demanding and unforgiving part of their psyche can be relentless and unyielding, leaving virtually no space for forgiveness and new beginnings.

Counseling with young people who have sinned must be responsible in two ways. First, it must lead teenagers into a very conscious awareness of their sin, with full recognition of the spiritual, psychological, relational and physical ramifications of their behavior. Confession to God, to the self and in some cases to others needs to be encouraged. Second, this type of counseling situation requires a very sensitive, empathic and non-judgmental approach. Adolescents need to learn to experience and deal effectively with their own sense of guilt. Lectures and other guilt-inducing tactics draw people away from their own internal experience and cause them instead to defend against the external pressure. It is far more valuable for them to focus on what is happening internally. A counseling relationship that can facilitate the confrontation of the internal self is an invaluable service to teenagers.

2. "My youth pastor sure talks a lot about cults. He's always telling us how bad they are and how their leaders are so evil. It doesn't seem like it to me that they're so bad. I think that they're really committed people. The cults seem to have a lot more commitment from their members than I see around our youth group, and even in the whole church."

Teenagers can be strongly attracted to radical and fanatical religious groups. Hare Krishna, the Unification Church, the Children of God and other cults possess several characteristics that draw adolescents' attention to them. They have very charismatic leaders who are able to elicit and coerce complete loyalty from their youthful followers. Their radical and sometimes revolutionary nature provides a natural image for adolescent identification. Teenagers are normally involved in rebellion at some level of intensity. They rebel against parents, school officials, government policies, church traditions or against anything regarded as normal and expected. Identifying with a strong "champion" for a cause appeals to teenagers' needs of personal justification and power. Cults' alleged ideals catch the imagination of idealistic and searching young people. The quest for excitement and adventure also lures teenagers into cults.

Educational programs are very helpful for informing young people about cults' backgrounds and practices. When a teenager does express interest in a cult, the most spontaneous adult response is to condemn the cult as absurd or evil. Although this approach works for some, for many adolescents it simply reinforces the cult as an attractive way to rebel. A more effective counseling approach is to invite the young person to express more fully his or her feelings and attraction toward the cult. Listen attentively and make special note of the unmet needs that are being expressed. Instead of criticizing the group, gently refocus the counseling attention on these unmet needs and their accompanying emotions. Encourage and accept their expression. When the relationship and a sense of deep understanding has been well-established, then the counselor can gently probe and draw out the teenager's perceptions of the cult and its leaders. Test these perceptions against the reality of the cult in order to assess their accuracy. This is a vital but difficult task. Take care not to raise too much resistance or stimulate defensive reactions. Instead, suggest that certain questions might be important to answer about the cult, its leader and its practices. The counselor's task is to encourage and support the youth's efforts in this self-searching process. Valuable insights, observations, facts and feelings about the cult should be offered by the counselor. However, introduce these with patience and sensitivity. Then, encourage response to this new input, gently confronting any inconsistencies.

Notes

1. James W. Fowler, *Stages of Faith* (San Francisco: Harper and Row, 1981).
2. Ibid., p. 201.
3. J.B. Phillips, *Your God Is Too Small* (New York, Macmillan, 1969).
4. Dan Baumann, "Are We Really One in the Spirit?" (San Diego: Sermon presented at College Avenue Baptist Church, February 12, 1984).

■ A Final Word

The role of counselor with teenagers is an adventuresome ministry that is exciting, demanding and always personally stretching. Adolescence, a transitional life stage, is characterized by rapid change, widely fluctuating moods and dramatic growth. There is an endless variety of challenging and stimulating counseling issues and situations. Yet counseling adolescents also demands a great investment of energy, creativity and caring. Working with teenagers will test lay and professional counselors to the limits of their skill and experience. It is at this point that we are most vulnerable to discouragement and frustration. But these moments also help us to grow, to reach beyond ourselves. With the courage to be imperfect, we recognize our own humanness. And with the decision to care actively for young people, we have the opportunity to entrust ourselves and the situation into God's hands.

Through reading this book you have furthered your understanding of adolescent psychology. You have expanded your knowledge of the psychology of counseling and have learned a general approach to counseling with teenagers. You have also gained some specific suggestions about how you can effectively counsel with teenagers who are experiencing a wide range of problems. The primary purpose of *Counseling Teenagers* is to stimulate your growth: professional, personal, relational and spiritual. Remember: *You* are the main ingredient in counseling. A constant purpose of this book is to serve *you* as a reference—to enable and equip your ongoing work and ministry with teenagers.

■ Index